T0201093

Barefoot in Babylon

The Creation of the
WOODSTOCK
MUSIC FESTIVAL, 1969

BOB SPITZ

FOREWORD BY GRAHAM NASH

PLUME

PLUME

An imprint of Penguin Random House
penguinrandomhouse.com

Previously published by W. W. Norton & Company, Inc.

Copyright © 1979 by Robert Stephen Spitz
Introduction to the 2014 edition © 2014 by Robert Stephen Spitz
Foreword © 2019 by Graham Nash
Penguin supports copyright. Copyright fuels creativity, encourages diverse voices, promotes free speech, and creates a vibrant culture. Thank you for buying an authorized edition of this book and for complying with copyright laws by not reproducing, scanning, or distributing any part of it in any form without permission. You are supporting writers and allowing Penguin to continue to publish books for every reader.

Pages 443–44 constitute an extension of this copyright page.

PLUME IS A REGISTERED TRADEMARK AND ITS COLOPHON IS A TRADEMARK OF
PENGUIN RANDOM HOUSE LLC.

LIBRARY OF CONGRESS CATALOGING-IN-PUBLICATION DATA
  Spitz, Bob.
Barefoot in Babylon : the creation of the Woodstock music festival, 1969 / Bob Spitz.—
2014 edition.
    pages cm
  Includes index.
  ISBN 978-0-14-218087-7
  1. Woodstock Festival (1969 : Bethel, N.Y.) I. Title.
ML38.W66S64 2014
781.66078'74735—dc23   2014021099

Printed in the United States of America
10 9 8 7 6 5 4 3 2

Set in Baskerbille MT Std Regular
Designed by Eve L. Kirch

In memory of John Roberts

Contents

Foreword by Graham Nash   vii

Introduction   x

Cast of Characters   xvii

Part I: The Nation at Peace

One.   Four Champions Fierce   3

Two.   Estranged Bedfellows   14

Three.   An Assembly of Good Fellows   38

Four.   The Seed of Commonwealth   74

Part II: The Nation at War

Five.   Home Again, and Home Again   119

Six.   The Long Arm of Justice   185

Seven.   Back into Battle   243

Eight. Loose Ends and Long Shots 267

Nine. Aquarius Rising 305

Part III: Alas, Babylon!

Ten. Friday, August 15, 1969 349

Eleven. Saturday, August 16, 1969 383

Twelve. Sunday, August 17, 1969 416

Afterword 437

Acknowledgments 440

Credits 443

Index 445

Foreword in Celebration of the Fiftieth Anniversary of Woodstock

BY GRAHAM NASH

All I knew was that we finally had a gig.

It was to be our debut as a group. After a few months of riding high on the charts we were going to perform in front of our first audience with a new look—and a new name. Our album *Crosby, Stills & Nash* had been released in May 1969 and set the trajectory of rock music on a different course, featuring killer songs, uniquely blended harmonies, and a laid-back California vibe. It was a game changer, no doubt about that. When it came time to promote the record, Ahmet Ertegun, the president of our record company, Atlantic Records, suggested we raise the bar, slotting Neil Young into the group—an idea born of what could only have been an ill-fated acid trip. Like Crosby famously said: "Juggling four bottles of nitroglycerin is fine—until you drop one."

Too late: Crosby, Stills, Nash & Young. Word of it beat along the jungle drums. Just like that, we'd become what some were calling a supergroup. That had a nice ring to it, but we were basically just recording artists. Nobody had ever seen us. We were dying to hit the road and show what we could do.

And, finally, we had a gig.

The booking was for Sunday evening, August 17, 1969, at something called the Woodstock festival in upstate New York. Sounded good to me. I loved New York, and being outside the city in a little fresh air would be a tonic for the spirit. We'd been cooped up in the Village Gate, teaching Neil our songs, then rehearsing our asses off at Stephen's house in Studio City. Turns out Neil was a nice little fit. We came out of that stretch on fire, raring to go.

A week or so before, we started hearing rumors that this Woodstock festival was picking up steam. Maybe twenty thousand kids were due to show. That was cool. I was used to nice, raucous crowds, having cut my teeth performing with the Hollies. And Stephen, Neil, and David were festival alumni, having played Monterey Pop with Buffalo Springfield and the Byrds. The way I read it, a sleepy country festival was nothing we couldn't handle.

Still, we decided a dress rehearsal was in order, so we warmed up the night before in front of a crowd at the Chicago Auditorium and the show went down like prairie fire. My girlfriend, Joni Mitchell, opened for us, which is like saying Picasso opened for Gauguin. We had to pull out all the stops and we came out swinging, launching right into "Suite: Judy Blue Eyes" before even introducing Neil. Needless to say, the place went ape-shit. Three and a half hours later they finally let us off the stage.

We were ready for Woodstock—or so we thought.

Joni was supposed to come with us, but an important TV appearance with Dick Cavett shanghaied her at the Carlyle Hotel in New York City. She was bummed big-time. We'd been hearing reports that one hundred thousand, even two hundred thousand, kids were making their way onto the festival grounds, and suddenly it became essential to appear on that bill. This was going to be epic, historic, a cultural flashpoint. We wanted to be part of it. We couldn't wait to get there.

There was no way to drive to the event—cars were backed up for twenty miles on the New York State Thruway in every direction and the National Guard was directing traffic, so we helicoptered in, a convoy of metal birds flying up the Hudson into the unknown. As we hovered over White Lake, the spectacle was awesome, surreal. It looked like the invasion scene from *Spartacus*, with masses of humanity mobilized on the plains below Vesuvius. Plumes of smoke rose from campfires, bodies packed like sardines as far as the eye could see. The enormous scope of it took my breath away—nearly *forever*. As we prepared to land, the tail rotor failed on the helicopter me and our drummer, Dallas Taylor, was riding in, causing the craft to spin in the opposite direction. The landing was, shall we say, less than ideal; Crosby, Stills, Nash & Young almost went back to being a trio.

Thankfully, emergency aid was standing by: John Sebastian arrived with some amazing dope, taking the edge off the whole mind-blowing affair. The act on before us, Santana, was making its major festival debut, and they brought down the house playing some of the finest music I'd ever heard. The roar that accompanied them was fucking frightening. It wasn't just the crowd, which appeared infinite; we were staggered by the pantheon of rock gods cavorting in the wings: Janis, the Band, the Airplane, Jimi, Sly, Joan Baez. When Stephen announced to the crowd, "We're scared shitless, man," it wasn't about the number of kids on that field; it was about performing in front of these incredible artists.

Needless to say, we thought we killed it and, in the process, established our cred as a group to be reckoned with. We rolled out a set of songs that would see us through the next fifty years—the "Suite," "Helplessly Hoping," "Guinevere," "Marrakesh Express," "Long Time Gone." They were not only expressions from our hearts—they also came with political statements that we hoped would stand up to warmongering and injustice. Our harmonies clicked, Stephen's guitar leads were razor-sharp, Neil contributed a few gems of his own. Only our second-ever show, and it was one for the ages. But the music was merely part of the Woodstock saga. The expectations by the establishment had been so low—that the festival would descend into chaos, that there would be violence, outside agitation, a freak show that discredited the entire youth movement. Yet we fooled 'em all. The seemingly wistful ideals this generation had been dreaming about—peace, love, understanding, living with acceptance and harmony, not to mention mind-bending drugs—came to fruition that weekend on a muddy field in upstate New York. It was a lesson for all of us.

Teach your children.

January 2019

Introduction to the 2014 Edition

I t's taken all of forty-five years to get the mud out of our pores, but there are some things about Woodstock that won't wash away. Forget about the vibe; vibes come and go. The effects of the brown acid have finally worn off. Peace and love? A noble, albeit archaic, concept. They even managed to get traffic moving on the New York State Thruway again—though just barely. Yet for all the event's remnants eroded by time, Woodstock remains the cynosure of a generation with a conflicted identity.

A great many hippies morphed into a species that swapped their bell-bottoms for a Prada suit, their VW vans for a BMW SUV, and spare change for a 401(k). Others craving more civil liberties became libertarians, while those prophesying free love wound up prostrate, in divorce court. Who of us vowing to share the land ever suspected we'd land a jumbo mortgage? Or vote for a guy who pledged to end welfare (well, maybe not him)? In any case, a lot of screwy stuff has come down the pike.

Boomers persist in embracing Woodstock as a warm, fuzzy keepsake; a special moment from their past that continues to burn in their loins like a first love. There is ample justification for it. Woodstock sets them apart from earlier generations that followed a narrow, buttoned-down script for their lives. It establishes them as rebels, lovers, *freaks*, allowing them to say to themselves (as mortgages and private-school bills pile up), "I'm the kind of person who once took off for three days to camp out in the mud, listen to music, and let it all hang out."

What a difference four decades make.

Real life distances us from what happened at Woodstock in August 1969. The festival that weekend was one of those cosmic markers that defined a generation. The fabulous sixties had a glutton's share of 'em—JFK, the Beatles, Dylan, Warhol, MLK, *Easy Rider*, Vietnam, sit-ins, be-ins, Jimi, the moon landing, among others—but Woodstock celebrated it all. It brought the decade's true believers together for one last lovely blowout, where anything and everything seemed possible. All the rapturous idealism and exuberance that had been fermenting since the counterculture reared its scraggly head culminated in the free-form rendition of "The Star-Spangled Banner" that all but capped the festival's program.

However, on Monday, August 18, 1969, when the clean-up crew moved in to clear away the detritus, the spirit of the sixties seemed set to disappear in the mists of time. What eventually became known as the Woodstock Generation said its good-byes, hit the road, and buckled in for a bumpy ride. The intervening years have not been kind. We may have been stardust and golden, as the poet proclaimed, but getting ourselves back to the garden has been one hell of a grind.

Music remains the touchstone. It was the promise of music that lured us to that field in White Lake, and it is the music that endows its legend. No lineup of acts has been assembled before or since that defined an entire generation, not only for its groove, its taste in music, but its attitudes and politics as well. Sure, the gods—Dylan, the Beatles, and the Stones—were absent, but their apostles certainly delivered the goods. Looking at the festival's roster of performers today, it becomes clear that the music is a soundtrack for the ages. But hold on a sec, I'm getting ahead of the story.

That Friday morning, August 15, 1969, I got up early to see two carloads of my friends off to points unknown in upstate New York. The Woodstock Music and Arts Festival was in everybody's ear. It seemed like the whole world was headed there. I was nineteen, a few weeks away from starting my junior year in college and smack in the middle of the rock and roll culture. An especially agile guitar player, I'd done my share of gigs and had a record collection that earned as much attention as my class books. There was a seat reserved for me in any one of those cars. All I had to do was say the word.

A note of full disclosure: I didn't go. That's right, the guy who wrote the book about Woodstock—the guy who, at the tenth anniversary party, was fingered by those responsible for putting the festival together as the only person in the room who knew the entire picture and had all the residual poop—was home, in Reading, Pennsylvania, that weekend, mowing the fucking lawn. And seething. Oh, was I in a deep, dark place! I'd spent hours in front of the tube watching news reports of the most incredible event of my life go down . . . *without me*. Worse, I was going to hear about it ad nauseam from my buddies on the ground.

I can't tell you why I didn't go. Suffice it to say, Woodstock caught me flatfooted. Perhaps I didn't realize how big it was going to be—or how important. By the end of that weekend, following hours worth of soul-searching (and not the least bit of self-flagellation), I had a new perspective on the culture—and on my life. I fully understood Woodstock's significance and the transformative quality of the performances. There was something spiritual, otherworldly, about the festival's essence. The crowd, the scene—it was messy and loud and teetered on disaster. There wasn't a legitimate game plan from one moment to the next. But the chaos was its own kind of poetry. The vibe there, like our collective vibe, ran on its own good steam. No one knew where this was headed, nor cared. The audience, to borrow from Jack Kerouac, was made up of "the mad ones, the ones who are mad to live, mad to talk, mad to be saved, desirous of everything at the same time . . . but burn, burn, burn, like fabulous yellow roman candles."

Studying the news feed as it evolved that weekend, I saw in the faces of those on the screen a wide-eyed, irrepressible abandon. I know, I know—they were stoned (just for appetizers). But most of us that age had grown up under the threat of nuclear annihilation, hiding under our school desks and looking to the skies. At Woodstock, however, they were under the stars, looking outward, heaven-bound, just two weeks after the first men had walked on the moon. The cosmos from that vantage was limitless and secure. There was a feeling that things were moving in the right direction, that a sane and rational voice meant enough to matter.

So much had shaken us in the intervening years: the assassinations of JFK, Malcolm X, Martin Luther King, Jr., Bobby Kennedy; a war in Southeast Asia that continued to claim our closest friends; civil unrest in our colleges and communities; the draft, protests, race riots, Agnew; the Chicago Seven; Chappaquiddick; the demonization of John Lennon by J. Edgar Hoover. Ideology pitted neighbor against neighbor, children against parents. America's soul, its fundamental quality, was turned inside out. Its Norman Rockwell image had grown ugly and nightmarish. No matter what, we weren't headed back in that direction. A new order would no longer be Rockwellian, but there was hope that it would be replaced by something equally upbeat.

Woodstock was certainly a legitimate template. The temporary community that formed on Max Yasgur's farm functioned on welcome, camaraderie, cooperation, respect, joy, and peace. It was utopian in every respect, a pop-up society whose flash, spontaneous origin precluded status or disunity. Michael Lang, Artie Kornfeld, John Roberts, and Joel Rosenman were its perfect architects. Dipolar opposites—hippies and suits—they had come together, rife with suspicions about one another, and stumbled on this idealized scheme. From the beginning, their crew labored with harmony and purpose, and from that arose the festival's core. There is no doubt in my mind that their spirit was contagious. Max's farm was consecrated ground.

Years after the festival ended, I couldn't shake my sense of stupidity for missing the experience. It had become clear that Woodstock was a moment, an aberration, not the linchpin of a new world order. It happened—and it passed. Attempts to replicate the magic fell short. Woodstock was followed by Altamont, the breakup of the Beatles, Kent State, and the deaths of Janis Joplin, Jimi Hendrix, and Jim Morrison. The society that formed in the aftermath wasn't the conformist society that preceded it, but valued passion, creativity, individualism, and freedom from stultifying restrictions. Yet it was beset by other conflicts. The "we" that was the Woodstock Generation began to splinter. Hippies fought for their own piece of the rock. There was still a sense of doing something important, working toward a goal, but it became individualistic, as opposed to an ensemble effort. All of which left me scratching my head.

I dearly wanted to attend Woodstock, I wanted in. In an effort to recapture those three days in August 1969, I decided to retrace the steps that led to the festival. Ten years after the last chord rang out over Max's farm, I set out on an odyssey—a personal reclamation project, if you will, that brought me into contact with practically everyone responsible for getting that remarkable weekend off the ground.

My timing couldn't have been better. Peoples' recollections of the event remained relatively sharp and, perhaps more important, free from the upholstery that often pads our memories decades later. Better yet, most were still alive and eager to talk. So many hands had contributed to the cause, and it wasn't until years afterward, when the shock of the festival had finally worn off, that they understood the important roles they had played. It was finally time for them to reflect, to make sense of this impact.

Two of the principals, John Roberts and Joel Rosenman, had already written a memoir about Woodstock, a funny little book called *Young Men with Unlimited Capital* that read like a CliffsNotes account of their experience. The cast resembled amiable cartoon characters; many were hidden behind pseudonyms. The narrative was humorous but myopic. I immediately gleaned this version was thin, at best, and had a bone to pick with their hangdog colleagues, Lang and Kornfeld.

Both Roberts and Rosenman were accessible. They were involved running a fairly successful New York recording studio that I had actually worked in on occasion, and a phone call brought them into the fold. They had offices in a building adjacent to the studio, on West Fifty-Seventh Street, which is where I found them one morning in 1979. Together—they were always together. This was no partnership of convenience, but something much deeper and true. They had the kind of friendship that I envied, lacking rivalry or ego. And they had each other's backs. Roberts was a big bear of a guy, more

Gentle Ben than Smokey. He had a buttoned-down conservative facade that clashed with his personality; the short Haldeman haircut, oxfords and chinos, and wire-rim banker's frames belied a playful self-image that endeared him at once. Rosenman, wiry and darker, had a harder outer shell. He struggled to play the éminence grise, but succumbed to an inner tug. While Roberts traded in common sense, Rosenman had the passion. He'd done some amateur acting and was a musician of note, and I got the sense those qualities constituted his demons in the venture-capital circle in which he and Roberts traveled. In any case, they made an enviable team.

They had also just emerged from an extended period of grieving. For longer than either man had expected, they'd shed tears over the ruins of Woodstock, which had cost them dearly. Roberts had lost his inheritance to its creditors. And the tangle of post-festival legalities, from licensing to endless lawsuits, short-circuited their livelihoods. Just when it seemed they could put it all behind them, I waltzed in the door.

"Gentlemen, prepare to relive the festival all over again."

I didn't actually say that to them, but you could see it on their faces. Instead of balking, they ushered me into a closet-sized room down the corridor with wall-to-wall file cabinets. "Welcome to what's left of the Woodstock festival," Roberts said. "It's all yours."

Everything, they'd saved everything—all the memos, schedules, blueprints, ledgers, even the contracts with the bands. Tickets, thousands of them, lay wrapped in rubber bands. I had almost forgotten that tickets were superfluous. Ultimately, hardly anyone paid their way into Woodstock; John Roberts had picked up the tab. Sifting through folder after folder, I realized what a bonanza this represented. Collectively, it was a blueprint for the festival, from its inception to its last futile gasp.

But Roberts and Rosenman knew they weren't off the hook. If the story was going to be recounted with accuracy, they'd have to endeavor to walk me back through the details. It meant reliving the whole exasperating mess, at least from their points of view. They were willing, at last, to get it off their chests.

Artie Kornfeld and Michael Lang were tougher customers. Unlike Roberts and Rosenman, who strove to put the festival behind them and move on, Kornfeld and Lang continued to ride high on its fumes. They had more invested in preserving the legend and portrayed it in a gauzy, mythic light. Kornfeld, whose Woodstock responsibilities were more ceremonial than hands-on, had more to lose by cooperating with me. As a member of the presiding quartet, he'd achieved hip celebrity that refused to vaporize after the initial fifteen minutes of fame. Woodstock was burned into the cultural consciousness. Artie reigned as one of its cocreators. He was the self-professed "Pied Piper of Woodstock," a name partly derived from the 1965 hit song he'd written for Crispian St. Peters, but also indebted, I suspect, to the itinerant Hamelin musician who led children away, never to return.

When we eventually met, he was all of that and more. Artie was one of the happiest and go-luckiest men I'd ever encountered. Woodstock, to him, was a total hoot, all about altitude, getting high on the vibe and the music and whatever else came one's way. He was childlike in his objectivity, a proponent of the rose-colored glasses he actually wore. Still, Artie had an insider's frame of reference that was offered in good faith, and I mined his knowledge at every turn.

Michael Lang, on the other hand, was elusive. Sneaky elusive. He knew, from the others, that I was closing in on the story and opted to make me chase him for his side of facts. "Give me a call after you've spoken to everybody else," he said, when I presented my credentials in an early phone call. Okay, I agreed to play by his rules. For months afterward, I combed the country, tracking down and interviewing his crew until, eventually, he had to take me on. Not so fast, buster. If I wanted to interview Michael, I had to do it 35,000 feet above the site, on a coast-to-coast jet. In first class. Fasten your seat belts.

The festival had been Michael's baby from the get-go. He was a crafty guy, with a vision as big as Montana and a determination not to let anything stand in his way. But Michael's chief asset was his cunning. He had the ability to knock anyone off their stride, to make one feel as if they were somehow inauthentic but could gain street cred by gravitating to his way of thinking. It was chilling to watch him in action. He could simply look at an opponent with his beatific grin and feel them get smaller and smaller. Both John Roberts and Joel Rosenman explained how they were putty in his hands, even when they felt he was screwing them into the ground. It's Michael Lang's unique power and he played it for all he was worth.

Woodstock became Michael's trump card. Ten years after the festival, he had parlayed his Woodstock fame into a record label deal and fronted a management company that included Joe Cocker, among others. Moreover, he'd become the face of Woodstock, the star of that gorgeous documentary film of the event, and its chief benefactor. Early on in the weekend, he'd detached himself from the backstage machinery of the festival—thus, from the mounting responsibilities—and lost himself in the groove. It wasn't in his best interests to have that story told.

Still, all four promoters devoted themselves to my quest, and once that happened, all the dominoes fell. As the months passed, the missing festival crew members who had slipped back into civilian life or gone underground or just plain disappeared began calling me to relate their experience, to make sure I got the story *right*. It was like working on a paint-by-numbers canvas. I knew what the festival looked like in my mind, its general outline, but the subsequent interviews began filling in the bigger picture. Finally, when the last story was told, I was able to allow myself a stroll across the site, across Max's farm, which was an experience that, trust me, I cannot put into words. I'll leave it to your imagination. Only one thing remained for me to piece it all together.

Which brings me back to the music. From the opening chords of Richie Havens's epic version of "Freedom" to Jimi Hendrix's chilling national anthem, there is hardly a finer anthology of rock music anywhere on record. Woodstock was a city of sound, and the roster of performers who graced the festival's stage remains, with some notable exceptions, the essence of sixties rock and roll. The mix of acts, much to Michael Lang's credit, was quirky, quirky perfect. The performances were quintessential, heroic. For many, their appearance at Woodstock was career-making and enduring. Consider that the festival introduced Joe Cocker to the States, served as the debut of Crosby, Stills, Nash & Young, put Santana on the map, all of whom continue to pack houses forty years later. Imagine listening to Janis Joplin at the top of her voice, thinking that no one could follow such an act, before she ceded the stage to Sly and the Family Stone. Picture the Who, destroying everything in sight, while several hundred thousand kids, zoned out of their minds, watched in goggle-eyed awe. Tim Hardin, the Band, the Dead, Joan Baez, Creedence . . . they summed up what was happening in music at a time when music was the cultural currency. It gave voice to what the generation was thinking.

The story of Woodstock is an adventure—and an artifact. There is much to be learned about dreamers and their dreams, about who we were and what we handed down. It's not so much a nostalgic trip as a rite of passage. Take it from me, after ten years' worth of regret and retribution, I eventually got to experience the festival from a vantage point that few get to see. Now it's your turn.

Go on—sit back, drop on a few well-chosen records (if you still have 'em), and light up a fat one. For god's sake, don't take the brown acid! Turn the page and enjoy the ride.

Cast of Characters

WOODSTOCK VENTURES

THE PRINCIPALS

ARTIE KORNFELD, *Publicity and Subsidiary Rights*
MICHAEL LANG, *Executive Producer*
JOHN ROBERTS, *Financier*
JOEL ROSENMAN, *Administrative Troubleshooter, Advertising*

THE EXECUTIVE STAFF

STEVE COHEN, *Production Stage Manager*
DON GANOUNG, *Community Relations*
STANLEY GOLDSTEIN, *Headhunter and Campgrounds Coordinator*
PETER GOODRICH, *Concessions*
CHRIS LANGHART, *Technical Director and Designer*
MEL LAWRENCE, *Director of Operations*
CHIP MONCK, *Stage Lighting and Technical Designer*
JOHN MORRIS, *Production Coordinator*
WES POMEROY, *Chief of Security*

THE STAFF

THE BASTARD SONS, *Construction*
TICIA BERNUTH, *Production Assistant*
THE BLACK SHIRTS, *"Heavy" Security*

KIMBERLY BRIGHT, *Office Assistant*

JAY DREVERS, *Staging Supervisor*

KAREN EAGER, *Security Assistant*

BOYD ELDER, *Art Crew*

JOHN FABBRI, *Security*

CAROL GREEN, *Staff Cook*

OTIS HALLENDALE, *Office Dog*

HOWARD HIRSCH, *Art Exhibit*

THE HOG FARM, *Spirit, Construction, and Security*

JOE KIMBLE, *Security*

PETER LEEDS, *Art Exhibit*

LENNY, *Director of Heavy Security*

RENEE LEVINE, *Bookkeeper*

RON LIIS, *Art and Playground Design and Water-Search*

LEE MACKLER, *Security and Administration*

JOYCE MITCHELL, *Office and Administration*

KEITH O'CONNOR, *Assistant Ticketing Operations*

JERRY POMPILI, *Administration*

BONNIE JEAN ROMNEY, *Hog Farm Coordinator*

HUGH ROMNEY, *Hog Farm Leader*

JEWEL ROSS, *Security*

PENNY STALLINGS, *Administrative Assistant*

INGRID VON WILSHEIM, *Purchasing*

BILL WARD, *Director of Art Crew*

JEAN WARD, *Art Crew and Administration*

INDEPENDENT ASSOCIATES

DR. WILLIAM ABRUZZI, *Medical Director*

BILL BELMONT, *Artist Coordination*

BERT COHEN, *Office Design and Coordinator of Underground Advertising*

TOM DRISCOLL, *Land Evaluation*

TOM EDMONSTON, *Construction*

FOOD FOR LOVE:

CHARLES BAXTER, LEE HOWARD, JEFFREY JOERGER,

STEPHEN WEINGRAD *(their lawyer)*

MICHAEL FOREMAN, *Program*

JANE FRIEDMAN, *Public Relations*

DICK GERSH, *Public Relations*

DONALD GOLDMACHER, *Medical Committee for Human Rights*

BILL GRAHAM, *Artists' Reps.*

JAMES GRANT,
Executive Director, New Mexico Governor's Crime Commission

MANNY GREENHILL, *Artists' Reps.*

TOM GRIMM, *Telephones*

ALBERT GROSSMAN, *Artists' Reps.*

BILL HANLEY, *Sound*

MALCOLM HART, *Preliminary Filming*

ABBIE HOFFMAN, *Atmosphere*

INTERMEDIA SYSTEMS, *Transportation and Efficiency*

EDDIE KRAMER, *Recording*

DAVID LEVINE, *Performers' Food*

CHARLES MACALUSO, *Trash and Carting*

MICHAEL MARGETS, *Preliminary Filming*

BOB MEURICE, *Motion Picture Producer*

DAVID MICHAELS, *Legal Rights Advice*

HECTOR MORALES, *Booking Agent*

LEE OSBORNE, *Recording*

ARNOLD PUFF, *tri-county citizens band radio club,*
Communications

BILL REYNOLDS, *Portable Toilets*

ALFRED ROBERTS, *John Roberts's father*

TOM ROUNDS, *Land Evaluation*

RIKKI SANDERSON, *Medical*

ARNOLD SKOLNICK, *Festival Poster*

TRI-COUNTY CITIZENS BAND RADIO CLUB, *Communications*

THE UP-AGAINST-THE-WALL MOTHERFUCKERS,
Threats and Excitement

MICHAEL WADLEIGH, *Motion Picture Director-Producer*

THE WARTOKE CONCERN, *Public Relations*

LANDOWNERS

HOWARD MILLS, JR., *Wallkill*

MR. SHALER, *Saugerties*

ALEXANDER TAPOOZ, *Woodstock*

MAX AND MIRIAM YASGUR, *Bethel*

THE LAWYERS

SAMUEL W. EAGER, JR., *Wallkill*
RICHARD GROSS, *Bethel*
MILES LOURIE, *New York City*
PAUL MARSHALL, *New York City*

ACCOMMODATIONS

THE DIAMOND HORSESHOE, *Bethel*
THE EL MONACO MOTEL, *Bethel*
THE RED TOP, *Middletown*
ROSENBERG'S, *Bullville, New York*

POLICE

RALPH COHEN, *NYPD, Festival Recruitment*
JOE FINK, *NYPD, Festival Recruitment*
HOWARD LEARY, *Commissioner, NYPD*
GEORGE MCMANUS, *NYPD, Chief Inspector*

WALLKILL

DENNIS COSGROVE, *Innkeeper*
IRV COULTER, *Town Clerk*
RICHARD DOW, *Concerned Citizens Committee*
HERBERT FABRICANT, *Attorney for Howard Mills*
HERBERT FREER, *Town Father*
LOUIS INGRASSIA, *Town Councilman*
HENRY ITZLA, *Town Councilman*
PAT MILLS, *Howard Mills's Wife*
JULES MINKER,
Attorney for Concerned Citizens Committee
JOSEPH OWEN, *Town Attorney*
CLIFF REYNOLDS, *Concerned Citizens Committee*
BRENT RISMILLER, *State Trooper*
AL ROMM, *Editor*
ETHEL ROMM, *Writer*
JACK SCHLOSSER, *Town Supervisor*
THE TIMES HERALD RECORD

BETHEL

MORRIS ABRAHAM, *Real Estate Middleman*

DANIEL J. AMATUCCI, *Town Supervisor*

JUDGE GEORGE L. COBB, *Heard Citizens' Complaints Against Festival*

HARRISON DUNBROOK, *New York State Transportation Director*

WILLIAM FILIPPINI, *Landowner*

LOUIS KOMANCHEK, *Town Father*

JOHN MONAHAN, *State Trooper*

CHARLIE PRINCE, *Branch Manager, Sidlivan County National Bank*

EMILY ROSCH, *Civil Defense Administrator*

CHARLES RUDIGER, *Superintendent, Monticello Schools*

FREDERICK W. V. SCHADT, *Town Attorney*

ELLIOTT TIEBER, *Motel Proprietor, El Monaco Motel*

KEN VAN LOAN, *Bethel Businessman*

TRAIN

GARLAND JEFFERIES

DON KEITER

BOB LENOX

PERFORMERS

JOAN BAEZ

THE BAND

BLOOD, SWEAT AND TEARS

CANNED HEAT

JOE COCKER

COUNTRY JOE MCDONALD & THE FISH

CREEDENCE CLEARWATER REVIVAL

CROSBY, STILLS AND NASH

GRATEFUL DEAD

ARLO GUTHRIE

TIM HARDIN

KEEF HARTLEY

RICHIE HAVENS

JIMI HENDRIX

THE INCREDIBLE STRING BAND

IRON BUTTERFLY *(failed to appear)*

IT'S A BEAUTIFUL DAY *(rejected)*

JANIS JOPLIN

THE JEFF BECK GROUP *(canceled)*

THE JEFFERSON AIRPLANE

THE JOSHUA LIGHT SHOW

MELANIE

MOUNTAIN

THE PAUL BUTTERFIELD BLUES BAND

QUILL

SANTANA

JOHN SEBASTIAN

RAVI SHANKAR

SLY AND THE FAMILY STONE

BERT SOMMER

SWEETWATER

TEN YEARS AFTER

THE WHO

JOHNNY WINTER

JOHN V. LINDSAY, *Mayor, New York City*

NELSON ROCKEFELLER, *Governor, New York*

HOWARD SAMUELS, *Lieutenant Governor, New York*

CHALLENGE INTERNATIONAL

MEDIA SOUND STUDIOS

Miracles are propitious accidents,
the natural causes of which are too
complicated to be readily understood.

—*George Santayana*

We are the music-makers,
And we are the dreamers of dreams,
Wandering by lone sea-breakers,
And sitting by desolate streams;
World-losers and world-forsakers,
On whom the pale moon gleams:
Yet we are the movers and shakers
Of the world forever, it seems.

—*Arthur W. E. O'Shaughnessy, "Ode"*

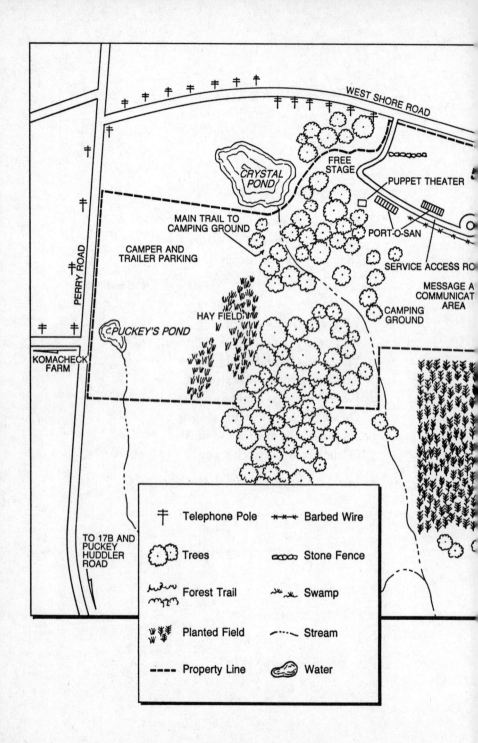

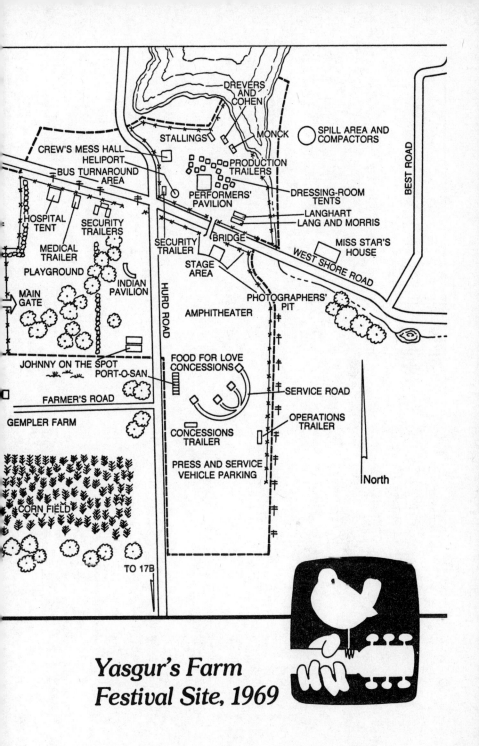

**Yasgur's Farm
Festival Site, 1969**

PART ONE

The Nation at Peace

CHAPTER ONE

Four Champions Fierce

From the beginning, the script reads like an MGM musical
comedy of the 1940s . . .   —*BusinessWeek*

— 1 —

A shrill alert penetrated the apartment's unruffled silence, startling the
two young men inside. John Roberts, who had been dialing a long-
distance call, vaulted toward the wall intercom and slapped the Talk button.

"Yes?" He automatically switched fingers to Listen. The doorman's heavily accented response crackled: "Meester Mike and Meester Arth."

Roberts peered over his shoulder to the velours couch where his friend
and partner, Joel Rosenman, was probing the circuitry of a disabled transis-
tor radio.

"Don't look at me." Rosenman shrugged, looking up from his surgery.

Roberts depressed the Talk button again. "Just a moment," he said, and
walked over to his desk. He flipped open a tan leather binder and ran his
finger over a dog-eared page. The cryptic entry in his appointment book
read simply: Lang/Kornfeld, 3:00. It was scrawled across the bottom of a
page dated "Thursday, February 6, 1969," a day that Roberts and Rosenman would forever inscribe as the moment of maculate conception, the birth
of the Woodstock Generation.

"These are the two guys Miles sent over," Roberts remembered. "I forgot
all about it."

"Me too," Rosenman said. "They're looking for money, right?"

Roberts said they were and instructed the doorman to allow their guests
into the building. He and Rosenman had halfheartedly agreed to see Lang/
Kornfeld on the recommendation of Miles Lourie, a prominent music-

business attorney, who represented an impressive roster of contemporary recording artists that included Ray Charles and Paul Simon. Lourie had heard through a mutual acquaintance that Roberts and Rosenman were rolling in investment capital and had called them a week earlier with a proposition.

"My clients have a unique approach to a recording studio," Lourie had said, holding back on the details. An old legal hoofer at heart, he played his cards slowly and with a dealer's reserve. Lourie, in fact, considered his clients' concept to be both economically sound and enticing, so much so that he was willing to represent it on a contingency basis. With the proper pairing of individuals, he envisioned everyone—including himself—profiting quite handsomely.

"All I'm asking is that you spend a few minutes with them, listen to what they have to say. And by the way, John, don't be put off by their appearance. They look a little different than the type of people you and Joel are accustomed to dealing with, but I think you'll find what they have to say refreshing."

The last thing John Roberts and Joel Rosenman wanted to do was to waste time listening to would-be tycoons with a penchant for sound systems and superstars. A few months before, after several false starts in private enterprise, they had been referred to a similar cartel intent on building a recording studio; that liaison had resulted in their involvement in a project called Media Sound (in which Roberts and Rosenman had become partners), that was now underway to their utmost satisfaction. Why should they waste their time mulling over an identical proposal?

Still and all, Miles Lourie was considered a moving force in an industry they were entering. It wouldn't do them any harm to be in his favor in return for a few minutes of their time. So John Roberts had consented to see Lang/Kornfeld at their convenience.

"You know anything about these guys?" Rosenman asked his partner, straightening up the pile of electrical scrap on the coffee table.

"Only that their first names sound like Meester Mike and Meester Arth—whatever the hell *that* means," he said, shaking his head discontentedly. "And . . ." *And, by the way, John, don't be put off by their appearances.* The lawyer's words came back to him as he straightened a few things on his desk. It was a peculiar statement for a lawyer to make about his clients.

"And?" Joel waited for Roberts to continue.

"Uh, nothing," Roberts said evasively as the door bell rang. "It wasn't important." And he moved in front of Rosenman to answer the door.

It wouldn't be Roberts's last appointment with this mysterious duo, although many of their subsequent encounters would not be arranged so easi-ly—*so exasperatingly easily!* For years to come, there would be moments when he would wonder in how many ways the course of his life might have been altered had he politely refused Miles Lourie's request. How indescribably empty it might have been—the colossal dream, the creativity, the excite-ment, the gamble, the recognition, the fame. Each memory invaded his senses the way a tilt-a-whirl whips a screaming child in and out of environ-mental focus. And after the legendary ride was over—when all contrasting recollections of enchantment and chaos had been sifted by perspective, by time—the inconceivable conclusion he always reached never failed to as-tound him: that given the chance, he would pull the magic lever and take the ride all over again.

Oliver Goldsmith once wrote that "friendship is a disinterested commerce between equals." If, in reality, there was ever an invisible line of demarcation drawn to define their worth to one another, neither John Roberts nor Joel Rosenman paid it any mind. Their friendship from the start was a genuine marriage of trust and admiration, neither lopsided nor doubted. If one of them needed advice, the other became father confessor; if there was a differ-ence of opinion, a compromise was eventually reached. It was that sort of give-and-take relationship, with impregnable bonds.

Roberts, a solid, bullish young man with pink dimpled cheeks, twinkling brown eyes that were dead giveaways in a poker game, and tousled, chestnut hair parted to the side, was three years younger than his friend. He had been born in New York City in 1945, four days before the German armies surren-dered to the Allied forces, and grew up in a small New Jersey army town. John's maternal grandfather, Alexander Block, was one of the early East Coast pharmaceutical empire builders. When he died in 1953, Block Drugs was divided among his children. Elizabeth Roberts, his only daughter, in-herited one third of a company grossing upwards of twenty million dollars a year behind such nationally renowned products as Polydent Toothpaste, Te-grin Medicated Shampoo, and the Pycopay line of accessories. But Elizabeth herself had been sickly, and it was not long after her father died that she, too, passed away at the age of thirty-nine. She was survived by three sons: Wil-liam, born in 1937; Keith in 1943; and John, her third and last child. John, who was eight years old at the time of his mother's death, with his two broth-ers, became a beneficiary of the Block Drug wealth.

Alfred Roberts, John's father, was left somewhat unprepared for the task of raising three sons, and he attempted it with diffidence. He was forty-six when Elizabeth died and never felt comfortable around Keith and John. "You're going to wind up *a bum*," he'd constantly berate John, who regarded school as primarily another social event.

In 1961, John preserved the Roberts family's Ivy League tradition without fanfare, and enrolled at the University of Pennsylvania. His going to college was merely intended as "doing the right thing" and, thus, he exhausted four years away from home, "having a great time and sliding by." Anyone evaluating his years at college would have summed them up in two words—*fraternity* and *friends*.

While an undergraduate at Penn, Roberts befriended a senior predental student named Douglas Rosenman, whose academic bravura complemented Roberts's open contempt for discipline. It wasn't long, however, before John came to realize that beneath the academically polished, all-American exterior, his new friend was tortured by a streak of insecurity. He was obsessed with the versatility of an older brother named Joel who seemed to have the aggravating habit of excelling in everything he attempted—and, to hear Douglas tell it, Joel had attempted everything at least once. It was not spite that Douglas nurtured, but jealousy, born together with love and admiration, the most painful kind of all.

Roberts soon tired of hearing about Joel's exploits and was determined that if he ever got hold of this living legend, he'd seek revenge for the number he had done on his friend Douglas.

All things considered, facing graduation, John Roberts was already a man of means in search of ways. He had inherited a cache of four hundred thousand dollars on his twenty-first birthday, and he was entitled to three separate payments of one million dollars on his twenty-fifth, thirtieth, and thirty-fifth birthdays. Accordingly, money, in the ordinary sense, was not a concern. However, he didn't care merely to live off his inheritance. But the question of what to do with his future remained. Oh, he was a talented horseman, could shoot eighteen holes in the low seventies on a good day, read about as many books as any member of his family, had an easy time acquiring and holding friends and, if one were to base an estimation of his coeducational finesse on the number of dates he had, an expert with women. But, while most of his friends (and women) devoted their full time to preparing for responsible careers, John Roberts was tensely biding his time. In the end, he was just another college kid burdened by millions of dollars.

— 2 —

The summer of 1966, what *Newsweek* billed as "the longest, hottest summer . . . the roughest in years," was the watershed for rebellion against the status quo. From then on, America's youth emerged as a group to be reckoned with. Suddenly, complaisance was designated as a treasonable offense by the young vocal masses: you were either for the draft or you evaded it; you supported the black power movement or you were a racist; you advocated the legalization of marijuana or you were a redneck. You took a stand and defended it. Everything had the potential for erupting into a passionately fought cause, and "right on!" provided the perfect wash. Within weeks, the lines were drawn across all traditions. It was child against parent, youth against the Establishment. No one knew what to expect.

By early June, for example, just before the University of Pennsylvania staged its graduation exercises at the wonderfully prehistoric Civic Center, the United States publicly admitted that it had conducted the first tactical bombing missions over Hanoi. Responding to Senator Fulbright's charge that the country was "succumbing to the arrogance of power," President Lyndon Johnson countered by advocating that "we must continue to raise the price of aggression at it's source." Students, who saw that price as being fixed relatively high in Washington, answered him by raising a phalanx of middle fingers. They saw themselves as apostles destined to change the course of history. And they were fired with determination.

Roberts watched this awakening skeptically, but he was a worried skeptic. He was cautiously amused by the movement's electricity but wondered where and how he would fit into it. He walked through commencement exercises shell-shocked, as one who had been abandoned in a crowd of strangers. Wherever he looked, his fellow Penn classmates filed past him, swelling with the pride of decision—an emotion he sorely lacked.

To others, John acted confidently. It was time, long past time, in fact, to make a few decisions about his future. He acknowledged to himself that if he made a clean break from the past, he'd be well on his way to standing on his own. At age twenty-one, it was something less than a prophetic revelation.

Graduation left John Roberts a displaced person on uncharted seas. He had no ambition, not even a glimmering of a concrete objective he could genuinely pursue. That was his singular punishment for inherited wealth. And he'd overcome it, he was convinced of that. His family harbored the hope that he might elect law as being as likely an alternative as any, but John put an immediate end to that; law placed too much emphasis on personal discipline.

Instead, he applied to the Annenberg School of Communications in Philadelphia on a part-time basis to study writing and literary criticism. He would have preferred entering Annenberg as a full-time student, but to escape being drafted and shipped to Vietnam, he had joined an army reserve unit at Fort Monmouth and had no idea when he would be called up to fulfill basic training. To keep him busy the other three days of the week, he accepted a position at a Wall Street brokerage firm as a research assistant.

Roberts tried to be a conventional businessman. He dabbled in the stock market, but his trading of securities was purely amateur ("speculative" being a term reserved for professionals who take *educated* risks) and took on a frightening, albeit recurring, characteristic: John handed Wall Street his money, and they handed him even less in return. Still, there didn't seem to be anything else looming in the future with which to occupy his time.

One afternoon John picked up the phone and was surprised to find an old friend on the other end of the line. Douglas Rosenman invited John to spend the weekend at the Rosenman family home in Long Island. "We could play a little golf, take in a few movies—you know, just take it easy, like old times. My brother, Joel, is out here. He's taking his bar exam, but will be finished in time to play golf with us. He's dying to meet you."

The name caught John completely off guard.

He was tempted to tell Douglas to make it another weekend; however, his curiosity got the better of him.

"You've got a deal, Douglas. Let me finish up here, and I'll see you Friday evening."

Joel joined them at a nearby golf course on Saturday morning. Much to his surprise, it was a thoroughly enjoyable interlude for Roberts. His apprehension was abated somewhat when he discovered that Douglas had come to terms with their previous rivalry. John, in fact, found himself enchanted by Joel. On the basis of previous descriptions of the older brother, he had expected an egotistical snob who would swagger across the course with them while playing his own unblemished game of par golf. Instead, he was charmed by Joel's friendliness and good-natured self-mockery; a young man of ordinary appearance and modest self-respect.

Joel Rosenman was of average height with active moonbutton eyes that seemed to balloon with excitement; Joel's aquiline face resembled a Shakespearean actor's chiseled, expressive features: cheekbones set high above gaunt cheeks, a jaw jutting forth from a thin, tight mouth. His black curly hair flopped along the sides of his temples and, from afar, he gave the impression of a shaggy dog playfully loping across a field. John was overwhelmed by Joel's carefree spirit, and they immediately struck up a relationship. By the end of the weekend, they had agreed to share an apartment in New York, where Joel was going to work at his uncle's law firm.

A month later, John Roberts and Joel Rosenman scoured the city in search of a place of their own. It took them two days to find an apartment within Joel's relatively conservative budget. But, more important, they spent most of that time locked in conversation. They opened up to each other in ways they had never thought existed. And at the end of those two days, John was convinced he knew Joel better than anyone else who had ever touched his life.

— 3 —

As a youngster, Joel Rosenman had developed a reputation for being a wise guy, rollicking in devilishness. He was a highly intelligent child, perky and aggressive, whose drive was shifted into high gear when it came to calling attention to himself in any manner possible. In school, at community functions, in a group of friends, Joel was constantly "on"—entertaining the way a comic creates his own applause, mostly at the expense of those around him. He had great energy, though; it billowed like contagious laughter and he drew others into this wonderful, fantastic child world with indefatigable verve.

There was hardly a time in his life when Joel Rosenman had *not* attempted to buck authority in one way or another. As a child in Cold Spring Harbor on Long Island, he was coddled by parents who indulged him the way one overlooks a genius's eccentricities. His father was an orthodontist, constantly on the move between his three suburban practices, and had precious little spare time to devote to a hyperactive son. As a result, Joel became a serious behavior problem, and he was bumped around from school to school in order to keep him slightly off balance.

When it came time to consider college, Joel's first reaction had been to put an abrupt, premature end to his formal education. But, like John Roberts, he succumbed to social pressure and enrolled at Princeton in the fall of 1959. Four years later, though, he was faced with still another leg of this now familiar dilemma: what to do after school was finished. The idea of continuing on to graduate school was not an appealing one and, yet, there was nothing more tangible on the horizon. He had no desire to teach, no attraction to commerce; though he was an artist of considerable merit, he foresaw the limitations of art as a profession. Law attracted the majority of his classmates, and Joel, totally oblivious of his stake in the future, decided to go with the flow.

In 1962, Joel Rosenman entered Yale Law School for many of the same reasons he had entered Princeton four years earlier. It had a good reputation, he could "bullshit his way through" with a minimum of effort (although while at Princeton he had to buckle down), and it would delay his having to make a decision that, he thought, would handcuff any future independence. Before long, he formed a college singing group that entertained at local clubs and hotel bars and was good enough to be booked as a lounge act at the Showboat Hotel in Las Vegas during summer breaks.

His current situation was not much better than John's. After law school was finished, he had been stranded on the podium, diploma in hand, waiting for inspiration to strike him.

It was common practice for recently graduated lawyers to comb New York's gray-flanneled firms and to grovel for the chance of filling some deserted cubbyhole where they could apprentice their trade. Joel, however, had exhibited nothing but disdain for the tradition—and he could afford to. While his classmates knocked on doors, opportunity beat its own path to Joel Rosenman; his uncle's practice was well respected and well connected, and he was welcomed there with open arms. But, like Roberts, he did not enjoy having success handed to him.

The Princeton Trio, as Rosenman's college group was called, was in demand on the coffee house circuit. They performed at a few celebrated New York clubs and were even scouted by Columbia Records' talent acquisition genius John Hammond, Sr. Hammond quietly took Joel aside one day and told him that Columbia would be interested in having him sign a record contract—but without the rest of the trio. Rosenman pondered the offer but eventually turned Hammond down, not wanting or *willing* to put in the necessary time or face the frustrations of a career in professional entertainment. Instead, he decided to slug it out as an associate in his uncle's prestigious law firm. He could still sing on his own time, and with a little luck, he might be able to settle down for a while.

Joel found that this pleasant picture of life was overturned by this reality: practicing law was even more dull than studying it. It was mundane, it was disciplinary—burdens he had so carefully avoided in the past. The thought of sharing an apartment with someone possessing the "sporting vitality" John Roberts exhibited was galvanizing to him. Here at last was the answer to some of his problems.

It wasn't long before John Roberts, too, realized the scope of their relationship, their interdependence, and upward mobility. He was certain that Rosenman was the one person on whom he could rely for friendship and motivation; Joel was assertive, a bit too cocksure of his own potential, skeptical of the counterculture—all qualities John was convinced were essential to his own growth.

The decision of Roberts to leave the Annenberg School of Communications in March 1967 and to pursue a business relationship with Joel Rosenman was anticlimactic. Joel, in turn, resigned his position at his uncle's firm with the hope of never returning to law. In all, he had been there less than six months.

Roberts was determined to continue his writing in one aspect or another. He had received rejection slips from all of his magazine submissions to date, but he got personal gratification from his work and was willing to wait patiently until some astute editor stumbled onto his talent. Joel also thought that writing would suit him, and they ascribed to the theory that two heads collaborating on manuscripts were better than one unpublished writer banging his brains against the wall. Furthermore, they reached the decision to write for television. That medium, they agreed, had the greatest potential for easy riches and instant fame, and it was a respectable career choice—one that their parents would be able to understand.

Joel had recently seen the movie *The Landlord* starring Beau Bridges and had identified with it from beginning to end. Its story line went something like this: A young man from a wealthy Westchester family inherits a tenement in Harlem and decides, against his parents' vehement protests, to become the resident slumlord. The young man's cunning soon wins over his angry tenants. And, of course, the predicaments he finds himself involved in from one extreme to the other are hilarious. Joel surmised that this was a universal concept, and they could adapt a similar story line for a series format. *Their* show would be about two men in their early twenties who pursue nutty business ventures and always manage to get themselves in over their heads; as the hour reached its end, the pair would be extricated by the miracle that somehow *is* television. (A year later, this farcical scenario would come back to haunt them in living Technicolor.)

It took Roberts and Rosenman about a week to write a proposal, which they rushed off to a television series packager who loved the idea. All he needed to cement a deal was a half-dozen episodic themes.

The only problem that stood between the amateur screenwriters and their creating a television dynasty was that, when it came to business, they were so inexperienced that they couldn't come up with a single insane business venture for the show. Everything they tried looked flat on paper.

At one point, however, John remembered that his brother, Billy, had at one time or another placed an advertisement in the newspaper looking for business capital.

"You'd never believe the assholes who responded," he told Joel, barely able to contain his laughter. "Every wacko in the county—no, excuse me, in the *world*—wrote in with their get-rich-quick schemes. It was a fiasco for Billy, but it kept us hysterical for weeks.

"Look, who *says* lightning doesn't strike twice! We compose an ad to lure these guys back out of the woodwork, and we're bound to wind up with the same type of idiotic schemes Billy got."

Joel finished the thought. "Instant zany business ventures for the series."

"Exactly."

Three days later, on March 22, 1967, the following ad ran in the "Capital Available" classified section of the *New York Times* and the *Wall Street Journal:*

> Young Men with Unlimited Capital looking for interesting, legitimate investment opportunities and business propositions.

The box at the respective papers to which reply was to be made was held in the name of Challenge International, Ltd., and, although the inquiries were to be "treated in the strictest of confidence" as protocol required, no disclaimer was made concerning the irreverent manner in which they were going to be used. The entire affair, as far as John and Joel were concerned, was to be played strictly for laughs.

The result was as expected: a prized collection of featherbrained offers. Sexual apparatus outdistanced the other inventions by nearly two to one. A man in Des Moines tendered an electric gadget guaranteed to bring about an orgasm with "shocking results." There were edible golf balls with subpar aftertastes, flying telephones that would land in one's lap upon ringing, a refrigerator that was programmed to inform its owner when it was out of certain staples, and an account of a proposed instrument designed to induce woodchucks to sing. John found one claiming that, for a mere $150,000, its author could tap the power from the eighth dimension. It was a carnival of absurdities. On the basis of the amount of preposterous mail they were receiving, they'd have enough material to get them through six years' worth of shows.

But not all of the ideas were laughable, and John and Joel found themselves intrigued enough by the feasability of some of them to investigate further. Eventually they realized they had stumbled onto a career. They had thoroughly enjoyed researching the plausibility of an investment and recognized that there had to be thousands of similar undeveloped opportunities waiting to be spawned. They were already endowed with perhaps the most scarce natural resource: John's money. And with a little help from their friends, Roberts and Rosenman let it be known around the New York business community that they would entertain any idea exhibiting commercial promise.

By early 1968, they had looked into a variety of business propositions, but nothing had come of it. Just when it seemed that they'd have to abandon Challenge International for something more concrete, a singing coach told Joel about a friend of his who was involved in an interesting project that needed completion capital. He sent Rosenman and Roberts to a man who, with a partner, had raised $66,000 for a planned recording studio. They explained that there was a severe lack of studio space in midtown Manhattan compared to the amount of contractual work offered by the recording companies.

Joel and John researched the material that was presented to them, greatly expanded on the concept to insure its financial soundness, and decided to see it through. It was something they would, indeed, be able to finance and *finish*; and it was both reasonable and secure. Their ensuing investigation substantiated that it was a long-term business, one that would regenerate itself in terms of profit. After checking further with John's investment counselors, they decided to accept an equal partnership in Media Sound Studios and, by the fall of 1968, construction was underway in a renovated church that they had purchased on West Fifty-seventh Street.

It was during this time, while supervising Media Sound's design, that they began to consider what their next project would be. Appointments had been made and kept regarding an assortment of ventures, but so far, nothing had turned up that interested them. The old anticipation began to creep up on them again, the way firemen get jumpy when it's been quiet for too long between fires. And just when it looked as though they needed a vacation away from the financial war zone, Miles Lourie called.

CHAPTER TWO

Estranged Bedfellows

What wretched—what miserable monster have I created?
                                        —*Dr. Frankenstein*

— 1 —

On February 6, 1969, already a few minutes late for their three o'clock appointment, Michael Lang and Artie Kornfeld got out of a Checker cab on Lexington Avenue and walked the short distance along Eighty-fifth Street to the new apartment building where Challenge International Limited had its headquarters. It was a crisp winter's afternoon, one of those days when people moved briskly from the pavement to warmer enclosures.

Once past the doorman, Lang and Kornfeld took the elevator to the thirty-second floor where they spent another minute or two picking out 32-C from a maze of numerical sequences over the apartment doors. John Roberts answered the door and invited them inside. As Michael and Artie stepped into the narrow foyer and removed their coats, the four boys exchanged an embarrassing rush of introductions to circumvent the culture shock they simultaneously experienced. Roberts wore a tailored, navy blue Brooks Brothers suit; Joel, dressed more comfortably, had on a yellow V-neck sweater over a white shirt and tie and gray slacks. Michael and Artie were hippies! Artie was "head shop mod," a suburban hippy, the diehards would call him, polished and practiced. His leather vest was expensive and covered a tasteful multicolored shirt with a pointed collar open at the neck. His bronze hair was long but sculptured, resting delicately on the back of his collar. As East Coast director of contemporary music for Capitol Records, he dressed so that he could attend conferences with artists as diverse as the Beatles and Nat King Cole without going through a costume change.

John and Joel were startled by Michael Lang's very presence. He was . . . well, in his own words: "real groovy," like Saint Exupéry's Little Prince. He seemed to glide when he crossed the room, in a shuffle that allowed him to slink unnoticed into the nearest corner but, in fact, drew attention by its very peculiarity. John, leaning against the piano, stared open-mouthed as Michael crossed in front of him and took a seat on the couch. He had seen kids like Lang hanging out on street corners asking for change and in newsreels about the hippie movement, but never before had he come into such close contact with anyone of Michael's ilk in a business dealing.

Lang, like Kornfeld, was dressed casually, although Michael's eclectic appearance was heavily accented by the coarseness of his street clothes: worn, faded jeans ripped and patched at the knee, scuffed sneakers, and a frayed leather vest draped over a T-shirt. His small, round face looked twice its size framed by a garland of long brown curls—like an Elizabethan actor's wig, Joel thought—and he carried a leather bag in place of a briefcase. John sized him up as an urchin. It would be a topic of amusement for the cocktail party he was going to later that evening.

"Uh, Miles told us that you gentlemen have an interesting proposition," John said, following them into the living room.

"You got it!" Artie said, cocking his thumb and forefinger like a loaded pistol. He settled into the couch along the far wall next to Michael. "We're onto somethin' so dynamite it can't miss. Man, it's so *involved*, so fuckin' outta sight."

John and Joel chose armchairs on either side of the couch. What could these people possibly want from us? Roberts wondered.

"You guys oughta know what we mean right away, your doin' a studio and all," Artie continued. "We have this far-out brainstorm for the same type o' scene but with an altogether different concept; different vibes, y'know: soft and groovy. A retreat."

Joel's eyes asked his partner what two hippies could possibly want with a monastery.

"Michael's like really into this already, man. Really. He's got his eye on this piece o' land up in Woodstock, a place upstate where this whole load of musicians hang out. It's pretty groovy—real rustic and laid back, y'know, and guys like Dylan, Tim Hardin, the Band, and the Spoonful live up there. The thing is, man, they've got no place to put down their tracks, no place where it's cool to act natural, do a few j's, y'know. They've gotta travel two hours into the city to make a new album and that's no good for their heads. We figure we can open a place up there where they can record and where other artists can sleep and eat and just groove on the magic."

Michael smiled in agreement. "And with Artie's situation bein' what it is at Capitol, he can send a lotta other dudes our way."

John and Joel exchanged an impassive glance.

"Michael's livin' up there doesn't hurt, either. He can hang out with all the music cats and make sure they work with us, y'know, bring their friends around for a little sweetening. Pretty soon, word'll get around that Woodstock's the scene to make. Like, *wow*, man, what a great place for musicians, bein' there and not havin' to leave and doin' whatever they want *when*ever they want. They can bop into the studio any time they get the urge and don't hafta leave until they come up with somethin' dynamite. As a producer, man, I *know* it's a group's dream."

"How did you and Michael come up with this idea?" Joel asked.

Artie waved the question off as though it was a well-known fact. "Simple, man. We have this thing goin' down together at Capitol. Michael laid a group on me and I was knocked out by them—a group called Train that he's managing—and we got to know each other super-well. We're like brothers, man. It took me a while to realize that, when it comes to the rock business and groovy music and all, well, Michael's a genius at gettin' things together. He's one of the real moving forces around rock today."

Michael smiled again, although this time he was faintly embarrassed. "Artie comes on a little heavy. He's the guy, though. He's been around and knows the score. Just havin' him along on this thing'll attract the biggest names in the business. We've *gotta* score big on this one. Can't miss."

"How long have you been in the music business?" Joel asked Lang.

"Not long. I did some shows in Florida, a festival too. But other than that, I've only been here a few months."

"But he's got it all down, man. He knows everything there is to know," Artie interrupted. *"Everything."*

"How would you handle something like this with your other job, Artie?" John asked.

"I don't intend to carry 'em both for long," Artie said more soberly. "I've been tryin' to unload my gig at Capitol for a while now. And this looks like the thing I need to tell 'em goodbye."

"Don't you think a studio such as this in a place like Woodstock is shutting yourself in?" asked Joel. "You're asking every recording artist to travel and bring their business to you. And that's a risky proposition in any book."

"No way, man. Once word circulates, artists'll make it their business to get up there and we'll be booked solid for years to come. It's outta sight, man. Just what they want."

Roberts and Rosenman looked skeptical, but Michael assured them that he was "in touch" with what was "going down in Woodstock" and how perfect a community it was. He knew what he was talking about and wanted to make his point. "A good top-of-the-line studio and a private lodge is novel. You don't have to be a Wall Street dude to understand that. It's innovative, and I don't think it can lose."

"Look," John interjected, "we really don't make it a habit of getting involved with something unless we can see it on paper."

Kornfeld assured him they would have something for his inspection in a few days' time.

"Just out of curiosity," Rosenman asked, "what do you think something like this retreat of yours would cost?"

Michael seemed to have all the answers. "About a half million bucks. Not a lotta bread for a gig that'll pay itself off in a year or two and'll then be pure gravy."

"And we can expand this sorta thing," Artie suggested. "I have a place in Eleuthra that's right on the water and real peaceful. It'd be a natural for a second retreat."

"Uh, yes. Well, thank you for coming, fellas," John said, standing up to signal an end to the meeting. The others followed his lead. "Joel and I would like to have a look at the entire dimensions of your studio idea when you get it down on paper. Why don't you give us a call, and we'll get together again?"

"No need," Michael stopped him. "We'll have it for you in two days."

"A complete proposal? With cash flows and equity splits?" Joel asked. His business acumen told him this was impossible.

"Sure thing, man," Artie agreed, slipping into his jacket. "How 'bout if we set something up now? Say, maybe, on the tenth—that's Monday—at the same time?"

John and Joel looked at each other with some degree of trepidation. "All right," they agreed, unable to give them a definite no. It was the only way they knew of getting rid of these characters.

Without another word, the meeting disbanded.

If John and Joel were the least bit intrigued by Michael and Artie's proposition, they kept it well hidden. The notion of tackling another recording studio after getting Media Sound off the ground bored them. It wasn't at all challenging. John thought it wondrously strange that Joel didn't just dismiss the proposition out of hand. And, yet, Joel seemed to be of a mind to keep the second appointment with Michael Lang and Artie Kornfeld rather than begging off and moving on to something with more inspired muscle. Joel, on

the other hand, was equally surprised that John hadn't immediately pronounced Michael and Artie "crooks" because of the way they were dressed
and their colorful, if somewhat incoherent, vernacular. In his estimation, the
deal was uninteresting. But Roberts, though he lived conservatively, was
envious of the cultural revolution and secretly wished to be a part of it. Nonetheless, they both agreed that the proposal lacked any new direction for
Challenge International. Their problem was they had never learned to say
no to anybody. Now they were committed to sitting through another meeting
with the hippies.

Monday afternoon, when Challenge International resumed its discussions with Lang/Kornfeld, the definition of the project was steered slightly
off course because of an item in the prospectus. Near the bottom of the
typewritten sheet itemizing the costs of the retreat, there was a random notation, an additional expense of a few hundred dollars curtained by the
heading: "Concert/Press Party."

By this time, John Roberts had succumbed to impatience and fidgeted in
his seat. He was totally opposed to becoming involved with this venture. He
felt the entire presentation—the motives, the concept, the physiognomy of
these so-called confederates—lacked a professional complexion; he and Joel
had already agreed not to undertake a duplicate project. He could not
fathom why Joel continued to pump them for additional information.

"What's this entry here about a press party?" Joel asked, dipping curiously over their papers.

Artie explained that in order to provide the opening of the retreat with a
festive atmosphere and an equally generous helping of publicity, he and Michael thought that a party for the media and other members of the rock
music community was in order. They would make an event of it, in true rock
tradition. They'd convince the local celebrities to attend and, if they were
extremely lucky, to perform. They had also toyed with the idea of putting
together some kind of concert with these artists, which would have the potential of financing the entire studio operation.

"This has real possibilities," Joel said, completely taken by the subject. "If
everyone could be persuaded to be there—Dylan, the Band, *everybody*—Jesus,
it could very well turn into a spectacular!"

Joel, unwittingly, had succumbed to Michael's devious talent for seizing
an opportunity. Now Lang was off and running with Joel's enthusiasm for a
concert of some kind. Along with Artie, he had tailored the press party to
Roberts and Rosenman's measurements. From the very beginning, Michael
Lang had envisioned a full-scale music festival to rival the likes of anything
ever put on in the world. The largest facilities available, the most awesome

gathering of rock talent on any stage, a massive turnout of people *(his* people) as thick as a blanket of autumn leaves covering the earth; his own personal party, the likes of which would never be forgotten. Now the opportunity presented itself. Michael's planning and outlining of a blueprint for promoting such a show had already taken up several months of his life; Artie's participation, the retreat, and his maintaining a low profile during these preliminary meetings were merely devices for achieving specific results—any results. The elements essential to his master plan, especially complete financial indemnification by a third party, were starting to fall neatly into place.

John Roberts was slowly (but very carefully) drawn into the fold. At first, he was merely an observer who graduated to being an inquirer. As the afternoon progressed, Roberts began actively participating in the formation of the game plan, often interrupting to make a clear point regarding the financing of the operation. He performed mentally a series of multiplications and arrived at some extremely tantalizing conclusions. Assuming a well-publicized event, with a super-talent drawing card, then according to the information Michael had fed them about previous festivals, they could expect upwards of fifty thousand people to attend their show. In 1967, Monterey Pop had attracted a crowd of forty-five thousand, and Newport, limited by a relatively small jazz audience, still managed to draw twenty thousand people a day. At five dollars per head, they could take in a quarter of a million dollars a day; if they were bold enough to put on a two-day show, he reasoned, they could double or triple their take, depending on the turnover.

"We can make a goddamn fortune!" John exclaimed in amazement.

Michael continuously fed the fire, dropping off bits of information like hot sealing wax to cement the even tenor of their conversation. He estimated that the cost of talent—if they went after every top group available—would be somewhere in the area of one hundred thousand dollars with a corresponding amount to cover the rest of their expenses. That would leave them a net profit of over three hundred thousand dollars, not including what they could gross on concessions, parking, and any number of ancillary businesses that they could put together along the way. Why, there might even be a film and a record sale from the concert (like at Monterey Pop) whose profits could exceed their wildest expectations.

The apartment had come alive with excitement over the prospects of putting on a Woodstock music festival to finance the retreat. Ties and jackets came off, shirt sleeves were rolled up, legal pads were brought out on which the four boys furiously scribbled their notes. As evening shadows crept across the living room, Joel got up to turn on some lights and casually put a record on the stereo as background music. "Inna godda da vida, honey/don't you know that I love you . . ." Michael's voice was an intoxicant in contrast to the droning of Iron Butterfly. With a master's sense of storytelling, he divulged to them his organizational resources as if they were facts, and not self-aggrandizement. He assured John, Joel, and Artie that he could handle the production. His experience promoting concerts in Miami had acquainted him with an expert staff of technicians and, with a little persuasion, they could be rounded up and brought on board to assist him. Artie's inherent sense of promotion, coupled with his industry connections, was more than sufficient to handle publicity and open record company doors; his experience in negotiating record contracts would also come in handy when and if the time came in which they had to consider a festival record deal. John and Joel would control the flow of money and arrange for ticketing. Their symbiotic relationship was, as Michael put it, "a natural."

The first order of business, they decided, would be to form a corporation for the mutual purposes of promoting a festival.

"Isn't that losing sight of our original concept?" asked Artie. "I really wanted to do the retreat we talked about. This festival stuff is a super idea, but the retreat, man, well—it's a full-time gig."

"Look," John said, "we'll get things moving for the festival, and the studio'll be a piece of cake."

Michael quickly came to Roberts's defense. "The festival'll help us to make a reputation for the retreat, man. These music cats'll get to know us at the show, and we'll hit 'em with the studio on the way out. Trust me, man. One follows the other."

Reasonably satisfied, Artie suggested they take an option on the land in Woodstock just to insure that it would still be available to them when the festival was over. Everyone agreed.

"Aren't we getting slightly ahead of ourselves?" Joel cautioned. "We're talking about money, land, festival, talent, studios. It's a little much to bite off in one afternoon's time. How about if we think things over for a while, jot down ideas and improve on our suggestions, and get together again in a couple of days to hash things out."

"Good idea," Michael agreed softly. "Where?"

Joel suggested Miles Lourie's office, but depending on everyone's mood, it could just as well be at their apartment or at Artie's place. "Let's keep it loose. But, by that time, everyone should have given some additional thought to how we should proceed."

Again, Michael edged to Joel's side. "Yeah. It's important we get rollin' as soon as possible. This thing'll sneak up on us before we know it, and timing's gonna be real crucial to pullin' it off before anyone else moves in on our action. Every fucker in creation's gonna want a piece for himself and we gotta be prepared to steamroll over 'em."

Everyone's head turned to Lang, half-stunned by this Napoleonic pronouncement of strategy. He had been casually restrained to a point of shyness, a timid prince seeking refuge in the shadows of outspoken kings. There were moments during the discussions when he withdrew completely, following the repartee with his silent eyes. Now, Michael revealed himself to the others as a seasoned guide, and Roberts and Rosenman reacted with astonishment. Michael caught their surprise and, with what was to become a familiar and recurring symbol of their consternation in the months ahead, held them at bay with a tight-jawed, childlike smile of defiance.

Somewhat uneasily, the four men stood up and shook hands on their future polity. This time, their physical differences were palled by unified aims and ultimatums. The Age of Aquarius was closer than even they thought.

Artie was ecstatic over the meeting's resolution. He blithely pranced out of the apartment building and into the street like a child who's just been told he is being taken on his first visit to the circus.

"This is it, man! These cats are goin' all the way down the line with us. Jesus, Michael! Didja see the way that guy Joel's eyes lit up?"

Michael smiled, more broadly this time, and held out his hand, palm upwards. Artie smacked it with all his might and returned the gesture.

"Yeah, they got it bad, man," Michael agreed. "Roberts is a goner."

"I saw him starin' at you with those big, wanting eyes of his. He was flippin' out. Shit, man—he wants to be hip in such a bad way, I thought for a moment he was gonna come over and sit on your lap." They laughed and slapped each other's palms again.

Slouched down securely in the back seat of a taxi, Michael lit up a joint, took a long, hard toke on the pulpy stump, and passed it over to Artie. He let his head fall gently against the torn leather seat cushion and closed his eyes. The rush of adrenaline Lang experienced bouncing on the back seat was fast and fluent. He let his mind wander, but his words were programmed with cold accuracy to summarize the matters at hand.

"They're only part o' the trip. We got it all this time, man. Music, movies, finance, recording studios, hotels, land. Man, the fuckin' world's at our feet. We're locked. Know what I mean?"

Kornfeld's giddiness signified his absolute elation, an intoxicated delight, and he was reconciled to facing a future of predominant well-being with the full tide of grace. This Woodstock venture—the retreat, the festival and who

knew what else would come out of it—would just about insure his future independence.

— 2 —

Artie Kornfeld's autonomy, in point of fact, unfolded from a time when he
was very young and growing up in an assortment of cities along the eastern
seaboard. His father, the eldest of eight children born to Russian immi-
grants, had become a policeman during the Depression as a means of supporting the family. Artie's mother was a self-educated woman unsparingly
dedicated to blind-alley liberal causes. Together, they moved from precinct
to precinct, from crusade to crusade, faithfully climbing each rung of the
social ladder and "bettering their American dream." When Artie was born
in Coney Island in 1942, they were caught in midstream of fulfilling their
ambitions but continued to move forward with intransigent fascination for
what life would bring them. By the time he graduated from high school,
Artie had attended fourteen schools, and as a result, he found himself able to
assume any cultural attitude for which the situation called.

During the middle-1950s, the Kornfelds moved their home base to
Charleston, North Carolina, where Artie got his first taste of grass-roots rock
and roll—not the kind that was bleached of its energy and recycled for white
audiences up north, but the Negro rhythm and blues culled from gospel
music and field chants. He was overwhelmed by its wildness, the screaming,
unintelligible choruses that rang over and over in his head. It affected him
perhaps more than anything else he had ever experienced. The Chords,
Ivory Joe Hunter, the Gladiolas, Stick McGhee—magic voices that pumped
out 45 rpm records audibly defining what another favorite of his, Little Richard, called "the healing music—the music that makes the blind see, the
lame, the deaf and the dumb hear, walk and talk." For Kornfeld, it was all
so evilly irresistible. Before long, he had wheedled his way into a job carrying
buckets of ice and soda at the Charleston Coliseum where he was exposed to
artists such as Chuck Berry, Little Richard, Buddy Holly, and Fats Domino.
It was a far cry from his other part-time work, organizing the mailing lists
for Harry Golden's Carolina *Israelite*, which his mother had arranged for
him. The two, however, managed to coexist until it was time, again, for his
family to pull up stakes for the move back north.

Once back in New York, he became totally immersed in city blues variations on the southern rock phenomenon. Electric blues had crept into the predominantly white ethnic neighborhoods in such a way that it was becoming popular for teen-age quartets to gather on playgrounds and in front of luncheonettes in the Bronx, Brooklyn, and Queens where they improvised four-chord melodies. By the time he was sixteen, Artie was writing music and playing with the top local bands.

Artie continued making demos of his songs while in school. By 1963, it was monopolizing so much of his time that he transferred to night sessions at Queens College and worked on his music during the day. It was there that he met Charlie Koppelman, a songwriter who, along with two friends, had just recorded a tune as The Ivy 3, called "Yogi." Koppelman suggested Artie meet a friend of his—a young music publisher named Don Kirshner.

A week later, Kornfeld took the subway into New York City, met with Kirshner and signed a contract with Aldon Music to write songs for $125 a week advanced against future royalties. He would have accepted payment in glass beads, but he didn't tell Kirshner that. It was the music business; he had dreamed of this happening to him for ten years. Now he had become part of it.

Kirshner's office at 1650 Broadway was considered the nucleus of New York's burgeoning rock empire. The building housed the archives of the Tin Pan Alley era—the publishers, the indignant cigar-smoking managers, roving songwriters, and independent record companies—and was in the process of making the much-resisted transition from swing to rock. When Artie began work there, writing teams such as Neil Sedaka and Howie Greenfield, Barry Mann and Cynthia Weil, and Carole King and Gerry Goffin were churning out hits faster than Kirshner could locate singing groups for them. Five music rooms constituted the creative wing of the publisher's suite, and each morning, the young resident writers would fight over who got what rooms. Space was scarce and everyone wanted to work. By ten-thirty, Kirshner would frantically pop into each room pleading for material.

"We need a song for the Shirelles in *two days*, a song for Dion in *three!* Let's hear those pianos going!"

Before long, Artie had several hits on the charts. For the Shirelles, he wrote "Tonight You're Gonna Fall In Love With Me" with Toni Wine, and "I Adore Him" for the Angels, which he penned with a handsome, blond-haired boy from California named Jan Berry who later formed one half of the singing group Jan and Dean. Jan subsequently introduced Kornfeld to a surfing buddy named Brian Wilson, and the three collaborated on the classic hit "Dead Man's Curve" and an additional four songs for Jan and Dean's *Drag City* album.

Artie married a girl from Forest Hills several years younger than he, with whom he had been going steady, and decided to look for security. He accepted a job as director of Artists and Repertoire for Mercury Records, and stumbled across a family act named the Cowsills whom he thought had immeasurable potential as superstars. He contacted his current writing collaborator, told him about the group, and together they sat down to write a hit for the Cowsills.

They wanted to write a "flower song" to commemorate what was happening on the West Coast. That spring of 1967, a youth crusade for peace and love was emerging from San Francisco's rock underground and was spreading eastward. Everyone, young and old, was seduced by its ingenuous rallying cry: "Flower Power!" "It can't miss," they agreed.

The lyric that emerged from their collaboration entitled "Rain, the Park, and Other Things," was about falling in love with a young hippie girl and was originally planned as a ballad:

> I love the flower girl,
> Oh I don't know just why,
> She simply caught my eye,
> I love the flower girl,
> She seemed to have the way
> To find a sunny day.

The song was an immediate hit and Artie left Mercury to enter into an independent production deal with the Cowsills, for which he also received a percentage of the management and control of their music-publishing interests. He stayed with them through 1968, producing and writing the group's material. When he left, he emerged from his Cowsill Connection independently wealthy; he had produced two triumphant albums on the heels of successive gold singles for them and would continue to earn royalties from the existing product on the market. Therefore, earning a livelihood didn't appear to be a problem; a spate of related projects would see him handily through the next few years. Soon thereafter, however, his old friend Charlie Koppelman, who had also been making a name for himself producing teen-oriented acts for various labels, insisted upon introducing Artie to Alan Livingston, who, at the time, was the president of Capitol Records.

Livingston and Kornfeld hit it off so well that Artie was offered a job at Capitol on the spot. They created a special position for him and a title to suit his luminous ego: Director of East Coast Contemporary Product. His chief function, concealed somewhere beneath the grandeur of that label, was to seek out and sign new hard-rock groups—a specialty they sorely lacked. To protect himself and to guarantee some job security, Artie asked to be placed under a two-year contract with the company, and Livingston agreed.

Capitol was a Mormon-owned company that, most industry insiders agreed, had been relatively lucky in putting out records by the Beach Boys and the Beatles in the years between 1961 and 1968. But once he was firmly installed into their corporate machinery, Artie found Capitol's problem to be far deeper than anything money or appearance could correct. He discovered they already *had* the types of groups they were looking for under contract; the Band, Bob Seger, Quicksilver Messenger Service, Joe South—all were artists who appealed to the flower generation's electric tastes. The company's antiquated focus, however, was more sharply directed at maintaining the supremacy of their stalwart sellers, the Lettermen and Guy Lombardo and his Royal Canadian Orchestra.

It was a more difficult task than even he had imagined. Whenever he registered a complaint with the company's board of directors about all the promotion given the Lettermen, he was punctually shown the accounting department's balance sheet on them. "These young men have been making a lot of money for us over the years, Mr. Kornfeld. You can't argue with success." For Kornfeld, it was a rude awakening about the realities of the business of rock and roll.

One afternoon, in late November 1968, Kornfeld's secretary buzzed him over the intercom and announced, "There's some kid out here who wants to see you. He says his name's Lang. Michael Lang."

Because of his earlier experience at 1650 Broadway with hordes of incredibly talented songwriters roaming the corridors trying to get their material heard, Artie's policy was to interview everybody who approached him with a tape. He also felt that since Capitol Records was the beneficiary of millions of dollars yearly from young people he would like to spend some of it on New York kids to give them a start.

Artie was amused by Lang's cherubic appearance—"like some kind of magic pixie," he later told his secretary. Artie was growing used to having hippies with long, stringy hair down their back ushered into his office, but although he was a product of the same culture, Michael Lang was noticeably different in his approach. He was not overly confident or demanding like his counterparts. If anything, "he was very shy and timid" and approached Artie as if he had been granted an audience with the king.

Lang had been around—*that* Artie was sure of. He carried himself in the manner of a vulnerable kid who possessed the mystical ability to beat others at their own game by the power of suggestion. Artie warmed to him imme-

diately. There was something about Lang's presence he found totally disarming. He was a phantasm, both real and deceptive, and Artie wanted to learn
more about him.

Lang told Artie that for the past couple of years he had been hanging out
wherever the scene was fast and then moving on, trying to elbow in on the
local action and make a few bucks. Like Kornfeld, Lang was originally from
Brooklyn. He had scraped around there for most of his twenty-three years,
but when he experienced the new, free spirit taking hold in Greenwich Village, he moved to Florida and opened the first head shop there in Coconut
Grove. His idea was to carry the spirit with him and spread it across the land
as if it were a religion. He held Artie transfixed with stories about the characters he met there—smugglers, dope dealers, two-bit gangsters, bikers
musicians—and about his dabbling in the local rock and roll scene. He had
sweet-talked his way into the Miami concert circuit and had put on a few
minor shows there, including a small festival. But he decided to "bag it" for
management because "that's where the real bread" was Lang had found a
hard-rock group called Train, which he had signed to a management and
production deal, and he was now working on getting their act together. He
lived in upstate New York in a small arts and crafts village called Woodstock.
Artie had never heard of it.

"This band's outta sight, man," Michael opined in a manner that seduced his listener into agreeing with him even before hearing the band. Artie
found himself nodding in agreement. Lang projected an image of being in
touch with what was happening and with what was vital. "They're gonna
blow you away!"

Artie wound the tape onto a recorder behind him. When he turned back
to inquire at what speed the material had been recorded, he found Michael
holding out a lighted joint to him. The gesture of friendship caught Artie
off-guard and he was visibly shaken.

"It's cool, man," Michael advised, smiling warmly. "It's nothing to get
uptight about."

"I'm not uptight," Artie protested, accepting the joint and dragging on it
as though it were an everyday occurrence. He choked mildly on the smoke
as he tried to hold it down. According to Artie, not only had he not done any
grass before, he had never experienced anyone smoking dope in the Capitol
offices. It just hadn't been a part of the record scene as he knew it; the groups
smoked, sure, but *never* while they were in the building. The whole thought
of getting high in his office was exhilarating to him. Wouldn't it only serve
to heighten his perception of the music? Wasn't that his job—to be totally
"turned on" to what was going down in the music scene? If those Mormons

could only see him now, Artie thought. They'd head back to Salt Lake City faster than they could count their Lettermen profits.

Lang's grass was far superior to his band. Kornfeld thought Train was "awful, very untogether." They tried to combine too many strains of music on top of one another: jazz, blues, acid rock, free-form synthetics. It just didn't work.

"Uh . . . nice," Artie said when the tape had run out. "They're, uh, innovative, really different, man. Let me think about it, listen to it a few more times, and we'll see what we can do. In the meantime, whaddya say you come over to my place for dinner tonight. I'd like you to meet my wife, and we can hang out awhile."

That night, the two boys, along with Linda Kornfeld, stayed up until long after midnight trading stories about music, drugs, the war, the impending revolution, the music business—Michael devoured tales about the music business like a child with an ice cream cone—and cemented a relationship they all pledged to continue. Artie "saw a very sharp mind, someone who has the power to see beneath the surface of everything and who was also fun to be with." He saw their friendship as a vehicle for making some of his own dreams come true.

Before the evening ended, Kornfeld had committed Capitol Records to enter into a business arrangement with Michael Lang for Train. Artie considered it to be a fair trade; he would teach Michael about the music business, and in return, Lang would teach him about the street. Kornfeld informed him that he could arrange an immediate ten-thousand-dollar advance for Lang so he'd have some money to live on, and they could probably swing the whole deal for something in the vicinity of one hundred fifty thousand dollars. Artie, of course, would produce Train's albums.

Michael offered his hand, which Artie shook vigorously and without hesitation. He looked directly into Michael's eyes and knew he was on the brink of an important step in his life.

"It's only the beginning," Michael said, and he disappeared into the night.

— **3** —

Michael Lang was convinced that Kornfeld would come through with the proposed contract for Train. He considered himself a good judge of character and had an intuitive line on Artie which he believed was invincible. The day after their introductory meeting at the Capitol offices, Lang called the group's drummer, Don Keiter, and casually dropped their good news in his lap.

Kieter listened to Lang's otherwise convincing hyperbole with reticence. More times than he cared to remember, he had been enticed by Lang's "sleight of hand" into taking part in some sort of flamboyant moneymaking scheme. The only person who ever profited from these schemes seemed to be Michael. Their last commercial adventure, a psychedelic poster business in Miami, was a depressing memory. According to Keiter, Michael had "conned" him and a woman artist into designing a series of Day-Glo posters that the three of them would subsequently distribute to gift shops as equal partners. After a few months' inactivity, Keiter began seeing their posters displayed for sale in store windows around the area, but neither he nor the woman ever realized a cent from the project. Nor did he find out who *made* money from the deal. But he had his suspicions.

Michael continued to promote his relationship with Artie Kornfeld, spending each available evening at the record executive's Manhattan apartment playing bumper pool and getting high until there was just enough time for him to catch the last bus back to Woodstock.

One of their few bones of contention was the fact that Artie refused to attend rock concerts. Michael found this wildly sacrilegious coming from a guy who was supposed to be on top of the music scene. Artie attemped to defend himself by explaining that he had more creative matters at heart, especially an idea for a Broadway show.

"It's called *The Concert,* and I'm gonna write it with Anthony Newley," he boasted. "It has to do with this composer, see, who is a truck driver and leads a Walter Mitty–type existence. He drives during the day but is really composing this fantastic rock symphony in his head all the while."

"Outta sight," Michael said, infatuated by the concept.

"It gets better. Y'see, no one really pays much attention to him. They think he's pretty flipped out, but he never gives up. Then, one day, outta nowhere, this record cat gives him a break. The whole thing goes down beautifully. Like, he cuts the rock symphony—right?—and it blows everybody's fuckin' mind. It's sensational. And that's the whole second act of the play."

"What is?"

"The concert, man. Dig it! This cat just stands center stage and lays down the whole rock symphony in sequence. Y'know, two hours of solid music. And the audience spaces out. I mean, they walk outta that theatre hummin' the whole fuckin' score, man. And the next thing you know . . ."

"They head for the closest record store and pick up the sound track."

"Right fuckin' on!"

"What a trip!"

"And I'll give you one guess who writes the rock symphony, owns all the publishing to it, and produces the original score."

Michael shook his head and laughed. "You got it all together, huh?"

"Bet your ass. I been runnin' this thing through my head for at least a year. A rock concert and a Broadway show squeezed into one and tossed out there onto the street—man, it's gotta be the hottest thing goin'. We'll do the place up in strobes and lasers and send 'em into orbit."

"Shit, man—it's got incredible possibilities," Michael stroked his smooth chin and looked up at Artie. "Who you gonna get to be the truckin' dude?"

"Dunno. I been playin' with a few angles. Hell, could you dig gettin' someone like the Beatles or Dylan—or even Sly, man—to do it? It'd be the fuckin' Who's Who of hard rock. It could run forever!"

Lang pondered the concept. "Y'know, I worked on this thing in Florida where a buncha us got together, rented out this race track, and had something like twelve or fifteen groups show up for a two-day gig. A rock festival, sorta. It was a pretty heavy trip. I was just thinkin' . . ."

"Yeah?"

"Now, this is just an idea. Like, we use what you just told me—the show thing—but we do it outdoors and have twenty fuckin' groups do different parts of the symphony. At a stadium, or someplace that can hold a lotta people. And we do it over a whole weekend. Whaddya think?"

"You kiddin'? I think it'd be the biggest fuckin' bash anyone's ever seen before. A monster. I don't know anyone who *wouldn't* wanna be there."

"And kids could crash there and do whatever the hell they wanted to do without gettin' uptight that some ol' fucker next to 'em's gonna blow the whistle on them."

"You're fuckin' amazing, Lang. But y'know, the thing to do is to buy the land and keep the show runnin' in cycles. Have the symphony goin' on for a few days, give the crowd a day or two to clear out, and then do it all over again. Hell, we could even put a recording studio on the property for during the week to keep the groups busy. We'd be booked forever. What an in-fuckin'-credible idea!"

"It's not so incredible," Michael said with a straight face. "Think about it. We get a couple o' dudes to go for the bread and we're halfway there. It won't be any problem gettin' the groups to go along with it. All you gotta do is pay 'em enough and they'll materialize outta nowhere."

"Think so?"

"I *know* so. You start spreadin' around big bucks, the kinda bread that stuns even these fat cat musicians, well—you'll wind up holdin' most o' the cards. You oughta know, man. Offer someone like Richie Havens a bundle and see if he doesn't start singin' round your door."

"You got the music business down better'n I thought."

"It's just *smart* business, man. It's how you play the game."

"We've gotta pull something like this off, Michael." Artie grew intensely serious. "We could record every top name in the business and they could live right there until they got bored with it."

"Like a retreat."

"*Right*—a rock retreat. It even makes good sense. These acts could make money comin' from both ends without movin' so much as two feet. It'd be a dream come true for them. But it's gonna take a fuckin' money machine to float a thing like that."

"Not really, man. Truth is, you've probably got the bread right at your fingertips."

"I couldn't swing it, man. Linda'd kill me."

"No," Michael said. "Not your own money. Record company money. You got all the connections."

Kornfeld clapped his hands together and jumped in the air. "It's so logical, it's silly!"

"How 'bout Capitol? Think they'd go for it?"

"Not a chance. They're too fuckin' straight for something like that, man. We'd be forced to bring the Lettermen up there and that'd blow our deal, for sure. No. But there's a couple music heavies who'd go for it. At least, I know 'em well enough to ask 'em what they think of it. I've only gotta know the answer to one question before I lay it on 'em."

"What's that?"

"Where we're gonna have this retreat."

Michael only smiled.

— 4 —

Nobody is quite sure about how Michael Lang came to settling in the village of Woodstock in 1968. Some say he simply appeared out of thin air, like Merlyn, and proceeded to cast a spell over those whose lives he chose to touch. Mothers wanted to mother him, lovers fought to make love to him, pigeons flipped coins over who would take a dive for him. And all the while, Michael Lang kept his mouth shut and smiled warmly; by the grace of guile, he glided through introductions to Woodstock's charmed circles with unassuming restraint. He had not, however, been there more than a week before he began soliciting money to promote rock shows. Rock was the coming messiah, he proselytized, and five'd-get-you-ten that backing outdoor shows featuring the hottest groups in the country was the quickest route to cornering a substantial piece of the rockpile.

Lang was the sideshow barker, the charming virtuoso whose every angle had a sterling silver hook attached to it. No one willingly put their full trust in him, yet everyone was eager to take a flier that his friendship would produce excitement for their success-starved existences. And, yet, Lang had nothing tangible to offer these ready-cash customers. What he effortlessly dispensed was a commodity ten times more potent than psychedelic music or marijuana. It was an aromatic blend of personality and dreams, a Utopian illusion for which the common herd sold their souls. It was pure and simple Michael Lang, and, in the words of his father, "Nobody sells Michael better than Michael."

Michael was well aware of his gift for creative inveigling. From the time he was ten when the patent for an invention called the electric toothbrush was pulled out from under him, Lang's ethic (a childhood friend claims) was catch-as-catch-can with a dash of smile and a flash of the eyes. He had what it took, and he took what he could.

High school was a thorn in his side. Michael's IQ was exceedingly high, but he rejected any subject that did not come easily for him. He had an inventor's mind and a mule's disposition. If it didn't come to him, he wasn't interested.

When he was seventeen, Michael began fantasizing about running away to Florida. He had relatives there, including a cousin, Al, whom he idolized. His mother was pushing him to go to college, but Michael quashed that argument when he failed to graduate from high school with his class. New York University still agreed to accept him, pending his taking a makeup course during the summer, because his aptitude tested so well, but Florida had become something of an obsession. And now his dream entertained a new twist: He wanted to open up a head shop there.

His ambitions were intensified by two related influences: the cultural revolution that was unfolding in the Village and a twenty-year-old girl named Ellen.

Hippies had run the Beatniks off MacDougal Street with unpardonable reproof. They replaced that dark era of black turtleneck sweaters and bongo drums with rainbow gaiety, strobe lights, and a softness of dress and emotion never before exhibited by Village inhabitants. Rock usurped jazz, drugs supplanted alcohol and adolescents swarmed in from parts unknown. Michael plugged himself into the eye of the hurricane with a tireless enthusiasm. He'd walk the streets into the early hours of morning turning on to the lights, the pulsating music coming from the cafés and the general environmental excitement.

Michael begged his parents to help him get started with his head shop. He had estimated an investment on their part of about ten thousand dollars to get him off the ground. He'd relocate in Miami where, he was convinced, he could capitalize on the college and tourist trade. Pretty soon the whole world would be hip to psychedelic paraphernalia—pipes, T-shirts, leather vests, black-light posters, incense—and he'd have the South virtually sewn up.

His mother was against his going. Two years before, Michael had pleaded with her for a sports car, and she was still blaming that extravagance for his failure to graduate from high school. But Michael threatened to go anyway and to sleep in the street until he found his metier. His parents had no other choice and soon gave in. He could have the money, but they advised him to use it wisely and to make all arrangements for his enterprise before he left Brooklyn. That way, he could change his mind if he found it to be impractical.

Michael, along with his new partner, Ellen, packed up the car with all the merchandise they had collected and headed toward Florida. But Michael was tired of his little turn-on-a-dime sports car and, instead, rented a spotless new Cadillac with power steering, power brakes, power windows, the works: a perfect vehicle for a hippie out to establish himself among his peers. No particular destination, just Florida. Maybe Miami, or Coconut Grove, whatever carried the most appeal once they arrived.

Florida, as Lang soon discovered, instead of being the land where dreams came true, turned out to be a state filled with such paranoia and hatred for hippies that they almost turned around and headed back to New York. But they found a beautiful little gift shop for rent in Dade County across the street from the University of Miami and they set up a store called The Head Shop.

The night they officially opened for business, the street had been cordoned off and a rock group played on the front lawn. The Head Shop was the first establishment of its kind to open in the Miami area, and the students treated it as a sacred event. Business was spectacular; Michael had become a neighborhood celebrity.

At about eight o'clock, in the heat of the festivities, several patrol cars pulled up to the Head Shop's entrance. Cops emptied out carrying sledgehammers and descended upon the crowd.

"Where's your license?" they demanded. Of course, all Michael had to show them was a temporary license that had been granted by the city a few days before the opening. "Well you can't open until you have a license. You broke the law and you've got to pay the price." Within an hour, they had completely demolished the store and everything in it.

The next week, Michael and Ellen packed the car, took what little money they had left and opened the Head Shop South in Coconut Grove, an artist's community twenty miles from Miami Beach. They were still harassed by the local police, but so were all the other store owners, and as long as they behaved, they were allowed to remain open for business.

One evening in 1967, Michael and Ellen closed the store early and took an acid trip together. Michael had the tendency to babble profusely while under the influence of LSD, and this night, he talked at length about his "concept of a Nation" which he had set out to create, similar in structure to that of a tiered cake. His visions about it were quite lucid. "The first tier was the store with all the paraphernalia, nice karma, peaceful music. The second floor would have subtle changes, the sound and the texture maybe. The walls would begin to lose their shape, items that had a substantial feel would feel different on the next level. Everything would begin to shed its former skin as you climbed higher and higher. As you became accustomed to one experience, you'd want to seek the next. And by the time you got to the top, you were, in fact, free. Nirvana. A floating feeling and sounds, sensations, tastes—all free. A total environment. A nation away from war and racism, where drugs were easily accessible. With rock music and toys everywhere you turned."

Ellen became so excited by his discourse, she thought it was going to take place right then and there. When they finally came down from the trip, they continued their discussions about this "Nation" concept and about how it could become a total media environment. "We can do it, kid," he assured her. "I know it was just a trip, but it can be done. I know it."

But it wasn't to be done with Ellen. Soon thereafter they separated and Lang decided it was time to make his move on the Miami rock scene, to branch out into other directions. He met a dapper older man named Peter Goodrich who catered to Lang's fancy for stories about scams and cons in which Goodrich had been involved.

To Lang, Goodrich represented all the things that were appealing. He led a life of intrigue, spent money on the finest clothing and food, spoke several languages fluently and travelled in fast company. And, above all, Goodrich presented himself as an international playboy. "The guy has style," Lang observed after making Goodrich's acquaintance. "He's got plenty of bread, and he knows people with the right connections."

Through Goodrich, Lang began laying his own groundwork for a move into the music business. It didn't take him long to organize a clique of investors under the corporate title of Joint Productions whose purpose it would be to stage a series of rock shows at the Gulfstream Racetrack on the fringe of Miami Beach. One of his partners in the co-venture was Don Keiter who introduced Lang to agencies handling rock bands and to an entirely new population of road managers, equipment men, and groupies. Gulfstream was organized much to the dismay of the local government and featured such performers as the Mothers of Invention, Jimi Hendrix, the Crazy World of Arthur Brown, John Lee Hooker, and Chuck Berry. Unfortunately, two of its three scheduled days were rained out and promoters suffered a sixty-thousand-dollar loss. More instrumental in the corporation's dissolution was the ugly scene going on backstage during the final day of the show. Lang had hired an ex-cop from Fort Lauderdale to act as a private security official to guard the box office receipts. He, in turn, hired several other men to assist in that task. When it became apparent that the promoters stood to lose their shirts, the private security force attempted to stop a Brinks truck from entering the gates so that they could transport what money there was to a local bank. The head of security had an alternate plan; he was going to lock his men in the money room and make sure they got paid first—in cash—before any money was taken from the track. The Brinks forces managed to reach the counting room at the same time as the private patrol and both sides drew their guns. It was up to Michael Lang to settle all accounts.

Michael made one phone call. One of his associates was a prominent Miami businessman with "connections" and, within minutes, he had the entire matter under his control.

Lang, to no one's surprise, made a beeline for New York until things cooled off back in Miami.

Once there he found himself drawn to a place upstate called Woodstock.

He had read a few articles about the village's arts and crafts reputation and about how it was opening up to the popular arts because of rock musicians who had recently made their homes there. Among the names mentioned in the articles were Bob Dylan and his backup group, the Band. The name Woodstock had a strange mystical ring to it, Lang thought, some kind of hip allusion to fertile land and rivers. Woodstock was synonymous with nature in his mind. He didn't know why, and therein lay its allure. It must carry some spiritual significance. The Promised Land: *Woodstock*.

In November 1968, Michael was reunited with Don Keiter, who was then part of a band called Mandor Beekman after a Manhattan apartment house. Lang "got off on the group" and welcomed them as a possible entree for him into the music business. He offered his services to them as a professional rock manager and professed to be able to sell their services to a major label. Falling flat for the Lang charm, they agreed to sign a management contract for which Michael would be well compensated if he brought about all he promised. His only suggestion upon hearing them was that they change the name of the band. They decided it was to be called Train.

Within three weeks after the management papers had been signed, Train was committed to a long-term deal with Capitol. Lang had performed some sort of magic as far as they were concerned. What Keiter couldn't figure out was "how the curly-haired kid managed to get his foot inside the door" so quickly. He knew that Lang's only approach was to go knocking on doors hoping that some tired executive's will would finally be broken down.

That was exactly what Lang had done. After a few curt rebukes at other record companies, he had gone to Capitol Records, where he was soon shown to Artie Kornfeld's office by one of the division assistants. When she opened his door and Michael "saw Artie giggling and diving off his desk," he knew his problems were over. According to Michael, he was not the one who introduced Artie to psychedelic drugs.

— **5** —

Kornfeld felt that the second meeting with Challenge International had been most successful. All indications pointed to some sort of formal offering being presented to them at their next rendezvous with Roberts and Rosenman.

As far as the budget that John and Joel had requested of them was concerned, Artie and Michael decided to improvise. "I've got a general idea what we spent on some of the gigs I did in Florida," Michael said. "What I don't remember, we'll just make up. They won't know the difference, and by the time they suspect anything, we'll have produced the genuine goods."

The two boys pasted together a superficial budget, consisting of one typewritten page of lump sums, which they presented to Roberts and Rosenman at the next meeting.

"You've got to break some of this stuff down for us," Roberts advised them. "Otherwise, Joel and I are ready to go ahead with the project. I think we'll all have a lot of fun with it."

"And get ourselves filthy rich in the process," Joel concluded. They all laughed and slapped palms.

"Before you rush off," Joel said, "I think we'd better discuss the corporate structure."

It was decided that, in proportion to what each participant had already brought to the project—Roberts and Rosenman, the money and necessary financial experience, Lang and Kornfeld, a unique knowledge of the rock culture and production technique—they should share equally in the corporation. Each would receive a twenty-five percent share, including ancillary income.

"But there's a hang-up, guys," Kornfeld interjected. "I can't legally sign any contracts until I'm free and clear of my obligation with Capitol."

"You've got an exclusive contract?" Joel asked.

"Right on. Isn't it a pisser?"

"We can work it out, man," said Michael. "Look, all you gotta do is make me a fifty-percent partner. You're almost outta that gig anyway. As soon as you get your freedom, I'll sign half of that over to you. At least that way we won't hafta wait to get things movin' and you won't get the shaft. Anything illegal about that?" he wondered, looking around the room.

"Not that I can see," Roberts said. "As long as Artie doesn't announce to the rest of the music business that he's connected with us in any way. It's a simple transfer of stock. That's all."

"Whaddya think, Artie?" Michael asked.

"As long as I don't stand a chance of getting fucked by Capitol, it's okay by me."

"Settled," Michael said.

Before they disbanded that afternoon, they chose a name for the new corporation. It was to be called Woodstock Ventures Incorporated. Its officers were to be decided at a later date.

Miles Lourie, acting as the new corporation's counselor, however, did not approve of his client's entering into an agreement whereby one of the parties was under exclusive contract to a major record corporation. "Artie is being paid by Capitol. It's a very dangerous situation if that gets out," he warned Michael, but Michael just smiled, and Miles felt as though he might be acting too lawyerlike. This was a different breed of client, he cautioned himself. Often, what applied to one was way off course for another. Maybe he was overdoing it. The matter dropped quietly, and never resurfaced.

CHAPTER THREE

An Assembly of Good Fellows

Their feet through faithless leather met the dirt,
And oftener chang'd their principles than shirt.
—*Edward Young (1683–1765)*

— 1 —

By the end of March 1969, the acquisition of land for an adequate festival site was presenting Woodstock Ventures with its first major problem. Weeks of dreaming and hanging-out, of informal organization and visionary planning, of feeling out the intentions of new associations, of fruitless expeditions into the hinterlands of upstate New York on motocycles and horseback had failed to turn up a sanctuary suitable for three days of peace and love.

The town of Woodstock, while undoubtedly possessing the atmosphere conducive to just such an event, had been ruled out early as being too small to accommodate the expected turnout. After a few scientific projections were made, the forecast for daily attendance had climbed to over one hundred thousand. Had there been even the remotest possibility of squeezing that many people onto a site slightly smaller in scale, Lang might have pressed his associates to consider doing so to preserve their namesake. But the largest available plot of land was a manicured pasture that, he realistically estimated, would hold not more than thirty thousand at tops, and that would not do at all. In addition, access to the community was limited to one major thoroughfare, a two-lane macadam boulevard badly in need of repair, that ran through the center of the sleepy hamlet and, besides promising traffic congestion, was too narrow to handle heavy vehicles bringing construction supplies to a site.

Michael meanwhile had made a number of tours around the countryside evaluating the feasibility of holding the show in a nearby community and weighing their options. There were few alternatives open to them considering the specifications they had mapped out beforehand—size, aesthetic beauty, access, proximity to Manhattan—and each abortive orbit around the area narrowed the possibilities even more.

On one of his expeditions, Lang had spotted what he thought to be a natural amphitheatre etched into a wooded area from the New York Thruway right off Exit 20. Upon further inspection, he discovered that it was part of six hundred acres of farmland, owned by a frankfurter magnate named Shaler, in the town of Saugerties. "It's got everything you could want to put on a site," he deliriously related to Artie after scooting back to the city. "There's acres of trees lining the property, seven permanent buildings already up and—get this, man—it's got a natural fuckin' bowl. It's *perfect!*"

Michael met the landowner and considered him to be a strong-minded, solid individual, whose reputation might provide Woodstock Ventures with the link for excellent community relations, and agreed on the lofty rental price of $40,000 for twelve weeks' use of the premises, pending the approval of his partners.

In practically no time, Michael, Artie, Joel, and John rented motorcycles, biked north to Saugerties, and spent an afternoon surveying the Shaler land. It *was* perfect, they agreed unanimously. It would take some renovation, but with the proper development and police assistance, it could easily accommodate one hundred thousand or more for the weekend. The exit right off the Thruway and its octopuslike appendages provided excellent access, and the permanent facilities—drainage, plumbing, wells, electric power—solved a number of outstanding questions about where to house the crew, situate the concession stands, toilets, and offices.

A week later, however, Lang asked John and Joel to intercede with Shaler on his behalf.

"I just don't know what's goin' down with this dude, man," he puzzled. "Only last week he was goin' for the whole scene in a big way and now I can't get the guy on the phone to save my life. I think the town got to him, y'know—leaned on him kinda heavy *not* to get involved with hippies, man. What a bummer." Michael gave them the phone number of Shaler's New York attorney, and John and Joel made an appointment to see him on March 29. "Maybe they'll dig dealing with some straight cats like you guys," Michael said optimistically. "You speak the same language."

The meeting though, which lasted less than a half hour, was abrupt and cataclysmic. Shaler's attorney, a Mr. Holmes, was a diminutive man who succeeded in intimidating Joel and John by posing questions that under-mined their maturity and their ability to manage his client's land in a re-sponsible manner.

After what seemed like an unnecessary inquisition, Joel brought the dis-agreeable attorney directly to the point. "Look, we were led to believe your client, Mr. Shaler, wished to comply with our offer to rent his land for a brief period in order that we might hold our festival there. We agreed to the price, we agreed to post a bond for any damages, we even agreed to return the land to its former state after we're finished with it. Now, that doesn't seem unrea-sonable to us, sir."

But, he informed them rather casually, it *did* to Mr. Shaler. He never had the slightest intention of renting his property to Michael Lang for a music and art festival, nor had he made Lang any promises of the sort. "I must tell you that my client wishes to keep this land inviolate for his sons, gentlemen. As far as I know, he'll never rent it to anyone whomsoever."

Michael was distraught by the news of the meeting. Instead of supplying his usual whirlwind optimism, he lapsed into moodiness and picked at their lack of progress.

"It's not happenin'," he told John dejectedly in Miles Lourie's office later that week. "The whole thing's not goin' down the way it should be, man. We don't have the land, we don't have personnel, there's no adequate staging proposal, we don't even have our own offices. It's gonna go down the tubes unless we get on with it."

Joel decided it was time he and John took a greater interest in acquiring land. Until now, he had made it a point to stay out of Lang and Kornfeld's designated areas of responsibility, but Michael was right—if there was no site, they would have no festival. It was time, as Michael would say, to "get it on" at any cost.

On March 30, a beautiful translucent Sunday morning, John and Joel got into their car and drove north along the Major Deegan Expressway, which bypassed Harlem and the Bronx and led onto the New York State Thruway toward Woodstock.

Joel reasoned that they would do best to consult local realtors who knew the area and what was available rather than driving blindly from farm to farm looking for owners.

Locating realtors on a Sunday afternoon was equally difficult. This was churchgoing country populated by large sects of Lutherans and Methodists who found it particularly offensive to discuss business on God's day. "Call back on Monday, son," they would say, only to do a quick about-face when they heard the proportions of the land desired. "Six hundred acres? Whew!

Meet me at the office in half an hour. I've got just what you're looking for."
But invariably, they were being corraled by small-time agents out to take
some of that free-flowin' city money into their pockets. They had nothing
that remotely resembled the amount of space the boys were asking for.

They were about to give up and head back to New York City when they
came across a concern representing an industrial park on the fringe of Middletown, a small farming community about fifteen miles from Woodstock
and part of a larger town called Wallkill. The realtor told them that the land
comprised several square miles of acreage in various degrees of development
and was owned by a man named Howard Mills. Mills was preparing to offer
it to manufacturers as a place to build their offices and was planning to construct a housing community of his own on a small adjacent portion. There
was, he told them, a good possibility that Mills would lease it to them for a
definite period of time before he was ready to show it to the industries. If they
would like to see the land, the realtor offered to call Mills and arrange for it.

Roberts and Rosenman hesitated. Michael had insisted that their site be
bucolic, the type of place where music and surroundings would complement
one another and induce feelings of peace and love. Industrial parks hardly
embodied that sense. On the other hand, their backs were to the wall. They
couldn't afford *not* to look at everything that was available. They informed
the realtor they would like to see the land as soon as possible and were taken
quite literally. The agent picked up the phone and called Howard Mills, who
made an appointment to see them at his house within the hour.

— **2** —

By the time Roberts and Rosenman pulled their green Porsche off the newly
cindered road in front of Howard Mills, Jr.'s house, the anxious landowner
had been awaiting their arrival for close to three hours. The boys had made
a wrong turn in their attempt to get from the realtor's office to the industrial
park (where Mills resided with his family), and then found themselves cruis-
ing along the New York Quickway toward Albany without being able to exit.

When, at last, they unfolded themselves from behind the wheel of the car,
it was almost dark. An astral blanket of twilight appeared to float mysteriously several feet above the large sloping roof of the Mills house. All that
remained of the day was in between the house and the infinite night dark-

ness—a milky-gray haze that outlined the large structure and cast translucent shadows over the periphery. Except for the innate feeling of expansiveness that land exudes, it was difficult for John and Joel to make out the surroundings. Nothing, however, could have detracted from the unusual and disarming symmetry of the house, a swaggerish piece of architecture—ridiculous, yet foreboding.

Howard Mills, a craggy man of about forty with slightly stooped shoulders, a receding hairline, and sharp facial features, met them at the door. Perturbed by their lateness, he treated John and Joel with much the same impatience a self-absorbed father inflicts upon a wanting child.

"What's all this hubbub I hear about a music and art fair?" he asked curtly, leading them through the wood-paneled family kitchen and down a flight of stairs to his office.

John and Joel took seats in front of Mills's metal desk and cautiously explained their undertaking. Their scenario was less than forthright; they guarded their words so that implied information would be interpreted to each party's liking. The four partners—John, Joel, Michael, and Artie—had discussed previously with Miles Lourie how to approach prospective landowners: with kid gloves, so as not to scare them away. It was an important tactic in their negotiations. Howard Mills, Jr., was a country farmer, a man of modest worldliness, and they knew full well that he would never go along with their presenting a rock festival of *any* proportion on his property; in fact, they assumed that rock music, to Mills, meant hippies, drugs, sex, and violence, all four of which the local papers had been devoting much unsympathetic space to throughout the past several months. So they discussed their proposition in terms of an art fair that would appeal to all members of the community and "would also encompass some music, probably small concerts, featuring a few of the area's finer musicians."

Mills, listening attentively, clasped his arms behind his head, dropped his feet on the desk, and tried to find a hole in their story. He thought they were crazy to assume people would wander through a field looking at pictures and listening to chamber music, but if he could rent his property for a function of that sort—why not? It was like found money, and he was not about to turn it away.

He described his property for John and Joel, occasionally referring to a map taped to the wall behind him. The lot comprised seven hundred acres of open farmland, which included a small barn and a few temporary installations used to aid construction crews in land development. But aside from a road he was putting in and several houses in the vicinity, there were no obstructions that might hinder this "cockeyed festival idea" of theirs.

Then Mills ushered John and Joel to his new Cadillac parked outside and drove them over to his property. While they bounced over gullies and partially developed terrain, Howard Mills told them about his life as a fruit farmer and about how he had arrived at the decision to divide his family's land. It had not been an easy decision for him to make; it meant his breaking a two-century-old Mills family tradition of farming, dating back to his great-great-great-grandfather, Jacob, who made shoes for General Washington's Continental Army. In 1963, Howard had decided to convert a large portion of his property into an industrial park. It wouldn't take much more than a minor face-lift on what he already owned and it would be up to those who leased it from him to provide their own facilities.

While Mills rambled on about his objectives as a developer, Joel studied him with unabated relish and deduced that underneath the crusty exterior, there was the soul of a complex man fashioned from pride and determination. It would be difficult for Woodstock Ventures once Mills caught on to the magnitude of their project, but Joel was sure he would eventually come around to viewing it as they all did—a financial investment with exceptionally attractive rates of return. He and John could talk to Mills as businessmen, appeal to his ambitions. Mills would be a pushover for Michael if he could get past what Joel was certain were the farmer's prejudices toward hippies. It would take a group effort to win him over to their side, but it *could* be done with finesse.

As their eyes adjusted to the night they could see what looked like miles of endless plain that rose in a conical hillside overlooking a plateau of level ground. It seemed like an ideal place for kids to spread blankets and watch a concert without crowding one another. There was some wooded area, though not foliage enough to satisfy Michael, and from what they could determine in the dark, a reasonable means of access that could be improved upon by their own crews. In time, *anything* could be amended by money and machinery. The only disconcerting features were two turquoise water towers that surged from the earth like massive, hulking missiles on each side of the site. Joel was certain that Michael and Artie would view them as monuments to the Establishment. But while they did pose certain cosmetic drawbacks, they also solved a major headache for the promoters: where to get enough water to satisfy both the living requirements of fifty thousand people a day and the local health ordinances. Mills told them that the larger tower, built in 1963, held 1,500,000 gallons, and the small one, built as recently as 1967, could accommodate 600,000 gallons when filled to capacity. They supplied the entire township with water; however, he assured them that they would be able to tap the tanks for their function if they agreed to pay the standard county rates for water.

It was barely fifteen minutes later when the Cadillac had gone full circle and returned to the entrance of the Mills residence. By that time, although John and Joel, independently, were considering making Mills an offer to rent the land, neither did. Instead, they told him that his property was the best place they had seen so far, but the decision to make a binding offer for it—or even to discuss price—had to be the unanimous decision of all four partners. Mr. Lang and Mr. Kornfeld, they said, would make appointments in the very near future to see the field and, after they all had had ample time to consult on its feasibility, they'd get back to him. Then they thanked Howard Mills, Jr., for his time and, for the forty-minute ride back to the city, traded ecstatic prophesies about what was to be their newfound home for the festival.

Neither John nor Joel could contain his excitement over their discovery, but when they arrived back at their apartment, they couldn't locate either Michael or Artie. The news waited until the next morning when John reached Michael who shared his enthusiasm, with the reservation that he would have to see the place for himself.

Michael drove up the next afternoon in a white Porsche the company had leased for him as part of their corporate agreement.

After a routine stroll over the barren grounds and a friendly chat with Howard Mills, he returned to the city in time for an informal meeting with Roberts and Rosenman. His attitude was less than joyful.

"It's not where it's at, man," he announced softly, passing verdict on their efforts. "I'm really bummed out about it too. Here I got all excited about this site of yours and it turns out to be a fuckin' hole. I mean, *nothin'*, man. It's just a big pit."

John and Joel automatically assumed that a large part of Michael's attitude could be attributed to the fact that it was *they* who had run across the site and not he or Artie. But after talking to him about it, they learned that Michael's objections indeed had to do with the fact that Mills's land was going to be converted into an industrial site, and that plain offended him. It "wasn't laid-back enough, wasn't rustic."

They had, however, been prepared for just such a reaction and launched into an explanation about how they were up against the wall as far as property was concerned.

"We're runnin' outta time, man," John countered, appealing to Michael's sense of immediacy. "We can't afford to be choosy anymore—not if we expect to get this thing moving by the end of the summer. You're the cat who said we gotta start things happening no matter what or it wouldn't go down at all. And, anyway, we can make this place in Wallkill work for us."

"Yeah," agreed Joel, jumping quickly to his partner's side. "It's not as bad as it looks. It's *real* damn big. Why, I'll bet we could get over a hundred thousand people a day onto that land if we needed to. *More!* The terrain is suitable for a show. There's a natural place to put the stage so that everyone can see, the roads are pretty good, and Mills is gettin' ready to unload the place so we can do whatever the hell we want to it and not worry about destroying any property. Hell, I think it's a gift, Michael. We oughta grab it while we can."

"I agree with Joel, man," John said.

Michael hesitated, weighing their judgment against his own concept of what the show was supposed to represent. "I don't know," he said glumly.

"Look, I think we should take an option on it," Joel offered. "That way, at least the place is ours if we decide we want it. We put up a few hundred bucks, and if we don't take it, we don't get hurt real badly. But that way it won't get pulled out from under us either. If you don't like it, you can keep looking for another place. Find something better, and we'll take it. An option's not a lotta bread."

By mid-afternoon, as Joel and John continued to rationalize some of the land's lesser qualities, pinpointing to him how they might overcome each disadvantage, Michael began feeling comfortable with the notion that it could be restructured to suit them. By day's end, Lang had agreed with them that taking an option on the Mills land would be their most logical alternative to having no land.

"Gimme some time to warm to it," he acquiesced. "I got a lotta thinkin' to do about it. I guess you guys are right about it. We got nothin' to lose but a little scratch if it doesn't work out. And"—he flashed his patented closed-mouth grin—"it's your dough."

— **3** —

During the eight weeks or so since the partners had first conceived of the festival, an air of playfulness swept through the Woodstock headquarters (which had temporarily been given a mobile home in Miles Lourie's suite at 250 West Fifty-seventh Street). The informal, carefree attitude of summer was instituted as office policy, and the activities of "doing" and "dreaming" overlapped with the business of the working day. Roberts, Rosenman, Lang, and Kornfeld would gather there every morning at about eleven o'clock. Together with a few "secretaries" they had hired and several assistants who were thrilled to be a part of all the excitement, they began sculpting the festival's skeletal substructure as casually as one assembles the pieces of a jigsaw puzzle.

Every so often when he was between clients, Miles Lourie would poke his head into the cubbyhole he had allocated for their use and inquire how the plans were going. "Far fucking out!" was the usual response from one of the myriad volunteers who passed through on a strange current of drug-induced euphoria and inflated importance.

Occasionally, Miles took some time out to join in the conviviality; Record Company Monopoly became a favorite office game wherein Artie would own Capitol Records, Michael would be dealt RCA, Miles would begin with Columbia, and they would vie to outsmart (and outfuck) each other in putting lucrative deals for artists on their respective rosters until the winner emerged holding all their artists as one massive rock conglomerate.

John and Joel were not immune to the attractiveness of this relaxed, alien atmosphere. The three-piece Brooks Brothers suits, the cardigan sweaters, the ties and monogrammed dress shirts were replaced by jeans, leather vests, wide-lapelled flowered shirts, and beads; in a daring display of independence, John and Joel allowed their hair to creep over their ears and their language to extend beyond their cultivated Ivy League puffery.

Joel seemed to adapt to this new lifestyle more quickly and easily than John, often "grooving" to strains of acid rock and related psychedelia preached by bands like the Airplane, Joe Cocker, the Who, and Cream. But it was John who was turned on by the feminine hippie mystique—that vacant, far-away look and dreamy smile offered often and unselfishly by lissome young women in soft, frayed jeans and threadbare T-shirts. Their casual lifestyle was so unlike anything he had ever experienced before that he left himself wide open for the sucker punch. His desires did not go unattended, either; the office soon overflowed with eager young assistants shuffling through in moccasins or bare feet. All of them saw to it that the stereo amplifiers continuously thumped hard rock, the ventilation wafted complementary fragrances of Acapulco Gold and strawberry incense, and their generation's credo of Peace and Love (emphasis on Love) was observed at all times. All things considered, the atmosphere was more conducive to turning on than to turning out a high degree of constructive work.

During this time, Michael Lang had been anything but idle. While the land search and other corporate structuring had been underway, Michael had inched farther and farther away from his responsibilities to Train, leaving Artie to fend off their increasing demands for more faithful career management. Many of the band's members were already beginning to suspect that they were being used to finance their manager's outside interests. But Michael was working on a power play whereby he and Artie would be able to unload the group and not be held responsible by Capitol Records. It would take a little time to complete, but it would free him to pursue his ultimate concern: The Woodstock Festival. Meanwhile, he began compiling an organization staff from past associations so that when the time came to begin work at the site, they would be ready to move into action.

The first person he hired was a man whom he had worked with at the Miami Pop Festival, named Stanley Goldstein. Goldstein was a bearlike young man who had just turned thirty, hypnotically articulate, and tenacious. He had thick black curly hair that seemed to continue around his head and to melt in a brillowy Smith Brothers–type beard. A former sound engineer at Criteria Recording Studios in Miami, Goldstein was passing through New York on his way to a similar job in Los Angeles, hoping to avert the long-distance move by convincing A&R Studios in New York to take him on.

Michael needed Goldstein's assistance desperately, for while Stanley could no doubt aid in the technical planning of the festival, his hidden talent was in locating resources—*human* resources—and, right now, qualified people were considered by Lang to be as good as gold. Rumor had it that, given a football stadium filled to capacity, Goldstein could pick out the two men or women there who were capable of fulfilling a specific need and somehow convince them to drop everything else and to work for his cause.

Through Goldstein's estranged wife, Lang traced him to a small, tumbledown hotel on Forty-ninth Street west of Broadway. He caught him just as Goldstein was preparing to leave for the Coast the next day. But not if Michael had his way.

What ensued was a conversation between two grand masters of persuasion, neither willing to compromise. Michael, however, was at his most convincing as he descriptively bore into Stanley's softest spot with promises of high times and prosperity.

"Listen, man," Michael said at last, "we'll get this thing out of the way in a flash and the studio's yours. The whole thing'll be a trip, anyway. We're gonna get Dylan and the Band and Hendrix and the Beatles and just about everybody—and for three days we're gonna throw the biggest fuckin' party this world's ever seen."

"Okay," Stanley said nonchalantly.

"You'll do it?"

"Um-hmm. When do I start?"

"Uh—tomorrow, man. How's tomorrow?" Michael asked in a flutter, trying to conceal his excitement.

"You're on. I'll see you at your office first thing in the morning."

Goldstein and Lang met the next day in a vacant office in the Capitol Records complex on Sixth Avenue, which Artie had placed at Michael's disposal. It was a dingy New York morning, callous and impersonal, the kind that often betrays the city's brittle, subliminal self.

Michael went into more detail than he had over the phone about his plans for the festival, explaining Roberts and Rosenman's "unfashionable" presence in the promoters' clique as "concessions we hadda make to get the bread away from 'em," and citing the studio retreat as their ultimate goal. But it was clear to Goldstein from the first breath that the retreat was and would always be secondary, if not to be completely forgotten. Michael's grand design would be no ordinary festival, at least not a repeat performance of the Miami fiasco, and, for lack of a better offer, he wanted to be a part of it.

They discussed the festival for more than two hours, outlining several concepts and projecting some rather spectacular "supposes." *Suppose* they did actually attract fifty thousand people a day for three days; *suppose* it was more; *suppose* Dylan, the Band, and the Who did sign to play at Woodstock; *suppose* they got the Beatles. *Suppose* they got lucky and actually pulled this thing off without a hitch, changing a lot of people's minds about hippies and rock music; *suppose* it became an annual event. *Suppose* they made a million bucks—think of all the power it would give them. *Suppose* . . . they were lapsing into a hallucination over the infinite possibilities this venture could create for them, a natural high.

Michael wanted Goldstein to get moving on technical matters immediately so that he could devote all his time to getting the talent together; at present, Lang was trying to land contracts with a few of the top recording acts, to "give the festival an air of authenticity" in the public's eyes and to create excitement within the record industry. He hadn't had much initial luck. Stan's presence in the organization would undoubtedly relieve Michael of related pressures and allow him to concentrate on the program. They agreed on a salary, a system whereby Stan would get a substantial cash advance and be reimbursed for his expenses, and a list of priorities demanding his immediate attention. Lighting, sound, and communal facilities were top priority. After Stan had had enough time to investigate them and develop a prospectus on how to put them into practice, they would meet again and decide how to facilitate the electrical layout. Michael assured him that he had a free hand when it came to getting the best of everything and backed it up with the three words that would become Lang's vocal trademark over the course of that summer: "Money's no object." Whether or not it was the emphasis or throwaway casualness with which he uttered the phrase, no one ever questioned Lang's solvency. Money flowed more freely than rain. By the end of August, that comparison would be considered ironic.

Goldstein went straight back to his midtown residence and began making a series of routine investigative calls regarding lighting. It soon became apparent to him that, for all his effort, he was not receiving any return messages. The hotel switchboard, he found, was run with about as much care as was afforded the establishment's maintenance. So he worked out a deal with hotel management whereby he could run their main switchboard and make his calls at the same time, thus assuring that incoming calls concerning festival business would reach him.

Principally, Goldstein contacted General Electric, Westinghouse, and Sylvania, all with main offices in the New York area, to discern what lighting levels were required to illuminate seven hundred acres of land. Very early on in his conversations, he had to make the delineation between *stage* lighting, which is aimed at a very specific target and requires its luminosity to be extremely aesthetic as well, and *area* lighting, whose purpose it would be to keep a crowd from falling down on the rocks while, hopefully, still retaining some of the intrinsic beauty of the surroundings. This part of his task was comparable to planning the lighting for a small village, including not only the purchasing of sufficient bulbs and lamps, but requiring that he map out above- and below-ground wiring between the lights and the master circuit. Goldstein also determined that it was essential that he develop a pattern of electrical "buzz words" before meeting with electric company representatives, in order for him to establish his credibility and to get a more comprehensive understanding of the information from those conversations. To accomplish that, he spent two days in the New York Public Library reading as much trade literature as was available and digging around in the archives for blueprints or specific guidelines used to stage other large-scale ventures. The files on the latter were, for all intents and purposes, nonexistent.

That led Stanley to calling on and researching places in the news that had just been, or were currently being, lit. Utilizing the first of his requests for expense money, he flew to Canada to get a firsthand look at the Montreal Expo, which was in the process of being completed. It provided him with a preliminary perspective on just what it was going to take to outfit the festival grounds; but none of the exposition's plans were made accessible to him. The concept, however, steered him toward a similar, more cordial group of impresarios located in a familiar neck of the woods. Upon returning to New York, Goldstein telephoned the people who had contracted lighting for the New York World's Fair, and they were sympathetic. In fact, they immediately discerned from his starched pitch that Stanley had absolutely no idea what he was talking about and helped draw up a rudimentary plan to put him on the right track. That, coupled with the information he received about pole lighting from the electric conglomerates and what Stan referred to as his "backup rationale," established a prospectus for lighting the Woodstock Music and Arts Festival that he knew would suffice until an electrical engineer was called in to implement the design. After consulting with Lang and whoever else had to approve the budget, it would only be a matter of a firm coming in with the best bid.

Next, Goldstein attempted to tackle sound. In this matter, Lang's demands had been explicit. He had advised Stanley that if they were to be successful this time and wanted to do a second festival sometime in the future, it meant keeping the groups happy. One way of doing that would be to utilize the best sound system available today. "Let 'em see that we know what we're doing," Michael told him. "No fuckups with sound, man. It doesn't matter what it costs to do it—just get the best cat in the business to handle the gig." It was not as easy as it sounded. There were few specialists who knew how to mike rock music effectively, and fewer whose equipment was diversified enough to amplify seven hundred acres. Looking ahead, Goldstein determined that they would most likely go over budget in order to put in an adequate sound system. In fact, it might take their putting somebody in business and supplying that person with equipment and personnel.

If anything, the technical inefficiency and lack of precedents regarding large-scale functions provided Goldstein with a terrible handicap, and he was forced to waste much precious time that might have been better spent bringing in personnel.

No one, it seemed, had the slightest idea of how to go about providing sufficient sound amplification. Most companies were groping in the dark when it came to handling sound, managing staging, coordinating microphone placement, and recording with interlocking systems. There was no call for it—no professional guidelines; when the various concerns heard the plans were based upon attendance of one hundred thousand people, it overwhelmed them. Goldstein telephoned a half-dozen companies across the country and not one gave him any indication that it would be able to accommodate him. They all, however, suggested he get in touch with a man in

Massachusetts named Bill Hanley who, some said, was one of those eccentric, head-in-the-clouds geniuses capable of turning a simple car stereo speaker into a veritable thunderburst. Each time he received a similar description of his talents, Stanley smiled smugly to himself. Bill Hanley, he realized, would fit the bill nicely.

Goldstein got Hanley's phone number from a friend who had contracted the sound company to provide amplification at a previous southern pop festival. Hanley "could do anything," the friend avowed, and owned a stock of equipment powerful enough to simulate an aural reenactment of World War II. But he also warned him that "the guy's a real bastard to work with, a real irascible dude who doesn't even want to know from your concept. He thinks he's goddamn Pablo Picasso. Just tell him what you want and stay out of his way. He'll deliver."

Goldstein had no trouble getting the sound engineer on the phone. But after explaining the magnitude of the undertaking and the dilemma he already faced in trying to enter into some kind of agreement with a sound company able to meet their requirements, Goldstein was abruptly cut off.

"You say you don't know what you want?" Hanley inquired in a mocking tone of voice. "I don't have time to give you a Dick-and-Jane primer in outdoor sound right now, Goldstein. You see, I'm a busy person. Everybody wants me to bail them out of trouble, but nobody knows what they want. I'll talk to you when you get your scene together. Just decide what it is you need, call me back, and I'll come down there and plug in my equipment, one-two-three," mercifully leaving out "'cause you've got no place else to turn."

"No, man, you don't seem to understand what we're building and what it's gonna entail from . . ."

"Hey, Goldstein—you're a fine person to tell me I don't understand. Get it together, pal. I'll be hearing from you."

Goldstein had little doubt that Hanley was their man; besides his sterling reputation and his already having the necessary equipment, Hanley's unflagging confidence and his posture that the festival was a simple job placed him high in Goldstein's esteem. It was Hanley's ego that troubled him. In exchange for the promise of competent services, he was being forced to play a waiting game, which was comparable to a sophisticated version of Russian roulette, by Hanley's offhand rules of trade. At this point in his dealings, however, he was so overjoyed to find someone out there who *knew* it could be done that the other drawbacks were overshadowed by his temporary relief. Goldstein's intuition had never failed him before. They would use Hanley Sound, Stan assured himself, and the Boy Wonder (if, indeed, he lived up to the reputation) would perform like a supertrooper. If he thought long and hard enough about the whole matter, he was positive he could come up with a surefire plan for putting Bill Hanley's name on the dotted line and everyone else's mind at ease. Stanley Goldstein, for the time being, was a contented man.

— 4 —

Throughout most of March and early April, the business concerning Train had somehow gotten switched onto the wrong track. Instead of merrily chugging along in the blissful "marriage-type relationship" Michael Lang had projected when signing the group to a personal management contract in 1968, they were headed toward the divorce mill faster than a speeding locomotive. No one was happy. Michael was making himself scarce—not picking up the group's calls or showing up for prearranged meetings. Artie could not have cared less about making a record with Train; the band wondered what had happened to the $125,000 advance from Capitol Records their manager was administering for them; and Capitol Records, everyone's benefactor, wanted to know who this group called Train was that kept phoning their corporate offices. The multitudinous voices fighting to be heard above the Train wreck resembled a modern-day Tower of Babel. Something had to give.

Something did.

Michael was on the verge of lying down and giving up where Train was concerned. The festival preparations were at a crucial stage, and he was well aware that if he left details in the hands of anyone other than Stanley Goldstein, he was in big trouble. He considered John and Joel to be harmless as long as they were kept out of sight. But Joel was beginning to check in with him more often—always at the wrong time; he was "becoming one royal pain in the ass" and was the one person Michael considered a threat to his aspirations. That made Rosenman an adversary. And maybe he should have taken Miles Lourie's advice and severed his ties with Artie long ago. Now it was too late, and he'd just have to make the best of a bad situation.

Train was another costly mistake. Once his ticket into the music business, they were old news. Putting Train on tour, no matter how successful their album became, was chickenshit compared to what he stood to make from Woodstock. In all fairness to them and to his own career it was time to cut them loose.

Together with Artie, Michael approached Roberts and Rosenman with a rehearsed act designed to bring the Train to a grinding halt. They explained that they were suffering from acute guilt inasmuch as they were engaged in an outside project that was a clear conflict of interest under their existing partnership agreement. Leo Gorcey and Huntz Hall couldn't have staged a more convincing charade of false brotherhood.

"It's just not right, man," Artie confessed, hanging his head, "that we should be equally involved in a music-oriented venture such as the festival and still have our gig with Train on the side. We're gonna score a fortune with them, and so far, we've cut you guys out of the take."

"So we got a better idea, man, something that really makes sense," Michael offered. "We're gonna bring you in on the deal. You know, make Train a part of our enterprises and that way we'll still be a unified brotherhood."

Joel and John were reluctant. Partly because of the enormous sum Michael requested from the corporation as reimbursement for his past expenses incurred in getting Train started and partly because they felt they were beginning to spread their talents (and bankroll) too thin. Management was a risk. There was no assurance that Train would hit. Would John, on a lifetime diet of the Johnny Mann Singers and Perry Como, have the magic touch for picking the next Vanilla Fudge? For that matter, would Joel fare any better having only recently severed his ties with the Yale Glee Club and a Las Vegas–style folk quartet? Hardly. But, after tossing the idea back and forth between them for a few days, they agreed on a mutual belief that "Michael and Artie were the apostles of a new awareness who saw and heard things too finely" for their mild palates. It was like speculating on an obscure stock, John rationalized. The payoff could be equally great. And so, for a hefty five-figure buyout of Lang's former company, Woodstock Kalaparusha Management was formed—the name originating from a twenty-minute diatribe by Michael, who told them that kalaparusha was the wheellike symbol that encompassed all the signs of the zodiac and would therefore guide their new endeavor under the universal spiritual order.

Somebody, however, should have informed the members of Train that they were no longer under the Lang stranglehold. Their further attempts to link up with Lang had proved futile, and guitarist Bob Lenox, in an effort to locate his manager, half-jokingly gauged that he had already spoken more to Michael's father on the telephone in one week than he had conferred with Lang himself during their entire relationship. Finally, out of a sense of utter frustration and as a precaution against resorting to physical violence to find out where Train stood, Lenox called the parent company at the Capitol Towers in Los Angeles hoping to get a comforting answer from them.

"We're a band called Train," he calmly explained to an officer of the company. "We have these tapes that we've recorded under our contract with your company—a very sizeable one, at that—for over $125,000 a year. We'd like to know what we should do with them now that they're finished and since we cannot find our manager."

An uncomfortable silence followed. "Are you still there?" Lennox asked, not quite knowing the required protocol in business situations like these.

"Uh—yes, I'm here," a voice responded. "Hang on a second, okay?" the official asked and came back onto the line after what Lenox determined to be time enough for him to have had a brief conference with an associate standing nearby. "Uh, I have a suggestion. Why don't you send us the tapes you've already made so we can hear what we bought for that impressive sum. We'll get back to you after we give them a listen. And, uh, Mr. Train—I mean, Mr. Lenox—thank you *very* much for bringing this to our attention."

Then, very quickly, Capitol Records swept their executive quarters from inside out.

During this siege, Artie Kornfeld was systematically able to negotiate his release from the exclusive contract Capitol had with him. After months of captivity, he was, at last, a free agent able openly to ride the festival to new personal heights.

Train would have welcomed the chance to negotiate so much as a cheeseburger for lunch. Instead, Bob Lenox, representing the band, was called before the Capitol leaders in an inquest regarding the future of their recording contract.

Unable to find Michael Lang, Lenox elected to attend the meeting by himself. Like a condemned man awaiting the final sentence of death, he wanted to get the whole thing over with as soon as possible.

Often the final blow never quite manages to come down hard enough on its victim to extinguish the misery. And Capitol Records kept Lenox twitching long after the guitarist had been subdued. One of the newly elected corporate vice-presidents came to that meeting balancing an armload of legal-sized folders and proceeded to point out to Lenox why it was that the company was deeply concerned about its rather enormous investment in Train. Their auditors had determined that entirely too much money had been wasted on the project in respect to the recorded evidence. Someone, it seems, had sold Capitol a bill of goods. He sincerely hoped there was some way their interrelationship could be resolved and, subsequently, dissolved.

A day later, when the initial shock of being released from the recording contract had begun to wear off, Bob Lenox finally got in touch with someone close to Michael Lang. Lang had asked this person to relay a message to the members of the group: They had been sold, through Michael's power of attorney, to a company in New York called Woodstock Ventures. Should they be interested in assessing their contractual obligations to that company, they were advised to get in touch with Messers. John Roberts and Joel Rosenman.

The Train ride was over.

Lang found it next to impossible to convince top-draw groups to sign on to the festival roster. At most of the major booking agencies, his requests for talent were met by polite snubs. "Sorry, the Airplane will be on an extended European tour when you want them." "Hendrix is holding that very weekend for a promoter in Cleveland." "Try us again next week. We'll probably know something by then." Such was Michael Lang's plight.

Lang knew that once a top act was signed up he could use it as a lever to convince others to join the show until being included on the festival bill became a much coveted trophy.

With the help and advice of Hector Morales, a hip music agent at the William Morris Agency who saw something extraordinary in Lang's festival design, a game plan for landing a big name or two was devised. Overpayment. If Lang would agree to offer an outrageous sum of money for a group's appearance and to comply by putting that entire amount into escrow, it would be difficult for an act to refuse the invitation. Groups could always manage to pull in those one-night-stand fees of a couple thousand dollars, but chances for the big money were still far and few between. He had to make it worth their while to take the risk.

A week later, after the line had been baited with what was considered to be a king's ransom in performance fees, Hector Morales called Lang to say that he had received a few nibbles. If Michael would remain patient a while longer, it would not be long before they had themselves a prize catch.

— **5** —

Stanley Goldstein passed what little free time he had in much the same manner most troubleshooters tackle their assignments: by holding theoretical conversations with himself in which he could air all sides of potential problems in the months ahead.

One of those very first self-dialogues occurred at the hotel while he was waiting for a lighting contractor to return his call. It went something like this: "What is it here we're dealing with? What are the impressions, be they positive or negative, that one will walk away with? What are the places I've enjoyed being, and what is the first thing I'd say about a place that I didn't like?" He thought about it for a while, pacing around his small room, before arriving at any conclusions. After a period of introspection: "I'd say, 'It was scuzzy, man, the toilets were fuckin' filthy, overflowing, the sinks were dirty, it smelled like a shithole.' We've *got* to have clean and sufficient public rest rooms." That, he determined, would have to be his next order of business: to find a quantity of portable toilets to handle the weekend's natural flow.

It took only a few random calls before Goldstein began to appreciate the convenience of permanent sanitary facilities in established arenas. He had assumed that the portable toilet business was similar to that of operating a regional McDonald's: A person applied for a franchise and, upon being accepted by the parent company, was then required to attend a seminar taught by trained personnel so that the novice manager could learn how to run his concern down to the last screw holding together the cash register. That, compared to the level of performance exhibited by the existing sanitation companies, would have been like holding a Ph.D. in hygienic engineering. Goldstein found that the local men were tantamount to career speculators; they put up a total of five thousand dollars to go into the portable toilet business, took a franchise by filling out a simple questionnaire about their financial assets, supplied a brief personal history showing they had no arrests, and were anointed Mr. Johnny-on-the-spot for the New York vicinity. First man in, so to speak, had the territory wrapped up. And to complicate matters, these men were dealers, not mechanics versed in the operation of the individual unit. What they *did* know was that you deliver it, you flush it, you take it back after the event, and you collect your check. Their minimal knowledge provided Stanley with virtually no assistance in plotting a sanitation program.

Nor could they aid him in calculating the amount of units he would need and the staff necessary to service them. Temporary toilets, he discovered, were basically designed for construction site usage where the number of units is determined by the relatively small number of bodies using them on a daily basis; servicing was only necessary, in those instances, once a week because a supply of decomposing chemicals contained in the base eats up the waste over a period of time. But at a large public gathering where the population demands a continuous turnover at the rest facilities, detoxification by chemicals makes absolutely no difference whatsoever. The disinfectant then becomes the most important element in sanitation because the level of waste matter very rapidly exceeds the level of water in the tanks, producing a terrible stench and destroying the antibodies that prevent bacterial infection.

Out of desperation, Goldstein contacted health department officials to tap their knowledge and to provide himself with the fundamental understanding of exactly what precautions would have to be taken by the festival coordinators to avoid dysentery. Much to his surprise and consternation, he found that despite the Department of Health's supposed understanding of effluence and of the possibility of typhoid arising from an inferior waste disposal system, their expertise did not extend to crowd dynamics.

The situation called for firsthand observation to establish a set of standards by which he could function. Goldstein, therefore, spent the next week visiting places like Madison Square Garden, Yankee Stadium, Kennedy Airport, movie theatres, concert halls—any facility where rest rooms were expected to service sizeable captive crowds over a number of hours. Armed with a stopwatch and a clipboard, he timed people's health habits and compared data to arrive at an average length of time he could adapt for his own purposes. One interesting phenomenon he deduced was that during the first period of occupation under one roof—be it one hour or one day—people tend *not* to use the rest rooms; they expressed a subliminal shyness of them. People accustomed themselves over the years to use the bathroom either before leaving home or at a local gas station on their way. The element of excitement in attending an event also often results in constipation. Sometime between the second and third period (or day) of the event, the situation reverses itself, and diarrhea sets in. Goldstein attributed this to a combination of things: the excitement, a change of living circumstances, water, junk food, long hours, etc. But one thing for certain was that the lines punctually formed like Friday afternoons in a bank, and it was going to be up to him to make sure those anxious people were accommodated.

Goldstein reported back to Lang that he wasn't quite sure how they were going to go about securing enough portable johns for a three-day event but, if it meant his digging a trench and covering it over with topsoil when it was full, Michael could count on his providing an adequate lavatory system. He also gave Lang a thumbnail sketch of his activities concerning sound and lighting and suggested to Michael that he hire someone to put all this information he was gathering to good use.

The problem of finding an operations chief had been Lang's most immediate order of business. The candidate had to be familiar with the fundamentals of grand-scale concert production and able to commandeer the crew's technical reins at the site; he also had to possess enough common sense and perspicacity to keep the locals at arm's length. Lang had envisioned a concert tour manager filling the gap, but most, he found, had already committed themselves to tours extending through Labor Day or were vacationing and could not be reached. He had even toyed with the idea of dropping the entire predicament into Goldstein's lap in the same manner one disposes of an unwanted child on a doorstep. He realized, however, that by doing so, he would only succeed in strangling his lifeline to the festival's already heavily mortgaged heart. Lately, Michael had been experiencing pangs of doubt with regard to Goldstein's ability to function smoothly under the gun. Stanley was the ideal "people-finder," but when faced with a number of overlapping responsibilities, all of which were complex and laborious, Michael watched him "go off the wall, seeming only to be able to work in desperate situations." Overloading Goldstein now was a serious mistake. Lang determined he would need at least one, if not two, other supervisors to assume the task, especially since time was becoming an important factor.

A few people had already put in their bids to control the show, including a jack-of-all-trades named Bert Cohen, who had worked on Michael's Miami show to less than overwhelming reaction. Cohen told Lang that his firm, Concert Hall Publications, would gladly handle the staging, publicity, public relations, concessions, anything he wished; Lang was pretty sure that, for a price, Cohen would have also performed with a rock band as their talent as well as hung the wallpaper in the festival production office. But Lang was more interested in a specialist and informed Bert that there would be more than enough for his company to do in the near future without taking on such a load. In fact, Lang had been mulling over a suggestion of Goldstein's that a friend of Stan's named Mel Lawrence be considered for the omnipotent position. Lawrence had worked on several other festivals, had designed the grounds and supervised the building of those facilities, and proved himself an able administrator in all those capacities.

At the age of thirty-three, already extending well beyond the over-thirty demarcation that separated the Love Generation from those not to be trusted, Mel Lawrence was considered a "brother." He carried himself with the ambiguity of a tireless revolutionary student able to communicate with faculty as well as the masses. Those who knew him well still found it difficult to believe Mel was a day over twenty-seven: trim, golden-brown from working under the western sun, and so easygoing. Mel, it was rumored, knew how to "hang out" better than kids half his age.

Mel Lawrence was, in fact, born Melvin Bernard Lachs in 1936, the son of a window-cleaning operator, who grew up in the Bay Parkway section of Brooklyn. After graduating from Lafayette High School in 1952, Lawrence attended Brooklyn College for a short time, electing speech therapy as his major area of concentration.

Six months later, though, he was back on the street with a diploma from the Church of Scientology. He had become a church auditor, assisting individual parishioners in locating their areas of spiritual distress and cleansing them. Armed with a Hubbard Electrometer—a little wooden box with two tin cans attached to either end by wires—he practiced "clearing" subjects by holding the tin cans to the person being purged of sins and repeating over and over again something as mundane as: "What did you do today?" When the needle on the e-meter finally registered no reading, it meant the subject was telling the truth, the person had been "cleared" of evil spirits.

Lawrence became one of church founder L. Ron Hubbard's favorite disciples and, together, they explored the latter's theory of dianetics, which dealt with the study of psychosomatic illnesses resulting from the "reactive mind." However, in 1966, Hubbard resigned from his position as head of the church and, by that time, Lawrence found his best interests leading him elsewhere.

His destination, this time, was Hawaii. There Lawrence honed in on the first tremors of cultural faddism, and this time it appeared he had latched on to a winner. Joining a friend named Tom Rounds, Mel began doing radio work, progressive rock broadcasting, and in a relatively short period of time, he, Rounds, and two other associates became the sole rock and roll promoters in Honolulu, importing top attractions from the mainland.

In early June 1967, Lawrence and Rounds were hired to organize a spectacular radio promotion in the San Francisco area—a large outdoor concert designed to combine rock and roll with the Bay Area's psychedelic ambience. "Intertwine all the colors of the culture into the show," they were advised by their employers, "to represent what's taking place with the kids today. Make them feel at home, as if the show belongs to them." Called the Fantasy Fair and Magic Mountain Music Festival, it was put on as a benefit for the black community at Hunter's Point for a nominal contribution of two dollars per person. Amazingly, and quite unexpectedly, forty-five thousand people stormed the gates to see an eclectic roster of bands including the Jefferson Airplane, Dionne Warwick, the Fifth Dimension, and the Grateful Dead. Musical lines had not yet been drawn between progressive and pop sounds, and a number of styles blended harmoniously in the spirit that carried this first rock and roll festival.

The word "festival" soon began cropping up in every active promoter's vocabulary. Festivals were loosely defined as venues held in stadiums or racetracks; some of the more adventurous showmen were even considering beach shows where capacity was, for all intents and purposes, unlimited. By clustering several popular acts on the bill, a festival could send the box office profits soaring beyond anyone's wildest expectations. The industry joke was that some ambitious promoter should negotiate for the right to rope off the state of Maine or, better yet, to fly a group over the United States and to charge an entertainment tax to anyone who looked up at the sky. The market was an agent's dream.

Monterey Pop, Atlanta, Atlantic City—the festival sites became overnight bywords of nirvana for the hippie masses. And Lawrence and Rounds were on hand for most of the big ones.

In the fall of 1968, having moved their base of operations to Los Angeles, Rounds and Lawrence were contacted by radio station mogul Bill Drake to produce a pop festival at the Gulfstream Racetrack in Miami.

Practically every rock act with a gold record was signed to appear there: the Grateful Dead, Iron Butterfly, Canned Heat, the Turtles, Richie Havens, Chuck Berry, Joni Mitchell, Marvin Gaye, Steppenwolf, Paul Butterfield, Flatt and Scruggs, Country Joe and the Fish, Buffy Sainte-Marie, Fleetwood Mac, John Mayall, Jose Feliciano, and fourteen others with burgeoning reputations. It was to be held on three successive days—December 28, 29, and 30, 1968, when the Florida beaches were teeming with college vacationers—and forecast phenomenal wealth for the promoters.

With only two months to go, however, Drake pulled out, citing the rising $280,000 production cost as an omen of runaway escalation. Not having that kind of money in their possession and thinking $280,000 just about all the money there was in the world, they called a stockbroker acquaintance in San Francisco in the hope that he might know where some money was just lying around collecting dust.

"Who is your funkiest, hippest, craziest client whom you think would be willing to risk about three hundred grand on a rock festival about to take place in two months' time?" Rounds asked. Without hesitation, the stockbroker replied, "Tom Driscoll," and a *shidduch* was made. Driscoll backed them with unconditional support.

Miami Pop, as their festival came to be known, was somewhat less than spectacular. The college kids, they found, could not be pried away from the beaches as they had hoped, and they were only moderately supported by the small youth population that remained in Miami during the height of the tourist season. Instead of taking a purse of $750,000 back to Los Angeles to wave in Bill Drake's face as they had hoped, they were fortunate to break even.

Tom Rounds thought they were lucky enough to escape Miami with their heads intact. From the very start, he and Lawrence had been apprehensive about security measures. The producers were afraid that a police presence would ignite an already explosive situation. But Miami insisted: no cops, no concert—it was as simple as that. Driscoll, the newest partner, was referred to Chief of Police George Emerick of the Hallendale Police Department to resolve the matter, although nothing moved quite as expeditiously as they wished. Emerick himself was under indictment at the time, and getting him to devote his time exclusively to a rock festival was something of a joke. As the festival drew dangerously close, Emerick finally consented to provide two hundred uniformed men to police the three-day event, and it all went down without incident. But battle lines had been drawn between the kids and the police, and more than a few times an hour, either Rounds or Lawrence had overheard a cop elucidate his wish to "break a few of those long-haired hippie skulls." The cops were merely waiting for their first available opportunity to step into the fray.

They got their chance soon enough—although it came to them in a somewhat more civilized and subdued manner than they had hoped. After Miami Pop, the promoters applied for another license to hold a concert at Gulfstream and were granted one by the Hallendale city government. A few days later, though, on March 2, 1969, Jim Morrison of the Doors was arrested for indecent exposure on a Miami stage. The Miami *Herald* picked up the story and sent it out on the wire services, crusading against the "dangers" instilled in contemporary youth by rock music, lambasting rock concerts, which exposed kids to drugs and sex, and making a strong plea that it should never be allowed to happen again in Miami. The city government sympathized with the *Herald*'s hysteria and revoked Lawrence, Round, and Driscoll's license for their repeat performance. Pretty soon, the city's "dignitaries" jumped on the bandwagon. On March 23, 1969, Jackie Gleason and Anita Bryant staged a Rally For Decency at the Orange Bowl sponsored by the Greater Miami Youths For Christ. Thirty thousand people, half of them adults, turned out in support and heard a teen-ager read from the stage a letter of support from President Richard Nixon who professed that "This is a very positive approach . . ." But the promoters were one step ahead of the fanatics. In a moment of divine wisdom, they had allied themselves with the Greater Miami Youths For Christ as their front for "musical piety." With that group's aid, they picketed the Hallendale City Hall, asking for restoration of their license, and it was granted. But the three men, while exulting over their victory, pledged to be mindful of their public image in the community's reproachful eye. To that end, they milked any available publicity, including commendations they had received for the architectural aesthetics of the festival site.

While in preproduction for Miami Pop, Mel Lawrence had fashioned an artistic environmental concept to suit the natural lines of the land. He had hired a crew of students and teachers from the University of Miami's art department to produce natural stone formation sculpture and to construct playgrounds from wood debris found in the area. It enhanced the festival atmosphere immensely and was written up in several periodicals, one, in particular, congratulating the promoters for "their daring architectural concepts and life-sized sculptures that dressed the grounds with more care than most of those in attendance showed toward attiring themselves."

One such person impressed by Lawrence's festival design was the bearded sound engineer from nearby Criteria Sound Studios, who had been dispatched to the site to record the show. Stanley Goldstein observed Mel Lawrence's performance at Miami Pop with the same outward admiration he expressed for the other coming-of-age professionals who worked there—like Bert Cohen and Chip Monck, the stage and lighting consultants. He recognized that the demand for such expertise in the rock concert market was greater than it had ever been before and knew it would only be a matter of time before they all worked together again on a related project with more encouraging results.

Lawrence needed little prodding from Michael Lang to bring his partners to New York City to look over the Woodstock Music and Art Festival plans. Lang had hinted at the possibility of making the show a joint effort between Woodstock Ventures and Lawrence's production firm. It sounded to Lawrence to be "one helluva undertaking" that he "couldn't afford to pass up if Lang's hype was on the level." He had been told that the festival budget would adequately compensate them for their expenses and, he explained to his partners, they might even walk away holding on to the deed of what appeared to be the largest festival yet. It had been four months since Miami Pop, and he thought they could stand a little excitement for the coming summer months. Lawrence phoned Lang back and said they would arrive in New York during the second week in April.

They disembarked at Kennedy International Airport on April 12.

The next morning, in surging rain, a caravan of limousines left the Plaza Hotel and transported Tom Rounds, Mel Lawrence, Tom Driscoll, Bill Hanley, Goldstein, and Lang north along the deserted Palisades Parkway toward Orange County.

On the way over, Tom Rounds asked Michael how many people he was preparing for. Without batting an eyelid, Lang replied, "Half a mill'—at least."

"It'll never work at that size, Mike," Rounds objected. "You cannot possibly entertain that many people at one time even if you squeeze them all in. The crowd scale is too big for a festival to be effective. I don't think you're being reasonable."

"It'll work, man," Lang insisted, smiling. "I got it all worked out. You'll see."

By the time they had arrived, Rounds's enthusiasm for getting involved with Woodstock Ventures and its proposed festival in August had waned considerably. He was not too keen on Lang's concept of responsibility and saw a major conflict looming in the distance over that very point. Michael's intentions were clear to Rounds; he wished to create a colossal happening regardless of the practicality or business advantages. Either way, Lang would profit, and that was not Rounds's cup of tea.

Lawrence immediately liked the way the site looked. He didn't allow himself to get overly excited in front of the others, but as they walked over the property, he pointed out that "the land was manageable despite the roads being in only fairly good condition. If the state moved its ass and got the bridge and repair work [that was in progress] completed in time, we can get trucks in to deliver the necessary materials for putting this thing together."

Back in New York, the California Connection approached Lang with their proposal. They needed insurance. Rounds and Driscoll asserted that the likelihood of the festival ever coming off was slim from what they had seen. Michael was going to have to make it worth their while for them to chance coming in with him. A figure had been decided upon, Rounds said. They wanted a nonrefundable guarantee of fifty thousand dollars apiece up front as a consulting fee and an additional five percent of the box office gross.

Michael drew out a breath, smiled and shook his head. "No way," he said softly. "You guys aren't even in the ballpark."

Toward the end of the day, Michael cornered Mel in his hotel room with a definite proposition. "Unload these dudes and come to work for me. They're not happenin', man, and you know it. You can do a lot of small-time Miami Pop shows, but mine's gonna make history. I got the bread, and I'll make it worth your while."

"I'd like to," Mel confessed, "but Driscoll and Rounds . . . we've been through a lot together."

"Time to move on."

"Yeah, I know, man. It sounds like an incredible thing, Woodstock. But I'll feel like a *schmuck* deserting them." Mel looked Michael in the eye. "How much you offerin'?"

Michael smiled. "How does seven grand sound for three months' work?"

"Make it eight and you got a deal."

They shook hands. Michael had his chief of operations.

— 6 —

Miles Lourie had been nagging both Roberts and Rosenman to cement their relationship with the Town of Wallkill if they indeed intended putting the festival on the Mills property. He suggested that they approach the town council with a formal application to hold a public gathering within the town's limits as soon as possible. "Just get it over with so we can all breathe a little easier," Miles advised. Granted it might very well open a can of worms, but it would make it a lot easier on everyone concerned with the festival if they knew where they stood with the town now rather than to have to contend with difficulties as the date closed in.

Through a Middletown attorney they had placed on retainer to represent them locally, John and Joel made an appointment to confront the Wallkill Zoning Board of Appeals on Friday afternoon, April 18, at four o'clock. After a brief debate between their consciences and their best interests, they chose to make the trip without Michael and Artie.

Until 1966, the Wallkill Zoning Board of Appeals and the town council held their monthly meetings in the town's small battery of firehouses. These were more akin to gatherings of friends and family than political meetings. Because of the growth that was providing towns and villages with metropolitan-sized headaches, firehouse caucuses rapidly became history. They could no longer accommodate the growing population and its corresponding problems, and Wallkill was no exception. The town was booming and it needed room to move.

A faction of its inhabitants had been screaming for years for a permanent structure of some kind, a town hall, where they would be able to get adequate representation on issues that concerned their families and their land. Most of those in favor of such an edifice were the farmers who had the most at stake. For the past few years, they had stood by and watched while the state and county governments sanctioned new roads and shopping centers, which ate up acres of fertile land that had, at one time, been productive. Now industry had begun creeping into their neighborhood too, and it was time for the farmers to be heard or to retire, victims of that which they euphemistically called progress. They wanted not only a place where they could meet to debate these pressing issues, but also a permanent home for the growing membership of a town government that supposedly had their best interests at heart.

The Wallkill Town Hall was completed in the spring of 1966, a one-story, gray cement block-and-glass structure that resembled a mini-version of the archetypal modern high school springing up in suburban communities across the country. Its stark interiors were as unadorned as the plot of shrubless land on which it sat, painted brick walls and white room dividers creating a labyrinthian network of small offices designed for productivity—except for the general meeting hall. It reflected the lofty self-esteem of the town fathers and their aspirations to gold-plated greatness. Walls were coated in dark veneers; the folded chairs that made up its nucleus faced a raised presidium-type podium where the councilmen sat. Directly in front of the podium was another lower level of superiority reserved for those with business on the meeting's agenda, like the UN General Assembly. That was where John and Joel sat as they awaited their turn to address the board.

After an hour's time of preliminary business John and Joel were asked to state their business. Striking their best poses of innocence, they gave a description of the festival that sounded remarkably like the ad copy for the Orange County Fair, long a community institution. "A sort of fair, with top-flight musicians and art exhibits," was how John phrased it.

The board of appeals spent less than ten minutes picking over the scant details. As long as it was going to be held on Howard Mills's property and they were fully covered for liability, then the board had no objections. The only provision was that no building was to be done more than seven feet above the ground. Both John and Joel rushed to assure them they would comply with that statute, never taking into consideration construction of a stage or speaker and lighting towers. If they kept their mouths shut, they were on the verge of securing the town's blessing for their extravaganza.

"Well," the chairman of the board sighed, "I guess there's no problem. Pending these boys getting their insurance, we'll say that the zoning board has no objections to what they're planning."

It was in the bag. Roberts and Rosenman slumped into their chairs and relaxed in victory. No board study of the proposition, no public referendum, no strings attached at all as far as their movement was concerned—all obstacles they had dreaded in advance. It seemed too good to be true.

It was.

As Joel and John began gathering their belongings to leave, one of the men on the board grew inquisitive.

"Say, son"—he pointed a wagging finger at Joel—"what kind of music you going to be putting on up here?"

The entire room's bustling activity seemed to freeze as everyone turned his attention to the young promoter. Joel looked at his associate for some kind of support. Their faces remained impassive. He was going to have to go this one alone.

"Well"—he paused, stalling to compose his performance—"I guess the best way to describe it would be, uh, folk. Basically folk. A little swing, too, maybe. A little jazz. You know."

No, the board member admitted, he *didn't* know. And he was concerned about the town's peaceful existence. Like a sleeping child, it was not to be disturbed.

Joel assured him that the promoters of "the fair" shared his concern. (This old codger's going to be trouble, he thought, trying to maintain his painted smile.) "After all, Wallkill's going to be like our home while we're up here."

That seemed to pacify the board member, who was nodding his head in approval. He turned to the rest of the panel, half-shrugged, and nodded again. "Okay," the chairman agreed. "If there's nothing further to be said, this meeting stands adjourned."

Ten minutes after his gavel fell on the desk, Roberts and Rosenman were headed back to New York City in a funnel of cool rain and the key to the Town of Wallkill firmly clutched in the palms of their hands. It was the second time they had come away from that community triumphantly, and it was beginning to look as though they had a certain flair for engineering the smiles of fortune.

Bert Cohen described his Philadelphia-based company, Concert Hall Publications, as "an advertising agency, and also a production company—an amalgamation of everything." And, in fact, Concert Hall would and could accommodate one's most intimate desires—for a slight percentage of the gross. Everything had its price, and Bert, a master of hyperbole, claimed he knew how to go about finding anything and where to buy it to save his customers time, trouble, and money. For a while he had existed as a middleman, buying and selling advertising space for school and underground newspapers. His ultimate dream was to convert them into an organized network of small revolutionary presses his company would control, "like Hearst and Gannett." But, in 1967, when the festival concept caught fire, Bert smelled smoke before anyone else. He somehow wheedled his way into Miami Pop as a production designer ("the most inaccessible staging ever devised," Mel Lawrence later reflected) and attempted to promote this new division of Concert Hall Publications with a vengeance.

Cohen, along with his "chief salesman," Michael Foreman, had made a profession out of courting Woodstock Ventures' bottomless bank account since its inception in mid-March. He was always in attendance when the four partners gathered, offering suggestions based upon his "gargantuan experience in the field" and joining in the rap sessions that ultimately led to defining the festival's superstructure. One thing was for certain: Bert wanted in; it didn't matter much to either him or Michael Foreman what Concert Hall's role was to be. Bert saw his "rightful place in their machinery," and he wanted a firm commitment from them in the way of money and means. "After all," Bert boasted, "who knows more about doing festivals in this country than me and Michael? You fellas can't do this without us." Lang wasn't so sure, but he wanted to hear everything that Bert could tell him about putting a show together, and allowed Cohen and Foreman to entertain the organizational meetings with tales of past escapades. Lang listened attentively and made notes.

During this time, it was decided that the group's aim was to convey to kids across the country that their festival was to be a place to escape the burdens of conventional society. "Look, you can sell 'em on the music and be like everything else that's gone before," Cohen asserted. "But if you really want to do as you say—create something that resembles a nation of people helping one another and getting high on life—then you've got to set the mood before others set it for you. It's got to be prevalent in your advertising; you're gonna hafta take some of the emphasis off the music and place it on the vibes."

Michael Foreman and Goldstein agreed that the name had to convey a sense of freedom, both of thought and of physical presence. It had to imply that kids could come to the festival to get away from being leaned on at home, could roam around the land without being confined to boundaries, could be free from all Establishment rules.

"That's why we gotta keep the name *Woodstock*," Lang insisted. "It really has a mystical feeling about it, everything that's there in the Band's music, y'know—country, woodsy feelings. I think all the hippies are into that. Our gig's gotta be called Woodstock no matter where it goes down."

"But Woodstock alone won't do it," Goldstein said. "There's a lotta people out there who won't be turned on to the depth of the word like you, Michael. And you can't say, 'Fuck 'em,' because we can turn those kids on to the whole trip by getting 'em to come in the first place, and we can't afford to lose them."

"I know," Lang agreed. "I been thinking about it and we gotta have something more. Like calling it an 'Aquarian festival.' That's it, man, 'Aquarian.'" He was pleased with the effect the word had.

"You could be right," Cohen said. "It's got a great hook to it."

"What does it mean?" Joel asked.

Michael chortled. "It's all about us, man. Y'know, the age of Aquarius. Our enlightenment, the order of man and nature. It's *gotta* be called an Aquarian festival." He folded his arms in front of him.

"The Woodstock Music and Arts Fair, An Aquarian Festival—I really dig it," Bert said admiringly.

"How about 'An Aquarian Exposition,'" Goldstein suggested, and everyone applauded his motion.

"It's got everything," Bert said. "Nature, art, the counterculture, music, freedom, tripping—it's terrific. And it'll look great in the underground papers. It's got no Establishment ties to it."

Everyone was in accord. Over the course of the next few get-togethers, Cohen presented the group with ideas for ticket distribution at a network of head shops and record stores. John and Joel, it was decided, would handle ticketing, and Goldstein knew someone who worked at the Fillmore East's box office who was willing to give them a hand. The only things to be worked out in that respect were prices for the show and how many tickets to order.

"We've gotta be careful not to give anyone the idea we're rippin' em off," Lang pointed out.

"Right on," Artie agreed.

"Well, you've got to set a fair price, one that's going to turn a profit at the gate and yet won't offend the hippies," Cohen said instructively. "It's not a tough thing to do."

"But can we do it by offering a combination of prices depending on the amount of days they attend?" Joel asked. "I mean, it's to our advantage to offer them a discount for taking a multiple-day ticket because they remain on the premises and are paying more up front."

"You mean, like givin' 'em a break for stayin' longer?" Lang asked.

"Sure. And also for buying a ticket beforehand and not at the gate. It'll save us a lot of time and trouble to get their money in advance."

Cohen tossed in another point. "It'll also lower the risk of gate-crashing." It was the first time anyone had ever brought that up, and it had a startling effect on the boys. "Look," he said, "I'm not gonna paint you a pretty picture of a stampede, but that's just about what's gone down at other festivals. A buncha kids start pushing at the gates, and before you know it, you've got a ton of kids running over the wall and it's a free-for-all. You're not gonna try to stop 'em by force, because then you'd have a fuckin' riot on your hands. So you take a beating. Joel's got the right idea. You encourage 'em with everything you've got to buy an advance ticket, even if it means giving up a couple bucks in the end."

"But we can't hit 'em with the hard sell, man. Everyone'll be comin' down on us for that," Michael protested. "It's gotta be low key."

Before that session was over, it was decided that the price of the show would be $7 for a one-day ticket, $13 for any combination of two days, and $18 for the package of three days and camping. Tickets would be printed in a variety of colors relative to the day of the show and a code of crescents and stars was to be imprinted behind the ticket legend to make the counterfeiting of tickets a virtual impossibility. Once they were ordered and printed, Cohen would organize the hippie outlets and John and Joel would work out a method by which to handle mail orders.

Pretty soon, Lang found it nearly impossible to exclude Concert Hall from the upper echelon of the festival team. Cohen had ingratiated himself into their plans, and yet there was something discomforting about his presence. It was pushy and irritating, like the hard-sell pitch of a garment center salesman, and since Lang had gotten just about all he could out of Cohen, there was little to justify his always being around. Eventually Lang decided that it would be more constructive to his purposes to give Cohen and his gang something trivial to do rather than to have him hanging around complaining all the time. So they struck a deal for Concert Hall to put together a festival program book and, possibly later, to buy air time to advertise the festival on the underground radio stations and in its press. The trouble was, Bert contended, all that was a long time off. He wanted some action to keep him busy *now*, and he was making it extremely difficult for Lang to say "no."

Michael finally figured out a way to sidetrack Cohen until he was ready for him (or until Cohen just went away and disappeared). Woodstock Ventures had found office space in a building on Fifty-seventh Street, a few blocks from Miles Lourie's office. If Bert wished to make a bid, they would entertain his firm's designing the new offices. Bert more than wished; he refused to allow them to offer the opportunity to an "outsider." After all, he asked, weren't they all family?

The offices were located on the fourth floor of a narrow building facing south so that one could observe the continuous stream of beautiful people flowing through the revolving doors at Henri Bendel's all afternoon long. The entire floor was laid out so that after getting past the reception area, all private offices extended off a central corridor like vertebrae attached to a spinal cord. John and Joel immediately staked their claim to the front room with the floor-to-ceiling picture window; Artie chose the very dark back of the floor; Michael displayed little or no interest in selecting his space. "How about it?" Joel had asked him one evening when they were evaluating the layout. "Which room do you want?" But Michael only replied, "I'm cool, man. Don't worry about me. I kinda roam free."

On April 17, Michael and Joel cosigned a check in the amount of $10,000 over to Concert Hall Publications to begin construction on the interiors of Woodstock Ventures' new offices. Bert Cohen was ecstatic. Pulling John Roberts aside after an inspection of the premises, he exclaimed, "It'll be great. Just beautiful! I'm going to create a total environment for you."

Something in the back of John's mind did not quite take to Cohen's terminology: total environment. "Are you sure we need something that drastic for day-to-day working space, man?"

"John, baby—you're in a new-wave business," he said, "dealing with hip capitalism. Your joint's gotta adapt, create its own environment. You'll have artists and other non-Establishment types popping in to hang out, and it's important that they feel at home and see that you're not stereotyped as *straight guys.*" Cohen made it sound as though they were lepers. "Wait'll you see what I have in store for you. You'll freak!"

That same day, another check was drawn on the Woodstock Ventures account, this one made out to Alexander Tapooz for $4,500 as a deposit on the property for the Woodstock retreat. Michael was adamant about "grabbing it 'fore some other dude whips it out from underneath us," and Artie categorically supported him. "It's our lifeline, baby, the future. We don't score that property and this whole festival gig goes up in smoke. Poof!" He snapped his fingers. Lang nodded his accord.

Roberts and Rosenman exchanged glances of alarm. Was it all that tenuous? The Mills property, their $400-a-week salaries, the contracts with Mel Lawrence and Stan Goldstein, the new offices, the $10,000 advance to Bert Cohen, the dozen or so other expenditures they had made since forming the company—did Michael and Artie take their investment *that* lightly? *Poof?* Did it all hinge on the retreat? John mentally totaled his investment and figured they had spent roughly $67,000 to date on the festival with, at least, an equal amount promised in future assignments. He blanched at his partners' indifference to their monetary commitment. Their motives were becoming better defined, in John's estimation, as time passed.

He had good reason for alarm. The money being used to underwrite their commerce, while John's in name, was not exactly his in the eyes of the bank that had advanced it into his personal account. It was true that his inheritance had been more than substantial—it could probably float two or three festivals—but, at his parents' discretion some years before, a stipulation had been inserted into the trust providing that he could not put his hands on the full amount until he turned thirty-five. The rest was in a time-released account that made portions of it available to him at three intervals over a fifteen-year period.

The money he had used since he turned twenty-one was merely interest that had accumulated on the trust fund, and that had been petered away by indiscriminate stock transactions, high living, and other intemperances. Little, if anything, was left of it. The next transfer of funds would not occur until his twenty-fifth birthday, and that was nearly a year away.

It had become clear to John Roberts some years before that if he was to enjoy independence in the financial world, he would have to devise a way of getting his hands on the major source of his inheritance. Three million dollars could perpetuate a lifetime of ventures. He tried everything, even going so far as to ask his father to alter the terms of the trust, but with no success. Then, in early 1969, Billy Roberts approached his brother with a roundabout route to their riches. It was all very aboveboard, Billy assured him. As it turned out, Billy had found an elderly gentleman officer of the National Bank of North America who, in return for a high rate of interest and reasonable guarantees, would provide the Roberts brothers with an enormous line of credit against their future inheritance. The bank, a staid Wall Street investment house, recognized their destined wealth as tangible assets and decided that their reputations and family background were enough security for reciprocity. Anyway, the boys had agreed to sign an agreement that constituted the bank's holding a lien against their trust funds for all outstanding debts. When the trusts became free and clear, the bank could legally attach their debts to the trusts as straight collateral. There was relatively little risk on the bank's part. And John would be given unrestricted access to his fortune.

His initial appropriation against that agreement was for $50,000, an amount he considered substantial; by mid-April, however, it had all but run out. John took it as an omen. Woodstock Ventures' funds had trickled away like liquid mercury, with no end to the spending in sight. If anything, it was clear to him that budgets had been seriously understated, that there would be a wild proliferation of expenditures before next month came screeching to a halt—money spent to protect their already hefty investment. He had observed snowballing before. It was a vicious monetary cancer, which signalled virtual bankruptcy. But it could be controlled if diagnosed soon enough and amended in time. Time was their worst enemy now, and the only method of speeding up the process was to pay through the nose for services. Catch-22. Something was not going according to plan, and John Roberts was distressed.

*　　*　　*

John, Joel, and Artie were tactically reduced to curious onlookers regarding Michael's progress with the entertainment program. When asked whether he had received any firm commitments from top groups to play at the festival, Michael would pat that person reassuringly on the shoulder and say, "I'm working on it, man. Don't get uptight." Their reaction at that time was exemplary considering everyone's livelihood was riding on his booking prowess. Had it been at any other point in contemporary history, he might have been lynched, but the motto of Peace and Love (*über alles*) was indelibly tattooed on each partner's psyche and they behaved like a band of brainwashed apostles en route to Hamlin. And nobody smelled a rat. "Right on, Michael," they'd nod, trustingly; however, as each day passed, the obligatory salaam took on a less loving tone.

Michael's first big break came in the middle of the second week in April. Hector Morales called to say that for $10,000 he believed Creedence Clearwater Revival could be enticed into being the first group to go to contract with him. Michael was openly relieved. "Do it, man," he ordered. "For any price. Do it. Just nail 'em down."

That much money for Creedence was preposterous considering they only had to perform for sixty minutes instead of having to do an entire concert. But the group had been getting between $5,000 and $7,500 for a two-hour show and were selling out wherever they played. Their popularity was unchallenged. Since 1968, when they dusted off a 1950s hit called "Suzie Q" and turned it into a hard-rock smash, they were consistently represented high up on the rock charts. The follow-ups to "Suzie Q"—"Proud Mary" and "Born On The Bayou"—were well on their way to becoming generational standards, and Morales predicted that their soon-to-be-released single, "Bad Moon Rising," would keep them hot. A sixty-minute term policy for $10,000 cash. Instant credibility. It was what Lang had been waiting for all along.

Hector Morales was also now in possession of that long-awaited lever with which to pry the lock off the tightly bolted record industry door.

"Whaddya mean, you don't wanna be the only supergroup on the program?" he'd confront a doubtful manager whose obstinancy was practically visible over the long-distance phone lines. "We got Creedence and we got plenty of bread. You wanta hold out? Fine. We got a dozen other acts waiting to approach us. Shit or get off the pot, pal."

The rock clouds having been seeded with capital, it was not long before the heavens opened up and the gods descended. On April 18, Hector called Lang with a confirmation that he had received a confirmation from folk singer Tim Harden to appear for $2,000. Michael thought Harden a good act for the Friday night show, which would cater to a soft-rock sound. April 21 landed Canned Heat for a whopping $13,000. They were off and running. The week of April 28, however, was his *pièce de rèsistance*. First, Johnny Winter's manager, Steve Paul, called to say his artist would perform for $7,500, an act that would draw the hardcore electric blues fanatics. Winter was becoming something of a legend, being the first albino guitarist who sounded black. Then, only hours later, a contract was signed guaranteeing Woodstock the Janis Joplin Show for $15,000. No one except the Beatles, Bob Dylan, and Jimi Hendrix was more controversial and in more demand. The booking of the Jefferson Airplane, perhaps the purveyors of the American culture shock-front, for the same $15,000 was, for the most part, anticlimactic. The tossed coin, having balanced neatly (and dangerously) on its edge for the past two months, had suddenly pitched its fate. For $62,500, Michael Lang had assured himself immortality.

CHAPTER FOUR

The Seed of Commonwealth

The true security is to be found in social solidarity rather than in isolated individual effort. —*Fyodor Dostoyevsky (1880)*

I was worried about security from the start, knew that if one thing was going to fuck us it would be everyone's total disregard for the law. I wanted a heavy cop. —*Michael Lang (1969)*

— 1 —

Even as Wes Pomeroy cruised past the White House, past the caravan of buses emptying mute demonstrators onto the barricaded esplanade that ordinarily would have solicited his attention, he was raking over the scraps of an earlier conversation. Reevaluating the unfinished thoughts dropped in the course of a three-minute phone call. Qualifying, double- and cross-checking any premise for its underlying implication. Interpreting motives. It was the cop in his blood; after twenty-five years in law enforcement, you *always* looked for a motive. Only then, when he had ascertained what it really was that someone wanted of him, would he be clearheaded enough to discuss it. And be in total command.

It was a pure May 6 morning. The sun reflected off the gentle Potomac, just within reach of the approach ramp, as Pomeroy edged his car into the outer lane of the parkway for the twenty-minute drive to Dulles. The week before, he had received a phone call from a man identifying himself as Stanley Goldstein, Operations Coordinator for the Woodstock Music and Arts Fair, in New York City. Goldstein told him that his name had been recommended by the International Association of Police Chiefs to head up security for a rock festival he and a group of people were putting on in August. Something about expecting a couple hundred thousand kids to turn out for the weekend and would he be interested in talking about it. What the hell? Pomeroy thought, staying a fraction below the fifty-five-mile-an-hour speed limit. He had been embroiled in one sort of controversy or another throughout his career. He'd be damned if age would soften his curiosity. Sure he'd talk.

At fifty-six, Wes Pomeroy was every inch the gilded rooster he had been as a police cadet. Even in the box-cut, slightly dated blue suit that had recently become his civilian uniform, he represented unmistakable authority. He was a broad man, built like a wrestler, meaty and powerful with a prominent chest that gave more than one associate the impression that he wore a bulletproof vest beneath his shirt. Pomeroy's physical presence was unquestionably awesome. His intense blue eyes were direct and piercing, yet radiant like sapphire chips. His tobacco-colored flat-top seemed uncompromising for the times. His appearance, however, was a contradiction of the man's temperament. Totally sympathetic to the problems of youth and their static environment, Pomeroy was a listener whose interpretation of the law was dictated by common sense. No one, it was said, ever crossed Wes Pomeroy's path with anything but respect.

Pomeroy had enjoyed a long and distinguished career as a civil servant, beginning in the Office of the Sheriff of San Mateo County, California, where he served for sixteen years, eight of them as under sheriff. His treatises on peaceful law enforcement were legendary and, as a result, he was called in to consult on a variety of interrelated activities, most notably the 1964 Republican National Convention in San Francisco, for which he directed outside policing and internal security. Ramsey Clark, then Attorney General of the United States, spotted Pomeroy's talent there and plucked him out of public service to act as his special assistant in Washington, after which he became associate administrator of the Law Enforcement Assistance Administration at the Department of Justice for the Johnson administration. It was no small wonder that the International Association of Police Chiefs had singled him out for the Woodstock job.

Pomeroy's term with the LEAA was nearing its end when Stan Goldstein called. Richard Nixon had been inaugurated as President six months earlier, and it was only a matter of time before he cleaned house of the last vestiges of Democratic rule. Pomeroy, not wishing to be released from his post like an aging ballplayer, had tendered his resignation in March—to take effect June 1, 1969—and was in the process of starting a private consulting business. Woodstock, he decided, could provide him with an interesting transition.

Goldstein's Eastern Airlines shuttle from New York was right on time. The two men made brief, perfunctory introductions and settled on the airport's terminal restaurant as the place where they could best confer. Gold-stein had worn a navy blue gauzy shirt decorated with white stars over his jeans "to see how it would affect this cop." It bore a distinct resemblance to a portion of the American flag, and Goldstein predicted that if anything rankled a cop more than long hair, a beard, and blue jeans, it was a hippie draped in the flag. "If he can live with this, I know he's our man," Goldstein told a friend on his way to the airport. Pomeroy smiled, shook hands with Goldstein, and didn't so much as bat an eye over his apparel.

The airport lounge was dark and noisy, but they separated themselves from the rest of the crowd by choosing a small table away from the window overlooking departures. Goldstein didn't waste precious time reiterating his employer's undertaking; Pomeroy had already heard it on the phone, and if he was there, he was interested.

"We've got a peaceful setting where people can enjoy themselves," he began. "I think it has the potential to become the first successful, nonviolent festival of its kind. And the largest."

Pomeroy raised an eyebrow at the last remark.

Goldstein smiled and nodded lazily. "Look, man, I don't want to bullshit you. It wouldn't do either of us any good. We've got a lot of bread behind us, and we intend to put on the biggest, most complete rock happening ever held."

"You think you fellas can handle something as ambitious as that?" Pome-roy asked.

Stanley's smile widened. "Not really. That's why I'm here talking to you. I'd be a fool to think we could do it ourselves. It'd wind up being the biggest fiasco this side of Vietnam. But one thing we *do* have is this enormous source of cash, and we don't intend to skimp. No, let's put it this way: we can't *afford* to skimp on doing it the right way. We're going to invest the money in getting ourselves the best of everything. Rock groups, traffic controllers, sound engi-neers, lighting experts—you name it. After seeing you this morning, I have an appointment at the Pentagon to consult with a staff of army engineers about sanitation. The facilities, staff, acts, *everything*—all the tops in provisions and personnel. I'd like to include your name in our next staff press release."

"Well, it sounds interesting," Pomeroy admitted, staring him squarely in the eyes. It was uncomfortable, and Goldstein eventually had to look away. "What would you want me to do?"

"Handle all phases of security, from police coordination right down to crowd control."

"It sounds like you're expecting trouble in both those areas."

"I always expect problems," Stan said. "Trouble can be avoided."

This time, it was Pomeroy's turn to smile.

"Crowd control." He said it as though jotting down the two words on an index card and filing it away. "Tell me what you mean by that."

"Okay. We're gonna have a lot of people up there in Wallkill, and it's gotta be orderly or else it's gonna get bloody. Remember—I said no bullshit. All right. It's up to everyone involved to make absolutely sure that doesn't happen. We've gotta have security, but it's got to be suggestive, subtle. No uniforms, no weapons, no angry authoritarian faces, no shoving people around. I don't want anyone in that crowd to be aware of our security, but I want it to be felt." He looked at Pomeroy for a reaction. The cop was smiling, his eyes alive. "My idea is to promote security from within. Encourage some of the bigger kids to lead the way without being abrasive."

"Have you been reading my manuals?" Pomeroy asked with a note of sarcasm to his voice. "I'm convinced—always have been—that one cannot preserve order by the use of force. It's contradictory by definition. If a couple hundred thousand kids see a wall of cops around the grounds, they'll suffocate. And when they begin to choke, they fight back; it's their only defense. No, Goldstein, I agree with you on that. But it's going to take a helluva lot of planning to pull it off. You're not talking about refereeing a football game." Pomeroy pulled his chair closer to the table and folded his hands. "Look, there's one thing I've got to get out front right now. I don't believe that conventional ways of trying to control people's behavior work anymore. There is one absolute—and on this, I think, we already agree, but I want you to hear it from me—is that *nobody*, I mean not even the man watching the gate receipts, will have a gun or a weapon. I want that very clear before I even talk to you about coming on staff."

Goldstein nodded soberly.

"If I get involved," Pomeroy continued, "it won't be with the conventional cop security approach." He related to Goldstein his theory that people are either innately violent or nonviolent, and that crimes are committed because a host of social and tacit contracts that usually regulate human emotions are broken. "This isn't a whole lot of baloney, believe me. It's checked out over the years. And it is central to my whole concept of security. Whether or not I'm your man is one thing. But I'll tell you right now—if you don't build your security system around that concept, you don't stand a chance of coming out of this thing alive. You've got to build security on the foundation of making everyone who attends feel good about their neighbors."

"It sounds like common sense," Goldstein affirmed. "How can I help but like it?"

"It *is* common sense, but that's something we seem to be short on these days. Yeah, look—I'm interested, but I'm expensive."

"That's a quality no one's short of these days. How much?"

"Two hundred dollars a day plus expenses and a per diem living allowance. That's not including a full staff of top advisers who I'm gonna have to bring in on this."

"Sounds reasonable to me. When can you start?"

"June 1. That's when I'm done here in Washington."

Stan shook his head. "No good. I needed you yesterday. There's too much work to be done and too little time left in which to do it."

"Goldstein, we've got ourselves our first problem," Pomeroy said. "I have a responsibility to finish my work here, and I'm not about to throw away my reputation for two hundred bucks a day. You got any suggestions?"

Indeed Goldstein did. He wasn't about to allow this treasure to walk away from him without his first agreeing to join the festival staff. Stan suggested that Pomeroy fly to New York next week, take a look at the site, and meet Michael Lang. "We'll work out a way to fly you in for a day or two each week until you're free. Naturally we'll pick up all costs. Then, it's full time. How does that sound?"

"Better," Pomeroy said approvingly. "I could rearrange my schedule now so that my absence in Washington won't make a difference. Meanwhile, I'll make a few calls for you and see if I can get another police chief or administrator up there in my place to do some of the initial leg work. You'll need someone who carries the same weight and outlook as me. I'll see what I can do."

The sun was directly overhead as Wes Pomeroy swung the car back onto the parkway toward the distant Capitol Building. The motives had been revealed and had panned out to what he believed were forthright. And exciting. The kids—he could handle the kids and all their idiosyncrasies. He had never let stereotypes influence him or stand in the way of things before. Not even Goldstein and that horrendous shirt he had on. They seemed to know what they were doing, they were paying their way, and that was all right by him. Their notion of what they were trying to do, Pomeroy thought, was not all that outrageous. Why shouldn't kids be allowed to congregate on a farm, listen to music, even get high, and expect an Establishment-free weekend? And if he had his way, Wes Pomeroy would be right there in Wallkill to help them bring it into focus.

Goldstein knew that relying solely on conventional methods of security to carry them through the festival was a sucker's game; if they, indeed, intended to barrel through the three-day free-for-all without incident, he was going to have to come up with a means of preserving the peace with which the counterculture could directly identify. Curiously, something in the back of his mind told him that this particular task would not be as difficult as he imagined.

Goldstein was searching for an organized group of people—preferably communal—to assist with a variety of security-related measures. He anticipated one hundred thousand kids from the city coming to Wallkill to listen to rock and roll who hadn't the slightest conception of how to get out of a rainstorm, let alone tend a cut foot. He needed a self-sufficient group used to crowds who knew how to care for people under a variety of situations, who could be "raggedly" disciplined and who knew how to contend with the Establishment forces in residence.

He remembered that Bert Cohen's partner, Michael Foreman, mentioned something about a group called the Hog Farm of whom Stanley had not heard. They were a core group of fifty men and women, led by ex–Beat poet Hugh Romney, whose communal expeditions in California and New Mexico were based on sharing all worldly possessions with one another and entertaining the public with pranks and carefully staged acts of guerilla theatre. The Hog Farm was an offshoot of Ken Kesey's Merry Pranksters, with whom Romney had been closely allied in the early sixties, and the Juke Savages, a California commune whose members lived outdoors in Indian-style tepees. Their self-sufficient lifestyle had permitted them, somewhat more easily than better qualified medical practitioners, to become involved with the intricacies of the experimental drug culture and the people who experienced bad acid trips; and they had a thorough understanding of what it took to care for those people.

Through a columnist at the *Village Voice*, Goldstein traced a faction of their members to a loft in New York City. He called and was delighted to discover that Hugh Romney himself was in attendance and would see him the next afternoon if he got his body over to their "hole" on Houston Street.

The description was apt. Their apartment was indeed a hole, a single room measuring one hundred by twenty-five, which housed over seventy-five people at the same time. The Farmers were dressed for the occasion, most resembling pictures of the kids Goldstein had seen wandering through the Haight.

Hugh Romney, a certified "freak" with a wide toothless grin, greeted him at the door with a great bear hug and asked Stan to join the members of his "family" around the table in the center of the room.

Goldstein explained briefly what Woodstock Ventures was trying to accomplish, suggesting the festival would truly be a party for the people—one of the Hog Farm's primary tenets. Instead, Romney's "family" reacted to

Goldstein's pitch with vehement distaste. They saw the festival as "political opposition"; it was a capitalistic venture and they were communally oriented.

"This alley cat's obviously a con man, Hugh," a couple of the family members said. "He's trying to fuck us over. We don't want your money, buster."

"Well, I hope that you'll change your mind. And if you do, you can't come unless I pay you."

"Whaddya mean?"

"I mean that there are going to be about two hundred people involved in making everyone comfortable, and they'll all be working for a salary. I don't want anyone to say that some are getting paid and others are not. You could give the money away for all I care, but you gotta take it before you shake it." He smiled.

"Whaddya got in mind?"

"Well, I'd like you there for a multitude of reasons, a few being crowd control—but you can forget about police assault, I'm talking about health and safety—the clearing of land, maintaining a 'free kitchen' to feed those who come without money, a 'free stage' behind the main stage where those without tickets could be entertained. . . ."

"Hey, you're really serious about making this a people's event," Romney said.

"Of course I mean business, but I'm by no means serious." They appreciated Goldstein's reference to their comic approach to life. "Look, I recognize the fact that if there *is* a crowd problem, we'd be better off having a bunch of pretty girls without brassieres running after the culprits with seltzer bottles than machine guns and tanks."

"Now you're talking!" Romney chortled. "We'd need about fifty cases of seltzer bottles and three truckloads of chocolate cream pies as ammunition for security. I knew we were talking the same lingo, Goldstein. What else you got in store for us?"

They talked into the late afternoon and, again, two days later with Michael Lang at a restaurant called the Kettle, about how it was imperative that the Hog Farm keep peace by discouraging troublemakers. If they kept everybody happy—either by donating food or medical attention or by playing pranks on one another—then they would reduce the possibility of trouble breaking out, as it had at previous festivals.

Goldstein wanted Romney to bring his family to Wallkill a month or two before the festival took place. They were to live on the land and work with the University of Miami art group in getting the site into shape, chopping wood for the playground and gathering crews from the interested kids who were sure to stop by for a job.

"How the hell do you expect me to get eighty of our people from New Mexico, where most of 'em are at right now, all the way to New York? Our bus won't make it, man. Not carryin' all eighty of 'em and equipment and stuff."

They worked out an agreement whereby fifteen men would come with the bus to Wallkill by the beginning of June, and the rest would be flown to New York in a specially chartered jet. They could load the essential equipment onto the plane. Everything else could be purchased in Wallkill.

"Meanwhile," Stanley pointed out, "I'd like you to prepare some kind of estimate of what it'll take to get the free kitchen off the ground. How much food you'll need. What kind of equipment. Anything at all you can think of that we'll want to have on the site. We'll make sure you get it. How does that sound?"

"You're forgetting something, friend. The money. You said we'd be paid and we might as well discuss it now before it gets messy."

Romney proved an able negotiator. Before the day was out, he had wheedled a promise of $8,000 in cash plus all equipment and living expenses to be turned over to the Hog Farm immediately after the festival. Peace, love, and, most of all, money. It was all beginning to fall into place.

— **2** —

A gentleman named George Lax owned the dark beige sandstone office building at 47 West Fifty-seventh Street, which had been designed in the early 1920s to complement the string of townhouse-style buildings joined to either side of it. Stretching a mere seven floors into the Manhattan skyline, it had provided a temporary home for some of the most prestigious New York firms, a high-rent address in the heart of the nouveau entertainment and art district.

Bert Cohen had promised John Roberts that the Woodstock Ventures offices would be ready for occupancy on Monday, May 19, in time to begin a full-scale advertising blitz in the underground press. They also wanted it ready in time as a place equipped to sort the rush of mail orders they expected. An auxiliary staff of sixteen people had been hired to handle ticketing, promotion, bookkeeping, and general office work, and their individual departments were beginning to get cramped on Roberts and Rosenman's living-room floor. The weekend before the move, however, it was clear that Bert was stalling them about taking possession of the premises, and they wanted to see why for themselves. After several minutes of begging them not to enter the place before it was completed, Bert caved in to their demands and agreed to take John and Joel on a premature tour of their new digs.

Cohen had entrusted the office decoration to a young industrial designer fresh out of school named Barry Reischman. Reischman had been in Concert Hall's employ for something under six months and, in his boss's judgment, was "bright, creative, stoned-out, functional hip—a real prototype of the late 1960s." In the case of Woodstock Ventures' new suite, the emphasis of Reischman's architectual prowess was unmistakably on *stoned-out*.

John and Joel's communal office, which looked out over Fifty-seventh Street, was built on a series of wooden risers, graduated in tiers and covered in royal-blue carpeting. The middle of the room had been hollowed out, the rugs dropping off into what looked like a huge pit. When filled with pillows, it was to be their conference area. There were no desks or chairs in the room; wooden crates had been randomly inserted beneath the carpeting to create "seating bumps" and "free-form nooks and crannies, which could be extremely functional if they used their imagination."

John Roberts's first impression of his new quarters was nausea. "What the hell are you doing, Bert?" he exploded. "We've gotta have space to work, not a place to loll around on the floor in our suits. This is the most uncomfortable-looking stuff I've ever seen."

"Oh, it'll be great, man. It's a little far out," Cohen admitted, "but when it's done, it'll be beautiful and you'll love it."

"It's done, Bert—and I don't love it."

But Cohen hadn't heard him. He and his staff were already swinging down the hall continuing their funhouse tour.

The next room, a spare office, was draped from floor to ceiling in stretched nylon—"so there are no sharp angles," Bert pointed out proudly. "No need to worry about sharp angles while you're working." All lighting was concealed behind the satiny walls, which cast a back-lit theatrical effect over the work area. Rosenman was convinced no Woodstock employee would get any work done there. It was the most *un*functional mess he had ever laid his eyes on.

The accounting office next door was in a transitory state of several shades of turquoise. Only a week before, they had hired a bookkeeper named Renee Levine, an older conservative woman from Brooklyn who was not about to pass her working day toiling in whorehouse decor. "You're crazy!" she screamed at Roberts when she entered the office. "If you think I'm going to work with numerical figures while looking at a room like this, you're completely off the wall!" Fearing she would bolt out the front door never to return, Roberts ordered the immediate repainting of the room in more sedate tones.

The ticket office toward the back of the floor was painted alternating stripes of red, white, and blue in a high-gloss finish. A net extended over the ceiling and diffused the fluorescent lighting so that weblike shadows danced on the walls. Some early mail orders for the event had already started to arrive based upon word of mouth, and they were being attended to by Keith O'Connor, a bearded, disheveled young man who had been coaxed away from his job at the Fillmore East box office. The room was being prepared for his specialized accounting "system," a procedure only O'Connor seemed equipped to comprehend. Predicting close to fifty thousand mail orders in the upcoming weeks, his system consisted only of a spiral notebook and a pencil. If they were correct in assuming an advance order of nearly two million dollars, Keith's abstract system would undoubtedly give Roberts's accountants palpitations.

Beyond the ticket office was Michael's shadowy sanctuary, a low-keyed cubicle painted silvery-gray to complement the charcoal area rug and tasteful oversized desk already in place. In view of its intended occupant, both Joel and John were somewhat taken aback by the room's conservative trimmings. No black-light posters, no peace signs etched into the wall, no stuffed animals or toys on the floor, no saying from Chairman Abbie taped to the wall. What they had feared most was that they would open the door onto a Turkish opium den with beaded-mirror pillows slung in front of mammoth hookah pipes laden with brandy and hash. Ironically, what they found was both a shock and a disappointment; they thought they had Lang pegged as a heathen, but perhaps they had been wrong.

Getting past the shocking red and green bathrooms flanking either side of the back hallway, Bert prepared his "guests" for his final and most fabulous creation. "Artie's pad, man. This office'll knock you out. It's just . . . it's just . . . well, beyond words. It's too groovy to describe. See for yourself."

Joel and John meekly entered the office and soared into the twilight zone, an excursion best described by the ingenuous gasp from John's mouth. It was like a scene out of Walt Disney's *Fantasia*. The walls, paneled in a light veneer, did little to distract from the gaudy, bright purple carpeting. Hanging from the canary-yellow ceiling was a berry-colored veil that dropped across the top of the room, creating a tent effect, whose purpose it was to focus the eye down onto an immense rosewood desk where Artie Kornfeld was to conduct his business. Artie's chair was anything but functional, a highbacked throne lathed in various shades of velvet—although it did put him within reaching distance of a bank of sound equipment positioned against the rear wall and seemingly powerful enough to blast a family of deaf mutes out of their minds. Directly opposite the desk was a raised platform under a panel of spotlights where one was asked to lounge when "hanging out" with Mr. Kornfeld.

"Very psychedelic, Bert," Joel managed to get out before asking to be excused.

"Whaddya think, John?" the designer inquired.

"Uh, yeah, Bert—psychedelic. Incredibly far out. I, uh, never would have conceived of such a layout in my most bizarre fantasies. You have some, uh, imagination."

"Thanks, man. It was a trip. My guys should be outta here in a few weeks. . . ."

"A few weeks!" John was annoyed. "We've got to get started in here now!"

"But we can put the finishing touches on while you're doing your thing. Just pretend we're not even around." Bert Cohen always had the right answer in his hip pocket.

Roberts and Rosenman were more disturbed by the implications arising from the decoration of Artie's psychedelic hovel than they were about the overall fiasco in their offices. "It's something out of a three-year-old's fantasy," John commented. "Just bizarre! And what's more, Artie *loves* it. He's like a little kid whenever he goes in there. It's fuckin' scary."

Kornfeld's entire existence since leaving Capitol Records had been regulated by his constant experimentation with drugs. Artie's previous enthusiasm for the record business had been considerably numbed and he began to function in quick, spasmodic movements accompanied by slurred speech. There was strong evidence offered by his closest friends to support the theory that Artie was firmly entrenched in the world of psychedelic drugs with plenty of money at his disposal to support a thirsty curiosity.

One afternoon, soon after Woodstock Ventures had moved permanently into the new offices, Artie encountered Bert Cohen alone in the reception area, inspecting his staff's work. The conversation eventually turned to drugs, and to Bert's virtual abstention every time something was offered to him.

"Why aren't you into grass, man?" Artie asked. "Grass is great, hash is even greater. But y'know what I'd really get off on? Mesc."

Mescaline, to which Artie referred, was a psychedelic hallucinogen rapidly growing in street popularity. Artificially produced in a laboratory, its source was peyote, a cactus whose crown is sliced off and dried to form a hard brownish disc known as the mescal button. The high one received from it was fast and fluid in much the same kaleidoscopic way that LSD parachuted its users into colorful dreamworlds. Its source, though, was scarce and expensive.

Two weeks later Bert came across Artie as he came stumbling out of his purple and yellow kingdom, head in the air, holding a conversation with nobody in particular, and realized he had found a source.

"Hey, man—anyone know where I can score some more great mesc?" Artie mumbled. "Time to buckle in and take off for space. Whoooosh!" Then he noticed Cohen standing by the receptionist's desk. "Bert—hey Bert, baby." Artie fell into the bigger man's arms and draped a languid hand around Cohen's back. A young girl in jeans and bare feet sitting at the desk looked on in bewildered embarrassment. Artie caught her expression of concern and tightened his clasp on Cohen. "Don't worry. Bert's my brother, baby. My *brother!*"

Artie slapped Cohen good-naturedly on the back a few more times and smiled. Pointing at Cohen again, he put his head on Bert's shoulder and closed his eyes. He muttered something about great mesc.

And laughed. And laughed. And laughed. And laughed. And laughed. And laughed. And laughed. And laughed. And laughed. And laughed. And laughed. And laughed. And laughed. And laughed. And laughed. And laughed. And laughed. And laughed.

— **3** —

Michael's blueprint for technical expertise was by no means a doctrine of probity. It was hunting season—hip music people were a rare species and Lang needed his staff completed. Everything that walked, talked, flew, or glided was considered fair game.

Nor was there honor even among the hippest of thieves. Lang recognized that the only qualified personnel in the field with any kind of track record worked for Bill Graham over at the Fillmore East on Second Avenue and he worked hard at making himself known around the backstage area.

Graham was the undisputed sultan of psychedelic rock. Since 1964, he

had nurtured San Francisco's acid rock arietta into an empire of countercul-
tural dialectics to the sweet tune of millions and gradually drew it eastward.
With it, he developed a corps of hippies who kept the machinery humming.
He taught them about dramatic lighting, amplification, balancing and mixing sound (which was simultaneously carried over as many as sixteen microphones), staging, and group travel. He had even gone as far as divulging his
methods of negotiating for talent and reading contracts. Of course, what he
was really doing was training the future competition, making sure that when
the time came for rock to emerge as a major industry, he would have cloned
the master race who helm the controls. And they would owe him. Graham's
children.

Graham pulled his road show into New York in late 1968, a city in which
he was not exactly welcomed with open arms by the local promoters. His
idea was to bridge the east-west cultural gap with a common denominator,
which he, of course, would establish. The result was Graham's opening a
carbon copy of his San Francisco rock emporium, the Fillmore, on the
Lower East Side in an old, dilapidated vaudeville house. Called the Fillmore
East, it was another huge success from the moment Bill Graham opened its
doors.

Lang had sanctioned midnight raids on Graham's staff almost from the
word go. Bill Hanley had blasted the Fillmore's sound senses and Keith
O'Connor had manned the box office; both were now securely within the
Woodstock camp. But there were more urgent, more complex duties to be
assigned, and Lang had his eye on several of Graham's most prized generals.

E. H. Beresford "Chip" Monck was one of the few acknowledged professionals among the expanding rock forces, and he had been firmly implanted
there for some time. He had started his career in New York in the late fifties,
providing lighting for folk performers like Odetta, Josh White, Harry Belafonte, and Geoffrey Holder at the Village Gate. In between stands, he took
several of those acts on extended tours across the country and subsequently
found himself in Africa with Miriam Makeba, and Australia with Peter, Paul
and Mary.

Most women found Monck strikingly handsome. Waves of dirty-blond
hair tied back into a ponytail and great muttonchops that grew the length of
either side of his face made him the embodiment of the great Southern California dream. He was strong, cocky, and overpowering.

After returning to California in 1967, Chip was introduced to Lou Adler
who hired him to stage Monterey Pop. Performers became more demanding
as the money grew, and by 1968, most acts were concerned with the theatrical components of staging—penny-ante dramatics controlled by technicians

stationed at control decks in the audience. Monck had been doing that for over a decade and when the demand became great, he found himself besieged by offers to do lighting for every top rock group. Naturally, Bill Graham had to have someone as talented as Monck under his roof, and it wasn't long before Chip became technical coordinator of both the Fillmore East and the Fillmore West.

Hector Morales first approached Monck about joining Woodstock backstage at the Fillmore East after a characteristically late show (many groups played five-hour sets that lasted until four o'clock in the morning). Chip was only mildly interested, citing that "everyone and his mother was planning" a similar event. He did, however, reluctantly agree to meet with the promoters as a favor to Morales.

The meeting took place a few blocks from the Fillmore at the home of John Morris, a garrulous twenty-four-year-old graduate of Fillmore East management who was in the process of raising capital for a multimillion-dollar Virgin Islands resort. Lang handled the sales talk with the usual savoir faire, pausing occasionally as Stan Goldstein added an unnoted virtue or two, and before long, Monck's indifference was a thing of the past.

"The only trouble is," he explained, "I've got a slew of commitments for the summer, paying gigs for Graham and a couple of other guys. My blocking out a couple months to do your festival might put me out of commission too long. It'd hurt my credibility. It sounds great though." He pondered it for a few seconds. "I'll try to work it out. Meanwhile, you might want to talk to John Morris, here, about a place on your staff."

Morris appeared flattered by the suggestion but, in Goldstein's estimation, was overly eager to get involved with the festival for someone caught up in a monumental land development deal. Woodstock had to be small peanuts by comparison. There had to be a bit more to his enthusiasm than met the eye, Stan deduced. And there was. Morris, as he later discovered, was a coattail surfer who rode a regular wave of bad luck. He always seemed to have his hands in a half-dozen scintillating projects controlled by close friends, only to be dumped as each one took off.

Still, Lang and Goldstein liked Morris. There were a number of ways he could be of value to them, especially when it came to dealing with performers. Because of his experience with Graham, he knew how to examine contracts, could execute the attached riders, and had a talent for being able to deal civilly with that nefarious species called the road manager, many of whom had remained friends after Morris left the music business. Morris had been a road manager himself for the Jefferson Airplane, and Lang assumed that he could learn from watching Morris operate. But, most of all, Morris was Michael's link to the ubiquitous Bill Graham. Graham had most of the world's major acts under contract for summer tours, and Lang knew that if he was going to penetrate those tour schedules, to lure the bands to Woodstock on one of their "open" days, some form of conciliation was going to have to be worked out with Graham. A trade-off of some kind. Michael might consider volunteering his staff's services free of charge for a Graham promotion, or donating ad space in the festival program book—anything. But something had to be arranged, and fast. Otherwise it'd be like pulling teeth to attract those sought-after groups who were not about to risk alienating Graham for one day's work. Michael was forced to seek the promoter's blessing, and John Morris could wind up being his ace in the hole.

Lang chased after Chip Monck without shame. Soon after their meeting in Morris's apartment, Lang called on him again to toss around some ideas about lighting a show of Woodstock's dimensions. As with the other experts Lang had seen, his primary interest was to tap Chip's knowledge so that, one day, he could ably challenge Graham's heavyweight title. Michael never gave instructions or even offered suggestions to his compatriots in those early meetings. Instead, he established an affinity with the creative people by asking: "Whaddya think we should do?" and making mental notes. It was a street leader's method of self-education and, ultimately, survival.

Lang and Monck began to hit it off as friends. The two were "movers" in a microcosm of followers, young men full of confidence and purpose who could lay back and unwind over a joint and still take care of business with unyielding tenacity. Here was that beautiful irony indicative of the generation's anti-Establishment heroes who wallowed in the splendors of cutthroat capitalism—fighting to excel in the very thing the movement rejected. They masqueraded as hippies although they also shared an affection for spending large sums of other people's money. But an even stronger bond was their abnormal respect for one another: one could look into the other's eyes, realize a lie was in progress, and still place unabiding trust and well-being in his judgment.

As their friendship progressed, Michael asked Monck to lay out a lighting design for a six-hundred-acre city and not to give cost a thought. "I want it to be very colorful, like an acid trip," Lang advised him, "much more than the usual alternating shades of red and blue. I want the audience *involved.*"

Chip suggested they hire the Fillmore's resident light-show designer, Joshua White, but Michael shook it off. "That's old news, man. Nobody's turned on by light shows anymore. No, I want something new and unique, something that produces a natural high. Can you do it?"

"Without worrying about bread? Yeah."

With that agreed upon, Monck signed a five-page contract guaranteeing Chipmonck Industries Corp. the sum of $7,000 for Chip's semiexclusive services and an additional $13,000 for "the said Mr. Monck" to employ a stage manager, designer, and construction foreman at his sole discretion.

The next day John Morris was hired as production coordinator. His only stipulation was that neither he nor Chip earn more than the other. It had something to do with a duel of egos that had been going on between them for years. Michael agreed, and presented John with a contract for $6,000. Based upon an element of trust—one of the Love Generation's principal commandments—John waived inspection of Chip's contract and committed his name to the binding agreement, thus becoming the tenth member of the festival's executive staff.

While trust and slogans of Peace and Brotherhood were enlisted to front the hippies' public call to unity, it was a combination of those very qualities that ultimately turned their euphoric dream into a nightmare of paranoia. Bruce Cook in his book *The Beat Generation* attributes much of the souring process to the pseudomystical lyrics of rock music, which, he asserts, had "begun to load them with such heavy intellectual fright." But, more so, there was strong evidence that the movement had overdosed on its own idealistic double-talk. Love. Peace. Beauty. Truth. Spiritual togetherness. Brotherhood: the hippies revolted against the Establishment and suspected anyone over thirty. "Fuck the system! Fuck the pigs!" When they began to tire of those unifying threads, their shopworn togetherness converted to enmity, and brother began fucking brother. It was all one could do to survive out there on the streets. Much of that had managed to seep into the hippie hierarchy as well. There were the power struggles to determine who was the most peaceful. There was a war going on in America with "Peace" as its battle cry.

None of this, of course, escaped the upper echelons of Woodstock Ventures Incorporated. For some time, Michael Lang had been worrying about how he was going to bring his newly acquired staff of groovy, laid-back, very together dudes under the same roof with "uptight cats" like John Roberts and Joel Rosenman. Cohabitation had always been one of Lang's primary objectives, but this was carrying it to extremes. As far as he was concerned, there wasn't a prayer that cool personalities like Chip Monck and Mel Lawrence were going to feel loose around the office. What's more, Michael himself was growing uncomfortable there. He found Roberts too regimented, too convinced there were proper business practices one had to subscribe to in order to succeed, and that was contrary to Lang's concept about how the Woodstock operation should be run. He felt it should represent the new, relaxed way of bringing business people together. Wasn't that why they had told Renee Levine, their bookkeeper, to come in each morning after she woke up—that's when the office officially opened for her? Hadn't they dispensed with dress codes for the same reason? Wasn't inner peace their universal aim?

Joel and Michael's personalities were about as compatible as those of a clergyman and a hooker. Joel did not trust Lang to so much as make a bank deposit without finding a way to siphon off part of it, much less to represent the best interests of the company in which they were partners. Nor was he subtle about his distrust. According to Michael, it was Joel's manner, the way he condescendingly spoke to Lang and Kornfeld as one orders a dog to "sit" and "stay." He seemed openly contemptuous of their hippie mannerisms, looking sideways at John throughout group conversations as if to say: "Get a load of this nonsense." Michael interpreted these nuances as threats and, in retaliation, began complaining to Goldstein that "Joel never told anyone the truth about anything." He felt as though Rosenman would tell him one thing and then run to Roberts with another story about how Michael was up to no good. "Joel lies, man, and I just can't get into that shit. He's also an imcompetent—bad news."

Michael was in a bind. He knew that if he brought the music and press people to the office, it would destroy the ethereal image of the festival; they would see through John and Joel's plastic hippie veneer and would be immediately turned off. Additionally, it would reduce his own credibility as a spokesman for the generation to that of a media joke. But even more important, he would be forced to defend his partners' attitudes to Mel and Chip—and he just could not bring himself to do that.

The third week in May, Michael took steps to alleviate his quandary by negotiating for alternate office space in a building around the corner from John Morris's apartment in Greenwich Village.

It was a measure of separation that perplexed John Roberts. Roberts had been under the impression that he and Joel had made sweeping strides in their personalities as a means of bridging the generation gap. He had even assumed, perhaps prematurely, that Michael and he were friends. There had been many occasions when they took long walks together around Manhattan discussing their divergent ideologies and comparing upbringings. And they weren't all that different.

Now Michael wanted them to remain apart.

"Why?" John asked him, hurt by the suggestion. "What's going on? Why do you want to take an office way down there when it will be impossible for us to remain in constant contact?"

"Because it won't happen uptown," Michael answered quietly as if it were as plain as day.

"I don't understand. What do you mean 'it won't happen uptown'?"

"It just won't." They stood silently, facing each other for a moment. Michael smiled, assuming he had made himself perfectly clear.

"Michael—we've just finished taking these offices, spent a lotta bread fixing them up to suit you guys. We don't *need* another office."

"Not we, man—me. The production staff. We need a big place to spread out and get in the groove. Y'know, where these guys can draw and work on stage plans and be creative and everything. Your place isn't even finished yet. Like, I need a place right away for my staff to get to work. Otherwise, we're nowhere." He also mentioned that ticketing wasn't being handled properly by Joel, and *his* gang needed a productive atmosphere although, in fact, Joel had nothing to do with ticketing. "Artie'll stay up here with you cats and handle publicity, and that way one of us'll always be around. I'll be poppin' in all the time, too. Relax, man."

John considered Michael's argument for the separation of powers and saw nothing particularly wrong with it. Nor did Joel. They *would* need a lot more room than the Fifty-seventh Street offices offered if they wanted to construct staging modules and to be able to work on those oversized drafting tables Michael said they needed. There were only two empty offices in the back of the uptown office, and those would eventually be taken over by the mail-order operation. What did it matter anyway if Lang and his crew were downtown? They were all working toward the same end.

Weren't they?

— *4* —

On May 20, 1969, Michael Lang, Mel Lawrence and his assistant—an attractive young blond girl from Texas named Penny Stallings—Chip Monck, an administrative office manager they had hired for downtown named Joyce Mitchell, John Morris, and several assistants moved into the second and third floors of a small commercial building at 513-A Avenue of the Americas between Twelfth and Thirteenth streets, a few blocks from the heart of the Village. That same night, Chip Monck stole onto the premises with a few tools and planks of wood, and when the office opened the next morning for its first day of business, the staff found handmade oak desks and draftsman's tables built into the walls. Michael's aim was to provide his specialists with a twenty-four-hour-a-day production facility, a place to which they would each have a key, without specific hours, where they would come to work when the spirit hit them.

Chip laid claim to the front part of the second floor as a design department and hired a young man from the Philadelphia Folk Festival production committee named Steve Cohen to work out a stage design. Chip was working on one of his own, but so were Bert Cohen and Chris Langhart, the latter a prodigal genius who taught technical design at nearby New York University and worked nights at the Fillmore East. Michael had requested an unusual stage design, something "rustic" to complement their surroundings and to contribute to the all-around "good vibes," as well as being functional. Also, the stage had to accommodate enough equipment for two bands at the same time so there would be no break in the show while the roadies set up and broke down the gear. It was a tall order for them to come up with a perfect blend of those ingredients and required that more than one person contribute to the design. So Chip made a contest out of it: the most ingenious design would be used as the stage.

John Morris requisitioned the middle section of that floor and settled down to coordinating activities with the various bands that were already under contract.

Each act had a rider attached to its contract that stated the additional services the producer of the festival was required to provide for them in addition to salary: equipment, exotic pitches to which the pianos were to be tuned, assistants for sound and equipment, microphones, food, modes of transportation—each was spelled out down to specific brand names that were to be on hand or else the contract could be nullified. Morris performed an overall breakdown of the riders to see what communal equipment could be rented to mutually satisfy a number of acts; that would trim costs considerably and prevent the festival's making arrangements for many of these things with too wide a variety of outside contractors. Then, he mailed each performer's manager a form letter inquiring as to the band's expected time of arrival and the number of rooms required for hotel accommodations. It had been decided by Lang that band members would have to double up in rooms, otherwise they'd never find enough hotel space to accommodate everyone. There was also the task of ordering bank checks for one half of each performer's salary as a deposit to satisfy contract requirements (the remainder was to be paid by check immediately preceding the performance). It seemed endless, but Morris was used to addressing these details with almost automatic execution and had things pretty well under control.

The third floor primarily belonged to Lang. It consisted of a wide entrance area governed by Joyce Mitchell and enclosed space directly behind here where he continued to barter by phone for the services of outstanding performers. As of May 21, the Band had agreed to join the show in a Sunday afternoon slot for a fee of $15,000, a signing that no doubt delighted Michael as he considered that group to personify the Woodstock ethic—cultural rogues who hung out in the country, did their music without regard for commerciality, and projected a homespun, backwoodsy feeling by just being around. They had also been Bob Dylan's backup band, and Lang was hoping that their playing at the festival would attract The Man himself. Michael had talked to Dylan's manager, Albert Grossman, about that possibility, but so far, he had not gotten so much as a nibble. Lang had also sent a letter to John Lennon pledging any sum if the Beatles would put in an appearance; however, Lennon wrote back that he could only guarantee the services of the Plastic Ono Band. Lang let the whole matter quietly drop.

To round out the cast of production office regulars, John Morris hired Kimberly Bright, the nineteen-year-old daughter of a New York State senator, as the festival's "spiritual adviser." Attired in the barest of essentials, Kimberly had such duties as buying fresh flowers each morning for the staff's desks, keeping incense burning in the ashtrays, and leading daily yoga exercises on each floor, for which she was paid one hundred dollars a week. Michael, it was said, considered her contributions vital to the tranquility of the working atmosphere.

Lawrence and Goldstein were not downtown office regulars, each preferring to work out details on his own. Mel Lawrence spent most of that third week in May assembling what he found to be his most valuable tool on a weekend music project: a checklist. "You don't have a checklist, you don't have shit!" he'd say to anyone asking how he intended to begin his work. He spent hours going over accounts of past festivals and large gatherings, making note of their most minute details: water, food, roads, the going rate for manpower, heavy equipment rental, taxes, security, licenses, insurance— everything. And once the list was assembled, he would not let it out of his sight for the duration of the assignment. It was like having his eyesight; without it he was as good as lost.

By May 28, Lawrence had developed a rough first draft of his checklist. It ran nearly four typewritten pages in length and was limited to generalized headings that would have to be broken down further into specific assignments. That would come with time, after he and Lang had had a chance to assess each major division of their crew, after theories had been tested and retested. But for now, just seeing the outlined scope of his mission on paper was enough to jolt Lawrence's presence of mind. Coming into this project, Mel had allowed himself to become imbued with the festival spirit, assuming responsibility with a capricious, offhand enthusiasm. It was the attitude of the hour. Everyone shared it. The checklist, though, provided a mild sedative to the fun. It resembled a complicated city planning brief and, in a funny way, it frightened him. He, like the rest of the executive staff, was an optimist when it came to putting together a show, but the checklist—its depth was awesome. It extended far beyond the limits of a music spectacle, beyond show business itself. They were implementing plans for an entire life support system capable of servicing hundreds of thousands of kids.

The checklist defined what Mel had dubbed the Designation of Area Responsibilities—a written treaty of sorts that divided operational responsibilities between him and John Morris. Lawrence would have overall control of the festival grounds; Morris would handle functions pertaining to the area immediately around the stage: performer and production facilities, personnel to operate transportation for performers between the hotels and the site, backstage security (to be coordinated with whomever Stan Goldstein eventually selected for that position), and the construction, materials, method, and crew for the building of the stage.

Lawrence's first concern had to do with finding accommodations for performers and staff. Performers were Lang and Morris's worry; his more immediate problem was where to quarter several dozen crew members due to be hired and to begin work in a week's time for a period of two months. Hotels were scratched as being too expensive, and no one wanted to be the one to tell a squadron of tired, sweaty workers that they had to camp out in tents after completing a ten-hour shift of heavy labor. Luckily, as a teen-ager, Mel had spent his summers working as a busboy in the Catskills resort hotels; the area surrounding Wallkill was like a second home to him. From what he remembered, the countryside was also cluttered with family-run bungalow colonies—smaller, less luxurious inns that catered to middle-class Jewish families on a budget. Most of them had died out in the early sixties, a consequence of the shift to the nuclear family. The ones that survived were half filled and starving for business. With a little imagination, those very colonies could provide an answer to his housing problem. He made a notation on the checklist to have Penny Stallings ride around the Catskills scouting bungalow colonies that would not be averse to a hippie work force mingling with its guests. Beneath that, he jotted down: (a) staff trailers, (b) food, (c) laundry, (d) housekeeping, (e) transportation. It was Lawrence's idea to organize a self-contained staff operation in order that site construction would be everyone's primary interest once the move north was made.

Transportation, being the second area of concern on the checklist, was subdivided into: commercial vehicles, buses, trains, and airplanes. Lawrence knew from experience that the situation demanded several types of vehicles to be on hand at the site. They would need to rent pickup trucks for transporting raw materials and supplies, station wagons as escort vehicles to take performers to and from hotels. One patch of land near where he intended to erect the stage was marshy and called for a road to be built through the bog, in which case they would need a swamp buggy. He added that to the list and put question marks in front of "horses" and "Hondas"; they were just "far-out thoughts," but he had made up his mind to check into rental costs anyway. The only other vehicles he thought they would need were approximately twenty courtesy cars for the staff and hired escorts, which they could probably rent in some kind of package deal from Hertz or Avis.

Bus and train scheduling was no problem once he was in possession of the schedules, but air transportation was tricky because it meant obtaining permits from the Federal Aviation Agency if they wished to use private planes for importing performers. There was a small airfield just outside of Middletown, and Mel decided to check with officials to determine the feasibility of landing planes there from Philadelphia, Boston, Chicago, and Los Angeles. There were also certain restrictions governing the landing of helicopters, a number of which he planned to have on hand in case of emergencies. He didn't think it would be too much trouble bringing helicopters into the Middletown airport; however, he also wanted to ascertain the laws regarding the building of a heliport right there on the Mills site. He made a note of that, and added a reminder to get "information on gliders and balloons"; this *was* going to be a festival, and the very definition of the word called for special effects to put the audience in the right mood. When he found time, he would look into the mechanics for assembling a tremendous helium-filled balloon to hover over the crowd.

Sanitation, in Lawrence's words, was "going to be a bitch." It represented the lengthiest and most complex section of his checklist and had to be strictly adhered to lest "it turn the site into a stinking sewer." Beneath its heading, the first item on the agenda—and perhaps to become his biggest headache— was the boldface caption: Health Department. Lawrence had worked with health department officials at his previous festivals and found them to be either excruciatingly difficult nit-pickers whose white glove inspections could unnecessarily delay the show, or men who, for the right price, looked the other way when it came to infractions. There was such a conglomeration of health-related details that any single minuscule item could put a stop to the show's ever being held. So, right up front, Lawrence knew that he and the county inspector would be dealing in trivialities and would have to reach some kind of agreement on how they would compromise. Each side would relinquish certain elements in its specifications to gain an advantage in others. It was an annoying game in which he wished he didn't have to participate. First things first, though; he would have to get a copy of the Orange County Health Code so they could conform as much as time permitted to the local ordinances while preparing for the show.

He knew that the amount of health precautions they'd have to take into consideration would be as boundless as the sea. A hundred thousand kids sitting on a field for three days—"it could turn into a fuckin' mess," he told Lang. There would have to be an unlimited abundance of food and toilets as well as an enormous supply of water, all of which were vulnerable to disease-producing organisms. "We're gonna have to think of *everything* to combat those problems, and it's gonna take a small fortune to do it. No fuckin' around where that's concerned. We can't take any chances." Lang reassured him the money was available and told him to get anything he needed to do the job effectively.

Lawrence made subheadings under "Sanitation." The first, "Performance Area," included having Goldstein check with the Pentagon in Washington, D.C., to observe how the U.S. Army handled waste and portable toilets when they were on field maneuvers. If they were lucky, the army would convey to him a list of distributors from whom they could rent a huge quantity of portable facilities for the festival. If not, Lawrence made a note to look into building their own and, beneath that, left a reminder to have someone check into costs for the construction of latrine-type wooden bathroom frames and the price of chemicals necessary for waste decomposition. They would need the same for the campgrounds, so it had to be a solid, effective method of disposal which could be transported into a wooded area.

"Sanitation" also included "Clean-Up." He'd designate someone on the staff, probably Goldstein again, to put out feelers for a carting concern to come in after the event and get rid of the inevitable mountain of garbage. That included the wood from the frame of the disassembled stage, lighting towers, and concession booths. Before that, they would have to provide recepticles for policing the area before and during the shows. At other shows he had done, they used fifty-five-gallon cans and upright trash containers with PUSH swinging lids. But those overflowed as quickly as they were moved into position. They'd have to find someone in the upstate New York area who had enough on hand to get them through the weekend or else they'd run into trouble early. Either way, it had to be done. And he'd have to hire a proportionate number of trucks to pick them up, empty them, and compact the trash intermittently throughout the weekend.

Concessions had always been the primary source of filth at Lawrence's other promotions; spoiled food and wrappers were strewn across the grounds without regard for health ordinances or announcements from the stage. It was an uncomfortable kind of mess and, he knew, by the third day the discarded waste would become rancid, especially if it was a warm weekend. This time, he'd attempt to alleviate some of his staff's responsibility by having Miles Lourie include a clause in the contract with a food emporium that legally required them to keep the area tidy. There were other points he knew he'd come across for inclusion on his "Sanitation" file but, for now, the only other thing he jotted down was a reminder to check with the health department for standards pertaining to water storage and drainage. All he needed to find out after the festival was that they had polluted the county's streams! That was one disaster he wanted to avoid from the very start.

The notes under the heading "Construction" were few and consisted mainly of names. Mel had reached an agreement with Bill and Jean Ward, from the art department of the University of Miami, to supervise ground clearing and beautifying the land. He'd also asked Bill Ward to assume the job of construction foreman. The young husband and wife team would be bringing a small crew of art students along with them and were scheduled to arrive during the first week of June. Lawrence had also met a man at the Miami Pop Festival named John Levitt and asked him to form a work crew to assist the Wards; when Levitt responded affirmatively, Lawrence added his name to the list. He also penciled in the name of Boyd Elder. Mel had met Elder in California and thought him to be one of the finest sculptors he had ever seen. He convinced Elder to fly out and to create giant sculptures along the paths and also to supervise the building of a playground from fallen trees taken from Mills's orchard that was to include swings, see-saws, monkey-bars, and environmental rides. Elder would be designated in charge of environment.

The field area would need a considerable amount of electrical primping, which Lawrence grouped under the heading "Electricity." The first thing he noted there was to have Chip Monck mimeograph some forms to simplify requests for power. They would be distributed to everyone involved with the festival requiring electricity for their area of concentration, and that way Mel would know exactly how much power was required and where to bring in lines when he hired an outside contractor to do the job. They'd need juice going to the stage area for sound, lights, and backstage accoutrements (such as a self-service elevator to lift the performers and crew onto the stage). They'd also need power for lights on the perimeter fences, on trees, and on poles to define access and area. The campground was totally unimproved land, and it needed a primary source tapped in, as did the designated parking lots. Because the festival would continue throughout the night, alternate lighting would be required in every feasible sector where kids might wander.

Parking had a separate heading all its own. It was not complete, as Lawrence still didn't have a plan worked out to his satisfaction on how to get a hundred thousand kids a day onto and off the site. He did know, however, that he'd need machinery for grading, rolling, and leveling the parking lots. He'd also have to mark parking spaces with a device similar to the one used to line football fields—a machine on wheels that releases lime every few feet. The only additional notation under "Parking" was a reminder for someone to price stanchions and rope enough to block off specific areas so that people wouldn't drive into the parking lot from different angles.

Concession stands weren't an immediate problem inasmuch as Lawrence would eventually contract a professional to bring in a seasoned operation— someone like Howard Johnson's or Nathan's—and the layout would be up to their discretion. Lang had flown in a friend from Florida named Peter Goodrich to look into concessions, and he was presently screening those corporations with fast-food divisions about taking on the account. But Lawrence would ultimately have to make sure that booths were built and ample power was brought into that area for cooking and refrigeration. The arts and crafts exhibits also came under "Concessions" and here Lawrence's only note was to have Miles Lourie draw up a set of rules for exhibitors that gave quality control to the festival staff. One thing he wanted to be absolutely sure of was that they would not be exhibiting a lot of amateur junk.

This version of the checklist was still a long way from being complete. Aside from reminders to check on available water lines with Howard Mills and to call the telephone company regarding the installation of equipment so they would have public and staff service at various points in the field, Lawrence was convinced that a lot of pertinent information had been overlooked. He would add pages to the dossier as time progressed and, by the time the show began, his checklist would resemble the Middletown telephone directory.

That afternoon, after running off several copies of his budget and distributing them to the rest of the production office staff for analysis, Mel met with Lang in a coffee shop below the office to review the estimates.

"It's pretty steep," he warned Michael, spreading out the outline on the counter amidst coffee and rolls. "I'd say judging from what I've got on these pages and enough to cover us for additional expenses that're bound to crop up—roughly six hundred grand."

Lang arched his eyebrows and blew out a noiseless whistle.

"That much, huh?"

"At least. I've really gotta see what it looks like when I get up there. We might find out that it's gonna take a lot more than what we thought to get that place into shape. From what I remember about it, Mills has really dug it up to shit. We may hafta put in a road or two, which'll push the budget up another hundred thou' or so. I'm not sure." He looked at Lang's surprised reaction. "You want me to see if we can trim it, cut a few corners?"

"Nope. If it takes six hundred big ones, well—just get it on. I don't want to cut corners. Not now. Hell, we got the land, the staff, and we're well on our way to getting the acts. Then, none of this'll matter. You've got my okay. Just get it on."

— **5** —

Getting it on was, indeed, becoming a basis for some concern. The month of May was rapidly drawing to a close. At the most, not taking into consideration rain days and other unavoidable delays, they had two and a half months left to complete preparations and to work everything into a semblance of reasonable decorum. At that rate, there wasn't a moment to waste.

On May 27, Lang confirmed with the festival's new public relations firm, the Wartoke Concern, a press release stating that the production staff for the Woodstock Music and Art Fair was now completed. In two-sentence paragraphs, it said that "Chris Langhart, Keith O'Connor, Stanley Goldstein, and Jerry Pompili (another Fillmore worker brought in at the last minute to help Chip) completed the staff of production executives . . . for the two-day contemporary music and arts festival being held in Wallkill, New York, on August 16 and 17 [they had decided to spring the third day on the unsuspecting public in a future press release to maximize their domination of available space]. Heading the production staff for Woodstock Ventures, Inc., under the direction of Executive Producer Michael Lang, are Production Coordinator John Morris; Production Manager Chip Monck; and Head of Operations [a title formerly used to describe Goldstein] Mel Lawrence." Michael had approved the release by scrawling his name across the top of the original document. No mention was made of John, Joel or Artie.

The next afternoon, May 28, Lang called Kornfeld at the uptown office to tell him that he had snagged the Incredible String Band and Indian sitarist Ravi Shankar for $4,500 each.

"Far out!" Artie sang into the receiver. "They'll be dynamite to open the evening's shows, soft, moody. Yeah, man! It's really shapin' up, huh?"

Michael laughed. "Yup. It's outta sight, baby. Really outta sight. It's a fuckin' groove. We got enough top acts to keep the place shakin' for a good two days, and I think I'm starin' a couple of the biggies right in the face. There's a pretty good chance of grabbin' the Who, and some dude says he can get me in to see Dylan."

"Holy shit! Can you imagine havin' Dylan? Oh man!"

"He's in Middletown campin' out at his doctor's." Lang was referring to Dr. Ed Thayler who had been nursing Dylan back to health after a motorcycle accident a few months earlier in Nashville. "And I'm still workin' on Hendrix, BS&T, and the Moodies. Even fuckin' Joan Baez. Manny Greenhill's playin' hard mother for her and Arlo, but he'll come around. We got a ways to go yet, and I got my fingers crossed for a few more groups to fall. No sweat our fillin' three days."

"You're too much, baby."

"Thanks. How you doin' on seein' about a film deal? Any luck?"

"Nothin' yet, but I'm workin' on it."

Artie had been given the assignment of negotiating subsidiary rights deals with record and film companies. Lang was convinced that once such arrangements were made and they had tangible advances from the respective companies, Roberts and Rosenman would sleep a lot easier knowing their investment was being recouped. And more important, they would stay off his back.

"Look, Artie, it's real fuckin' important that we ice this shit quickly. How about Miles? Have you talked to him about his contacts?"

"Nah," Artie whined. "He's too fuckin' soft when it comes to makin' deals, man. I'm seein' Paul Marshall about it tomorrow." Marshall was Kornfeld's personal attorney. "*He's* a deal maker, a real son of a bitch. Fuck Miles."

"Okay. Just get it movin'. And, Artie—don't say too much to our *other* friends. You know those guys. They don't know what the hell is goin' down and are forever fuckin' things up. I don't need that right now. So keep it cool, okay?"

"You got it, m'man. Just between brothers."

"Between brothers."

The budget, by this time, had crept well beyond the $500,000 figure origi-nally predicted by Michael and Artie back in February. Taking into consid-eration Mel Lawrence's $600,000 operations estimate (which had since been pared to a more reasonable, although equally inaccurate, $175,000), a talent expenditure that had already exceeded $93,000 and was rising every time Lang picked up the phone, land transactions, money spent on lawyers, pub-lic relations, the dormant management of Train, offices and existing con-tracts with ten executives, a more realistic statement might well have put Woodstock Ventures Incorporated over the $1,200,000 mark in cash outlay.

Somewhere along the way, Roberts and Rosenman had lost touch—or were cunningly being prevented from remaining in touch—with their com-pany's transactions. The Woodstock Music and Art Fair grew up and around them and expanded into a financial monster that, all of a sudden, began squeezing the life out of their venture from all sides.

Roberts vacillated on a day-to-day basis between pulling the plug on the financial drain to consolidate his losses and giving the staff a vote of confi-dence by reinforcing the dwindling bank account with another generous advance from the Bank of North America. It was a decision that had to be made soon but was delayed by the realization that either way he approached this mess, he was bound to lose. And that was only the beginning of the nightmare from which he awoke each night twisted with anxiety. Artie and Michael were holding him securely by the shoulders as the Bank of North America burned to the ground. They were laughing hysterically, and as he tore loose and ran toward the inferno, he caught sight of a neon sign blinking in the building's fiery glare; what remained of the sign said: WOODST.

— 6 —

Joel's relationship with Michael and Artie was rapidly deteriorating. What had begun four months earlier as an uncomfortable, although promising, merger of dipolar attitudes had dwindled to impassive tolerance between them, severely hindering their once fluent channel of communications. Michael went out of his way to avoid putting in an appearance at the uptown office; the less he saw of his nemesis the better. Artie, for a while, just seemed to have evaporated into thin air. He, too, stopped coming into the office on a daily basis. It was assumed that Artie was scouting potential movie and record deals, but no apparent progress was being made in either direction and his absence aroused suspicion.

None of this was lost on Joel. He sensed their contempt and grew inhibited when they eventually came around. If he entered into a discussion with them, his words and thoughts became confused, never making their intended impact. He lost his former confidence, electing to feel that they had a clearly developed philosophy that elevated them to an ethereal understanding of what was and was not important in society; and every time Joel opened his mouth, he felt he was betraying himself as a person who was concerned only with petty issues.

He discussed this insecurity with John, who did everything in his power to allay his friend's complex. "Why do you bother?" he asked Joel. "We're mixed up with a bunch of bumbling children who just happened to get their hands on our money."

But as the days passed, their displeasure with their associates was further provoked by stories that came filtering back to them through Stanley Goldstein, John Morris, and other downtowners: Lang was imparting specific orders to his staff that were contrary to their mutual business interests. Expense money was being squandered, often falling into the hands of people who had nothing at all to do with the festival, or was being used for the purchasing of pot and acid. Trips were being taken in limousines and helicopters as a means of entertainment or to impress those who hung out in the downtown office. One of the publicity firms handling the festival called John Roberts and requested that he "not make Kornfeld responsible for any press deadlines or, for that matter, *anything*. He is so spaced out, he has no idea what's going on around him."

Joel also began noticing changes in the way festival publicity was being released to the press. He and John had put Burrelle's press clipping service on retainer. Each morning, an envelope would arrive from Burrelle's containing the previous day's clippings, and Joel would begin his morning reading them over coffee and danish. Pretty soon, he found that his and John's names were being left completely off all press releases.

"Hey, get a load of this," he called to John one morning while sorting through the envelope from Burrelle's. He held up a mimeographed piece of paper and began reading. " 'The Woodstock Music and Art Fair has found a home this coming August 15, 16, and 17 in Wallkill, New York. Co-promoters Mike Lang and Artie Kornfeld announced today that . . .' They're all like that," he said, paging through the packet on his lap. " 'Mike Lang and Artie Kornfeld, the festival's producers announced . . .' Looks like you and I have been ditched."

"It's probably just a mistake, Joel."

"Not a chance, pal. It's the same thing in each article and there are papers here from all over the country. 'Mike Lang and Artie Kornfeld; Mike Lang and Artie Kornfeld . . .' Someone's pulling the ol' behind-the-back switcheroo, and I'll lay five to one with you that I know who's behind it."

John went through the remainder of the clippings and became as upset as his partner. "I don't know what the hell they could gain from this. It's like they think we're fools, we won't notice or something."

Joel called Miles Lourie who cautiously warned them that after the festival was over, the show's producers could write their own ticket for just about anything they wished. The fewer the producers, the fewer ways to slice up the post-performance rewards. But, he told them, the entire incident might be traced elsewhere, perhaps to publicity firms handling the Woodstock account who didn't know any better. "You'd better check there first," he advised.

A hasty call to Wartoke and Dick Gersh's company confirmed Joel's worst suspicions. He was told that two weeks before, Artie had called with instructions to delete Roberts and Rosenman's names from further releases. According to Artie, the four partners agreed that it was in the festival's best interests that the moneymen's names not tarnish the festival's unmaterialistic doctrine. No Establishment connections. "Michael told us that from now on only he or Artie was to approve each release before it was issued."

Roberts and Rosenman were furious. "We must look like a buncha schmucks," John said. "We've been bustin' our humps to establish credibility as businessmen, telling each account we set up about our involvement with the festival, and the fucking *New York Times* carries a column announcing to the whole world that it's Michael and Artie's personal show. Christ, am I pissed off."

Roberts telephoned Arnold Koppelson, the Challenge International lawyer who had done their work on Media Sound, and Koppelson said, "Fuck 'em, kill the deal." He hadn't trusted their association with Lang and Kornfeld from the very beginning. But Rosenman and Roberts thought about it, and decided that splitting up was too harsh a conclusion. They wanted to resolve the situation, not dissolve it.

By June 1, though, the very thought of Lang and Kornfeld working out of their sight was driving Roberts and Rosenman mad with suspicion.

At eleven o'clock that evening, John telephoned Michael and asked if he and Joel might meet with him to go over some mutual problems that needed their immediate attention. It was decided that they would get together around midnight at the Excellent Restaurant on Lexington Avenue, downstairs from their apartment.

Michael was half an hour late for the appointment, alluding to a traffic backup from Thirty-fourth Street down to the Village. He appeared relaxed; his eyes were limpid and guileless, and when he dropped into his seat, he seemed to curl up like a contented cat. Even while they sat there and watched Michael surrender to their soft impeachment, John and Joel knew they were defending a lost cause. Michael, merely by showing up, was in complete control of the mood; it was his masterful forte.

"How's it goin', guys?" he asked in a high-pitched, casual tone.

John folded his hands formally on the table and regarded Lang the way a personnel director interviews a prospective job applicant. "That's what we've come to ask you, Mike."

"Far out!" He seemed amused. "Well, shoot."

Joel had something along that line in his mind.

John cleared his throat nervously. All of a sudden, he felt foolish. Especially glancing over at Lang's expression of patience. Michael had succeeded in reducing the climate of the meeting to a fraternal get-together. "We, uh, seem to be seeing less of you lately," he began.

Michael smiled. "Been busy."

"Yeah, well, we've all been busy, Michael," Joel said, "but it's not that at all. What's going on? You've got this downtown office and everything. You never come around to our place anymore. It's like we don't exist as a team."

"That's not true, man. We're like the Four Musketeers, you, me, Joel, and Artie. We just gotta keep movin' forward. Make the scene beautiful."

Joel looked away. He saw Michael setting up his smokescreen and wondered how he was going to hold back his temper.

John tried to maintain their original direction. "Speaking of Artie, what's he been up to lately? Has he been downtown with you?"

"Hey look, guys," Michael said, waving his hands in front of his face, "my major *problem* is Artie." John and Joel did a double take and fastened their stares directly on Michael. They were both stunned by his statement. "That's why I took the downtown office in the first place—to get away from him. He fucks up everything he comes into contact with. I just can't be around him."

John felt his heart slip into his lap. They had suspected all along that Artie Kornfeld was incapable of handling responsibility but that Michael exercised some mystical power over him that brought about positive results and kept Artie in check. Either that, or Michael covered for him. Now, Michael was confirming their worst fears.

"Look, I love Artie like a brother, man. I owe him; he's the dude who taught me all about the record business and gave my band a contract when I knew he never liked them. We hung out and had great times. But I've always known he was totally out of it when it came to gettin' things done. You gotta do me a favor and keep him away from me."

"What do you want us to do?" Joel asked sternly.

"I don't know, man. Take the responsibility away from him. That way he'll be harmless. If he gets involved, he's sure to fuck everything up. You guys are gonna hafta handle it. I can't deal with it. Whatever you decide to do is fine."

"Maybe we should all sit down and talk things over with him," John suggested.

"Oh no, man. I couldn't do that. I couldn't get through it. It'd kill Artie, too. You gotta understand, he's like my brother." Michael almost sounded convinced of it. "Just do me a favor and keep him away from me."

"Well, it seems to me we've got to have a talk with Artie about his attitude and draw the line on his involvement," Joel said. "It can't go on like this; we've got too much at stake."

John agreed. "Whaddya think, Mike? Should we approach him directly and say these things to him?"

"No, we couldn't do that," Lang protested. He seemed genuinely concerned for the first time that evening. "It'll kill Artie, man. It'll show him that we've lost confidence in him, and he'll go to pieces."

"That's tough shit," Joel said. "If we don't talk to him, then the festival and all our other plans will go to pieces. We can't allow Artie's feelings to shoot that all to hell."

"That's right," John said. "Someone's gotta talk to him. How about it, Mike? Will you do it?"

"No, I told you, man. I couldn't get through it. It looks like you guys'll have to take care of it."

The next afternoon, around 2:00, Joel observed Artie stealing into the office and caught up with him halfway down the hall.

"Hey Artie, got a minute?"

"Sure, baby, for you?—always. What's shakin'?"

"Uh, why don't we go into your office," Joel offered. This promised to be difficult enough for him. He didn't want to humiliate Artie by reprimanding him in front of the employees.

Inside Artie's rainbow-colored domain, the two boys made themselves comfortable in the conference pit. Artie turned on the stereo and offered Joel a joint, which he waved off.

Joel proceeded to tell him about the conference with Michael and John the night before: They were unanimously agreed that Artie wasn't performing his responsibilities up to par. The problem had to be reconciled before too much damage was done.

Artie's face wilted as he listened. Later, he would tell a friend, "A piece of me died right then and there. I just couldn't believe it."

"I'm just the spokesman for the three of us, Artie," Joel continued, "but I feel that way, too. It's not a hopeless cause or anything. If you start coming into the office and doing your job, we can pull off the festival the way we originally planned it to be. Together. I'm sure it's all going to work out."

"I can't believe it. I can't fuckin' believe my ears," Artie moaned. "I always assumed I had it together. But what really gets me is that Michael said those things. Are you *sure*, man?"

Joel nodded.

"Wow, man, like—you know, we always had decent communications, him and me. I'd do anything for him. I thought that went both ways. But I'll tell you the truth. I don't think we can take any of this too seriously."

"Whaddya mean?"

"What I mean is that Michael's been dealin' me the same story about you guys."

"What?" Joel was startled.

"He told me to keep you guys out of his way. Dig it, man. He said, 'If any of my cats gets a look at Joel and John, they'll freak right out. They're so fuckin' unhip about everything. They just can't get anything together.' You know, something like that."

"That son of a bitch!"

"Yeah. He's doin' a number on all of us, man." Artie stood up. "We gotta stick together to make this thing work. Look, I want you to know that I can dig how hard it was for you to stroll in here and give it to me straight. You were the only dude with enough nerve to talk to both sides." Artie put his arms around Joel and gave him a hug.

Joel stumbled out of Kornfeld's office dumbfounded. He had gone into that meeting hoping to put Artie in his place once and for all. In fact, there had been a point in the proceedings the night before when he was relieved about what Michael told them; finally, he surmised, he could bank on his instincts with those two and not feel like he was out of touch with the culture. But now he saw the con game for what it was, with him, Artie, and John as the pieces to be moved in and out of place at Lang's will.

"He's more clever than I thought," Joel brooded. "Now the game's being played on a level on which I can participate as an equal."

Later that afternoon, Joel relayed the minutes of his meeting with Artie to John who was no less thunderstruck by Michael's audacity.

"That little fuck!" John fumed, astounded by the amount of venom in his own voice. "I'm gonna take care of him. You'll see." He picked up the phone and rummaged for the number of the downtown office. But Joel dissuaded him from taking any kind of immediate action. He argued that they had too much money and time invested in the project to blow it away right now. They owed it to themselves, he maintained, to wait until Michael showed his face to expose his pie-faced antics so that everyone could have his say. That way, they could lay the matter to rest and get on with their business at hand.

Another two hours passed before Lang strolled in humming. John cornered him in the reception area, immediately divulging the news that the Musketeers had compared notes and were beginning to doubt strongly the fourth's loyalty to the cause.

Michael played dumb. He feigned not having the slightest idea what they were talking about. "I just want to get the gig done," he offered.

John asked him to "define exactly what the fuck" he meant by that. Up until now, he had been fairly tolerant of Michael's shifty tactics; there were times when they even amused him. This, however, was not one of them. He was not about to stand there and be lied to when everyone present (Artie and Joel had wandered into the room) knew the truth.

"It means I just want to get the gig done," he echoed. John could sense he was getting nowhere, and only succeeding in raising his own blood pressure. "What's the problem, man?"

The problem, he explained at the top of his voice, was that Michael's juvenile games and office politics were destroying their trust in him. If he continued in the same way they would never "get the gig" or anything else done.

To everyone's surprise, Artie interceded on Michael's behalf. "Wait, man. I don't think we're being entirely fair to Michael. Seriously, I can dig what he's saying."

Both Joel and John contemplated strangling him. Joel didn't intend to let him get away with the about-face. "Now, hold on a minute, Artie. You were just as pissed off as we were about this whole thing a minute ago. What the fuck is going on?"

"It's just that I see what Michael's saying, man. We're all in this together, and if we run around worrying about who said what to who every second, we're just gonna fuck ourselves."

"Right on!" Michael yelped. He gathered up the momentum that had somehow been inverted and turned it in his favor. Coolly, he delivered a speech about how they had gotten bogged down in matters unrelated to the festival. According to Lang, by being so petty, they were all responsible for interfering with progress. It was time they put aside such trivialities and, instead, put their noses to the grindstone.

Artie gave him a resounding cheer of support and promised to get his "publicity program" moving. Michael slapped him encouragingly on the back.

In a state of disbelief and shock, John and Joel reaffirmed their support and drifted back to their office. Lang had bamboozled them again. They had been prepared to crush his wayward enthusiasm, but their desire had been stronger than their stamina, a blank cartridge. They lacked his killer instinct. And worst of all, they knew the time would come when they would pay for their mistake.

That same afternoon, Lang kept an appointment in the downtown office with a career cop they had flown north from the South who was interested in regulating security for the festival. The former chief of police had recently been under indictment regarding his well-publicized ties with organized crime and had either retired or been eased off the force to save both sides unnecessary embarrassment. His name had been one of those that Stanley Goldstein had been given by the International Association of Police Chiefs, and he wanted Michael to meet him before the next day's get-together with Wes Pomeroy.

A half hour before that appointment was to take place, Stanley informed Lang that there was a young lady waiting on the second-floor landing who Stanley considered to be a prime candidate for personal assistant to Michael. The entire office had been assigned the task of finding such a person at Michael's request. They jumped at the opportunity primarily because they desperately needed a responsible person to stay by Lang's side, making sure he got to scheduled meetings on time and reminding him about problems requiring his notoriously short attention span. Michael grumbled something about being swamped with work, but told Goldstein to send her in anyway. He'd get it over with quickly and move on to more important matters.

Ticia Bernuth was a tall young woman as lissome as Tennyson's hazel wand. When she sat down across from Lang's desk, her limberness dropped her flush against the curved chair support, misrepresenting her actual height.

Michael judged her to be close to six feet tall and around twenty-two years old. Her most striking characteristic, though, was her hair, which was the color of the scarlet halo that surrounds a flame and plummeted to a point below her shoulders without so much as a comma or a wave. The intensity of her hair gave her boyish face an uncommon chalky nakedness; her tight compact figure, small breasts, and long tapering fingers added to her extraordinary appearance, all of which Michael found quite sensual and bewitching.

Ticia explained to him that she had just returned from spending six years traveling abroad. She romanced Lang with tales about her adventures in Saudi Arabia and Iran, about gallivanting across the desert sand on a camel, about sheiks and kingdoms and splendor he never thought existed in modern times. It was astounding reality carved from the very pages of the Arabian Nights tales, and Michael was sold.

"You got the job," he told her, "starting immediately." Her first assignment was to pick up Wes Pomeroy at LaGuardia Airport the next morning. Stanley was to give her a description of the Washington law enforcement official, and it would be up to her to locate him as he came off the plane. She had been asked to remain in the office that afternoon "to sit in on a meeting that was gonna go down with another cop."

That meeting lasted less than a half hour. The cop, a big, burly man with a wrenched nose and a furrowed brow, was shown in by Goldstein and assured them that he had a fail-safe security plan worked out that would not only maintain order but would "keep the little bastards seated in one place for as long as they were on the grounds." Ticia looked nervously at Lang, who smiled and shook his head. The policeman's plan had to do with building two barbed-wire fences six feet apart around the perimeter of the site. "The area in between," he explained, "would be filled with hundreds of snarling Doberman pinschers right out there in the open as a warning for them to sit down and shut up—or else! Any time you want, all you have to do is cut a hole in the fence and let the dogs go charging out. Believe me, there won't be any trouble at all if you let me handle it this way."

"Sounds great," Michael quipped. "I'm sure you and Stanley can continue this discussion later. Right now, I'm already an hour late for a meeting with my financial advisers, so if you don't mind, we'll discuss your plan among ourselves and call you with our decision." He stood up as Goldstein ushered the disgruntled cop from the room.

"Do you believe that asshole?" Michael asked Ticia. "He'd love to get his hands on the kids at the site. Whew! Was that great. There's millions of guys like that walking the streets, that's the scary part. Look," he said, changing the subject, "head out to LaGuardia tomorrow and make sure Pomeroy gets back here in one piece. It looks like we're gonna be dependin' on him more than I thought. Somebody's got to protect us from these fuckers, and I think he may be just the guy to do it."

Ticia had no trouble picking Wes Pomeroy out of the crowd that poured off the Eastern Airlines shuttle from Washington the next day. She had been told that he resembled Ward Bond, the star of *Wagon Train*, and that he "looked like a cop"—nothing more. It was all she needed. She immediately hooked his arm, and within twenty minutes he was back in the Woodstock production office on Sixth Avenue waiting for Michael Lang to arrive.

Lang showed up an hour late without an apology. There were a few matters that he had to tend to upon walking through the door, but he asked Pomeroy if he would follow him into his office while he got those things quickly out of the way. Pomeroy watched Michael carefully as he returned a few calls to booking agents and managers. He was impressed that, although Lang did not come close to resembling an executive, he was able to make decisions swiftly and see them through with an authoritarian tone of voice. Nobody really gives these kids a chance, Pomeroy thought.

Stanley Goldstein, barechested and frenzied, came in to say hello and was asked to remain by Lang as he hung up the phone. Ticia, catlike, curled up in a chair in the corner of the room.

"Stanley tells me that you're interested in headin' up our security operation at the festival," Michael began.

"Well, I'm interested in hearing more about it first. I may very well not be the right person to handle it. Then again, I may find your whole proposition offensive and objectionable." Pomeroy smiled politely.

"Right on." Lang appreciated his direct approach. No pressure. No commitment. No fucking around. "I guess Stan told you pretty much about what we're trying to do. I'd like to hear your ideas on it. Then again, I might find *your* ideas crude and too fuckin' Establishment-oriented to suit *my* purposes." He returned Pomeroy's smile, and they were even.

Pomeroy reiterated his concept of a nonviolent security force—"a peace force"—made up of kids and off-duty cops uniformed in T-shirts and jeans. "I don't want to see anybody hurt like in Chicago," he stated emphatically. "That was a crime committed by stupid people."

"Stan said you were involved in Chicago."

"I can't say I'd go along with being 'involved,' but yes, I was there and saw the bloodbath that was going on with my own eyes. It all could have been avoided, you know, had Daley and the others not been so damned pigheaded."

He had captured Lang's absolute attention; Michael's eyes danced like a little boy's awaiting a bedtime story.

Pomeroy explained to Lang that in 1968, he had been appointed the special assistant to Ramsey Clark, assigned to coordinate "a federal presence" at both the Democratic and Republican national conventions later that year. Pomeroy was left in charge of just about everything including the army, the advance cadres of the remaining branches of the armed services, the state police, liaisons to the National Guard, the Secret Service, and the specially augmented Secret Service that consisted of agents borrowed from all other federal agencies to help in their "mission." Unfortunately, he only had the services of one other man at his disposal to organize the entire affair, and when Clark asked Pomeroy how many additional peace officers he'd need to get the work done, Wes astutely told him that he wanted to use what was available—to coordinate his two-man team and see if they could handle it on their own. He thought it would be foolish to attempt to set up a peacekeeping system that was entirely different from what everybody was used to.

Sometime just before the Democratic convention in Chicago, he continued, Rennie Davis contacted the Attorney General's office and requested federal assistance in organizing a peaceful demonstration to run concurrent with the convention. "We're putting together a mobilization committee and we're going to protest against a number of issues," he informed Clark, "Vietnam being the most important. We've been trying to negotiate with the City of Chicago to get parade routes and specific meeting places allotted for our purposes, but nobody in the administration will deal with us. We're getting the runaround, and we wish you'd use your office to persuade Daley to at least *talk* to us because we don't want any violence there."

Clark asked Pomeroy and Roger Wilkens, the Director of Community Relations, to assess the situation and to report back to him so they could avoid an angry confrontation between the hippies and the politicos during the convention. If there was a way around it, he wanted to know so his office could take steps to avert a street war.

Wilkens and Pomeroy conducted their investigations separately and, in the final analysis, drew the same conclusions. They told Clark that it would be utterly unfortunate if Daley held the hard line and didn't deal with these people. "The mobilization organization has a diverse number of interests that represents the feelings of a considerable number of the populace," Pomeroy told Clark. "If Daley communicates with them, I think it would be possible for the leaders of the movement to develop self-regulation and a self-policing responsibility." In his estimation, there would be no need for extensive policing from the federal reserve in Chicago, nor was there any real possibility that violence would occur. "These are kids with a desire for peace; that's their whole purpose in demonstrating in the first place. I think it's our responsibility, and in the best interests of the country, to get Daley to change his mind."

Ramsey Clark agreed with him wholeheartedly. The next week, he dispatched Pomeroy and Roger Wilkens to Chicago to confer with the stubborn mayor. Daley reluctantly agreed to see them. Once they were securely inside his office, he told them that if the U.S. Department of Justice really wanted to help him, they would let him know in advance "who the subversives and radicals were when they crossed the town line" so his "local boys can prepare for and deal with them."

They tried desperately to get Daley to negotiate with Rennie Davis and several of the other leaders of the movement, to bend in the slightest way so they could achieve the common purpose of a peaceful political convention, but Daley waved them off. "I told you my permit people are already dealing with them," he said, losing his patience. "Look, we have all kinds of special events planned for people in the neighborhoods of Chicago during the convention. There won't be any trouble in *my* city, because I know Chicago and the people wouldn't dare embarrass me by causing any problems."

After the meeting had concluded, Pomeroy and Wilkens shared an elevator to the lobby floor. "You know, it'd be more useful if we had been speaking different languages," he confided to Wilkens, "because then we'd *know* we didn't understand one another. That asshole Daley's gonna blow things sky high."

"You really called Daley an asshole?" Lang asked excitedly.

"Oh, I might have." Pomeroy smiled. "I was in an ornery mood and, then, anything is possible."

"Don't stop now," Michael pleaded. "What happened after that?"

Pomeroy and Wilkens got professional runarounds from Daley's people for the two weeks preceding the convention. They would receive printed announcements in their Washington office issued by the Chicago city government advising the public that "we are putting you on notice that there will be no violence in Chicago." And one was indiscriminately worded to the effect of: "Stay out of Chicago or we'll take care of you." It was exactly the opposite of what Wilkens and Pomeroy had advised Daley to do.

Upon Ramsey Clark's request, Pomeroy made a second trip to Chicago, this time accompanied by Warren Christopher, the Deputy Attorney General, a very quiet, efficient, principled man. Daley met with them and was more obstinate than he had been with Pomeroy and Wilkens. He wanted names of subversives and he wanted them quickly. Pomeroy and Christopher returned to Washington, D.C., that same evening and impressed the mayor's attitude upon Clark who, they felt certain, knew what the implications were.

Lang squeezed out a lazy, high-pitched whistle. "Fucked up, man. Couldn't'cha lay it all on him, like, let him know the fuzz'd be bringing sticks down on skulls if he didn't do something?"

"He knew," Wes continued. "I heard that a day or two before the convention, Ramsey had a meeting about it with Lyndon Johnson and Hubert Humphrey. Ramsey supposedly told Johnson: 'You're the only one who can stop it by getting Daley to back off. If he doesn't, we're going to have ourselves one hell of a disturbance here in Chicago.' But it was no use. They needed Daley's support to carry the state of Illinois and didn't want to make waves. In the end, they came back to him and told him that they would not interfere with Daley. It was his city and he could ably handle the situation."

"Couldn't you see what was happenin', man?" Lang asked.

"Oh, I could see it all right. Anyone who wasn't blind could see what was about to occur. It was frustrating as hell."

"Well, whaddija do?"

"Nothing," Pomeroy said. "We just sat back and watched as the local cops turned into thugs. You can't imagine how that feels being a cop all your life and watching them embarrass a time-honored tradition of law enforcement. And, you know, the whole demonstration was the biggest goddamned put-on in the world, and these idiots in Chicago took it seriously. You take a guy like Abbie Hoffman; he's only a street theatre guy with a lot of humor in him who tries to put a lot of people on whenever he can. I remember watching Abbie doing a snake dance in the park outside the convention hall; it was hilarious. And the next day, the Chicago papers billed it as a diversionary tactic to propel a riot. Bullshit. I know it wasn't. I was there."

Wes told Lang and Goldstein that the police department had gotten all of its ill feelings and direction from Daley. "In effect, Daley had emasculated the top command of his police department. Even if they wanted to have aided in pulling off a peaceful demonstration and maintaining civil order, they couldn't have done much about it. The whole thing was preventable. It was just a crying shame."

Lang knew now, more than ever, that they had their man for the security detail at the festival and there was no way he was going to allow him to walk out of the office before agreeing to take the job. Attitude was the key. Without it, one could bring in any form of crowd-controlling device and not get desired results. But Pomeroy's attitude was enough to instill a feeling that everything was going to go down in a peaceful manner. He was compassionate, and he had a true understanding of the people's right to carry on without fearing police intervention. Moreover, Pomeroy lacked the fear of the generation that other cops had.

Pomeroy sensed Lang shared his concern for the audience's safety and was somewhat convinced that, despite their unmatched appearances, they both had the same interests at heart.

"You know, Michael," he explained, "in almost all cases you can assume that groups of people *don't* want violence. If you can persuade them that you're not going to oppress them and will help them express their own points of view, the potential for violence is almost nil. You'd better get one thing straight, too: you *do* have that power. The Establishment *always* has the power. And anyone running this rock festival with all that money behind them is going to wind up being the Establishment, whether you like it or not."

Michael made the first move. "We really want you on our side at the festival. I think you could help bring about some kind of unity between the kids and the cops."

"And use some of my pull to land you guys local respect."

"Right," Michael acquiesced.

"Well, the more I talk to you, the better a chance I feel there is of actually accomplishing what you've set out to do. I've worked out a situation with my personal affairs that'll let me out of Washington two days a week until the middle of this month. If that's all right with you, I can make a few calls and have someone else I trust set the preliminary security system into motion up in Wallkill before I arrive."

"Who do you have in mind?"

"There's any number of people who could do it. I've got a friend in New Orleans who's pretty competent and who I'll be seeing next week. There's also John Fabbri." Fabbri was the chief of the roughneck South San Francisco police department, a precinct constantly at odds with the rebellious working-class kids who, each Friday, converted their factory wages into alcohol and went on a tear. Fabbri had kept the peace there; he understood the kids and had developed personal relationships with many of them. Fabbri and Pomeroy had become friendly when Wes was the San Mateo County under sherrif, and they had published a book together on police personnel selection. "Fabbri would be a godsend in a situation such as this. If we can get him away from the force for a few months, you fellas'll be very lucky indeed."

Pomeroy also suggested they give him authority to hire Don Ganoung, a man from San Francisco with a background diverse enough to confuse even

Nero Wolfe. Pomeroy had met Ganoung in 1964 while policing the Republican National Convention at the Cow Palace in San Francisco. Ganoung was an Episcopal priest, having been one of Bishop Pike's street priests. He was attending the convention representing the Christians for Social Action, a coalition of mostly religious groups who intended to protest about the rights of the people being revoked at the government's whim.

"When I heard the Christians for Social Action were going to be an entity there, I contacted them and arranged a meeting with Don Ganoung at the Good Samaritan parish house on the Patrero." The Patrero was the troubled Chicano and Samoan district in greater San Francisco. "Ganoung and I began to establish ground rules for the demonstration. No one had ever tried to do this with protesters before, and we worked out a mutual agreement whereby they could express their opinions and expose their problems to the public. That's all they wanted. I also became their advocate in a strange way because I was their only line of communication to the outside Establishment of which I was a part."

Pomeroy and Ganoung became good friends and pursued mutual goals in the area of civil rights and humanities. During this time, Pomeroy found out that Ganoung had a degree from the School of Criminology at Berkeley, was the recipient of a master's degree in a related area, had been a CID officer in the Korean War, and a juvenile probation officer thereafter before becoming a priest. Pomeroy brought Ganoung into the Law Enforcement Assistance Administration where he worked on personnel selection and screening candidates for the Attorney General's staff for several months.

"You need a guy like Ganoung at the festival. He can become invaluable in community relations. Ship him up there a couple weeks ahead of time, and let him mediate matters for you."

Lang didn't hesitate. "Grab him. Offer him anything he likes, but don't let him shuffle out of our reach."

"Tell him we can use him as soon as possible," Goldstein interjected. "We're moving up to Wallkill on the sixth, and I'd like him along to smooth the rough edges. If he agrees, I'll work out an airline ticket for him and a place to stay once he gets here."

Pomeroy nodded, and made a note in his appointment book to phone Ganoung. "What do you want me to begin with once my staff is firmed up and out of the way?"

"I'd like you to organize and coordinate a written security plan, something we can show the town and the rest of the cats helping out around the site. It's gotta include some way to handle security without seeing security—y'know, like you were sayin' before."

"I'm gonna run him up to the site so he can see what he's dealing with before tackling the security plan," Goldstein told Lang.

"Good." He turned to Pomeroy. "Then, when you've had some time to give this thing some thought, we'll get together up in Wallkill and begin work."

Lang, Pomeroy, and Goldstein stood up and exchanged firm handshakes. As Pomeroy and Goldstein left, Michael turned to Ticia who was beaming her approval. Michael gave her the high sign and collapsed into his chair. It was the first time since beginning this project that he actually felt relaxed about giving up some of the authority. By having this Washington cop at their side, they would finally be recognized as a force to contend with in the eyes of the Establishment. They had been legitimized; Wes Pomeroy had sealed their fate.

PART TWO

The Nation at War

CHAPTER FIVE

Home Again, and Home Again

The landlord's laugh was ready chorus.　　　*—Robert Burns*

— 1 —

On a palmy, summer afternoon in 1969, there was no better place in Wallkill to measure the pulse of the community than the graded space in the Burger King parking lot on Route 211. It was there one came to rubberneck and exchange confidences. Whether they were nursing a chocolate shake or car-hopping along a row of jacked-up Mustang convertibles that were so popular with teen-agers there, it was possible to keep one eye posted on the traffic that rolled off the Quickway exit directly across the street. The light there, suspended above the pavement by a girded cable, marked the crossroads of the town. It was a regional landmark used for directing visitors anywhere within town boundaries, much like the old school-house or bronze statue or white brick church in other tank towns across the United States. Sooner or later, everyone was bound to cross that intersection, and when he did, the occasion would be noted with telltale speculation.

If one was patient and withstood several hours' worth of Whoppers and lukewarm French fries, he could conceivably unravel the town's innermost secrets— that is, if there were any knotting up at the moment. One eye on the bite; the other on the light. That summer, though, an astute front-seat detective would observe little to finance a whispering campaign.

The ennui and apathy of rural existence set in like a contagious disease infecting the town's anemic youth. To hear the kids' chatter through open car windows, they were the living sum total of the past. The intersection in front of Burger King told the whole miserable story. From a point just over the dashboard, they watched what was the only show in town: a cavalcade of grunting diesel trucks whose familiar inscriptions—Sunoco, Agway, International Harvester, Consolidated Can Corporation—supposedly kept the community alive. "They're proof to the rest of the country of our productivity, our *strength*," a Middletowner lectured his son. Civic pride, however, is not an inherited trait. While the old guard persisted in rambling on about maintaining the status quo, it dawned on the younger generation that, culturally, they were dying.

That June, those who maintained the vigil at the Burger King/Quickway intersection noticed a sprinkling of brightly colored vans mingled in with the steel-gray truck flow. No one reacted at first; no one realized its significance. No one suspected their small town would ever be singled out as an arena for commercial hijinx in much the same way Professor Harold Hill stole into River City with his satchel full of band uniforms. A transformation, however, was taking place in front of their very eyes, and as time wore on, they watched, transfixed by the excitement before them. First came the vans, then the flatbed trucks piled high with plywood planks and wire fencing, then the heavy machinery. Then it was too late. Babylon had descended upon Wallkill, and with it, like River City's commotion, came trouble—with a capital T.

The festival stopwatch had been set on June 5 and was immediately activated. Like a time bomb, it could not be defused without exploding. There were no allowances in the schedule for mistakes; excuses would surely prove fatal. With only seventy days allotted for preparations between the move to Wallkill and August 15 when the first guitar would strike a note for eternity, time was everything. Each action had to be negotiated with forethought, every plan carried out with precision. There was no stopping time.

Mel Lawrence had reached an agreement with a faltering bungalow colony in Bullville, a Catskill Mountain adjunct, to provide housing for the twenty-person crew due to arrive in Wallkill to begin work on June 6. Rosenberg's was a family retreat known for its Kosher cuisine and was once removed from the mainstream of Catskill celebrity haunts. Its provisions were the solemn, rhymeless necessities that catered to a solid working-class clientele. Each summer, finding themselves handcuffed by inflation, the same faces trudged back to escape fleetingly the humdrum, dispassionate city grind. They carried their green-and-white-striped beach chairs to the pool's edge, where they passed two weeks locked in expressionless gin rummy tournaments while their children splashed nearby. Lawrence, nonetheless, had remembered it from his teen-age days as a waiter in that region and knew it to be clean, congenial, and accommodating. He had cajoled its owners, an elderly Jewish couple, into making it available to Woodstock Ventures by passing off his band of hippies as a "bunch of nice Jewish kids who promise to be good while they are guests of the colony." The next day, the Rosenbergs and their annual summer lodgers gawked shamelessly as a congregation resembling a faction of Hell's Angels dropped its backpacks in the Main Lodge reception area while awaiting their room assignments. Religious families whose men wore yarmulkes on their heads gathered around them as "Funny, you don't *look* Jewish" became a much repeated salutation.

The first to arrive were Lawrence, Michael Lang, Penny Stallings, a woman friend of John Morris's named Lee Mackler who was hired to assist the security honchos with police selection, and the five University of Miami artists led by Bill and Jean Ward. They swept down upon this unassuming little hamlet like a tropical storm, and after being transferred to their rooms in unembellished cabins dubbed "The Apple," "The Berry," "The Cherry," and "The Grape," they squeezed into two rented station wagons and drove over to the Mills property to acquaint themselves with their forthcoming task.

The site looked like an overgrown picnic area. A knee-high jungle of grass covered the acreage as far as the eye could see, an olive green blanket checkered with dandelions, milkweed, and chicory. Every few hundred yards, a dead tree jutted forth, its leafless limbs stretching like a haggard hawk on descent. The once productive orchard had receded to the road. Mosquitoes glided inches above the soft marshy spots and nested in the disregarded piles of dried ashwood. Nevertheless, its unadorned soul shone through. It was a stunning example of how man botched natural beauty by reckless neglect.

The hippies wandered across the meadow like pioneers validating a lost deed. They set to work analyzing their respective jobs without a day's delay. Everyone possessed an identical sense of urgency regarding the festival's incarnation. Michael did well to heighten that feeling by disclosing to them that, since the first run of festival advertisements had hit the papers last week, mail-order requests averaging twenty to thirty thousand dollars a day were pouring into the uptown office. History was in the making, he assured them, and it was up to each one present to see that the hippie canon was inscribed in the annals with significant import.

Lawrence set up festival headquarters in a miniature red barn covered with gray slate shingles on the perimeter of Howard Mills's property, which he had rented from their landlord for a slight additional charge. (Everything not specifically mentioned in the lease, they were informed early, would carry a "slight additional charge.") Desks and swivel chairs were shipped upstate from the production office. Mel's desk occupied the hayloft, which permitted him an unobstructed view of what was happening on the site through a second-story window. Penny Stallings was stationed directly beneath him. The other desks and architects' tables situated across from Penny were reserved for assistants who would gravitate north as their schedules allowed.

From the first day of occupancy in the barn, Lawrence was buried beneath a tangle of blueprints and structural designs commissioned months before. From here on in, he had to attend to the physical construction of the site; channels for electrical lines had to be plotted, coordinates were set for the sinking of the concrete stage supports, a system of piping to carry water from the towers to the field was pending his approval, lumber had to be ordered for building the stage and lighting towers, county diagrams were unrolled and tacked on a bulletin board to accelerate the festival's request for additional roads to be laid by the art and field crews. Lawrence then shuttled the sheaves of paper onto Penny's desk so that she could begin working on deals for ordering hardware and machinery. No one was afforded a moment's rest, and everyone worked on impulse.

Michael was on hand for the first few days' activities, strolling across the grounds with a tattered paperback copy of *The Electric Kool-Aid Acid Test* stuffed into his back pocket. He and Mel fantasized about the crowds that would descend upon the very spot they stood on in slightly more than two months' time. "You see that hill over there, kid?" Lawrence asked him, cradling Michael with an arm and pointing to the bowl's grassy knoll. "Fifty thousand kids, m'man. Fifty thousand of those little fuckers are gonna bound in here to see this show." They'd slap each other's palms and cap off their elation by sharing a joint. Together, they walked off approximate measurements for the campgrounds, which were to be cut from the remains of the orchard. Some of the dead trees would have to be chopped down; they decided to prune them for camping firewood and to use what was left for a playground. They also conceived a network of paths, which had to be tramped through the trees, to facilitate getting from one section of the site to another.

One problem was obvious from the onset. "We're gonna run into trouble with parking," Mel advised Lang on one of their morning jaunts across the field. "We've got just enough room to stash a few hundred cars around the entrance, but after that, we're in for nothing but headaches. You know as well as I do that we're gonna be bombarded with wheels—maybe up to twenty thousand a day."

"How about parking 'em on the ground behind the stage and having 'em walk from there around to the gate?"

"Good thinkin', pal. Tell you what: I'll appoint you to go out there at night with a flashlight and try to coax fifty thousand half-crazed hippies through a ten-foot entranceway. Ever see a stampede from up close? Try that, and I guarantee that you will. There's no access to that area. There aren't enough adequate roads to keep the cars moving without creating a goddamn traffic jam."

"Can we build one?"

"Not in the amount of time we've got. A two-lane road wouldn't help. What we need is enough access to handle more than the twenty thousand cars a day, several roads leading into that area so we can convert them to one-way drives. That way, at least we'd have a little control over the flow. But that'd take too much time. You gotta remember, we're gonna be rollin' over people's land and they're gonna be screamin' their fuckin' heads off about that. We'll be tossed outta here on our asses so fast we won't know what hit us. What we *can* do is to rebuild and pave the road above the site so that it gives us another means to get 'em in the front door. Beyond that, I think we're gonna have ourselves a helluva problem."

Lawrence informed Lang that he was investigating various methods of alternative busing. Hopefully, he'd locate one or several large fields within the town, which he could rent and where people could be directed to park their cars before they ever came within proximity of the festival grounds. They'd have to contract a private bus company to shuttle those with tickets from the parking lot onto the site. "It'll be expensive," he contended, "but it'll avoid creating a devastating situation with the traffic."

"That's cool," Lang approved. "Don't worry about the bread. It's more important that we let it happen."

"Yeah. I figured that'd be your reaction. Hey kid, you sure you got the bucks behind you? We're in over our fuckin' heads with this thing. I'm no longer playin' bingo with a sack full of nickels and dimes. This gig could float a major political campaign."

"Don't worry, Mel. It's no hassle. I got it all under control." Michael smiled and gave him the high sign.

"All right. I just hadda say it once now that we're goin' for broke. I'll ride around later this afternoon and see what I can dig up in the way of fields. I talked to Goldstein a little while ago. He's latched onto this company outta Cambridge that is some kinda hip efficiency organization. They drop in, look at the layout, and determine how we can slide through it with a little more breathing room. Maybe they can do something about the traffic situation. Meanwhile, I suggest you tack on to the ads some kinda warning that kids should leave their wheels at home and take public transportation. If we can encourage that and it works, we'll reduce the risk of a fiasco by a helluva lot. Otherwise we're fucked."

Michael made a note of it and slipped it into the front cover of his book.

"What's the latest word on bands?" Mel asked.

"The contracts just came in for Sweetwater, and I signed BS&T yesterday."

"Hey, far fuckin' out!"

Michael had spent a considerable amount of time searching for another headliner. Blood, Sweat and Tears was considered of superstar magnitude. Their signing was a conspicuous feather in Lang's frumpy leather cap. By mid-1969, their second album, *Blood, Sweat and Tears* (minus founder Al Kooper), was firmly stationed at the top of the charts, and their unique sound—a synthesis of electric blues and jazz—began to dominate commercial rock music. All of the up-and-coming recording artists were incorporating a horn section like BS&T's into their bands and were similarly experimenting with more spontaneous chord progressions. Chicago Transit Authority, another progressive group who captured the teen-age market, followed suit but had not yet worked their way into matching sales figures. Lang went with the proven commodity. Blood, Sweat and Tears had just come off a series of Top Forty hits. He banked on the percentage theory of their still being hot in mid-August.

"They hit us for fifteen grand, man."

Lawrence whistled. "That's a shitload of bread. They oughta direct traffic, work the concession booths, and do lights for that kinda money." They both laughed.

"They'll pack 'em in, though. I checked it out, and they're selling out faster than almost any other American group on the road. They also got a lotta class with Clayton-Thomas, and all. And Sweetwater'll be a good act to stick on Friday's show."

"How about Sly?" Mel asked.

"I don't know, man. They're jivin' everybody. Shit, Sly didn't show up for his last two gigs and the promoters almost had a fuckin' riot. Cops, dogs, the works. Who needs that kinda shit. I can just see a hundred thousand kids stormin' the stage when we announce that Sly hadda cancel. He's bad news."

"But can you afford *not* to have him?"

Michael shook his head indecisively. "I don't know. I wish I had some kinda guarantee that he'll show. I'm just not sure yet."

Lang had made splendid headway in booking the show. Like a chain reaction of egos, once a top act deemed the Aquarian Exposition a worthwhile date on its tour, those feverishly trying to hang on to celebrity begged their agents to get them on the bill. The few gaps left in the three-day extravaganza would eventually fill themselves. All Michael had to do was to sit back and wait for the phone to ring.

The most important thing now was the preening of Mills Heights. The industrial site needed a dramatic face-lift nothing short of an act of God. The staff was raring to go, but nobody had yet picked up a shovel.

Bill and Jean Ward spent hours pondering the lay of the land in an attempt to determine a starting point for their group of sculptors. During the first week in Wallkill, they took several long walks with Mel Lawrence crisscrossing the field, wandering through the woods, sitting in the orchard. They wanted to design a visionary model city. Within this city, they'd emphasize the symbols of the festival nation by creating communities: places where people ate, slept, cared for their health, performed their bodily functions and entertained themselves. Each facility built on the site somehow had to convey the message of a brotherhood working toward the common initiative of peace. At the same time, it was essential that they maintain the earth's natural beauty. Their original concept had been to create gigantic metal sculptures such as they had done at Miami Pop. That type of art—roughhewn, fierce, and larger than life—was, however, inappropriate for Woodstock. It carried no message, instilled no feeling of tranquility; it was brash and arrogant and would only jolt the senses of those who came to unwind.

"We've got a terrific opportunity here," Jean explained to the artists back at Rosenberg's. "We can attempt to tackle something that all of us have been taught in theory but which we've not had access to: land and heritage. You guys saw the scenery on the way up here. This part of the country is positively beautiful. I think we should forget about sculpture and allow the land to dictate what we do."

"It means that you'll have to concede to us more of a responsibility in preparing the festival grounds," Bill Ward specified to Lawrence. Likewise, the artists would be compelled to participate in interrelated, practical matters such as paving the roads, clearing brush, and excavating stone paths through the woods since every stroke would affect their finished canvas.

Bill spent several days hidden away in a corner of the field office sketching their ideas for Lawrence's approval. Working from an aerial photograph of the field, which Mills had taken a year before, he subdivided the land into parcels, added paths, removed natural obstacles, and penned in a variety of wooden structures where stands were planned. Lawrence studied the renderings, making several suggestions; however, for the most part, he and Ward were on the same wavelength. Once the designs were resolved, Bill took a day off, drove Mel's car into Brooklyn and purchased work gloves, machetes, hammers, hatchets, and sledgehammers for the crew to get started.

Jean turned her thoughts to productivity and came upon an unforeseen problem almost immediately. On one of her trips through the field, she had left the barn and walked in a direct line about three quarters of a mile up the side of the hill where the audience was slated to sit. All of a sudden, she noticed that the weeds covering it changed color; their dull leaves turned pointed and shiny. It was covered with poison ivy. Her heart sank. There was another massive patch of it flourishing over the rise of the hill and continuing on back into the area designated for camping. It had to go—every last stitch of it—before they got started with the actual sculpting of the land, otherwise it would be ground into the dirt and just as contagious as if still on the vine. Along with several of the art students, she tried cutting it with a hand mower, but there were too many trees in the vicinity and they couldn't get close enough with the machinery to complete the job. The only thing left for them to do was to get down on their hands and knees and to pull it physically out by the roots. Since this was not quite the type of job for which everyone readily volunteered, turns were assigned and rotated so no one person was exposed to the ivy more than anyone else. Not that it really mattered. Within a week, everyone except Jean was covered with a rash and had to be taken to a doctor in Middletown to receive shots.

Once most of the poison ivy was eliminated, the rest of the overgrown field had to be sheared. The work load was monumental in comparison to the retinue of co-workers. There was no time to screen personnel or even hire experienced landscrapers. Instead, Jean practiced on-the-job training with a pickup team of vagabond hippies. She and Mel hired kids who were drifting by and stopped to see what was taking place on the Mills property. None of these kids, called hippies by preference, had any money, nor did they seem to care about being able to afford such luxuries as motel rooms or sumptuous meals. They weren't overly industrious by any stretch of the imagination. All, however, were quick to accept a job at Woodstock, which, in return, would provide them with "a place to crash," three meals a day, and pocket money to help send them on their way to the next destination. A continuous flow of hippies subsequently joined the field crew and put in a day's honest labor before partaking in the partylike atmosphere after dinner. They pulled their brightly decorated Volkswagen vans and campers off the road by the barn, picked up a sickle, a clipper or a scythe (or merely improvised and used their hands), and set to work manicuring the festival grounds. The results were immediate and immensely gratifying.

*　　*　　*

Howard Mills, Jr., remained aloof from his diligent tenants. He did, however, quickly adjust to playing the role of lord of the manor by, each day, swinging his Coupe deVille off the road and bouncing it across the field to inspect their progress. Mills had no complaint. His original plan had been to unload the family land; now he could simply sit back and collect an unexpected bonus while waiting for the right industrial concern to make him an appetizing offer. The land, in his eyes, had outlived its agricultural purpose; so, in fact, had Wallkill; now, he had to make a move that would elevate his lot and, naturally, his net worth.

Mills had told a neighbor at a party that the "Woodstock hippies were going to make Howard Mills, Jr., a household name—not only in this town, but in the state as well." The woman, who had known Mills most of his life, almost dropped her drink; the vacant smile on Howard's face had the lifeless quality of a wooden puppet. "You'll see. First I'll run for county supervisor," he bragged. "Then, when all this nonsense is over with, I'm going to run for governor of New York. No one will be able to resist Howard Mills. No one."

The couple who owned the bungalow colony, the Rosenbergs, derived no such satisfaction from the alien beings who had invaded their quiet haven. The hippies had become, if anything, a nuisance. They refused to come to the dining hall with shoes on their feet; the sweet pungence of strawberry incense had a discomforting effect on the traditional Sabbath dinner of boiled chicken and soup; and the psychedelic vans surrounding the entrance, in which the crew members slept, were beginning to scare off potential guests. Those who were already there for their summer vacations were grumbling. They resented having to share the shuffleboard block and swimming pool with the hippies, and their kids were being chased from the basketball court while Mel Lawrence went one-on-one with his staff. Within two weeks after Woodstock Ventures' arrival in Bullville, the Rosenbergs intimated that they'd feel a lot better about their business if the hippies looked for another home.

They were not the only ones with a grievance. Their reaction, in fact, was subdued and respectful in comparison to other reactions from outsiders. A prominent Middletown politician who was in the midst of a campaign for reelection must have blanched when he saw them arrive. He pulled Goldstein and Lawrence aside the afternoon they opened the field office and said, "I just want you to know that you're not welcome in this community, and I'm going to do everything in my power to see you don't remain here." (His ardor might have been violent had he known a prominent member of Woodstock's staff was having sexual relations with his daughter.) It was one issue on which both he and his constituents agreed. The next day, the threatening phone calls started; not many at first, but enough to instill feelings of paranoia and fear in their peace-seeking hearts.

"If you hippies don't get the hell out of our town, you'll be sorry." Click.

"We don't want you filthy pigs in Wallkill." Click.

"You've got two days to move out of here or we're going to burn that barn down with all your people locked inside." Click.

"If you don't clear out, you're going to die." Click.

Penny had taken most of the calls during the first week. At first, she was reluctant to tell anyone about the incendiary messages for fear it would interrupt the headway they were making on the site; she also did not take them too seriously. But the increasing venom in the anonymous voices frightened her. She had to tell Lawrence.

"Shit!" he snapped. "I figured we'd run into a fair share of rednecks up here, but I didn't think they'd come on that strong." He thought about it for a few moments while Penny watched him. "You're right, Pen," he said finally, "it's fuckin' scary. I'd better call the kid."

Lang had gone back to New York that morning. With time closing in, and urged on by the beginning of work on the site, he stepped up booking negotiations. Michael was in the uptown office when Lawrence finally tracked him down.

"Circle the wagons, man," said Michael. "It looks like we're gonna have a helluva fight on our hands. Sounds to me like those assholes want blood."

"Hippie blood, Michael. They made that real clear on the phone. Think you oughta tell Pomeroy?"

"Not yet. He'll be up there this weekend, and the two of you cats can kick it around. Try to ignore it for now. If it gets any worse, call me and I'll get in touch with him. Got any idea who's pullin' this shit?"

"Take your pick. How many people did you say live up here?"

"Very funny, man."

"No. No it's not."

"Hey, Mel, you guys *clean* up there?"

"As best as can be expected. No heavy stuff. Everyone's doin' their share of grass, that's all."

"Well cool it, okay?"

"That's gonna be tough, Michael. Most of these kids aren't gettin' much bread outta this deal. You can't ask 'em not to get high."

"Just tell 'em to be cool about it. Nothin' on the site. We can fight those assholes all the way down the line if we stay clean 'cause we aren't doing anything wrong and we got permission from that zoning board or whatever. If anyone gets busted, we're done for. Even if it's not one of our own guys. They'll make a whole scene out of something like that. And we'll be guilty no matter what. Not only that, I'll bet anything they're dying to get the goods on us. Once they do, we're blown."

"Yeah. You're right."

"Hey—and Mel, keep your eye out for a narc. It could be any one of those kids."

Lawrence hung up the phone and asked Penny to gather everyone into the barn as soon as possible. He could not afford to let this matter slide. The same thing had happened to him in Miami. Every cop was looking over his shoulder just panting to make the bust that would close them down. It was all they could do to stay calm and follow through on their jobs.

It took about fifteen minutes for the crew to wind down their jobs and find their way back to the barn. When they arrived, Mel was leaning against the railing in the hayloft.

"Sorry to have to call you guys in here in the middle of the afternoon, but we've gotten some bad vibes from our neighbors and it couldn't wait." A chorus of groans rose from the gallery below him. "It seems they don't want any of our filthy, dope-smokin', mother-fuckin', hippie rapist kind up here in their God-fearin' community." The profanity skipped along like a tuneful children's song and drew a laugh. "Now, I know we haven't given anyone any reason to come down hard on us like this, but they're afraid, and we gotta let it slide by so we can get the gig on. So I gotta ask you to lay off the dope for a while and to be on your best behavior. And if you're ballin' one of the local chicks, for God's sake just make sure it's not some politician's daughter." Several of those below him laughed less than the others. "A lot of these redneck fuckers are gonna be lookin' for anything to jump on us with, so we gotta play by their rules. You're gonna be stopped whenever one of the local pigs is in the neighborhood. Just be polite. So if you're cool they'll pat you on the head and send you on your way. And, for Christ's sake, don't ever carry any dope on you. That's the first thing they'll look for. They're gonna search you from head to toe every chance they get. You get busted, we're gonna get the shoe and you better like prison food. If you're clean, there's no charge they can make stick. You wanna get high? Just be cool about it. Keep it around your bedroom and only light up if you know everybody who's in there with you. We're gonna fight to stay here, and we're gonna win."

Two days later, on June 9, a visitor in a black three-piece suit carrying a briefcase arrived at the barn to "speak to the man in charge." Penny referred him to Lawrence.

"What are you people doing here?" the man asked with practiced insouciance.

"What's it to you, pal?"

"I'll tell you *exactly* what it is to me, wise guy. I represent the Wallkill Town Council, and anything that takes place within the town's limits is our business."

Lawrence apologized for his ill-mannered behavior. "It's been a rough two days for us," he said. "We've had some pretty bizarre calls lettin' us know that we're not exactly welcome around these parts, and I'm a little on the defensive side." Mel introduced himself. "What can I do for you, uh . . ."

No reciprocity was forthcoming. The man offered no clue as to his identity. "You can start by telling me what you're doing here."

"Sure." He climbed down the ladder from the loft. Lee Mackler was at her desk by the door and kept her eyes trained on the stranger. "We just broke ground for our festival, the music and art fair we're having in August. It's gonna take us about two months to get it together and . . ."

"How about your permits? Do you have zoning board permission?"

"We don't need permits. Two of our guys went before the zoning board a couple of weeks ago, and they were told that it was beyond that body's jurisdiction. In effect, they gave us their blessing. Mr. Mills told us the same thing."

"I'm afraid you're mistaken. Under no circumstances are you allowed to make any renovations on property in this county without the proper permits. From the looks of things," he said, swinging his nose in a half circle, "you've broken the law. I suggest you cease what you're doing immediately. I've got to report this back to my committee. There may be a fine."

Lawrence shook his head in disbelief. This guy was putting him on, he thought. Someone—probably Goldstein or one of the others—put some clown up to playing a practical joke on him. But they wouldn't do that knowing how pressed he was for time. "Don't fuck around with me, pal." The man took a step back toward the door. "You go tell your committee that we don't intend to move a foot off this place. We paid to rent this land, and that zoning board of yours told us it was cool to proceed. We're proceeding. Now you can beat it unless you've got a warrant."

"Then I think we'll have to seek an injunction to teach you your rights."

"You do that! Interfere with our plans and we'll slap a suit on you guys so fast you won't know what hit you. Go on—get outta here, and don't come back without eighteen bucks for a ticket to the festival."

Lee Mackler was already dialing Lang at the production office.

"Asshole," Lawrence muttered when the man was out of hearing distance. "What are you doing?" he asked Lee.

"Trying to get the curly-haired kid." She tried several numbers, but Lang was not to be found.

"Never mind. Put through a call to John Roberts. I want to find out just what rights we've got up here."

Roberts shrugged it off as an oversight on the town's part. He told Lawrence that the zoning board of appeals, the group Mills had him see, had given him and Joel their complete approval. "There's been a breakdown in communications somewhere along the way. It's only a matter of time before that group representative gets it straight. Don't worry about a thing. Just to double-check, I'll put our lawyer on it right away and get back to you."

Lawrence got in touch with Stanley Goldstein who decided it was high time to begin a public relations drive in the town. He, in turn, contacted the *Times Herald Record,* the Middletown newspaper with the largest circulation, and offered to give them a story about a major event that was going to take place in their community. The story, a short piece outlining the festival, appeared the next morning in the June 11 edition of the paper. It defined their association with "Howard D. Mills, Jr., of Scotchtown, a well-known land developer," as Goldstein hoped it would. It was essential that their efforts be linked with local names and places to soften their impact on the residents.

The article quoted Goldstein as saying that certain members of the staff were setting out to contact the residents of Scotchtown to "reassure them we are doing everything in the right way. We want to be good neighbors . . . not just dump twenty thousand people out here. We will answer any questions about the festival and will do all we can to make sure no one is upset by our festival plans." Goldstein tried to accrue a little sympathy to offset some of the staff's anticipation. "It is regrettable," he went on, "that there are already rumors and fears. We will hire experienced people to direct the festival . . . people who know what they are doing." He identified the Reverend Don Ganoung, Wes Pomeroy, and Mel Lawrence, giving brief descriptions of their respective qualifications. When asked by the reporter to identify any of the principals from Woodstock Ventures, Goldstein offered only: "Mike Lang of Florida."

The remainder of the article was devoted to a listing of the acts already committed to appearing on the bill and included heretofore undisclosed names such as the Moody Blues (who had not yet signed a contract), Crosby, Stills and Nash, and the Iron Butterfly.

Goldstein was not completely satisfied with the story's appearance. While it might serve to pacify some of their opponents, he knew it would undoubtedly aggravate others. That morning, he telephoned Lang and asked him to get Ganoung and Pomeroy up to the site as fast as possible. He considered it of utmost importance that Ganoung slap on his collar, visit with anyone in the community voicing displeasure over their presence, and solicit their advice in lieu of action. Michael informed him that Ganoung was due to arrive in Wallkill within a few days' time and "not to get uptight about it." The whole thing, he contended, would blow over in a few days' time.

A headline, though, in the next edition of the *Times Herald Record* substantiated Goldstein's prudent state of alarm. In bold, black screaming letters, the paper announced: WALLKILL FACTION GIRDS TO BLOCK FOLK FESTIVAL. According to the paper's account, a residents' group and town officials were joining hands to rewrite the Aquarian Exposition's horoscope. It included a vague interview with Town Supervisor Jack A. Schlosser, who expressed concern for the safety of town residents and vowed to propose new legislation to protect his constituents from "the various things that might occur" [at the festival]." Some definite action was promised at a town board meeting scheduled for later that evening. "I don't oppose anything like this in principle," Schlosser hedged, "if the promoters can meet all safety requirements." From the administrator's insinuating tone, it was clear the august town board would see to it that that would be highly unlikely.

If that was not disheartening enough, the article went on to identify the self-appointed spokesman of a "citizens' ad hoc committee" opposing the festival as Richard Dow, also of Scotchtown. Dow was quoted as saying, "We do not want 20,000 of those hippie-type people in the area. A hippie influx into the city of Boston last summer caused a large increase in hepatitis, venereal disease, and drug abuse."

Goldstein was flabbergasted. How could anyone attack something they knew absolutely nothing about? he wondered. Stanley read the article to Lang over the phone and told Michael of his plan to represent Woodstock Ventures at the town council meeting later that night. Lang agreed. Goldstein was impressive in front of a crowd. He could deal with all types of people and was eloquent. He could conceivably quench the heated Wallkill temperaments before they erupted. Michael's appearance there could only produce added stress in a situation that was already coming apart at the seams. "Take along as many blueprints as you can, man. Those cats love people who look official." Goldstein said he had already borrowed the topographical maps Mel had drawn for his crews and would "wave them around for the politicos."

"We got a visitor down here this morning who you might also want to take along with you," Michael said more cheerfully. Don Ganoung had arrived, and not a day too soon.

— 2 —

In his mid-forties, Don Ganoung was a hippie lost-child grown-up, an amal-gamation of every Damon Runyon character whose life bordered on delin-quency but whose salvation was his heart. Ganoung had a heart and wore it proudly on his sleeve. He was an imposing individual, a hulking, six-foot-three-inch titan. His features, however, were softened by pearl-white hair, a dense beard to match, and sad, compassionate eyes. Those who knew him intimately, and even those who were merely introduced, were taken by his graceful, almost poetic approach to life; he could quote from the Scriptures and Dylan in the same sentence and possessed the ability to bore straight through to the emotional source of a man's soul. But for all his sagelike bear-ing and being a man of the cloth, Ganoung was a self-confessed rascal like the others.

"A lusty man," was how Wes Pomeroy described his friend. Pomeroy had first encountered Don Ganoung in San Francisco when the latter was a pa-role officer in Alameda County, a neighboring district off Pomeroy's turf. "He had a deep commitment to religion, was one of the most religious men I've ever known," Pomeroy recalled, "but he liked to raise a little hell every now and then, and Don could do that just about as well or better than anyone around."

Ganoung's ministry was in San Francisco's run-down Patrero district where religion had all but disappeared in the early 1960s. Poverty had usurped faith and, in an attempt to keep religious spirit alive in the Patrero, Ganoung combined three failing congregations, took over the Good Samar-itan Settlement House on the peninsula, and immediately did away with Sunday services. Don took the practical approach. He organized a get-together at "Good Sam" each Wednesday night and played on the people's guilt to get them to attend. Wednesday mornings he would buy a few bottles of wine and a loaf of bread for the sacraments, and the people chipped in for food, for they all ate together after a short prayer service.

Ganoung's intentions went beyond pure religion. Because of his congre-gation's low post on the social ladder, he was determined to educate them as to ways of elevating their lives. In the wooden pews, where one expected to find hymnals, Ganoung would place literature on subjects like birth control and social service agencies. He brought in minority leaders from the com-munity to speak about things that affected them directly. Pomeroy remem-bers first hearing the words "black power" there at a time when racial pride was soft-pedaled as heresy. But the Wednesday night gatherings were far from solemn affairs. After dinner, there was lots of singing. People were encouraged to forget their troubles for an evening and to enjoy the pleasures that were still, and would always be, theirs. Ganoung led the revelry. "He couldn't sing worth a damn," Pomeroy said, "but he walked around smiling at his people, bellowing at the top of his voice. He wanted to convince them he was just like every one of them."

He was, indeed. Don Ganoung, like the blacks, Puerto Ricans, and South Sea Islanders who came to his church, was a mere mortal. When Pomeroy called him to find out about his interest in joining up with Woodstock, Ganoung was having marital difficulties and had only recently licked a drinking problem. In the long run, he, too, would profit from the festival's doctrine of fellowship, and without hesitation, he told Pomeroy he would arrange for a leave of absence and fly to Wallkill.

On June 12, Goldstein and Ganoung entered the paneled public assembly room of the Wallkill Town Hall a few minutes past seven o'clock and had difficulty finding a pair of seats together. The room was never more than a quarter full for most meetings. Now, it was jammed with people of all ages who had presumably come to express their opinions concerning the coming of the Woodstock Music and Art Fair.

Goldstein had called Town Supervisor Schlosser's office earlier in the day and, without much difficulty, had his and Ganoung's names inserted into the evening's agenda, which provided them with the opportunity to defend themselves against any opposition should that be necessary. As he took his seat near the back of the room, Goldstein had become convinced that his addressing the mob of citizens was inevitable. The agitated crowd was growing more impatient with each passing minute, and all because of one threatening word: festival. Their work was cut out for them before they even opened their mouths.

Jack Schlosser, a beefy, tenacious man with a biting disposition, entered the room carrying a manilla ledger a few minutes before the meeting's seven-thirty starting time. Neither Goldstein nor Ganoung had any idea of what to expect from him, although the supervisor's obstinacy was no secret. It was said that Schlosser's manner was curt and his temper equally abrupt; if one wished to make a contradicting point in his presence, it had better be louder and more vehement than his own.

That attitude was, perhaps, what had sustained Schlosser's appointment as supervisor in an oppositional town for so long a time. He had been elected in 1961, the first Democrat ever to hold that post in a staunch Republican stronghold. His overwhelming victory had come about from the uncovering and exposing of a political favoritism scheme some months before. He ran for election not so much to forge a career in politics as to put up such a good fight that the Republicans would be forced to clean house and put some law-abiding men into office. Within months, though, he found himself occupying a position in need of a strict constitutionalist and a strong arm; he had become, in effect, the presiding official in the town of Wallkill and he intended to exercise his power to bring about change in what had become known as an antiquated New York bedroom community.

Schlosser learned quickly. In his first term of office, he had managed to obtain a half-million dollars in federal aid for construction of Wallkill's first public sewer system, established a lower tax basis to attract industry, thus lowering unemployment, and reorganized the fire protection services that established Wallkill's independence from the city of Middletown. Those refinements had not come about without long and drawn-out battles contesting Schlosser's actions. But they were nothing, he imagined, compared to what this festival business promised to bring him. He was not looking forward to it.

Schlosser's first order of business that night had to do with the rezoning of certain areas of Wallkill township. After that had been taken care of, he shuffled a few papers and noted the time. "There's been a lot of jabbering about this rock folk festival that's supposed to be held up on Howard Mills's place," Schlosser announced coolly. Goldstein interpreted his use of the passive *supposed* as an inauspicious omen. "We're going to hear from the people who are putting on this thing and then from a few people who aren't so happy about it. Hopefully, we'll reach some conclusion about what to do with it."

"I'll tell you what to do with it," one red-cheeked man cried out from the back of the room. "First we oughta shave those hippies' heads so we can tell whether they're boys or girls we're dealing with. Then we ought to rub their noses in the dirt for what they're doing to this country." The room broke into strident applause.

Schlosser pounded his gavel on a gnarled block. "I'll have no more of that," he ordered, "from anybody. This is a town meeting, and it's going to be conducted in an orderly fashion. If you've got anything to say, you can raise your hand and we'll get around to calling on you. Now, we've got a rough thing on our hands, something that bears a lot of thought and discussion. As some of you already know, a bunch of young people have begun work preparing for a music festival on Howard's land."

"You bet we know," a woman shouted. Schlosser gaveled her down. His face wore the expression of a condemned man realizing there would be no eleventh-hour reprieve from the governor's office.

He began again. "Tonight we're going to hear from a representative of Woodstock Ventures, the company promoting it. His name is Mr. Stanley Goldstein, and he's seated over there." Three hundred heads turned and glowered in Goldstein's direction. Schlosser motioned him to the bench. "He's going to tell us a little about what this group is planning and what we can expect."

There was a murmur of general disapproval as Goldstein made his way toward the front of the room.

In as controlled and authoritative tone as possible, Stanley laid out the plans for the festival emphasizing the proposed art exhibit, a dance program, the presentation of experimental and underground motion pictures, and repertory theatre. No allusion was made to the Aquarian Exposition being a rock festival. Goldstein stressed that the crowds would be handled by a staff of highly skilled, competent professionals. When he had finished, he smiled at the stony faces and asked if there were any questions he could answer for them. Several people shouted for the right to be heard. Schlosser patted their hands down.

"I have to be honest with you, Mr. Goldstein," he began. "We're a small town that has never experienced anything like what you are proposing. It's not the music or the type of people that we're worried about . . ."

"Like hell it's not!" someone screamed.

". . . it's the amount of people you're expecting. We're just not equipped to handle as many people and cars as you're predicting will show up. We're only a small town with limited facilities." Goldstein assured him that the promoters did not expect more than four thousand cars a day, but Schlosser deferred to his better judgment. "You can't be sure of that, and besides, with all the work being done on the roads up there, you'd create something of a disaster. No, Mr. Goldstein. I'm going to recommend that the town council pass legislation restricting public assemblies larger than one thousand persons to make sure that does not happen. I'm sorry."

Goldstein asked him to clarify his statement. What kind of restrictions did he intend to provide for in this so-called ordinance?

"I don't quite know how the phrasing will read," he said, "so I'm limited with respect to giving you more information. But I seriously doubt it will read in your favor."

Schlosser recognized Richard Dow, who was seated in the second row of the audience, and invited him to stand and be heard.

Dow waved a leaf of legal-sized paper in the air and presented the town council with a petition from fifty-five residents of Wallkill who were "violently objecting" to the festival's being held. "I can't tell you how much we fear the kind of hippie-yippie crowd this thing'll attract," he said to rousing applause. Schlosser allowed it to continue for longer than it should have before pounding his gavel. "We're forming an ad hoc committee and we're going to see that something as dangerous as this festival never takes place in our community."

"We don't want your kind here! Get out of our town!" someone from behind him shouted at Stanley. A clamor of voices echoed a similar sentiment.

"Look, we've got a considerable investment in your community," Goldstein said in the festival's defense. "Like any other company that comes here, we're going to be employing local people, entering into negotiations with Wallkill contractors and developers. We're going to be bringing business *into* your community, not taking anything away."

"Not if we can help it!"

"You goddamn hippies aren't coming anywhere near our people!"

"I don't think there's anything to get this excited about," he yelled. When people had calmed down, he tried another angle. "We welcome your advice and knowledge."

"Take some advice and *get lost!*" Derisive laughter filled the hall for about thirty seconds.

Schlosser put the gavel aside and banged his hands on the table. The meeting was slipping away from his control. "Let's have some order here. Mr. Goldstein has the floor. I don't expect another outburst like this one." He nodded for Stanley to continue.

"Where do you intend to put all these kids who show up here?" someone called from the floor. Stanley was having some trouble seeing where the questions were coming from and began talking to the wrong side of the room. "Over here."

"Excuse me," he said, pointing to his glasses and smiling. "They're not what they used to be." A few people chuckled sympathetically. At least they're human, he thought. "They'll all be on the festival grounds. Most are planning to camp in an area which will be provided for overnight accommodations there."

Until this time, no one had seen Howard Mills make his entrance and take a seat in the back of the room. Following Goldstein's statement about camping, he stood up and attracted the attention of the crowd.

"I don't know anything about this part of it. I'm telling you right now, there is to be no camping on the property of the proposed site of the Aquarian Music and Art Fair. I won't allow it."

An undercurrent of commotion filled the room as though a momentous decision had been made. Goldstein looked soberly at Don Ganoung who squinted his lack of understanding.

"We allegedly had permission to camp on this ground and this information is a new development to me. Therefore this information must be held in question."

"You want me to explain it to you?" a woman shouted contemptuously. "*No camping!*" she spat. Again applause and laughter resounded from the crowd. Goldstein ignored her as best he could and launched into an explanation of auxillary accommodations. He said the festival staff had already reserved two hundred motel rooms in the vicinity. "We could accommodate fifty thousand people tomorrow if we had to."

A resident of Wallkill reservedly inquired about the provisions the festival staff intended to make for dealing with the extraordinary number of people expected to attend the three-day affair. Goldstein said that Don Ganoung would be a better person to explain their security measures and introduced him.

Ganoung's age and background acted as a buffer to subdue temporarily the distressed townspeople. He walked to the dais slowly, with visible confidence, never allowing the faint din of voices at his back to distract him. Ganoung, poised at the lecturn, delivered a summary of the security program like a sermon, modulating his voice to underscore particular points he wanted brought home. He was magnificent at the lecturn. Even Goldstein momentarily lost vision of Ganoung's real purpose in being there. Unfortunately, the thought of a hippie congregation only minutes from their homes failed to temper the assembly's social hatred, and what religion had prevailed in their lives was momentarily extinguished.

"You think one man's gonna be able to control all those wild hippie kids up there?" a man taunted. "You gotta be kidding."

Ganoung unfolded a piece of paper on which he had written some specific details earlier that afternoon. "You didn't hear me correctly, sir. I believe I said that Mr. Pomeroy would *helm* our security force. Let me explain. We intend to employ several hundred men drawn from the existing forces in New York and Washington. Men who have had police experience in crowd control and peace-keeping procedures."

"You expect the police to cooperate with a buncha hippies?"

"Well, Mr. Pomeroy is not a hippie, although he understands their problems and knows how to deal with them. Neither am I. But to answer your question—yes, I have full trust in Wes Pomeroy's ability to mobilize a security force, although no contracts have been signed at this time."

The last part of that sentence appeared to satisfy the Wallkill questioner who sat back in his chair, folded his arms, and smiled smugly.

Goldstein interjected that these same people working on Woodstock had staged similar festivals in Florida and California. "In Fort Lauderdale," he said, "police called the crowd we assembled larger than the annual influx of riotous college students but better behaved than any group they had ever seen. We are planning this event to be just as orderly."

"That don't fool me," a man halfway back said. "I'll tell you this: I'm going to be sitting on my front porch with a loaded shotgun, and the first hippie that sets foot on my land—I'm gonna shoot to kill."

Goldstein and Ganoung exchanged glances of disbelief, not so much on the strength of the threat but on the accord that filtered throughout the hall. Schlosser was equally appalled and savagely pounded his gavel to alleviate his own aggravation as best he could.

"There'll be no more talk like that, Joe," he warned.

"A man's gotta protect his land."

"You won't have to worry about that," Goldstein said, somewhat shaken. "We have more than enough land at our disposal and, according to my information, we are insured up to one million dollars per incident."

Schlosser asked, "Can you substantiate that?"

"I'm uncertain as to the exact terms of the policy, but I've heard such rates quoted."

"Well, I expect you to present to this board a facsimile of your existing insurance policy so that we might examine the extent of its coverage. I think the zoning board of appeals might have taken better care of this whole matter with a proposal of the existing zoning laws on the issuance of special permits. There should have been a hearing concerning this matter. I don't know how the hell the zoning board said a special permit wasn't necessary. Look, as far as I'm concerned, the town board is now ready to entertain a motion limiting assemblage to protect our community rights."

A flurry of hands fought to be recognized.

"Why don't you give the kids a chance before you condemn them?" Goldstein pleaded. "Just because they have long hair and are against the war . . ."

Schlosser lost his temper. "I'm upset about public safety, not about the kind of people who will be here," he shouted. "I'm only interested in insuring public health and safety, something I'm afraid you have not given much thought to."

Goldstein shook his head in disgust. He had laid out specific measures the festival staff had taken regarding sanitation and medical facilities, but they obviously had not made any impact on the board. And the people were only interested in one thing: that the hippies not be allowed into their town.

Until they were assured of that, it was doubtful they would listen to anything he said.

"Hey, Jack," a man caught Schlosser's attention, "is there any chance of our breaking this ridiculous lease they have with Howard?"

Goldstein did not give Schlosser a chance to answer. "If you tried to come between us and an existing agreement we have already made with Mr. Mills, we would take that to the highest court in the land because of the large amount of money already invested. *That,* my friend, you'd better be sure of before you decide to interfere with our plans. Now, we've come before the town council to make our position clear and to answer any questions. We've let it be known that we look to you of the community for your help and guidance. But we intend to stay here. We intend to have our festival as scheduled. And if you wish to turn it into a battle, then we're ready to fight you down to the last clause in your town charter."

To his surprise, a smattering of applause broke out in scattered points around the room.

Schlosser looked at the clock. The meeting had gone on for nearly four hours. Nothing more could be said without first examining certain documents the festival committee claimed to have in their possession so he could determine the town's degree of commitment.

"The zoning board of appeals is a quasi-officiating group," he explained, "which interprets already existing zoning laws made by this council. The town board will now take up the question of knowing and voiding the zoning board's decision with our attorney."

One rational citizen asked him if it would be possible for the festival principals to meet with both the town board and the zoning board of appeals with finalized plans for the festival.

Goldstein used that as a lever for compromise. "That sounds like a good idea. I think my employers would agree to that. If we do not satisfy the regulations imposed upon us by the Town of Wallkill, we will agree to shut down."

"Why don't you do us all a favor," someone called, "and do it now!"

Schlosser asked that Richard Dow hand him the citizens' petition, and he gave it to the town clerk. "Mr. Goldstein, I'd like to request that sometime next week, you appear in my office with the proper insurance policies, a copy of your lease—in fact, maybe you could persuade Howard to come along with you—your director of operations, the festival's principals, and I think it would be to your benefit to have your lawyer in attendance. If there is no further discussion, this meeting stands adjourned."

— 3 —

After listening to Goldstein's recounting of the events of the previous night's town council meeting, Michael Lang's attitude remained doggedly unchanged toward "getting it on" in Wallkill. He called Roberts and Rosenman and, together, they determined it would be to their advantage to continue preparing the site and to slug it out with the town. After all, they had a binding contract with Howard Mills, and the April 14 blessing of the zoning board of appeals was a matter of record. After he presented the staff's credentials and the board had time to study the facts, they were certain the Wallkill councilmen would see the futility of attempting to bar them from the area. The law was undoubtedly on the festival's side.

To Goldstein's astonishment, the local paper had not been too hard on its reporting of the hearing. The *Times Herald Record* admirably presented both sides of the argument without bias. In a related editorial, they chose to "reserve final judgment" on the matter until they had ample time to conduct an investigation into "the credentials of the promoters and the experience of other communities where such events had taken place."

Roberts conferred that afternoon with Miles Lourie on their right to remain in Wallkill. The attorney assured him of their compliance with the law; however, he advised John that Woodstock Ventures would do well to retain local Orange County counsel to see them through the remainder of their negotiations with the inhospitable town. "The last thing they want to see is some slick New York City attorney come up there supposedly to outsmart the country farmers. My presence there will only ruffle their feathers, and, anyway, I'm not a real estate lawyer. You need someone more well versed in local law." Lourie offered to interview several Middletown lawyers by phone to help narrow the choices down to the best man. Roberts gladly accepted. "You also need additional public relations within the community," Miles advised him. I suggest that you limit Wartoke's involvement to the rock press and some of the other media and get that guy Ganoung moving up there. Have him set up some meetings with the local press, leading citizens, politicians, and anyone who is opposed to your being there. Let him answer their questions and establish relationships whereby you might pick up a few more champions of your cause."

Roberts told him he thought it might be a good move to apply some political pressure on the Wallkill councilmen. A friend of his had suggested that they petition the Orange County legislature for an endorsement or, better yet, for that same body to proclaim the festival an official exhibition of the arts. Maybe they could go as far as having the New York State Council on the Arts give it a stamp of approval. That would tie the town's hands. Miles agreed. A step in that direction, he said, would be an admirable move for them to make.

"How about your dad, Miles?" John asked. Felix Lourie, like his son, was a prominent Manhattan attorney with political influence. "You once told us that he was well connected. Could you get in touch with him for us?"

Miles did not think he would have too much trouble convincing his father to go to bat for them, and he made the call.

Felix Lourie was a patriarchal, white-haired gentleman in his late sixties who, Joel thought, resembled the old man on the Monopoly "Community Chest" cards. Felix told them that Miles had explained their plight and that they should not worry about a thing. He thought he might be able to get them in to see Lieutenant Governor Malcolm Wilson, the second-in-command to Nelson Rockefeller. Wilson had an office close by—on West Fifty-fifth Street in Manhattan—and although he was most certainly a busy man, Felix presumed he might call in a few old favors to help the boys out.

The next morning, Roberts, Rosenman, and the elder Lourie met in the lieutenant governor's chambers only two blocks from the uptown festival office. A bear-hug greeting between the two older men confirmed that they were, indeed, old friends. However, not even friendship could coerce the state leader into taking a stand for the festival. Wilson arbitrarily explained that the state's hands were tied as far as its providing financial support. As far as an endorsement was concerned, his office could "under no circumstances fund or endorse a private venture."

Felix Lourie was undaunted by the setback. Later that afternoon, he called Albany and made an appointment to see one of Governor Rockefeller's aides at the State Capitol Building to discern whether or not it was worth pursuing at a higher political level. While not completely satisfying, that meeting in Albany between Roberts, Felix, and Rockefeller's secretary produced an outside chance that they might be extended a letter from Rockefeller himself, "praising artistic endeavors in general and welcoming" the Woodstock Music and Art Fair to the state of New York. It was considerably less potent a document than Roberts had anticipated, but it would give them time until someone came up with an idea to curtail the town council. Roberts knew what they really needed was a top-seeded con man to pull the wool over the eyes of the Wallkill town fathers. And for the first time that month he relaxed. Filling that job would not cost him more than a dime. All he had to do was to call the downtown production office.

*   *   *

Two days after the town council meeting, John Roberts and Joel Rosenman received a certified letter from Town Attorney Joseph Owen. Owen had not wasted a moment jumping into his newly appointed chair and had conferred upon them, on behalf of the town board, a detailed list of fourteen divisions of production plans that were to be submitted for his obvious dissection. Specifically, he asked for: a map of the area they intended to occupy and a description of what each area would be used for; a statement of purpose; a sanitation facilities blueprint; the parking plan; the food and beverage plan; the water plans; the schematic for electricity and lighting; outdoor public address system diagrams; camping arrangements; medical facilities to be implemented on the premises; the type of entertainment; the security plan; and the festival's extent of liability to the public and to the town. The task was mindboggling. It would probably take the full seventy days to accumulate the paperwork.

Monday morning, June 17, Woodstock Ventures issued a statement to the press defending its position in the town, which was buried in the Classified Announcements section of the late edition of that day's *Times Herald Record*. It was designed by Stanley Goldstein to explain and expose the external pressures that had been leveled against several members of the festival's executive staff and Howard Mills, Jr.

The article also made public the incessant harassment to which they had been subjected since arriving in Orange County. This was a dangerous step on Goldstein's part. By making accusations against "certain members of the community," they were, in effect, condemning a portion of the town's residents without identifying anyone in particular, thus alienating and inviting protests from those wrongly accused. Those who *had* made threats to staff members could use this indiscretion as a weapon in their defense. Goldstein consulted Roberts and Lang on this section of the article, and they decided not only to support it, but to expand it. "These same uninformed persons, who claimed that we did not inform them of our plans made no attempt to gather any information but rather issued . . . statements, made assumptions, twisted and lifted out of context comments made related to our activities, that they have fabricated—for what purpose we do not know—what we can only consider stories designed to intensify the concern of area residents. . . . These persons created an atmosphere that forces officials to worry for their political lives. . . . Certain businessmen in the area have been told that if they cooperate with us in any way, certain people will be aware of it and will do everything within their power to make certain that the impact of their disapproval will be felt in business and personal relationships, and that they will do everything possible to assure that these businessmen will not be able to conduct their normal activities."

The latter charge was an ex post facto impeachment of local commerce based upon a number of related incidents in which Jean Ward had been involved. Soon after she and Bill had drawn up their equipment list, Jean began scouring the countryside for provisions. Wherever she attempted to make a purchase, she encountered antagonism. The merchants didn't want to rent to the hippies. Many refused outright to sell to Woodstock Ventures while others soothed their consciences by simply charging her three and four times the regular price of goods. Those in town who treated the crews fairly or sympathized with their right to be in Wallkill were awakened in the middle of the night by anonymous callers and subjected to "questions, slanderous and malicious statements, to vituperative harangues"—all, of which, the article stated, "ain't being very neighborly!"

What had really incited Goldstein was the story he heard from Howard Mills's wife, Pat. She told him that a vigilante committee of neighbors and one-time friends took turns calling the Mills residence throughout the daytime warning that if she and Howard did not put an end to the festival, their "house would be burned to the ground with [their] children in it."

The remainder of the statement was an impassioned declaration of intent and an invitation to "other reasonable and responsible members of the community" to meet with the festival staff to discuss the plans and goals of the Aquarian Exposition. The article was signed by twenty-six of the people employed by Woodstock Ventures. Only the name of Otis Hallendale had been added to the document without the co-signer's prior consent, and it is doubtful Goldstein would have received it had he asked; Otis Hallendale was Mel Lawrence's dog.

They couldn't leave Mills Heights now. Too much had already been accomplished in the short time in which they had occupied the land. Within a week, tractors had cleared and mowed most of the open fields. Paths had been chiseled through the woods. After Lawrence had sufficient time to study the practical effect of the paths on that part of the land, he turned it over to the art crew. They lined the trails with rock fragments and pieces of dark brown wood. Windchimes were made out of broken glass and clay and hung from the tops of trees. At night, beneath a star-filled sky, the wind would strum through the orchard producing a natural harmony that echoed across the open flatland; it would have a tranquilizing effect on a crowd of one hundred thousand people. Dead trees were hauled out of the marshes, stripped and piled in the stage area to be used for construction. Bill Ward had rented a bulldozer and built an access road for service trucks leading from the barn around to the left of the entrance toward the bowl, up a hill and through the woods to another road that ran behind the site. That way, they would not interfere with local commerce and be conspicuous to Mills's neighbors. As one observer casually noted, "The preparations were a picture of meticulousness. No one could utter a word against their industry." That person, unfortunately, could not have been farther from the truth.

That Sunday morning, June 15, the telephone rattled Jules Minker out of a perfectly satisfying dream. Minker was a young attorney with NBC-TV in New York City, and between the two-hour commute from Wallkill each day and the hammering pressure of his job, he was pretty well worn to a shadow by the time the weekend rolled around. Sunday was *his* day, the only time he could sleep. But by nine o'clock that morning some message-carrying linebacker had broken through and waited breathlessly on the other end of the wire until Minker put himself in touch with the new day.

"Jules, you gotta make it out to my place as soon as you can," the voice insisted. It was Dennis Cosgrove, a high school friend of Minker who owned a bar called the Circleville Inn just outside of town. Fearing that his friend was in some kind of trouble with the law, Minker promised he would get dressed and be over within a few minutes.

When he arrived, Cosgrove alarmed him by mentioning that two state troopers were waiting inside. "Christ, Big D., what kind of trouble did you get yourself into?"

"It's nothin' like that. These guys are friends. You'll see."

Cosgrove led Minker into the dark bar where two ordinary looking men were seated on wooden stools enjoying tall glasses of beer. He looked around for the state troopers. No one else was present.

"These are two guys you should get to know," Cosgrove told him, pointing to the drinkers. "Cliff Reynolds and Brent Rismiller." The two men stood up, shook hands with Minker and invited him to join them at a table.

Reynolds, a blond man with a cold, scrubbed face, did most of the talking. He asked Minker if he had heard about this festival that was moving into the community.

"Sure. It sounds great, doesn't it?"

Reynolds studied him expressionlessly for a moment longer than was necessary before answering. "It's a goddamn disgrace is what it is. We want it out of here." Reynolds erupted. He proceeded to spew out flecks of venom almost as rapidly as submachine gun fire. He was incensed that the town had approved the festival without realizing how many "goddamn hippies" would attend.

Minker listened attentively as Reynolds unwound. Cosgrove had pulled up a chair and voiced his own concern. They were dedicated to putting a stop to the hippie conclave if it meant "going up there to the Mills place with a few shotguns and scaring the hell out of those bastards."

"Take it easy, Cliff," Minker advised. "You have some legal recourse here. There are several ways to approach it, but violence is not one of them."

"Then you do it. Just get those hippies out of here for us—whatever it takes."

What it took, they decided that morning, was a court-ordered injunction against Woodstock Ventures, which Minker agreed to bring for them for a fee of $350. "I think you have a good chance of stopping this thing if you do it the right way. But you've got to do it the *right* way."

"Okay. We'll play by your rules for now," Reynolds agreed. "But if that doesn't work out, we'll handle it ourselves."

— *4* —

The chain of disorganized underground movements lurking in the New York metropolitan area had done their own inimitable share to prickle the inner wheelworks of the festival machinery. As soon as the downtown production office had been established, Lang started receiving visits—"raids," Michael called them—from Abbie Hoffman, self-styled bad boy of the New Left who periodically descended upon the office shouting anticapitalist war cries and retreated before anyone could invite him in for a smoke. To Hoffman's utter dismay, the staff there found his guerilla-theatre warfare quite amusing; it was part of the ambience Lang had striven so hard to instill in his undertaking—a type of pseudorevolutionary atmosphere, even if it was played strictly for laughs. Hoffman had been a Village mainstay since his spectacular stage performance in Judge Julius Hoffman's Chicago courtroom. He had spent his between-trial appearances that year staging rallies against anything that stank of Establishment hype. According to a confidant of his, Abbie was purported to have written "Prankster" in the space allotted for his profession on a department store charge account application. Lang welcomed Hoffman's camouflaged participation with equally camouflaged opened arms, although neither one would dare admit it to the other for fear of losing face.

One afternoon during the second weekend in June, Lang and Rosenman were walking through another "friendly chat" in the midst of their ticketing cold war when the phone rang. Michael jumped to answer it before Joel could pick it up. It was Abbie Hoffman.

"Do-Lang Do-Lang—hey, man, listen. We gotta get together."

Michael recognized the voice. "Okay," he said pleasantly.

"Just like *that?* Ho ho, you're the one I been gunnin' for, m'man. You got any idea what I want?"

"No."

"I want *money.* Bread—and plenty of it. Or else."

Michael laughed at the absurdity in Hoffman's voice. He sounded like some cheap gangster on a television detective series. "Or else what?"

"Fireworks. You're rippin' off the people, man. You guys are chargin' country club prices for street music and that's a fuckin', capitalist ripoff. You're gonna pay, Lang-o."

"You jivin' me, man?"

"Jive *ass,* I'm jivin' you. Who's jivin' who, man? You're gonna be one rich dude in a couple of months, and I think it's about time you start contributin' to the cause. You can pay on the installment plan if you like, but you better open up your heart awful quickly if you know what's good for that little festival of yours."

"I repeat: Or else what?"

"Or else it'll be one bad scene up there in Wallkill, man. Just try and collect any of that rich-kid bread without us on your side of the gate. You'd look awful silly tryin' to explain to the pigs how all that acid crept into your water supply. What a trip! How's that for openers?"

"Uh, yeah. Fine. C'mon over and we'll talk about it."

"Not a chance, man. Why don't you and your playfriends take a stroll over our way and we'll play house. Say, next Thursday afternoon—threeish?"

"I gotta make an *appointment* with *you?*"

"Sure, man. I got a big fuckin' secretary who sits on my knee and lights my joint."

"You mean joints."

"Sure. Anything you say."

"I'll be there."

"You're a sweetheart."

*   *   *

Hoffman and his merry band of thieves lived in a slovenly tenement on the Lower East Side, just around the corner from the Fillmore East. On June 19, Joel, Michael and Artie trudged up the stoop to the building with suspicious smiles plastered across their faces. Even Lang was admittedly out of his element going in there: he had no idea what to expect from Hoffman's phone conversation and knew this crowd could get tough if they had to. The meeting could go any number of ways.

Lang had been on his guard from the moment he agreed to the meeting. What's more, he was worried about having Joel along for the ride. Joel's idea of hanging out, Lang thought, was an afternoon on the Princeton Club's squash court with a well-placed colleague. He was certain Hoffman and his cronies would smell Joel's manufactured hipness from underneath his slip-covered jeans and sculptured short hair. If Rosenman so much as uttered a logical word, he'd "blow the lid off Abbie's scam." They all had to be cool.

"We need these cats on our side," Lang had pleaded with him the afternoon when the call had come in. "They're pretty groovy guys to have around, and they have a direct line to the underground which'd be invaluable to us. If they're in our corner, we can't miss."

"I thought Bert Cohen was taking care of the underground press for us," Joel said, recalling the fifteen-thousand-dollar check he had countersigned over to Concert Hall Publications back in April for that very reason.

"Well, yeah—Bert's handlin' the underground and all, but we need to take our message to the streets and that's where these guys come in. They'll put the word out that it's cool to come to the festival."

"And if they don't?"

"Whew! I don't even want to consider that, man. It'd be a bummer."

"What do they want?"

"I don't know what they'll ask for, man. They're weird dudes. Could be anything. Free tickets, maybe, or a booth for their leaflets and shit. Fuck it! They may even want some stage time."

But as with everything else he had done concerning the festival so far, Michael had sorely underestimated Hoffman's avarice.

"We want fifty grand, man," he said emphatically. They were seated around a small table in Abbie's apartment with Michael, Joel, Artie Kornfeld, and a few members of Hoffman's ragtag entourage. "That's not askin' too much, is it?" He smiled.

Lang chuckled and shook his head. "Come off it, man. We don't have that kinda bread."

"Don't give me that shit, pal. You motherfuckin' capitalist bastards are swimmin' in cash. Me?—I just want enough to bathe in. I gotta pay the bills for my trial, man. All the time I was up on that bench in court representin' the people, the accountants were puttin' it down on my tab. I figure I got it comin', man, seein' as how I was speakin' for all of us."

"Look, if you're really *for* the people, man, we'll give you some bread to do work," Michael conceded. "If you want to come up and distribute information—great— I'll make sure you get some space and some booths. But fifty grand is out of the question."

"That's it, huh? Well, we'll take you up on those booths, but it won't do you or us any good if there's no festival, will it?" Hoffman laughed raucously and encouraged his friends to join him. "I'll save us all some time, man. No negotiatin'. No jerkin' each other off. We'll take ten G's and not a cent less. Or else."

"Or else what?"

"Or else that fuckin' festival is gonna end up around your ass."

Joel was furious over Hoffman's demands. "That's fuckin' extortion, man," he declared walking back to the downtown office. "They can shove it if they think we're gonna be a party to that."

"We don't have any choice, man," Michael said. "They got us over a barrel. We *have* to pay it. Ten G's—just look at it as insurance."

"I'm lookin' at it as ten thousand dollars down the drain, Michael. You know damn well where that money's going—into Hoffman's pocket."

"You're probably right, but it doesn't make any difference. We've still gotta pay it. Lemme explain something to you. As much as they're all for peace and love, man, they'd as soon nail you to the wall if you tried to fuck with them. See, if we don't shell out the bread for Abbie, man, they're gonna turn the kids off to the festival. They can do it, too. They'll pass out leaflets callin' us assholes, they'll picket the festival and, who knows, maybe they'll even storm the gates. We can't take that chance. We'll have a fuckin' riot up there. Anyway, they'll add color to what we're doin' if they're on our side—a nice sidelight to the music and all. It'll be worth ten grand. You think I *wanna* give 'em the bread? Shit, man, I'd rather put it towards another band or something. I'd have been real happy if they left it alone like it was none o' their fuckin' business, which it's not. But it's too late for that. If you think ten grand's a lotta money, let me tell you—it'll cost us a lot more than that to fight 'em off."

In a bizarre way, Michael's reasoning made good business sense to Joel and John. It was like renting an apartment in New York City, they thought: It was outrageous to spend four hundred dollars a month for a one-bedroom apartment, but if a person waited too long, he would eventually have to swallow his outrage and settle for the same thing at five hundred dollars a month. Supply and demand. Anyway, Michael said they *had* to do it, and he obviously knew how to handle this bunch.

Throughout the remainder of that week, substantial bundles of petty cash were drawn on the Woodstock Ventures account. When ten thousand dollars had been accumulated, it was sent to the downtown office for Lang and, later that night, turned over to Abbie Hoffman. For ten thousand dollars the New Left had taken a considerable turn to the right; hip capitalism was in vogue on the Lower East Side. Years later, for a considerable advance from a major publishing house, Hoffman would attribute the festival's destruction to "the egocentric greed of the Rock Empire itself . . . the stealing from each other." He had an inside track on that information and had, at last, earned his recognition as that culture's leader.

The same afternoon the powwow took place in Abbie Hoffman's East Village lair, Stanley Goldstein, recognized as a duly employed representative of Woodstock Ventures, Inc., was served with a summons ordering the festival's principals to appear before the State Supreme Court in Goshen, New York, on July 7. At that time, a motion, brought by several Wallkill complainants, would be heard for an injunction restraining the Aquarian Exposition from being held in that town.

The action was initiated by two families, Mr. and Mrs. Martin Nowack and Mr. and Mrs. Adam Papuga, who owned tracts of land adjoining Mills Heights "on behalf of themselves and all other residents and property owners in the Town of Wallkill, County of Orange, New York." The papers had been filed that morning by their attorney, Jules Minker, who, it seemed, was making a career out of representing people opposed to the festival.

According to papers signed by Minker's clients, they charged that the "security force planned for the event [was] inadequate, that their lives and property [would] be in jeopardy, and that local roads [would] be so obstructed that emergency travel [would] be impossible." The *Times Herald Record*, however, was quick to point out that "the plaintiffs must prove a clear and present danger exists, for which monetary compensation could not be given."

One of the plaintiffs' earliest public supporters was Cliff Reynolds, who had been busily collecting over two hundred signatures on a petition that condemned the festival.

Goldstein immediately telephoned Samuel W. Eager, Jr., a Middletown attorney who, only two days before, had agreed to represent Woodstock Ventures locally. Eager was the meticulously mannered, gaunt son of a local judge whose family had long supported Republican causes within the immediate community. He was highly respected for his unemotional, staunchly conservative practice of jurisprudence, and several residents who had known the family for as long as they could remember were surprised to see Sam take the case.

Eager advised Goldstein to send the papers over to his Dolson Avenue office and to go about festival business as though nothing had happened. He would make all the necessary calls to those involved with the action and would immediately begin drafting their defense. Meanwhile, he had been gathering information concerning his new clients' dilemma. Only a day before, he had called Jack Schlosser to request an informal meeting between the members of the town board and the four Woodstock officers. Schlosser consented, setting aside Thursday evening, June 19, at 7:30 in his office; it was the same day on which Goldstein was served with the complaint.

Eager meant business. Normally, he was not one to jump to a conclusion, electing instead to pore over every shred of available information until his position, based on legal precedent, became clear. This time, however, he had formed an opinion about the conflict before he even agreed to take Woodstock's account. Aside from the fact that holding such an event in the Town of Wallkill seemed personally attractive to him, it appeared to Sam Eager that a legal wrong had been done the boys. No matter how he personally felt about rock music and long hair (and he detested both), it was his duty as a lawyer to defend a person or a group of people against such injustices.

"Sam was sticking his neck out further than he may have realized," a friend of the family's declared. "It was an admirable gesture from a legal standpoint, but one which most people around here found foolhardy. If he lost the case, he could slowly reinstate himself into the mainstream here in Wallkill, but if he won, if the town was forced to hold the festival as scheduled against its will and Sam had caused it, he would be ostracized and possibly even run out of town."

Eager's first test of resolute endurance came that very evening at the informal board meeting to review the festival staff and their method of operations. Eager had instructed his clients to be prepared to present a cohesive, fully documented explanation of their plans. The men they would be facing that night were considered by him to be "probing analysts," a label Eager substituted for something more critical of their celebrated bellyaching. He wanted them to be able to justify their every move under cross-examination.

The council's biggest grievance lay with traffic. Not only did they disapprove of the number of cars slated to enter Wallkill for the weekend, but they also opposed any amendment to the transportation problem. Construction had begun that spring on Route 211, the main access to the Quickway, and that was the main thoroughfare in the festival shuttle scheme. "That road is a hazard now," Schlosser pointed out. "It's the main route for getting to and from all the shopping districts. Right *now*, it's an intersection to avoid. How do you expect me to allow you to use that road to bring in twenty thousand cars a day? You load something like this festival onto it and it'll be a complete mess."

Then, one of the other board members asked what would be done about sanitation. Three days, to him, seemed "like an awfully long time for somebody to go without taking a shit." It drew a hearty round of laughter from his colleagues.

Mel smiled through the raillery. He explained their negotiations with two companies, Port-O-San and Johnny-On-The-Spot, to provide one hundred transportable toilets for the event. "These are companies with years of experience in large-scale sanitation, and they have been advising us on proper use and care of the units. We'll have a fully trained staff to oversee that phase of the operation by the time August rolls around."

"Where do you intend to get rid of the waste?" asked a man who was dressed in baggy overalls.

Lawrence answered without hesitation. "The two companies I mentioned will have tank trucks standing by. They'll empty what has not chemically decomposed into the trucks. Don't you think *they* know what they're doing either? All your goddamn construction crews use the same facilities I'm talking about, and I'll bet my last nickel you don't ask your builders how they intend to get rid of the waste. I ran down to take a look at that new Sears that's coming up in Middletown, and what I saw was pathetic. Their sanitation facilities stink—literally. Why, every goddamn infraction of your existing health codes is being taken advantage of by those guys and you don't even give it two minutes of your time. Instead, you want us to *schlep* our entire plans in here because you're afraid of hippies. Why don't you cut us a break and stick to what's relevant? I didn't intend to have to answer for us and all the professional companies involved, and I shouldn't have to. You want to know if Port-O-San can handle the festival—*you* give 'em a call. If you used your heads in the first place, you'd know they could handle their part of the act."

Sam Eager nervously tried to smooth things over by indicating that the councilman was simply trying to get the whole picture.

"Sure," Mel said faithlessly.

"You young men talk about cooking, sanitation, camping—all things that require a great deal of water in their operation. Where do you intend to get that much water from?"

"Whaddya mean?" Mel asked indignantly. "There's plenty of water on the site."

Schlosser walked to the window above his desk and drew the pleated curtains. "Is that the tank Howard said you could tap?" he asked, pointing to the larger of the two turquoise towers nestled in the trees.

"Yes."

"No, you can't. That's the town water supply. It can't handle anywhere near an additional fifty thousand people's needs. You tap into that and the existing district will be without water."

"We'll be glad to pay for what we use," Lang offered.

"That doesn't make any difference. Howard's awfully generous with other people's water. I can't let you get into those tanks at any price."

Lawrence had been prepared for just such an intrusion. He explained that the festival offered him two alternatives to a potential water problem, and they were willing to take action on whichever solution the town board preferred. Firstly, they were prepared to finance and construct a water-processing plant on a portion of Mills Heights, which they would donate to the town at the conclusion of the festival. Schlosser immediately negated that proposal by explaining the town council would have to investigate its feasibility—which meant calling in state and county supervisors at a great expense to advise them on zoning and tax regulations—and then they'd have to put it to a referendum for approval. That would take up to six months or a year before he could even give them an answer. The second option, and one which Lawrence had Stanley Goldstein exploring at that very moment, was for them to import water from other municipalities. They would bring it in in large tankers under the supervision of the board of health. Goldstein had spoken with a number of dairy farmers and local army divisions about renting their water transportation equipment for that purpose. The problem, Goldstein had reported back, was not accumulating the vehicles, but actually getting his hands on that much water. By mid-June, he had still not come up with a large enough source, and the prospects were diminishing. But he and Lawrence decided they would proceed along this line of reasoning until they could come up with another plan.

"I think you fellas either ought to head over to the Orange County Fairgrounds where they can handle all this for you or look for a different community because we're not going to allow you to hold your festival here under these conditions," Schlosser said.

"What about the zoning board's approval?" Michael asked somewhat belligerently. He was growing impatient listening to Schlosser destroy his plans.

"I have a pretty good idea that you young fellas misrepresented your intentions when you went before the zoning board. If that's the case, well then, I don't think we're going to have to stand by that decision. I'm not saying that's what we've decided, but you have to understand our position. It is our job to provide for the health and safety of the community. If we ever think that's in jeopardy, then we have to take measures to prevent it from getting any worse."

"These boys are trying very hard to work alongside the town, Jack," Eager said. "They're trying to work out a solution to these difficulties."

"I realize that. This meeting tonight is for the purpose of expressing our mutual cooperation." Schlosser's perspective was inimitably that of a politician. "If they can meet the standards we impose on them—the same set of standards we impose on *everybody* who puts on an event up here—then we won't stand in their way. We've got to have some time to study this thing."

Lang agreed to have the festival plans in Schlosser's hands early the following week. He had actually been holding off sending that information for as long as was possible. It was certain to provide the key to their downfall— not that it wasn't a comprehensive and accurate representation of the crew's superb efforts. The very fact that it *was* so precise worked against them. It would place in the hands of the town board that many additional details to debate, delaying progress while Woodstock awaited their consent. They had, indeed, spent a considerable fortune to start the ball rolling, but nothing, it seemed, cost them as much as time. If the town board got their way, it would be the one commodity Woodstock Ventures would never be able to afford.

— **5** —

Michael chose not to impart a play-by-play account of the Wallkill court martial to his staff in the downtown production office. The activity there had advanced quite expeditiously; there was rarely an evening when the two floors went unoccupied by a working staff, and he took great precautions not to foreclose on their industry.

Emphasis there had, in the past few weeks, shifted to the building of actual working models based on their previous brainstorming. Some of the staff divided their time between New York City and the site so they could effectively plan their details; others hung out with the Fillmore East staff and discussed the contrasting ways of staging an outdoor event. From this, a tangible working plan evolved.

Chip spent four days in Wallkill staking out the field in order to determine the best place to put the stage. Using a 100-meter tape measure, he marked off a succession of geodesic angles with stakes and twine to locate the most tractable bowl for acoustic resonance. He took into consideration that part of the land that offered the widest focal span before any trees were removed or the existing grade was rescaled. After that, he strolled along its periphery identifying any obstacles in the line of sight. Remarkably, there were none. His selection, of course, would ultimately be influenced by the plans for security and human traffic flow, but he had established enough of a theoretical foundation for where the stage should sit that he could begin working out lighting and power configurations. The symmetry of the land was such that he would not be off the mark by more than a hundred feet either way when the location was finalized.

Back in the New York office, Lang called a meeting of the production executives for the purpose of getting the design and construction of the stage underway. This was one of the most fundamental aspects of the production since all physical structures on the site would derive their utility from its functional design. The person who would undertake this had to be able to consult with and accommodate all other divisions and heads of the production staff without compromising his task. And he had to be able to withstand mental fatigue; the job at other festivals had proven to be irksome and, at times, overwhelming.

Chip Monck, Steven Cohen, Bert Cohen, and Chris Langhart had been working independently on designs for the stage. Their guidelines consisted only of Michael's request that it be both rustic and practical.

The situation, however, had created an unnecessary rivalry among the staff. Bert Cohen had designed the stage for Miami Pop and was under the impression that, by rights, his firm would inherit the same assignment for Woodstock. Chip and Mel, however, considered Cohen's job in Miami a travesty, one that was neither aesthetically nor functionally suited for this festival. They were categorically opposed to Bert's having a hand in this production and said so.

Cohen was characteristically persistent. He frequently cornered Lang in the office and complained that it was he and Michael Foreman who had spent so much time with the four principals in the early stages of planning and had, in good faith, provided them with expertise. Because of that, he had assumed that when it came time to apportion the enterprise, he and Foreman would be afforded first choice of the prime assignments. Now, however, Concert Hall's involvement had been reduced drastically to the point where they were doing little more than supplying ad copy to the underground press. He was calling in a debt; he wanted Lang to give them the stage assignment.

For the first time, Cohen's request was met with open resistance. Michael contended that Concert Hall had "fucked up the uptown offices" and was doing an uninspired job coordinating the underground media. That very morning, he had received a call from Jane Friedman at Wartoke complaining that festival ad copy wasn't getting to radio stations on time—a crucial part of Concert Hall's job. Additionally, Jane didn't think Woodstock Ventures was getting its money's worth in underground print ads. The promoters had advanced Bert a substantial sum for that purpose, and now Lang found himself in the position of having to ask his friend for an accounting of the money. The staff would revolt if Michael awarded Concert Hall the stage. He'd lose their support, and right now, he was banking on that very commodity to see him through the next two months.

The disaccord was not limited to Bert Cohen. Chip Monck campaigned for his friend Steve Cohen to oversee the stage design based upon the latter's experience building platforms for the Philadelphia Folk Festival. Cohen, a stocky, balding youth with a drooping moustache, was a graduate of Carnegie Tech and had a background in the technical arts as well as being a skilled draftsman. But John Morris crusaded even more vigorously for Chris Langhart whom Morris (and just about everyone else on staff) considered a technical genius. Langhart, too, was an alumnus of Carnegie Tech, but whereas Steve Cohen's skill was acquired while he was a student there, Langhart's began in grade school and developed over the years to the point where he was offered a position teaching scenic design, technical directing, and lighting at New York University.

Lang wanted to maintain harmony more than anything else. The disagreement had blown up into a contest of personalities between Monck and Morris, both of whom were devoting too much time to the campaign. The best thing to do, Michael decided, was to make a formal contest of it. He'd examine each entry, and the best one would be built on Howard Mills's land.

Within a week, miniature models of stages had been submitted to Lang by Bert Cohen, Chris Langhart, and Steve Cohen. Bert's was a replica of the design they had used without much success at Miami Pop. It consisted of two 40-foot circular platforms linked by a trolley track. Both circular stages were constructed to detach in the middle so that while a group was performing on one, another band could set up and tune their instruments on the platform across the tracks. That would eliminate the unnecessary thirty-minute intermissions between each set for equipment changes. Lang had been worried about the crowd's getting restless during those interruptions; Cohen's method would certainly solve that problem. When one act had finished performing, the back half of their stage would detach and carry them away while the front part of the other one would bring the next group, ready to play, to the fore. The trolley would then swing into operation and transport any other essentials from one performing area to the next one. Two shafts between the platforms rose into the air and spanned outward, covering both stages like a giant umbrella. Beneath that, lights would be fastened and could be controlled from backstage. The top of the tentlike covering was encircled with twenty-five colorful flags and a twirling top. Lang thought it "looked like a cross between a birthday cake and a carousel" and dismissed it out of hand as being too slick.

By comparison, Langhart's stage model was prosaic and considerably more practical. It was a single-pitch platform, circular, with a spiraled springlike canopy balanced on top of two 80-foot telephone poles. The crossbar above it was shaped like a gigantic peace sign. A cable was attached to each part of the covering from both poles so that it would not twist and sway in the wind. The base was fashioned from plywood 2-by-10-foot planks, and raised off the ground by a herculean white pine scaffolding. As in Bert Cohen's design, a system of multicolored lights would be contained in a niche around the inner seam of the soft covering. It did, however, lack a mechanical device for changing bands without a lengthy layover. Langhart was not overwhelmed by his own design. It fell short on originality, and he knew that Lang aspired to something more imaginative, something with a Woodstock signature to it.

At first, Michael could not figure out what to make of Langhart's scale model. He had not been prepared for something so plain, and yet it fit his needs perfectly. He called Langhart into his office and asked him if it were possible to use more natural wood in his design. He wanted something that adapted to rock and roll performance, but resembled a log cabin. Langhart thought about it for a few minutes and consented to reconstruct his model, but with the expressed instruction from Lang that it would be used as the performers' pavillion. As far as the stage went, Langhart had struck out. Strike two.

Steve Cohen's design was the only one left to be judged. He and Chip Monck had spent several nights formulating its elaborate mechanical skeleton, a 100-foot turntable based on the Japanese-style horticultural tent in Sacramento, California. The turntable was constructed from two detachable semicircles attached by a central core with bearings and wheels underneath it. While one group performed on the front half of the moon, the next act would be setting up behind them, after which an electrical switch would be thrown and the semicircles would reverse. Two 70-foot telephone poles were lowered through the floor of the stage and sunk into a 6-foot cube of cement in the ground. Guy wires were attached at various points along the poles and stretched outward to absorb the incredible thrust of tension supporting the platform. The most spectacular feature, however, was a mushroom cap balanced on top of the poles which was devised by Monck to hold a bank of 280 individual lighting units. As one imaginative observer remarked, it looked like a scheme for increasing the illumination of Yankee Stadium. It was dazzling.

Michael made a few suggestions for a more woodsy effect, but as far as he was concerned, Steve Cohen had his vote. The young Philadelphian would assume the responsibility of constructing the Woodstock festival stage—the largest one anyone on the staff had ever been asked to assemble. A budget was submitted along with the design; it would cost almost twenty thousand dollars to build.

Langhart, meanwhile, had presented another working model to his employer, which was unanimously approved for the performers' pavilion—a design which had, by far, come closest to Lang's ideal. It was a Lincoln Log–type structure of thirty-four telephone poles; seventeen were to be sunk into the ground, and the rest were perfectly balanced on top of them to create an open roof over which cheesecloth would be draped. After discussing layout with Mel, it was decided that the pavilion would be constructed behind and to the left of the stage for easy access. They had hired a man named David Levine, who owned a restaurant across from the Fillmore East named David's Potbelly, to cater food for the performers' exotic palates. It was hoped that an atmosphere of relaxed conviviality would predominate there throughout the festival.

John Morris spent most of his free time filling in the few gaps left on the performing bill. He and Lang had arrived at a formula for sequence whereby Friday evening would showcase folk-oriented artists to build the audience's enthusiasm slowly and to ease them into their new surroundings. Presenting an acid rock show the first night might whip the kids into an uncontrollable frenzy, and, at all costs, they wanted to avoid a riotous mood. Joan Baez had finally given her consent to appear (for a very convincing $10,000 fee) on Friday, and Lang hoped her performance carried enough of a political message to pacify Abbie Hoffman and his cohorts. In addition to Richie Havens, Tim Hardin, Arlo Guthrie, Ravi Shankar, and the Incredible String Band, who were already under contract, Michael had commissioned a friend named Leon Auerbach to fly to Scotland to persuade Donovan to round out that night's activities. Donovan was something of an international phenomenon, and Lang and Morris felt they could justify the added expense of sending a man overseas for that purpose.

Saturday's show was to feature American bands from the Bay Area—most notably the Jefferson Airplane, Creedence Clearwater, the Grateful Dead, and Janis Joplin, all of whom were already booked. Although the Grateful Dead were being counted on to contribute one of their typically hypnotic five-hour sets, Morris calculated that there weren't enough groups scheduled for the second day to take them from late morning on through to the middle of the night without a break. They had room for three or four more groups without overloading. Lang was still hoping to attract Bob Dylan, whose music could be integrated nicely into that afternoon's show, but even Dylan's appearance wouldn't serve to lengthen the presentation by all that much. Simon and Garfunkel, another superstar choice of Lang's, were having personal differences and had not scheduled any personal appearances for the summer months. Lang had several conferences with their manager, Mort Lewis, but not even Lewis could persuade them to change their minds.

Morris looked to Bill Graham, his former employer, to bail them out. Graham, at the time, was artfully soft-peddling several acts from San Francisco that he claimed were heirs to the throne of rock gods. Two months from their conversation, he contended, these acts would undoubtedly be pulling in king's ransoms for stadium-size appearances. Timing, he reminded Morris, was everything in the rock music business, and if John acted promptly, he could have them immediately for a pittance. Graham noted that if Morris exercised his intuition by taking the groups he offered him, John would be recognized as a true booking genius in six months' time. It was one of the oldest ploys in the book, one which Morris had watched Graham use effectively over and over again while working for him. But that was just it—Graham was extraordinarily convincing, such a master of hyperbole that Morris bought the whole pitch without question. He jumped up, and ran into Lang's office proclaiming Bill Graham their official savior.

"We can sign these groups and lay back. It's the answer we've been looking for."

"Hey, take it easy, man. I'm not signin' anybody until I hear them—and, even then, I gotta at least *like* them."

"You've gotta do it. You've gotta appease Graham."

"Cool it, John. That's a crock o' shit. I don't *gotta* do anything. Graham's not doin' anybody a favor except himself."

Bill Graham, however, knew how to deliver the final blow and sent tapes of the two groups to Michael's attention. Both groups impressed Lang.

"I don't know," he told Morris a week later. "They're both pretty good, but nobody's ever heard of 'em. I mean, we'd look like schmucks adding both It's A Beautiful Day *and* Santana when we could get two other groups that *mean* something. I'm gonna hafta pass."

Still Graham refused to give up. He called Morris again and implied that if they didn't take Santana from him, he'd pull the Grateful Dead off the show. Lang was furious when the veiled threat was repeated to him, but he knew that Graham was capable of such a move. Graham was known for picking fights with promoters and holding grudges that often lasted years and prevented promoters from booking his acts. He was quoted in a December 1968 Sunday *New York Times Magazine* article as saying, "I give you a chance, you don't deliver, I'll kill you; in my head, you're dead." Lang decided that for a few dollars more, it was not worth cutting his own throat. He called Bill Graham and, by process of elimination, chose the unknown group, Santana, to open Saturday's show for $1,500. Two months later, it would prove to be one of the highlights of the Aquarian Exposition and would establish Santana as one of the most exciting and influential groups in contemporary pop music. Graham, indeed, had the magic touch, and Woodstock Ventures was, as Graham had predicted, acclaimed as a booking genius.

Michael Lang and Bill Graham had another score to settle. Michael had booked many of the groups for the festival that Graham was promoting in the New England and New York areas that summer. The festival was picking up a lot of steam, causing a lot of the young kids to take notice of what was happening in Wallkill. If Woodstock was a box office success, Graham's shows in the area would die. He reasoned that the kids would not pay an additional five dollars each to see the Airplane or Creedence or Richie Havens or a half dozen other acts he worked when they could buy one ticket to see them all at Woodstock. His summer schedule was in trouble.

One afternoon in mid-June, John Morris ran into Lang's office and closed the door. "We got trouble, man. Bad news. Bill just called, and he says he's gonna buy you out."

"What!?"

"He's gonna buy out the festival or make it impossible for us to put it over. And he can do it, too, Michael. You've gotta take him seriously this time."

"Sure," Michael said, giving Morris the high sign. "Why don't you go into your office and cool off. I'll take care of Graham."

"All right, but make it quick. He can stop us dead."

Lang assumed correctly that Morris had overreacted. When it came to Bill Graham, Morris's negotiating steel became molten. But Lang was smart enough to take the premise seriously. Graham was not about to let Woodstock get away with ruining several millions of dollars in regional gate receipts without a fight. They'd have to make some kind of a deal.

Lang called Graham, found out the San Francisco impresario was about to fly to New York, and arranged to meet him for lunch at Ratner's, a famous Kosher dairy restaurant on the Lower East Side of Manhattan. There, over a tiny table laden with bowls of hot onion rolls, sour cream, and blintzes, they worked out a formula whereby Lang would wait until a month before Graham played his acts in the area to advertise the same groups appearing at Woodstock. The festival already boasted close to fifteen acts that Graham had planned to showcase at the Fillmore during the summer, and Graham worried that it would kill his business.

"You've got nothing to worry about," Michael assured him. "We'll wait. It's not going to make any difference to us." They shook hands on the arrangement.

As Lang got up to leave, he was swept with divine inspiration. "Hey—I got a great idea. You should come up for the festival and emcee it for us. It'd knock everybody out."

Graham was flattered, but he didn't want to share Lang's spotlight.

"That's too bad. I was really hopin' you'd be there."

Graham looked up from his plate and smiled without any humor. "You don't have to worry about that, my friend. I'll be there, I'll be there."

Sunday's show was the most incomplete of the three days. Only the Band, Blood, Sweat and Tears, and Johnny Winter were firmly under contract, and those names remaining on Michael's list of available top stars (and *only* the biggest names were being sought to cap off the event) were rapidly filling in their schedules with other dates. A good two months' lead time was absolutely essential for wrapping up negotiations with managers, and that date was approaching with alarming speed. The Moody Blues had decided not to play the festival because of the long haul it would take to get them there and the obvious financial loss they would incur by doing so; Michael had offered them $5,000—a figure that barely covered their plane tickets from London. They had to pass. Jimi Hendrix, who had performed for less than $5,000 at Miami Pop only a year before, was demanding $50,000 to put in an appearance at Wallkill. Michael told Morris: "We don't need him at that price, but keep all channels open to Mike Jefferies [his manager]. He'll come around sooner or later."

"There's always Sly," Morris suggested, knowing Lang had already rejected that idea twice before.

"We'll see. Don't make any deals for him yet. The way things are going, he'll have plenty of free dates left for the summer. No one's taking a chance with him. Keep Sly hanging as a last resort."

One chance that Lang *had* decided to take was with a virtually unknown performer whom Artie had brought to his attention a month before the staff's move to Wallkill. Artie had disappeared for a few days without telling anyone where he could be contacted. When he resurfaced, he casually told Lang that he had "gone to the Islands to do a little gambling" and had met a "real together cat" named Denny Cordell at one of the casinos. Cordell was a rock manager who insisted that Kornfeld listen to a new act he was producing.

"Send me a record," Artie said, a typical record-executive response.

"I'll do better than that, man,—I'll give you the single we've just done and you can tell me right away what you think."

Artie feigned enthusiasm and halfheartedly accepted Cordell's invitation. He soon made a complete about-face.

The record was called "Feelin' Alright," and Artie thought the singer, a growling Englishman named Joe Cocker, was just about the most exciting new voice he had ever heard.

"You gotta get into this guy, Michael," Artie insisted. "We gotta grab him to do the festival before he gets hot."

Lang listened and was "blown away." He agreed that Cocker would make a great "discovery" for them to introduce at Woodstock and instructed Kornfeld to make introductions. Artie had one of Cordell's business cards and, within a few days, Joe Cocker had signed to open Sunday afternoon's show at a mutually acceptable price of $2,750. It was perhaps the first bargain, other than Santana, they had gotten since putting the show together.

Sunday's format was shaping up to include "the rest of the world"— groups who were hard-rockers and mostly English. The Beatles were still a possibility—even though Lennon had suggested otherwise—and Lang had kept a spot open for them should they eventually be convinced of Woodstock's eminence. But there was room on the bill for three more acts, and "they had to be killers."

Morris called Frank Barsalona who was head of Premier Talent, the most influential hard-rock booking agency in the United States. Barsalona quickly sold him the Jeff Beck Group and Ten Years After for a combined price of $18,000. Beck had earned his reputation by replacing Eric Clapton as the lead guitarist of the Yardbirds. When that group broke up in 1967, Beck formed a new band featuring a young singer named Rod Stewart who belted British blues standards more powerfully than anyone else on the scene. Ten Years After was an equally up-and-coming progressive blues band, having made their first American appearance a few months before with a dazzling guitarist named Alvin Lee. Some critics invested Lee with the title of Clapton's logical heir, which aroused national interest in the group. Lee, the Woodstock people were informed, had a bad back and was canceling unimportant dates to recuperate, but his manager, Dee Anthony, guaranteed he would be at Woodstock ready to play if he personally had to bring Alvin in on a stretcher.

With Jimi Hendrix temporarily in cold storage, they still needed a headliner, a group or performer whose appearance would be welcomed with mounting anticipation and would send the audience back to their respective cities reeling with delight. Barsalona had mentioned that the Who would be in the United States during that time, but he seriously doubted that they could be convinced to add another city to their overcrowded tour at that late a date. They were slated to close out their American obligation two weeks before Woodstock, and then they were leaving. They desperately needed a vacation, he told Morris, after which they were prepared to begin work on a long-overdue album. After some gentle prodding, Barsalona consented to ask anyway.

In the meantime, Morris learned that while the Who were going back to England when they were through in America, they had to return two weeks later to put in a promised appearance at Tanglewood for Bill Graham—the same weekend as the festival. He called Barsalona and said that if they would do the festival, Morris would arrange to have a helicopter pick them up at Tanglewood, shuttle them to Woodstock and then directly to Kennedy Airport for their trip back—*anything*, as long as they said "yes." Unfortunately, it was to no avail. Peter Townshend, the group's leader, wanted nothing to do with another American date.

"We need them badly, Frank," Morris begged. "I'll do anything. Can't we work out some kind of deal where Graham and I both get them for some fantastic sum?"

Morris was told that a few thousand dollars more meant nothing to a band that made millions yearly. They preferred their sanity, and that meant a quick escape back to the motherland.

"Look, I know I shouldn't do this," Barsalona said, "but my wife and I are having Peter over to our house for dinner tomorrow night. Why don't you come too, and we'll see if we can work on him. It's your only hope."

Morris hung up with Barsalona and simultaneously informed Joyce Mitchell that he was going home to sleep. "In the middle of the afternoon?" she asked. John explained that it was a well-known fact among rock execs that Frank Barsalona was an incurable insomniac; people knew that if they arrived for dinner at Barsalona's house at seven o'clock in the evening, they might not leave until nine the next morning. "I need all the rest I can get. This looks like it's going to be the toughest fight yet. Barsalona may very well set a new Guiness record for Most Hours Awake."

Barsalona and Morris had agreed beforehand they would combine their talents to "do a number on Townshend." But as they sat down to heaping bowls of spaghetti and meatballs, the Who's guitarist made his position clear. "We're not coming back, and that's all there is to it."

"You've got to," Barsalona protested. "First of all, you can't fuck Bill Graham. And secondly, you really should do Woodstock. It's going to turn into one of the biggest events in the world. It'll be fantastic, and you'll kick yourselves later for missing it. You'll have the prestige of playing Tanglewood one night, and doing the biggest festival in history the next."

"I'm exhausted, man, and I want to get home."

The subject was dropped for the moment, but Barsalona and Morris had only begun their windup for the fast pitch.

After dinner, the guests and their host moved into the living room; Frank and John sat facing each other in armchairs while Townshend took up a position on the floor amidst Barsalona's pre-Columbian artifacts. Talk turned to the Who's future projects—an album, a new rock opera, perhaps even a motion picture. Every time Townshend was permitted to explain one of those areas, Barsalona brought up the festival.

"You guys are trying to get me to give in, aren't you?" Townshend asked. "Well, it's no use. We're not gonna do it."

The Who's manager, John Wolff, arrived at one o'clock in the morning and shifted the conversation to anecdotes about the current tour. Somehow, Barsalona always led them back to Woodstock without being too pushy. No more dates would be considered under any circumstance, Wolff said. The group was on the verge of physical collapse; they needed an immediate rest; they should not even play Tanglewood. Barsalona "practically had to sit on him." He and Morris then had to work on the irascible Wolff for a few hours to "calm him down." Without his support, the Who would never appear at Woodstock.

Through all this, Townsend was slumped in the corner, asleep. Barsalona shook him every few minutes to keep him awake. It was a modernized version of rack torture, Morris thought. Sooner or later, their victim would "break" and agree to anything—which was not very far off from what actually happened.

As the clock struck eight the next morning, Barsalona and Morris's filibuster was still raging. Townshend's resistance was crumbling. Finally, he looked up at both of them with red eyes and dark shadows above his cheekbones. "All right—I give in. I'll do it. As long as you let me go home and go to bed."

"How much?" Wolff asked.

Morris swallowed. Price was one thing they hadn't discussed beforehand. There *was* a problem. Lang had told him that, in case it took the full $50,000 to get Jimi Hendrix, Morris could only spend another $10,000 *total* on bands. Not a cent more. Graham was giving the Who $12,500 for their Tanglewood performance. How was he going to be able to tell them that "the biggest rock festival in the world" could not match Graham's price?

"Ten grand. That's all we can do."

All of a sudden, Townshend was awake. "What!? Are you kidding?"

Assuring him that he certainly was not, it took Morris another two hours to convince the guitarist that the Woodstock Music and Art Fair's funds had been depleted by exaggerated costs. By ten o'clock that morning, however, everyone left Barsalona to his sleep. Promises had been made, hands shaken. The Who would play Woodstock on Sunday, August 17, 1969. The price they had agreed upon was $12,500. Bill Graham had struck again.

— **6** —

Wes Pomeroy arrived in Wallkill on June 15 amidst all the pandemonium between his young associates and the town board. Michael briefed Pomeroy on the trouble, assured him everything was under control, and asked to see the budget Wes had been assigned to prepare for the security operation.

"I couldn't come up with a budget."

Michael's eyes became inquisitive slits. He had counted on Pomeroy's dependability, had not given the assignment a second thought since their earlier meeting in New York City. Lang needed a security breakdown urgently to wave in front of the board's frosty stares. The residents of the town, he explained to Wes, wanted to be assured of police protection from the hippies before anything else; *that* was really the issue—not drugs or sex or even loud music.

"I know what you're saying, but that doesn't help me to arrive at a more conclusive proposal. We don't even know that we have any land. You say you can get that overpass finished quickly; if you don't, we're in real trouble. We're also being pushed by people who are frightened. You see, we're dealing with several levels of human comprehension here, and I just can't come up with a budget because I haven't been able to figure out how many men I'm going to need to appease them. We certainly won't need many. If our idea works about a central culture that encourages peace-keeping among the people themselves, we don't need cops. *At all.* But we cannot say that publicly because people are scared. They'll climb the walls with fear if our plan is exposed."

John and Joel made a rare visit to the site and walked in on the middle of Pomeroy's discussion. Wes greeted them warmly and told them he appreciated that the majority of the festival's principals were on hand to hear what he had to say. "I've got to say something once to you, and then I'll never mention it again," he began uncomfortably. "What I'm saying is not judgmental. It doesn't mean a damn to me what anybody uses here. I'm no longer in the police business, I'm a consultant. But I *do* know that drug enforcement is so important to a lot of police agencies and police officers. And you guys are really quite vulnerable. You've put a lot of money on the line and have a lot of things riding on this festival—not to mention your professional reputations. The whole thing could be blown out of the water with one chickenshit little marijuana bust. So I strongly suggest that you make a hard and fast rule that there be no use of any drugs by any of your staff during the planning process, anywhere near this site or anywhere we go together."

Michael explained to him that he and Mel had already made speeches of that nature to the staff.

Pomeroy's eyes narrowed. "Then make another one. They're playing games with you. Don't pussyfoot around it. It's your necks, not theirs." Later, he expressed a desire to meet with the three of them along with Stanley Goldstein, Don Ganoung, and Mel Lawrence sometime that evening so they could become acquainted and go over his plans. Everyone agreed upon midnight for a field office rendezvous. The hour, someone said, seemed a fitting time for them to conspire against the town. No one laughed at this statement.

Several members of the town had done a little extracurricular plotting of their own. A week or so after the festival crews began work in the field, Pat Mills was busy in the kitchen feeding her baby when the phone rang.

"Mrs. Mills?"

"Yes, speaking."

"Listen carefully, Mrs. Mills. You've got two days to get those slobs off your land and out of our town before we start throwing rocks through your picture window to give you some encouragement. Understand?"

"Who is this?" she demanded, but the line went dead. She told herself it was someone's thoughtless practical joke and fought to put it out of her mind. But when she resumed feeding her child, she had to wait for ten minutes for her hand to stop trembling.

She had decided not to tell Howard about the call. Enough pressure was being brought against him by some of the neighbors to renege on his lease with Woodstock Ventures. Several of his close friends had even gone so far as to sever their relationship with him until he "came to his senses." The call would only serve to worry him more.

The next morning, though, another call disrupted her day, this one jarring her beyond all imagination. It was the same voice.

"They're still there, Mrs. Mills. Those goddamn hippies are still in your field. You're not taking us seriously enough. You'd believe us if you woke up in the middle of the night and found your house on fire, wouldn't you? Your beautiful children, Mrs. Mills, they . . ."

She was not listening anymore. The house, the children—*they had actually threatened her with something that inhuman?* People whom she most likely knew! This is insane, she thought.

That night, as they were preparing to go to bed, Pat Mills was undemonstrative. Howard sensed something was wrong and asked how she felt.

"I'm okay," she lied, turning down the bedspread. Mills accepted his wife's taciturn mood and went about getting washed. When he returned, he found her ready and willing to talk about what was on her mind. "Howard, I'm scared. I feel as if we're being watched by someone very close to us, and I have no idea who it might be." She told him about the calls.

"I've gotten the same ones at the office," he admitted. "*I* didn't want to frighten *you*. I don't think it's anything we should worry about."

"My God, Howard, what if they actually do what they say?"

"They're not going to do anything of the kind. Look, maybe you and the kids should take a vacation until this thing is over. That fellow, Goldstein— the one from the festival group with the black beard—he said they'd be willing to pay all costs if we want to get out of here for the rest of the summer. What do you think?"

"All of us?"

"You know I couldn't run out and leave my property in the hands of those kids. No, just you and the children."

"Absolutely not." She refused to leave her husband while he was receiving threats on his life. "We've got to do something about them. Isn't there some-one we can notify, someone who could watch the house?"

Mills remembered reading in the paper that the festival's security chief was supposed to have checked in a few days before. He called the barn and the woman who answered the phone told him that Wes Pomeroy was staying at a local motel.

"I'll call him now," he told his wife.

"It's the middle of the night, Howard. You can't wake someone up at this hour." It was minutes after eleven o'clock.

Mills was already dialing Pomeroy's number. "I want us to be able to sleep in our own house without worrying that some disaster is going to strike. Leave it to me."

Mills caught Pomeroy minutes before he was ready to leave for the secu-rity meeting. Pomeroy spoke to him for ten minutes and got a fairly good picture of what was going on. He knew what was expected of him in such a time of crisis, accepted the commission without demur, and promised to be at the landowner's home within half an hour.

Pomeroy was deeply concerned about his meeting with Mills. More suc-cinctly, he was disturbed by his own impotence in dealing with the situation. He felt he should be able to step resolutely into the eye of the storm and alle-viate the man's alarm, yet he was not plugged into the community well enough to assess how seriously the threats should be treated. He could not, however, ignore the possibility that Mills's life was in danger. He wished he had the chance to discuss the situation with Don Ganoung. He tried tracking down Ganoung before he left the motel, but the community relations man was already on his way to the security meeting and might have stopped off at any one of ten places to kill some time.

Fortunately, Pomeroy was not unprepared. He had encountered this type of recalcitrant community response before in his career. He knew only too well that there were people who thrived on pumping fear into those whose opinions differed from their own, and that it took only one such person to create a distressing situation. It was a sickness, and he recognized the symptoms immediately. The cure was an automatic response. More than anything else, Mills needed reassurance that his family would be safe, and it was up to Pomeroy to see that he got it.

Mills ran it down for Pomeroy again in his living room. He was visibly shaken and needed to talk. This time, he admitted his panic; he was terrified of anything happening to his wife and children and took the threats at face value. Pomeroy assured Mills that he understood his concern—Wes had a wife and two daughters who were due to arrive in Wallkill in two weeks' time—and he intended to take measures to prevent anything from happening.

He had devised a plan, one based on the principle that not much crime occurs on a well-lighted street. He instructed Mills to take five minutes and to turn on every available light outside his house. "Right now, Howard. I'll wait."

"What good is that going to do? It will just help whoever's been threatening us to make sure they have the right address when they toss the torch."

Pomeroy told him that he was going to have the field crews—"big, husky guys"—grab a few sleeping bags and camp out in the yard. "Believe me, Howard, it will discourage anyone from setting a foot on your property. We'll circle the entire house. Now, I suggest that you go back upstairs and tell your wife that we'll have sentries posted outside your window all night, and *every* night until this foolishness stops or we catch who's been making the calls. Assure her there's nothing to worry about." Mills thanked him and did as he was instructed.

A circle of fluorescent light cast an eerie fence around the mansion. Howard Mills pulled back a curtain and peeked out at the spectacle it made. No one could possibly approach within a hundred feet of the house without being spotted. By the time he said good night to the security chief, he was openly relieved.

From his bedroom window, Mills could see the detail of hippies sleeping on the ground in his backyard. He was sure they were out front as well; he didn't need to check. It was enough for Mills to know that Pomeroy had given his word they'd be protected. He climbed back into bed and slept soundly that night.

It may very well have proved to be his last peaceful night's sleep. The next morning, the voice on the other end of the line informed him that they were turning the matter over to a professional, someone who would see to it that the situation was put to rest once and for all. Howard Mills, they said, was to be shot and killed.

* * *

The security meeting began an hour late. Wes didn't arrive at the barn until well after midnight, and he spent some time filling in the executive staff on what had taken place at Howard Mills's house. He instructed Mel Lawrence to keep in constant touch with Mills and, if necessary, to have "one of the bigger guys" on duty at their house all day. "Mills is on our side," he said. "Despite everything that's happened to him and his family, he is deeply concerned about honoring the contract he has with Woodstock Ventures."

He suggested that it would be a good idea for Don Ganoung to put his collar on and make random visits to neighbors and concerned citizens in town. "Keep your ears open, Don. There's no telling what you might pick up inside someone's home. We may be able to get to the bottom of who's making these calls." Ganoung assured him that he'd begin setting up appointments the next morning.

Mel took over from there. He spent a few minutes recounting what had transpired since they began work, stressing the excellent job done by the University of Miami crews. "They've cleared most of the land, and we're at a point now where we can really throw all of our concentration into setting up the rest of the facilities. The first thing we ought to discuss is fencing. We've got to establish a means of securing the grounds whereby everyone who enters the site will come in through the front gate." He looked at Wes Pomeroy. "You've gotta let us know what you want so we can begin ordering supplies. And a lot of that depends on how high you think they ought to be."

Instead of offering an immediate opinion, Pomeroy suggested they spend some time discussing what a fence meant, both to the crowd and to the promoters. Lawrence stated that they "needed a fence high enough and strong enough to keep people out."

"No fence can keep people out," Pomeroy replied. "Not if they really want to get through. Even at maximum security prisons where they use two fences twenty-five feet high and a few yards apart. The only purpose in having a fence at all is to slow people down so that someone else can do something to change their minds."

"Then how do we keep people out?" Michael asked. "It'll be impossible."

They discussed the dilemma for another hour and arrived at the conclusion that they would symbolically destroy the fences. They'd *have* a fence bordering the site, but it would be constructed so as not to keep anyone from scaling it if they really wanted to. In fact, Pomeroy told them he didn't care what it was made out of. "We'll sell them on this idea: 'We'd appreciate it if you did not go beyond this fence. Please go to the gate and pay for a ticket.'"

To accomplish that, they'd have people stationed every hundred feet or so around the grounds whose duty it would be to talk to the crowd. If someone desired to crash the gate, the staff person was to say: "We wish you wouldn't do that. Everyone else has bought a ticket. You shouldn't ruin it for the rest of the crowd." But if they insisted and went over the fence, the sentry was not to go after them.

"I don't like it," Lawrence said. "It means we're going to forfeit a lot of income from lost gate receipts." No one seemed to pay much attention to his objection. They were more concerned with putting the show on and making sure that no incidents occurred except those they could easily control.

The meeting lasted well into the morning. Each man contributed ideas as to how trouble could be avoided, with Lawrence consistently the most conservative of those in attendance. He was voted down on almost every point of added security and tighter control. After another hour or so, he gave up and adopted their theory. He could see there was realistically no way around it. The festival would most probably lose money, but it would be peaceful. He just needed some time to reconcile himself to the decision.

Before they disbanded, an elaborate security program had evolved based on the theory of nonconfrontation. Wes was in favor of busing people onto the site as a measure against potential gate-crashers. Everyone coming to the festival would be met in assigned parking lots by a staff member and escorted onto buses going to the site. The guides would talk to the people without tickets and explain where they could purchase them. If the kids had no tickets or money, they would be told various ways they could earn admission.

It would be possible for those who came empty-handed to be allowed into the grounds for free if they promised beforehand to help clean up after each day's show. It was to be an honor system. No names would be taken, only words of good faith. After the show, they would meet at a prearranged place and begin to rake the area. If that failed to meet with their approval, the festival worker would issue them a staff armband and ask them to help load new arrivals onto the buses; once they did that, they would travel to the site with the full bus and explain where the people were to go, eat, and camp. That way, they could assure everyone that there was plenty of food, could point out that a playground for children existed, and could provide anyone who wished with a map of the area.

They decided to call the security force the Peace Service Corps. It had a soft sound to it, yet it suggested regimentation. They had to be well organized, Lawrence insisted. Everyone pledged his best to see they were able to collect as much money from the festival goers as possible.

Wes said that he'd always have a couple thousand tickets to the festival on his person. If anyone tried getting past members of the Peace Service Corps stationed at the gates, Wes would be alerted by walkie-talkie and would negotiate with the gate-crasher until he finally gave in and handed him a free ticket. For those who simply had to force their way inside, the executive staff decided to make some kind of arrangement with Ken Kesey's Merry Pranksters to act as its representatives in aiding the obsessed. The Pranksters would arrive early and camp right up against the fence so no one would see the hole they had dug underneath. The Pranksters would then let those determined to enter illegally crawl under the fence as if they were helping them pull off a scam. Indirectly, they had arrived at a system of institutionalized gate-crashing that would avoid ripping out the fences.

It was a brilliant plan, everyone agreed. No one would ever be compelled to fight his way into the festival, and each person would think he got in on his own initiative.

"What are we going to tell Roberts and Rosenman when they want to know how we intend to keep people out?" someone asked.

"We don't tell them anything," Michael said. "No need to upset 'em. They'll make out all right, and we'll all come out smelling like first-class heroes. The most important thing is to protect the show. Everything else'll fall neatly into place."

Goldstein requisitioned the services of one of the members of the Miami art crew, a tall, strapping man named Ron Liis, to accompany him on an expedition for some 750,000 gallons of water for the festival.

Water—purified water, the hardest to find—seemed to be emerging as the festival's common currency. It was the base ingredient for most of the recipes they were preparing in the Hog Farm's free kitchen, it was required for boiling cooking utensils and rinsing stoves. New York State, like most other regions of the country, required running water in all commercial kitchens before its agency granted the restaurateur a proprietary license. The flushing of toilets entailed enormous quantities of it, as did the washing of hands, brushing of teeth, taking of medication, and cleansing of cuts and bruises—all priorities on the board of health's list of prerequisites. And, of course, there was drinking. How in the world were they going to predict and accommodate the number of gallons necessary for consumption? There was no precedent on which to base an estimation. And with time closing in, their inimitable monetary system was on the verge of collapse.

It would have been so simple for them and solved many of their problems had they been given permission to drill for wells on Mills's land. Chris Langhart was friendly with several instructors at New York University who were familiar with the intricacies of pumping mechanisms and could erect small, homemade water wells to their specifications within a few weeks' time. He had made a few informal inquiries and could most likely have them on the site with a few days' notice. But Schlosser had perfunctorily waived their request for on-site natural resources, and there did not seem to be any way around the red tape. That solution was sadly but swiftly abandoned as being hopeless.

Goldstein and Liis determined that the only alternative open to them was to buy water elsewhere and have it trucked in, a procedure that proved, on paper, to be both complicated and costly. Because of the precarious nature of such an enterprise and the susceptibility of their delicate load in transit, stringent codes were enforced to supervise the moving of water from one place to another. Additionally, New York City was battling one of the most severe droughts in its history. Mayor John Lindsay had declared a state of emergency, going so far as to issue a proclamation that prohibited the placement of water on restaurant tables unless it was specifically requested. Their water department was drawing off the surplus of every neighboring county at an incredible rate. As envied and hated a place as New York City already was, it was doubtful its needs would be shunned to accommodate a gathering of hippies in Wallkill. Still and all, it was the only method left at their disposal and they had to investigate the outside chance that they could find a donor.

The two men spent the first week calling all conceivable sources. With a phone in one hand and a crinkled tristate map in the other, they tried every municipality in an expanding circle.

Most of their calls were met with unqualified refusals or solicitous, profit-driven schemes that indirectly made the sale impossible. Others merely quoted them outrageous prices; a particular city to the east of Middletown set its price at ten cents per gallon of raw water, nearly five times the going rate.

Trucks, too, seemed to present them with an insurmountable problem. If, indeed, they were able to arrange for the rental of voluminous trucks from dairy farmers, they had to contend with health department-approved cleansing procedures that adhered to converting the vehicles from milk to water carriers. This necessitated the installation of stainless steel linings and proper purifying elements within the metal stomachs. All of that was inordinately expensive. Even if they eventually got the trucks and agreed to make the conversion, they still couldn't fill them. Catch-22.

They finally stopped looking.

Goldstein spent a number of conscience-searching days pondering the dilemma and arrived at a seemingly hopeless conclusion. Astonishingly enough, that verdict was to drop the whole matter, to just ignore it. They'd act as though they had either made a deal with another source of water or would go through the motions of looking, being "on the verge of a deal" whenever the water inspector came snooping, but it would be put aside until the last possible moment. However irresponsible Goldstein's plan seemed, it was not entirely without merit, nor had he arrived at it without being absolutely convinced of its practicality. He had reexamined a section of the local zoning ordinances and discovered that once a concern was licensed by the Town of Wallkill to open its doors, water was *not* a legal requirement for operating a business. The responsibility was completely undefined. Therefore, they didn't have to submit a plan of that nature to the town board for inspection. And once they were a duly recognized part of the community, they could not be refused water, fire protection, or police services. They were taxpayers like anybody else and were covered by existing rights under the law.

Goldstein was certain the town would capitulate and allow them to tap the water supply in the turquoise towers as an emergency backup. If not, they would be within their rights to appeal to both state and federal agencies to assure they received the same services as any other taxpaying institution. All they had to do was sit back and wait. Water would be flowing as freely as emotions on the Mills property yet if Goldstein had interpreted the law correctly. And, for the moment, it was worth the gamble.

— **7** —

The *Times Herald Record* had discreetly supported the festival's arrival in Wallkill inasmuch as it had refrained from taking a swipe at its character, as everyone else was doing. The paper's editor, Al Romm, an unpopular individual because of his liberal and fastidious approach to covering local news, was skeptical of the promoters' claims of pulling it off without a hitch. There were too many inconsistencies, too many variables in the plan as it was presented to the town board, and he knew they would receive minimal assistance from local merchants. Still, he recognized their attempt to bring culture into an artistically lifeless community and wanted to let that attractive proposition breathe for as long a time as possible. Maybe, he speculated, some of its fanciful intention would rub off on the town's gentry and move them to support the classical arts more than they had before. There was nothing to lose by waiting before he took a stand.

Romm nevertheless had papers to sell and baited his readers on trumped-up headlines the size of billboards impeaching teen-agers' susceptibility to drugs. BLOW YOUR MIND: THREE WHO DID was the star caption hoisted above the June 14 *Times Herald Record* banner. It related, in exaggerated detail, the "painful truth" about a few Orange County youths "hooked" on speed and marijuana. One of the accounts in this particular article involved a teen-age boy who, because of his drug involvement, "giggles a great deal at private jokes . . . and floats off on his own universe. . . . Pride in his appearance is gone and black stains are on his teeth from irregular dental care." On June 18, another front-page feature blazoned LSD TRIPS UP 3 TEENS, SULLIVAN [county] MAN DIES OF 'H,' and was followed the next day by a story calling for community support to "stamp out drug abuse," which had infested the local school system. While there was some validity for editorial concern, the sensational manner in which the stories were presented created a voyeuristic thirst for more. LSD FELLS THREE TEENS directed attention to three Monticello High School students "who became ill after *apparently* taking LSD." HIPPIE GUNMEN ROB ORANGE TOPLESS HAVEN recounted a robbery involving two men of indeterminable age with long hair who, while holding up a bar, wore bell-bottoms and "large hippy-type glasses." Rampant innuendo was unleashed on the Catskill communities, which adapted and repackaged it as effective ammunition to be hurled against the Aquarian Exposition's presence in Wallkill.

Guilt by association was another factor that was stacking up against the festival's public image. On Sunday, June 23, while the staff nervously awaited the town board's decision on whether or not they could proceed based upon its inspection of the ground plans, another festival in Northridge, California, a suburban community near the San Fernando Valley Fairgrounds, was erupting in violence. Northridge had attracted 60,000 paid admissions, most of whom were hippies from the Los Angeles and San Diego area. When police attempted to disperse a relatively small group of roughnecks who intended to rush the gate, thousands of sympathizers flocked to their aid, flinging rocks and bottles at anyone in an official blue uniform The police arrested a total of 165 hippies. Forty-five were charged with assaulting a police officer; an additional ninety arrests were made for drug and marijuana-related offenses; there were 402 injuries reported in all. Monday morning's edition of the *Times Herald Record* carried an item on the disturbance, describing it as a "battle" and citing (again) *alleged* charges of "attempted murder and assault with a deadly weapon." It was not exactly the sort of publicity the festival had been hoping for.

Pomeroy called an old friend of his, Joseph P. Kimble, the newly appointed police chief of Beverly Hills, and asked him, if it was at all possible, to drop whatever he was doing and look into what had caused the Northridge chaos. Kimble had worked under Pomeroy in the San Mateo County Sheriff's Department, and Wes knew he could rely on the younger man's judgment in gaining a fair, unbiased appraisal of the disturbance.

Kimble informed Pomeroy that Cliff Reynolds had also contacted the LAPD seeking the same information. Reynolds was champing at the bit to turn the unfortunate incident against his rivals in Wallkill. His intention was to present the unrelated information to a New York State court as precedent and ostensibly convict Woodstock Ventures on slurs and innuendo.

Kimble's investigation turned up little to discredit the crowd. He found that those who had gained admittance to the performance area were very well behaved. Internal security, however, was disorganized and disruptive. The men who were hired as a peace-keeping force were inexperienced in crowd control. Many came to work armed, and others became stoned and drunk on site as the day progressed An ancillary force, consisting of thirty-five UCLA football players performed their jobs with more insight into the young audience than was exhibited by experienced security personnel, but even they could not hold back several hundred rebels outside the fences. When it became apparent that the security force was in jeopardy of collapsing, the LAPD area commander, Captain Al Lembke, detailed fifty tactical squad men to the area to contain the assault. By that time it was too late. Lines had been drawn, and war was declared.

Pomeroy sent a detailed memorandum concerning Northridge to those on the Woodstock staff. It summarized Kimble's findings and prepared them for a confrontation with Reynolds and his spurious Concerned Citizens group over the matter.

Kimble affirmed what they already knew: that camping facilities were a must and that "monitor policing should exist around the clock." In addition to cataloguing what Pomeroy already had in his security plan, Kimble recommended that "first-aid stations should be established in advance and a sufficient number of ambulances [should be] standing by. Pre-event arrangements should be made with local hospitals." Wes took that last bit of advice to heart and directed Don Ganoung to put out feelers for a staff doctor. He would assume the task of opening relations with local hospitals. Pomeroy was convinced there would be a standard amount of bad trips and drug-related problems that they could attend to with the help of the Hog Farm, but with an expected attendance of well over one hundred thousand, there was no telling what other emergencies might arise. They had to be prepared for everything that might crop up along the way.

What Pomeroy neglected to mention in the memo was that he had asked his former colleague to join the security team at Woodstock. Pomeroy desperately needed trained individuals who shared his outlook on peaceful crowd control and youth to assist him in all phases of the show's organization. Kimble would be a treasured asset. He was responsible, well liked by other peace officers, and in control of his emotions enough to deal with both the kids and the more conservative local law enforcement officials whose assistance was eagerly sought. It would mean Kimble's asking for a leave of absence from a job that he had only recently assumed. Wes hated to put him in that position, but he needed his help.

It is perhaps a measure of Wes Pomeroy's stature and the respect afforded him by his peers that Kimble unswervingly accepted the job. If all went according to plan, he would arrive in New York on August 11, in time for the festival.

The festival's public relations efforts in New York City had fallen off considerably and were in about as unhealthy a state as the smoldering remains of hospitality originally extended them by the zoning board of appeals over three months before. An odious wind blew through the Village streets. Word had come down through the ranks of hippiedom, by way of underground radio and the "scene," which, at this time, included the Fillmore and the Central Park, be-ins, that all was not well in Wallkill. Things, it was said, were coming apart at the seams, and among the "cool," the "groovy," and those generally in the know, there was serious doubt that Woodstock would ever see the light of July let alone the glory that was to be August.

Wartoke, whose very existence was born out of their sharing the Woodstock Ventures account, had relied heavily on the affinity established with the underground press to provide a send-off for festival "hot tips." Whenever the embers needed a vigorous fanning, a Wartoke representative called one of the more prominant biweekly tabloids—Boston's *Avatar*, the Berkeley *Barb*, New York City's *Rat, Realist,* or *East Village Other,* or any of the remaining 451 underground presses in the country publishing on a regular basis—and "leaked" a story. The information was passed from paper to paper, like a hippie wire service, and established what became the foundation for Woodstock's publicity. Even a peace-oriented organization like Woodstock, though, soon wore its welcome thin.

The underground press had amassed its strength from a common bond of radical politics and pop music. Constant foes of big business (capitalist pigs, for the sake of atmosphere), the editors began to smell a colossal "ripoff" in the making. *Hype*—the word sat in their stomachs like acid indigestion. It had not taken most of the editors long to digest a few of Wartoke's "hot tips" before they deduced that not only did someone stand to make a substantial fortune promoting "3 Days of Peace and Music" in their papers, but that the press was being primed to help do it. By continuing to print stories about this wonderful Aquarian Exposition, they were aiding an enterprise whose prime interest was separating The People from Their Bread. This was not part of their ethic. Their open door policy in respect to the Woodstock festival, they decided, had to be slammed shut if they intended to peddle their agrarian ideals. Woodstock, all of a sudden, had become bad news.

Wartoke was right on top of the situation. Catching the scent of rebuff from their peers, they foiled any collective attempt by the underground press to break off relationships with Woodstock by calling for a seminar to discuss exactly what it was that Woodstock should signify. It was a stroke of divine inspiration on Wartoke's part; in addition to averting an organized boycott of the festival, they would instill in every editor who attended the feeling that his paper had played an integral part in the planning of the event. It would serve to bring the festival that much closer to the media and guarantee them total support from the counterculture's accredited spokesmen.

Several drafts of invitations to the seminar were made and passed on to Michael Lang for his approval. After a number of rejections, one met with unanimous acclaim from the executive staff:

> The Music Festival is not a battleground. If we are to seduce the music festival back from the California battleground, we must formulate new and sure methods of preparation to provide for safe and nonviolent amusement. You are urged to participate in a special meeting to develop and set ground rules for outdoor peace and music programs. Thursday, June 26th, 11:00 A.M. Village Gate. Bleecker Street.
> We are all responsible.

Sixty-six rock media luminaries were invited to attend, including reporters from such aboveground publications as *Life, Newsweek,* and *Time* as well as a representative from UPI and camera crews from the three major television networks. It was to be a truly spectacular rally, as flashy a laid-back, hip meeting as one could ever hope to stage. For vanity's sake, it was not promoted under the auspices of Woodstock Ventures, nor was it touted as a festival arm, although its underlying purpose, as everyone knew, was to mobilize support for the August 15 bonanza. Instead, it was thinly disguised as a forum in which participants would examine the Northridge disaster and attempt to preserve the concept of "festival" as an authorized conclave of the stoned generation.

Wartoke knowingly, and without hesitation, then took a considerable risk by attempting to cover up their account's stake in the seminar. After the invitations had gone out, someone at the public relations firm took it upon himself to inform the editors by phone that one of the council's primary functions was for those in attendance to vote on whether or not Woodstock should become a political arena to encourage antiwar protesters. If they voted affirmatively, then the heads of every movement would be allotted a predetermined period of time on stage to promote their righteous causes; if their decision was negative, then all political fronts would award themselves a three-day holiday and come out for what promised to be an unparalleled rock concert. The response to that proposition was overly enthusiastic; the editors would abide by the wishes of the majority.

Of course, Lang and his partners had no intention of endangering either their prospective monetary landslide or their reputations by imposing such a damnable blockade on the show; the thought of sponsoring the most expensive political convention since the Continental Congress was utterly insane and beyond question. Wartoke was banking on the various radical groups backing down. They believed that, despite the individual commitments made by the movements to destroy The System, all anybody really wanted to do was to tune in and have a good time. If they were wrong—and they insisted they weren't—then they were prepared to tell "everyone there to fuck off and to do the festival anyway." Either way, Wartoke guaranteed the skeptical partners, Woodstock would go down exactly as they envisioned it. Unfortunately, that only seemed like a promising image to half of the corporation.

The turnout at the Village Gate was better than even Wartoke had anticipated. Some two hundred underground editors, radio disc jockeys, reporters, rock executives, and street leaders pushed into the pocket-sized club to take part in the great debate, to see who would be brave enough to fire the first shot at the hip imposters' artful dodge. Many had hitchiked from as far away as Texas to state their case while those with less vocal sentiments hid among the smokey shadows of the austere room. It was enough for most just to *be* there, to sit among their generation's most quoted spokesmen, to have a hand in cultural destiny. They had come out of curiosity, and they would return home enlightened by what they had heard. This, they had been told, was history in the making.

The room had been arranged to suggest some kind of loose structure to provide for those who wished to speak from the floor. A long, cloth-covered conference table was set up on the elevated stage where the Gate's jazz artists performed nightly. Behind it were six folding chairs, and in front of every speaker's position was a microphone. Those who came as spectators or secondary participants were shown to seats in the sunken audience gallery. By 10:45, every seat in the house was taken or being shared, and the spillover improvised on radiators and window sills.

Jim Forad, a local movement leader, had volunteered his services as a moderator. Forad was an articulate, soft-spoken young man who had amassed a great deal of respect among the New York underground community. He knew most of the people in the audience that morning by sight, which, if things got out of hand, would allow him to single people out and settle them down. It was hoped that his participation would be limited to short, impromptu introductions.

Michael Lang was first on the dais. As he pulled the microphone closer to his chest, the room came alive with excitement. Here he was at last, Lang the enigma, the man-child whose name had been carried across press releases like a dignitary's thrust into the limelight with the velocity of a buck-shot politician with a ten-dollar smile. He had a magical quality about him that touched everyone who slapped palms with him. Even those who had yet to meet him felt an attraction on the basis of a description or a quote attributed to him in the press. Karma, Michael called it. He had the uncanny ability to reach out and touch someone with spiritual telepathy and claimed he could read it in others equally well. One evening in March he tried to convince John Roberts that Karma had prevented his being busted.

"One time I was going to see a friend. And I couldn't get in the door." His friend was on the other side in the process of being arrested for possession. "The door wasn't locked. It was just that I couldn't open it."

"Michael," Roberts scoffed, "You mean that the . . . vibes coming from inside stopped you? Actually prevented you?"

"Yeah."

"But that's impossible. Anybody can open . . ."

"It's not impossible, man," Michael said sotto voce.

"Michael is the devil," Ticia had contended when asked about his charisma. In the six weeks since she had been hired, Ticia and Michael had become lovers, and her perception of him had been heightened by their relationship. "He has two little bumps high up on his forehead where his horns used to be." Now he was working his satanical charm on the small audience below him and he had yet to open his mouth. Lang's pitch was unchanged. He explained Woodstock in terms of the utopian adventure meant for peace-loving people and emphasized the concept of "togetherness and understanding through music."

Indirectly, he pointed out, everyone who bought a ticket to the festival was contributing to a united front against the war in Vietnam. "We're showing the world how it's possible for a lot of kids to get along peacefully under the same roof. And we'll do it, too, as brothers." He assured the audience that a strong antiwar sentiment would pervade the festival's nonaggressive atmosphere. It would be equivalent to staging a massive political protest felt round the world without anyone having to utter an objectionable word.

Michael then went into detail about an art show that would coincide with the concert to introduce the work of young ghetto artists. A rock manager named Peter Leeds was in the process of assembling the exhibit, and he would announce within the next two weeks the rules governing submission of art. He also described the playground being built by the University of Miami art crew, the free stage where those who came without a ticket or enough money to buy one would be entertained throughout the three days, the puppet theatre (which was still in the discussion stage) and, of course, the concert itself. He gave them a quick update on the most current list of acts and alluded to "a few surprises."

Wes Pomeroy took over. He spent several minutes reviewing the festival's ultraspecialized security program with the temerity of a Supreme Court justice. Pomeroy casually sidestepped the audience's questions pertaining to the handling of the drug busts. It was a delicate gray area in their security program and he had not figured that one out yet for himself. But, he assured them, they were "taking every precaution to guarantee each and every person who attends their rights under the law as an American citizen." An undercurrent of hissing followed his patriotic pledge.

"Some good that'll do us," a spectator called out. The rest of the young crowd chimed its displeasure.

"Look, it certainly won't be a sanctuary for illegal behavior any more than a city street is," he said, taking a harder line. It did nothing to improve his position.

A dissatisfaction with any type of regulation grew in the dimly lit room. A few of the movement leaders who were scattered in the crowd requested permission to speak and were invited up to the podium. They were angry, they said. They felt that they, as well as those for whom they spoke, expressed a valid political philosophy that was being purposefully suffocated by those who held the power. Right now, the promoters of the festival held that power and had turned their back on their own brothers. With respect to the war, their pleas for its immediate end went ignored, their protest fell on deaf ears; their interests *as American citizens* were being subjugated by "political fools" who refused to honor their rights; they were beaten over the head by cops who clearly exhibited an intense hatred of their individuality; they were thrown in jail by "social alcoholics" for smoking pot; they were forced to accept and defend all this absurdity by consenting to being shipped over to Vietnam with a gun and told to kill an unknown enemy. None of it made any sense to them. They were scared. Now, their own cultural looka-likes were attempting to silence their views at an event where they had the potential to reach several hundred thousand who would listen. It was getting scarier all the time.

"You talk about fair treatment in the eyes of the law," accused one young man in a blue and orange tie-dye T-shirt. "Those eyes are *blind,* man! That's a lot of fascist bullshit you're tryin' to lay on us. You want everybody to come up to Woodstock on your say-so, to listen to the music, turn on to the vibes. Sure, it sounds great, but there's more to it than that. I'll tell you what I think; I think that one of us takes a step in the wrong direction and they're gonna bring those fuckin' sticks of theirs down on our heads. Where's that gonna leave us? Nowhere, man! That's where we are now, and that's where we're gonna be up there in the country with all those pigs breathin' down our necks. A fuckin' festival isn't the answer unless it's gonna help bring about the revolution."

Pomeroy looked at Lang with a tightly clenched jaw. He wanted some kind of sign from his young associate to tell him how to proceed. Michael only smiled; he seemed to be thoroughly enjoying himself.

Wes attempted to alleviate a measure of their exasperation by explaining that no member of their security corps would be permitted to bear arms. "The only one you're going to have to answer to for your actions there is the person sitting next to you." He stressed that the 300-man team helping him would consist of hand-picked off-duty policemen from the metropolitan force. They would be chosen for their coolness in tight situations and their ability to communicate with hippies. "The Peace Service Corps will *not* be there to make on-the-spot arrests for the expected pot smoking, fence jumping, nudity, or sex. They will have been instructed only to inform the wrong-doers that such actions are frowned upon by their brothers, that they should be done in a more discreet place, and that the wrongdoer might be liable to arrest."

"What about narcs, man?"

"You'd better expect them to be there, son. In fact, if the narcs are doing their job, they may very well be sitting next to you right now." A drone of nervous laughter stuttered across the room. Heads comically swiveled to get a better view of their neighbors. "I've got no control over federal undercover narcotics agents, but I have it in good faith that no bust will be made on the grounds without my permission—and I don't think that's going to be easily had. There'll be uniformed cops there—state and local cops, you can be sure of that—and they'll be looking for drugs, but they won't be permitted inside the festival grounds without a warrant. It's up to each and every one of us to see we keep things under control so that won't be necessary."

Pomeroy's speech had a decided effect on those members of the media who were lucky enough to attend the meeting. The promoters could sense a collective sigh of relief from their guests. *Rat*, perhaps the most radical of the underground papers and certainly one highly suspicious of Woodstock's cultivated image of peace and brotherhood, would later write of Pomeroy's words, "Chief Pomeroy knows where it's at. No redneck this one. No nigger-pinko-jew hater this one. No curl of the upper lip. His middle-aged graying hair sports appropriate but not too long sideburns. His smile is easy, his eyes open and frank. If it ever entered your mind that an officer of the law might be your adversary, chief cop Pomeroy is a worthy one." *Rat* did, however, plead with its readership not to be taken in by the promoters' slick, hip business tactics. "Remember always, a pig is a pig is a pig. As far as cops go, these are the better ones. We salute them. But they are playing a role, they are wearing foreign costumes, they are engaged in theatrics. We will not be fooled."

Finally, after four hours of rhetoric when everybody had had his say, after grievances had been aired, philosophies propounded, accusations flung, banners waved, the proposition of suspending politics at the Woodstock music festival was grimly put to a vote. Morally, they all agreed that they had an obligation to keep politics in the forefront of every action they undertook, every event in which they participated, until either the war was ended or the system destroyed (or both). But, they conceded, they were exhausted. The battle they waged was physically taxing and costly. It had been a politically active winter and spring; the sit-ins and activist rallies had proved successful. More and more of the masses had been won over to their side. There was still a lot to be done, much to say that had not already been said. At that point, though, they were under such intense pressure from law enforcement agencies and experiencing such a knot of tension in their personal lives from the struggle that they needed to give themselves a rest. The weekend of August 15–17 was just about as good a time as any, one bearded boy argued. They would come up to the festival, hang out, have a good time, and rest up for the long struggle ahead.

CHAPTER SIX

The Long Arm of Justice

They had hoped to find a home, and they found only hatred. Okies—the owners hated them because the owners knew they were soft and the Okies strong, that they were fed and the Okies hungry. —*John Steinbeck (1939)*

Public opinion's always in advance of the law. —*John Galsworthy (1922)*

— 1 —

Miles Lourie called Woodstock Ventures' uptown offices late that afternoon after word had filtered back to him about the morning's conference at the Village Gate. In the background, he detected the bustle of celebration and did his best not to sound overly official. The call was, nonetheless, business; it could not wait.

John Roberts, who took the lawyer's call with resignation, informed him that the meeting had gone the way they had hoped it would. It was receiving excellent press and television coverage with most local stations running in-depth interviews with Lang and Pomeroy. "The press," he said jokingly, "seems to be the *only* group that doesn't want to take a bite out of my ass. Thank God for small favors."

"I'm glad you feel that way, because I've just heard from Sam Eager in Middletown, and he's just been handed a copy of the proposed legislation the town board's written to regulate public gatherings."

"For Christ's sake, Miles. Why didn't you say so?"

"I wanted to ease into it as much as possible."

"Aw, shit. It's that bad?"

"Well, let's put it this way: it's not exactly what I'd call a key to the city. But it's not prohibitive."

He read the text of it slowly over the phone, stopping every so often to clarify some ponderous legal terminology.

It was a formal document designed by the town attorney to discourage assemblies of more than five thousand people to be held within the Town of Wallkill. Under the proposed law, a corporation seeking the right to hold an event first had to be granted a permit by the town board twenty days prior to its commencement. The preliminary requirements for such an application were fairly standard: the name of the owner of the property, the expected number of visitors, cars and similar vehicles, the proposed dates and hours of the function, its purpose and admission charge all had to be submitted along with an application fee of one dollar (refundable if the application was turned down) to the town board. Maps had to be included along with that information, clearly denoting any roads, buildings, and property on or adjacent to the site that might be affected by its use. Likewise, plans had to be presented detailing systems of water distribution, sewage disposal, food preparation, parking, and access routes.

As far as John could tell, they had already provided Town Supervisor Jack Schlosser with all of the above except for conclusive water and concession plans. Goldstein had several water alternatives working, and they were having a meeting concerning the retail sale of food at Paul Marshall's office in a few days' time. Roberts surmised, however prematurely, that, so far, the list of requirements ("impositions" was more suitable a word) could be coordinated in record time should the town board put the squeeze on them with a time factor.

The root of obstruction, however, began to twine tightly around the festival's already weak heart as Lourie continued his spiritless recitation. Ambiguities, obviously grafted on to conventional statutes as well-timed afterthoughts, provided Wallkill with an airtight alibi should the town want to close down a function on the slightest of whims. Roberts listened mournfully as Lourie repeated a paragraph prohibiting music to be played "in such a manner that the sound . . . shall be audible beyond the property line of the place of assembly nor in a manner which either annoys, disturbs, injures, endangers, or tends to annoy, disturb, injure, or endanger the comfort, repose, health, peace, or safety of other persons or the public." Not to be misunderstood, the author of the document was quick to point out that the provision included "loud, unnecessary, or unusual noises."

"You've *gotta* be kidding!" Roberts was baffled by the extent of the interdiction. Woodstock Ventures could theoretically be run out of town for so much playing a radio too loud in the field office. All a town board member—or any other "concerned" citizen, for that matter—had to do to thwart their endeavors was to get Howard Mills to declare the noise level emanating from the festival was disturbing his family. No formal indictment was necessary. That was all it took.

But, in fact, there were supplementary regulations, the length of which seemed unending, should the noise deterrent not prove disuasive. The promoters had to promise that "no soot, cinders, smoke, noxious acids, fumes, gasses or disagreeable or unusual odors" would be permitted to emanate from the property "so as to be detrimental to any person or the public." So much for campfires, food concessions or even automobile exhaust pipes. "In addition, no light on any part of the property of assembly shall be permitted to shine unreasonably beyond the property line of the property," nor could they permit any "unreasonable glow" to shine beyond the site.

The proposed law further stated that, before granting a permit to any outside concern petitioning the town board to stage an assembly, the board had the privilege to require the approval of any or all government agencies that had jurisdiction over any phase of the event. Those included the county health inspector, the town sanitary inspector, the town health officer, the state Water Resources Commission, the town building inspector, the county highway department, the state Department of Transportation, the sheriff's office, the state police, the chief engineer, and the local fire commissioners, the town fire advisory board, the zoning board of appeals, the town police department, and the county fire coordinator. If any of the hundred or so officials who were employed by any one of these august bodies wished to do so, he could sign the festival's death certificate without entertaining an appeal.

The barriers seemed insurmountable. Woodstock Ventures could, of course, make a halfhearted show of compliance with these various clauses and hope they could drag legislation through until September before anyone got the better of them, but that was highly unlikely and beyond objective reasoning. A provision setting forth stiff fines for offenders discouraged John from giving it any serious thought. Fines were set at one hundred dollars for each offense and Howard Mills could also receive a concurrent fine for permitting the infraction to take place on his land. If too many citations were issued for the same assembly, the local court reserved the right to impose a jail sentence on said culprits for up to six months.

John relayed the news to Joel Rosenman who shared his partner's abject dismay. Their hands were tied, they agreed. They could shut down production and swallow a half-million-dollar loss or, in a moment of daring, challenge the law and elect to pay the fines. Either way, they lost. The decision rested with them; nonetheless, Roberts felt he had to confer with other members of the festival staff before passing a verdict. He tried unsuccessfuly to reach Michael Lang and finally got hold of Sam Eager in his Middletown office.

"It's not a law yet, John, just a proposal for an ordinance. For it to become law requires, if my memory serves me correctly, that a public hearing on the matter be held and that two thirds of the town board ratify it. That could take time. And, of course, we'll oppose it."

"What do you think our chances are of stopping its passage?"

Eager answered characteristically, "I don't know."

The attorney did say, however, that if they were still willing to go on with their plans, an application had to be made to the board no later than July 2. That was the day on which the council convened, the only such meeting scheduled before the festival was to take place. If they were late, and the ordinance was adopted into law, they would most probably forfeit their right to hold the event in Wallkill. Roberts suggested that Eager speak to Mel Lawrence and Stanley Goldstein regarding the feasibility of the field crew meeting the stipulations. He had not yet reached Lang, but Roberts was reasonably certain of what Michael's position would be. "We'll fight it," he told Eager. Too much time and money had already been expended. Besides, they were being railroaded, and that infuriated the hell out of him. War had been declared by the enemy, and John Roberts rose to accept the challenge.

The *Times Herald Record* also viewed the proposed ordinance as a declaration of war, an action that, it said, was a "monstrous decision . . . a time bomb" so severe that "it is inconceivable to us that [the Aquarian Exposition] would survive even casual court scrutiny." On June 27, the morning after the text of the law was released to the press, editor Al Romm published an editorial lambasting the action of the board. "The Town of Wallkill has declared war on the proposed rock-folk festival August 15–17 on the Howard Mills property in Scotchtown," he began. "We regard the proposed ordinance as an example of flagrant misuse of governmental power. . . . It is, in our opinion, highly improper to prohibit one event in the guise of regulating it."

The editorial cited several "ludicrous" sections of the bill, and raised a question pertaining to its ultimate effect on the community. The Town of Wallkill, Romm pointed out, may have inadvertently given the ax to one of its oldest and most respected traditions: the Orange County Fair. "The Orange County Fair, scheduled in late July, could not possibly meet the light-noise-odor test Supervisor Jack Schlosser and his associates devised. For another, the privately operated stock car races at the fairgrounds, which spread their noise pollution 10 miles away . . . would be out of business. The latter result would be a blessing, but we don't imagine that the town fathers had it in mind."

The promoters regarded the editorial as an encouraging sign that all was not lost. As long as a single Wallkill voice sounded in their behalf, they felt they had "a shot at beating the bad rap." The *Times Herald Record* was a very loud voice, indeed. It serviced practically all of Orange County and many cities in neighboring Sullivan County that relied on its insight into and advice on local affairs. Romm would have to be courted for his support.

While Woodstock Ventures prepared a defense against the proposed ordinance, Mel Lawrence continued primping the grounds as though nothing unusual had occurred. Michael had advised him against putting up any kind of permanent structure; likewise, he told Chip Monck not to pour the concrete for the stage supports. If they were forced "to split," they would do so with the least amount of inconvenience. Otherwise, they were to proceed as originally planned. "We're gonna beat this rap," Lang declared. He asked Lawrence and Monck if they could maintain the crew's morale through the legal fight. They assured him they could.

The crew's morale, in fact, needed the least boosting of all. After they moved from Rosenberg's into a motel called the Red Top, a few miles away from the site, a unique, communal social structure unfolded which instilled in them the kind of noble temptation necessary to view every predicament with high hopes and self-assurance. Everything to them was "beautiful" and "far out"; if they were being "fucked over by the Establishment" as the newspapers claimed, it was because certain "uptight individuals hadn't yet learned how to express feelings of love and brotherhood." They were the Family of Man, the last, best hope for peace and the forebears of civilized society.

The Woodstock family in Wallkill now numbered over seventy hippies and was growing by tens and twenties every day. Most of the late arrivals had heard about the "fabulous festival in the country" from friends or in underground newspapers and were tempted by the cultural dictate of Total Involvement. Hans Toch, the noted psychologist, in a *Nation* article entitled "The Last Word on Hippies," attributed their "unfettered freedom and unconditional reward" to their being spoiled. "It insures that the world view from the crib will last undisturbed through sobering experiences that usually overlay infancy with the veneers of civilization." But the hordes of roving children who wandered into the field offices weren't looking to be pampered or reimbursed for their time. They volunteered to work, to help out, to run errands—anything that, in some small way, would further the great festival and increase the hippie's providence.

Many of them had come from as far off as Texas and New Mexico in search of "a place to fit in," and they were welcomed aboard with open arms. Some were draft resisters on the move who knew they wouldn't be betrayed, others were runaways or dropouts. Mostly, however, they were happy and young, between the ages of fifteen and twenty, with wholesome, angelic faces and serene dispositions. After they answered a few routine questions about why they wanted to join the festival team, one of the executive staff members would take down some general information about them for payroll purposes—name, address, social security number (Roberts and Rosenman's accountants had insisted upon that), age, emergency reference—and introduce them around until they felt at home. After a reasonable grace period not usually lasting more than a day or two—during which time they hung around the Red Top, got high with the other kids, exchanged stories about travel and trauma (the latter most certainly about their run-ins with law enforcement officials)—they were asked to join one of the field crews and get to work. No one took advantage of the festival's cordiality; everyone participated in the physical labor according to his ability and, for the most part, without complaint.

As much as they had attempted to abolish traditional role playing in the crew's quarters, family members were assigned specific domestic tasks for which they were directly responsible. They all had their "old lady" or "old man" to whom they "swore" allegiance. There were strictly enforced territorial rights in the motel established by various couples to assure them of privacy in their relationships. Within a week after they had moved in, the Red Top resembled the epitome of organized, denominational society, hippie-style.

Those who chose not to work on one of the field crews were asked to cook, do the shopping, run errands, or keep the area clean. Michael made sure that all out-of-pocket expenses were assumed by Woodstock Ventures and gave Mel Lawrence, Penny Stallings, Lee Mackler, or one of the other executives enough cash each week to keep a well-stocked pantry. Whatever money was left over was spent on provisions or put to some other use like clothing or dope. If one of the kids needed new blue jeans or a T-shirt, all he had to do was to inform the designated supply agent on his way into town and enough petty cash would be put aside for it. Windbreakers, blankets, sleeping bags, "everything up to and including Tampax was supplied by the expense fund."

A routine unfolded from the daily chores. Each morning, a designated person would get up at sunrise and wake the staff cook. Once breakfast preparations were under way, they would knock on each bedroom or car door, making sure that everyone got out of the sack with enough time left to eat breakfast and hitch a ride out to the site. Fraternization between most crew members was standard fare and subject to change on an almost daily basis (unless small children or one on the way dictated otherwise, and even then, propriety was often overlooked). It was always a game for the wake-up brigade to guess who had spent the night with whom as casual sex was neither frowned upon nor refused (although during the poison ivy epidemic relations were somewhat diminished by incompatible rashes). Breakfast, cooked by two teen-age girls, consisted of eggs prepared a different way each morning, every dry cereal on the market, hot oatmeal, an array of fruit juices, coffee, and tea. Milk and fruit were staples at every meal as they were readily accessible from one of the many dairy and produce farms in the area.

As soon as everyone left for the site, the two cooks, Carol and Linda, washed the utensils and went shopping. Their trek to the supermarket about a mile and a half down the road rarely went unattended by the local police force. Halfway there, the girls would invariably be pulled over to the side of the road, where they would be ordered out of the car, told to put their hands on top of their heads, and frisked—including Linda, who was six months pregnant. Their car was habitually ransacked by state troopers who ripped out the back seat cushions and tore wiring from underneath the dashboard in an attempt to find a hidden cache of drugs. Nothing was ever found, nor was an arrest recorded in the police blotter concerning the festival staff over the two-month period, but it was the sheriff's own little way of warning the crew against making a wrong or suspicious move in his territory.

Between noon and one o'clock each day, work stopped for lunch. Carol and Linda prepared several hundred tuna fish and egg-salad sandwiches in the late mornings and brought them to the site, whereupon assistants would take them out to the various crews. Dinners consisted of hearty dishes—roast beef, stews, turkey, with plenty of mashed potatoes and rice to supplement the strenuous work they did during the days. Occasionally, the diet varied with the crew's mood. A wave of experimental vegetarianism washed away any romantic illusion the staff had about not eating meat. Another faction of workers flirted with the notion that they were the living incarnation of western desperadoes. "We want grits!" they demanded quite abruptly, sitting down to dinner in full cowboy regalia. Carol, the cook for that evening's meal, started to laugh. Before her very eyes sat a contingent of middle-class suburban kids whose childhood fantasies of being Roy Rogers or Hopalong

Cassidy had finally gotten the better of them. The next day, she served them heaping platters of a mush substance they had never seen before. "This stuff tastes like shit!" one of them complained, propping his spurred boots on the table. "What is it?" Why, it was grits, she replied. Isn't that the cowboy's favorite dish? "We're not gonna eat that shit. Bring us some real food." The deal she made with them, of course, was that they take off their silly Halloween costumes and become hippies again before she brought them *real* food.

After dinner most of the kids went into town or stayed around the motel playing shuffleboard and watching television. Many of the local Middletown teen-agers—those who had quietly begun dropping acid or smoking dope in their bedrooms—would spend their evenings at the Red Top begging the festival staff to tell them what was really going on in "the outside world." They treated crew members like gods and goddesses and promised to talk their parents into keeping the festival in their home town. Each night after dinner, the staff would retire to a local dealer's bus where they got high and made love. No one could have asked for more; no one thought there *was* more to life than that.

The festival women spent their afternoons at the Red Top doing laundry and tending to an endless procession of cuts and bruises that disabled their men. Each morning Mel Lawrence sketched out what he wanted done that day and sent the crews into the field nodding aimlessly while he disappeared into the barn. Before long, one boy mowed off his toe, and another lost a finger trying to operate an unwieldy chain saw. Someone in need of medical attention (it occurred to such an extent that a system of immediate treatment had to be devised) would be tossed into the back seat of a rented station wagon and transported to the lobby of the Red Top where one of the girls, notified by phone of the emergency, would sew him up with as much surgical expertise as the patient had demonstrated with the heavy machinery. Before anyone knew that an accident had occurred, the kid would be back on the job.

The only group with any operational expertise whatsoever was the art crew. By the last week in June, they had maneuvered three tractors back and forth across the site, mowing the tall grass and plowing the underbrush free of debris, until Mills Heights looked like a neatly manicured ball field. Large clefts of the orchard were cleared for the installation of additional sculpture and an area where the playground would be constructed was tilled with backhoes and trenchers. Lawrence had hired a subordinate crew of youngsters to assist the artists with incidental grooming efforts. One morning, after a walking inspection of the site, he sent them crawling across the land to pick up rocks, twigs, rotten apples, and anything else that might interfere with the crowd's sitting there comfortably on a blanket. During Pomeroy's security meeting, the crowd's comfort had been equated with its capacity to remain tranquil and orderly throughout the event, and every facet of production, right down to the contour of the land, was being taken into consideration to insure a motionless, unencumbered atmosphere. The campgrounds were segregated from the rest of the site by a single line of trees and left virtually untouched. Their sculpture awaited Stan Goldstein's direction, and he was still tied up with petty administrative functions that had to be resolved before he could be present at the site. The area designated for concessions, too, was left unfinished as its landscape would be greatly influenced by whatever firm was eventually brought in to oversee its operation.

The only other headway made concerned aesthetic enhancement of the grounds. Bill Ward had arrived at a decision concerning the festival's decorations, which he hoped would reflect the artists' understanding of the Catskill environment. He and Jean spent a lot of their spare time driving around the country roads studying the farmland architecture and, in particular, old wooden barns. Wherever they went, they noticed old tractors and other barnyard fixtures—case plows, cultivators, balers, and hayrakes—neglected and rusting in heaps behind the barns. The Wards regarded them as antiques and began making the farmers lucrative offers for the useless scrap. They purchased a number of ancient John Deere tractors, planters with unique cast iron flanges, and a variety of metal wheels on which were imprinted legends of ancient companies; these were randomly scattered around the festival site in place of the originally planned metal scuptures. If the kids tired of listening to the music, Bill Ward contended, they could always entertain themselves by climbing over the ornamental machinery or use them as bleachers.

"We are such stuff as dreams are made of," Shakespeare had written almost three hundred and fifty years before the first hippie ever set foot in Orange County. Psychedelic reveries had replaced some of the dreams, but everything else had pretty much remained the same. The seeds of ingenuity planted many months before had sprouted roots whose potential knew no bounds, and with a scant six weeks left until the festival finally burst forth, only the stone-cold wall of reality stood in its way.

— **2** —

The Hog Farm had rolled their bus out of New York City heading west back in April. Their now familiar cry of: "The United States, driver, and step on it!" as they cruised through the Lincoln Tunnel drew a curtain of uncertainty across the odds of their honoring their commitment. For all anyone knew, they were on their way to the outer reaches of civilization with just enough gas and money left to get them there. Stanley Goldstein was worried about their turning up in time to be of any use to him, and justifiably so.

Goldstein's presentiment had to do with his own credibility, not theirs. When he last discussed the Hog Farm's participation with Hugh Romney, he had been purposely vague about tying them to any sort of binding agreement so as not to come on too strongly. Unfortunately, he might have underplayed his hand. In an attempt to appear only mildly concerned about the business aspect of their arrangement, he had failed to mention to them anything about time schedules, supplies, cash advances to transport them to the site, and a hundred other significant matters of interest to each party.

The last Goldstein had heard, the itinerant commune was temporarily settled on the Tesuque (pronounced: Teh-soo-kee) Indian Reservation in Aspen Meadows, New Mexico, where they planned to celebrate the summer solstice before heading back east (or west or . . .). Because of the inchoate living conditions there, it was virtually impossible to contact anyone on the reservation. He could send them a letter or put in a personal appearance, the latter of which required making an expeditionary drive into the wilderness hours from any major city. Nonetheless, a large portion of the festival's success hinged on their complete participation in it, and a few days' sacrifice would be worth the peace of mind. The most logical way of reinstating himself in their good graces, Goldstein decided, was for him to make an unannounced run out to New Mexico, and he easily convinced Lang that Woodstock Ventures should foot the bill for his trip.

Before he left, Goldstein discussed his impending visit with Wes Pomeroy. Together, they reexamined the purpose of having the commune take part in the festival and slowly created a distinct area of supervision for which the Hog Farm would be directly responsible. Pomeroy made a salient point of reminding Goldstein that they were not to think they were being transported halfway across the country simply to provide atmosphere for a gathering of middle-class hippies. If anything, they were being counted on to help prepare the land, establish and supply provisions for a free kitchen capable of feeding one hundred thousand kids in an emergency situation, lend their knowledge of the effect of psychedelic drugs to help administer first aid to the expected overflow of bad trips and narcotics overdoses, and help the clean-up crew restore the land to its natural condition after the festival was over. The failure of the Hog Farm to take any one of those crucial areas seriously could result in the loss of hundreds of thousands of dollars and, possibly, lives.

Pomeroy called a man named James Grant, the executive director of the New Mexico Governor's Crime Commission, who agreed to meet Goldstein in Albequerque on June 21 and navigate the trip the rest of the way. Together, they would spend the weekend with the Hog Farm and file individual reports on their findings, which would then be reviewed by Wes. That way, the police chief would be afforded two observations of the Hog Farm's potential from divergent personalities and would better know how to work them into his security plan.

Goldstein flew to New Mexico on Friday, June 20. He met Jim Grant at the airport and began the journey that would take them high into the Pueblos and on toward Aspen Meadows.

He had been forewarned that if he failed to evince at least a modicum of unassailable authority, be it the elucidation of their duties in Wallkill or, at best, an airtight plan for bringing them to New York, the Hog Farmers would treat him like a simpleton. They'd behave much like incorrigible inmates of an asylum for the duration of Goldstein's visit as if to mirror the absurdity of their heretofore welcome guest. One's self-esteem could be obliterated with a single wrong word.

No one walked away without being undone by them in some way or another. But the supreme mistake one could make, the fatal error and, at the same time, the tip-off to their double-faced personality, was to assume they didn't take *themselves* seriously. That would swiftly eliminate any chance of a relationship with them. In fact, members of the Hog Farm considered their cause the ne plus ultra, a faultless existence devoid of life's authoritarian impurities. Nor did they much care how their actions affected those with whom they came into contact. The Hog Farmers masqueraded among their own (or anybody they could get to accept their harebrained stories) as educators of "the psychic consciousness." More aptly, they were a self-seeking band of opportunists more interested in filling their pockets than other people's minds. If after having been shunned, one persisted in chasing after them, they often became hateful, nasty instigators and, if provoked, vengeful. Theirs was a game of only winning combinations. Goldstein knew about the falsehearted pledges they made to their employers, had weighed their worth to the festival, and was prepared to gamble—again.

The Hog Farm was unprepared for Goldstein's unannounced arrival. It was as though he was a spectre who had mysteriously emerged from out of their not-too-distant past, and he was, thus, greeted with mild shock and apprehension. Hugh Romney had attached little relevance to Goldstein's pitch in New York. Romney was used to hearing all sorts of wonderful offers from promoters in need of assistance who never delivered on their word. One such impresario with an impressive office and even more attractive offer had pledged one hundred thousand dollars to the Hog Farm's favorite charity (themselves) if they agreed to supervise a show he was putting together. After spending months acquiring a staff and traveling one thousand miles to get there in time, they found that the show had been cancelled and their benefactor had disappeared. When Romney had asked Lang how he intended to get the Hog Farm from New Mexico to New York, Michael had casually replied, "Well, we'll just get ourselves a plane and pick you up there." *Riiight!* Romney thought; it was just as he had suspected all along: the old soft-shoe, and from that moment on, he simply tuned them out. Goldstein was henceforth regarded by him as another in the succession of "long-haired charlatans pimping for big business." Stan's flying to Aspen Meadows, however, augured in them a long-suppressed expression of faith that affected members of the Hog Farm almost as sincerely as a cash deposit. This time, they assured him, they would listen to his offer more carefully.

Goldstein's approach was direct and uncompromising. "I don't want any hero-fuckers to make the trip," he told Romney, his wife Bonnie Jean, and a few family members who sat in on the meeting. "It's gonna be tough enough without the usual bunch of groupies. Your gang is going to have to set an example every step along the way—not only during the festival, but also in the course of our preparations. It's not going to be glamorous. If you have any designs about hanging around the stage or making the scene with the production staff, well, stay here."

They discussed the Hog Farm's taking over the administration of the festival campgrounds, which Goldstein wanted to relinquish so that he might devote more time to looking for water. He believed that their years of experience living under the stars and knowing how to set up and maintain makeshift living quarters could very well be the cornerstone for cultivating campgrounds. Romney insisted that their role be more meaningful than building trails and chopping wood. Once that was out of the way, they didn't want to sit around on their haunches for six weeks until they were paid.

"How about the free kitchen you hit us with in New York? Was that on the level?"

"Sure. In fact, it's already been worked into the security and provision plan. All we'll need from your people is a budget—what you think the food and utensils for cooking are going to cost us."

"We're gonna have to get your approval on everything we do?"

"No. Look, you're making this tougher than it's gotta be. You've only got to give me a rough estimate of what you'll need so I can free the bread. Once I get the okay on the overall budget, one of your people is going to have to take responsibility for purchasing all the supplies. We wouldn't know our ass from a hole in the ground as far as that stuffs concerned, and, frankly, we don't have the time."

As for the staff, Stanley asked they gather a crew of eighty-five of their people to make the trip. Since only fifteen Hog Farmers actually lived together, Romney and Bonnie Jean agreed to tap the circle of existing communes in the New Mexico area. They had already established good relationships with the Juke Savages and the Buffalo Commune, and with a little persuasion, they assured Goldstein that they could complete the conscription in time.

"We need a dozen of your strongest men right away," Goldstein said. There was still a lot of heavy labor to be done. "If you can send them east in the Road Hog [the Hog Farm's bus], we'll see they're handsomely paid for their services."

"How about the rest of the people we get together? How do you expect us to get them to New York without wheels?"

"By plane. Look, we weren't kidding about sending a plane for you. We've already made some tentative arrangements with American Airlines to charter one of their smaller jets to bring you out." He opened his briefcase and showed them pieces of correspondence with American's charter division. They were visibly impressed by Goldstein's handiwork. "As soon as you can let me know when the staffing arrangements have been completed, I'll arrange for a plane to pick you up in Albequerque."

It was the "most idiotic scheme" the Hog Farm had ever heard of, but somehow Romney trusted Goldstein enough to pledge their total support. Bonnie Jean was appointed Goldstein's liaison. She would walk two miles to the closest phone each afternoon at two o'clock and call him, using one of several bogus credit cards the Hog Farm had picked up along the way, to fill him in on her progress.

The only thing left for them to discuss before the business could be adjourned was compensation. Stanley had promised them that, in addition to picking up all of their expenses, Woodstock Ventures was prepared to pay them a decent wage for their time spent on festival business. Romney, however, insisted on a lump-sum minimum guarantee in the area of twenty thousand dollars. Their bus was in bad shape, he said, and they'd have to buy another one soon; it would take practically as much as twenty grand to get one in decent condition. Anyhow, as long as a lot of money was going to be made by the promoters, he felt no remorse about asking for so much. No one was particularly choked up about making some twenty-year-old hippie from Miami a millionaire. Goldstein thought that twenty thousand dollars was too high, and said so. They could have what was left of the food and all the heavy cooking utensils, but they'd have to lower their fee considerably for him to make such a deal. After an hour of honest bartering, it was agreed that the Hog Farm, in return for being the Woodstock festival's special task force, would receive one-way transportation by chartered jet to New York, food and lodging for as long as they were employed by Woodstock Ventures, an hourly wage for the men who worked in the field, all edible leftovers, all cookware, and fifteen thousand dollars in cash. They had Goldstein over a barrel, but he knew the festival desperately needed their assistance and therefore accepted the terms. If they actually accomplished as much as he thought they would, fifteen thousand dollars would be a bargain.

Jim Grant was not even remotely as satisfied as Goldstein had been. Grant's evaluation of the trip, sent to Wes Pomeroy in a letter dated June 23, 1969, was predicated on a previous personal respect for the Hog Farm's orderliness that had come undone by this visit to their camp. He had devoted much of his time in Aspen Meadows to making an inspection of the site in relation to the extent of the commune's management of it. According to the New Mexico bureaucrat's impression, "the entire affair appeared to be completely without organization or management." He was particularly repulsed by the seemingly nonexistent hygienic conditions. "The only sanitation facilities observed," Grant reported, "consisted of a garbage disposal pit being dug some ten feet from the well and the cooking area. . . . We arrived at the campground during the dinner hour and found different groups preparing their dinners over open fires under what seemed to be quite unsanitary conditions."

Pomeroy was not really that interested in the Hog Farm's health habits; Lawrence and Goldstein were capable of handling sanitation on their own. He was, however, expressly dismayed over Grant's evaluation of their muddled organization. "There were no means for crowd control in the event it became necessary," Grant continued. "There was no attempt to provide information services. There was no traffic direction or control. There was a certain amount of mammarial exposure [which, according to Goldstein's account, was a gross understatement: "I never saw so many bare tits flaunted so casually before."]. It may be that when these people do their 'thing' for themselves," he concluded, "the circumstances are completely different than when they stage a production strictly for profit."

Pomeroy was now forced to reexamine his security arrangement and, perhaps, restructure it to exclude much of the Hog Farm's predominance. After an intense study of his working plan, during which time he consulted frequently with Goldstein, Lawrence, and Ganoung about their corresponding divisions, Pomeroy settled on relying on his basic working plan, however padding the Hog Farm's participation in it with the services of experienced professionals.

Pomeroy's first alteration had to do with maintaining channels of communication between Security Command and all other areas on and around the site throughout the three-day event. Originally, some method of interaction utilizing members of the Hog Farm as messengers was to be worked out, but Pomeroy could no longer count on their soundness to carry it off. Don Ganoung had done some preliminary scouting around the county and stumbled upon a group of ham radio operators whom he recommended to the head of security. The Tri-County Citizens Band Radio Club, a seventy-five-member organization, was interested in hearing what Pomeroy would offer them, and Ganoung set up a meeting between the two parties at the group's headquarters in Middletown on June 28.

Eleven of the club's members showed up for the meeting, all of whom voiced considerable interest in participating in the Aquarian Exposition. The festival, as they saw it, presented them with a real challenge and, as Tri-Co's president, Arnold Puff, confided to several associates who were radio equipment dealers, "I think we can sell these guys a few walkie-talkies in the process."

Their function, as Pomeroy described it, would be manifold as the weekend progressed. At this time, he and his staff had outlined several responsibilities that had materialized from hours of discussions and included manning posts inside the festival area, reporting to a Command Central any and all difficulties on the site, handling communications with the bus dispatcher in charge of routing transportation between the parking lots and the gates, dispatching buses when necessary, patroling the perimeter of the site and calling for assistance when and if they found spectators camping on lawn owned by residents. Tri-Co would, in his estimation, be the sole force that connected security to all outlying areas of the festival and was highly regarded in his formula for success.

As Pomeroy prepared to leave so the men could resume their normal business meeting. Arnold Puff raised a possible conflict of interest that might prohibit his men from taking part in the festival security plans. The club, it seemed, had scheduled a jamboree for the same weekend as Woodstock. Its purpose was to raise financing for a much-needed clubhouse and could not, at this point, very well be put off. He expressed a desire, and, of course, he spoke on behalf of the entire membership, for Woodstock Ventures to make it worthwhile for Tri-Co to cancel their event so they could fulfill an obligation to the festival instead.

"How much do you expect to clear from this jamboree?" Pomeroy asked suspiciously. If experience was any indication of what was about to happen, they were going to hit him with an astronomical figure with which he would have to comply.

"All told, about two hundred dollars," the president replied.

Pomeroy tried not to disclose his utter relief, but had to laugh. "Oh, I think we could see our way clear to cover you for that. If your members vote to support our function, we'll see you receive a comparable amount."

Nothing more had to be said. Pomeroy grabbed his sport coat and headed for the front door before anyone had a chance to interpret his laugh as a lease on life. He headed straight for his hotel room where, for the next few days, he revised the pile of false starts that had been made of the security budget. He itemized the costs he thought they'd incur with Tri-Co's field stint, tacked on a round figure to include John Fabbri and Joe Kimble's fees and computed his own expenses on the basis of an estimate taken over the past few weeks since he moved to Wallkill. When he finished, the security budget, so far, was a three-page balance sheet with an accurate accounting of his divisional costs. The only element lacking was security.

In 1969, the New York City Police Department was still viewed as an exceptional organization of courageous men dedicated to preserving and defending the law in a greatly troubled city. The hippies, of course, looked upon them as a savage bunch of rednecks with a license to harass them, but for the most part the unit of 28,000 officers was reviewed quite warmly by the average Joe. It was said that there was no more honorable identification card in all New York City than the glint of a silver-plated shield with the forceful letters NYPD embossed across the top. This was before the commission headed by Wall Street lawyer Whitman Knapp moved in in 1971 to weed out a widespread virus of corruption that had been infecting the force for longer than anyone cared to remember. And Woodstock Ventures wanted that uplifting group of men on their side of the turnstiles—even if it meant allying themselves with their cultural foes. Some things, as Michael Lang knew well, could not be avoided if the festival was to succeed.

Wes Pomeroy was also depending on their assistance to supplement his principle of self-regulation. He had initially spoken to Chief Inspector George P. McManus, who sat at the helm of the city's patrolmen, about recruiting off-duty security personnel from within the department. For all his efforts, though, Pomeroy had never been able to extract a clear-cut statement of policy from McManus and, thus, turned that responsibility over to John Fabbri, hoping for better results. Fabbri and McManus knew each other from various police conferences attended over the years and had established a respect for one another's methods of law enforcement. When Fabbri arrived in Wallkill the last week in June, he placed a call to McManus and, in one conversation, managed to elicit a promise of cooperation from the department. McManus suggested that they notify the captains of the city's individual precincts about the festival, have them put some kind of circular spelling out the assignment on their bulletin boards and refer them to his office for approval.

Pomeroy, Ganoung, and Fabbri spent several hours discussing and drawing up the announcement calling for extracurricular police assistance that would be posted in every Manhattan station house the first week in July. Originally, they had gone in the direction of a clever ad designed to catch the eye; that was soon abandoned as sounding too much like a television commercial for a new detergent. Pomeroy wanted something more reserved and less polished, something that would enable him to put forth the job description and still have built-in devices that would discourage cops not suited for the position. After much deliberation and several revisions, they settled on the straightforward approach:

> The Woodstock Music and Art Fair seeks to employ many New York City patrolmen who will be available from August 14 to August 17 inclusive (preferably on vacation), to act as guides, ushers, and monitors during this weekend festival.
> Salary—$50 per eight-hour day. Overtime at $6.25 per hour.
> Food and lodgings will be provided at resort facilities. Transportation and clothing furnished. No law enforcement duties.

Interested parties were directed to pick up an application from Woodstock Ventures at the downtown production office, or to see their duly appointed representative in the precinct.

The applicants, as everyone connected with the festival knew, were going to have to be carefully screened. If, during an interview, a patrolman gave any indication of a personal prejudice toward hippies or the desire to use force in any manner whatsoever, he would be swiftly eliminated. A cop would also be judged on his facial expressions; if he habitually snarled when he talked, if he gave the slightest impression that he had something to prove or displayed a *macho* attitude, his application would be dropped into the dead-letter file. Even the secretary at the desk who accepted the applications was brought into the screening process. She noted how the cops came dressed to the production office, how they reacted to seeing incense burning in the ashtrays and psychedelic posters on the walls, the manner in which they confronted the attractive, braless secretaries. These telling traits, as Pomeroy had rightly calculated, were the first step in sifting out strict enforcers, hippie haters, and those with an obvious chip on their shoulder. There would be similar levels of questioning at a later date until the stack of applicants dwindled to between 300 and 350 men. Those who made the cut would probably be hired and eventually become members of the Peace Service Corps.

Before he could begin step two of security screening—a process that included hours of intensive psychological grilling of the candidates—Pomeroy had to recruit his own command force from among the available experts in the field. "A tight cell" was how he liked to refer to this unit, with the equivalent ranks of "sergeants" and "captains" who would report to him at the festival and would interview and ultimately select all personnel. Ganoung, Fabbri, and Joe Kimble were automatically placed in the cell and made commanders, the highest grade. Ganoung and Fabbri already knew the staff and procedures (and had developed relationships with many of the local residents), and Kimble would arrive in time for an intensive orientation that Pomeroy himself would conduct. The way he laid it out on the topographical map, he needed someone to direct "inner security" and someone to direct "outer security," mobilizing the nonuniformed force in each of those areas. The third commander would be assigned a functional duty, such as "transportation/ parking." Pomeroy considered the last to be the most critical responsibility because of "the almost impossibly inadequate road access to the site." Whoever assumed that role could not allow the roads to become bottled up with traffic; otherwise, they'd have a certified disaster on their hands.

Pomeroy's first choice to join the expanded security force was his old friend Jewell Ross, a retired Berkeley Police Department captain with whom he had worked on numerous occasions. Pomeroy wanted Ross for his wisdom and intelligence, which the old man expertly applied to his methods of officiating. An even-tempered Irishman with a thick, tuneful brogue, Ross had directed fourteen conferences on civil disorder for the Department of Justice in 1968, all of which emphasized the human element involved and urged policemen to respond to distress with compassion. This was the type of educated philosophy that Pomeroy wanted carried over to his own "Indians" (as he called the off-duty cops) in their dealings with the young crowd. Ross consented to join the staff. He'd arrive a few days before the festival and leave the moment it was over. For a consultant's fee of $150 a day plus expenses and accommodations, he became the newest and most experienced of the cell.

Pomeroy wanted the third position filled from within the NYPD to afford him easy access to McManus and Police Commissioner Howard Leary. A high-placed New York City cop's presence would also exercise a certain amount of influence over the "Indians" insofar as, once they returned to their ordinary jobs in the city, they would be required to salute and answer to him. Someone recommended he hire Deputy Inspector Joe Fink whose turf was Greenwich Village and who frequented hippie hangouts there such as the Fillmore, the Electric Circus, and the Cafe Au Go Go. It was not until much later, after Fink joined the cell, that several of the festival staff members admitted having dealt with Fink in unofficial rendezvous. Those who had been associated with the East Village music scene claimed Joe Fink was the police official who somehow ensured that busts would not be made in their establishments. A popular story was that Circus owner Jerry Brandt made him wear a pig mask when he entered the club. Pomeroy, however, was unaware of Fink's alleged participation in these matters and welcomed him aboard. Fink was to be compensated for his services at the rate of $12.50 an hour (a considerable supplement to his NYPD salary) and the fiat fee of $100 a day while on duty at the festival site. Pomeroy suggested that Fink hire himself an assistant for the three-day ordeal and he, in turn, commissioned Ralph Cohen, captain of Manhattan's ninetieth precinct, for that position.

It had taken Pomeroy almost a full two months to finally select the upper echelon of his security pyramid, all men he felt had the emotional flexibility to hold down the fort and whom he trusted to respond to the hippies' whirlwind animus with equally disarming finesse. Their real test of equanimity would come in the week immediately preceding the show when a force more potentially destructive than anything the hippies presented to them threatened the festival's peaceful existence. Their reaction to that danger would be viewed with varying opinion; some would accuse them of falling down on the job while others would see their behavior as the only rational way out. But for now, the top law enforcement minds in the country were pondering the festival's fate, and Pomeroy's cell seemed, for the most part, positively charged.

Slowly but surely, a definitive security plan came more clearly into focus. Pomeroy, who, in the past, had been reluctant to prepare an unyielding departmental budget for Lang's approval, now set to it with a prompt, methodical willingness. The greater perspective afforded by the days spent on the site and in observation of the Wallkill community provided him with new enlightenment on which to base his calculations. Security now meant not only protecting the local residents from the hippies but had expanded to include protecting the hippies from the irate townsfolk. Extra men would have to be put on shifts to keep an eye on Cliff Reynolds and his sympathizers to make sure they did not attempt to sabotage the festival's tranquility.

The first draft of the security budget called for only seventy-five officers of "patrolman" rank (sixty-four men and six women) to report for four days' work at $75 per day and an additional stipend of $20 a day for expenses. Ten first-grade supervisors, three shift supervisors, an assistant chief (Fabbri), and an attorney made up the rest of the team with graduated increments in pay based upon rank and tenures beginning as much as two weeks before the weekend. This estimation was, of course, drastically conservative and, when examined a few days later, abandoned.

Pomeroy went back to his room and drew up a revised budget, a headier document which reflected a more realistic assessment of what the situation called for. This time, the itemization of manpower included 215 "monitors" (formerly "patrolmen") at a lower base rate of $50 a day with a per diem of $17.50 for expenses. The number of supervisors was, likewise, bolstered to 25 and the number of command officers to 6, bringing the combined payroll of 246 Peace Service Corps employees to a wolloping $72,100. The price of hiring the four consultants alone (Pomeroy, Ganoung, Fabbri, and Kimble) added roughly another $15,000 to the package. Simple arithmetic at this stage in the budget's preparation made security appear overblown and excessive. Still, Pomeroy increased the total by $69,000 more before everything necessary was accounted for. That figure accounted for additional personnel (three secretaries, forty radio operators, six radio dispatchers, five social workers, a social worker supervisor, three doctors, five nurses, four firemen, two fire captains, a personnel coordinator, and six security advisers starting on July 15), and related equipment (two rented ambulences, a rented helicopter, a tow truck, radios, several security vehicles, bullhorns with sirens, barricades, telephones, medical equipment, fire extinguishers, plastic handcuffs, plastic whistles, flashlights, rented trailers and furniture for the trailers). Social security, workmen's compensation and insurance premiums brought the final figure to $156,156, approximately one third of the initial financing figure for the entire festival submitted to Roberts and Rosenman by their hip partners back on February 6.

Money did not matter much anymore to the technical crew. It had no real value; like Monopoly money it was acquired from an amiable banker and mindlessly spent. "Only the best" became the crew's slogan. Why buy Baltic Avenue when Park Place could be had with almost as little effort? Why not roll out the red carpet and pass "Go" with revolving-door regularity? The cost of what it was taking to get the Woodstock festival into production had moved far beyond reality. As Ticia told a friend over the phone, "We're involved in a true cosmic experience, man. This show belongs to the people." And when Wes Pomeroy placed his security bill under Lang's nose, it was approved without so much as a simple question. It was, after all, only money.

— **3** —

Those who awoke early on the morning of July 2 were treated to a satellite-relayed broadcast from Great Britain. Queen Elizabeth bestowed the crown of the Prince of Wales on her son Charles, thus designating him her heir apparent. Michael Lang slept through the ceremony. He awoke at 10:30 A.M. to a phone call from Ticia Bernuth begging him to "get his ass into the office."

He was worried about the apparent turn of events in upstate New York. Mel Lawrence had called him to coordinate Michael's arrival in time for the town meeting and to fill him in on the latest news, neither of which bespoke propitious solutions.

The *Times Herald Record,* a last bastion of support, had run an article that morning that aired a wide range of opinions from county residents and Mel read it to him with reluctance. Aside from a few meek voices that accused the town board of railroading the promoters, angry residents were lining up to get a clear shot at the hippies.

Michael winced on the other end of the line. From the sound of things, they could expect more of the same when the town board convened its special session later that evening. Mel couldn't have agreed with him more. What should have been a moderate debate on the ordinance, he contended, was destined to be a three-ring spectacle.

He was pleasantly surprised, then, when only seventy-five Wallkillians filed into the paneled assembly hall to hear both sides of the argument present their case. The room was filled with an unmistakable air of apprehension as the executive staff of Woodstock Ventures arrived and took their seats together, in the first row of the spectators' gallery. Almost immediately thereafter, the elegant double doors to the hall parted and Jack Schlosser strolled to the podium, followed by Councilmen Henry Itzla, Louis Ingrassia, and Samuel Mitchell, all wearing dark suits and white shirts.

After the town clerk dispensed with the minutes of the last meeting, Schlosser spent half an hour reading the legal document concerning the right of assembly (which included a few changes the board had decided to insert).

Sam Eager appeared poised with his clients, often jotting down notes on a yellow legal pad balanced on his briefcase. Michael Lang sat at his elbow wearing a neatly pressed sport shirt in place of his traditional leather vest and beads. Mel Lawrence was flanked by Lang and Don Ganoung, and Stanley Goldstein brought up the phalanx of festival dignitaries. Only Wes Pomeroy was absent, working on a traffic plan with a few men from the department of transportation. The festival representatives appeared in good spirits despite the imminence of reprisal, and joked quietly with one another, while they waited for Schlosser to finish with the formalities.

The hour approached nine o'clock when Sam Eager finally took the floor. He was a discreet practitioner of the law and not many of those gathered in the town hall assembly room knew he represented Woodstock Ventures. Everyone quieted down in order to hear the advice from this favorite son.

Eager's poker face concealed his intimate line of attack. "Most of you here tonight know who I am. I'm an attorney, I'm over thirty"—the crowd laughed easily—"and I'm the father of four. Unfortunately or not so unfortunately, depending upon how one looks at it, my family's convinced that I'm a conservative Republican." He shook his head in wonderment and attracted a heartier laugh. The tenseness in the room relaxed. Eager's droll sense of humor had a disarming effect on the crowd, and he began to build his defense on their bonhomie. "I'm real pleased and proud of the way everyone's conducted themselves at this meeting. And I think it's only fair that you know I'm representing Woodstock Ventures."

Gasps of disbelief conveyed the crowd's resentment. Eager was forced to raise his voice over their anger to be heard. "I'm also your neighbor and, as such, I'm afraid that, with this ordinance, the Town of Wallkill may be about to commit a wrong." Schlosser furiously pounded his gavel, and the crowd settled down a bit. "You know, in one way or another, we all invited Woodstock Ventures to come to Wallkill. On April 14, the zoning board of appeals told Woodstock Ventures what they planned to do was legal and they needed no permit. We owe something to the principals of this young corporation who have given their personal funds, totaling over $450,000, to the entertainers who have signed contracts with them, and to the executive staff who have based their professional lives on what happens to the festival. This proposed ordinance—which does not regulate the fairgrounds and, at the present time, can only regulate the festival—is prohibitive and, in parts, cannot be complied with."

The town attorney, Joseph Owen, was moved to defend the board's platform and lectured the festival representatives on proper legislative conduct. "There is no misrepresentation by any [governmental] body of this town. If there is misrepresentation, it is by Woodstock Ventures. If you search the records, you will find that what was represented at the April meeting [of the zoning board of appeals] and what is represented here today is not the same."

The promoters had, in fact, attempted to examine the transcripts of that meeting, which had supposedly been filed by the town clerk; however, the minutes had curiously disappeared from the record books. As far as the register showed, that meeting never took place.

"And let me make it clear," Schlosser added, "that this ordinance would apply for any gathering of over five thousand people even if President Nixon wished to come and hold something in an area where facilities were not available."

Owen nodded his agreement. "The fairgrounds is equipped for large assemblies. They have proper facilities for sanitation, parking, and water. It would be desirable for President Nixon to go to the fairgrounds."

Mel Lawrence, who had jumped to his feet, thought he knew where else it would be desirable for President Nixon to go, but refrained from making a comment.

"I'd give President Nixon a lot more credit for choosing the fairgrounds than an open field," Schlosser boomed.

"How about leaving Nixon outta this thing?" Lawrence said. "I've got enough of a headache without having to hear his name mentioned. I've also had a look at your fairgrounds and I'll tell you this: it's nothing to write home about. We're providing better services than they are, and you know it. Our intentions are good. If you'd give us the time of day, you'd see that we're only trying to make our affair a safer one."

"In other words," Schlosser asked, "you're saying that you intend to comply with our requirements?"

"Yeah—I'm willing to say that."

Schlosser chuckled and shook his head.

The meeting stretched on for another hour during which Jules Minker launched a reprehensible attack against the promoters.

As other residents addressed the board, patience wore down considerably until Schlosser decided to put an end to the proceedings. "Now, before we adjourn for the evening," he broke in, "there are a few pieces of information we have to get out of the way. First of all, I still think you boys ought to consider moving to the Orange County Fairgrounds. We'll even help you out and provide you with a justice of the peace at no extra cost.

"As far as the proposed law is concerned, this board is prepared to hold a special session immediately after this hearing tonight to decide whether or not it becomes a law. If it does, and if Woodstock Ventures so wishes, they can make application to this council for a permit, another public hearing will be held after we've had time to examine their application, and a determination will be made on the basis of all best interests of the people of the Town of Wallkill. If there are no further questions. . . ."

He looked around the room as a few hands flew up. Several people took up another twenty minutes congratulating the town board and Woodstock Ventures for their cooperation. After a reasonable number of repetitions, Schlosser pounded his gavel and called the public meeting to a close. It was 10:15 P.M.

It took an additional half hour before the meeting hall was cleared of spectators. A few residents stopped by the podium to pump Jack Schlosser's hand and praise him on a job well done. The supervisor responded warmly to the well-wishers, most of whom he knew by their first names. This was the Town of Wallkill's biggest night, and he was their man of the hour. Civic pride had never loomed so brightly.

The methodical, dispassionate account of the special session of the town board as taken down by the town clerk in shorthand and later inserted into the minutes of the regular meeting is, perhaps, the most accurate description available of the wearied session:

Mr. Schlosser opened the meeting. A lengthy discussion ensued concerning various aspects of the proposed Local Law #1 of 1969 Regulating the Assembly of Persons in Public Places.

Mr. (Louis) Ingrassia moved, seconded by Mr. (Samuel) Mitchell, for adoption of the amended proposed Local Law #1 of 1969, Local Law Regulating Assembly of Persons in the Town of Wallkill, Orange County, New York, as read with the added exceptions and corrections of Section 3.2, paragraph h. will read: All garbage, trash, rubbish or other refuse shall be stored until removed at an unobtrusive area of the premises. . . . The rest of that paragraph remains the same except the words between the hours of 11:00 P.M. and 7:00 A.M. instead of the words 9:00 P.M. and 7:00 A.M.

The other exception and correction is with reference to Section 3.4, paragraph c will read: No permit shall be issued unless the applicant shall deposit with the Town Clerk cash or good surety company bond, approved by the Town Clerk, in the minimum sum of $100,000.00, and conditioned that no damage will be done to any public or private property. . . . The rest of that paragraph remains the same.

A roll call vote on the proposed Local Law #1 was as follows:

Supervisor Scholosser	Voting Aye
Councilman Mitchell	Voting Aye
Councilman Itzla	Voting Aye
Councilman Thompson	Voting Absent
Councilman Ingrassia	Voting Aye

The Supervisor declared the Local Law adopted.

Mr. Schlosser moved, seconded by Mr. Itzla, that the meeting be adjourned. The meeting was adjourned at 11:30 P.M.

— 4 —

The next morning, news of the town board's decision to adopt Local Law #1 skipped across Orange County like a brushfire. Radio stations repeated the lead story every twenty minutes.

The inflated banner that rode across the July 3 *Times Herald Record* was a doleful assessment of the facts. It proclaimed: WALLKILL VOTES TO CURB AQUARIAN FESTIVAL, and, indeed, most residents of the peaceful little town heaved a sigh of relief upon reading the paper's terse account of the public hearing. From the tone of things, it was highly improbable that the promoters would get a permit from the town board for this, or any other, rock music pageant. At last, they could resume their uncomplicated lives out from under the threat of a hippie invasion.

Of all the parties influenced by the legislation, the festival staff was probably least affected. The young workers were so full of quixotic fortitude that they thought they could overcome any obstacle in their path. "It's nothing to get uptight about," crew chiefs told their teams, "we'll work it out." And no one doubted that would be so. The security, the insurance, the sanitation, the water, the permit—somehow it would all materialize at the last second, and the show would go down as planned. "I see my light come shining," they sang in the field, "from the west unto the east. Any day now, any day now, I shall be released."

The executive staff was more pragmatic. They assured themselves of success on the basis of one significant fact: the law was on their side. On April 14, the zoning board of appeals had sanctioned their enterprise, and should they ever be forced to go to arbitration over it, they were convinced the court would uphold that decision. It was as simple as that. If that, however, was not enough ammunition, they had another barrel loaded and ready to be fired. Social prejudice had been recently thrust into the public eye and viewed as one of the most heinous of iniquities that could be inflicted upon an American citizen. If the town board so chose to test opinion, they were prepared to scream "discrimination" across the pages of every publication and on every television network from Wallkill to Waikiki to preserve the festival.

"Just keep on working as if nothing has happened," Michael Lang directed his generals. "We're gonna fight this thing to the end, and we're gonna win." He had, in fact, discussed that line of action with two of his partners and they concurred with him. John Roberts and Joel Rosenman, like Michael, believed that, come August 15, the Woodstock Music and Art Fair would announce its first act from a stage on Mills Heights.

Where they differed, however, was on their perception of a realistic approach to the situation at hand. Roberts saw the new law as a serious, although not fatal, problem. It was just another problem in line for his and Joel's attention. His initial reaction was anger. He was particularly disturbed over the influence of people like Cliff Reynolds and the other concerned citizens inasmuch as they were decidedly interfering with his constitutional rights as a competitive businessman. The ordinance, he reasoned, was discriminatory and aimed specifically at Woodstock Ventures. They had two means by which to fight Local Law #1 and prevail: (1) to challenge it through the court system, in which case he was certain they would win; and (2) to complain loudly enough so that the dilemma might be resolved fairly and quickly. Either method was fine by him, as long as it produced a settlement in their favor.

Rosenman was more skeptical. As an attorney, he had already seen how flexible the law could be when it came down to passing final judgment. In this case, he felt "there was a series of extralegal maneuvers with legal clothes on" going on about them and bringing considerable weight to bear on the outcome of their endeavor. By virtue of the money already invested in the project and the verbal commitments issued in front of witnesses, he thought the net result would produce an understanding between Woodstock Ventures and the Town of Wallkill enabling them to proceed as scheduled. Concessions would have to be made; they'd undoubtedly have to come up with a better security plan and post a substantial bond for damages, but when the smoke cleared, they would still hold the festival in the Town of Wallkill.

A secretary in the field office had been instructed to canvass a sampling of the larger metropolitan dailies for coverage of the town board meeting. The appearance of negative publicity might discourage the advance sale of tickets (which, until July 2, had been overwhelming). In order to head off any misleading information, it was imperative they check out all related news stories as they appeared. Wartoke was to issue a public statement later that afternoon; however, by the time it was in print, it might conceivably be too late.

By noon the next day, most of the papers had been examined and had turned up nothing. Only the *New York Times* remained. The front section was chock-full of items on the coronation of Prince Charles and not a word on Woodstock. Then, as the secretary worked her way through the theatre pages, her attention was drawn to a familiar picture at the top of the page.

"Aw, shit," she said, folding the paper commuter-style to get a better look.

A member of the art crew was standing nearby, working on a blueprint of the staging area. He had heard the secretary's reaction and walked over to her desk. "Bad, huh?"

"Worse. Brian Jones is dead."

"What! That's impossible!"

But, in fact, it wasn't. A small item sandwiched in between a human interest story on Lou Brock and the Broadway theatre directory related how the Rolling Stones' twenty-six-year-old rhythm guitarist had been fished unconscious out of his swimming pool and had died later that night. The coroner's report ruled that Jones died as a result of "drowning by immersion in fresh water associated with severe liver dysfunction caused by fatty degeneration and ingestion of alcohol and drugs." Further studies had turned up traces of pep pills, sleeping tablets, and alcohol in his bloodstream.

"What a waste. He was my favorite Stone, too. I just can't believe it," she said, tossing the rest of the newspaper onto the pile at her feet.

The artist compassionately rubbed her shoulder and eased himself up onto the corner of the wooden desk. "Everything's coming down on us all at once. I'm not feelin' real good about our future here," he said.

"It's probably just a coincidence."

He smiled and kissed her on the forehead. "Or maybe it's a sign of the times."

Preparations for the Woodstock Music and Art Fair continued without interruption. If the town board's new law was simply a stumbling block, then the outcome depended heavily upon their maintaining forward progress at all times. Money continued to be "no object."

Jim Mitchell, the purchasing agent, had been given the go-ahead on the proposed advertising and printing job that he had submitted to Lang for approval. A few weeks before, Lang and several of his cohorts in the downtown office had decided on utilizing two posters to promote the festival. One, depicting a naked young woman pouring water from a jug hoisted upon her shoulder (the servile Aquarian), was the official souvenir poster. Patterned after the garish, psychedelic posters that announced the Fillmore West's concert schedules, the limpid figure was ensconced in a nervous maze of traditional red and blue curliques and dazzling flowers. Across the bottom was printed: "An Aquarian Exposition, Wallkill, New York, August 15-16-17." Nowhere did it say who would be appearing there, nor did it inform potential customers where they could purchase tickets. This poster was the chaser— the "artistic" follow-up to all the hoopla about the grandest festival of all time, the poster that could be taken home and framed without the legend scrawled across the front. Mitchell had ordered ten thousand of them to be printed, along with a smaller postcard version of which twenty thousand would be made.

To hawk tickets, Lang had commissioned an artist named Arnold Skolnick to do artwork for a publicity poster that listed the performers, described events at length, in terms of an art show, crafts bazaar, campground, and gastronomical delight, and informed people where they could purchase tickets. Skolnick's concept was to incorporate the dove of peace into a design that would also convey the musical ingredient of the festival. Together, its simplicity served to offset all the information that had to be plugged into the surrounding space and to give it a gentle push from behind the garble of print. Skolnick came up with just the right blend. His original sketch of an expressionless dove perched on the neck of a guitar had the right feel to it and was adopted as the logo for all future Woodstock festival literature. The dove, whose only discernible feature was a red beak and a tenuous, yellow claw, was printed in white. It was well contrasted against the red matte background and still retained some of the psychedelic texture of the genre. The guitar was bright shades of blue and emerald green, and a pale yellow hand reached around the neck of the instrument to form a chord over the stunning list of performers. It was a memorable design worthy of its distinction.

Jim Mitchell ordered 35,000 copies of the Skolnick poster, which was used as a garnish for store windows and bulletin boards in schools around the area. Additionally, the posters were to be slapped on the wooden fences that surrounded every construction site in New York City and on lamp posts and street signs. Wherever one looked (if all went according to plan), one would be greeted by the dove and guitar until the logo became synonymous with the event. Of course, that kind of identification would cost money. Appropriately, when Mitchell submitted the bill for the posters, along with the printing of 100,000 brochures and envelopes, it totaled $8,917.

The ever garrulous John Morris, in between duties of executing the performers' contract riders and arranging for their lodging, took it upon himself to troubleshoot various arrangements that were underway in other departments.

"We have the opportunity through this festival to do a great deal of good," Morris said in a report to Lang commenting on festival publicity, "as well as put on a good show and make money. That is through the charity record." Several weeks before the public hearing on Local Law #1, Morris had brought up the idea of negotiating a Woodstock record deal and then turning the proceeds over to a charity. At the time, a few staff members in the production office expressed their interest in hearing more about it and sent Morris on his way with a sniggering pat on the back. Little did they know he would carry the idea to such extremes.

Morris met with the people at UNICEF to determine their interest in participating with Woodstock Ventures in such a project. UNICEF, he reasoned, was a safe charity as far as the counterculture was concerned inasmuch as the contributions went to children and not to support big business. They'd also provide the festival with a touch of institutionalized class— something of which he thought they were in dire need considering their frosty reception in Wallkill. As he had suspected all along, his proposal was received cordially by the United Nations organization, and he soon went flying off to see Jac Holzman, the president of Elektra Records, to begin his drive for record industry support.

Holzman was even more gracious than the people at UNICEF had been. He agreed to provide them with Elektra's record-processing plant, which would press the festival albums at cost. He also volunteered to distribute the album gratis, but advised Morris to call Clive Davis, who presided over the Columbia Records Group, to see if CBS was interested in distributing it.

That way, he said, more than one record company would be involved, so as not to alienate the rest of the industry. Considering the excessive number of Columbia artists on the bill, it would accelerate Morris's obtaining permission to record their sets.

Morris's negotiations for the charity recording never got much farther than that. In order for him to authorize anything concrete regarding a record deal, Lang not only had to be consulted but be in agreement with the terms. One can only imagine Michael Lang's reaction to Morris's proposal, but certainly, it must have been one of absolute horror. Here, Lang had spent months working toward a future of infinite wealth, and now Morris proposed to donate perhaps the largest chunk of his nest egg to the United Nations! That was about as half-assed a plan as he had ever heard in his life and he discounted it without another word. He simply ignored it, pretended that Morris had never mentioned such a curse, and instructed Artie Kornfeld to step up negotiations for their own lucrative, profit-sharing deal. He also directed Morris to secure permission from the artists' managers for record and film rights to their Woodstock performance. If necessary, he was to offer them an additional fifty percent of their booking fee for the record and another fifty percent of that for motion picture rights. It was essential that they be able to represent to a movie or record company that the performers were under contract to them, otherwise they had no package.

Undaunted by the rebuke, Morris renewed his labored analysis of the production, striking out at the festival's deceptive appellation. "What concretely is being done to turn people physically headed for Woodstock to Wallkill?" he wanted to know. No one had given that likelihood much thought. Was it even necessary, what with all the publicity their efforts were receiving in Wallkill? Morris, in fact, had contested the use of the name *Woodstock* on their posters and brochures since he had joined the executive staff. "It's misleading," he argued, "not to mention dishonest. We're going to give the kids the impression that the festival is a tribute to the performers who live in Woodstock—*including* Bob Dylan—which just isn't so. Half the ticket holders are going to wind up there looking for our show, and they're gonna be pissed. We're going to be held responsible for making good on their tickets."

Again, Lang treated the objection as simply another display of John Morris's skittishness. All indications are that he dismissed it without further ado (however, a sign was finally erected in Woodstock to deter those people who had not figured it out for themselves). Morris persisted, though, in his effort to do away with the name *Woodstock* altogether until Michael was forced to confront him head-on about it. Lang advised him to drop the matter quietly before he was compelled to take more drastic measures that would tie John's hands. Morris had been nothing but trouble for him of late. A few nights before, John had researched the employment files, making a thorough study of Chip Monck's contract with Woodstock Ventures. Needless to say, he had discovered that Monck was not, as he had been assured, receiving a fee equal to his own. There was a $1,000 discrepancy in Chip's favor, and something had to be done to put them back on a matching pay scale; Morris's suggestion to Lang the next morning was that he be awarded a $1,000 boost in salary.

Michael was furious. For the first time during his tenure as a producer, he lost his temper. He warned Morris about snooping around in matters that did not concern him. He said that if John persisted in creating political situations within the office structure, he would be dismissed. Lang had been on the verge of firing Morris for some time. Lang was particularly irked by Morris's insistence on importing a council of American Indians from Santa Fe, New Mexico, to provide atmosphere for the festival. Not that he was opposed to the idea. On the contrary, he thought it was a wonderful suggestion and authorized Morris to give him more details about it. In this case, John had learned about the Institute of Indian Art from a writer for the *Village Voice*. *Time* had also run a story on the school, and on a trip to Los Angeles, he stopped off in Santa Fe to see for himself what all the excitement was about. He was completely fascinated by what he found: hundreds of paintings done by Indian students that were overlooked by the commercial art world. Without hesitating, he made a deal with the school's director to bring twenty-five Indian artists—mostly those who came from Shongopovi, Second Mesa, a thousand-year-old Hopi village, consisting of stone dwellings cut into the side of an eroded desert bluff—to Wallkill where they'd be given the opportunity to exhibit and sell their wares. The festival was already sending a plane to New Mexico to pick up members of the Hog Farm; he was certain they could arrange for a few additional passengers on the same flight. John organized the exhibit with an Apache named Billy Soza, and before long they had assembled the artists who most represented the spirit of American Indian art.

Back in New York, it seemed to Morris that everyone had a comment on one aspect or another of his plan. Where would the Indians be lodged? How were they to eat? Would they help out with grounds construction? Were they going to be paid a salary? Who was taking care of getting liability releases from their parents? Was it absolutely necessary to get involved with this when there were so many other important things yet to be done? Morris felt as if there were an organized conspiracy to squelch the ideas he proposed. "Our reward for diligence in financial areas has been rewarded with argumentation on each point," he complained in a memo to Lang, "and . . . it seems we must fight like hell to try to add an individual artistic effort by bringing an Indian crafts exhibit to the festival."

"Stop being such a crybaby," Michael admonished him. "Bring your Indians in with the Hog Farm, but for Christ's sake, John, be cool about it, will you."

Lang had more important business to transact. Time was running out for them to prepare and submit an application for a permit to the Wallkill Town Board. They had to come up with something that merited widespread acclaim to counteract the united front of opposition that was armed and preparing for legal war against them. Their wearied troops couldn't withstand another defeat. They had one discernible shot left: the permit had to be secured.

Lang was prepared to do battle on all sides. He and Don Ganoung arranged for a Boston rock group called Quill to play benefit performances at the state hospital in Middletown, the Catskill Reformatory in Ellenville, and the Mid-Hudson Rehabilitation Center in Beacon. Their hope was that the gesture would establish Woodstock Ventures as a civic-minded organization willing to make its contribution to the county's social service institutions. Moreover, the places ultimately chosen for Quill's concerts were selected on the basis of their unassailability. "Who in their right mind would come down on us for entertaining the inmates of a mental hospital?" Ganoung asked wryly. "This will be one event from which we emerge smelling like heroes." He must not have picked up on the scent, however, as he also arranged for the group to play weekend dances at the Middletown Teen Center and similar socials in neighboring Goshen and Monticello. The general consensus around the field office was that this was one act of kindness that could not be overextended. Quill would perform as often as the situation warranted.

While community relations were being fostered on the bandstand, the executive staff's attention turned to the areas of security and traffic, clearly the two dominant obstacles that separated the promoters from inheriting the much-coveted permit. Pomeroy contended it would be an uphill struggle for them from here on in, more a game of cat-and-mouse than one of forthright representation. There were certain facts that had to be kept in the background of their talks with town officials if they were to continue on in Wallkill. It was up to all of them, he said, to keep moving at all times, to become inaccessible if they had to, so that the board never was afforded enough of an opportunity to pick apart their proposals.

Pomeroy's badly shaken confidence in gaining the town's formal approval teetered on a growing disenchantment with their site. If indeed, their success hinged on convincing the town board of a trouble-free flow of traffic, their future in Wallkill was in serious difficulty. As far as he could determine, the roads around Mills Heights would most certainly be congested, if not completely choked off, by the number of cars they expected. He discussed this problem with Lang and Mel Lawrence, both of whom assured him that the festival's crew were doing everything possible to forge new roads in and out of the grounds. It would be taken care of by August, in plenty of time for the first arrivals. If, on the other hand, they could present the town board with a plausible method for vehicle control, one that looked better on paper than it actually worked, they could buy time to figure out a solution so that, come August 15, traffic would appear to be under a semblance of control. It was decided they would go with the latter plan of attack and pray that it would buy them a permit.

They determined that shuttle bus transportation would make a better first impression on the councilmen without arousing too much skepticism on their part. On Saturday morning, July 5, Ganoung and John Fabbri, Pomeroy's second-in-command, were dispatched to New York City where they met with transportation representatives from the All-State Bus Corporation, a private chartering company, and Murray Vidockler, president of Intermedia Sound, which the festival had retained for traffic coordination. (Vidockler was related to the principal owners of All-State Bus Corp.) Fabbri explained the festival's traffic predicament to them, utilizing a map of the site and its surrounding roadways to explain the restrictions. All-State's people examined the alternatives and told them it wouldn't be a problem to meet the transportation needs of the festival.

"We've already made plans to handle shuttle services from New York City to Wallkill for the three days of the show," they said. "It won't be difficult adapting what we've already planned to meet *your* needs."

All-State had arranged to have several pickup locations and terminals scattered throughout New York City. They had busily been advertising their service through community bulletins and in daily newspapers and were waiting for their tickets to be printed so that they could begin selling seats to the festival. At that point, all they had to do was to coordinate all their activities with a Woodstock representative so that everyone's customers could be serviced with the least amount of complications.

As far as shuttling people from parking lots to the site was concerned, All-State estimated that they could handle up to thirty thousand people an hour, depending, of course, on their evaluation of the physical layout. This calculation was based upon an allotment of an hour and a half prior to show time to board their passengers on the bus, travel to the gate, and allow everyone enough time to disembark comfortably before the buses returned to the parking lot. They also agreed to provide transportation for the security personnel between New York City and Wallkill, and between the site and housing areas. Woodstock need only assign a person to coordinate bus dispatching with the firm, and the rest would be worked out to their satisfaction.

Fabbri was pleased with All-State's response and notified Pomeroy of his intention to consolidate their efforts. As far as he could determine, it would help with traffic control and might very well appease the town board's concern.

Pomeroy had also set up a meeting for his two commanders that same afternoon with representatives from the New York City Police Department in an effort to mobilize the Peace Service Corps. Wes and Fabbri had discussed the arrangements to be gone over with Joe Fink and Ralph Cohen beforehand and had outlined the following objectives: (1) to urge Cohen to bring in an officer of the Patrolmen's Benevolent Association, the bargaining agent for police officers; and (2) to have Fink and Cohen come to Middletown immediately.

Chief Inspector McManus, who still refused formally to grant police help to the festival, told Pomeroy that if the request for patrolmen to work at Woodstock came to him both from someone within the department *and* from a member of the PBA, he would give his approval; it was a safeguard designed to absolve McManus of any future blame that might be pointed in his direction.

Fink assured Fabbri and Ganoung that he would have no problem obtaining proper clearance for the hiring of police personnel from the NYPD. He'd follow McManus's guidelines by coordinating his own departmental request with that of a colleague from the PBA. Cohen, meanwhile, would begin the preparations for the recruitment and selection of personnel to be transported upstate.

Fabbri agreed to provide the two officers with application forms for screening the men, a complete listing of what they would be required to bring with them by way of tools (map, flashlights, etc.), and information regarding the form in which salary would be paid and the type of tax deductions taken from their wages. They would handle the rest at the precinct level.

As far as Fink and Cohen's instant deployment to Wallkill was concerned, they would have to clear that with their immediate supervisors. That would be more difficult to arrange because they were high-level officers. However, they pledged to give it their best efforts. If all went well, they'd let them know if they could in a few days—when a Woodstock representative got back to them with the requested information.

It had all gone down smoothly, exactly as planned. The New York police were going to cooperate with a group of hip promoters staging a rock festival. It was unbelievable. Not only would the cops be on hand to insure the peace, but they would be incognito without intending to bust the kids. The promoters were also delighted that they could link their name with the NYPD. New York's Finest were on their side. How could the Town of Wallkill possibly balk at that? Ganoung and Fabbri were completely satisfied that the recruitment of security personnel was under responsible, professional control.

— 5 —

The week that followed was a hip publicist's nightmare, deluged by a cascade of stories reporting developments along the troubled American festival front. If the public's expectation of rock music events had, indeed, become one of quasi-gladitorial lust, as the hippies claimed, their craving was satiated by bountiful descriptions of wantonness, over-the-counterculture drug dispensaries, and violence. The papers were full of it; the National Affairs sections carried the sordid details, the Community Culture pages analyzed them as social phenomena, the TV-Theatre sections advertised upcoming festivals directly above commercials for "Oh Calcutta!" and "Che!" ("Tasteful Nudity," the ads proclaimed) and, curiously, all the stories were carried over into Sports. What better combination than dope and doom for a send-off of The Biggest One of Them All in scenic Wallkill? The Concerned Citizens Committee would surely feast on the spoils for weeks to come, the promoters were convinced. It was a dreadful position for anyone to be in. With their backs against the wall, faith became the hippies' placebo to stave off the ides of imminent defeat.

The seven-day blowout was kicked off in Atlanta with a weekend Pop Festival that attracted 125,000 long-haired kids onto the red clay infield of the International Raceway. The drawing card—fourteen unbroken hours of music a day—featured many of the same groups slated to play Woodstock in August, as well as newcomers to the star-studded rock galaxy, such as Chicago Transit Authority, Pacific Gas & Electric, and Led Zeppelin. And while the musical jamboree went down without noticeable incident, the *New York*

Times chose to present it as a convention of counterculture merchants and drug dealers. The "underground industrial complex," it was termed, a culture that supports "an impromptu but efficient commodities exchange in marijuana and LSD, where buyers and sellers let supply and demand establish prices."

The next day, the sixteen-year-old tradition of the Newport Jazz Festival in Rhode Island was "invaded . . . by several hundred young people who broke down a section of the 10-foot wooden fence surrounding Festival Field and engaged in a rock throwing battle with security guards." Sly and the Family Stone were on stage at the time (not exactly a group capable of producing a settling effect on an angry mob), which led the festival's producers to place the blame for the depressing circumstances on their allowing rock music to be represented on the program. To rectify their mistake, the remaining rock groups on the Newport festival's agenda were cancelled.

Then, two days later, a Smokey Robinson and the Miracles concert in Boston's South End resulted in scattered incidents of stone throwing and window breaking. According to a witness, the melee began when the audience rushed the stage to hear better after the amplification system had failed. When local police asked the crowd to move back, the Miracles left the stage and six thousand teen-agers rushed into the streets breaking everything in sight.

Bad timing, the Woodstock staff claimed, was killing their act. The *Times Herald Record* continued to litter its pages with accounts of local drug busts and overdoses. "Five Fined on Drug Charges" one story began; it was small, but somehow managed to jump out of the page like a neon billboard. "Two Seized in Ulster Drug Raid," "Nixon Calls for Crackdown on Drug Abuse," "Fish Urges Marijuana Probe"—they appeared one on top of the other until the most unsuspecting reader got the message. And while the *Times Herald Record* remained an editorial ally of the Aquarian Exposition, its sense of newsworthiness was kicking the festival all the way to the seamy depths of the Hudson River. The handwriting, if not yet on the wall, was in the works.

The defenders of the faith were the Wallkill kids themselves. Parents, whose homes had been sanctuaries from the Hippie versus Establishment title bout going on elsewhere in the country, were suddenly besieged with pleas from their children to defend the festival's right to remain in their town. "Nothing ever happens here "that we can relate to," they complained. "The result is going to be that, once we leave Wallkill for college, we're never going to return. You've got to allow us the right to our own events. Please—*please* don't let them do this to us. We want the festival to remain here. It's our only hope." The editor of the Bush *Telegraph,* a local high school newspaper, wrote a letter to the editor of the *Times Herald Record* in which she discounted traffic and security as the main reasons for expelling the festival. "The real reason . . . is that a few reactionary people are afraid of anyone and anything that is different from them and from the way they are accustomed to living," she said. "The problem of people being so narrowminded that they can't accept anything new and different is a serious one. These people have to be made to see that the people they term as 'hippies' are not dangerous, inhuman, or anything like that. They are people, just like anyone else, who have the right to be judged on their individual worth, and their ideas, rather than be lumped together in a group and classified as 'dirty hippies.'" As far as prohibiting loud music was concerned, her brazen voice lapsed into plaintive notes of resignation. "There isn't really that much a teen-ager in this area can get for entertainment without having to go to [New York City]." There was something pathetically sad, yet proud, in her expression, the way an appreciative sister smiles at her hand-me-down wardrobe. "I think we deserve the opportunity to be able to hear these artists without going to all the expense of going to the city. It's not a lot to ask."

Cliff Reynolds, however, took exception to the young woman's way of thinking. Having made no effort to tour the festival site nor indicated any interest in the preparations, Reynolds announced to the press that he intended to bring a complaint against Woodstock Ventures for operating a place of business in a residentially zoned area. He had apparently done his homework. He found that the barn on Howard Mills's land, which was being used as the festival's headquarters, was within 1,600 feet of the road and therefore, according to existing records, a gross violation of the zoning ordinance. Such a violation was punishable by a fine of $50 a day, and Reynolds was quick to note that the promoters were already responsible for $1,500 in penalties should the zoning board of appeals take action on his complaint.

Reynolds also let it be known that the Concerned Citizens Committee had decided to go on with their suit against the promoters, and that it was likely to come before a State Supreme Court justice as early as Friday, July 11. According to Jules Minker, two informal meetings had already taken place between his group (which, as far as anyone knew, consisted *only* of Reynolds) and Woodstock Ventures. "But *nothing* more than promises come from them," he said. "We have yet to see a single piece of written evidence, although we would adjourn the suit if the defendants produce proof of their commitment to protecting public health and safety."

The promoters found Minker's last bit of sophistry the most exasperating dig of all. They'd *never* be able to satisfy his or Reynolds's demands. It all seemed to depend upon their adversary's mood at the time, a toss of the coin.

What were they expected to do—spend an additional ten grand on security only to discover it was not substantial enough to suit Reynolds? Do they purchase 300,000 gallons of water only to find that his gripe about transportation stops them cold? Or consult him on the color of festival T-shirts? Go for the yardage or punt? The whole thing was that ridiculous. The paranoia was unrelenting. Yet, it continued to haunt the Woodstock team with an even greater intensity as the days progressed.

In the meantime, several "older" members of the festival's executive staff swung into action. They took an assortment of operational problems to outside interest groups capable of providing them with added vocational muscle, not to mention imagination and influence.

On July 7, Wes Pomeroy and Don Ganoung drove north to the state capitol in Albany to meet with Harrison F. Dunbrook, the director of traffic operations for the New York State Department of Transportation. By 10:00 A.M., eight men, all of whom bore titles the length of a grocery list, were settled into the fourth-floor conference room in the main office of the state campus. The purpose of the meeting, in addition to presenting the Department of Transportation with a formal statement of purpose, was for Ganoung and Pomeroy to urge vigorously state support of the Aquarian Exposition in the form of highway alterations throughout the festival weekend.

Ganoung gave the state brass a list of eight points they sought to carry home. It had been Pomeroy's ardent hope to persuade the Department of Transportation to provide them with emergency openings off the Quickway at the Scotchtown Road overpass and at the intersection with Route 302, which cut across Circleville and snaked onto the back end of the Mills property. Both could be easily tapped, and while neither road was in any kind of shape to accommodate the number of cars Pomeroy was contemplating, they'd serve to lessen the strain at Exit 120. At this point, Exit 120 was the only major artery leading directly onto Route 211, across from the Burger King, and on toward the site. If that remained the case, cars would be bunched up for miles trying to get in and out. They desperately needed more access; Pomeroy thought two more exits would do the trick.

To Pomeroy's chagrin, the request was denied straightaway. Besanceney, the state director of engineering and safety, pointed out that, should their highway division approve additional exits, the traffic turning into them would slow the normal movement of high-speed vehicles on the Quickway, thereby crippling travel upstate and beyond. That was out of the question. He did agree, however, to send an investigating committee to Exit 120 in order to determine what could be done about the construction work that was presently going on there. The factfinding expedition would also discuss with the contractor the possibility of opening Industrial Road and Egbert Drive, two narrow roads that traversed Mills Heights, onto Route 211 during the exposition. That, for the moment, was all they could offer. It wasn't much, but it was an improvement.

A request for posting festival signs on the Quickway was met with somewhat more enthusiasm, although not enough to produce the permits necessary for the security staff to begin work. The state officials agreed to entertain such a motion, but only after certain requirements were met. First, the promoters had to submit to them a sampling of the legends to go on the signs; secondly, the locations where they were going to be displayed had to be thoroughly mapped out and registered with the State Highway Commission; and, finally, facsimiles of color and how they were to be lettered had to be offered for approval.

But there was more about which they had to agree before they could relax. Once granted a permit, Woodstock Ventures had to adhere to age-old statutes that forbid signs to be fixed on the shoulder of the road. Pomeroy shrugged, defeated by the complexity of it all. That more or less restricted them to fastening wide directional markers to staff vehicles or to signs already positioned in exit lanes. It was a lesson in legislative futility. Their only recourse, one which Ganoung and Pomeroy considered both practical and attractive, was to contact the State Thruway Authority and work out a system whereby directions to the parking lots and site could be handed out at toll booths where the Thruway intersected with the Quickway.

One of Ganoung's primary interests in addressing the Department of Transportation had to do with acquiring additional parking lot space in the Wallkill-Middletown vicinity from which he could conduct his shuttling operation. Several parcels of land had already been examined for rental. While scouting prospective property, Wes had come across a four-mile stretch of nearly finished highway to the north of Middletown that was part of the Interstate Highway 84 project connecting the New England states. It was called the Road To Nowhere by the local residents because of its abrupt halt a few miles out of town. As far as Pomeroy knew, it wasn't scheduled for completion before the end of the year, and he wanted permission to lease it from the state as a parking facility for four thousand cars. Woodstock Ventures, he warranted, would assure them that the piece of road would be properly protected and insured, and that all refuse would be removed before they left the area.

The representatives from the state agency took everything in stride. The red tape involved was agonizing. All of Pomeroy and Ganoung's requests for special privileges would necessitate further examination by one aide or another before any decision could be made. Pending everyone's satisfaction, the festival security officers would be referred to specialized deputies further on down the legislative ladder for final approval on each matter. And to make matters worse, no one could give them an estimate of how long that might take. It could be a matter of days; it might even take weeks!

John Fabbri had better luck. While Pomeroy and Ganoung were struggling through the ineffectual traffic meeting in Albany, he was huddled with four representatives from Tri-Co to iron out the specifics of their communications job at the festival. Arnold Puff had discussed the organization's chance to work at the site with the rest of his membership and had come away with an eager vote in favor of supporting the outing. Now, all that remained was for them to work out a strategy with Fabbri that would enable them to estimate the amount of equipment and manpower they'd have to supply.

It was decided that the members would be divided into three groups to man the Communications Command Center, the Mobile Security Patrol and the Parking Lots Control Communications. Tri-Co was to provide their own four-base station transmitters with a total of six frequencies, one each for Headquarters Command, the Inner Command, the Outer Command, Transportation and Parking Command, outside law enforcement agencies (which included the New York State Police and the Wallkill Fire Department), and a frequency left in reserve for any emergencies that might crop up along the way. They would also attempt to lease an additional channel from nearby Newburgh for the purpose of coordinating the transportation of performers between hotels and the backstage area.

Luckily, Tri-Co had access to radio-equipped vehicles that, for ten cents a mile, would compose the Mobile Security Patrol. In addition to walkie-talkies, each car would be manned by a festival staff member who'd work in tandem with a representative from the club. The ground force would be outfitted with two-channel crystal handkie-talkies connected to the Communications Command Center trailer. Puff suggested they use sixty-four such radios, which Woodstock Ventures would have to purchase from one of three member retailers for $120 per unit.

Tri-Co agreed to take care of all of the preparations so that when they arrived for work, they'd be ready to go. They requested that Mel Lawrence have a trailer prepared prior to Friday, August 8, so they'd be able to commence with the installation and testing of equipment on the ninth. The rest would depend on the crowd.

Like Pomeroy, Ganoung, and Fabbri, Peter Goodrich spent the second week in July hopping from one corporate boardroom to another trying to convince a fast-food concern to handle concessions at the festival. The legalities behind Woodstock Ventures operating a public kitchen by themselves proved too complicated indeed, so Goodrich had been dispatched to discuss some form of limited partnership with the leading Manhattan-based vendors. He had a relatively easy time making appointments with executives from Restaurant Associates, the Harry M. Stevens Company (who fed hundreds of thousands of sports enthusiasts weekly at places like Madison Square Garden, and Shea and Yankee stadiums), Chock Full 'o Nuts, and Nathan's Famous. His plan was to listen to their sales talk, perhaps sample a menu of their wares, and award the account to the company willing to part with the greatest share of the profits. The prerequisite was that a company be able to provide a diverse bill of fare that was simple to prepare, and inexpensive. Goodrich wasn't looking for anything fancy, just a hearty combination of the usual concert grub: hamburgers, Cokes, possibly corn on the cob, potato chips—it didn't have to be nutritious, just filling. The size of the crowd demanded that they be able to produce a quick turnover so no one spent two out of the three days in line waiting to get a drink. That didn't seem like a difficult request. Goodrich expected the vendors would jump at the chance to get in on lucrative action like that.

He was therefore stunned by the indifference with which his proposal was greeted. Here he thought he was dangling a multimillion-dollar plum in front of their eyes—the opportunity to feed a captive audience for three days without the slightest hint of competition. And, yet, the reply that most commonly followed his explanation of the festival was: "We'd rather not be bothered." Of the four food powers he approached, only Nathan's indicated passing interest in handling the refreshment stands, and that was only if the promoters agreed to certain requirements beforehand. Their most emphatic stipulation was that Woodstock Ventures provide them with the services of three hundred auxiliary firemen to feed the estimated one hundred thousand people a day. If that could be arranged, they'd be willing to turn the negotiations over to their lawyers who would prepare the necessary papers.

Goodrich forlornly explained the situation to Michael Lang and urged him to grab Nathan's offer before they changed their mind. It had nothing to do with profits, he noted, and there is some doubt that Goodrich even got around to discussing finances with the hot dog wholesalers. His advise was based strictly on *availability*. Nathan's was the only game in town, it was as simple as that.

Michael found Goodrich's evaluation a little hard to believe. He, nonetheless, told him to go ahead with the deal. Six weeks didn't leave them with a helluva lot of time to shop around. Besides, there was a peculiar charm to having Nathan's cater the festival's concessions. The company had more or less been associated with local New York amusement parks since anyone could remember, a bright, happy yellow logo plastered on every boardwalk and beachfront sign. And Woodstock represented the future of teen-age entertainment. The more Lang thought about it, the more Nathan's was perfect for the festival's image. Simple food—the *people's* food: hot dogs and orange drink. It was made in heaven.

The cosmic illusion, however, went right on past the people in Wallkill. When Goodrich approached the Middletown Fire Department to enlist their help, he was politely, but firmly, turned down. The firemen unanimously voted against the offer, objecting to the long hours they were expected to work (from 6:30 P.M. to 4:30 A.M.) and to the wages offered (a measly $1.75 an hour—they could earn more sitting around the firehouse playing cards). Nathan's, in turn, cancelled the deal.

The food situation was mounting into a serious problem for the promoters. They realized that without a professional concessionaire in their employ, they'd never be granted a permit from the town board, the health inspector, or any other agency empowered to wield the ax. The companies that remained in the Yellow Pages who claimed they could "cater any affair" had dwindled into a handful of second-rate appetizer brokers with a fleet of pickup trucks and three cheerful assistants.

Goodrich became panicked. His former sophisticated, wily manner turned sour and abrupt. His schemes became vengeful instead of manipulative and humorous. A great many of his phone calls to inquire about a fast-food chain's potential ended in shouting. He had to come up with a company in a matter of days, before they applied for the permit, and that did not look possible.

Lang put an end to his friend's despair. Pulling Goodrich aside in the downtown production office one afternoon, he suggested to Peter that he forget about trying to hire a professional for the job and work on another angle. "Put somebody in business," he said. Michael's proposition was to find a few people with a flair for organization, to pass them off as experts and work them into the overall scheme as concessionaires. After all, how hard could it possibly be to buy supplies, cook the food, slap it onto a plate and ring up sales? There must be hundreds of capable people willing to give it a try.

It is difficult to determine whether or not a plan to skim a percentage of the profits off the top of such an arrangement was discussed; however, there is evidence that Goodrich certainly gave it a try. For the moment, though, it appeared as though their problems were over. The town board could be held at bay long enough for him to work out some kind of package deal; if he had to, Michael would allege a tentative agreement with one of the national food corporations, which he could later say fell through. But the important thing was for Goodrich to find a syndicate to front the refreshment interests, and the Miami art hustler had just the right gang in mind.

By July 9, it looked to John Roberts as though their position in Wallkill was rapidly deteriorating. The night before, Pomeroy and Ganoung had met with the town fire advisory board in the Silver Lake Firehouse to discuss the festival's fire protection needs. That meeting, like the others before it, was interrupted by protesters whose insults carried a sinister undercurrent of vigilantism. Nor was its administrative outcome any more promising. Instead of evaluating the festival's requirements and coming to an informal arrangement, the advisory board decided not to act on the promoters' fire plans until it was asked to do so by the town board under the new local law. Roberts understood the implications of such a decision: the advisory board would not commit themselves without a permit, and a permit would not be given them without first having fire protection services.

That same morning, Joel opened a letter addressed to the Woodstock Music Company from the Town of Shawangunk in upstate New York. Margaret Y. Tremper, the deputy town clerk, had written to bring to their attention an oversight on their part in publicizing the festival's location.

"Gentlemen," she began, "I wish to inform you that the incorrect address used by you in your advertising for the Aquarian Exposition has caused considerable confusion and created a nuisance in our community. The address given on your brochure is Wallkill, New York, which is a small town in Ulster County not remotely connected with the place in Orange County where your exposition is to be held." Mrs. Tremper was concerned that thousands of hippies would arrive on their doorstep on the morning of August 15 searching for the festival. She "strongly suggested" that the promoters correct their advertising to avoid "further confusion to all concerned."

Joel checked an atlas. Running a magnifying glass across the northern region of New York State, he came upon what he knew he would find all along: Wallkill, New York, population 1,215, smack in the middle of Ulster County. It was a good twenty-five miles from their own site. It took only a short telephone call to discover that they had been incorrectly using Wallkill, New York, as an address for the festival. It was Wallkill, all right, but it had to be clearly represented on posters and in ads as Town of Wallkill, Orange County, otherwise it was improperly labeled.

Their logical reaction to the letter was to call Miles Lourie and discuss its legal implications in light of the advertising having already gone out. Could they be held responsible for any inconvenience in Ulster County's Wallkill should some disgruntled hippies express their indignation at not being in the right place by lobbing a few pop bottles through an authentic Wallkill window? Would they have to make good on unused tickets should some of their prospective audience wander farther upstate than they should have? These were all questions that had to be answered before they corrected the inaccuracy; as an attorney himself, Joel knew that, often in a legal action, the most damage was done to one side's position by its impulsive endeavor to admit blame. The seat of the problem, however, was their reluctance to give Lourie a call. John Roberts was of the opinion that Miles "had become a pain in the ass" during the past few weeks. By calling him, Roberts felt they would only be leaving themselves wide open for one of the lawyer's self-aggrandizing lectures. They liked Miles and wanted to avoid another bitter confrontation with him at all costs and hoped that the problem would solve itself.

It did. The next afternoon, a messenger arrived at their door with an envelope containing Miles Lourie's resignation as counsel for Woodstock Ventures. It was a courteous, dignified letter to the four partners, explaining in rather vague terms his sense of being slighted by their recent appointment of Paul Marshall as additional counsel for the festival. The final straw had been Marshall's assignment to represent Woodstock Ventures at the temporary injunction in Newburgh on Friday—an action Lourie clearly interpreted as a lack of faith in his ability. "Paul has requested that I continue to work with him on this and, subject to your approval, I will be reviewing whatever papers he prepares to defend the motion and to give whatever advice I can," he wrote. In fact, the two attorneys had met in a coffee shop across from Marshall's office a few days previous to Lourie's formal withdrawal, to iron out professional differences over who was officially representing Woodstock Ventures. "Don't be a *schmuck*," Marshall claims to have told his colleague, "there's a fortune to be made in legal fees from this festival— plenty for the both of us without squabbling." But, for Miles Lourie, it was also a matter of pride. He had put the principals together, offered them his office as their own headquarters before the corporation had been established, and sweated with them over each preliminary decision in giving the festival substance. He had an emotional stake in their enterprise that, he felt, should not be compromised. Making his position clear to his former clients, he spelled out his future involvement in no uncertain terms. "Inasmuch as I was not consulted concerning this [injunction] until the last moment and inasmuch as it is my opinion that a lawsuit should be handled by one attorney primarily, I don't think I should do any more than I have indicated above."

Miles Lourie had become Woodstock Ventures' first casualty. In the five months since the company's synergistic beginnings, several of its visionaries had come to near-blows and survived the test of brotherhood. Words had been exchanged, philosophies had been assaulted, goals had been reexamined, and associations had been damned. No one, however, had suffered more than a mindful slap on the wrist until Lourie departed. And while no one was willing to admit it, his leaving had a pronounced effect on their spiritual objective for it had broken the unbreakable bond of unity and served as a warning that all was not peace and love in hippieland.

— **6** —

"Goodrich has found us some food cats." Michael Lang was his old jubilant self as he waited on the other end of the line for John Roberts's reaction.

"Well, great. That's really good news, Michael. Who are they?"

Lang said that he wasn't sure, he didn't know them personally. Goodrich, however, had assured him only yesterday that "they're heavy."

Heavy—oh shit, that was always a sure sign of trouble. Roberts prayed that they were not the three men he and Goodrich had spoken about some weeks back. During a moment of seemingly honest revelation (a moment that Roberts felt represented the *only* truthful exchange in their short relationship), Goodrich had told him, "I have these three guys that I know we can use in a pinch. I'd prefer not to do that if we don't have to, but if we can't get ahold of Restaurant Associates or Stevens or one of the others to come in with us, we can go with this group."

"This is bullshit," Roberts had remarked. "Here it is the end of June, and we have no food concessionaires. It's just insane. I can't risk waiting much longer. How are these guys?"

Goodrich was uncommonly candid. "They're fine—I just can't stand them personally."

Roberts had defensively put that discussion out of his mind, so convinced was he that it was only a matter of time before vendors would be beating down their door in an attempt to land the account. Now, having experienced a dozen or more rejections from the major food concerns, he had a sneaking premonition that the worst had happened, that they had hit rock bottom and he was about to be introduced to Goodrich's three stooges.

"The thing is," Michael went on, "we gotta close the deal with them fast—like tomorrow. They need bread, and they've gotta get started." He had taken the liberty of arranging a meeting at Paul Marshall's office on the morning of July 10. Peter Goodrich would meet him there to make the proper introductions. As Joel was tied up with festival advertising and publicity, Roberts reluctantly agreed to attend alone.

At precisely 10:30 the next morning, Roberts found himself being squired into Marshall's dark, mahogany office, a room so regally furnished that John thought it befitted a distinguished Supreme Court justice. Besides their newly appointed lawyer and Peter Goodrich (who looked apprehensive), four other men were settled into various armchairs positioned around the room. They were fleetingly introduced to him as Charles Baxter, Jeffrey Joerger, and Lee Howard—the partners of a new corporation called Food For Love—and Stephen Weingrad, their attorney.

Roberts's head was still spinning from the swift and scrambled presentation of these men. The whole thing had happened so quickly that he had missed the imparting of their credentials. All he had left to go on were appearance, and he did not like what he saw. The three men looked no more like fast-food executives than Michael and Artie, and perhaps it was that resemblance that bothered him most of all. Baxter, tall and spare, bore a strong resemblance to Ichabod Crane. He was young, somewhere in his late twenties, and Roberts would later learn that his experience had been limited to selling souvenirs at the New York World's Fair and managing a Gimbel's toy department. Joerger looked like a suburban roughneck. He, too, was young, although somewhat shorter than Baxter, and had long dark hair that was combed over to one side of his head. Joerger was dressed in faded jeans and a T-shirt, his usual work garb, for he had interrupted his routine, selling antiques in the Village, to attend the conference. Howard was the shortest member of the isosceles triangle, whose quill-like long hair provided a comic relief to his dumpy, short-legged physique. He owned and operated a small film rehearsal hall in the Village and was known to run with a tough crowd. Together, they looked like the characters in a Rodo-Boulanger lithograph and had about as much collective experience operating a restaurant facility as a coffee shop cashier. Roberts had a sinking feeling that he was up against another one of Goodrich's schemes.

Weingrad, their nattily dressed lawyer, barreled into the meeting with a plethora of revealing information. From what Roberts could gather, Goodrich had committed the festival's concessions to Food For Love as many as three weeks beforehand. Joerger, acting upon what he thought to be a firm deal, worked out provisioning with a line of suppliers and was now in need of about seventy-five thousand dollars to assure him of delivery in time for the festival. Food For Love, however, had no means of financing such an arrangement. Goodrich had implied that Roberts would underwrite their fledgling operation. It smelled to both Marshall and Roberts like cronyism of the worst kind.

It was, in fact, Charles Baxter who had first approached Goodrich about being given the food concession. He had wandered into the downtown production office in late June, got what he thought was a vote of confidence from Lang's henchman, and set out in search of suitable partners to finance him along. Somewhere along the line, both Joerger and Howard represented to him that they could put up the money. Baxter's previous relationship with them was professional, and even then, spotty; he'd rented furniture from Joerger's store and had been involved in photographic "shoots" at Howard's studio. But he desperately needed their backing. By the time he discovered their pots were as empty as his, they had formed a formal partnership, Joerger had done a great deal of comparative pricing on food, and Howard had arrived at a cloying name for their new company to ingratiate them with the hippie promoters: Food For Love. None of the partners liked the name, but they agreed on its underlying purpose. The only one left to convince was Peter Goodrich, and that was easier than they had imagined it would be. Goodrich told them right out: "I'll make sure you get it if you take care of me." A price was set that everyone thought was respectable for his consideration—$10,000—and Goodrich passed their names on to Lang as frontrunners in the concession competition. Considering there was no one else in line for the job, they stood to capture the purse.

Weingrad proposed an "equitable deal" whereby Food For Love and Woodstock Ventures would become partners. Roberts would sign over to his clients a check for $75,000 that would be used for the purchase of food, soft goods, shipping, and wages. The first $75,000 that came in at the festival would be returned to Woodstock Ventures and everything else would be split fifty-fifty.

Marshall was "appalled" by the terms of the deal. He thought, "There's not going to be any food out there." Moreover, he was concerned that his client was about to embark on a "messy, ugly deal with such horrible people."

It was John Roberts, though, who sealed their fate. In a moment of diversion, while Marshall asked Weingrad a few questions, John leaned over to Peter Goodrich and asked: "Do we have any other possibilities open to us?"

"None, man. These are the only cats. Everyone else has passed."

Roberts dejectedly agreed with Weingrad's proposal. He would advance Food For Love $75,000 and sign a contract with them whereby the festival staff would build the refreshment stands, make certain there was proper plumbing and electricity with which to operate a health department-approved restaurant, and guarantee them a minimum number of customers against fifty percent of the gross. It *was* a horrible deal for Roberts. For the same money, he could hire himself a competent staff, put them on salary, and pocket one hundred percent of the profits. But he felt as though Woodstock Ventures had "dilly-dallied around on the food" too much, and if he waited any longer, they'd be left without concession stands and without a permit from the town. His back, as so many times before, was up against the wall. An hour later, he signed a contract with the inexperienced firm and gave them a check to cement the deal. Food For Love had become another mouth for him to feed.

The entire production staff had been asked to attend a meeting that night at 9:00 P.M. at the Wallkill site office to go over all progress that had been made since they began. It would also provide them with an opportunity to take stock of their position with the town. A day later, they were scheduled to go before Judge Edward M. O'Gormon in Newburgh, New York, and three days after that, they had to appear before the zoning board of appeals in what would prove to be the determining factor in their application for a permit. It was a wise idea, Lang thought, to discuss thoroughly the plans again so that if any person was called on during these sessions to represent a point, it would, in fact, be the official position of Woodstock Ventures and not merely a personal opinion.

The meeting might very well have been the first time since groundbreaking that everyone had a chance to get together. John Morris, Peter Goodrich, Chip Monck, Jim Mitchell, Steve Cohen, Joyce Mitchell, and Lang represented the downtown staff; Artie Kornfeld, Roberts, and Rosenman were there from corporate headquarters; and Wes Pomeroy, Mel Lawrence, Don Ganoung, Stanley Goldstein, Penny Stallings, and Lee Mackler carried the weight of production central—the site staff. It remains a wonder that a full-scale war did not break out from those contrasting personalities simply being under the same roof. From the notes of the meeting, however, it appears to have been conducted as a model of decorum, one in which everyone had a chance to learn what was going on in other areas of the production and was allowed to speak his or her piece.

Mel Lawrence kicked things off by explaining that the ground preparations were well ahead of schedule. Eighty percent of all paths leading from the bowl to the outlying areas of the site had been cleared. The dead apple trees had been cut down, and the remaining part of the orchard had been treated so that kids could pick fruit from the trees during the exposition. Using a map, he showed his colleagues how a fence was to encircle the entire region of Mills Heights with two main entrances positioned somewhere close to the field office. That way they could keep an eye on who came in and out of the performance area from a position in the hayloft. The only thing they had not yet decided was the height of the fences. Someone suggested that it be ten feet to insure fortification from within; however, Lawrence pointed out that if it was six feet or less, no permit was required from the zoning board. Everyone agreed that should bear considerable weight when Security made their final decision.

Two campsites were being groomed on either side of the bowl, and Lawrence mentioned a larger one on Route 211 that was also available to them if the situation called for more space. Sixty percent of the people attending the festival were expected to stay throughout the three days. With only 3,000 motel rooms in the Wallkill-Middletown area, they were going to have to accommodate everyone without a reservation. It could be a zoo, someone suggested. Lawrence explained that was precisely why they were keeping several adjacent pieces of property in reserve for any last-minute overflow. Additionally, they had planned to make the camping area as amusing as possible with the help of antics from the Hog Farm, the Merry Pranksters, and a few other communal groups. The Wards were taking care of building the playground for the younger kids, which would include swings, sandboxes, and jungle gyms; that was near completion and would be ready in a matter of days.

Don Ganoung noted that he had entered into a tentative agreement with nine area farmers to lease tracts of land for parking lots, and that it would relieve a great deal of gate pressure during congested hours. The lots were located six and seven miles from the site, which would allow dispatchers to regulate the flow of people on their way into the festival grounds, and were expected to hold up to three thousand cars each. From what he had seen on inspection, there would not be a problem with the amount of cars expected to attend.

Electricity was to be supplied to all areas of the grounds, a detail that would be farmed out to a local contractor. Chip Monck was making sure that floodlights reached into all nooks and crannies, and a television contractor had agreed to provide three cameras for videotaping the event, which were to be appropriately placed in front of the stage.

Goldstein reported that approximately one hundred and fifty sanitary units would be installed near the road later on in the week. Some would be placed directly behind the stage for direct access by performers, while the bulk of toilets would be located in back of a wall of hay on the other side of the playground. He had spoken to a fire inspector earlier in the afternoon and was informed that the hay would have to be fireproofed. Jim Mitchell was assigned the task of finding a substance to be sprayed on the hay, which would have to be done before they could hope to pass inspection for a permit.

Goldstein was not as at ease about the statutory water requirement. The situation, he said, was still a major problem, and could lead to a legal snag lethal enough to halt production. Thus far, ten trucks had been located from as far off as West Virginia, each one capable of transporting 60,000 gallons of water in one trip. The trouble was that they still had nothing to fill the trucks with, nor had they any additional leads. It seemed to him that water would be a last-minute conveyance and that they all ought to keep their fingers crossed that it would elude the town board's attention. He could provide them with no better solution than fate.

There were more conclusive provisions made for first aid. They had rented a trailer partitioned into variously sized compartments where doctors and nurses could attend to patients on a twenty-four-hour-a-day basis. Wes Pomeroy had hired a staff of seven doctors and half as many nurses to work in eight-hour shifts and had contracted a local hospital to provide around-the-clock ambulance service. He pointed out that studies of other festivals had prompted him to take into consideration such emergencies as insulin shock, freakouts, and sunstroke, all of which could be anticipated during the course of the Aquarian Exposition. Because of the expected crowds, he had directed Jim Mitchell to double the quantity of medical supplies they had originally called for, and had put out a request for a supplementary first aid staff in case they were inundated with casualties.

As far as security was concerned, Pomeroy announced that, to date, 240 off-duty New York City cops who applied for a staff position at the festival had passed through the first phase of screening and would be interviewed by a panel of festival security officers before the month was out. They were still accepting applications in the downtown office and on the site, and he expected to hire a total of 300 men and women to become the Peace Security Corps. They were to be teamed with representatives from the Tri-County Citizens Band Radio Club in what Pomeroy considered to be an invincible peace-keeping influence.

Steve Cohen briefly described his committee's plans for the stage, and John Morris closed the meeting with a summary of the accommodations

being made for performers and their road crews. A schedule of which acts
would perform in what order had not yet been completed as there were still
a few outstanding time slots to be filled on the bill; however, with the recent
addition of Sly and the Family Stone, they were fairly close to closing the
booking. He had hired a helicopter to shuttle the groups from the Holiday
Inn in Goshen to one of twelve dressing rooms available for their use off to
one side of the stage. He'd send around a memo to all festival employees as
soon as he and Michael had worked out a suitable sequence. Like the rest of
the committee's feedback data, everything was beginning to fall neatly into
place.

It was well past midnight when the meeting finally disbanded. One by
one, the wearied mythmakers pulled themselves up off the blanket-covered
floor and drifted back to where individual sleeping arrangements awaited
their return. Tomorrow was their long-awaited day in court when they were
certain they'd put an end to the menacing spectre of Cliff Reynolds and be
left to see their dream through with rightful peace of mind. No more harassment, no more spiteful demands to be met, no more hatred and bigoted
disregard of personal rights. Yes sir—things *were* falling into their proper
place. Nothing could stop them now.

There were some members of the festival staff, however, who weren't as
freely convinced of their clear sailing. Mel Lawrence, whose perpetually
suntanned face was drawn and haggard, showed signs of extreme mental
fatigue and uneasiness. Standing beneath the canopy of crusty wooden pil-
lars that supported his office, his expression bore the icy chill of discontent
one notices in terminally ill patients. The smile on his face did not register
the confidence of the others, the blind trust in Lang's motto: "I got it covered." The number of details being left to chance boggled his mind; there
were too many "ifs" and not enough easy solutions. Being rid of Reynolds
would certainly help their cause, but it wouldn't lead them to water or devise
a fail-safe traffic plan, nor was it likely to induce the Department of Health
to give them the white flag. The pressure of fighting back was beginning to
take its toll on him.

Stanley Goldstein was seated across from him on the corner of a secre-
tarial desk trying to place a long-distance phone call to Bonnie Jean Romney in New Mexico. Goldstein's anguish was unconcealed. He had been
under inordinate pressure these last few days to produce a source of water,
and his once-solid relationship with Michael Lang had steadily crumbled.
Michael had thrown them to the wolves for a stab at celebrity. In what
Goldstein viewed as a last-ditch effort to rescue their sinking ship, he had
visited Lang at his home in Woodstock and pleaded with the "Kid" to take

charge. "It's slipping away from us, Michael, you're losing sight of what's going on and, I can tell you—it's not good. We're gonna lose this fight. John and Joel are complete washouts as far as our ticket operation is concerned. They don't have the slightest idea what they're doing, and it's turning into one big mess. The festival checkbook bounces from one hand to another like an abandoned puppy; everyone's forging the officers' signatures with alarming regularity. You're not around; nobody can reach you. What the hell's going on here?"

Michael managed to convince Goldstein that things were under control and that he'd make more effort to be involved with the legal fight in Wallkill. But the settling effect he had on Goldstein was only temporary. He tried to convince the others of his alarm but nobody believed him. They were finished, outta there, a festival without a home. Even Bonnie Jean Romney wasn't at the proper place for their prearranged phone conference. He hung up the phone after the fifteenth ring.

Then Goldstein swiveled around on the desk and saw Mel Lawrence staring off into space. Lawrence—the most conservative of the bunch, who wanted an impenetrable system of fencing strung around the grounds so that his employers could make back their expenses and, perhaps, hire him again. It was an admirable thought, however altruistic, and would never see the light of day. He knew the inner turmoil Lawrence must be going through, the inability to come to grips with the inexactitude of his detail. As their eyes met, they exchanged a commiserating nod in regard to the job before them. It was at that moment that Goldstein knew that, after the frivolity and carefree spirit had been exorcised from their midst, he was no longer alone.

— 7 —

Sam Eager's good news preceded the promoters' ordeal in the State Supreme Court by a matter of hours and left them feeling the least bit cocky. In a memo to Michael Lang, dated July 10, Eager meticulously outlined their position in each of the upcoming legal contests and suggested the festival had an unexpected ally in their landlord. Or, at least, salvation in light of Howard Mills's recent declaration of noninvolvement. Eager reported that Mills and his attorney, Herbert F. Fabricant, "take the position that they will neither abet nor hinder you in the injunction." It was strictly a gratuitous position for Mills to assume considering he had signed what amounted to an ironclad contract with Woodstock Ventures. Mills, however, *was* a co-defendant in the pending case and, had it benefited him to protect his own interests, he would have been advised by counsel to file a cross-claim against his tenants, thereby safeguarding his being branded an accomplice. By remaining silent, he stood to profit no matter which way the judge saw fit to rule. If an injunction was granted to Reynolds and the rest of the complainants, Mills could pocket the $1,500 deposit he had received from Woodstock Ventures and would most likely sue them to recover any loss he suffered as a result of a broken contract; if the injunction was dismissed, Mills would continue under his present agreement with them and, come September 1969, reap the $15,000 harvest. All he had to do was keep his mouth shut and watch the action. Nonetheless, the promoters heaved a sigh of relief in knowing they would not be challenged by their landlord.

Eager warned them, though, of putting too much faith in Mills's generosity. "They suggest there may be no lease because of a lack of description in the written instrument and apparent omissions from the purpose clauses thereof." Should Mills need a back door to crawl out of during the proceedings, his lawyer would undoubtedly allege that his client had been duped, first by Roberts and Roseman and then by Lang, in their representation of the Aquarian Exposition. It was a possibility that worried Eager since there was no way to reconstruct or prove conversations between the two parties that led to the agreement. It would boil down to Mills's word against theirs, and that didn't sit well with him.

For the time being, neither party was forced into making any hasty allegations. Acting State Supreme Court Justice Edward M. O'Gorman, after hearing remarks from both sides of the dispute, reserved his decision for an injunction against Woodstock Ventures. He was told by Wallkill Town Attorney Joseph Owen, who appeared "amicus curiae" (friend of the court), that "no application has been applied for, and no permit has been issued." Subsequently, O'Gorman informed Jules Minker that the injunction attempt was "premature," since the zoning board of appeals had not moved to accept or deny a permit that the promoters would need to construct a stage. He would be glad to entertain a similar motion after the Town of Wallkill handed down its decision, but, at this point, he would not grant the injunction.

The postponement was Woodstock Ventures' first taste of victory since migrating into Orange County in early June, yet there was still little cause for celebration. If anything, the temporary delay would afford Reynolds and his committee more time to sharpen their teeth, and there was another predator with whom they had to tangle before they could rest: the zoning board of appeals. No one was kidding himself. The zoning board had hoped that the Concerned Citizens Committee would do their dirty work for them. As it turned out, they were the last vestige of resistance to the Woodstock Music and Art Fair's remaining where they were. The irony, of course, is that it was that same civic body that started all the commotion when they first granted approval for the show back in April. Monday, July 14, 1969, was the Town of Wallkill's last chance to preserve the peace they had known for so long— Armageddon; by Tuesday, it would be history.

A large crowd of residents had gathered outside the town hall assembly room as much as an hour before the start of the public hearing "to get a good seat" (or, as one spectator ingenuously observed, "to get within firing range"). Unlike previous encounters in which a thirst for knowledge had cut through their wrath, the mood this time was strangely quiet—one might even have gone so far as to call it cold fury. Very few words were exchanged among those waiting to get in until the moment when, at approximately 8:15 P.M., the plate glass front doors swung open and Sam Eager led his charges through the corridor and into the boardroom where they monopolized a front row of folding chairs. Then, the crowd's apathy broke loose. As they scuttled to the remaining seats behind the festival contingent—Eager, Don Ganoung, Mel Lawrence, Michael Lang, Stanley Goldstein, and Joel Rosenman—a volley of tasteless barbs rushed forward to express their abhorrence. The days of restraint were over; Wallkill wanted a divorce.

Joseph Owen, the acting town attorney, had been chosen to preside over the hearing. Dressed in a severe dark suit, his perfectly knotted tie in place, Owen made his way to the center of the speaker's podium where he nodded to the zoning board's secretary, Herbert Freer, who read the Notice of Public Hearing with great deliberation.

Sam Eager then delivered a brief, unemotional preliminary statement summarizing his clients' activities since they took possession of Mills Heights. Michael Lang, who, like his young associates, wore jeans and casual clothing, listened with an outward show of boredom as Eager recounted the facts. Lang had become callous to the Establishment's mandatory show of sovereignty, the gothic ignorance of political power. He remembered how they had destroyed his first head shop in Miami and knew that they were out to do the same thing to his festival. As far as rights were concerned, they were impotent, and that defeat was visibly etched on his face.

Eager called Stan Goldstein as his first witness, then Mel Lawrence, and

Don Ganoung, all of whom diligently answered his questions concerning their respective duties. Yes, they had fixed traffic posts and area mobile patrol units for inner and outer security. No, there weren't any fences around the camping area, but a six-foot-high chain-link fence surrounded the festival grounds. Yes, the traffic and security personnel had credentials—all outlined in detail in Exhibit #20. The painstaking itemization seemed endless.

"Mr. Chairman," Eager said, checking his watch to let the board know he was mindful of the hour, "I have two more witnesses."

As Michael Lang rose and walked to the front of the room, the gallery erupted with a barrage of insults and hissing. "Isn't he pretty?" one man called, cupping his hand around his mouth, and then falling back in hysterics. "A he? Why, I thought it was a *she!*" someone answered from the other side of the room. Two or three men, seated near the front with their arms folded over noticeable paunches, chimed in with kissing sounds.

Owen let the mockery run its course before calling for order. He, too, seemed to derive pleasure from the sheepish grin on Michael's face, which they wrongly read as embarrassment. It was indulgence.

Michael, like those witnesses before him, provided the board with a thumbnail sketch of his background. "And you are now one of the principals of Woodstock Ventures and production supervisor?"

"That's right. The others are Mr. Joel Rosenman, Mr. John Roberts, and Mr. Artie Kornfeld."

Eager continued with his examination as Joseph Owen quietly got up from his chair and walked over to the American flag stand.

"Mr. Lang—can you please tell us what was done between April 14 and June 13, 1969, by Woodstock Ventures?"

"I'm not going to allow him to answer that." Everyone's head swiveled to where Owen was standing. The intended image of the town attorney defending the flag against a band of conspiratorial hippies was farcical, indeed. "This has nothing to do with the hearing at hand."

Eager argued that the activities during that period revealed the nature of the event and the precautionary measures the staff had taken to insure a professional, safe festival. To deprive them of that right defeated the entire purpose of a hearing. The rest of the board overruled Owen's denial.

Reading from a slip of paper in his hand, Michael related how he and his partners had firmed commitments with contractors, booked performing artists, employed a full staff of experts and prepared plans and and designs, which amounted to an outlay of over $457,000.

"I want that list of expenses put into evidence," Owen said, pointing to Lang's crib sheet.

"I'm sorry, Joe," Eager interrupted, "but I cannot allow that to be done. There are notes on the bottom of that paper that are not intended for any-body else's eyes."

"I don't care. I demand, on behalf of the zoning board of appeals, that the whole piece of paper that Mr. Lang read from be inserted into the rec-ord."

Eager shook his head. Owen was making a fool out of his office, yet it only cast suspicion on his clients. "This is only a memorandum used by Mr. Lang to refresh his memory. I'm going to leave it up to him to decide whether he wants it submitted or not."

"I'd prefer not to have it submitted," Michael said.

"Mark Exhibit #25 refused in evidence," Owen growled.

"We're totally committed to the plans, the event, and the site," Michael continued. He explained that after June 13, when they realized there was going to be contention from local residents, they slowed their progress a bit. "Now, we've gotta commit ourselves to finishing the project. We've got a responsibility to the people who are coming to the show. I hesitate to think what would happen if forty thousand people came to Wallkill and there was no event."

The statement, according to an account the next day in the *Times Herald Record,* "unsettled the audience." Several gasps were heard as residents turned to one another in utter horror. The thought of reconciling forty thou-sand disappointed hippies had not occurred to them. Why, it could almost wind up worse than allowing the festival to take place on Mills's farm.

"I think, with the help of the town, we can provide something everyone can be proud of and something that the town would want back next year."

"Don't count on it, y' bum!"

"Look in the mirror, and then talk about pride!"

Sam Eager motioned him off the stand, and Michael slipped numbly back into his seat.

At 10:50, with tempers badly frayed on both sides of the controversy, Owen called for a five-minute recess.

When the hearing reconvened, Herbert Freer announced that it was now the townspeople's turn to fire questions at the festival representatives.

And so it went, for another two hours, with local residents picking over facts that had been given them two or three times already during the course of the meeting. Everyone who wanted a shot at the hippies was given a chance, including their most dependable arch-rivals, Richard Dow and Cliff Reynolds. Reynolds was actually quite timid in his approach, lingering on the subject of arresting people during the festival. He insinuated that whenever one hundred thousand people get together there is a possibility of trouble occurring and that the state police would be on hand to deal with perpetrators in the proper manner. Reynolds, though, was emerging as a master in the art of scare tactics. By leading the audience's attention to the eventuality of trouble, he added that "a citizen's arrest could be made for anything from a traffic violation on up."

"That's all this crowd's got to know." Lawrence wondered if that law applied to his arresting Reynolds for attempting to incite a riot.

By 1:00 in the morning, half the people in the spectators' gallery had either left or stomped out to emphasize a point that had been made. A woman named Ann Kelsh was the last to make a dramatic exit. Raising a clenched fist at Sam Eager, she bellowed: "Now there will be three days, twenty-four hours a day, of interference. I will call you every time I am bothered. Perhaps you should pay for my baby sitter for the hours I wasted here tonight. People should go and visit their neighbors around the area!" Then she flew out the door in a rage.

There was one more point of order from the floor before Herbert Freer called for a motion to adjourn. As the last Wallkill citizen reclaimed his seat, two board members jumped at the chance to end the ordeal. The rest of the board members so moved to grant their request, and by 1:20 A.M., the last car turned out of the town hall parking lot onto the deserted highway.

The Wallkill Zoning Board of Appeals passed judgment on the status of Woodstock Ventures' application for a permit the next morning, July 15, 1969, in a closed session at the town hall. By 3:00 that same afternoon, most everyone within a ten-mile radius had heard their decision.

Mel Lawrence was standing in front of the field office signing a bill of lading when the phone on his desk rang. The truck driver, holding the clipboard on which Mel was writing, was in a rush. He had driven all night to deliver the seventy Georgia-pine telephone poles that were to be used for the stage support and wanted to head back south while there was still enough daylight.

"Penny, will you get that," Lawrence called, putting the finishing touches on the receipt.

"It's for you," she called back.

"Can't you see that I'm busy! Take a message."

"It's Michael. He says to tell you it's urgent."

Lawrence handed the clipboard back to the driver. "You can drop the poles just over that rise where the crew is standing." He waved his thanks, climbed the ladder to his loft office, and picked up the phone. "Hey Michael—what's shakin'?"

"It's blown."

"What's blown? What the fuck are you talkin' about?"

"I just got the word. Listen to this: 'In a unanimous decision, the five-member board handed exposition promoters their most serious setback to date by refusing to allow them to build anything on their 200-acre site.'"

"Ah shit! You mean those fuckers turned down our application?"

"That's it, man. We're gone. We gotta start lookin' for another site."

"Fuck 'em. Let's stay and fight."

"Well, I'm gonna talk to Eager about that later, but the vibes I'm gettin' aren't too good, man. It looks like we're gonna get the boot. Just do me a favor—okay?"

"Sure," Lawrence said dejectedly. "Name it."

"Don't put anything on the site we can't take with us."

"Don't worry, there's nothin' here we've gotta—oh shit, hang on a second."

The logs! he thought. *They're gonna drop the fuckin' logs!* "Hold it!" he screamed out the second-story window of the barn. "Don't drop those logs!" *They couldn't hear him.* He knocked over half the accessories on his desk trying to get to the ladder and out to the staging area before three tons of telephone poles could be dumped across Mills Heights. How could this be happening, he wondered, flailing his arms in the air as he ran up the embankment that looked out over the bowl. Lang had said nothing permanent. Those poles were practically as unmovable lying on the ground as they'd be after they were sunk into cement. No one on the staff was big enough to move them without the proper machinery, and it would cost a fortune to have them professionally loaded on to a flatbed truck.

As he came up over the rise, he could see the driver climb back into the cab of the truck and drop his hand to the discharge mechanism that would slide the load off the rear platform.

"Don't drop those logs! Wait! *Noooo!*" Lawrence screamed. But a second ill wind was about to hit the Town of Wallkill that afternoon. As he ran toward the truck, a strong country breeze rushed through the barren orchard and muffled his cries. It was not substantial enough, however, to dampen the clamor as the telephone poles rolled off the truck and tumbled onto the soft grass. Lawrence dropped to his knees and watched in horror until the last pole came to rest on the heap. The driver's aim had been precise; he had delivered the Parthian shot.

CHAPTER SEVEN

Back into Battle

Darkened so, yet shone
Above them all the Archangel: but his face
Deep scars of thunder had intrenched, and care
Sat on his faded cheek, but under brows
Of dauntless courage, and considerate pride
Waiting revenge.

—*John Milton*, Paradise Lost

— 1 —

Thirty-one days—that was all that kept ringing in Mel Lawrence's head as he paced across the floor of what, only yesterday, had been his production office. That morning, an eviction notice had been posted on the front door of Howard Mills's barn telling Woodstock Ventures to pack up its belongings and clear out. No one was certain whether or not it was a legal document, but it raised a perfectly legitimate point: What was the purpose of maintaining headquarters in the barn if there wasn't going to be a festival? Since word had leaked out about the zoning board of appeal's decision, contractors and suppliers had stopped by to collect outstanding accounts and the attorney general's office had phoned to ask whether they intended to make good on tickets that had already been purchased. It was as near to a disaster as Lawrence had ever been in in his life. And, yet, when Lang asked him if he could still get it together on another site in time, he heard himself answer, "Yes." Was he out of his mind? He only had *thirty-one days* left.

Mel picked up a late edition of the *Times Herald Record* from off a desk. There, under a story about the Apollo 11 blastoff, was an update on their own uncertain destination, entitled "Festival to Sue Wallkill." Much good it'd do them, he thought, as he skimmed the article. It began: "The promoters of the controversial Aquarian Exposition, which has drawn nationwide attention, ordered their lawyers . . . to prepare a damage suit against the Town of Wallkill Zoning Board of Appeals and unnamed individuals who have opposed their proposed three-day folk-rock festival." There was a slew of promises from John Roberts to the effect that, come August 15, a festival would take place on Howard Mills's property as planned; they had no intention of moving or canceling the show. Lawrence's stomach wrenched as he read an opinion the reporter had gotten from Cliff Reynolds. "These people are in complete disregard for the laws of the town," he said. "They come in with the pretension of upholding the law and are now in flagrant violation of it." As far as Reynolds was concerned, his own lawsuit was still pending, and that would finish the festival off, once and for all.

Mel hated to admit it, but he agreed with the state cop. As of last count, they had sold close to fifty thousand tickets for each day and had spent just over a half-million dollars, but without land, it was practically hopeless. Even if Michael managed to produce another site, how was he expected to prepare and construct the grounds in three weeks' time? In a practical sense, the feat was impossible.

As he refolded the paper and flung it down on the desk, the phone rang. It was Michael Lang in Manhattan.

"We're gonna make a move."

"Are you kidding?"

"No, man. We'll find another place. Look, don't worry. I'm comin' up."

Within two hours, Lawrence and Lang were securely belted into the cabin of a rented helicopter and swinging over the sylvan New York countryside in search of a new home for the festival. They made a half-dozen stops, touching down whenever they saw a large, unplanted field, but the land proved to be either too swampy or provided no access to the site. When they got back to Wallkill, Ticia was waiting for them in the barn.

"Some guy named Elliott just called," she said. "He said that he lives in the town of White Lake, about twenty-five miles away, and that the whole town wants the festival moved up there. And get this: he says he's got the most perfect property for us! I told him we'd be up there this afternoon."

"Groovy!" Lang said, slapping Lawrence's palm.

Ticia kissed them both on the cheek. "Stanley's already up there looking at it. I told him that you guys'd meet him as soon as you get back." She gave them directions, and, within minutes, they were on their way.

White Lake, in the Town of Bethel, Sullivan County, had, at one time, been a small, fashionable resort that attracted Orthodox Jewish families

from all parts of the world. Its chief attraction, of course, was a sandy shored
lake, originally named Kauneonga by the Indians, around which lay a web
of rhododendron-lined lanes extending out to quaint cottages. In the 1940s
and 1950s, however, most of the summer clientele moved a few miles south
to the rejuvenated Borscht Belt, where Grossinger's, the Concord, Kutcher's,
and Brown's lured them with Las Vegas–type entertainment, and White
Lake, instead of competing, never recovered from the exodus. Even the
hordes of faithful anglers, who, each season, came to pluck carmine-spotted
brook trout and pike from out of the pure, clear water, disappeared. The
residents of White Lake had been too slow to respond to what was a simple
public relations problem, and their former prosperity plummeted to embarrassing, incurable lows.

Lawrence and Lang could not help but appreciate the rolling, uneven
fields as they pulled Michael's white Porsche into the gravel-topped parking
lot of the El Monaco Motel, where Ticia told them Stanley Goldstein would
be waiting for them. The roads were in good condition, the air was pine
scented and scintillating, and there seemed to be little enough commercial
activity in the area so they couldn't be accused of interrupting the livelihood
of the town's inhabitants. White Lake had been used to crowds of frenzied
tourists pouring into the community each summer; though it had been some
time since the town's boardinghouses had flourished, Michael and Mel
imagined they'd be greeted there with open arms.

Their fantasy nearly came true. As they stepped out of the car, the front
door of the motel opened and Goldstein and a young man, introduced to
them as Elliott Tieber, the proprietor of the El Monaco Motel, gamboled out
and, at once, were all over them. There was a site, large, it was available,
permits weren't necessary, no, Stanley hadn't seen it yet, but Elliott's description of it was tantalizing.

"Follow me down the hill," Elliott said, pointing to a sloping grade
around the side of the building.

Together the four young men trudged down the bank—Stanley in the
lead, Mel and Michael close behind him, and Elliott following a few steps in
back of the pack. Michael was the first to notice that the ground was soft and,
in places, slushy. A sloshing sound began to keep time with their pace, and
by the time they reached the bottom of the hill, the cuffs on all of their trou-
sers were splattered with mud.

"This place is a fuckin' swamp!" Lawrence said, pulling his foot out of a
puddle of spongy muck. "Where the hell is this site you're talking about?"

"Right through there." Elliott pointed to an archway that appeared to
lead into a jungle of vines and bushy overgrowth.

"Sure," Michael said sarcastically. "Are you puttin' us on?"

"No, really—it'll make a great place to hold a festival. You'll see. There's a natural bowl and everything!"

Goldstein, who had walked ahead of the group, suddenly emerged from the entranceway to Elliott Tieber's supposed fairgrounds, screwing up his face in disgust. "It's a swamp. You won't believe it."

"Aw shit, Elliott," Mel barked, "what's goin' on here, man?"

The young innkeeper appeared uncomfortable and embarrassed. "Nothing, man. I'm tellin' you, it's got incredible possibilities. You can bulldoze it out and drain the water off in hardly no time."

Michael leaned over and looked closely into Elliott's face. "What did you say?"

"I said . . ." His face flushed a dark shade of crimson. "Uh—I said you could bulldoze and drain it."

Michael shook his head in disbelief. "Sure, man—if we had six months and a twenty-million-dollar grant we might be able to do that."

Tieber began to tremble. "I, uh, think you guys oughta take a look at it for yourselves. I'll meet you back up in the motel." And, without further ado, he turned and tramped back up the steep slope, leaving them to fend for themselves.

Lawrence was livid. "Look the fuck what this guy's making us do, waste our day like this! This place is totally unacceptable."

"Not to an alligator," Goldstein said, smiling. "Hey, look, the guy only wanted to help us out. It's been a long time since anyone wanted to do much for us."

"I'm not so sure," Michael said. "This place sucks. It really *is* a fucking swamp. There's not really any chance of our using it, is there?" he asked Goldstein.

"Not on your life."

"Then let's get outta here."

When they reached the small reception desk, they found Elliott Tieber taking long, nervous drags on a cigarette. "I'm sorry, fellas. I just thought it was better than nothing. You know, we'd sure like to see the festival take place around here. It'd liven up the place a bit."

"Don't worry about it," Lang reassured him. "Listen, Elliott—is there anything else around here we should see—something a little dryer?"

"Not that I know of, but I have a friend, an older guy, who deals in country real estate. Why don't you guys hang around for a few minutes, and I'll give him a call."

Elliott picked up a phone and dialed someone he referred to throughout the conversation as Mr. Abraham. He briefly explained the promoters' plight and handed the receiver over to Michael, who took over from there.

"Well, I'll tell you, young fella, I just might be able to work something out to solve your problem if you make it worth my while." Lang assured Abraham that, if he could produce anywhere near six hundred acres of beautiful pasture that was suitable for a concert, he could name his commission. "Good, good. It just so happens that I know a milk farmer a few miles from where you're standin' right now, who, only last year, was willin' to rent his land to a herd of boy scouts for some kind of jam-*bo*-ree. Now, if he's still in the same frame of mind, I think we might have ourselves a deal. Why don't you boys meet me at the El Monaco tomorrow morning—say about 10:00— and I'll take you over to meet him."

"We'll be there, Mr. Abraham," Michael promised, none too excitedly. This guy Abraham sounded as though he was going to hit them for a stiff fee. "Just for the record, though, would you mind telling me his name."

"Why, no. Not at all. His name is Max—Max Yasgur."

— **2** —

Max Yasgur's name had always been mentioned in a tone that conveyed something more than respect by the people of Sullivan County—like that of an elder statesman or a community demagogue. And, in fact, Max Yasgur was a bit of both.

That summer of 1969, as he prepared to purchase still another barn to harbor his expanding herd of black and white Holstein cattle, beaming with pride as children from all neighboring schools and academies were conducted on tours through his processing plants, Max Yasgur was gearing up to celebrate yet another milestone in his illustrious career. He had been born in Maplewood, New York, a small farming community a few miles outside of Monticello, on December 15, 1919, fifty years before Michael Lang set foot in White Lake, and the golden occasion would be commemorated in grand style by a family reunion. Throughout the decades of his prosperity, Max, an outspoken leader, had immersed himself in every local fracas that came his way, choosing to raise a commanding voice above the buzz of dispute when it would have been more convenient to remain quiet. He continuously found himself at the helm of controversy, and if he wasn't negotiating a zoning regulation, it was a political debate or commercial polemics that caught his attention. But Max wasn't a fighter, he was a farmer who won the admiration and respect of his neighbors by unselfishly putting them ahead of his own pleasure.

Everyone within fifty miles of White Lake knew Yasgur's Dairy. Their children, and their children's children, had been drinking Yasgur's Pasteurized Milk since the day they were born, and Max saw to it that they never missed a day. He ran what was practically an around-the-clock operation, getting up well before dawn to be in the fields and taking calls at ungodly hours of the night from his employees to insure that production quotas were met. Many natives of Sullivan County worked at the dairy farm, either tending the milking apparatus or making deliveries throughout the county, and they always returned home talking about Max—never Mr. Yasgur, but *Max*—like he was one of the family.

His own parents had migrated to Sullivan County shortly before Max was born and bought a farm on the fringe of the Town of Bethel. His father had been a butcher, but poor health prohibited him from keeping up with the duties of such a rigorous occupation, and so he decided to farm, taking in enough of a crop each year to provide for his modest family. They knew, however, that it was nearly impossible to make a decent living from the farm, so, as most of the townsfolk did in those days, they built a small boardinghouse next to their own home where, during the months of July and August, they took in guests who delighted in the refreshing country air and showed their appreciation of Yasgur's hospitality by returning year after year.

Max grew up on that Maplewood farm, and when his father died in 1936, he took over the crops and helped his mother run the boardinghouse. Subsequently, he had little time to cultivate an athletic legacy in high school or as a student at New York University where he studied real estate law, intending to enter a family brokerage. But if physical fitness was the mark of able-bodied gentry, then Max Yasgur was a specimen of unusually sound refinement. The hours spent plowing the fields, bringing in the hay, sowing grain and husking corn added muscle to his tanned physique and enabled him to perform most any feat of strength. Though he was slight of build, he presented a dashing, affable appearance. He had a wide forehead, a statuesque chin, a Semitic nose, and dark, sympathetic eyes which attracted a respectable flock of admirers. Max married one of them, a vivacious girl named Miriam two years younger than he, whose parents had brought her, each summer since she was three years old, to the Yasgurs' inn at Maplewood.

They lived on the home farm, as it was called, until 1947, when Max decided that he no longer wished to enlarge the boarding house or go into the hotel business. He loved the farm, he loved the land, and he began looking around for additional property with which to expand his already well-grounded operation.

Before long, Max purchased a larger farm in Bethel, closed the boardinghouse, and pumped the profit right back into more farmland. He and Miriam ended up with nine different farms that were pretty much adjacent to one another. But they were not complete. Their original plan had been to convert the farms into a gigantic processing plant where they would eventually pasteurize and sell "the Cadillac of milks," as Max liked to call his product, and other dairy produce. It took them nearly ten years, during which time they battled New York State in a grueling act of endurance, until they were finally issued a license to purify and bottle milk—Max's greatest pride. He enjoyed his work, he loved walking the fields each night at sunset (which, by the time of the festival, had grown to nearly two hundred thousand acres), and he dreamt of the time when he could retire to Florida after having turned his dairy empire over to his two beautiful children.

The rigorous task of running the farms, however, had taken its toll on Max. By 1968, he had already suffered an inordinate share of heart attacks and never strayed further than ten feet from a jet tank of pure oxygen. Every time he got excited—which occurred at least three or four times a day—Max would excuse himself from any confrontation, lock himself into the nearest private quarters available, and relax under the oxygen tent. That may have been a strong factor in his decision *not* to rent a portion of his property to outside promoters when Morris Abraham called to inquire about its availability.

"It could wind up being a substantial rental fee. Are you sure you're not interested?" Abraham asked.

"Frankly—no. We're cutting hay, and we can't have people tramping around in our fields." Max thanked him for his interest and said that maybe sometime in the future the situation would be different and he would be more attuned to such a proposal.

The next day, however, Abraham called back and told Max that the group for whom he was inquiring was made up of those young people he may have been reading about in the newspaper who had been deprived of their site in Wallkill. Abraham explained the extenuating circumstances to Max and asked him if he would reconsider. Without a moment's hesitation, Max said yes, the sooner the better. If Abraham brought them around to the office, he would see them immediately.

*   *   *

Michael Lang spent the next morning of July 17 navigating the switchbacks around White Lake with reckless bravado. Running the white Porsche quickly through all five gears, he soared over barren stretches of country blacktop, up and down hilly ranges, across cattle paths, the way a child commandeers a penny arcade road game. Once inside the village limits, he sent Ticia Bernuth scrambling from the passenger side of the car to check the names on roadside mailboxes. He needed to be certain that he was not being led down another blind alley like the one Elliott had guided them into yesterday afternoon. What a colossal waste of time wallowing through that marsh had been, Michael thought. Everyone wanted to latch onto a corner of his star—if only for a moment. People offered to help without thinking of the consequences. The only way he could prevent that from happening again was by locating the Yasgur property before the scheduled one o'clock appointment and helping himself to a sneak preview of its untold bounties.

They combed the area for nearly an hour without much luck. Most of the farms were of a substantial size, and it was difficult to determine who belonged to what piece of property. Houses were set back quite a distance from the main road, which forced them to spend a ponderous amount of time backing the car down narrow driveways only to be greeted by the family German shepherd or some other snapping carnivore. On the verge of returning to Wallkill unrewarded, Ticia suddenly squealed with delight. "Look, Michael, that road." She pointed to a cutoff obscured by an enormous tree. "It's called Happy Avenue. Let's see where it goes."

Michael rolled his eyes skyward. Just what he had time for! Snapping dogs in White Lake, ferocious wolves in Wallkill, and she wants to skip down Happy Avenue looking for—what, fairies and elves? "Please?" Ticia asked with big, expectant eyes, knowing it would be impossible for him to refuse her. And she was right. Having passed the intersection during Ticia's appeal, Michael performed a neat U-turn, retraced the two hundred or so yards to where the tiny sign pointed left, and turned the Porsche into Happy Avenue and points unknown.

Almost at once, they came upon what they had been searching for all morning. Through a choppy band of hedges that barricaded a patchwork field was a wide, unobstructed meadow with a graceful incline that pitched toward a picturebook red barn. Michael almost plowed his car into a tree while he attempted to see beyond the hedge. He pulled off onto the shoulder of the road and climbed out. "That's it," he whispered reverently. "It's outta sight!"

Ticia and Lang sauntered over to the hedge and stared off across the field. It was magnificent. For as far as one could see, there was lush, green, virgin field—acres and acres of it—just sitting there, left untended. Oh, it was wonderful, they thought, holding hands and carrying on like children on Christmas Eve. The first hundred acres or so was, to some extent, level and formed a plateau that curved around the outskirts of the site like the upper deck of a baseball stadium. The remainder of the field was uneven, flowing like a sea of tiny moguls on a choppy ski slope. The miniature hills sat one on top of the other overlooking a ravine that appeared to be scooped out of a section of woods. Nothing could have been more perfect for an outdoor concert. There was plenty of room for seating, the stage could be placed at the bottom of the hill, and the trees would act as an acoustical backdrop off which the sound could reverberate. Access was freer than what they had been prepared to contend with at Wallkill; two main roads circled the property and joined larger, better equipped thoroughfares that bypassed the Town of Bethel. If Michael remembered correctly, the Quickway was only a mile or so down the road. Their staff people could more or less meet all incoming cars at the Quickway ramp and herd them toward the festival grounds without causing a traffic tie-up of any proportion.

"Michael, let's take a closer look," Ticia prompted, squeezing his hand in anticipation of their discovery.

"Unh-uh. Not now. I want to wait until later this afternoon—if this *is*, in fact, Yasgur's place. Otherwise, we've got two shots at grabbin' ourselves some land. Let's get back to Wallkill so I can hook up with Mel and the rest of the guys before we head back up here."

They hopped back into the sports car and slowly rolled down the street, never, for a moment, taking their eyes off the field. Ticia kept repeating, "Michael—it's on *Happy* Avenue. We're leaving a town called *Wallkill*. The signs, look at the signs, man!"

The signs were, indeed, cosmic. Only yesterday, their fate hinged on a legal technicality and seemed inevitable. Now, at least, Michael knew there was land to be had in the vicinity of their first site. They could move everything from one place to the other in a matter of days and still have time to meet their deadline. It all depended on the disposition of the man who owned it. Max Yasgur, or whoever it was who held the deed on that fantastic Happy Avenue piece of property, was about to come up against a tidal wave of bargaining stamina. He had nothing to lose (it was John Roberts's money he was spending). All it took was land, and by that evening, a lease would be in his hip pocket. Michael Lang was not to be denied.

Lang, with Mel Lawrence, rode back to White Lake that afternoon in a blinding downpour. Traffic slowed to a crawl on Route 17, the ultrahazardous New York Quickway, and the white Porsche was obliged to take its ines-capable place behind a bottleneck of trucks and trailers as they wound through the Catskill Mountain motorgap.

Elliott and Morris Abraham, whose features were obscured by a super-stratum of khaki raingear and a bulky scarf, hurriedly met them in the door-way of the El Monaco Motel. They hastened the Woodstock executives into the back seat of Abraham's car to carry them comfortably over to Max Yasgur's farm.

The rain had just about subsided as the realtor turned into a wide, paved driveway which pointed the way to the farmer's office (they were to learn later that Yasgur also maintained offices in town and at his home). Michael Lang's face was a study in disappointment. Their terminus was not the same piece of land that he and Ticia had explored earlier that morning, and he was shamelessly crestfallen. What could Yasgur offer them that was even remotely as superb as that field on Happy Avenue? Why hadn't he had the good sense to hunt out the landlord of that property right then and there and strike a deal? Now, he'd have to waste the rest of the daylight hours sightsee-ing with a group of money-hungry opportunists and wait until Saturday morning to return to Happy Avenue. It was a pity, considering that time was the biggest factor working against them.

Max Yasgur met them in front of his processing plant and offered to take them on a walking tour of his property. He was courteous in a business way that precluded intimacy and, without ceremony, marched his visitors off around the corner of the barn to the tract that was up for lease.

He showed them a parcel of 250 acres that had absolutely no contour whatsoever.

"This'll make a great parking lot," Lawrence quipped, "but don't you have anything else with some kinda definite form—a few hills, some eleva-tion? This just won't work for us."

"Yes. As a matter of fact, I do have a considerable alfalfa field, but it's in use. I'll tell you what—why don't we drive over there and you can take a look at it anyway."

The four men piled back into Abraham's car, and they cautiously plowed through patches of dense fog on their way to the other location. On the way there, Yasgur told them that he had heard about their trouble in Wallkill, and that he considered it an outrage, flagrant injustice. "I want to help you boys, if I can. You got the raw end of a deal." He felt that young people, in general, were being prejudged. In his book, everyone, either young or old, had the same rights. That included the right to congregate. If they abused that right, then they could endanger their position later on; however, that remained to be seen. He equated it to a fair trial. "How would it look if a jury had already made their minds up about a certain case before they heard any of the evidence? That's not what this country's about." Max went on and on about the doctrine of equality, but Lang was no longer listening. Something else had caught his attention. He had wiped away a section of condensation on the side window of the car and saw a vision that sent his spirits soaring.

"Excuse me, Mr. Yasgur," Michael said, interrupting the long-winded farmer, "but does all this belong to you, too?" He motioned to the scenery.

"Sure does."

Michael sat back in the seat and smiled as Abraham pulled the car off Happy Avenue and barreled down a service road toward the wooded ravine.

Lawrence couldn't believe his eyes and spun around in a circle trying to take in as much of the view as he possibly could in one glance. "I can't believe it," he gasped, "this is really great. It's just incredible."

Lang grinned and gave him the "high sign." Drawing Mel aside, he whispered, "Listen, you take care of Abraham. Keep him out of the way for a couple minutes. I'm gonna see what Max has got up his sleeve. I got a feeling he's a pretty slick dude."

Indeed, he was. At first, Yasgur was reluctant even to discuss this portion of his land. If it was disturbed by a group of young kids—or, for that matter, by anybody else—he stood to lose an entire crop.

"Look, Max, without it, we're sunk. We can lose close to three-quarters of a million bucks. I'm layin' it on the line to you. We need this land, and we'll make it worth your while."

Yasgur said that he wanted to help, but he could not afford to give up the crop. "You'd have to reimburse me for my loss," he said, looking sideways at Lang out of the corner of his eyes.

"How much, Max?"

"It's going to come to close to $300 an acre. Let's say, $50,000." Michael whistled. "And that won't permit you to use certain pieces of land until later on because I can still salvage some of the growth."

"You got it. Anything. We don't need most of the land until a day before the show. None of that matters. Let's make a deal."

"Hold on, now, young fella. This is valuable property, and I don't intend to risk everything I've worked for over the years to make a quick buck. This is serious. Now, I'm going to want your company to guarantee that I get my property back in the same condition it was given to you. And you're going to have to place a substantial sum—for safety's sake, let's say $75,000—into an escrow account in case there are any damages. Do you have that kind of money?"

Michael nodded meekly. The figures Yasgur was quoting made his head spin. Sure, they had the bread. But another $125,000 was an awful load to carry—even if it wasn't his money.

"All right then—why don't you bring your representatives around to my attorney's office tomorrow morning, and we'll discuss the fine points of this arrangement." He gave Lang his lawyer's name and address and agreed to meet them there a little before noon. "You fellas can roam around out here while Mr. Abraham takes me home. I'll send him back for you when he's done." They shook hands, and Max Yasgur slipped into the car with Abraham and drove off.

Lawrence practically catapulted onto Michael's shoulders. "Far fuckin' out, man! This place is even better than Wallkill. How'd it go?"

Michael, however, was still looking at his outstretched hand.

"What's the matter?"

"Oh, nothin'! Well, actually, it's gotta do with Yasgur's handshake." Michael scrunched up his face. "The cat's only got three fingers. It was really weird, man. I mean, I grabbed his hand to shake on a deal, and I only got three fingers."

"You mean—we got the place?" Lawrence asked.

"Uh, yeah," Michael said, staring at his hand.

"That's great! I mean—Michael, we're back in business!" He slapped Lang on the back five or ten times and, soon, they were hugging one another, dancing around in a circle. "I can't believe it! I can't fuckin' believe it!" Lawrence screamed. "Kid—you're incredible!"

"Thanks." Michael was grinning from ear to ear now, and the two men began to slap each other's hands so rapidly that their palms turned bright red. Lawrence collapsed in the wet grass, ecstatic. "C'mon, get up. Let's take a look around the place before ol' Abraham comes back." Michael pulled him up by the arms, and they wandered across the bowl, not quite really knowing where to go or what to look at first.

"The incredible thing," Lawrence said, pointing toward the section of land carved out from the woods, "is that this is a natural amphitheatre. In all my years doing shows, I don't think I've ever seen anything more suited to a performing arts center than this place." He explained acoustics to Lang, using his hands to show how sound would careen off the trees in direct/reflecting audio frequency and travel outward, in this case up the hill, in an ever expanding radius. "If we place our sound towers just outside the line of the reflected waves, everyone within a mile of this place will be able to hear as clearly as if they were listening to a record at home."

While they discussed the layout, the fog had lifted off a patch of ground to the left of the woods revealing a lake. Lawrence and Lang stared open-mouthed at the mist-covered body of water.

"Holy shit! Where did that come from?"

"I don't know, man, but if a voice comes from its depths, I'm cuttin' outta here."

"Do you believe this? Huh? *Do you fuckin' believe this?*" They hugged each other again. "Oh, this is really going to be good," Mel said. "It's perfect, perfect, perfect!"

"Are you gonna be able to put it together in three weeks?"

"Yeah. Don't give it another thought. Come August 15, you're gonna see one hundred thousand kids sittin' up there on that hill turnin' on to our show."

"Haven't I heard that before somewhere?"

"Yeah." Lawrence nodded sheepishly. "You have. But this time, I think you can pretty much bank on it, m'man. We got ourselves one helluva festival site."

"I think you're right, Mel. C'mon—let's get outta here. I think we could both use a rest."

They slapped palms again—once, this time, for good measure—and walked up the embankment, arms draped around each other's back, to where Abraham's car waited to take them back to the EI Monaco.

— **3** —

Since their ouster from Mills Heights, John Roberts and Joel Rosenman had shuttered themselves in the uptown office, juggling the torrent of inquiries from the press and other interested parties as to the destiny of the Aquarian Exposition. They had no idea *what* to tell their interrogators, except that the Town of Wallkill's decision to ban the festival was completely unjustified and, as far as their lawyers could determine, without regard for the law. They intended to stay and fight. Unfortunately, not only did that rationale *not* hold water with those who had already purchased tickets, but John and Joel didn't really believe it themselves. The festival's tortured soul was on the critical list, and John couldn't help but ponder the incredible medical bill he'd be picking up for its intensive care treatment.

The Concerned Citizens Committee certainly hadn't helped matters.

After the permit was rejected, they saw fit to call a press conference in order
to announce the verdict to the world. While they were at it, they also implied
that, since there would be no festival in the Town of Wallkill, all patrons of
Woodstock Ventures should seek refunds on their ticket investment. That
little thorn prompted their ticket vendors to curtail all future sales, brought
their mail-order activity grinding to a halt, and signaled the attorney general's office to call out the consumer complaint troops. There was little else
they could do but to lie. "Cancelled?" Roberts feigned astonishment. "Not
on your life! In fact, we've already got an alternate site lined up."

In light of that exaggeration, Michael Lang's phone call, which would
have ordinarily been held in dubious esteem, was greeted with vast relief.
"Well, Michael, I certainly hope you have some good news for us for a
change. We've been pretty fucking miserable trying to put people off. Where
do we stand?"

"Even better than our position in Wallkill," he said, and John had to do
everything possible to refrain from laughing. Lang, however, persevered in
his description of the White Lake site and topped it off with a testimonial to
their newfound benefactor. "Max is a prince, man. He's totally behind us
and the rest of the townspeople are in our corner. It's like—beautiful, man.
Listen, the whole thing's gonna go down tomorrow morning at Max's lawyer's pad. I think you oughta be in on it, and you'd better bring along a lotta
bread. Max drives a hard bargain." He told Roberts the terms of the agreement.

"I think I oughta see the place before I *buy* it, Michael. Tell this Yasgur
guy that we'll meet him on the site before the meeting, and we can all drive
to the attorney's together. I'll meet you in Middletown about nine o'clock."
Lang agreed, however reluctantly, and hung up.

The next morning, John and Michael drove from Wallkill to White Lake
in near silence. Their lack of conversation might have been embarrassing
had they not been absorbed by the news reports about Teddy Kennedy's auto
mishap in Massachusetts, which had evolved from a tragedy into something
of a national scandal. From what they could gather from the various broad-
casts, the senator had been driving home from a party the night before and
had plunged his car off the Chappaquiddick Island Bridge, and his twenty-
eight-year-old companion, Mary Jo Kopechne, had drowned. Speculation
abounded about the incident, linking the two accident victims as partners in
an illicit romance. Kennedy's failure to report the accident until the next day
served to heighten the suspicion.

"Unbelievable," John snorted, trying to appear as hip as he possibly
could be in front of Michael. "It goes to show you just how much we cannot
trust politicians."

"Well, you can't be sure, man. The way I figure it—they got John and Bobby. Ted's the only one left."

"Who, Michael?"

"*They,* man. Y'know, the Establishment. Sooner or later they pin a bum rap on all their enemies. That's why the revolution's just around the corner, man. This country belongs to the people, not the FBI and CIA, and one day they're gonna take it back from those dudes who hold the power. You'll see."

"Hmmm . . ."

"Right here, man," Michael said abruptly, pointing to the entranceway to Yasgur's farm. "There's Max up ahead."

Roberts was afforded the same professional treatment that Michael had received the day before. He found Max quite charming and an improvement many times over their former landlord, Howard Mills, Jr. Here was a man he found very much like his own father—middle-aged, well dressed, eloquent, educated, Jewish—and, yet, Max Yasgur exhibited more compassion toward young people than Alfred Roberts might have shown in the same situation, especially when it came to their being prejudged because of their age and appearance.

"That's great, Max," Roberts agreed, "but, gee, you're talking about an incredible amount of money for us to put up just to rent your land for a couple days."

"You're right. But, right now, it's the only thing you have, and I'm taking a considerable risk with my neighbors and my reputation. They're not going to like this too much."

"We're worried about that, too. We have no guarantee that once we move in, we'll be able to stay."

Max looked stupefied. "What do you mean—stay? Of course, you'll be allowed to stay. What I do with my property is my own business."

"I understand that, but we've just been tossed out of one place that told us the same thing. A lotta good that did us. Now, it's going to cost us another $125,000 to get ourselves situated, not to speak of publicity and another public relations campaign from scratch. What happens if the Town of Bethel decides they don't like what they see?"

"Don't you worry about a thing. I carry a substantial amount of weight in this town, and if I enter into a contractual arrangement with you, I intend to deliver my end of the deal. Anyway, I've taken the liberty of arranging a town meeting for you fellas next week—that is, if we have a deal."

"We do, Max, we do. You said it yourself: it's the only thing we have. And, anyway, I rather like it. I think we'll get along real fine."

Michael, who had remained a spectator throughout the proceedings, let out a comical sigh of relief.

"Good," Max said. "Now why don't you fellas come over to my house. I'll take you on a tour of my dairy, we'll have ourselves some chocolate milk"—he sardonically smiled—"and then we'll get down to business."

When the collective bargaining session was over, Max Yasgur had made himself a deal as shrewd as the one in which Peter Stuyvesant got New York in exchange for a handful of glass beads. Roberts had agreed to Yasgur's preposterous asking price early in the negotiations and prepared to take leave and compute his new indebtedness in the privacy of his Manhattan apartment. Three hours—and several gallons of chocolate milk—later, the two men remained locked in debate over the term of occupancy Woodstock Ventures would be entitled to by virtue of the lease. Max had prepared an intricately detailed map of his land featuring each crop, barn, cow, and, if one were to ask Roberts, every blade of grass between Happy Avenue and the great unknown. Beneath each notation, Max had penciled in a date on which that particular segment of the site would be made available to them. Several times during the discussion, John feigned breaking off the talks, and each time, Yasgur reminded his young associate of his recent heart attack until Roberts acceded to the farmer's demands. No one was permitted to disturb Max's crops until it was contractually all right to do so; any violation of the time schedule would draw a stiff monetary penalty.

"This is the best I can do, John," Yasgur contended. "I don't think you have many options open to you other than what I'm offering. You'd best think twice before you walk out of here without a deal." In other words: take it or leave it.

Roberts took it. By 10:30 P.M., both parties confirmed their accord with each clause (one party more enthusiastically than the other) and a deal memorandum was submitted to Yasgur's attorney for formal papers to be drafted. The Woodstock Music and Art Fair was back in business.

On their way back to New York City, Roberts painfully brought up a subject that, only recently, had provided him with sleepless nights: financing. "You know, Michael, we've said goodbye to the $500,000-mark we originally set. I think it's time we took a realistic look at what this thing's going to wind up costing us and work something out."

"Like what, man?"

"Nothing that will get you upset. Look, I'm going to have to come up with at least another $500,000 before the end of this thing. Okay—so it was more expensive than we thought. I realize those things happen. But I'm the guy who's going to be taking all the risks."

"And you want to adjust the percentages, right?"

"Wrong. I don't do business that way. We made a deal, and I intend to stick by it. We're equal partners."

"Outta sight, man. I can appreciate what you're doing, and all."

"But I do have to sign a promissory note with the bank for the rest of the financing within the next day or two. Now, I don't think your and Artie's guarantees are worth a pile of beans. But, at least to my way of thinking, it would be an act of good faith if you guys were to come in on this damn thing with me."

"You want us to *sign* on the loan?" Michael was incredulous.

"That's right."

"Well . . ." Lang's voice trailed off, "I don't know, man."

"What don't you know?"

"I mean, what good would it do?" Michael shifted his seat to face Roberts. "Let me see if I've got this straight. Now, if the festival goes into debt, that means Artie and I would have to bear a share of the responsibility—right?"

"That's right."

"Well, I don't know about Artie, man, but if I'm called on to come up with $500,000, I couldn't do it. Whew! What a bummer, man."

"I know you couldn't do it. You guys probably couldn't buy a newspaper on credit between you. But I just think that it would be a vote of confidence for me when I walk into the bank on Monday and ask for another half million. Anyway—it's not going to mean anything to you in the long run. Look at ticket sales. We're going to make a bundle on the festival. What do you think?"

"I don't know, man. Let me sleep on it, and we'll talk about it tomorrow."

"All right, Michael. But if you've got any second thoughts about the success of the festival, I hope to hell you'll let me know before I spring for the rest."

It was, however, the last time the subject was discussed between the partners.

The only person with an afterthought about his deal was Max Yasgur. Like Roberts, Max intended to honor his commitment to the promoters, and he was satisfied that the deal he had made with the boys was a fair one. But the reality of hosting the event on his land—well, something told him that he hadn't taken enough time to consider all of the consequences. He was confused, not only about the eventuality of the festival, but also about the young people who were likely to attend it. Yasgur was a conservative Republican farmer who took a strict line with his own children. Now, in a strange turn of events, he was about to assume responsibility for an entire generation whose social politics were a puzzle to him. In the most profound sense, he had been taken aback by Michael Lang's appearance—the dirty jeans, bare chest, beaded vest, rawhide wristbands, the long curls, the crazy leather hat, and motorcycle boots. Only a day before, he would have shunned a person like Lang had they passed one another on the street. There was no doubt he would have branded the boy a troublemaker had he not known him. But that afternoon, Max strolled into his house, found his wife, Miriam, in the living room reading a newspaper, and told her, "You wouldn't believe that a boy who looks like that could be so nice." He had been charmed by Lang's soft, polite voice and ingratiating smile—and that worried him, too.

That evening, Miriam Yasgur presented Max with several additional problems they might encounter along the way, namely property damage and the antagonism of their neighbors. "We don't want to distress anyone, Max. We're comfortable in our business, we make our own living. I'm not sure if it's wise to rock the boat."

"I agree with you," he admitted. "The only thing is, it's wrong to deny these young people the same right you'd give to older folks. I guess I'm the guy who's going to have to prove that. And, anyway, it's an excellent business deal. I'll tell you what: let's sleep on it and discuss it again in the morning."

Word travels fast in a small town. Thanks to the promotional instincts of Elliott Tieber, it was announced to the *Times Herald Record* that he would hold a press conference on Monday, July 21, "to reveal information about a White Lake Music Festival." Bethel residents began to investigate the rumor's validity, hoping to turn up the culprit before it was too late. By Sunday morning, they had traced its trail to the home of Max Yasgur.

Max was still in a quandary about his newly acquired role as the housefather to a swarm of bleary-eyed hippies when he left the house early Sunday morning. The points that Miriam had raised the night before began to swell in his mind, and he was now seriously in doubt as to whether he had taken a noble stand or had inadvertently made a grave and costly mistake. "Don't worry about it," she had advised him, so that he'd be able to conduct his business at the dairy with a minimal amount of mental stress, but it preoccupied him, nonetheless.

Whatever indecision Yasgur might have had at that moment was obliterated within minutes. As he backed out of the driveway, he came face-to-face with something that served to reinforce his partnership with Woodstock Ventures. There, nailed to a tree at the end of the lane, was a crudely lettered sign on which was painted: "Buy No Milk. Local People Speak Out. Stop Max's Hippy Music Festival. No 150,000 Hippies Here." Max was furious.

What person, in his right mind, would waste his time doing something that foolish? Whose business was it, anyway? *Stop Max's Hippy Music Festival*—the thought was preposterous! If anything had convinced Max that he was doing the right thing, that sign was the deciding factor.

Later, opponents of the festival would argue among themselves that anyone who knew Max should have realized that, from the moment that billboard was hoisted into place, the festival was "all systems go." He'd be damned if he was going to allow a bunch of hard-nosed bigots to eject the kids from his property.

Max sent two of his farmhands back to the house and had them remove the sign. Later, when he returned for breakfast, he discussed it with his wife.

"I have a feeling we're going to go through with this, aren't we, Max?"

"Well, if you agree, I think it's time we spoke out about the injustice being done to these kids. What do you say?"

Miriam smiled wistfully. What could she say? Her husband was stubborn as a mule. "I'm with you, Max," she said. "Just tell me one thing. Are you sure that you can handle this?"

He just shrugged. They had made up their minds thirteen years before, when Max suffered his first heart attack, that they would live one day at a time, without fear. That was it. The time was right, and Max had made up his mind: the Aquarian Exposition had come to White Lake. He'd be there to celebrate their success when it was over.

— 4 —

Joel Rosenman had been dispatched to White Lake as an emissary from the uptown office whose job it would be to keep an eye on the corporation's future disbursements. Too many questionable expenditures had come to their attention of late; several thousand dollars a week were being spent for which there were no receipts, and a flurry of checks on which John Roberts's signature had been forged crossed their bookkeeper's desk until it became commonplace for her not to recognize either of the co-signers' endorsements. For the longest time, Penny Stallings had held the on-site checkbook, but even her strict control of company funds was ineffective against the sophisticated methods of scamming. Hardly an afternoon went by when she didn't find Michael Lang holding a corporate check up to the window so he could trace

John Roberts's signature, or uncover a ploy for someone on the staff to filch a few bucks from petty cash. The only defense left was for Joel to regulate the bank account, and that didn't sit well with anyone except John Roberts.

Rosenman arrived in White Lake just a few hours before the Apollo 11 astronauts were scheduled to become the first human beings to set foot on the moon. His plan had been to settle into a production trailer behind the El Monaco (whose parking lot the festival agreed to repave in return for a temporary place to drop anchor), and then head over to the Red Top where the staff was gathering to watch the televised landing. On the way back to his car, Joel was intercepted by Michael Lang and a middle-aged, squat man with large, bulging eyes whom he introduced as Morris Abraham, "a cat with unbelievable connections." On some prearranged signal, Abraham excused himself so that Lang could have a few words alone with his partner.

"Look, Joel, there's a few things goin' down here that need, uh, special attention. Know what I mean?"

"Not really, Michael."

"You gotta deal with Morris, man. He's pretty heavy in the town. Like, he got the racetrack into Monticello when the people were against it. Right now, we need him on our side to keep things cool with the locals."

"How do you know he's on the level? Have you checked him out?"

"Oh sure, man. He's cool. Look, I had a check made up for him for $2,500. He wants $10,000 for 'expenses' for the whole gig; otherwise we're on the street again. We're gonna have to play ball, but I don't want to give him the whole thing in advance."

"There's no other alternative for us?"

"No way, man. You know what I know."

I only wish it were so, Joel thought. "Look, Michael, if you've been dealing with him so far, maybe you'd . . ."

"Don't sweat it, Joel. I'll work it out with the dude, and we'll be good as gold."

But before Rosenman could escape unnoticed, Abraham was at his trailer door circumstantiating the steep retainer and demanding the entire $10,000 up front. "I got expenses, Joel, and they can't wait." Lang had obviously placed the blame on Rosenman for their having to put Abraham on the installment plan.

"Sorry, Morris, but we have to see some results before we settle any accounts. I'm sure you understand our position."

The realtor pleaded for understanding of his own. He needed an expense fund at his disposal from which he could skim several thousand dollars in small bills to pay for "influence." Otherwise, it was going to be tough producing "the desired effect."

"But I'm sure you'll find some way to do it. If we're not here come August, you're not going to see another penny from us."

"You're the boss, Joel," Abraham surrendered. "You'll see, it'll go smoothly. Just let 'em give me any trouble, Joel. I'll ram this festival down their fucking throats."

There was something about Abraham's method of operation that did not sit well with Lang, either. That evening, after Neil Armstrong intoned "One small step for a man, one giant step for mankind" from the lunar surface, Michael and Stanley Goldstein paid a visit to Max Yasgur, at his home.

The boys were shown into their host's spacious kitchen where they were offered the house drink, chocolate milk, and a few hours of Max's time. The dairy business required that he be up long before dawn, and therefore he made every attempt to get to bed at a reasonable hour.

"That's cool," Michael acknowledged. "There's something that we gotta tell you, though. It won't take long. I just don't know how you're gonna take this. But we've been straight with each other and I think you oughta know."

Max propped his elbows on the kitchen table, folded his hands into a bridge, and balanced his chin on it for support.

Goldstein took over, choosing each word carefully. "While we were in Wallkill, we decided that we would not buy our way into the community." He hesitated when Yasgur's eyes narrowed, not certain how to proceed. He couldn't tell whether Max was interested in what he said or if he was growing impatient. "Had we not taken that position—who knows, we might still be there now. But whether we were right or not, we went with our instincts. Now, we've been approached by certain parties who have informed us that it's going to take $10,000 to 'buy' the proper authorities, otherwise they'll make trouble for us."

Yasgur raised both hands at once and brought them crashing down on the formica table. "My God!" he cried. "That's positively disgusting. I can't believe it. Who's this 'certain party' that you're referring to?"

"We can't tell you, Max," Michael said.

"You've got to. You said it yourself: we've been straight with one another, and I'll be goddamned if I let this kind of hornswaggling go on in my community. Why, that's bribery. Now, tell me who it is. Tell me and I'll go down the line with you."

Michael gave him Abraham's name quite willingly, as he had planned to do all along.

"That son of a bitch. He can't get away with that."

Lang shared Max's indignation. "Yeah, it's extortion, and I'd rather not be a party to it. But I don't see any other way out."

"You'd better find one, young man, or else you won't hold your festival on my property. Let me tell you something. I've never paid a bribe in my life, and I won't allow something like that to take place with my knowledge."

"I'm not gonna bribe him, Max. That's why Stan and I came to see you, your knowin' these people and all. I'd rather take that money and give it to the town somehow—in a way that will benefit everybody."

"We have the check ready, Max," Goldstein said. "We were prepared to pay it to these men, but we thought that since we were making so much of a commitment to the Town of Bethel, we'd like to give it to the hospital for their building fund."

"I think that's a damned good idea, boys."

"But we still have to deal with these guys who want the bread."

"You fellas leave that up to me."

Before the evening was out, the three men had worked out a plan whereby Max would make an appointment to see Morris Abraham and extract from him the name of the town official who stood to inherit a substantial sum from the scheme. Abraham, he was convinced, would tell him because the realtor knew that Max was capable of making trouble for him. Once that was done, he would need the four partners to sign a document attesting to the fact that they had, indeed, been threatened with expulsion from Bethel unless payment was made to this individual. Max would then confront that man, and instruct him that unless Woodstock Ventures was given complete assurance that nothing would interfere with their production, he was prepared to personally finance a campaign exposing the blackmailer in every newspaper in upstate New York.

"You know—I think it'll work, Max. I think it's just lethal enough to put the gag on these cats."

"It had better," he said, wiping his forehead with a handkerchief. The murky summer humidity, combined with the heated conversation, had turned Max's flimsy white shirt into a soggy towel. "You know, I've lived in this community nearly all my life and, even though I've heard some pretty scandalous stories, which I happen to *know* are true, I don't think that anything's ever upset me as much as the sinister business you've revealed to me here tonight. Why, you're talking about people whom I've entrusted to look after my own interests, people whom I've elected to office. I don't understand what could possibly have driven them to do such things, and, what's more, it eats me that they presumed they'd get away with it right in front of my eyes. It's just beyond me. But I'll tell you one thing, boys, and on this I stake my reputation as a solid, *honest* citizen"—he rapped his index finger on the table until it turned a bright red—"it's not going to happen here as long as I have the breath in my body to put a stop to it. I don't intend to be a party to dirty politics, and you should make it a point now, while you're both still young, never to participate in it either."

Yasgur rose slowly, then ushered Goldstein and Lang out onto his front porch with the finesse of a statesman. It was late. In a few hours he'd be expected in his barn to look after his prize bulls. "Tomorrow morning, before any of us gets carried away with our own affairs, we'll put this entire matter to rest. I expect you'll have that paper signed for me so I'll have some ammunition," he said, pointing to a folded sheet of paper in Lang's hand. "Right now, I think I'd better put myself to rest. I'll see you in the morning."

With that, Max Yasgur slipped behind his screen door, turned off the hall light, and went to sleep.

There is no indication that anyone involved in the attempted "favoritism" payoff made the slightest effort to refute the allegations. No mention of a confrontation was ever made public, nor were the details of such a meeting ever discussed between Max Yasgur and his new business associates. There is, however, a yellowed paper that exists, divulging the name of the town official who employed Morris Abraham as his go-between, attached to a deposition signed by the four principals of Woodstock Ventures that Max kept hidden in a bedroom dresser drawer for several years after the festival. From that, one may deduce that Max discreetly met with this individual, thrust his evidence in the person's panic-stricken face, and obtained a pledge from the offender to use the powers of his office to see that the promoters were given a fair shake when it came time for them to request permits.

Whatever promise Max received was kept that very same night. The festival's production executives were summoned before the Bethel town and zoning boards at 7:30 P.M. and, on the basis of the town attorney's advice, they were granted, by unanimous vote of council, permission to hold their event on the new, Sullivan County site.

The examination of Woodstock Ventures' credentials, including plot plans and insurance guarantees, proved less tormenting than their previous experience in Wallkill, although the Bethel legislative caucus was every bit as thorough. Presided over by Town Supervisor Daniel J. Amatucci, a committee of two town justices, a building inspector, two councilmen, four zoning board representatives and three planning board members listened patiently while Mel Lawrence, Wes Pomeroy, and the festival's *new* local attorney, Richard Gross, of the Liberty, New York, firm of Gross, Gross and Gross, presented an accumulation of their plans. Gross had been astute enough in his preparation of the case to have already conferred with Bethel Town Attorney Frederick W. V. Schadt over the weekend, in order to determine whether his clients would be in violation of local zoning ordinances during their tenure on Yasgur's farm. They were most certainly *not*, Schadt announced, which cleared the way for the board's unfettered cooperation.

Only a handful of residents attended the hearing in the unadorned town hall. Their conduct was courteous, although there was a distinct split of opinion concerning the festival's settling in White Lake for the rest of the summer. One faction, though restrained, was furious with Yasgur for his harboring of hippies in a resort area. "It will be worse than the grasshoppers in the grain fields," was how one disgruntled neighbor of Max's described the situation. However, those in favor of the celebrated addition to their town easily outnumbered the protesters two to one.

Daniel Amatucci told a reporter from the *Times Herald Record*, later that evening, that he "would not stand in the way of anything if it is legal." He had met informally with the promoters, and found everything they said to be in order. "We will welcome anyone to the town if they abide by the law, mind their Ps and Qs, and live within the law," he proclaimed nobly, and for the moment he was a champion to the residential youth who longed for such a celebration to take place in Bethel. "If they do this, there will be no problem."

Earlier, a writer had cornered Max Yasgur as he emerged from the town hall and asked him for a comment. Max was in his glory and played the role of Defender Of The Faith to the hilt. Hands on hips, head tilted ever so slightly upward, scholarly eyes looking off into the distance, he nodded his head a few times before answering: "All they are asking for is [meaningful pause] fair play." That line, overheard by a festival staff member, was repeated ten and twenty times during the course of the parties held later that night, each time drawing a more exultant response than the last. "All we are asking for is fair play! All we are asking for is fair play!" It was the catch phrase they had been waiting for all along.

When hours later, perhaps worlds later, word was carried into the celebration that Judge Edward O'Gorman had, earlier that day, handed down a decision from the highest court in the state of New York banning the festival from the Town of Wallkill, shrieks of laughter rang throughout the two camps. The fools have had their day in court, they sang, and we shall have our freedom! They were convinced that Max Yasgur, this messiah from White Lake, had led them into the Promised Land and, that night, the tenacious band of hippies was home at last.

CHAPTER EIGHT

Loose Ends and Long Shots

Go, sir, gallop, and don't forget that the world was made in
six days. You can ask me for anything you like, except time.
—*Napolean Bonaparte (1803)*

Don't ask questions, man. We can handle it, we can handle
it. Just get it together.   —*Michael Lang (1969)*

— 1 —

Bethel—the land of our forefathers, the ancient city in central Palestine
where Abraham built his first altar, the name given to Jacob's sacred
stone and where the Ark of the Covenant temporarily found sanctuary. The
Prophets had great plans for Bethel. It was destined to be the heartland of
Judaism, the place where religious ideology flourished, unsuppressed. That
is, until Jerusalem siphoned off its inspirational grandeur, and Bethel fell to
the likes of heathen worshipers and pagans.

On Tuesday, July 22, 1969, more than two thousand years after the Syr-
ians destroyed the temple, and only seven days after the Wallkill Zoning
Board of Appeals padlocked the gates of Eden, Mel Lawrence led his people
back to Bethel in a manner not unlike that of his scriptural ancestors. The
caravan of trucks, buses, station wagons, heavy machinery, vans, and motorcycles that journeyed from Orange County like interlocking circus elephants
was unlike anything the residents of the tiny town had ever witnessed before.
Crowds of befuddled villagers watched from behind half-shuttered windows;
those who were braver and more receptive to the hippies' arrival lined the
sidewalks as they paraded through the center of town on their way to Yasgur's
farm. Teen-agers cheered from their curbside outposts. For them, especially,

the festival staff were like conquering heroes. The local kids held both hands high in the air as peace signs were offered in a poignant, deep-felt reception, and most greetings were returned in kind by the vehicles' smiling passengers.

"This expression of love is a symbol of the generation," one young bystander told a local policeman. "No guns, man, no hatred, no inhibitions. These are our brothers, and they've come to spread the word. Peace and love, man."

Mel Lawrence, beaming as he looked on from the front seat of a staff car, hugged a reporter who had joined the entourage. "This is the way we've always hoped it would be. Look! Everyone is smiling and happy. Once we have established the festival, we are sure that it will grow to the satisfaction of everyone. It can be an entertainment symbol for the betterment of Sullivan County and the Town of Bethel."

The production staff set up their facilities just behind the natural amphitheatre, utilizing the dirt access roads Max had sanctioned off Hurd Road and West Shore Road, on either side of the site. Because of the time spent on finding new land and appealing to the town officials, the actual working days left to finalize the production had been drastically reduced to twenty-four, and that was not taking into account any unforeseen difficulties. Along the way, Lawrence had picked up another hundred or so workers who would be assigned to prepare the grounds, and seventy more to assist the stage and construction crews in what would have to be a selfless, harrowing commitment to getting the job done. Bill Ward had been prematurely summoned back to the University of Miami to teach a summer session, leaving his wife, Jean, and Ron Liis behind to supervise the aesthetic preparations, and his technical expertise would be sorely missed. That left most of the guidance in the hands of inexperienced corporals who, while presumably talented, were unproven quantities. A good deal more of the construction than they had thought would have to be farmed out to independent contractors, which would ultimately inflate the budget to near bursting proportions. It was going to take a consolidated effort from everyone involved with the show to pull it off, but Lawrence had no doubt that it could and would be accomplished in time.

His biggest worry was morale. The staff had spent the latter part of the last two weeks worrying about the festival's uncertainty, never really knowing if all the time and effort they were investing in it would go rewarded. Several kids had packed up and left when Wallkill looked doomed. Others, sensing eventual defeat, began to brood about starting over in White Lake. Lawrence knew that bad vibes could lead to their downfall and took every precaution to prevent them from infecting his ranks. His first act upon reaching the new site was to call a meeting of the entire staff on the lawn behind the El Monaco Motel. Close to three hundred people showed up, many of whom he had never laid eyes on before, to hear Mel, standing on top of a weather-eaten picnic table, deliver an old-fashioned high school pep talk. Some of the hard-boiled construction team, who snidely referred to him as "General Eisenhower" behind his back on account of his customary use of military terms, began to chuckle when Lawrence got underway with, "All right, you guys, we've got to get out there and hit those fields with all we've got." For the most part, however, his words were comforting and encouraging. "The most important thing to remember," he impressed upon them, "is that, if we keep the faith, we're gonna make it. It's true, man. We may have been fucked over back there by those cats in Wallkill, but, among one another, we've always maintained pretty good karma. Those who were uptight back there in Mills's place—the guys who tried to fuck us—well, they'll get it in the end. Guys like that always do. We've got good intentions, we have the capability to put it together, and I'll tell you I just don't think we can miss. It depends on all of you pitching in and helping out where you're needed. Because we're on our way to staging the greatest rock show ever held."

The executive staff members from the downtown production office— Chip Monck, John Morris, Chris Langhart, Steve Cohen, Jim Mitchell, and their special assistants—were hustled up to Bethel and assigned rooms at the El Monaco. They would eventually be moved to a separate staff house complete with private chef, along with Michael Lang, on the other side of town, but from here on in, their presence would be required on the site, and they'd be expected to oversee their respective areas of production. Mitchell had rented several trailers—for security, lighting/sound, medical, provisioning/ promoters, and staging—which would be circled behind the stage, and from where the festival's direction would be coordinated before and during the show. Only Lawrence's field location was different, Mitchell having positioned Mel's command trailer on the hill facing the stage.

Peering over the grassy knoll above the amphitheatre, one could see the full panorama of festival grounds, sense the breadth of the landscape, grasp the designless pitch of earth, all of which foretold the project's striking proportions. The task that lay before them was enormous. Six hundred acres of raw farmland called for refinement in three weeks' time, not to mention the precise implementation of life-sustaining services for one hundred thousand people a day. And even if that was miraculously accomplished, who guaranteed that the independent affiliate committees—those looking after publicity, tickets, concessions, and security—would live up to their obligations? Michael Lang? Hardly. Although Mel firmly believed that Lang was the motivating spirit behind the festival, he knew that Michael was busily basking in the national spotlight and cultivating a standing for himself in the exclusive rock music industry. That's cool, he thought. It was Michael's prerogative as the festival's creator. But there were so many unanswered questions left up to him. From what source would they be able to tap purified water? It was an old problem still in need of solving. Where would they park twenty thousand cars? How did they expect to man the gates? Who was arranging to meet the artists, check them into the hotels and get them to the show in time for their performances? What happens if they run low on food? These were only a few of the questions that clouded Lawrence's perspective and slowly, but surely, began to chip away at his once stable endurance.

All that night and throughout most of the next morning, a weary Mel Lawrence worked, uninterruptedly, on revising his timetable. Appropriating a corner table in the desolate El Monaco bar as an office, he met individually with the members of his executive staff to review their progress and to chart a chronological course that would enable each of them to complete his or her particular phase of production by August 14.

The budget, which he had discussed earlier with Michael Lang, he told each man was no longer relevant. Money was no object. It was to be used— liberally, if they must—as a catalyst for getting things accomplished in a shorter period of time. "Find out what it costs someone to put their people on overtime, and tell them, if that's what it takes, that we'll be more than happy to pay for it. The important thing is to get it done." Payment was to be made to suppliers and contractors by company check—half up front and the balance upon receipt of a bill immediately after the festival was over. If anyone hesitated about the method of compensation, an executive was authorized to have the office issue a substantial retainer to provide that person or firm with the necessary impetus. Money was the most convincing lever at their disposal. "With all due respect to our suppliers, you'll see how quickly a little cash will pry open a locked door," Lawrence slyly advised an aid.

Most of his staff, he found, had their departments well in hand. By the time they moved their work from Sixth Avenue to White Lake, all that was left was for crews to be appointed to put things in their proper place.

Steve Cohen and Chip Monck had completed the stage and lighting designs, and most of the supplies for both structures had been ordered. They had been waiting until the new site was confirmed before letting the truckers know where to deliver the hardware. Construction, they implied, would get underway as early as the next morning. Neither man voiced concern over what Lawrence thought was an insufficient amount of time to execute it.

Unbeknownst to Lawrence, Cohen had turned over his stack of blueprints for the stage, the performers' pavilion, and the lighting and sound towers to his twenty-one-year-old assistant, Jay Drevers, who was late of the Filmore East junior staff. Aside from being part of the auxiliary crew at the Philadelphia Folk Festival and a technician in Miami, Drevers had no prior experience directing such an assignment. The monumental job of interpreting Cohen's architectural diagrams, enlisting the support of a work force, and physically putting together the wood-and-steel framework was, nonetheless, dropped suddenly and quite recklessly into the youngster's lap.

Cohen chose instead to while away his afternoons in an air-conditioned trailer parked to the left of the staging area. He had become smitten with his own swollen sense of importance and was closing in on his aspirations of traveling in fast, celebrated company. There was talk of his joining up with Crosby, Stills and Nash when the festival was over, his going into partnership with Chip Monck, who was already well connected in the galaxy of rock stars. Whatever the reason may have been, Cohen made it clear that the title bestowed upon him by Michael Lang, that of stage manager, required him to organize activities on the stage during the festival—and nothing more. He would be available to consult on the various designs he had prepared, but otherwise, Drevers was the boss.

Monck was a bit of a high-flyer himself, content to lie back and relax while assistants worked diligently to preserve his sterling reputation. "Chip's knack for making himself look good was uncanny," according to one of his Woodstock co-workers. "That cool, offhand charm, phony smile, his ability to kiss someone on the cheek while reaching down to find their Achilles' heel was such clever deception, so well contrived, that he could have made a good impression on Dale Carnegie. But the truth is that he is a *schmoozer,* a professional mingler. He knew what to do, and when to do it—and everyone wanted him there to do it to them first."

That Chip Monck's burnished good looks and smooth personality had the power to create such jealousy among his associates was an old song vocalized by many amongst the rock elite. Others were put off by him. People like John Morris found themselves always having to compete for attention whenever Monck was on the scene, and even Wes Pomeroy remarked that he "would not trust that guy to walk across the street with my daughter."

What these same people chose not to debate, however, was Chip Monck's superb work with theatrical lighting, his ability to translate a rock group's tired antics into a scintillating performance with the mere overlapping of colored gels and follow-spots. He knew where each successive beat of music came, was friendly with most of the groups, got high with their managers, entertained their roadies with stories of his experiences on tour, was always prepared for a show, and kept his play-on-words nickname in front of the audience's eyes as if he were a performing artist himself. More importantly, Monck had excellent relationships with reliable concert suppliers from coast to coast. If it meant snaring a particularly hard to get mixing board or lighting console, or rounding up a last-minute gang of operators tuned into his graphically dramatic style, Chip would have them in a concert hall on a moment's notice. A promoter was more apt to put up with his Joe Cool swagger to insure getting professional and spectacular effects than to settle for second best.

Chip certainly hadn't disappointed Mel Lawrence. When the two men conferred over beers at the El Monaco, Monck reported that he had already located fifteen supertroopers to handle the long shots and had enough incandescent lighting coming to flood a small Eastern European country. "It's gonna bring half those little hippie chicks to orgasm," he joked, confident that if he had to show results, he probably could. The plan was to hang banks of colored beams on huge wooden trusses lodged into the sides of the stage. Two telephone-pole crossbeams would sit on top of the trusses, onto which additional lights would be hinged, practically tripling the luminous output of any normal show. Using a good balance of this apparatus, the spotlights would throw shafts of stark white light from four scattered locations in the audience, and the colored effects would flash from the sides and from directly overhead of the performers. It was a brazen concept, one that could be attempted only because of the money available to rent the glut of equipment. It was certainly worth the try, Monck reasoned, and if they pulled it off, it would be one aspect of the festival that would be talked about and imitated for years to come.

The system of lights, which he diagramed for Lawrence on a napkin, could not be bolted into place until, of course, the stage was built. Chip, meanwhile, agreed to prepare the intercoms that allowed his operators to hear his instructions from their remote locations and would help out with the installation of power until they were ready to dress the stage.

It was Monck's formal requisition of electrical power, in fact, that distressed another colleague on the Woodstock project—so much so that it had touched off a serious question as to the practicality of such a boldly devised lighting experiment. Chris Langhart had spent several days analyzing a topographical survey of Yasgur's land in an attempt to approximate the electrical and mechanical improvements they'd have to make on it before the show began. The most drastic nonentity was utilities. There was no plumbing on the site, no electricity, and, except for a few phone company accessories on the other side of Hurd Road, no communications equipment. The implications of that study, as Langhart told an associate, were "fantastic." They were going to have to find some way of running power to every reach of land. It probably meant setting up a few portable generators in the woods behind the stage and extending the cables to the outlying areas; however, that in itself could take the better part of a week and could only happen if they found someone who could engineer it.

Every division supervisor had submitted his specifications early for electricity, but they had been contingent upon the Mills Heights resources, a pillar of modern technology compared to the provincial state of Max's undeveloped hillside. In Wallkill, they had relied upon the close proximity of power lines to bail them out of a dilemma, but that was no longer possible. Virtually every plan now had to be reworked to conform to their present aboriginal situation. Energy would have to be conserved, or a method would have to be devised whereby power could be brought in quickly and efficiently.

Langhart, therefore, considered Chip's spectacle of lights an extravagance and, if need be, expendable. He'd have more than enough luminescence from the follow-spotlights without jeopardizing a power overload. If there was time, they'd make every attempt to accommodate him, but Langhart was making no guarantees.

Chris was more concerned with how they were going to put an entire plumbing system into operation in just three weeks' time. Just before they left Wallkill, he had devised a plan whereby four emergency water storage tanks, each a refillable fiberglass unit capable of holding up to 10,000 gallons, would be firmly implanted in sand beds at the top of the hill facing the stage. Then, fitting together several miles of plastic piping and elbow joints, crews would dig trenches across the site into which these channels would be laid and water could be brought from the tanks to almost anywhere it was needed. Goldstein had finally come to terms with two water transporting firms, one in Goshen and one in Schenectady, whose 5,800-gallon milk trucks were to make continuous trips between a reservoir and the site to replenish their source of supply.

There were, however, extenuating factors in the plan that did not sit well with Langhart. Chris had been in possession of a carrier table left over from the days when he installed the air-conditioning at the Filmore East. The carrier table was a handy plumber's device that helped to calculate the volume of water able to force its way through any variably sized pipes—taking into account the effects of temperature, pressure, and friction—in a certain amount of time. With it, he could assess the amount of water that would be necessary to keep several hundred spigots functional at the same moment without experiencing too great a loss of pressure. From his initial calculations, however, he deduced that it was not the pressure they ought to be concerned about, but rather the depletion of water. Water would be consumed at such a rapid rate that the tanks would have to be refilled nearly every other hour. And simple arithmetic told him that was impossible without a healthy fleet of trucks capable of transporting greater capacities of liquid.

"If I've figured correctly, we've got a number of ways outta this," he told Lawrence, unrolling a rudimentary relief map of the landscape. He pointed to a blue-tinted circle next to the amphitheatre. "This lake is a godsend. It usually signifies a wellspring, something beneath it acting as a source. If what I know of fundamental geology holds any weight, then there's sure to be enormous deposits of spring water seventy or eighty feet under the entire site. All we have to do is to get Max's permission to go after it, bring a rigger in, and begin drilling. We should hit water right away. If I'm wrong, then we can draw it off the lake."

"What! Are you shittin' me?" Lawrence quailed. "Kids are gonna be swimming in there. Anybody tries to drink that shit'll probably drop in their tracks."

"Not really. What we can do is to modify a large swimming-pool filtering system, chock-full of wonderful chemicals from our friendly health department, and pump the tanks full from the water in the lake. It'll be fine for drinking—probably a lot healthier than that shit they get out of their faucets in New York City. You don't have to worry about that. I've already checked into it and we're in the clear. But I think we've got a better shot at passing inspection if we open up a few wells. And our supply'll probably last longer."

"In other words"—Lawrence appeared still to be skeptical of Langhart's theory—"all we have to do is get Max to go along with it and we can stop worrying about water? That's all there is to it?"

"That's right."

"Then what're you waitin' for, man? Go track down Max and don't let him out of your sight until he says we can help ourselves to his subterranean private stock."

Max, to everyone's amazement, was delighted with the idea, tipped his hat to the young staff's ingenuity, lauded it as "an extremely resourceful solution to an overwhelming problem." How could he oppose something so promising, especially when it was he who stood to benefit most from its success? Why, if they actually found as much water as they suspected was quietly gurgling beneath his pasture, it would transform his unsound irrigation into an automatic sprinkling system. His crops would shoot up like guided missiles. Of course they could drill for wells—as long as he was consulted first on their specific locations and the work would be done by a professional contractor.

"There's just one thing I can't allow," he said, taking Langhart aside at the dairy, "and it might hamper the outcome of your plumbing adventure. It has to do with what's gone into the development of this place over the years. You see, I originally worked to get the land into shape myself. When we bought the farm, my son Sam and I spent a lot of time picking up all the stones that were laying in the field and reseeding it, over and over again, until all the grass you now see out there grew back. If you, all of a sudden, come in here with a dipstick and run a slot across the land, well—it's liable to ruin the soil erosion. Every time there's a downfall, the water will run down the hill, seep into those trenches, and I'll have furrows all over my field. Now, if you want to arrange for a plumbing system, fine, I'll go along with that, on the condition that all pipes are somehow kept *above* ground. That's it, that's the best I can do for you."

Pipes above ground—that was one of the most unusual requests that Langhart had ever heard. He wasn't even sure it could be done that way. How were the fixtures—plastic ones, at that—supposed to remain in place with one hundred thousand kids roaming around them? Was Max serious? And, if he was, would he hold them to it later on?

It is highly doubtful that the wily farmer expected them to follow through with such an ambitious proposal, especially after his dropping the bombshell about using unconcealed pipe. After all, most of the production staff he had dealt with up to that time had been unskilled youth under the age of twenty-five who, for the most part, had learned their trades (if one could, indeed, esteem them such) by trial and error. He couldn't possibly have expected them to construct such an elaborate system in less than three weeks when they hadn't a survey of the existing sedementary formations, or equipment, or a team of gifted engineers to direct the complicated process, or any idea of the type or amount of piping to purchase, or cost estimates or suppliers, or an excavating crew. The whole thing appeared quite hopeless.

He must have been baffled then when Chris Langhart knocked on his door the next afternoon asking to be shown the places where they were permitted to drill. They had decided to go ahead with the project as a last resort in their endless quest for water. It is a known fact that Max "went diving for the oxygen tent" when, two weeks later, Langhart proudly announced to him that they had opened eight individual wells between the entrance on Hurd Road and the campgrounds—and hit gushing spring water in seven of them.

— **2** —

One point the producers had neglected to keep tabs on was the deplorable conditions in the overcrowded staff quarters.

While members of the top guard were busy congratulating one another on evading the legal ax and hastily revising mechanical layouts that had been custom built for Mills Heights, clusters of hired hands had voiced disenchantment with their living arrangements. Rooms at the Red Top were jammed to capacity. When the festival had taken over the tiny motel, they found that it was ideally equipped to handle seventy kids on staff and could probably accommodate another ten or twenty latecomers as the situation called for it. But the crew had multiplied beyond anyone's expectations and, with the recent arrival of the Hog Farm advance crew and another eighty members of the commune expected on the August 7 charter from New Mexico, the grievances were ripening with indignation.

As many as 140 hippies congregated around the Red Top kitchen at mealtimes, many with special requests on how their food should be prepared or with confidential tips on how the cooks could improve upon their bland recipes. "It was a zoo," attests Carol Green, who planned most of the menus. "Everyone was a certified expert, but no one was willing to put on an apron and help out—except the owner of the motel, an Italian man named Jimmy, who insisted on seasoning everything we ate with oregano."

Housing was even more aggravating, a new-wave rendition of musical chairs, with losers in the free-for-alls having to spend the nights curled up on a couch or in a sleeping bag on the living room floor. And when friends or lovers showed up for the night and wound up staying a week, inconvenience became an absurdity even peace and love couldn't rectify.

Mel Lawrence was swamped with more important matters that demanded his immediate attention and, subsequently, turned over the housing hunt to his assistant, Penny Stallings. "Find any place you can," he instructed her, "it doesn't matter what it looks like as long as it'll hold 150 of our people comfortably. Only for God's sake, do it before I have a mutiny on my hands."

For two days, Penny drove around the Bethel–White Lake area investigating the local inns, many of which turned out to be yeshivas and Hasidic retreats and had to be disqualified for dietary reasons. She finally found a deserted, Prohibition-era hotel called the Diamond Horseshoe, a few miles down the road from Max's, which she entered by crawling through an opened window on the bottom floor. It reminded her of something out of the Twilight Zone. The interior looked as though people had been there that very morning and just got up and left. Scraps of food had been left on plates in the kitchen, personal articles were strewn around the spacious living room floor, the bathrooms were a mess. But with some creative repair work (and a healthy imagination), the place had a lot of possibilities.

"It's not real pretty to look at," she reported to Lawrence, "but it's huge. We can pack a couple hundred people into there if we have to. I counted about a hundred bedrooms, but I'm sure it's bigger than that." She had located the caretaker, a creaky, old man who resided in a cottage adjacent to the main building, who eagerly escorted her on a tour of the vast premises.

The Diamond Horseshoe, Penny discovered, belonged to a New York dentist who had bought the run-down hotel with the belief that, one day, legalized gambling would rescue the Catskills from its present desolate state. Until that time, which looked a long, *long* way off, he rented it out "at disgustingly reasonable rates" to any group that expressed interest.

It must have been exquisite in its day, she imagined, as they strolled around the grounds. Actually, the Diamond Horseshoe was several buildings that were situated on a campus of rolling lawns and thick-girthed weeping willows. The hotel itself sported a roomy reception area that opened onto the living room. The wallpaper was hanging down in strips and large sections of the floor were missing, but it was nothing a little touching up wouldn't fix. There were two dining rooms that would easily seat their staff, and a filthy kitchen with all its utilities intact. But the pièce de résistance was the arcade directly behind the inn. The backyard was defined by an Olympic-sized swimming pool surrounded by multicolored cabanas and a bar. The bar, which became the center of all evening activity, was completely stocked with liquor and had an old-fashioned, neon Wurlitzer jukebox that blared hits of the past. It was simply wonderful, and conveniently close to the site.

"I'll bet this place costs a fortune to rent," Penny backed off.

"Not really. But there are a few terms we have to agree to before I let you young kids in here." They included a thorough spring cleaning of the hotel and an overhauling of the dilapidated facilities—a deal Penny was quick to accept.

Under the direction of Chris Langhart and several instructors from the

New York University theatre department, a team of hippies rigorously swept through the old building, replacing decayed sections of galvanized piping that had been allowed to freeze by the previous tenants and filling gaping holes in the wall, floor, and ceiling. Where furniture was missing arms and legs, makeshift appendages were inserted. Pillows and cushions were sewn together, bookcases were dusted, tabletops were refinished. Floors were scrubbed, and dried food was chipped off the pots and pans until the inside of the hotel was livable.

That left the recreational area. A construction crew cleaned out the inside of the swimming pool, added several coats of rust-resistant paint to its cracked surface, changed the filtering system, and filled it with water. By the end of the week they had made noticeable headway. The Diamond Horseshoe was, by no means, returned to its pristine stateliness, nor could it be considered luxurious, but it was ready for occupation, and by Tuesday, July 29, with duffel bags and suitcases piled high in its reception area, 165 members of the Woodstock Music and Art Fair's production staff had agreed to call it home.

The wayfaring members of the festival troupe were not the only ones who found themselves in need of sending out change-of-address cards. It was decided, soon after the move to White Lake, that someone had better come up with an inventive way of cuing the general public in on the Aquarian Exposition's new location before too much time elapsed. Their well-publicized censure by the Wallkill town fathers was likely to touch off an epidemic of refunds that could be abated with the proper handling of the situation. Word had to be sent to the underground that *Woodstock Lives*.

The day after the crew dumped their gear into the Diamond Horseshoe lobby, the promoters called a meeting of their public relations advisers at Paul Marshall's office. It was the first time in over a month that the estranged partners—Lang and Kornfeld/Roberts and Rosenman—appeared under the same roof together. Hardly a homecoming—they sat on opposite sides of the room, barely on speaking terms as a result of professional differences. Regardless of the ostensible friction that permeated the meeting, wisely neither side exchanged an uncivilized word.

The first and most important order of business was how to communicate their survival to the public. On the advice of their publicists, they opted to place an ad in every newspaper they could, to impart: (1) why they were moving the site (a woeful tale of social injustice they hoped would evoke sympathy from the underground media); (2) the festival's new location; (3) that the three-day coupons now in the hands of ticket holders were still legal tender in White Lake; and (4) that the new site was twice as large as their former abode and, therefore, twice as beautiful.

Arnold Skolnick, who had designed the original posters, was invited to sit in on the meeting. He came up with a backhanded ad that ran in newspapers and magazines for a solid week. Across the top of the notice, in bold type, was the official proclamation: TO INSURE THREE DAYS OF PEACE & MUSIC, WE'VE LEFT WALLKILL AND ARE NOW IN WHITE LAKE, N.Y. Beneath that, Skolnick had drawn a cartoon featuring two hillbillies, one "fashionably" attired in a "Get Out Of Wallkill" T-shirt, and both armed with shotguns. The ornery characters just happened to bear uncanny resemblances to Howard Mills, Jr., and Jack Schlosser, although, the promoters claimed, that hadn't been their intention.

"Certain people of Wallkill decided to try to run us out of town before we even got there," the copy began, quite innocently. "They were afraid. Of what, we don't know. We're not even sure that they know. But anyway, to avoid a hassle, we moved our festival site. . . . After all, the whole idea of a festival is to bring you three days of peace and music. Not three days of dirty looks and cold shoulders."

Skolnick also unveiled a mock-up of a new poster, one featuring the dove and guitar logo against a red background. Unlike the flashy art deco placard that had been used to announce the Wallkill event, this one was an unelaborate, straightforward account of the various modes of entertainment scheduled for the fair, as well as an up-to-the-minute listing of the groups slated to perform. Jim Mitchell said he could have them printed and plastered in every head shop, record store, drive-in restaurant, and army-navy store within hours of delivery.

Marshall instructed Lang to get on the telephone and call every manager and rock artist he'd been dealing with, letting them know that the new site was only thirty miles north of Wallkill and that it would be as convenient to reach. "Act as though it's a minor point, spout the virtues of Max's farm, even imply that their dressing rooms will be more commodious—anything. But just before you're ready to hang up, let them know that you'll be sending out a rider to the contract affirming the new location." Woodstock Ventures would have to receive written acceptance of all performers' compliance to appear in *White Lake*, he said, otherwise a group could legally back out of their contractual obligation. He did not anticipate this becoming a problem; however, it did put the festival at somewhat of a disadvantage, and he warned Michael that he could expect a few of the managers to ask for "incentives." If adjustments in fees had to be made, they were in agreement to do so as long as they were reasonable.

After Skolnick and the publicity people had departed, someone brought

TO INSURE THREE DAYS OF PEACE & MUSIC WE'VE LEFT WALLKILL AND ARE NOW AT WHITE LAKE, N.Y.*

Certain people of Wallkill decided to try to run us out of town before we even got there.

They were afraid.

Of what, we don't know. We're not even sure that they know.

But anyway, to avoid a hassle, we moved our festival site to White Lake, Town of Bethel (Sullivan County), N.Y. We could have stayed, but we decided we'd rather switch now, and fight Wallkill later.

After all, the whole idea of the festival is to bring you three days of peace and music.

Not three days of dirty looks and cold shoulders.

Just one more word about those *concerned* citizens of Wallkill —

Our lawyers have been instructed to start damages proceedings immediately.

Now to something a bit more pleasant.

Our New Site. It's twice the size of our original site. (Who knows, maybe the people of Wallkill did us a favor?) That means twice as many trees. And twice as much grass. And twice as many acres of land to roam around on.

For those of you who have already purchased tickets, don't worry. Your tickets, even though printed Wallkill, will of course be accepted at our new festival site at White Lake in the Town of Bethel.

We'd also like at this time to thank the people of Bethel for receiving the news of our arrival so enthusiastically.

See you at White Lake, for the first Aquarian Exposition, Aug. 15, 16, and 17.

*White Lake, Town of Bethel, Sullivan County, N.Y.

WOODSTOCK MUSIC & ART FAIR

up the film deal and asked Artie how negotiations were going. At Stan Gold-stein's behest, Kornfeld had consulted with the principals at Cannon Films, the producers *of Joe* and other low-budget features. They were willing to put up $500,000 for the rights, pay the full production costs, and split the profits down the middle. Michael had also referred him to the Maysles Brothers, whose credits included *Monterey Pop* and *New York Meets the Beatles*. But Artie thought there were bigger fish to be had—especially if he could offer both the film and record rights in a package to a multimedia conglomerate capa-ble of promoting such a commodity. He was particularly interested in some kind of partnership arrangement with Warner Brothers, although, at pres-ent, the Hollywood dynasty was doubtful that a documentary film about rock music had any commercial potential. "You make the picture, and we'll be happy to take a look at it," they had told him, but Marshall encouraged his clients to have a distributor in tow before they began hiring and trying to support a film crew.

Artie, ever the optimist, assured them he was "on top of it," that making a film deal for Woodstock was "a cinch," and that something more conclusive would be forthcoming from him in a day or two.

"I certainly hope so," Roberts said, "but I've got a feeling we're in for a knockdown, drag-out struggle."

"You worry too much, baby. Hang loose."

But they had been left hanging for too long a period of time, Roberts thought. It was time he and Joel tightened the reins, possibly even took over Artie's responsibilities. He'd give it a little more time and see what happened. It couldn't get any worse.

The Town of Bethel was also keeping a vigilant eye on the proceedings in White Lake, not really knowing what to expect from the denizens of Max Yasgur's farm.

By July 24, Supervisor Amatucci reported getting about twenty phone calls from outraged residents, but, in his scrupulous estimation, it didn't seem like an organized campaign, nor had there been any threats of "legal entan-glement." Town Attorney Schadt had also been confronted by some mem-bers of the community wondering why a public hearing had not been held, but he told them that "there is nothing in the Bethel Town Law I could find that requires one." His office would not disapprove of the festival's presence in the town since no putative ordinance had been violated.

That, however, was not grounds enough to curb a handful of cranky residents from turning the festival's "apparent bed of roses," as the *Times*

Herald Record defined it, "into a briar patch." By Saturday, July 26, a committee, composed of a dairy farmer named Louis Komancheck whose land adjoined the Yasgur spread, two members of the local appeals board, Burton Lemon, the town historian, and an "interested" party of taxpayers (who had the decency not to adopt the label *concerned citizens*), began circulating petitions that opposed the festival, citing it as a "public nuisance, a health menace, and conductive [*sic*] to traffic congestion creating fire and health hazards."

"Our roads are dangerous at their best," came the committee's unvarnished appeal. "They are narrow, there is no parking. How can we handle 150,000 people?" It was, in the most absolute sense, a reasonable, uncorrupted qualm that deserved an answer from their tormentors. "We are contacting state officials, including our assemblyman. The attitude of the town administration is that there is no opposition."

So, Monday morning, bright and early, it began once again, like a recurring nightmare. The protesters, fearful of being ignored, mounted a new offensive to drive their point home (and, as one restless bystander so inelegantly affirmed, "the hippies *back* to where they came from"). During a meeting at the town hall, at which Michael Lang was called on to present an all-inclusive draft of the festival's intentions to New York State Health Department officials as well as representatives from the state police and the county sheriff's office, an angry crowd stormed the conference. Their purpose, as one retired schoolteacher told a reporter, was to disrupt the session, and, thereby, to prevent the authorities from issuing their respective lawful consents to the promoters. Instead, they were invited inside the supervisor's chambers to participate in the discussions.

The meeting, subsequently, lasted eight hours. Lang and Mel Lawrence, as one eyewitness noted, "gave the performance of their careers" as they were unmercifully battered by a landslide of procedural questions. The state health inspector repeatedly badgered them for more conclusive information, which they rattled off with knowledgeable versatility. ("Did you expect otherwise?" Mel later asked an onlooker who marveled at the production chief's deftness. "We've had a lot of practice at this sort of thing.") They also permitted themselves to be cross-examined, at times almost too obligingly, by members of the residents' council. Again and again they refused to participate in a public hearing, explaining that there wasn't sufficient time for them to do that and still finish the groundwork. "We are going ahead with our plans," Lawrence said, if not a bit too defiantly. "Our time is too short."

That same night, they got a shot in the arm from an unexpected ally. The ninety-member Bethel Businessman's Association, converging on the Ken-

more Hotel to assess the effect the festival would have on their establishments, voted to throw their weight behind the festival and its activities on
Max's farm.

"This is the greatest thing that ever happened to Sullivan County," ac-
claimed Ken Van Loan, the merchants' wiry spokesman, "and it just fell into
our lap. Besides, the festival will be a cloudburst and a great thing for the
area's young people since they're always complaining that they have nothing
to do." If the inquiries made that afternoon resulted in the board's ordering
a public hearing, Van Loan pledged to use the association's influence to back
the promoters to the limit. "The festival will boost money spent in Bethel for
lodging, food, and auto maintenance [the latter being Van Loan's forte]. We
want these people to be well received so they will make this an annual event."

Van Loan's tribute, while a welcome and timely endorsement, was, nevertheless, impulsive and excluded several regional enterprises whose stock
would not be enhanced by the festival's attraction of tourists.

The next afternoon, Woodstock Ventures was served with papers to appear before Judge George L. Cobb, in the Village of Catskill, in reference to
an action brought against the promoters by the owners of four area summer
camps—Camp Chipinaw, Camp Ranger, the Hillel School, and Camp Ma-
Ho-Ge—who charged that their businesses would be overrun by hippies.
Not more than an hour later, another process server appeared in a production trailer toting a second summons, this one sworn out by four co-owners
of a summer home adjacent to the festival site.

Paul Marshall advised his clients not to worry—that court actions took
time and that it was doubtful any case would come before a justice of the
peace before the festival was over and long gone from the Town of Bethel.
Just to be on the safe side, though, Marshall requested show-cause orders in
both of the outstanding actions.

When the plaintiffs arrived in Catskill, Marshall walked up to one of the
camp owners, vigorously pumped his hand, and said, "Hi, Uncle Davy, don't
you remember me? I'm Paulie Marshall. I used to be a regular at your
camp—let's see now, it was practically thirty years ago. You look great,
Uncle Davy." Much to his embarrassment, the owner admitted that he
hadn't recognized Paul under "all that white hair," and asked the attorney if
he would mind not referring to him as Uncle Davy in front of the judge,
which is exactly what Marshall did.

"Your Honor, I'd like to ask Uncle Davy why he hadn't contacted us before this?"

"Your Honor, would you please instruct Uncle Davy to answer the question."

For three hours Marshall directed questions at the camp directors and finally agreed upon an out of court settlement with them for an undisclosed sum.

The homeowners refused to be bought off. They wanted the festival moved out of the area on the grounds that Yasgur's farm was not properly zoned for commercial use. Claiming inadequate police protection, insufficient accommodations, and poor sanitary facilities, they asked the court to grant them an injunction restraining Woodstock Ventures from going ahead with the exposition.

It was a difficult decision, the judge said, considering that the promoters would suffer irreparable damage if their event was postponed. By now the festival's principals had laid out approximately $1.4 million on developing their site and promoting the rock shows. But if they were in violation of a zoning statute, then a motion would be granted. The law, contrary to popular belief, was not made to be broken.

Judge Cobb announced that he would reserve decision on the motion before him, pending further investigation of Bethel's intricate zoning regulations. That would require some time, he noted—reviewing, interpreting, coming to an equitable conclusion; it was a painstaking process for one man to preside over. He would most likely hand down a ruling two Thursdays hence.

Paul Marshall consulted a calendar and felt his pulse skate ahead, like the rush of adrenelin he experienced each time a verdict was about to be delivered. That date, circled in his appointment book as a reminder for him to leave New York, was August 14.

— 3 —

On August 5, 1969, less than twenty-four hours after Don Ganoung presented the Bethel Medical Center with the festival's check for $10,000, officers of the Peace Service Corps moved into their new headquarters, the recently vacated New York Telephone building on Lake Street in the center of Bethel. A crew of volunteers had spent four days refurbishing its corroded interior—chipping caked paint off the windowpanes, repainting the walls, rewiring the fixtures, installing desks and accessories—until, by Tuesday morning, it resembled a fairly accurate replica of a police station minus the harsh realities. That afternoon, Wes Pomeroy, Don Ganoung, Lee Mackler, and Joel Rosenman each claimed a desk there and began sorting out the last-minute appurtenances necessary to round out the program.

Pomeroy was exceptionally pleased with the new site in White Lake and considered it to be instrumental to the success of his security plan, Max's farm was decidedly more rustic than Mills Heights, a factor Wes thought would "help to create a relaxed atmosphere and elicit better vibes between the kids." The long extended entrance to the site off Hurd Road gave ticket holders a leisurely walk from remote drop-off points to the ticket booths, and then another similar distance to the amphitheatre, which would serve to temper their restlessness and allow Pomeroy's staff to weed out potential troublemakers before they got inside the gates. The site contained more ground than in Wallkill so there would be less need for kids to crowd one another, the campgrounds were more comfortable, the natural boundaries were more confining, the scenery more pleasant, the facilities more abundant. All in all, he could not have asked for a more adequate, practical, accommodating place to carry out his assignment.

Pomeroy had been inundated with applications from New York Police Department officers interested in working at the festival and notified the production office to stop accepting any more as, at last count, there were over 1,400 names from which to select. At his request, Lee Mackler rented a Manhattan assembly hall from City College for two days, and, with Joe Fink, Ralph Cohen, Don Ganoung and Jewell Ross (who had finally arrived from San Francisco to help organize the team), he spent a total of twenty hours interviewing candidates for the job.

The screening process took place over a weekend in late July, and the policemen arrived in droves, "like it was a casting call for the battle scenes in *Ben-Hur*." They sat around long lunch tables, drinking coffee until their names were called, at which time they were led away in groups of twenty-five to be briefed and observed by the festival staff.

At the beginning of each day, Pomeroy lectured the men on procedure. A number of cops walked out in a huff after Pomeroy's opening remarks, almost always the older men who resented anyone who wore his hair long or spoke out against the war in Vietnam. They had come out of curiosity, not really having any idea what to expect other than their getting a glimpse of the great Wes Pomeroy in action. Hippies disgusted them. They blamed America's youth for the alarming rise in armed robbery and rape, accused them of being traitors to their country, disrespectful to their parents, iconoclasts who personified all that was sick in contemporary society. They had no intention of babysitting 100,000 of these hippies while the kids made a mockery of the law. What kind of cop was this Pomeroy? they asked them-selves. How could he be a party to an orgy, a gathering of young criminals?

The younger cops, however, were willing to abide by Pomeroy's orders, and remained behind to audition for one of the representatives from Wood-stock Ventures. Seated behind card tables, Mackler, Ganoung, Fink, Cohen, and Ross called them one at a time and asked them their views on hippies, drugs, sex, and any other sensitive topic that came to mind.

"Tell me, Officer F——, what would you do if a bearded kid walked up to you carrying a lighted joint, called you a pig, and blew smoke in your face?"

"I'd bust his fuckin' head is what I'd do!"

"Thank you. Next."

Or: "What are your views on premarital sex, and what would you do if you saw two hippies fornicating in public?"

If their answer was, "I'd hang 'em by the balls from the nearest tree," they were asked to leave, and the application was thrown out. Otherwise, the men were rated on a numerical system and filed according to facial reactions.

By the weekend, they had narrowed the applicants down to 325 men. Fink was asked to hire those who had made the cut, and Lee Mackler took down pertinent information such as their precincts, social security numbers, and clothing sizes, as they would be issued jeans and T-shirts for the duration of their employment by Woodstock Ventures.

Pomeroy made sure that each policeman hired was aware that he was to leave all weapons at home. "If I see any guns, or sticks, or *anything* that even suggests violence—well, I promise you I'll make it damned tough on you when you get back to the city."

They were to check in at the telephone building in Bethel—Command Central—on August 14 for orientation. Shifts would be reasonably inter-spaced to give them plenty of time to rest up and call their families. The entire security force would be lodged at a dude ranch outside of Middletown, where facilities included use of both indoor and outdoor swimming pools, tennis courts, and rifle and trapshooting ranges.

"I think you men will enjoy this experience," Pomeroy said. "We're all looking forward to a peaceful weekend in the mountains, and I'm particu-larly pleased to be represented by such a fine group of men from NYPD. I'm sure you'll all make me extremely proud of our job in White Lake and of the time we spend together."

That night, Wes Pomeroy returned to White Lake alone. Now he could pull back a bit and give his full attention to working out the ever-present traffic problem. Aside from that, he couldn't foresee anything standing in the way of a successful festival. Nor did he ever dream he'd be betrayed by the one group whose integrity he had long ceased to question.

* * *

Don Ganoung's area of concentration had also shifted since the festival moved to White Lake, more drastically so than that of any of his companions. Formerly the director of community relations, Don's curious distinction was now mutated to that of supervisor of parking lots-medical, a concoction some thought only made possible through the auspices of LSD. The truth behind the interchange was that Joel Rosenman had grown disenchanted with what he believed was the minister's ineffectiveness as a troubleshooter for a company that seemed only to invite trouble. Ganoung had failed to persuade the good folks in Wallkill of the entertainment's merit, and the corporation's investers were worried that history might heartlessly repeat itself if Don was not removed posthaste.

Ganoung was prudently reassigned to the security unit and instructed to pick up where he left off in Wallkill with the shuttling operation. During his absence from the project, Intermedia Systems had designed a somewhat methodical concept for activating the ground arrangements and set about the preliminary steps for its effectuation. Several adjoining properties (as well as some heretofore undeclared tracts of Yasgur's land) were rented as parking lots at premiums unheard of on the open market. Acreage that had been *selling* for $15,000 only a week before the production staff moved into town was *rented* to Woodstock Ventures on a short-term lease for twice the price. But there had been no time to negotiate respectable terms. The areas expressly defined for parking had to be appropriated *before* Pomeroy could take his traffic itinerary before the Bethel Town Board and the New York Department of Transportation, which left them with a little under three weeks for everything to be approved. By August 18, there would be more than enough in the till to compensate their loss.

Ganoung discussed the setup with Stu Vidockler, Intermedia's chief consultant, and approximated that the cost of the satellite shuttling service would come in at roughly $82,000. For $82,000, it was conceivable one could start one's own nationwide auto-supply distributorship.

Ganoung supported Intermedia's theories. In a memorandum to Wes Pomeroy, he concluded, "I feel that while this is an extremely large expense, the urgency of securing this transportation system now belies the possibility of seeking alternative bus contractors." Pomeroy evidently agreed with him, as the next day, a map was commissioned by the chief of security displaying ten parking lots in juxtaposition to Yasgur's farm—one for buses, one to accommodate campers, another for motorcycles, and seven lots for cars.

By August 6, Pomeroy had stockpiled a surfeit of material that enabled him to present his conclusions to the town board of Bethel for their approval.

His requests were concise and well supported by logic. He argued that, because the surrounding roads were narrow and poorly kept, the flow of traffic would be severely impeded if they remained two-way. Pending the board's concurrence, he wanted the authority to change eight thoroughfares, leading and contingent to the site, to one-way, with the exception of Hurd Road between Route 17-M (off the Quickway) and West Shore Road. Pomeroy contended that the modification would practically guarantee quicker access to the exposition parking lots and keep the roads open for emergency vehicles.

His other wish was to limit access to the roads to residents who lived in the area, as well as to festival employees, shuttle buses, emergency vehicles, entertainers, and "various categories of people to whom passes are issued, including, but not limited to: doctors, nurses, reporters, displaying artists, and security and communications personnel." Wes pledged to man roadblocks at these intersections with off-duty New York City policemen experienced in this type of detail on a twenty-four-hour-a-day basis. Hurd Road, south of West Shore Road, would be cordoned off completely for exclusive use as a service road (primarily for concession service vehicles, water trucks, and trucks servicing the portable toilets). "By allowing Hurd Road to be used in this way," he reasoned, "the . . . vehicles in the categories enumerated above (many of them making several round trips daily) will be 'siphoned off' from other access roads and will thus reduce congestion on them."

The town authorities were sympathetic to Pomeroy's wishes. Their subsequent stance regarding traffic control was formulated on the notion that, since they had already sanctioned the festival's presence within their boundaries, it was useless to foil its smooth operation by withholding their consent. As long as he filed a prospectus with the New York State Department of Transportation, Pomeroy could proceed as requested.

Wes was pleased, although he was by no means content that these directional safeguards would forestall the stoppage of traffic. As a precautionary measure in case of their inability to get an ambulance or a fire engine through to the site while the festival was in progress, he instructed Ganoung to locate a helicopter service for standby emergency situations.

Don, sensing the necessity, had already contacted an aviation company in nearby Spring Valley, a small suburban community on the New York–New Jersey border, and suggested the pilot keep the August weekend free and clear for the festival's needs. The proposed cost for the use of a Bell 47G helicopter, including flight and ground personnel, was $45 an hour for daylight flights, and $55 during the evenings (evenings being defined as one hour after sunset to one hour before sunrise). And, of course, Woodstock Ventures would provide them with a heliport. Of course.

Ganoung spent no less than three days pleading with a neighbor of Max's, who owned the land directly behind the stage, to lease the negligible, unused portion of his property to them for a heliport. It was not until Don marched up to the man's house with a contract permitting Woodstock Ventures access to that fragment of land in exchange for $4,500 that the man was brought to his senses. The term of the contract was a pitiful four days in length. Any extension thereof violated the written instrument and, as Ganoung was reminded time and again, infractions would be settled in court.

The task of constructing the heliport was delegated to Chris Langhart, who knew nothing of aeronautics and hadn't the vaguest idea how to go about installing an air base in a farmer's pasture. Nor was there time for him to study the syntax of an existing operation at Kennedy, LaGuardia, or even the primitive airport in Westchester County. As with everything else that was growing up around him, Langhart was forced to improvise with the hope that his errors would be minimal and easily adjusted.

Common sense compelled him to mow the grass where it was expected the helicopters would touch down until that patch of ground resembled a masterfully manicured golf course green. Once that was done, however, he was lost. He couldn't be expected to build a control tower; in fact, he wasn't certain that air-to-ground radios would direct the slight traffic onto the mark. But something told him there had to be more to a heliport than a plot of mowed grass.

"Don't you guys need to be able to see at night?" he asked a pilot who had dropped by to inspect the facilities.

"Sure. We'll need to have some frame of reference from the air," he replied. "But do us a favor and make sure your signal is not a beam shining directly in our eyes."

Langhart remembered a truckload of Christmas lights that Jim Mitchell had brought back from one of his supply runs in the New England area. Most were to be used in the woods to light the paths between the performance arena and the campgrounds. Borrowing an immodest portion of the colored bulbs, Langhart drove stakes around the perimeter of the sheared land and strung the Christmas lights on them until it looked like a landing strip in an underdeveloped African nation. Its usefulness would be forcibly limited by the lack of available ground space and by the heliport's scissors-and-paste composition, but it was imaginatively functional (as observers were quick to admit) and would handily service the sole helicopter budgeted to take off and land there.

Of course, had Chris Langhart any indication then of the significance his handiwork was to play in the overall success of the festival, he would have surely thrown his hands up in the air and yielded to the engineering acumen of the Civil Aeronautics Board. Little did he suspect, as they ran tests on the lights, that his heliport would provide the only means by which anyone would be able to enter or leave the festival grounds that weekend, and, where, by Saturday morning, a squadron of some fifteen whirlybirds would wait their turn to land.

The security office, kept open eighteen hours a day, operated on a tankful of nervous energy. Logically, the staff's preparations were supposed to fall neatly into place as the festival approached, but it seemed that exactly the opposite was happening. Hard as they pushed, and as adept as some of them became at heading off defeat, the unsolved problems always seemed more numerous than before, their goal more distant and more futile.

Chief Pomeroy had unsparingly devoted a great deal of time in Wallkill to organizing a mobile medical unit made up of doctors from nearby Memorial Hospital. The two supervising physicians had consented to rent medical equipment and to purchase enough supplies to treat thirty thousand people, as well as to work out shift assignments for a rotating staff of residents and interns. But when relations with the town collapsed, the doctors followed suit. Fearing reprisals from hospital administrators and patients alike, they asked to be relieved of their command and quietly slunk back to the unassuming refuge of their practices.

Bill Ward heard about the predicament while in Miami and called Jean to remind her about a doctor he knew of, living in Wappingers Falls in Dutchess County, New York, who specialized in crowd medicine.

Bill Abruzzi was, in fact, one of the few medical practitioners in the world who had any practical experience caring for the masses without fretting over compensation. He was a humanitarian, Ward noted. And, to make matters considerably more appealing to the hippies, he was a recognized friend of the civil rights movement, a certificate of character that attested to his compassion for the underprivileged and downtrodden.

While doing graduate work at the Columbia School of Medicine, Abruzzi became interested in "the seemingly disjointed rights of some antisocial segments of the culture—like junkies in dire need of help." Subsequently, he spent his time between classes "dragging a lot of black kids who were stoned out of the gutter and trying to keep them from being jailed." Later on, as selective justice resulted in a cry of national outrage, Abruzzi immersed himself in the moral plight of the black man and actively participated in the 1965 Selma-to-Montgomery march, which, among his colleagues, branded him "a nigger sympathizer." Undaunted by the professional criticism, he pursued his convictions by caring for James Meredith in Birmingham, Alabama, marching alongside and treating Martin Luther King, Jr., and counseling members of SNCC on self-survival before settling down with his family a few miles from White Lake.

Abruzzi was immediately receptive to joining the staff of the Woodstock festival. He saw it as a logical extension of his work with minority groups, primarily because the only people he knew in the area "who treated young people in a drugged state did so by calling the police or by bringing them to a mental hospital or by calling their parents." As Abruzzi saw it, "Kids have their own rights as well, and it's not necessarily in their best interests to admit them to a medical facility only *after* they receive parental consent. Of course, that was the law, but the law isn't always just. You turn a freaked-out kid over to his parents, and it's often worse than confronting the medical problem."

Abruzzi's terms were sensible and pragmatic. He wanted to employ a complete staff of doctors and nurses for around-the-clock duty instead of utilizing a volunteer group as had been planned. "My experience with the civil rights movement indicated that volunteers are great—God love them for giving up their time and energy to help a worthy cause—but it becomes anarchistic," he told Don Ganoung during a meeting in the security office. "How do you tell someone who leaves his practice to come help out that he's got to do feet even though he's a dermatologist? Someone's got to be able to say, 'Do it now,' satisfied that it will be taken care of because they're in charge. So, we'll welcome volunteers and we'll try to integrate them into the medical care program, but I have to have a staff of trained nurses and physicians I know I can depend on, people who, if I have to, I can order around."

He calculated that the medical unit would require three separate facilities: one for analysis, one as a recovery room, and one for bad trips. On the basis of their seeing from five hundred to one thousand cases over a three-day period, he settled on a recruitment of two physicians and four nurses for each eight-hour shift—each doctor and nurse receiving $320 and $50 a shift respectively, as well as $17.50 per person for maintenance and traveling expenses. Additionally, a number of doctors from Thornton Memorial Hospital in Middletown had agreed to stop by when they could see their way free of other obligations, and they would require a fee of $20 an hour per man. Taking into account six physicians, thirty-six nurses, eighteen medical assistants (including medical clerks and aids), and a contingency fund of $500 in case he had underestimated staff costs, the total medical personnel budget came to $15,875. Abruzzi wanted the entire amount "up front and in cash," and cautioned Ganoung to "be prepared to pay for overtime on a pro-rated hourly basis." The only outstanding item left to be resolved was a stipulation that Woodstock Ventures provide the medical staff with a malpractice insurance policy by 8:00 A.M., Friday, August 15, as, Abruzzi warned, the doctors "will not go on duty before such malpractice insurance contracts have been made available to them."

The three facilities that were ultimately decided upon for the exposition's medical complex consisted of a trailer and two circus tents with eight or ten army cots and a refrigerator for storing and preserving drugs in each tent. Abruzzi had classified medication he wanted on hand by six categories— injectables, orals, eye and ear drops, suppositories, intravenous solutions, and ointments and creams—each of which were broken down further by generic variety. No possible emergency would be left to chance. This detailed list of drugs included painkillers, steroids, digitalis, antibiotics, antihistimines, cough suppressants, antidiarrhetics, muscle relaxants, hormones, penicillin, asthmatics, Vitamins A through Z, insulin, salt tablets, and several gallons of merthiolate tincture as it was anticipated they'd be overrun by cut feet. Abruzzi also asked for common first aid applicators such as Band-Aids, adhesive tape, splints, slings, Ace bandages, eye patches, syringes, and sutures. They would need a veritable warehouse of medical supplies on hand in case the roads were blocked and ambulances could not get through. A walkie-talkie system would be installed in ambulances, trailers, and hospital tents so Abruzzi could monitor his staff and patients and insure that all medical units were operating effectively at all times.

Abruzzi put three area hospitals on alert—Monticello General, Thornton Memorial, and Beacon—with another four in reserve in case they filled up quickly or were understaffed for the weekend. As a precautionary measure, he informed administrators at each of the institutions to be prepared for a crisis situation. "Please save a percentage of your beds for our kids, have beds sheeted and ready that you can set up in the corridors, and see what you can do about having a subsidiary facility with a roof that you can put up outside for transient care."

Ganoung was convinced that Bill Abruzzi had the situation under control and that their medical operation was in good hands, so that he could attend to several other matters that commanded his attention.

Twenty Courier CWT-50 Walkie-Talkie transceivers were purchased by Ganoung, along with one hundred crystal sets and two hundred Alkaline Energizer batteries with which to operate them. The radios and walkie-talkies were inventoried, cases and shoulder straps attached, and finally tested for accuracy. An antenna was installed on the roof of the Lake Street office that would enable them to transmit messages to and from the site and receive calls from mobile surveillance squads patroling the outlying areas.

Pinkerton guards were hired to handle, pick up, and count all ticket money, two thousand signs for identifying everything from refreshment stands to highway shortcuts were prepared and ordered, a sign production shop was set up on the site, and paper maps were prepared to provide all necessary graphic information concerning the layout of the grounds, color-coordinated to the actual booths and utilities, which were to be passed out at the entrance gate.

Two other areas that the minister had gotten into pretty good shape were a Clergy Assistance Program, made up of the Sullivan County Ministerial Alliance, the Sullivan County Council of Churches, and a coalition of local rabbis, to foster a program that offered advice to rebellious teen-agers and runaways concerning their domestic problems, and a Legal Assistance Service. This latter program, headed by a youthful, long-haired Wall Street lawyer named David Michaels whom Stanley Goldstein had met during a skirmish in Grand Central Station, was established to benefit young offenders who found themselves in police custody as a result of drug busts. Michaels had prepared a pamphlet to be distributed to ticket holders that included a summary of what to do if they were arrested and the rights of the arrested person, an outline of the state drug law, notes regarding the law on search and seizure, and a warning against violations of the law. Accompanied by a social worker and a team of five juvenile defenders from New York City, Michaels was primed to spend the three-day weekend behind a well-marked booth near the entrance gate where he would answer the kids' questions and, if the situation called for it, stand up for them in court.

Ganoung also saw to it that an employment office was opened on the site to hire an army of guides, seventy parking lot guards, three hundred Food For Love vendors, and two hundred attendants whose duty it would be to supervise the garbage clean-up detail at the conclusion of each day's show. Most of the people whom they hired were green—drifters or Bethel students, who stopped by for a progress report, volunteered their services, and wound up signing the daily payroll register next to an identification number in exchange for twenty dollars in cash.

By August 7, when Don Ganoung hurriedly left upstate New York in time to greet the Hog Farm and Indian artists arriving at Kennedy Airport, Woodstock Ventures' employment rolls exceeded a staggering fifteen hundred names. In less than two weeks' time, their staff had quadrupled. By August 15, he'd find it had doubled again, as the Aquarian Baby Boom stretched the festival's already lopsided budget further out of proportion.

— 4 —

"Just walking around the Hog Farm is an incredible trip," a reporter from the *East Village Other* observed while strolling through the commune's ply-wood homestead located at the north end of the festival campgrounds. "A few thousand of the absolutely most together and peaceful and loving and beautiful heads in the world are gathered in a grand tribal new beginning. This meadow, which drops off to a steep slope . . . had become a gypsy camp of heads. All the petty bullshit things that before kept us apart vanished, and for the first time we were free."

This idyllic rendering, a splendid and graphic example of how vapid Hip Journalism had become, was, perhaps, one of the grossest misrepresentations of festival life to appear in print since the Concerned Citizens Committee's smear campaign hit the Town of Wallkill.

"Everything *was* beautiful until those scoundrels arrived," a production assistant sneered, jerking a thumb in the direction of Movement City, as the newcomers had so named their stomping grounds. "They're the hogs, man—the greediest, nastiest, most loathsome human miscreants I've ever laid eyes on. People can call me a dirty hippie if that's where their heads are at, but those Hog Farmers are downright disgusting. They smell, man—I mean, they're downright foul smelling—and they've got every communica-ble disease known to modern science. Since they barreled in here, we've been missing wallets and watches and anything else of value they can get their hands on. Believe me, they'll swipe anything that's not nailed down. Peace and love, man—to them, it's one fat excuse for taking what they can get without working."

Penny Stallings wore a Mickey Mouse watch strapped to her left wrist that she'd been given as a little girl. A week after the Hog Farm made the scene, it, too, was gone. "One of their guys marched up to me and demanded that I give it to him," she recalled, shaking her head in disbelief. "And, fool that I was, I *did*. I actually took it off and handed it over to that ignoramus, quite pleased that I could contribute to their welfare. They had me totally brainwashed into believing that I was supposed to give away all of my earthly possessions to them. We all wish they'd never have shown up."

The American Airlines charter carrying the Hog Farm and their chil-dren taxied up to the arrivals gate at Kennedy Airport a few minutes past 5:00 P.M. on August 7, but, as Wes Pomeroy noted, "They were so high, they could have flown in without the plane." A cluster of reporters and television commentators appeared awestruck as they watched "the parade of sideshow freaks" shuffle down the ramp to the waiting room clad in "whatever mommy and daddy would find offensive." Men in dresses and top hats, in tattered pajamas, women wrapped in swatches of the American flag, carrying naked babies, and a pet black and white hog named Pigasus—all trailing behind their mentor, Hugh Romney, a toothless Gabby Hayes lookalike, dressed in a white nightgown and a Donald Duck aviator's cap.

"Hey, it's the God Squad," Romney said, waving cheerfully at the members of the press who swarmed around them, poised for a statement.

A man from the New York *Daily News* elbowed his way to the front of the crush. "I understand your group is here for security at the Woodstock festival," he began.

"Security, hey?" Romney rolled his eyes and flashed an audacious grin. "It's just you and me and there's all those other guys about ten feet away. Do you feel threatened? Of course not! I'm sure you're secure."

Members of Romney's party burst into laughter as reporters smiled nervously at one another. No one wanted to be the Hog Farm's next Establishment victim until a New York *Post* music critic finally spoke up. "What do you plan to use for weapons?"

"Oh yeah—like weapons, I almost forgot about them. Why, seltzer bottles. Seltzer bottles and cream pies," Romney said, flashing on the silly plan he and Goldstein had concocted five months before at their first meeting. "And we'll move in with that if anyone gets out of hand. They can face off like gladiators if they want." He grimaced, pantomiming the net and trident fighters of ancient Rome. "We just want to keep things together."

Sensing the carnival the press conference had become, everyone from the media began feeding Romney straight lines hoping he could turn them into quotable inanities. That became a signal for Ganoung and two other festival executives to herd their guests onto waiting buses parked outside for the trip upstate.

The plane ride had, indeed, been a "trip." The Hog Farm "did a couple tabs of great acid each" and the Indian artists, not particularly thrilled with their traveling companions, "got riproaringly drunk on airline samplers." According to a horrified airline official, the flight was a nightmare. Tepee poles cluttered the aisles, making it virtually impossible for the flight attendants to get through to the rear cabin. The tribe sang and screamed obscenities until "one of the stewardesses locked herself in a lavatory and refused to come out until they landed in New York."

Arranging the trip had not proved all that much easier to deal with. In addition to the difficulty of booking the charter—at an expense to the promoters which the New York *Post* put at around sixteen thousand dollars (although there is evidence it was considerably less)—a Hog Farm representative had called Penny before leaving New Mexico and insisted that they be served only vegetarian meals with a side of goat's milk while on board. That was not quite as time-consuming, she thought, as it would have been to fill the artists' order for authentic American Indian cuisine, a request that the airlines dismissed out of hand.

That night, the newest arrivals were reunited with the rest of their "family" who had come to New York weeks before as part of the labor crew. Paul Foster, a Merry Prankster who had joined the Farm's touring company, had constructed a geodesic dome from leftover scraps of polyethylene and branches in the campgrounds, and had set up a communal kitchen where the Hog Farm prepared individual assignments and ate their meals. "Houses" were built out of rolled plastic, and blankets were passed out among them for "roofs." In the morning, after family yoga exercises (which Wes Pomeroy attended as an avid participant) and a hearty breakfast served on picnic benches in front of the dome, a core-group of Hog Farm leaders examined the grounds, picked crew leaders, and lined up the rest of their members behind them in order of talents and capabilities: the kitchen crew, the cop crew, the trail crew, and the art crew. Romney was designated to coordinate the activities of each in the pages of *The White Lake Daily Weirdness,* a mimeographed newsletter he edited each night before they assembled for the family campfire.

"ROOLS FOR TOOLS," began one entry in the bulletin. "All right you tools, step over to the tool shed and see the Tool Man. Calling all flashlites for a check off." Another provided an undecipherable instruction for daily crew assignments. "The large benched circle in the field of last night's circle bong will be the work recruiting center. Please hang there if you are free. We will provide joys and toys." Romney had dubbed himself Captain of the White Lake Please Department, the Pro-Curer, and vowed: "There isn't a stone left unturned that I can't turn over again. Turn those stones, men! Rock on!"

Their playful buffoonery made it difficult for anyone to take umbrage with the Hog Farm's glaring incompetence as laborers. "They were fun to have around," Jay Drevers admitted, "but they were a royal pain in the ass, too." Drevers's biggest headache was keeping them away from the heavy equipment his men used to build the stage. "They played on that machinery the way little babies cavort on tricycles, riding around on giant forklifts until they ran out of gas. Then, instead of telling anyone, they'd simply abandon the machine in the middle of the field and take off. Once, after I'd screamed bloody murder about bringing back what they took, they filled all the gasoline vehicles with diesel fuel and filled the diesel engines with gas. That did it. I gave the crew orders to throw hammers at the Hog Farmers anytime we caught one of them stealing into the construction trailer. By the end of the second week in August, we wouldn't let them within fifty feet of our stage area."

From the beginning, complaints about the Hog Farm rained down upon production executives with growing fervor. "They've all got dysentery, man," a stagehand declared, visibly sickened by their abject neglect of sanitary conditions. "We're not going near those fuckers until they clean up their act." Romney was asked to restrict his followers to the use of specially marked portable toilets so as not to endanger the staff's health, but after a while, the appeals were ignored.

Under Goldstein's direction, the campgrounds, located on a moss-covered incline several hundred yards behind and to the left of the stage, had gotten off to a fairly good start. A contingent of Hog Farm members, in one of their more productive moods, drove a backhoe into the area and carved a huge drainage ditch into a level plot of the land, which they lined with rocks, filled with water from one of Chris Langhart's wells, and transformed into an inchoate bath-and-shower facility. Tepees were erected on either end of the campgrounds like goalposts; tents with floors were set up in between them and graded for drawing off rain seepage.

On the basis of a poll of ticket outlets, the promoters had learned that, of the 65,000 tickets already sold, about 85 percent were for the entire weekend's festivities. That meant they had to be prepared for a minimum of 55,000 campers vying for space, more probably 100,000. Several Hog Farmers cleared little nestlike compartments in the woods where they estimated another 2,000 people could set up a tent. More land, however, would be needed to provide lodging for the troops, and word was sent to Joel Rosenman, advising him to start buying up surrounding property as fast as he could.

Another group built knotty-pine frames for what were to become the Free Kitchen, a puppet theatre, a Free Stage, and a fourth medical facility—Big Pink (so named for the ghastly prominent blot it made on the green horizon)—which would provide shelter for those on bad trips.

The readying of the Free Kitchen was supervised by Bonnie Jean Romney who, each afternoon, assembled the Hog Farm women on the lawn in front of the dome to discuss menus and provisions. The entire kitchen, they decided, would be made up of five individual serving booths. Four units were designed so that there was sufficient counter space on three sides of the stand and an oak cutting shelf in the middle where the cold dishes and vegetables would be prepared. The open, back ends could then be usefully barricaded with bulging burlap sacks of wheat, corn, rolled oats, nuts, and other popular dry goods, allowing enough room for helpers to squeeze by on their way to the garbage compactors hidden in the woods. The fifth booth was twice the size of the others in order to make room for the five single-burner stoves, five pressure cookers, two sinks, and bank of hot water tanks used for boiling vegetables and a variety of blended beverages.

There was an organized effort by the Hog Farmers to serve only macrobiotic food at the festival—seaweed, dandelion, kelp, watercress, and unpolished brown rice ("enough to wipe out the entire healthy U.S. Olympic Team," according to a New York dietician), but it proved to be too great an undertaking for even the heady Hog Farm. That was quickly forsaken in favor of a well-balanced, nutritious selection of organic foods capable of being mass produced on a shoestring.

Gallons of unsweetened yogurt, thousands of eggs, and several hundred pounds of powdered milk were ordered from the local farmers, as was a great percentage of the fruit and vegetables. Stan Goldstein handed the Hog Farm an envelope containing $6,500 in cash, and two of their scavengers went on a four-day shopping spree of lower Manhattan's wholesale staple outlets.

They brought back a pickup truck loaded with a cross-section of supplies varied enough to confound even the most diversified restaurateurs. Twenty-five pounds of coconuts, 100 pounds of blanched peanuts, 150 pounds of sunflower seeds, ten 100-pound sacks of rolled oats, 100 pounds of wheat germ, 100 pounds of turbinado sugar, fifty 100-pound bags of bulgar wheat, seventy-five 25-pound boxes of currants, 30,000 paper plates, 2,300 pairs of chopsticks, 28,000 plastic spoons, an unusual assortment of serving utensils and condiment dispensers, and, not the least bit out of place in such a culinary conundrum, 200 onyx Buddhas. "Now I understand why they're called the *Hog* Farm," jibed one of the younger boys as he unpacked the groceries. "Who, in their right mind, is gonna touch any of this shit?"

It would later be said that no mass of humanity in history had ever been so well fed and well cared for as were those who practiced survival on Max Yasgur's farm. That claim, in essence, was undeniably true, in spite of the rumors of a dire food shortage or rampant injuries which, for years to come, echoed throughout sensational media accounts of the festival. However hypocritical the Hog Farmers appeared to their critics, however selfish their intentions or inexcusable their duplicity, they came prepared for the holocaust.

*   *   *

For the most part, the hippies, in the best interests of brotherhood, left their Hog Farm co-workers to themselves. As soon as work was finished for the day, the groups parted company, consciously washing their hands of one another until morning when their mutual goal made avoidance impossible.

Little was known about the individuals who belonged to the commune. They valued their anonymity, hiding behind aliases like Baba, Goose, Calico, Red Dog, and Gandalf, and it was generally assumed, although incorrectly, that they were empty headed and illiterate. Stan Goldstein, who grew to know them intimately and became a trusted friend, found that many of them were fugitives from universities and corporations. Two had been practicing attorneys who had become disillusioned with the law's due process and opted for anarchy, another had been a government physicist who saw no future for the modern world and dropped out. They had tasted success, found its price tag too high, and took off in search of inner peace. Others were refugees from the Movement's ruins; when the various student organizations fell apart, they ran up against an emotional void that needed to be filled and found what they needed buried deep within the Hog Farm's protective custody. Much like any other cult through the ages, they provided their members with a sense of belonging and, in an abstract way, a sense of order. The rest of the family gave purpose to their fuzzy existences. They depended on one another for survival, and, as one Hog Farmer jokingly admitted, for their sanity.

To the ordinary hippie at work on the festival, whose lifestyle was a watered-down version of the commune's, the childish conduct of the Hog Farm was of only marginal interest. They were easily ignored, and what little damage they did could be corrected without causing anyone too much inconvenience. They would be gone in a few weeks, anyway. For now, the work was progressing well on schedule. It looked to most of the staff that there would, indeed, be a Woodstock festival, morale was high, and August 15 was approaching much too rapidly for them to be distracted by anything else.

— **5** —

The one determining factor over which they had no control, and which could conceivably foil the festival's groundwork, was the weather. Everyone depended on the customary midsummer climate, the temperate breezes, dazzling skies, natural fragrances, the fresh, clear exhilaration of working outdoors, to carry them through August on a bed of roses. There was that unfaltering, blind confidence about the weather that one came to expect from the hippies. It rained eighteen out of the twenty-two days before the festival. Not simply intermittent showers, but steady, driving downpours that lasted five and ten hours at a time before taking the briefest of intermissions.

The newspapers and weathermen called the precipitation "a curious irregularity in the atmosphere," but there were few who wished it would end. Farmers cheered as their crops flourished. The parched metropolitan areas were rescued from earlier drought as reservoirs were replenished. Fire companies relaxed for the first time in months, no longer fearful of brushfires streaking through the baked mountain forests. Fishermen extolled. It was a good time for prosperity. Only in White Lake, or, more accurately, in the half-readied segment of Max Yasgur's farm, did anyone languish in the rainy weather.

Each morning, as the sky prophesied another inclement spell, several hundred hopefuls waded through the flooded gullies in front of the production trailers, praying they'd be selected for one of that day's crew assignments. Clusters of itinerant workers were interviewed between nine and ten o'clock by either Chris Langhart, Chip Monck, or Steve Cohen, to determine the extent of their skills, and then redirected to other areas around the site that were in various stages of development.

"Any of you guys ever welded before?" A few hands always responded to the challenge, even if they had never laid eyes on a welding gun before. "How about power? Do you know anything about electricity? Have any of you ever worked on heavy construction crews? Do we have any plumbers in this gang?" Those who were ultimately chosen were issued ponchos, a felt hat, and gloves, and led off in the morning mist to where they were lectured on the type of labor to be done and left to work.

The rest of the staff went about their tasks as best they could, considering the weather.

There was, to begin with, a need for administrative organization that would keep everything running at optimum strength. Not much had been done to bring the unrefined land up to date in terms of technology. One of the most difficult installations, in this respect, was the engaging of telephone lines in and around the production area. Someone had contacted the phone company as soon as their lease was signed and requested ten lines be put in backstage, six for each of the trailers, six in the security office, and one hundred pay phones scattered around the concession area. The person who took the order was dumbfounded and not only refused to believe there was a customer in need of that many lines in Max's farmyard but doubted the festival's ability to pay for that kind of service. An offer of cash and a sizeable retainer to insure payment of accounts was politely put off and the company said that they would call back within a few days.

They never did.

Luckily, Chris Langhart had a friend named Tom Grimm who was an executive with Ohio Bell and he was flown in to accelerate the somewhat sensitive situation. Grimm said that the phone company representative who had filed away the order probably did not fully understand the urgency or the complexity of the job; someone, namely himself, had to lay it out for them in specific terms.

Once Grimm had identified himself as a phone company employee who had been retained by Woodstock Ventures as a special consultant, previously locked doors were flung open with an almost despicable willingness to please. Certainly Mr. Grimm could have those lines as requested, a salesman assured him, but it would take a good six weeks to two months to put them in working order. Manpower had been severely depleted, their crews were all working overtime on account of the rain, and cable was in short supply.

No one is quite sure what Tom Grimm said or did to convince the phone company that time was of the essence. Langhart suspected Grimm contacted a friend at the Public Service Commission "to give them a little boot in the ass." John Morris heard a story that Grimm made an unannounced inspection of the phone company's facilities in White Lake, found "forty-eight violations of standard operating procedure," and "urged" them to lend him a hand in getting Woodstock Ventures their phone equipment.

No matter what really happened, the next morning, eight telephone crews showed up at the site with cable wire shipped in from as far off as Canada, and began banging up lines all the way down the road to the center of Bethel.

By the end of the day, there was a total of fifty-three men at work on the festival's communications network, not including the office personnel who arranged billing, cleared circuits, and assigned them sequential exchanges. Any reference to a six-week or two-month hiatus had been dismissed as bureaucratic nonsense. It had been proved that even hip capitalism could play by the Establishment's rules, and, within seventy-two hours, phones were ringing from every end of the site to everyone's complete satisfaction.

A week of uninterrupted rainfall had turned the site into what one crew member likened to a "hog wallow."

Much of the work around the concession area slowed to a crawl. Stage and lighting crews dodged the storms in an attempt to sink the concrete footings for their respective platforms. The fence gangs had momentary success driving posts along the boundary line; pretty soon, the metal standards sagged, then gave way in the syrupy dirt and had to be recovered from underneath layers of slime before they disappeared completely. No one, it seemed, was making any headway.

Two recently built roads—one behind the stage and another leading into the site from Hurd Road—were temporarily closed to all vehicles. Their unpaved surfaces became quicksand to anything weighing over three hundred pounds, and several times a day, Ken Van Loan's tow trucks had to free staff cars and dune buggies from the bog.

The meteorologists hadn't provided much hope either. The five-day forecast read like an angler's dream: More rain with little chance of clearing. It was a bad situation growing worse.

Mel Lawrence spent the time in his trailer up on the hill reconfirming sanitation and garbage maintenance for the festival with three independent contractors. In Wallkill, he had negotiated a deal with the Port-O-San Corporation for 252 "standard" portable toilets, which would be serviced by a fleet of five trucks and men at a cost of $21,578. That had seemed quite sufficient to see them through the weekend. But as reports of booming ticket sales streamed in, Lawrence agonized over their health provisions and placed a matching order with Johnny-On-The-Spot, which added an unforeseen $21,630 to his skyrocketing budget. He hoped the 500 toilets would suffice, as both companies had been cleaned out of their stock and there wasn't a company within 200 miles capable of bailing them out with more.

By comparison, garbage collection was a steal. Lawrence had run across a man named Charles Macaluso, from New York Carting, who presented him with a sensible plan for keeping the area clean. For a mere $12,720, Macaluso proposed to install two stationary compactors (which he claimed were the largest in the state) in the woods. They would be supplemented by a mobile compactor, several maintenance vehicles, 300 recepticle stands, and 20,000 paper-can bags. New York Carting would also store and transport all solid wastes out of the immediate area. In return, Lawrence was to furnish Macaluso's men with thirty supervisors who, at the end of each day, would organize a clean-up detail. Drawing a labor force from a contingent of non-ticket holders, admitted on good faith by Wes Pomeroy, they'd roam the site, remove and staple the one-way bags, and fling them into the jaws of the mobile compactor that trailed behind them. When that was completed, they'd insert an empty bag in its place and the entire process would carry over to the next day.

It was a well-conceived plan and might have worked, at that—had the crowd been amenable to clearing the amphitheatre after each day's show ended or was manageable enough to allow a truck to get through. As it was, only a small percentage of the garbage bags were retrieved, with the lion's share left to roast beneath the torrid sun.

Lawrence was also disturbed over their wavering rapport with Max Yasgur. Each day, Max arrived in the production trailer with a typed inventory of his ruined land for which he wanted them to make full restitution. "I don't want to interfere with your work, boys, but this wholesale demolition of my land has got to stop." Mel commiserated with the farmer and agreed to lend him a crew of hippies to help take in the hay or cut the tall stalks of alfalfa that surrounded the stage. "Oh, my cows!" Max grieved. "Look what they're doing now! What's going to be done about this?"

Lawrence felt that Yasgur had begun to regret his involvement with Woodstock Ventures. The further they got into production, the more frequently Max would come by the site to examine his land. He'd stand to one side of the action, hands on his hips, shaking his head in consternation as the work progressed.

Mel passed a lot of time attempting to keep Max from his real tormentors: the pipelayers. Langhart had run into several problems with pipe alignment and was left no alternative but to break ground on sections of property not yet under the festival's contractual control.

"Look," Chris warned Mel, "whatever you do, keep Max away from the campgrounds between one and four this afternoon. We've gotta get that pipe in there before we run outta time."

To avoid a confrontation, one in which Max always expressed indignation over having to play cuckold to a bunch of long-haired kids, Lawrence arranged to meet his car at the Hurd Road entrance of the site so that the director of operations could chaperone him on a tour of the concessions area or the medical complex or the performers' kitchen—*anywhere* but the campgrounds. It was what Lawrence referred to as "the Yasgur two-step."

Later on, though, after taking the prearranged excursion, Max would inevitably work his way to the campgrounds and, like Lot's wife, he'd stiffen with rage. "Oh, my God! Do you see what they've done! Look—they've laid pipe there."

"Gee, I had no idea, Max," Lawrence would plead innocently, "otherwise I never woulda let it happen. How do you suppose those guys snuck up here without me seeing them? I'm stunned."

Of course, while they were busy consoling one another, Langhart would move his crew to another off-limits section of the site that demanded his immediate attention.

This went on for several days before Max grabbed hold of Michael Lang and asked him if he'd be so kind as to accompany him on a casual walk.

"Max was a real pisser," Michael recalled later, smiling in what could only be interpreted as admiration. "He'd point out to me where we had violated the contract or damaged a particular crop. Then, quicker than the eye could follow, he'd whip a small tablet out of his back pocket, wet the point of a pencil in his fingertips, and compute what we owed him right on the spot. He didn't miss a trick."

Nor was he inclined to negotiate the bill.

"Max would fight you on a deal to the nth degree," his wife explained, "but once you settled on something and shook hands with him, that handshake meant more than a contract. If someone went back on their word with Max, he could make things very tough."

Woodstock Ventures fared no better than the rest of Yasgur's associates. Max kept a running tally of their transgressions, attaching a dollar figure commensurate to each one, and balanced the total against the festival's $75,000 security deposit that he held in escrow. It was certainly an equitable arrangement, seeing as how both sides profited handsomely in their own right. The production staff obviously felt comfortable enough to move in any direction they wished in order to meet their deadline, and each time they did, Max transferred another chunk of cash into his plus column of the ledger. By the end of August, when the two parties met to divvy up the balance in the fund, neither was particularly surprised to learn they were even.

CHAPTER NINE

Aquarius Rising

And what rough beast, its hour come round at last,
Slouches towards Bethlehem to be born?
—*W. B. Yeats, "The Second Coming"*

— 1 —

"**T**his is the time when the jitters hit us," Mel Lawrence told a reporter, noting that only a week remained until the festival officially opened its gates. "It always happens this way. You walk around the site taking stock of what remains to be done, and it seems as though you're not even close. You just want to freak or run away. But we always get finished."

Lawrence's assuredness seemed immutable as always. And for a very good reason. In slightly less than two days since the rains had stopped, the site had slowly, and quite wonderfully, begun to sprout life.

Several A-frame structures that were to become the concession stands had been erected on the brim around the hill; a tractor-trailer had moved rows of portable toilets into place on either side of the bowl; seesaws, swings, a maze, and a latticework climber adorned a corner of the campgrounds; the performer's pavilion approached completion; two sound towers, patterned after the giant cribs that surround oil wells, inched toward the clouds. And there, nesting in the gap of clover at the base of the hill, were the makings for the most fantastic outdoor concert stage ever built. Twenty-three yards of concrete had been poured for its foundation, the cable clamps that would later suspend the telephone-pole footings had been sunk into the floor, and an 18-foot wall of yellow scaffolding had been pieced together as a support for the gigantic rotating platform that was still a ways off. It was all reasonably encouraging.

Local interest intensified as word of progress spread across the county. The *Times Herald Record* devoted several columns a day to the young crews' astonishing advances, marking the festival's stride under such banners as 'Aquarians Race Clock As Crowd Grows," or "6,000 Festivalgoers Swarm Into Area," or "Age of Aquarius Dawns," accompanied by photo layouts depicting the wonderful spirit of brotherhood at work on the project. Carloads of sightseers converged on the farm to nourish their curiosity, and Monticello police reported that large numbers of youths had recently appeared in the city, most carrying backpacks and sleeping bags. The anticipation that had spun out as a result of all the publicity, both in Wallkill and now in White Lake, was unlike anything ever experienced before.

But beyond the dreamy spell the festival seemed to have cast over the country's youth, it had also generated intense admiration from many of the local businessmen who suddenly found themselves involved with the blue-jeaned production staff. Max Bender, a respected civic leader and chairman of the Sullivan County Planning Board, was overwhelmed by the headway being made on Yasgur's farm and urged the residents to throw their unqualified support behind the festival. "Perhaps some of the people are shortsighted and do not understand what these children are doing," he said, in a published interview, referring to the outstanding legal suit for an injunction still pending before the State Supreme Court in Catskill. "These people are bringing recreation to the county and should be given an opportunity to express themselves. The results will be good and if successful they will bring an economic boost to the county without it costing the taxpayer a cent." Bender's committee was directly responsible for bringing along two Sullivan County projects designed to pump new life into the area—a five-million-dollar airport, and a six-million-dollar convention hall—but he shrugged them off as undeveloped and distant rewards. Pointing to the festival's imminence, he declared, "We have something right now, tangible and real. Let everyone help and everyone will benefit."

A combined force of three hundred laborers was doing everything in its power to move them closer to that very end. Max Bender stood in awe of their remarkable success. "Some of those kids probably never saw a shovel, a sledgehammer, or a pick ax. Today they are using them and building something for which they will receive little pay but great satisfaction."

Max Yasgur voiced an almost identical amazement to his wife, although his high spirits were somewhat diluted by the current of events it took to produce such results. He thought the "kids were doing a tremendous job of erecting a stage in far less time than they should have," but they were dragging tractors and trees and all kinds of tools across his land, tearing up alfalfa fields and crops with little concern for their value. "To them, it's all grass," Max complained. "But you should see what they're doing! I can't believe it. They're working like beavers. I saw a huge tractor plowing across the field with a little guy perched on top controlling it, and when he came down, I saw that *it was a girl!* I've never seen kids work like this before. They're such a pleasure to have around."

For practical purposes, many of those crews were put on brutal, twenty-four-hour shifts to keep pace with the rest of the progression. For the stage and tower crews especially, life became one continuous rhythm of exertion from which there seemed no apparent relief. No one went back to the hotel at night. Their meals—a piece of cold chicken or a sandwich and a piece of fruit—were brought to them in the field by one of the girls from the Diamond Horseshoe. Occasionally, they'd be allowed an hour's rest in one of the production trailers or on the back seat of a staff car, but no one dared to take it, fearing they'd never want to return.

Endurance became a source of one's pride. Most everyone knew that if they could hold together for another week, they'd come damn close to being ready for Friday afternoon's show. Bill Abruzzi had arranged to give daily Vitamin B12 shots to the stage crew, which, he claimed, would accelerate their metabolic rate and, hopefully, keep everyone on his feet just that much longer. Most of the men, however, found the effect wore off in a matter of hours and made them even more sluggish than before. The ultimate remedy came directly from the top: Those who needed an extra lift were slipped tabs of acid or speed to keep them going. "Get it on at all costs" remained Michael's tireless motto. After five months of climbing over the enemy, exhaustion could not be permitted to stand in his way.

To build the stage, it took every ounce of determination left in the battered crew—a tinker from San Francisco, two teen-agers from Georgia (who, aside from having recently sat in the audience at a southern festival, had no practical experience whatsoever), and a pair of bikers from the town of Woodstock. Their foreman, an elderly Italian man whose scaffolding company had supplied them with raw materials, was of the opinion that they were all wasting their time by running themselves ragged. They'd never finish—he knew from experience. He subsequently retreated to the sidelines where he idly watched their "folly" as if it were some form of psychedelic entertainment.

Jay Drevers was in charge of the hapless platoon. Drevers related well to the men. A patient, team-spirited individual, he found it unnecessary to display patronizing fits of temper in order to bring about results. Instead, he approached the challenge with logic and self-restraint, expressed a reasonable amount of faith in its outcome, and unconsciously traded on his enthusiasm to motivate the rest of the crew.

By the middle of the second week in August, they had progressed favorably to a point whereby they were ready to put the deck on top of the stage's stiltlike foundation. The foreman, who had taken to sunning himself during the afternoons, was so stunned by their accomplishment that even he was moved to rejoin the group in their come-from-behind drive toward the finish gate. It was a long shot, he conceded, but he no longer bet against their success.

They started by laying narrow planks of wood across the upended scaffolding until it resembled a ballroom-size parquet floor with legs. Then, two layers of plywood were positioned on top of it and the whole wooden sandwich was fastened together with hundreds of sixpenny nails so that it remained rigidly in place.

The five roof trusses were built out of enormous pieces of wood weighing over 800 pounds each. These were to be held in place above the bandstand by a palisade of telephone poles and were to be used to support both the lights and the strips of canvas-covering for the stage.

The telephone poles were bolted into place early that Monday morning before the festival. Upon closer examination, most of them were found to be either split or rotten, but it was already too late to do anything about it. So, rather than scrapping the project, it was decided they would make due with what they had and hope for the best. To attach guy wires consisting of half-inch aircraft cable from the top of the poles to the cement footings, two stagehands crawled inside 55-gallon steel drums and were hoisted 300 feet into the air by a gigantic crane. The crane held the boys steady in midair while they leaned out of the capsule and yanked the wire through and around a metal cap on top of the poles before tossing it back down to a man on the ground. It was a foolhardy and risky way to secure their stage supports, but it finished that particular phase of the construction in less than six hours, a full day ahead of schedule.

A curious mix of ex-merchant marines and hippies who called themselves the Bastard Sons (as a result of always being served last at mealtimes) assembled a cavalcade of ten lightweight concession stands in the section of woods between the Hog Farm and the backstage area. Born out of Michael's concept of The Nation, the Aquarian Crafts Bazaar was to be the most exquisite head shop ever amassed in one location, where the Woodstock Generation could parade before an open mall of peddlers invited there to hawk their wares. Beads, handsewn moccasins, posters, T-shirts, water pipes, ceramics, belt buckles, drug-related accessories, and head bands—anything identified with the counterculture was there for the asking, and at prices low enough to conform to the hippie's economic doctrine of spare change.

A coalition of radical underground newspapers, as well as a political leftist outfit called the Up-Against-The-Wall Motherfuckers, had reserved one of the booths adjoining the bazaar to promote "the inevitable revolution." Durable platforms were buttressed into a rear wall of their stand that would amply support the weight of mimeograph machines and stacks of paper. Another horizontal ledge in the front formed the display counter where up-to-the-minute festival editions, philosophical pamphlets, and Marxist propaganda were to be given away free to their sympathizers.

Using a miscellany of hand tools, the Bastard Sons pruned the area immediately around the stands and notched comely paths through the rest of the thicket, which they padded with wood chips shipped in from Texas. The trails, shaded hideaways where one could conceivably come to escape the frenzy of crowds and hard rock, were marked by arrow-shaped signs pointing to Groovy Way, High Way, Gentle Path, and Easy Street. The remaining Christmas lights were strung across the stands and through the treetops, and footlights were blanketed beneath umbrellas of reconstructed pine cones.

There was still a great deal of work to be done on the main concession stands above the amphitheatre. Food For Love was due in there Tuesday afternoon to set up the kitchens, but Monday night, the Bastard Sons were still hammering away at their cumbersome birchwood frameworks.

The food stands were objects of art in their own right. Long lines of colored braided rope were knotted at the tops of the center poles to form a crown and wound down around the supporting posts like a hundred serpentine rainbows. Indian tapestries had been interwoven with swatches of mirror cloth to spawn exotic thatched roofs and were highlighted underneath by soft, yellow fluorescent panels. And colorful banners—advertising which stands sold hot dogs, soft drinks, French fries, ice cream, corn-on-the-cob, watermelon, or tacos—flapped from the pyramidal masts.

The interiors still remained to be furnished. Griddles had to be assembled, refrigeration appliances needed to be connected to generators, kettles for boiling corn had to be installed, and running water had yet to be tapped in from a nearby well.

Peter Goodrich frantically accosted members of other crews and begged them to lend a hand in the concession area. Manpower, though, was worth its weight in gold and at an unmatched premium. There was just too much still to be done elsewhere for production supervisors to relinquish their hold on crew members, and by Tuesday night, that extremely vital area of production had collapsed into utter pandemonium.

— **2** —

The developments from here on in moved very rapidly. By the end of the first week in August, it became apparent that the portion of West Shore Road that ran behind the stage was going to fill up with people as soon as the gates were opened. That meant the rock groups would not be able to reach the stage from the performers' pavilion and their assigned trailers without first wading through a mob of overzealous fans. The fence separating the two areas was unsturdy and, therefore, meaningless to the security of the performers. An alternative line of access had to be worked out to bypass the road completely.

On Sunday, August 10, Chris Langhart, assisted by a corps of technical people he knew from summer theatres in Syracuse, began constructing a footbridge over the road. Borrowing machinery and raw materials from the stage crew, they frivolously based their calculations for weight and size on whatever information was available to them. "It's got to be strong enough so that Janis Joplin can be followed across the bridge by a horde of roadies with everybody jumping up and down in time to the music," Langhart told his co-workers, who looked at him as though he were on a bad trip. Accuracy, they assumed, was not going to be an essential element in the building of their overpass. "No, I'm serious," he said. "Hey, John," Langhart called to John Morris who was on his way toward the stage from a production trailer, "what's the weight of the average roadie?"

It was also on the tenth that Howard Hirsch and Peter Leeds arrived at Yasgur's farm to begin setting up the exhibition of amateur artists along the festival's northwestern perimeter. All of the show's entries were to be hung on the fence and trees just beyond the campgrounds. The Indian artists, whose prime interest was to make an enormous profit from the sale of their handicrafts, elected to remain independent of the others. Langhart had built them a special pavilion on the way to the concession area—a setting more apropos for the type of fast-paced hustle they had in mind.

The next day, August 11, Langhart flagged down Joel Rosenman as the promoter wheeled his way around the stage on a quick tour of the site. It had become an unspoken pact between the two young men that whenever a particularly large expense loomed in the foreseeable distance, either Rosenman or John Roberts would be notified about it beforehand, lest Michael be given another go at the corporate bank account. This time, Langhart's emergency had to do with their most plentiful source of water—the large pond on the fringe of Max's farm; Max did not own it.

The pond belonged to an association of owners whose only visible proxy was William Filippini, an Italian farmer whose chicken farm was within shouting distance of the festival site. Filippini, Joel found, was like the rest of the farmers they had encountered since setting out. He claimed to be one of "the little people" who were always being taken advantage of by city slickers, expressed a good deal of resentment over the hippies' presence in his community, and speculated aloud how much it was worth to Woodstock Ventures for the right to trespass on his property.

Rosenman underwent several bargaining sessions with the old man, each one more frustrating than the last. And more time-consuming. Filippini grew to look forward to Rosenman's visits and never failed to break out a bottle of chianti over which, he said, it was customary in the old country to settle all differences.

But, as James Russell Lowell wrote, "There is no good in arguing with the inevitable," and, in this case, the inevitable was practically five days away. Filippini could have it whichever way he wanted, Joel thought. Come Friday, there'd be no stopping them. If a water shortage arose, they'd begin pumping the pond to avert a disaster with or without a written agreement. He suspected that any court of law would exhibit leniency under the circumstances.

Filippini, despite his tendency toward "countrified ignorance," reached the same conclusion as Joel, and delivered the terms of settlement with practiced finesse: $5,000 for the right to pump water, without restriction, from the lake for a period lasting not longer than ten days, take it or leave it.

They took it.

John Roberts spent that same evening, the evening of August 11, alone in his New York apartment, packing for Wednesday's trip upstate. Roberts was blissfully loose, perhaps even exploiting a touch of the old *sangfroid* kept in reserve for just such an occasion, as he tossed a few toiletries into a monogrammed overnight bag on the bed. An all-too-conspicuous maelstrom surged within a few hours of shattering his cozy world, but for the moment, Roberts felt no pain.

The balance sheet on his night table was responsible for John's current state of mind. As of that afternoon's accounting, Woodstock Ventures had posted receipt of advance ticket sales totaling $1,107,936. It was true that they had run through nearly twice that sum in order to produce the festival, and, yes, it had been somewhat infuriating that he had allowed himself to be taken in by those two, Lang and Kornfeld, but it appeared now as though the inequities would cancel out one another. From where he stood, they were in for a hearty gate, which would undoubtedly lift them into the black for the first time in months.

Roberts admitted to himself that as long as they broke even in this venture he'd be happy. For all the hassles he'd endured, despite the traumas and the tribulations that had contributed to his sleepless nights, for all the uncertainty and delusion, it had been a hell of a summer. He had finally wormed his way out from under the stigma of failure. He was caught up in the midst of an exciting, although somewhat notorious, cultural phenomenon. And his father, whom he had invited to accompany him to Bethel, would have to come to terms with John's emerging professional status or be damned by his narrow-mindedness.

Of course, Roberts attributed an even greater measure of optimism to their impending film deal, of which he expected to hear good news any day.

Some weeks ago, right after Wallkill caved in, the three active partners—Michael, Joel, and John—confessed that it was no longer expedient for them to rely solely on Artie Kornfeld to wrap up any movie transaction at all, let alone in enough time for a major studio to jettison a field crew to Bethel. Psychedelic drugs had shot Artie's personality full of holes. He was a human being only inasmuch as his heart beat steadily and his brain received electrochemical impulses, but otherwise, Artie was what the hippies referred to as a "deadhead" or a "casualty." His behavior paralleled that of a retarded child. He chose to glide through the summer of 1969 in a "purple haze," oblivious of the world at large. They'd have to cover for him. The only way they could keep a film deal from slipping through their fingers was for Woodstock Ventures to have its own camera crew standing in the wings while their attorneys raced against the clock to find a legitimate distributor.

Lang very swiftly hired two Englishmen, Michael Margetz and Malcolm Hart, to film the preliminary activity on and around the site, and that was proceeding rather nicely. For the concert footage, they commissioned a young team of filmmakers named Bob Meurice and Michael Wadleigh, whose studio on upper Broadway Lang had urged his partners to visit during the last week in July.

Neither John nor Joel had ever heard of Wadleigh-Meurice Productions before. Nor, for that matter, had any of their moviegoing friends who were usually well informed when it came to matching names to credits. The little they managed to dig up about them from industry associates was either irrelevant to their interests or circumstantial. As with the rest of their half-assed gambles, Roberts and Rosenman had to feel their way through this end of the enterprise with extreme caution and hope they wouldn't ultimately be taken to the cleaners.

Michael Wadleigh, they learned, was a medical-school dropout from Ohio whose honey-colored long hair, undernourished leanness, pious eyes, Zapata moustache, and wing-tipped beard invited comparison to a twentieth-century Christ. He shunned traditional Hollywood slickness and convention for an informal existence in the East. Wadleigh had made a documentary about the war called *No Vietnamese Ever Called Me Nigger*, which had received critical acclaim, but aside from that, he had relatively little experience or renown as a film director. Bob Meurice was the more conservative of the two, outspoken and fearless, and his credentials were as incomplete as his partner's. Nevertheless, Roberts and Rosenman found them enthusiastic about doing a film on the festival, and they had even volunteered to work on speculation. Since no distributor was involved as yet, they would pay for their own raw stock (which they estimated would come to roughly $100,000) and use their influence (whatever that might be) to place the finished product with a major film company for distribution.

That was indirectly what Roberts had been waiting to hear all along: there was somebody *else* out there, besides him, who was willing to invest money in the festival. Until now, the deals Lang had brought to them were sweet ones for everyone *but* Roberts and Rosenman. This was indeed a welcome change of pace.

Even so, money alone was not to be the determining factor that led to Wadleigh-Meurice Productions' clinching the Woodstock deal. Michael Wadleigh invited Roberts to screen a few reels of his experimental work so that John might get a better feeling for what the director had in mind for their film—should he be given the chance to shoot it. Wadleigh had heard that the reason the major distributors shied away from making a commitment so far was because they remained unconvinced that a documentary about a rock festival could capture the emotional, as well as the musical, excitement of the event. They felt—and rightly so—that a movie without those basic ingredients was clearly box office poison.

Wadleigh agreed with the experts who believed that a lot was lost in the translation from live concert to film, no matter how "in touch" the director and cameraman were with their subject. However, he also claimed to have found a way around it. He had been toying with the split-screen technique of editing and found it to be most effective in energizing a documentary. When two completely different scenes were projected onto the screen at the same time and shown side by side, the viewer was treated to much the same kind of superabundant, electrified thrills one experienced at a three-ring circus.

After sitting through a few examples of that type of filmmaking, Roberts was a firm believer that Wadleigh knew what he was talking about.

The deal they entered into as a result of that meeting was potentially advantageous for both groups. Wadleigh-Meurice Productions would raise all the necessary monies for the production of the film. In addition to their being awarded exclusive filming rights, they could retain artistic control by placing the finished movie with a distributor with whom they felt comfortable. That indirectly removed all responsibility from Artie's hands. Woodstock Ventures would retain fifty percent of the producer's royalty after the distributor took his cut, and Wadleigh-Meurice would share thirty percent of that. Everyone expressed satisfaction with his end of the package.

A week later, Bob Meurice called Roberts back to inquire whether or not John might be interested in renegotiating their deal. Meurice had second thoughts about bankrolling a documentary about a festival that might not take place. Woodstock Ventures, he pointed out, was still under the threat of an injunction, and, anyway, Meurice hadn't had much luck in finding investors to underwrite the costs of their production. He wondered whether Woodstock Ventures might put up the $100,000 to make the film, for which, in return, they could take one hundred percent of the profits.

Roberts was adamantly opposed to an alteration in the contract no matter what concessions were made. He told Meurice that he was already in over his head as far as his *own* company's financing was concerned. His personal accounts were drained. Woodstock Ventures needed refunding. This time it just couldn't be any other way—he'd have to pass.

John was relieved. It had been the first time he dared to say "no" to anybody since going into business with Lang and Kornfeld. He'd been a pushover these last few months; nobody knew it better than he. But, by politely refusing Bob Meurice's request, he had scaled something of a psychological hurdle that had been troubling him. Polite, but firm. It hadn't been so bad. He'd won for a change.

This time, however, Roberts had made a mistake—a very costly mistake. It would haunt him for at least a decade. Over the course of the next week, their film distribution deal would pass through the hands of just about every major studio in Hollywood, the terms would vary according to the offer,

Paramount and Columbia would renege on promises, and Meurice and Wadleigh would ultimately reach an agreement with Warner Brothers. And, in their haste, when the terms of the deal were set, the promoters of the Woodstock Music and Art Fair would lose points as rapidly as a dog sheds its winter coat. But John Roberts's decision not to stake Wadleigh-Meurice Productions to $100,000, after all the money that had been squandered on wasted efforts and bribes, on luxury sports cars and helicopter rides, on unused land and pointless legal battles, turned out to be the most unrewarding and, perhaps, the most tragic decision of his career.

— **3** —

Construction continued on the site throughout Tuesday, August 12, despite periodic showers.

Lang, Steve Cohen, Ticia Bernuth, and John Morris spent most of that afternoon galloping back and forth across the bowl on horseback, ignoring the hundreds of dedicated laborers in their path who worked to carry the preparations to their hurried climax. "At that moment," a bare-chested stake driver attested, "we felt humiliated, just blown away. It was like massah and the gentry had come down from the castle to ride among the slaves."

By Wednesday morning, though, the enervated crews had a fresh source from which they borrowed encouragement.

Cars, jeeps, buses, and trains had been arriving in Monticello throughout the night, all bursting at the seams with hippies en route to the festival. They came from as far west as California and Washington, from as deep into the south as Florida, Georgia, and Alabama, and, to the north, from Maine and Wisconsin—all lacking overnight accommodations. They hadn't given much thought to lodging before leaving home, and as they quite rudely discovered upon arrival, Sullivan County's motels were either booked solid through the festival weekend or off limits to hippies.

With no other option open to them, an estimated thirty thousand teenagers, "many barefoot and looking like pioneers," descended upon the site, and, by 11:00 that morning, were settled snugly into the open bowl on Yasgur's farm.

"My God," a stagehand exclaimed to a friend, as they struggled to keep the trusses from slipping, "it's for real! I never had time to stop and think about whether anybody was actually gonna show up for this thing—but there they are! Far fuckin' out, man—*there they are!*"

As he had promised Stan Goldstein and Michael Lang back in April, Bill Hanley pulled his sound truck into the service road behind the stage around the same time the crowds started arriving, plugged some equipment into a portable amplifier, and piped prerecorded music out to the sheer delight of the audience.

> Get your motor runnin', head out on the highway,
> Lookin' for adventure, and whatever comes our way . . .

Bulldozers roared in the background as they smoothed rock fill and gravel into mudholes. The rain had washed away a few trails in the woods and temporarily choked off the press and service vehicle parking lots above the concession area, but, aside from that, the land itself was in pretty good shape. In time, the sun would dry everything out.

What promised to be their biggest headache for the duration of the festival revealed itself quickly enough. By high noon, a staff technician noticed a severe drop in water pressure and made a spot check of the wells. Everything seemed to be in top working order. But the gauges continued to weaken. By 1:00 p.m., they were dangerously low. Ordinarily, that signaled a water emergency, but it was too early for that to occur. The water supply had hardly been in operation for two hours. The two 10,000-gallon tanks were full, and the wells were functioning at peak performance, yielding anywhere from 7 to 35 gallons a minute each, depending upon their size. It had to be something else, something incidental to the water supply that was causing the problem. That narrowed it down to only one possibility: pipes.

Chris Langhart got hold of a jeep and followed the fourteen-mile aquaduct around the festival grounds checking the flow of water in each of the plastic arteries. He was behind the wheel for no longer than five minutes, perhaps, when he came across several instances of trouble, each one identical in context and inherent to the problem of overall maintanance of the plumbing system.

Langhart had been looking for an occlusion of some sort, a chunk of debris lodged in a pipe joint or a wad of hardened mud balled up at a critical pivot. Instead, he found the problem to be a human one, which should have been evident when they began laying the waterline. The audience, who had begun milling around the area, stepped on the pipes without realizing how fragile they were and inadvertently pushed their feet through the soft plastic casing. Subsequently, the line had sprung leaks in, at least, ten different locations, thereby cutting off the pressure.

Luckily, Langhart had had the good sense to install emergency communications equipment along the way for just such an occasion. He had found a surplus outfit in Lima, Ohio, which specialized in reconditioning army crank phones, and had ordered a quantity of them for the festival. When they buried the pumping aparatus, Langhart also concealed a crank phone in a plastic case next to each well head, pilot valve, and fountain so that, in case of an emergency, a field technician could locate the problem and call it in to a central operator who, in turn, would dispatch a repair crew to the trouble spot.

Reaching into a crevice, he pulled up a crank phone, explained the situation to a voice on the other end of the line, and, within minutes, Langhart and two assistants were bandaging the broken slots with rubber sheeting and holding them in place with multiple radiator clamps acquired from an auto supply wholesaler.

"We need signs," he said to Mel Lawrence. "Have one of your guys over at the print shop run off a couple hundred warnings that we can plant every few feet or so. And while you're at it—Max is half-crazy over all those kids tromping through the crops and riding his cows. The poor guy's gonna head straight for the coronary care unit if we don't do something about it."

Lawrence radioed the request to the men from Intermedia who operated the silkscreen presses at the print shack. Like clockwork, they hand-stenciled 200 "Danger" signs, one which identified "Max's Barn," and another requesting that those who had recently joined the festival community "Please Let Max's Cows Moo In Peace."

"The crowd seems to be enjoying themselves and behaving rather orderly," Lawrence told a disc jockey from Rahway, New Jersey, who called to find out what was "going down in White Lake." It was to be the first of over 250 similar broadcast interviews the festival staff would give over the course of the long weekend. "There's plenty to eat, enough room to run around for three days without stopping, and probably the best vibes anywhere on the continent. These kids are in love, man. They're high on life. You oughta make it up here and see for yourself."

"So then, there will, in fact, be a Woodstock festival."

"You're damn straight! Whoops—I forgot, I'm on the air. Sorry. It just sorta slipped out."

"That's all right, Mr. Lawrence. Can you tell us something about the facilities?"

Mel went through the list of Woodstock amenities and rattled off the full

lineup of performers, adding that Jeff Beck had called that morning to cancel
because of sickness. "But he's the only one, so far. Most of the groups have
arrived or are on their way to the site. We've still got to finish the stage, but
aside from that, we're ready to rock and roll."

"We've had reports that traffic around the Monticello area is beginning
to become boxed up."

"Not from where I'm standing, man." Lawrence lifted a pair of binocu-
lars to his eyes and scanned the site approach from Hurd Road. A few cars
waited their turn to enter the parking lot, but, other than that, the street was
clear. "Which means that Route 17-B is also pretty decent. We're all set for
you. The state police have got it all under control, and we don't anticipate a
single car to be backed up from around here now until next Monday."

John Roberts met his father and his brother, Billy, at 9:30 A.M. on the corner
of Fifty-seventh Street and Sixth Avenue to keep them from seeing his psychedelic office. The ride to White Lake was as somber an occasion as any
Roberts family reunion since John had graduated from college. To an outsider, the trio might have appeared overwhelmed by the implications of their
journey, fully aware that young people from all over the United States were
on their way to the festival, but to John Roberts, it seemed like the instant
replay of a bad dream.

The three of us took refuge in the contemplation of our abundant neu-
roses. I reflected on the fact that I was more nervous about my father's
reaction to the site than I was about its actual condition, and I decided
to have myself committed as soon as the festival was over. Billy reflected
on the possibility that he was about to see evidence of incompetence so
overwhelming that his refusal to participate would be seen as culpable,
and he considered having me committed before the festival got started.
My father busied himself trying to adopt an attitude of benign resignation toward the calamities he confidently expected to unfold, and tried
to figure out a way of having everyone on the Woodstock staff committed before they could do further harm. It was a rollicking journey.

John nearly fainted from shock as their car turned into Hurd Road and
pulled up alongside the Indian artists' pavilion. "What the hell is going on
here!" he shrieked. He stared out at the mass of people swarming around
inside the bowl. "They're not supposed to be inside yet. I've got the tickets
for the booths with me! This is incredible!" He experienced a tremendous

sinking feeling, and slumped down into the seat. "Good Lord—there's no gates, there's no gates."

The ticket booths were in pieces on the ground. John watched in horror as a mob of potential customers filed through the entrance, careful not to trip over the turnstiles.

He looked nervously at his father, prepared to bear the brunt of the elder Roberts's indignation. His father's cynicism, however, had been transformed into support. "It'll work out," he said. "Just get out there and get those people of yours to build the gates, and I'm sure they'll be ready in time."

John leaped out of the car and ran practically headfirst into an exultant Michael Lang who was standing below the unfinished stage. Lang saw him coming and raised his right arm in order to slap John's palm. The look on Roberts's face, however, warned him that such a greeting would be in bad taste.

"Hey, far out, man—you made it. It's outta sight, huh?"

"What's going on here, Michael? The gates aren't up, the fences look about as sturdy as tissue paper, thousands of people were let in before we collected their money. I mean, shit—the *stage* isn't ready. What's the meaning of this?"

Lang waved his hands in front of Roberts's face. "Don't get excited, man. It's cool."

"Of course it isn't cool, Michael," he said, still wanting to believe what his easygoing partner pretended would come true. But that was exactly what had gotten him into this situation, and, from what he could see, it was a boldfaced lie. "There just aren't enough hands and bodies and hammers and nails to get all these things together in time."

"You worry too much. I'm tellin' you, man, it's gonna be cool. Our guys got everything under control. I just talked to Mel, and he . . ."

"I'm going to have a talk with Mel myself. Where is he?"

"I don't know, man. He's around here someplace." Michael shrugged. "The cat's got a lotta ground to cover. Listen, I just took some wheels around the site, and it looks to me like we're on the verge of gettin' it together. Hang loose, man. It's not worth doin' a number on yourself. That'd only be self-defeating." Roberts regarded Michael's sophistry with sharp-eyed contempt. "I'm tellin' you, everything's groovy. You'll see. By tomorrow, they'll have the gates up, these cats here'll be swingin' from the stage, and we'll be ready to take on the whole fuckin' world."

Roberts had regained a modest degree of composure by the time his father dropped him off in front of the security building. No one had said more than five words to him in the car, and he had had time to think about the senseless waste of energy that had been invested in this sorry muddle they called a festival. All his and Joel's hopes of striking out on their own, of making a big killing before slipping into the more structured sanctum of Media Sound—they all seemed to have gone for naught. There were thirty thousand people wandering around that bowl—*thirty thousand*, practically the entire population of Sullivan County—who not only got in on a full John Roberts scholarship, but now looked to him to sustain their welfare. The biggest irony was that he felt an incredible sense of responsibility to see they got what they expected, to insure them a *festive* weekend in the country. Was he losing his mind? It really didn't seem to make that much difference anymore.

And, yet, he was angrier than hell about the impasse they had reached. It wasn't the money. He'd still have a sizeable nest egg to tide him over the next few years. Nor were Michael and Artie the source of his bitterness. Holding them completely at fault for the corporation's scandalous mismanagement was like blaming a week-old baby for wetting its diapers. No, it was the generation with which he was at odds. The hippies. He resented their deceitful charade more than anything else, their sleepy-eyed grin, puerile demeanor, always with their heart open and their hand out. They had hoodwinked him into believing all the gibberish about brotherhood and peace when, all the time, they were only interested in self-gratification. Takers. The what's-in-it-for-me generation. If he hadn't envied their carefree lifestyle as a way around his own depression, he'd never have gotten himself into this mess. The only thing he could do now was to make the best of it until the weekend was over.

The mood inside the security office wasn't at all what Roberts had expected. Lee Madder, Wes Pomeroy, John Fabbri (who had returned from San Francisco with Joe Kimble), Jewel Ross, Karen Eager (Sam's teen-age daughter who helped out answering the phones), and two young people he had never seen before were in the process of celebrating good news. *Good news?* Roberts asked. What could possibly be good about the farce-in-progress at Max's farm? But there was, indeed, something to smile about. Richard Gross, their local attorney, had called a few minutes before John arrived to relay the news that the suit against the festival had been withdrawn. Gross had reached an agreement with the co-owners of that summer home; all Woodstock Ventures had to do was provide them with a few security men to protect their property and they'd back off from a legal action. Wes agreed to assign a squad of the New York City cops to stand guard around their place and keep kids a safe distance away. It was as simple as that.

John drew Pomeroy aside and asked him about securing the entrance to the amphitheatre. "We've got to do something quickly, Wes—not just about keeping people out, but we've got to figure out some way to empty the bowl so that I can collect their tickets. Maybe we can make an announcement from the stage or something along that order."

"What do you want, John, a riot? You try pushing thirty thousand people out of there, and that's exactly what you're going to have."

"What about pulling some of the crews off what they're doing and stationing them around the entrance until we can get the gates up? Or the cops—what about using the Peace Service Corps? They're obviously acquainted with things of this nature."

The police, however, were not due in White Lake until Thursday morning, and, according to Pomeroy, even they couldn't help at a time like this. The crews, he said, were understaffed as it was. "The stage has got to be finished before we can attend to anything else. It doesn't matter how many kids you have inside or outside of the grounds. If that stage isn't finished in time, *we'll* be. Those kids will be pretty upset that they came all this way and paid a lot of money *not* to be entertained." Pomeroy suggested that Roberts forget about the people who were already inside the fences and work on getting the gates up.

He received the same advice from Mel Lawrence. Roberts finally caught up with the director of operations in the command trailer around three o'clock that afternoon and asked him about their chances for success.

"They're pretty good," Lawrence offered, "but I'm not sayin' it's not gonna be a bitch bringin' it off." Lawrence was genuinely distraught over the inadequate condition of the fences but admitted there was nothing to be done about it. He had his hands full keeping the kids who were working the heavy assignments alive. "Do you realize that most of them are working on three days without sleep? The trouble is, I can't let 'em sleep even when they're done cause I need 'em all the way through the weekend. They're higher than a kite right now. I just hope they don't fall on their faces before we lift this thing off the ground."

Lawrence was also disturbed over the irresponsibility of his stage crew chief. An hour before, one of the younger assistants informed him that the giant crane they were renting at $200 an hour had been permanently built into the scenery. "We can't get it out without tearing down the stage," the boy had said. Langhart had built the bridge around it without realizing that the crane had to be first driven out, and now they were stuck.

"This is the kinda shit that I've hadda put up with," he told Roberts. "A lotta these guys stopped thinkin' when the people started rollin' in. You wanna hear the kinda nonsense that's going on with the lights? Well, I'll tell you. Chip spent a fortune on all those overhead spots, but we're not gonna be able to use even one of them. The telephone poles holding up the trusses are bending out of shape. I've gotta figure out a way to get a roof up there without damaging anything. If we load hundreds of pounds of lighting onto it too, those 800-pound babies are gonna come crashing down on some-body's head. I mean, *that's it,* man. That's what I've been doin' these last few days and there's not all that much time left to work it out. Sorry, John. I know how much those fences mean to you, but right now, we've gotta worry about the stage."

Roberts found his way back to the security office about four o'clock and briefed Joel on his discussion with Lawrence. Ten minutes later, Lee Mackler walked over to where they were sitting, her hands noticeably trembling.

"You're never going to believe this," she said in a voice barely louder than a whisper. "I just spoke to Joe Fink, and he said we've been screwed."

"What are you talking about, Lee?" Joel asked.

"Screwed, man—we've been fucked over by those goddamn pigs. Fink said that the police commissioner withdrew his consent for the cops to work at the festival. We're gonna have two hundred thousand kids up here without any fucking security."

"Oh my God!" Roberts screamed, covering his face with his hands. "It can't be. It just can't be. Tell me you're only kidding, Lee."

"I'm sorry, John. I wish I could."

The teletype that was sent to every New York City Police Department precinct earlier that afternoon was short and tersely worded:

> It has come to the attention of the Department that certain members of the force have been engaged to do various work assignments during the Woodstock Music and Art Fair. . . . The attention of all parties is drawn to the provisions of TOP320 of 1967 which pertains to off-duty employ-ment: . . . this type of employment must first be approved by the Chief of Personnel.
>
> . . . permission will not be granted for extra employment where, as a condition of employment, the police officer's uniform, shield, gun or exercise of police authority is not to be used. . . .

The language behind Commissioner Howard Leary's door had been even stronger. According to a police source, Leary was livid when he learned that three hundred of his men were engaged "to cavort with hippies." Where there were hippies, he contended, there was certain to be widespread use of drugs and illicit sex. He was supposed to have told his precinct commanders:

"If I find out that even one patrolman has participated in this crime, heads are going to roll around here."

Pomeroy walked into the security office a few minutes later, carrying three cellophane-wrapped sandwiches.

"You're pretty hungry, huh, Wes?" Lee asked him.

"You bet."

"Watch how fast your appetite goes away." She repeated Fink's message, careful not to leave out a single word.

Pomeroy stood speechless in the middle of the room, his head turning to each staff member present as if to say "Someone tell me this is a joke." When he realized Mackler was serious, his face flushed with anger. "Jesus Christ!" he exploded. "Let me call Joe." He lunged at the phone and dialed the ninth precinct.

Everyone respectfully left the room and went outside to wait for his decision. After a five-minute conversation with Fink, Wes told them it was all right if they came back inside.

"Fink knows how to get the cops up here," he said, still stunned by the news. "He'll handle it. It's just going to cost us."

"How much?" John asked.

"Probably double."

Pomeroy's original estimate for security had been $20,750. Roberts did not have to punch it up on the calculator to arrive at their new payroll. "Holy shit! That's a lot of bread."

"Is there any way we can conceivably consolidate the amount of men we hire?" Joel asked. "Perhaps pair a volunteer from the crowd with one of the trained patrolmen Fink sends us?"

"With a crowd this size?" Pomeroy's voice rose an octave. "Not a chance. And once word gets out that we've got a security problem, we're lucky if we don't have to double—or even triple—our personnel. My God! I can't believe this has happened so close to the festival. We supposedly had Leary's word—a cop's word. In my book, that's a solemn oath." He shook his head in disbelief. "You talk about brotherhood." Wes took in the young faces seated around him. "Well, cops have the same kind of brotherhood, although it's not as pronounced as what your generation's preaching. But it's every ounce as meaningful. For them to do this to us—" He slammed his fist on the table. "Goddammit! He can't get away with this. Lee—hand me that phone." Pomeroy dialed long distance. "Commissioner Leary, please. Tell him it's Wes Pomeroy." He waited a moment for the response. "What do you mean he cannot be disturbed. We've got an emergency on our hands." He paused again as the secretary on the other end of the line offered a perfunctory excuse. Pomeroy gave her his number in Bethel, said he'd be expecting Leary's call, and hung up.

He tried Leary's office twice more in the next hour and finally gave up. The same thing happened when he tried to reach Mayor John Lindsay and Governor Nelson Rockefeller.

"Fink had better deliver," Pomeroy muttered, looking out of the window as clusters of teen-agers headed toward the site. "Or God help us all."

"The pigs have been offed," a Hog Farmer told Michael Lang as he listened to a sound check that evening.

"What're you talkin' about, man?"

"The pigs, man. Like, we don't have any."

"You jivin' me?"

"There's your old lady," he said, pointing to Ticia, who was emerging from one of the production trailers. "Check it out, man. I'll bet she's got a line on it."

Ticia confirmed the story.

"I guess it's time to hold our breath," Michael said.

"I don't know. Pomeroy didn't sound all that uptight when he called," Ticia reported. "If I were you, Michael, I'd try to catch him over at the security building. He'll probably want to know what you want him to do."

Instead, Michael went into his trailer, locked the door behind him, and telephoned a friend of his named Lenny in Woodstock. Lenny had been recruited by Lang some weeks before to organize a group of four powerful-looking men whose job it would be to provide the festival with "heavy security"—Lang's euphemism for carrying a loaded pistol. The Black Shirts, as they were called because of specially designed T-shirts they wore, were expected to arrive Thursday evening and remain through Monday morning until the banks opened and all the cash was transferred there. For a man who had created a festival based on the ethic of "Love Thy Brother," Michael Lang didn't even trust his own shadow.

"Lenny," he spoke softly into the receiver, "it's Lang. Look, man, there's been a slight change of plans. It wouldn't hurt for you and the guys to make the scene as soon as possible. Yeah—like tonight, man. Make it eight guys instead of four, okay? Things might get a little hairy around here. And Lenny—don't forget to tell 'em to carry a piece."

Jefffrey Joerger harbored the rage of a charging bull as he inspected the half-finished concession stands that were supposed to accommodate his fast-food operation. He had arrived in Bethel late Tuesday afternoon to supervise the hiring of four hundred teen-aged vendors and, instead, found his installations in such a state of disrepair that he was unable to do little more than kick up a row. The Bastard Sons had been pulled off the job to assist an electrical contractor with the performers' pavilion, leaving Food For Love in the lurch. The interior appliances had not been assembled, counters were piled on the ground waiting to be installed, and tarpaulins still hadn't been fastened to the roof supports.

"What the fuck am I supposed to do if it rains?" Joerger screamed at Peter Goodrich. "Tell me—huh? What do you expect me to do? I've got a hundred grand's worth of food sitting out in the open that'll turn to mush if it so much as drizzles." He kicked a few cans of nails that were lying on the grass. "This is the worst! Somebody's gonna pay, man. Whoever's responsible for this is gonna get their ass kicked."

Goodrich attempted to calm Joerger down by having the Hog Farm put up a tent for the food until the booths were finished, but its effect was temporary. Within hours, Joerger was on the phone with his lawyer, Steven Weingrad, alleging that a conspiracy had been aimed at driving them out of business.

According to Charles Baxter, a Food For Love partner, an acquaintance arrived in Bethel a few hours later "with a case of mace and a trunk full of sidearms." Joerger and associate Lee Howard claimed to have spotted "known criminals" among the protection agency staff Goodrich had hired to protect the money, and they wanted something with which they could defend themselves in case one of the thugs tried to interfere with business. They were provided with exactly what they asked for.

Baxter was appalled by the sight of loaded weapons around so many kids. He nervously asked Joerger and Howard to get rid of them. He didn't want to upset them for fear they "would fire at anyone who disagreed with them," but he finally found the courage to issue an ultimatum: either they agreed to lock the guns in a file cabinet in the office trailer, or he'd leave for New York without another word.

"Cool it, Charlie," Joerger warned him. "This isn't time to play Crusader Rabbit. There's bound to be trouble, and we won't be safe without them. Now, if you can't handle the reality of the situation—well, then take off."

Baxter flew into an uproar that bordered on hysteria. "Okay, man, then that's it. It's very simple. I walk. I walk and I tell everybody why I left. I won't be around guns. I don't like them. And I'm not about to sit by and watch you shoot some innocent kid. I'm tellin' you guys—I'm gonna find a cop or someone like that if you don't lock those damn things up."

Joerger and Howard reluctantly relinquished their guns, over Weingrad's vehement objections. It wasn't just criminals they couldn't trust, the lawyer said, it was hippies as well. He considered them to be "the scum of the earth." Nevertheless, Joerger decided to continue on unarmed until a situation arose which called for them to take more extreme actions. "But we know where the guns are in case we need to hold off an attempted robbery," Joerger reportedly told an executive from Woodstock Ventures, "and we're not afraid to use them. You'd just better hope everything works out the way it's supposed to—or else there's going to be a war."

From 4 P.M. until 8:15 Wednesday night, the New York State Police manned a roadblock at the Harriman interchange to the New York State Thruway. Waving what they called a "random sampling" of vehicles over to the side of the road, they searched every car that looked as if it was on its way to the festival. Hippies were ordered out from behind the wheel, told to place their hands on top of their heads, and were frisked for anything that might implicate them in a felony. Most of the frightened kids had their cars systematically torn apart as they looked on in horror. Glove compartments were rifled, personal belongings confiscated, upholstery ripped apart, trunks opened and emptied. To a passerby, the scene might have resembled something out of a movie about Nazi Germany.

By the end of the stretch, two troopers had arrested six young people on nine drug charges, including possession of implements (a water pipe). "The law will not go unobserved," a statement from the law enforcement agency read, "and all violaters will be prosecuted to its fullest extent."

"You ain't seen nothing yet," was the weary comment of one officer. "If this is what it looks like today, even before it gets going, I don't want to think about Friday."

— 4 —

The state police continued issuing summonses well into Thursday night, racking up over 150 arrests for possession of marijuana, amphetamines, LSD, heroin, and other "suspicious substances."

The police had pledged not to interfere with the festival's own security regimen, but that promise was broken early in the day. It was no secret that the New York cops had been forbidden to participate in the celebration at White Lake. And, besides, the festival had expanded its territory to several miles of surrounding area not covered under the original agreement. The boundaries to the site were not well defined, many of the fences had been torn down by hundreds of hippies eager to gain admittance to the festival grounds without buying a ticket, and there seemed to be no order to the disorder; the cops deemed it to be well within their rights to make on-site arrests.

Two state police cars had cordoned off access to the main road coming into the site where they picked off would-be violators like jungle snipers. Before they knew what had hit them, hippies carrying blankets, picnic baskets, sleeping bags, changes of clothes, and perhaps a half ounce of grass were handcuffed, thrown into the back seat of a patrol car, and driven seven miles into Monticello where they were arraigned and, in most cases, held in lieu of bail.

Wes Pomeroy was furious with the conduct of the state police. Every outside group affiliated with the festival had done its job as planned except for the troopers. It seemed they were only out for one specific purpose: to prove that the hippies' degenerate society was an accurate assessment of America's youth.

This was the second time in two days that Pomeroy felt betrayed by his own kind, and it had a marked effect on his performance for the remainder of the festival. To others, it appeared that he walked through his duties as chief of security without power or purpose. The police had cut off Pomeroy's greatest source of strength—his authority—and in doing so, a security assistant summarized, "they had cut off his balls."

The lack of assistance he received from the state police was best represented by an exchange Wes had later that afternoon with Captain John Monahan, a former student of Pomeroy's who would later rise to notoriety as the man who led the charge against the inmates at Attica State Penitentiary.

"John," Wes asked him, during a moment of reflection, "what would you do now if you had to control disorder with this group?"

"I'd dig a hole," Monahan answered, without missing a beat.

And dig a hole they did. In their blind rush to intercept drug suspects, the state police inadvertently blocked off entranceways to the festival's two main parking lots with their patrol cars. Within two hours, traffic had backed up on Hurd Road and out onto Route 17-B, strangling most of the inlets to the Bethel-White Lake community. Nothing moved. Another hour passed, then two, and still no progress was made. The line of cars occasionally inched forward, but they never moved far enough to provide the travelers with hope of reaching the festival. So, the kids took the only remaining option: they abandoned their cars in the middle of the road and walked the rest of the way to Yasgur's farm while the parking lots, for which the promoters had so preposterously overpaid, stood barren and unavailing.

Mel Lawrence spent the latter part of Thursday morning in his trailer going over the checklist he had first compiled back in June. He smiled to himself as he recalled his conversation with Michael Lang that same week in a suite at the Plaza Hotel. "It sounds like a helluva undertaking," was how he had responded to Lang's graphic and extraordinary portrayal of the festival. "The biggest one ever"—it was the type of exaggeration that came effortlessly to Michael, and Mel accepted it without reservation. He still accepted it. "It'll work, man," the kid had said, confidently. "I'm gonna make history with this one." Now, he had twenty-four hours—thirty, at the most—to keep the festival from collapsing, and yet he still had every reason to believe it would be a dramatic and memorable success.

Lawrence had made a postdawn inspection of the site and came away with the impression that everything was just a few hours away from completion.

The campgrounds were as finished as they would ever be. Wednesday night, 11,000 people moved in there, most of them planning on a five-day stay, and 40,000 more were rumored to be on their way. If the need arose, a spillover could pitch tents in the adjoining parking lot on the other side of the road as it didn't appear that any additional vehicles would be admitted into the area. Otherwise, everyone seemed comfortable.

Lawrence checked the Port-O-Sans, which separated the campgrounds from the puppet theatre, and found all of them to be clean and in good working order. The Free Kitchen was also ready to go. Some of the Hog Farm women had been up since before sunrise, preparing cauldrons of gruel, which they mixed with black iron shovels. A wide selection of fruit had been sliced for breakfast, and mammoth kettles of cider were being warmed over an open flame in anticipation of 60,000 early risers.

An eerie calm pervaded the woods next to the campgrounds as Lawrence continued on his rounds. Electricity had been run in from behind the stage and thousands of tiny light bulbs glistened in the thicket. Birds darted in and out of the brush picking at garbage cans. Rabbits scampered along the paths. Lawrence tested a water fountain there and found its pressure to be a little too low for his liking. He'd send Langhart or one of the other plumbers over to adjust it as soon as time permitted.

The night before, an organized black market moved into the woods and did energetic business, openly trading in a variety of contraband. Signs declaring "Pharmacy Now Open For Business" and "Le Drug Store" were propped against tree trunks as consumers were lured there by the temptation of forbidden fruit. Current prices ("subject to change," a notice read) were posted in Day-Glo paint. One competitive wholesaler boasted "We Will Not Be Undersold." Another offered a mix-and-match plan whereby customers could concoct their own combination packages, much as one ordered a family-style dinner in a Chinese restaurant. It was more than he had bargained for, Lawrence thought, retrieving the discarded signs, but as long as the dealers maintained a low profile and didn't pose a threat to security, not much harm could come of it. The kids had to buy their dope from somebody. And so far, that activity was confined to the woods and away from the main entrance.

A few weeks earlier, Lang and Peter Goodrich had planned to corner the festival's drug market by bringing a shipment of dope through the Florida Keys by motorboat. On Monday afternoon, however, word was passed through the underground that their stash had been impounded by the Coast Guard. It looked as though the capitalist tradition of free enterprise would prevail after all.

On the other side of the woods, Lawrence veered off toward the stage area and the ever-expanding performers' colony, which had been under steady construction throughout most of the night.

The huge wooden box sitting at the foot of the sloping lawn had actually begun to resemble a stage. Early that morning, Jay Drevers and a crew of thirty men positioned the 40-foot turntable in the center of the bandstand and attached dozens of swivel castors to its plywood underbelly so that it could roll around upstage. A passenger elevator converted out of a giant forklift was latched onto the back end of the floor, and two young carpenters worked at fitting an asbestos roof over its exposed shaft.

Fifteen other men hammered away at a picket fence ten feet in front of the stage that was strategically designed to keep the audience at a safe distance and to create a photographers' pit for the press. The only thing yet to be completed was a roof, and Drevers hadn't yet decided exactly how they were going to put one up without overloading the trusses.

Lawrence spent a few minutes watching the sound crew as they worked at getting their equipment into place without slowing down the stagehands. Bill Hanley had flown in a staff of twelve young sound engineers from New York and Boston that morning who were familiar with the audio requirements of all the acts on the bill. They worked with a crane to get all the

speakers and horns on top of the towers and in focus before patching everything into the special 440-volt/440-amp three-phase power system that was
normally used only by sprawling industrial complexes. Hanley had built a
custom speaker to carry sound to the farthest reaches of Yasgur's farm, and
prepared revolutionary mixing boards to blend the sound "because nothing
straight off the shelf was capable of handling such an unprecedented and
remarkable job." All told, the setup required that Hanley Sound take out a
$3-million insurance policy to cover its equipment before leaving Boston.
According to one expert's cumulative eye, the hi-fi equipment in the bowl
represented the most expensive sound system ever assembled at one time in
any given location.

By 10:30 A.M., the cables connecting the speakers to the power were buried. Separate Crown DC300 monitors were bolted on to the front of the
stage, and the main current was turned on for the first time to test and set
microphone levels.

"Hey—good morning! Welcome to the Woodstock Music and Art Festival, gang!" John Morris's voice thundered across the site.

A clamor of 65,000 voices deliriously cheered his greeting in an ovation
that lasted nearly five minutes.

"That sounds great! Look—you guys sit tight out there. It's supposed to
be a gorgeous day, and we're expecting another 50,000 or so brothers to join
us in the next couple hours."

Another roar of approval drowned out the clatter of machinery encom-
passing the site.

"We've got a few things we've gotta finish up here, so pardon us if we're
a little inconsiderate. We know you're out there. You might want to check out
the playground or grab a bite to eat while you're waiting. But, whatever you
do, don't go away. We're gonna have ourselves a helluva party, and you're all
invited!"

The fanfare the audience gave Morris was deafening. Lawrence clapped
him on the back as he chugged down the stairs leading from the stage to the
production trailers. "That was outta sight, man. Keep it up. Every half hour
or so get back on those microphones and give this crowd some encouragement. We've got a lotta time to kill before the music starts."

And, yet, not a moment to lose, Lawrence thought. There was still a lot
of ground he had to cover before checking everything against his master
production list. He wanted to go around back to see how the bridge was
coming along, and also to have a look at the performers' pavilion and an
employee mess hall that Peter Goodrich was setting up, but something he
saw out of the corner of his eye stopped him in his tracks. The medical

trailer, which was supposed to have been in operation since Wednesday morning, was padlocked and dark.

"What is this shit?" Lawrence barked, tugging in vain at the front door. "Hey—is anybody in there? C'mon, open up. You've got people waiting out here."

A young couple sitting on the grass whom Lawrence judged to be around sixteen years old scrambled to their feet. "Hey, it's cool, man. We're okay. Don't get uptight." The pretty green-eyed girl with long braids smiled at him.

"I'm not uptight," Lawrence protested, "I'm in charge."

"Wow, man! In charge. Far out."

"Right—far out. Listen, did either of you guys see anybody enter or leave this trailer since you've been out here?"

They told him they hadn't and asked Mel if he knew when the doctor was due to arrive.

"Well, he shoulda been here by now, but I'm gonna give him a call just in case. Why? Are you guys hurt or something?"

"Not really." The boy smiled sheepishly. "Y'see, my old lady and I were ballin' all night, and this morning she looked in her bag and found out she forgot her pill. We thought maybe the doctor could, y'know, like help us out without her having to call home. That wouldn't be too cool."

"I can imagine," Mel agreed. "Yeah, look, I'm gonna get in touch with him right away, and I'll ask him to bring a bunch of contraceptives along. But you guys do yourselves a favor and keep your pants on till he gets here. Okay?"

"You're beautiful, man. Peace."

"Yeah, piece—that's what got you guys into this spot in the first place."

Lawrence made his way through the crowd to the top of the hill and called Bill Abruzzi at his office in Wappingers Falls. "C'mon, man, get it together, will you. You wait much longer, and you're gonna get caught up in all that traffic comin' in here." Lawrence told him about police reports of cars backed up all the way to Monticello, and advised him to travel the back roads.

"My wife and a nurse named Betsy Morris are on their way in now," Abruzzi said. "There's another woman from Wallkill named Rikki Sanderson who's en route and should be there within an hour or so. They'll be able to hold down the fort until I can close up here. I've got a patient now, and another one waiting, so I should get out of here by 2, figure 2:30 to be safe. What's the latest crowd estimate?"

"Well, the cops say 65,000, but I think there's that many in the bowl alone. My guess would be nearer to 85,000 with another 100,000 or so on their way. I know this sounds a little crazy, but I think we could possibly hit 250,000 before the weekend's out."

"Then you'd better get someone to triple my order for first aid supplies and find another ambulance or two that we can keep on standby. To tell you the truth, I could probably use another twenty hands or so if you think we're going to draw that large. I'd like to put out an immediate medical alert to round up more doctors. Can you handle the cost?"

"Whatever. Just get 'em here if we need them. I'll make sure they get paid. Oh yeah—one more thing. You got any birth control pills in the trailer?"

"Sure. Fifty-seven varieties. My wife'll know where they are."

"Okay, but I think you might want to bring a whole trunkload of them up with you. I've got a sneaky feeling that by tomorrow night, this place is gonna be Fuck City."

"We got trouble with the food." It sounded like Michael Lang's voice crackling over the walkie-talkie, but Lawrence couldn't be sure. "I can't make out what you're sayin'. You wanna do that again." "We got trouble with the food cats." It was Lang, loud and clear. "Get over to the trailer right away."

Mel shut off the radio frequency and left a note on the desk pinpointing his whereabouts in case anyone was looking for him. Trouble with the food could mean almost anything, he thought. It wasn't as if he didn't have his hands full with a hundred other problems. But it also wasn't Michael's style to sound the alarm unless tragedy was already upon them. Grabbing a walkie-talkie, he bolted out of the office and ran across the top of the hill to the concessions trailer.

When he got there, he found Lang, John Roberts, Lee Howard, Lenny, and another Black Shirt security tough standing in front of the camper watching Peter Goodrich trying to break down the door.

"C'mon outta there, you little cocksucker!" Goodrich screamed. "I'm gonna push those teeth of yours back down your throat! You're trying to sabotage the whole operation, and I'm not going to let you get away with it." Goodrich pounded furiously on the door's recessed handle, but only succeeded in denting the corrugated aluminum frame.

A temperamental inferno erupted from inside the trailer. "I want my gun, Weber! Get away from in front of that cabinet! I want to teach that son of a bitch that he can't fuck around with me!" The blistering howl bore a remarkable resemblance to none other than Jeffrey Joerger, Food For Love's impassioned spokesman.

"What the hell's going on here?" Lawrence asked the Black Shirt, whose name he didn't know.

"They're having a difference of opinion."

"Thanks. I can *see* that. What about?"

"Food and love—but mostly food."

Suddenly the door to the trailer was flung wide open and Joerger, unarmed and unruly, jumped to the ground. "This is your fault, you son of a bitch." He shook a fist at Goodrich.

"No, Joerger. Don't hand me that crap. You fucked up. You were so worried about slipping a couple extra bucks into your back pocket that you blew it. We've got 65,000 kids out there who are gonna be hungry in a few hours, and you're not ready. You're a kid, and I should have known better than to let a kid do a man's job. Get out of my sight."

"*You fucking asshole! You no good fucking asshole!* We did our part. You don't even have the goddamn booths built so we can get our stuff in. I've got $125,000 worth of food sitting out in those trucks, and all you're looking for is a bigger rake-off. You incompetent fuck!"

Goodrich's eyes flashed pain, and then widened with rage. With the quick, deadly strike of a rattlesnake, he lashed out a fist and caught Joerger on the side of the face.

"Oh my God—*he hit me! He hit me!*" Joerger crumpled in distress.

Lee Howard stepped forward to revenge his partner's humiliation, but thought better of it when the two Black Shirts moved menacingly in his direction.

"Aw shit, Peter. Did you have to hit 'em, man?"

"I'm sorry, Michael. He had it coming."

Joerger looked at Roberts with accusing eyes. "You saw that! You saw him hit me. You think we're going to stand for that kinda shit? Like hell we are. We're pulling out. You guys can go fuck yourselves."

"Now wait a minute," Roberts blurted, not quite sure how to cope with the situation, "It's obvious that things haven't been going well here, but I'm sure whatever problem you have, we can work it out."

"You bet your ass, man. You're going to have to make some real concessions to us—like changes in our contract. We've had it up to here with you," he said, running a bloody finger across his forehead. "And I'm tellin' you right now, man. If you don't square with us, if you think we're kiddin' around—well, then I feel sorry for you. Because we'll fix you. I mean it, man. We're not gonna take this shit!"

"Don't be a fool, Jeffrey," Roberts said. "Look, we'll meet again tonight— say, about 7:00 in your trailer—to talk this thing out. I don't want you to leave or do anything foolish until we've had a chance to discuss this rationally. Can you at least do that for me?"

"Yeah—all right. Fine." Joerger pouted. "We won't leave yet. But I'm warnin' you, man. You're gonna pay for this to the point where you're gonna wish that you never even heard of Food For Love."

"Jeff," Roberts said, fighting back a smile, "you must be a mind-reader. I don't think I could have said that better myself."

Michael returned to his stageside trailer tired and withdrawn. His face had the puffy, bloodshot look of an alcoholic who had just come back from an all-night tour of bars. He switched off the overhead light as he entered the motor home, opened a can of warm soda, and curled up in a plastic contoured chair by the window.

"That fight just wasted me, man," Lang disclosed to John Morris, who, still pumped up from his splash on stage that morning, was on the phone with the festival's press coordinator. Michael waited until Morris was finished and recounted the violent scene at the concessionaires' trailer in patchy detail, making it seem as though Joerger had thrown the first punch. "We got burned by those dudes. They're bad cats, and now Peter says that we're stuck with them. That's karma, man—we gotta ride it through. What's happenin' on your end? Are we okay for tomorrow?"

"I think so. Everything's pretty much ready to go," Morris said, sprightfully rocking back and forth on his heels.

"Hey, do me a favor, man, and stand still. I got enough trouble tryin' to keep my eyes open without watchin' you bounce up and down like a beach ball."

"Sorry, Michael. I'm just excited," he apologized, sitting down on the corner of a formica table. "The groups have begun drifting in over at the Holiday Inn most of this afternoon, and it's turned into sort of a homecoming over there. I've got Country Joe's manager, Bill Belmont, babysitting the performers, and he said the lobby's turned into a stage for a big jam session. Everyone's got a guitar, and Janis is singing duets with just about anyone who can carry a tune."

"Far out!" Lang's spirit perked up.

"Belmont's in the process of working out a schedule with the drivers of the limos we hired to move those guys over here in time to do their sets during the next three days. It might get difficult, what with all the traffic, but he's pretty resourceful. He'll figure something out. You heard from Jimi yet?"

"No, man. He's a weird cat. I talked to Mike Jeffries this morning, and he told me Jimi's freaked over the number of kids he heard are comin' in here. He doesn't want to do the show, but Jeffries is takin' it all in stride. He's given me his word that Jimi'll be here."

"How about Dylan?"

"Your guess is as good as mine." Michael shrugged. Dylan had granted an interview to Al Aronowitz of the New York *Post* in late July, in which he said, "I may play there if I feel like it. I've been invited, so I know it'll be okay if I show up." But Lang had not heard a word since from the counterculture's poet laureate. "If he does make it, just make sure and keep everybody out of his way. I don't want anyone hasslin' him."

Lang and Morris spent a few minutes going over a change of sequence for Friday afternoon's show, in which Tim Hardin was moved from the opening spot to sixth, behind the Incredible String Band. Hardin had arrived from his home in Woodstock a day early to let the promoters know he couldn't cope with going on first. "We'll open with Sweetwater," Lang decided, "then go to Richie Havens, probably Country Joe and the Fish next, Bert Sommer, the String Band, Tim, and we'll see how it goes from there. I got a feeling that a few other cats are gonna 'drop by,' and we'll have to let 'em do a few numbers."

"Yeah, somebody told me that Melanie showed up at the Holiday Inn last night."

"Outta sight! We'll work her in sometime during the night. Have you cooled off Josh?" Intentionally disobeying Lang's wishes, Morris had gone ahead and contracted Joshua White, from the Fillmore, to put on a light show, justifying the expense as a "religious necessity." When he found out about it, Lang demanded the show not last more than a few minutes.

"He's taking it like Josh—badly."

"Well, fuck 'em. Nobody gives a shit about light shows anymore," Michael declared.

"Speaking of which—Chip's shittin' a brick over the lights. Drevers came down with the final word on that today: no go. Chip's gotta be satisfied with a couple of follow-spots and some gels to get him through the show and he's pissed."

They both began to laugh. "All those lights sitting on the side," Michael cackled, "oh—it's too much, man. I think the bill for that system is even bigger than Chip's ego. Man, he must be goin' out of his skull seein' 'em sittin' there like that and knowin' he can't use them."

"He was stompin' around like Rumplestiltskin when Drevers laid it on him."

"Well, he'll get over it. I want him to share announcing chores with you, John. You guys work it out between you."

"Oh shit, man." Morris was shamelessly dejected. "You can't do that to me." He took it as a calculated slap in the face.

"I gotta. That's all there is to it. Look, how about cuttin' outta here for a few minutes. I wanta make a few calls, and then I'm gonna try to catch a few z's."

"All right," he moaned. "There's just one more thing we gotta discuss. It's about all those people out in the bowl, man. We gotta figure out some way of askin' 'em to leave."

"What!" Michael shrieked. "Have you flipped, man?"

"Be serious, Michael. We gotta find some way of collecting their tickets."

"I *am* serious. We're not collectin' their tickets. It's too late for that. They're like groovin' on the vibes, and you want to hit 'em with something like that! Don't be ridiculous."

"We're gonna take a beating then. I mean—hell, John Roberts has a fortune invested in this thing."

"He's got plenty of bread. I told you, man, it's too late for that. I can't worry about it."

"How about if we recruit a few guys from the crew, I'll go on stage and make an announcement about how we're gonna get *schlonged* by lettin' everybody in ahead of time, and these guys can pass a basket around the audience for contributions."

"Don't kid around with me."

"I'm not kidding, Michael. I think it'll work."

"You're out of your fucking mind. You try anything like that, man, not only'll Chip be making *all* the announcements, he'll also be taking home your paycheck. Now, get outta here and leave me alone." Lang tipped his chair back on two legs until it rested against the wall, put his hands behind his head, and closed his eyes.

"What am I supposed to tell people when they ask me where they can buy tickets?"

"You can tell 'em to c'mon inside and enjoy the show. This is a free festival from here on in."

Later that afternoon, six broad-shouldered, athletic-looking men dressed in jeans and army fatigue jackets entered the security office looking for "the General—the man in charge of the infantry." Their "friend," Joe Fink, had suggested they "get in contact with some guy named Pomeroy about a few days' work" at the festival.

"We are, uh, affiliated with—uh, how can I put this?—a certain well-known police bureau," their spokesman, a stout man with huge jowls and a piddling moustache, told Lee Mackler, "and we'd rather that our presence not be broadcast too loudly for fear of repercussions, if you get what I mean."

Cops! Like the cavalry in a Hollywood western, they had come to the rescue at the last minute, boldly defying Commissioner Leary's edict forbidding it. Lee assured them that she understood perfectly, and asked that they have a seat while she located Pomeroy who had gone over to the site to attend to a problem with the state police.

"How many of you are there all together?" she asked the leader, while she dialed the production trailer.

"About two hundred. More if you need them. That all depends."

"On what?"

"On the magic word."

Pomeroy could not tear himself away from the conference to meet with the cops but sent Don Ganoung in his place.

The magic word, Ganoung soon learned, was *cash*. The patrolmen, most of whom carried NYPD shields, wanted twice what they had originally been offered to work in White Lake, and they wanted it in *cash* at the end of each twelve-hour shift—"or else."

"I'm afraid of these guys, Wes," Ganoung reported back to Pomeroy over a cup of coffee in the employees' mess hall. "The way they're acting—well, they're talking crazy, not like cops but like thugs. I know a veiled threat when I hear one. They insisted that we meet their demands for pay, that they be given contracts because they don't trust us worth a damn, or else they said they'd raise all hell with the festival. They're organized, Wes, and that could spell trouble."

Pomeroy was furious, but he instructed Ganoung to proceed with the negotiations. "Give them anything they want," he sighed. "I'm afraid we've got no choice. They know that we need them more than they need us and, by God, *we need them*. I'd gladly pay for the opportunity to tell them to go fuck themselves, but, right now, that looks like it's out of the question."

Ganoung spent two hours with the renegade cops, listening to their list of inflexible and corrupt prerequisites, and he finally agreed to hire them under aliases.

"No names," they stressed, although it was more appropriately a threat, "or else we'll keep on running and never come back. As far as you're concerned, nobody's ever heard of us. We don't exist. No records, either. You give us a contract, but you get nothing in return. We don't sign any receipts for our pay, we don't talk to any reporters. You fuck around with those conditions, and it's all over."

At 6:00 Thursday evening, 276 "unofficial" members of the Peace Service Corps crowded into the security office for an improvised orientation program. Pomeroy and John Fabbri briefed them on their responsibilities, gave each man a walkie-talkie in case he needed assistance, and issued them special red T-shirts with the festival logo on the back.

For God's sake, just remember one thing: you men are here to *help* these kids," Pomeroy reiterated. "If you don't like the way they're acting, or how they look, even if one of them comes up to you and gives you the finger—*ignore them.* We're sitting on top of too explosive a situation to fool around. And just one thing more. You can do whatever the hell you like out there this weekend, but I'm warning each and every one of you: You lay a hand on one of those kids and, so help me, I'll find you and take you apart myself."

Before they left for an impromptu party with a few "hippie chicks" two of the men had corraled before orientation, the cops picked up their contracts made out to such distinguished personalities as Robin Hood, R. T. Tin, Deputy Dawg, Irving Zorro, and Clark Kent. Pomeroy signed each one as they went by. At first, he felt like a warden who had been coerced into paroling hardcore criminals. But as the procession moved on, as the fictitious names ranged from comical to ludicrous, he unwound. He no longer saw them as law enforcement officials, or, for that matter, as real people. Casper the Ghost, Barney Rubble, Wile E. Coyote, Elmer Fudd. No, they were artists in their own right, he thought—con artists—and he was the ringmaster of an egregious carnival who had just been given the signal to send in the clowns.

"Give them anything they want." Wes Pomeroy found himself imparting the same expression of defeat for the second time within an hour. "Do whatever they ask you to do. You're being extorted, and we'll be able to straighten it out after the festival."

"It might not be that easy," Joel said, wrinkling his face like a hand-puppet. "After all, they've got a binding contract with Woodstock Ventures that holds us responsible for providing them with adequate facilities for serving the food. I don't know exactly how faultless we are in this situation."

"And they're really prepared to take off," Roberts added. "I don't think they're bluffing, and I'm not so sure we can afford to call them on it."

"No, I don't want you to do anything that might endanger the welfare of those kids sitting out there. Hell, without food we'd have an absolute catastrophe on our hands. But it's extortion, nonetheless. They've got you backed into a corner whereby you've got to do anything they ask. Just remember, they've got clauses in that contract which they've got to abide by as well. Now they want to alter the deal or they'll close you down. I don't like threats like that, and anyway, I've got my suspicions about that bunch. Do as I said—give them anything they want. Tomorrow, I want you, John, and your lawyer to drive into Monticello with me. There's an FBI office there, and I intend to bring this matter to the attention of one of their agents. In the meantime, don't give those bastards any reason to walk out. Unfortunately, we're in desperate need of their services, however amateurish they may be. Now, you'd better get over there and see them before they jump to the conclusion that you've stood them up. And, by God, call me as soon as you get back."

John and Joel rode over to the site on spanking new motorbikes that had been gleaned from the corporate toychest to mollify their deep-rooted despair. During the course of their briefing, Wes had made it starkly clear to them that the gates and ticket booths they counted on to recoup their investment were no longer within the realm of reason. There were too many people inside the amphitheatre—110,000 was the latest estimate—and no politic alternative but "to allow the freeloaders to remain there in peace." It was a crushing defeat for the two promoters, one that meant the waste of seven months of their precious time, of professional disappointment, and, ultimately, failure. What had struck John at that moment was not the inevitability of the financial ruin he faced as a result of his gullibility so much as his realization that there was still an element of choice open to him. Instead of personally assuming a debt of close to $1 million, he could refuse to pour another cent of his money into the festival, forcing Woodstock Ventures into bankruptcy. That was the logical thing for him to do. Any financial expert would give him the same advice. After all, he was but one of four principal shareholders of a company whose creation had been legally streamlined to take advantage of corporate loopholes, should the occasion present itself. Why should he solely underwrite the loss when it seemed to him that two of his partners had gone out of their way to bring it upon them in the first place? There certainly appeared to be a decision to be made, and ironically, it seemed to have fallen entirely into Roberts's hands.

As they sped through the police barricade and pulled up in the press parking lot behind the concession stands, Roberts and Rosenman were confronted by what appeared to be a solid block of humanity coating the inside of the bowl like a swash of speckled paint. Scattered campfires had been started, over which hot dogs and marshmallows roasted. (*Life* reported spotting two East Village artists "trying to warm soup in a beer can suspended by string over a wastepaper fire.") The stage glowed like a sacred talisman, not yet consecrated by an uprighteous roof—but the crew was working on it. "Occasionally, music would come floating up," Roberts recorded in a memoir, "smells, too: meat, grass, excrement from the nearby Johnnys-On-The-Spot. Considering the exertions of the day—and what was still to come—it was a beguilingly peaceful moment. The armies were at rest, the battle . . . distant."

They met Lang and Goodrich in front of the concessions trailer and conveyed Pomeroy's instructions regarding compromises that might have to be made with the food concern. "We all just keep our mouths shut and nod our agreement," Joel cautioned them. "Let's not risk jeopardizing the festival on their account. We'll have our lawyers straighten things out with them afterwards."

That didn't seem at all satisfactory to Goodrich. He was personally insulted, he said, by Food For Love's failure to honor an agreement that he had made with them. It reflected poorly on his ability to carry out his responsibility, and he could not allow them to get away with that.

"Peter, there is no honor among thieves," Roberts said. "What are you getting all upset about? We've been *had,* that's all there is to it. Now, we've got to make sure that they don't do us any more harm. I can understand your being upset about it, but would you kindly keep your mouth shut throughout this negotiation? I've unfortunately got a lot more at stake here than your pride, and I'd rather not have to worry about pacifying you and these guys at the same time."

Roberts waited for Goodrich to remark that he'd respect his wishes, but, at that moment, the door to the trailer swung open and Stephen Weingrad, Food For Love's lawyer, slipped out.

"They're still too angry to talk to you guys," Weingrad said, gesturing his helplessness with an upturned hand. "They're talking crazy. They want to go home."

"Hey, they can't do that to us, man," Michael said softly. "We got a deal."

"Yeah, well, that's the way *you* look at it, but they're taking a completely different view of the situation. They claim you broke the deal, and that means there's no reason they've got to stay. There's nothing I can do."

"I suggest you make an effort," Rosenman said. "We'd like to come to terms with them. The concession stands are just about complete, so it would be a shame to spoil everything we've both worked for."

"I'll see what I can do."

Weingrad disappeared inside the trailer and returned a moment later, shaking his head. "They don't want to stay. I don't think there's anything you can do to make them change their minds after the way they've been treated."

"That's crazy!" Roberts shouted. He could feel the anger rising in his body, and he checked his temper. "There's a lot of money to be made here. They've done a lot of work to prepare for this, and they can walk away from this extremely well off come Monday morning. I think they should. But we've got to reach a settlement."

"You're right, Roberts, but, like I said, they're talking crazy."

"Well, settle them down. You're their lawyer. They'll obviously listen to you. Now, we'd like to meet with them, and we're not going to budge from this spot until we do."

Another few minutes passed while Weingrad huddled with his team. When the door to the trailer opened again, it was done so by Charles Baxter who invited them inside.

Joerger and Howard were seated around a small table in the rear compartment, reviewing a copy of their contract with Woodstock Ventures. Weingrad motioned for the visitors to have a seat, and Baxter propped himself up in the corner, choosing to remain apart from the negotiations.

"Hey guys," Michael greeted them cheerfully. "What's shakin'?"

"You know damn well what's shakin'," Lee Howard sneered.

"Look, man, we don't wanna hassle you. We know you're freaked over what happened this afternoon, and we're all pretty sorry about it. It's a bummer."

"It's fuckin' assault, is what it is," Joerger said.

"C'mon, man. We came to work things out with you guys. This festival's turned into too much of a trip to let anything like this fuck things up."

"Yeah," Roberts agreed, "and we want to know what it will take to smooth things out."

"Money, man," Joerger said. "We want the contract changed. You people have completely abused us. You haven't given us a place to sell our merchandise, we've had to build the stands ourselves, and Goodrich wants to be able to call the shots with the money. That's no good. We want total control of the money because we don't think this thing is going to work out anymore."

"What're you sayin', Jeff?" Lang asked him.

"I'm sayin' we want it all, man. We'll give you back the first $75,000 that comes in, and then we're gonna take 100 percent of the profits. No more partnership."

"That's not cool, man."

"I don't really give a fuck about *cool!*"

"Jeffrey, we're in trouble as is," Roberts confessed. "We put you in business because we thought we could make good money from an association of that type. But now, we're counting on our take from the food to keep us out of the hole."

"That's your problem, man. We gotta protect our own ass. And, anyway, there's no room here for discussion. We get 100 percent, or you wind up with no food at the festival."

"You've got us over a barrel."

"You bet," Joerger said, pleased with his position. "You've got no choice."

"Well, we'll have to do it your way, but we want it in writing, and we're not expecting our lawyer to get up here until tomorrow afternoon."

"That seems to be in accordance with what my clients want," Weingrad approved.

"Yeah, it's okay with us," Joerger said, "because, come Friday, if you haven't signed 100 percent of the profits over to us, we'll still walk out."

— 5 —

By nine o'clock Thursday night, the line of traffic stretched along Route 17-B looked like an uncoiled Slinky, eleven miles in length and four cars deep. "And Mike Lang's smile was as wide . . ." the New York *Post* ribbed. "That doesn't allow for too many lanes of automobiles, but then how bad could Mike Lang feel to be stuck in a traffic jam when every car that got past his happy face was actually headed for his pocket?"

Considering the pandemic inconvenience on the road, none of the hippies seemed the least bit annoyed. Tens of thousands of hitchhikers marched toward the festival on foot, passing wineskins among the ranks, chanting, laughing, holding hands, waving banners, generously offering joints to strangers, motioning for others stalled in their cars to join them in the pilgrimage to Bethel.

Journalist Gail Sheehy, recounting her impression of the processional in a *New York* magazine article, likened it to a national convention of the master race:

Ten million yards of blue cotton twill and striped T-shirting. The bodies coming out of them stop your breath with their beauty. Luxuriantly tanned, hair swinging free, muscled as though their skin is stretched over bouncing tennis balls. There are more beautiful, happy, healthy-faced young Americans than I ever remember seeing in one place. . . . The road with its thousands of walking feet resembles the main drag out of Delhi. . . . No one honks. No one shouts. No one shoves. It's unnatural.

A spokesman from the American Automobile Association declared the road situation an "absolute madhouse," and, in an interview the next morning with the *New York Times*, Wes Pomeroy cautioned: "Anybody who tries to come here is crazy. Sullivan County is a great big parking lot."

There were those, however, who thought that Pomeroy and the transportation agencies characteristically overreacted. Even among his staff, there was already serious talk that Pomeroy "had lost control over himself." One production coordinator glumly told an assistant, "Wes is gone, man. His mind just kinda fell apart when the cops did, and he still hasn't recovered from the shock. We'd better keep an eye on him for the next couple days. And tell someone to make sure Fabbri covers for him." It may have been a hasty judgment on the staff's part, but the loss of his security force, coupled with the bumbling inefficiency of the state police and the Food For Love affair, had temporarily rendered Pomeroy impotent. As for the alarmists, a local underground disk jockey said that referring to the bottleneck as an emergency was "like calling the week-old Sharon Tate murders an infectious conspiracy." He scoffed at any allusions the papers had made to Bethel as a combat zone and said that the immovable line of cars running through town was merely "an anachronism for the cloistered fate of American prosperity, the final flight of the middle class choked-off in its own exhaust."

The *Boston Globe* took it all in a lighter perspective and facetiously suggested that "perhaps someday this would be the way the world would end—in an endless traffic jam."

But that was an outsider's view, typically uncompassionate. The area's homeowners failed to see the humor in what they were calling "a human debacle." Some of the hippies tossed garbage into their yards on the way through, or paused to urinate against their trees "like common beggars." Others drove their cars up over the curb and attempted to reach the festival by shortcut, by wheeling across newly seeded lawns or vegetable patches. "This isn't the way we were told it would be," cried an outraged mother as she cradled her two children into the nap of her dress, "not the *Christian* brotherhood that Father Ganoung had described to us."

Along a two-mile stretch, residents leaned out of upper-story windows screaming at teen-agers who trespassed on their property or lined up their families in beach chairs in front of their homes. "It was all we could do to stave off the siege," a homeowner maintained to a state trooper, defending his right to spray intruders with a garden hose.

So much for practicality. The traffic, however, remained stranded on the roadways, an immovable bastion of hippie enfranchisement, closing off all access to the country village. No chartered buses were being allowed off Route 17-B and into the site area; hundreds had taken their place in line on the Quickway, and, according to reports, hundreds more were on their way from over thirty-five states. None of them, of course, would ever come within more than ten miles of the festival site.

Thousands of young people carrying specially stamped tickets patiently waited their turns behind yellow police barricades at New York's Port Authority Bus Terminal, preparing to board one of the Short Line buses to Monticello or Bethel. The company had to rent an extra twenty vehicles to even approach satisfying the inordinate demand for seats, and they interspersed departures every fifteen minutes, from 7:30 A.M. to 10:15 P.M. *New York Times* reporter Lacey Fosburgh chatted with some of the young travelers milling around the depot who, she said, "spoke with gusto about marijuana and music, and the weekend ahead."

"They were so upset," an eighteen-year-old girl from Philadelphia said of her parents' reaction to her trip north. "I've never done much traveling and they were so afraid of riots and police trouble and drugs. We had to sit down and talk it all out." A sixteen-year-old boy from Westbury, Long Island, construed his outing as an edification of life to extort his parents' consent. "My parents knew there'd be drugs there, that it'll be a bit wild. They didn't want me to come," he said. "I know there'll be drugs everywhere and I wonder what it will all be like. I've never been away from home before. I wonder what will happen to all of us."

Now, most of those same young pioneers were stranded on the dark Quickway, pleading with obstinate bus drivers to let them out so they could walk the rest of the way. "Driver Is Not Permitted To Make Unscheduled Stops," a white sticker read above the dashboard of each licensed carrier. So they sat, and they sat, and they sat—hoping for some small miracle that would enable them to be delivered at their destination in time to hear the opening bars of music. By midnight, however, it seemed unlikely that even a tank could barge its way through the unconquerable mess.

Closer to the site, fire engines forlornly retreated from an unanswered alarm, unable to pass through local intersections, as a crew of hippies desperately battled a blaze on the first floor of the Diamond Horseshoe Hotel.

John Morris grumbled to a dumbfounded reporter from the New York

Post that it took him and Michael Lang an hour and twenty minutes to reach their hotel rooms the night before the festival. It seemed to the reporter such an inappropriate, foolish claim for a festival leader to make—to squawk coquettishly about his discomfort, standing in the midst of seismic pandemonium. "Even if they had been able to get to their accommodations for some sleep," he asked his readers, "what dreams could Lang possibly have left?"

PART THREE

Alas, Babylon!

CHAPTER TEN

Friday, August 15, 1969

If these are the kids that are going to inherit the world, I don't
fear for it.   —*Max Yasgur*

The Lamb that belonged to the Sheep, whose skin the Wolf
was wearing, began to follow the Wolf in the Sheep's clothing. . . . Appearances are deceptive.   —*Aesop, from a "Fable"*

— 1 —

An unexpected cowl of fog had rolled in early that morning, bathing the
Hudson Valley in a shadowy ethereal film. Still, army helicopters, using
sophisticated infrared equipment, had been able to deliver clear reconnais-
sance data to State Department observers in Albany, obtained while flying
low over the restricted festival region.

The photographs must have resembled the aftereffect of an attack of
deadly gas on a densely populated city. It looked like a civilization in suspended animation. Cars were stalled on every highway, road, and lane in a
five-mile radius of the site. Open fields, parking lots, lawns, and even ceme-
tery plots were dotted with cars and tents. Teen-agers slept on the grass along
highway median strips and on the roofs of cars. But the most awesome sight
of all—an apparition so extraordinary that it must have jolted even the most
acclimated eyewitness—had to be the spectacle of 175,000 apparently lifeless
bodies draped across the wide open spaces of Yasgur's farm.

Promptly at 7 A.M., the governor's office phoned the command trailer on
top of the hill for the purpose of officially declaring White Lake in a state of
emergency.

"We've moved the National Guard into the area, and we're preparing to send troops onto the farm as soon as we've been given the word," a state aide to Nelson Rockefeller solemnly informed a volunteer phone operator. "If everything works out the way we hope it will, we should have the city cleared of young people by no later than noon."

Luckily the young girl assigned to hold down the phones in Lawrence's trailer did not panic. "Hey, wait a second, man. I don't think you want to do anything like that. Everything's under control here, really in good shape, you know. Just do me a favor, huh, and don't send in the troops or anybody like that until you've spoken to Mel Lawrence; he's our director of operations. I expect him any minute, and I think he'll tell you that everything's groovy up here."

Lawrence had gone back to the Holiday Inn to shower and freshen up about two o'clock in the morning and never returned.

"Excuse me, miss, but we've been informed by local authorities that the festival has turned into an all-out disaster. The governor is quite concerned about the health and welfare of, not only the people in that community, but also those of you attending the festival. We can airlift people out to safety in practically no time."

"Safety? Mister, this *is* safety. We've got 175,000 people sound asleep out on that field right now. Just sleepin'. It sure doesn't look to me like an emergency situation. I mean, you've got to see it to believe it, man. Everybody's layin' there asleep with a big grin plastered across their face. They're all dreaming, and when they wake up, they're going to find out that all their dreams have come true. It's beautiful. I think you owe it to all the people who've knocked themselves out over the past few weeks not to be taken in by lies, man. Really—we're all okay and having an outrageous time."

The girl immediately called Lawrence at the motel and filled him in on the details. "Wonderful!" he said, trying to shake himself out of trancelike exhaustion. "Okay, look, I'll call the security guys and have them handle it. If any other politicos like that call, just tell 'em the same thing. 'It's groovy, man, we're havin' a great time, wish you were here.' Try anything you think'll talk 'em out of sending in dogs. I'll be there in fifteen minutes to give you a hand."

Lawrence called the security office and got Lee Mackler. She informed him that Wes Pomeroy and John Roberts had left for Monticello about 6:30 A.M. and weren't expected back until the afternoon. "But there's nothing to worry about, Mel. We've been taking calls like that all morning. Fabbri and I have been telling everybody the same thing: 'Peace and love, man, we're cool, no need to get uptight about anything.' Fabbri gives them the official rundown and refers whoever's on the other end of the line to the sheriff. He's a real arrogant asshole, but he's on our side. God bless him. Ever think you'd hear me say such nice things about a pig?"

"You're all heart, Lee," Lawrence conceded. "All right. I guess we sit tight and take it all in stride. It looks like we're all in for a long, hot weekend."

With the assistance of a citizens' band radio and mobile security checkpoint patrols, Wes Pomeroy had managed to route himself and Roberts along the back roads around Bethel and into Monticello by 8:15 A.M.

The city's business district looked much like the main street in Bethel— lined with teen-agers, who skipped in and out of stores searching for camping supplies and nonperishable food. There had been some early reports of price gouging, and, as was expected, there were those smaller establishments who pocketed two dollars for a loaf of bread or a quart of milk. But most of the merchants were grateful for the surge of sales and went out of their way to help the kids pack their purchases properly for travel. There were also those who stood by signs reading "Free water" and gave away sandwiches to anyone who was hungry.

Pomeroy and Roberts located the local FBI office within minutes, and waited in a claustrophobic anteroom until one of the agents there was free to see them.

"I'm not going to tolerate this kind of muscle," Wes repeatedly mumbled to John. "No sir. Can't allow ourselves to be pushed around by crooks. By God, these guys are going to pay for this. They're criminals. Have to keep an eye on them."

Roberts listened somewhat uneasily to Pomeroy's lament, recognizing that "this was clearly a man in mourning for his security."

"We'll make sure they don't get away with this. Can't tolerate this conduct. Have to control these jokers."

Roberts found that the FBI agents "were like something out of the television series." They were very cordial, and listened to the promoter's story with polite concern.

"Why did you come to us?" the special agent in charge of the office asked Pomeroy.

"Well, there's two things I'd like you to do. One: Move fast enough to cool these guys off. Two: Cut off their attempted extortion."

"I'm not sure we can move as fast as you'd like, sir," the special agent said, "but be assured that we'll investigate your accusations and determine if there's any cause for prosecuting Food For Love. Our advice to you at this point is to go through the weekend with these people. If you lose their services, we can't help you get food to the audience. Meanwhile, we'll run a check on them—Joerger, Howard, Baxter, and Weingrad—and see if we come up with anything. You never can tell. One of them might be wanted for something else. Stay in touch with us, let us know what develops, and we'll try to get you some kind of an answer as soon as possible."

According to Pomeroy, Roberts was emotionally shaken by his encounter with the FBI. "In all my life, I never once thought I'd be dealing with criminals," he explained to the chief of security as they wound their way back to the site. "I mean—*the FBI*. I actually had to go to the FBI! It's unreal. They were never anything more to me than actors in a movie or in spy novels. Now, I've got to rely on them to help pull us out of this nasty business. I can't believe I've gotten myself involved in something as shady as this. How do you see it, Wes? Is there anything the FBI can do to bail us out?"

"You *bet* there is," he said, as if it were beyond question. "You'll probably have to wait until after the festival is over to take any action against our would-be concessionaires, but, for now, you can rest assured that it's all been laid out, and the Bureau's got it. If those guys try to hurt you, their ass is really in a sling."

Bill Abruzzi, dressed comfortably in a Lacoste T-shirt and Bermuda shorts, left the medical trailer shortly after 9:15 A.M. After stopping off briefly by the side of the stage to say a few words to Michael Lang, he took the increasingly popular shopper's route through the woods (careful not to appear overly interested in the drug trade along the way), and found his way into one of the Hog Farm medical complexes in the northeast corner of the campgrounds.

Attendance in Big Pink was already limited to Standing Room Only, brimming over with flaccid bodies on an assortment of bad trips.

"This place is a travel agent's nightmare," an emaciated, bare-chested member of the commune, who appeared to have taken charge of the facility, told Abruzzi. "I wouldn't go as far as to say we're doing a 'healthy' business, but . . ."

"It's an old joke."

"Right, man. Sorry to offend you. Anyway, the folks you see here are off in some other universe for a while, but they'll be comin' back down to earth in a couple hours or so. The acid floatin' around the scene is pretty good stuff. We checked it out ourselves." He grinned foolishly.

"That's nice to know." Abruzzi played along, deferring to his instinctive judgment. "As long as it's not laced with something harmful, there shouldn't be too many complications."

"Nah—the rat-shit guys haven't started dealing yet. They like to sleep late. Most of 'em are night cats."

"Uh-huh. Anyway—it's more crowded up here than I thought it would be. Do you fellas need any help?"

The young man's face tightened with obvious distrust. "You mean *trained* help, don't you?" he sneered. "Whitecoats whose job it'll be to peek over our shoulders and keep an eye on the goods—isn't that what you're tryin' out on us, Doc? Why didn't you just come out and say that in the first place instead of comin' on as some kinda friend of the freaks." He raised his chin in defiance, and, for a moment, Abruzzi thought the hippie was going to spit in his face.

"Take it easy, will you?" Abruzzi said too loudly, taking a step backward. The boy lowered his chin, and Abruzzi felt a bit embarrassed for revealing his trepidation. "You've got it all wrong, pal. I didn't come here to get myself into a political discussion with you people. And, anyway, you'd probably be shocked to learn we're coming from the same place. I only wanted to know if I could give you a hand or some extra space in my trailer, although, God knows, I'm about as overcrowded as you are. I'm not trying to step on anybody's toes. But we've got an interrelated job, and it's my responsibility to set up some kind of system in conjunction with you if we're going to survive the weekend."

"Hey, man—we know what we're doing. We've had a lot of experience with kids on bummers and we can run our own show."

"I don't want to . . ."

"You doctor guys—what makes you think we give a shit about your training, anyway? We don't trust the fuckin' medical profession, man."

"That's odd." Abruzzi snorted a laugh. "Three weeks ago, when one of your babies crawled into the commune's campfire, you ran to a doctor's house in Middletown and begged him to examine it right away. What happened, friend? Did you people do a sudden about-face on doctors? You treat people with respect only when and if you can get something out of them. Look, why don't you cut the crap? You run your trip, I'll run mine. But we've got to establish some bond of trust between us because we're going to face some real crises."

The Hog Farmer, caught in his own moral crisis, ran a hand along the side of his face while he considered Abruzzi's proposal. "What're your terms, man?"

"What do you mean—terms?"

"You know, the conditions under which we're supposed to get along."

"No terms, no conditions," Abruzzi said. "Look, I've heard nothing but good things from people who have seen you work with kids. From what they have told me, you're supergood at dealing with bad trips and talking people down from them. I was relieved to hear that you'd be working here, because, frankly, I don't know anything about that type of specialized counseling. You're the experts. So how about if I send you the kids who are having a bad time of it from some drug, and I'll personally guarantee that nobody from my staff will interfere with that part of the operation. In turn, you refer me all of the medical cases. There's no reason why we should compete. How does that sound to you?"

The young man continued to sandpaper the side of his face with the back of his hand. Then, he abruptly turned his back on the doctor and walked away without giving him an answer.

That's really clever, Abruzzi thought, staring after the insolent Hog Farmer without bothering to give chase. These kids aren't going to accomplish a damned thing by going out of their way to insult the members of the Establishment who *agree* with their philosophy. He had no idea what it was they wanted him to prove; he'd tried a number of approaches to gain their confidence, and nothing worked. He hadn't even come close. Peaceful coexistence seemed to be outside their convenient definition of brotherhood. They'd both suffer for it.

Abruzzi wandered around Big Pink for another twenty minutes, staring into the blank faces of teen-agers suffering through grotesque hallucinations. As many as sixteen youngsters at one time were treated during his first visit to the tent. Many of them, lying face down on the damp hospital cots, buckled in agony or defenselessly screamed while a member of the Hog Farm attempted to flip them over and bathe their foreheads with cold compresses. Others tossed on the ground until they could be restrained and helped onto a bed. But all of them eventually received what Abruzzi considered to be "superb paraprofessional treatment," mostly from Hog Farm family members.

He would have enjoyed working alongside the commune in this project. They'd have offset each other's deficiencies, and it would have provided him with an immense and invaluable indoctrination into the applied science of hallucinogenic drug treatment. The trouble was, there didn't seem to be any way of communicating with the Hog Farm. So be it. He was resigned to figuring out some way to work around them as best he could, and would keep his fingers crossed that the acid remained clean.

Abruzzi checked his watch and found that it was almost 10:30. He'd told Rikki Sanderson he'd be back by then to go over administrative procedure and to instruct her in the fundamental psychology of crowd medicine.

As he turned to leave, a girl dressed in a doeskin Indian dress and sandals grabbed his elbow, spun him around to face her, and stared up at him expectantly. Her pale blue eyes were dilated, and she pursed her mouth, as if wanting to speak but finding herself unable to get a sound out.

"Here," he said, taking her by the arm, "let me find somebody who can help you."

She began to giggle like an infant. "You got it wrong, man. I'm not one of the loonies. At least, not yet." She fingered a strand of colored beads around her frail neck. "I got a message for you if you're the great medicine man they been talkin' about."

Abruzzi introduced himself and asked the girl exactly who had sent her to find him.

"Paul, man. He said to tell you: 'It's cool.' "

"Paul?"

"Yeah. You know, man, *Paul*." She brought both hands to either side of her face as if to frame a definitive picture of the enigma, Paul. Abruzzi shook his head in bewilderment. "And—oh yeah, he said to tell you: 'No terms and no conditions.' "

At last, Abruzzi said to himself, they had struck up a simple, unofficial bargain. He and the Hog Farm—it wasn't the most ideal medical partnership, but, nonetheless, it *was* an understanding by which they could coexist. He was relieved, and he walked back through the woods with a discernible bounce, back to his own "scene," feeling as though, in some fragmented way, he had cornered the market on healing.

Mel Lawrence checked in with security a few minutes past noon and informed Lee Mackler that everything at the site had passed inspection with flying colors and was just about ready to go.

Bill Hanley's men had just completed their sound check, adjusting each microphone and speaker, correcting each buzz and hiss, replacing every faulty wire and cable, until the acoustics were, to his ears, as near to being impeccable as was humanly possible. The recording engineers—Lee Osborne and Eddie Kramer—were stationed in the paneled sound truck on the side of the stage and had started the tapes rolling to capture a couple reels of "crowd noises" hours before the show began. Even Bill Hanley's fossilized deadpan was cocked in mild amusement. "I'd like to see that stuffy Bahs-ton bastard split his sides laughing just once," Lawrence remarked. "Except I've heard a rumor that his chuckling is prerecorded at 33-1/3 rpm and played back at 45 to simulate human laughter."

The performers' pavilion looked like "a gourmet chuckwagon," Mel said, with its long cafeteria-style tables decorated with an array of colored table-cloths that rivaled Jacob's coat. A wall of tarnished coffee urns, antique refrigerators, and griddles lined the back of the tent where the celebrities were to be served their favorite dishes. Chef David Levine had rejected a number of "unpretentious" menus suggested by the staff as being too bland in favor of the ultimate in superstar cuisine: Woodstock Ventures had provided him with 400 pounds of prime steak, and Levine agreed to prepare performers' individual requests to order.

"We're having a bit of a problem getting electricity into the pavilion," Lawrence said, "but that should be corrected within the hour. It doesn't matter right now, anyway. We're having a helluva time getting performers through the traffic."

"What about Sweetwater? You mean to tell me they're not there yet?" Lee asked.

"Not *here* yet? They're not even checked in at the Holiday Inn. Last thing we heard, a roadie called to say the band was en route upstate, but that was last night and we haven't gotten another report since. Their equipment hasn't arrived either."

"For Chrissake, Mel, the show's only three hours off."

"Relax, babe. Lang's delivered the motto a half-dozen times already: 'Don't worry, man—we've got it covered,'" he mimicked. "The kid's as cool as ever. I gotta believe he either knows what he's doing, or he's certified insane. Hey, listen, I'd love to chat, but I've got company. Two hundred fifty thousand of my closest friends dropped in for coffee, and I've got to take the croissants out of the oven. Is Roberts around? I've gotta do another number on the poor guy."

"Yeah, he's right here," she said. "Go easy on him, Mel, will you? His morale is not exactly what I'd call buoyant. It hasn't been the easiest of weeks for young John."

"Well, then you'd better have a medic standing by. I've gotta sing the blues again, and my voice is enough to shatter glass."

Roberts got on the line a moment later. His voice sounded scratchy and slow, as if he had pulled a week's worth of all-nighters for a final exam only to learn that he'd studied the wrong material. "Who died, Mel?" he quipped.

"Hey, John baby—don't worry, man. We're disposing of the corpse before anyone finds out."

"Mel—have a heart! Only good news. Okay?"

"I wish I could, kid," he said seriously. "But I'm afraid we've got ourselves another humdinger of a decision to make." He explained to Roberts how, earlier that morning, he stood outside his trailer and watched as a gang of hippies shook what was left of the retaining fence around the site. They rode the poles back and forth until a portion of the fence buckled, and then drew imaginary straws to decide who would lead the march inside. "Then they started streaming in there like troops who had come to liberate political prisoners. And I saw people climbing the fence in other areas, too. Look, man, it's dangerous. Someone might really get hurt pulling shit like that. I know that, deep down inside, you're still counting on the fences to inspire ticket sales, but it's no use. I'd like your permission to take the fences down."

There was a long silence on the other end of the phone while Roberts contemplated the request.

"All right, Mel," he relented, "if that's the situation, let's do it."

"Thanks, man. I know how difficult that was for you, and I really appreciate it. But just for the record—it's already been done. As usual, you made the right decision."

— **2** —

An audience of "long-haired boy gypsies, their pretty 'old ladies' in pilgrim dress, the hip students, and the young rock rebels" had invented infinite ways of entertaining themselves with show time still a few hours off. By 2:30 Friday afternoon, under a magnificent sun-drenched sky, the long-awaited music, which had initially attracted most of them to White Lake, indeed became secondary to their ritual of self-abandon.

Participants of every size and shape twined through the packed amphitheatre; some danced to the accompaniment of strolling troubadors, others whistled as they hopped from blanket to blanket, hugging strangers, shaking hands.

"Peace, man. Where you from?" was the question of the day. The responses were as wondrous, and often incomprehensible, to the inquirer as the scene in which they were moving. Pittsburgh, Boise, Oklahoma City, Seattle, Bangor, Burlington, Miami, Des Moines, St. Paul, San Mateo, Montreal, Austin, Louisville, Omaha—the map of hometowns extended as far as one was willing to take it. "Far out, man. Howja manage to get here? I've never been out there; how 'bout tellin' me about what it's like?"

Undying friendships were established on a moment's notice and consummated with the exchange of an ounce of grass or a handful of multicolored pills. "Here, take some of these, man. They'll help you stay on your feet through the night." Eight-track tapes were traded, copied, edited, or over-dubbed to suit the most definitive collector's requirements.

"My cousin from Miami knows Stephen Stills, and he said he's a card-carrying' freak, man."

"No shit! Hey, Tinker—this guy's cousin hangs out with Stills! C'mere, you gotta meet this cat."

An entire collection of American flags was burned to rousing cheers from the onlookers. A photograph of Richard Nixon was tossed onto one of the red, white, and blue bonfires "to really give that fire somethin' to burn about."

"Hell, he's a lot better than ol' Lyndon B. Johnson, man."

"Here's to ol' Lyndon B.!" A boy in overalls arched his back and threw both his middle fingers into the air.

"Y'know what the 'B' stands for, dontcha?"

"Yeah—Big Motherfuckin' Asshole!" someone shouted, and the crowd screamed its approval.

While all this was transpiring, Tom Law, one of the Hog Farm "heads," sat center stage in the lotus position, guiding the receptive masses through a series of tranquilizing Yoga exercises. "That's it. Take a deep breath—c'mon, nice and deep now—and keep your spine very straight. That's where the main energy of your body goes," he instructed as many as 100,000 attentive students. "Now, let it out very slowly. Very slowly—like a desert breeze. Beautiful, man. That's it. Peaceful and beautiful, and you're all outta sight."

A splinter population of 85,000 others never even bothered to venture into the bowl, but, instead, chose to congregate in one of the isolated theatres of action adjoining the stage grounds.

The Indian art exhibit had been cancelled due to the size of the crowd, but a trio of young guitarists from Long Island moved their show into the Hopi pavilion and led those who gathered around them in a group sing.

> Just about a year ago
> I set out on the road.
> Seekin' my fame and fortune,
> Lookin' for a pot of gold.
> Things got bad, and things got worse,
> I guess you will know the tune.
> Oh Lord, stuck in Lodi again.

Behind them, voices chimed, "I've got acid here, mescaline, and hash!"

"Best Colombian dope in the campgrounds!"

"Rolling paper! Pipes and rolling paper! Can't beat these prices."

"Straight from Turkey—brainfuckers!"

The playground was initially conceived as a hip environmental nursery for infants and preschoolers, but it was soon taken over by a clique of hippies in no mood to share the facilities with anyone else. They coaxed the younger children off the swings and seesaws, took over the sliding board, and laid uncontested claim to the climbing maze, which Ron Liis had finished building only three days before. Vines had been tied to the tops of trees, and teenagers took turns on them, swinging out over the fields and dropping into cushions of loosely piled hay.

Yet the most popular of all recreation areas were the three lakes—one behind the campgrounds, one off Perry Road across from the hayfield, and another situated on the other side of the woods behind the crew's mess hall. Since late morning, they had become festive swimming holes. At first, the cool quartz water attracted only waders who longed to escape the tortuous August humidity. They shed sneakers or sandals, rolled their wide bell-bottomed jeans as high as they would go without cutting off the circulation in their legs, and eased into the shallowest ends of the lakes for a dip before heading back to the bowl. Pretty soon, however, the hippies grew more daring and clothing began disappearing, piece by piece. Shirts and halter tops were blithely cast on shore, then pants, and finally underwear, until heterosexual nude bathing became the instant Aquarian rage.

Young couples shamelessly caressed in the waist-high water. They lathered each other with soap, washed their mate's hair with warm beer, floated on top of one another until playfulness gave way to immodest lovemaking. A few of the more brazen bathers sunned themselves on towels, oblivious to the people who stopped to gawk.

FETE ON FRIDAY: FREEDOM, POT, SKINNY-DIPPING, a headline in the *Times Herald Record* capsulized the afternoon's events. Ethel Romm, the editor's outspoken wife who was rushed into service when the paper's team of reporters failed to show, questioned aloud whether or not the Aquarian Exposition would survive its own orgiastic indulgences and, if so, mulled over the possibilities that lay ahead in the two succeeding days. "Maybe there will be a riot today or tomorrow. Maybe it will all turn into a very bad scene. Maybe we'll all get dysentery or hepatitis," she speculated. "Right now, we're at a happy carnival with young children cavorting through inventive playgrounds and older ones swaying to rock and folk music."

And the music, itself, remained the biggest question mark of all.

As the afternoon wore on, word began circulating through the crowd that the promoters were in a bad way and were not to be trusted.

It was no secret to the hippies that most of the audience was inside the grounds on a free ride. The fences had been "liberated by the People," and it was beyond reason to even the most virtuous in attendance that the festival's backers would be able to collect money from their patrons without an organized system of gates and turnstiles. Woodstock Ventures, it was agreed, would surely take a costly bath, and that spelled nothing but trouble.

It was also common knowledge that security had fallen apart. No gathering of the counterculture had ever been held before where there was not strict enforcement of the law. There seemed to be no visible means of getting anyone through the clutter of abandoned cars on the roads around the site. People sensed trouble with the food; the "pirate" vendors from local luncheonettes who flanked the amphitheatre with their refrigerated pushcarts had sold out of ice cream and orangeade, and the snack bars were sorely understaffed. The frequency of stage announcements had drastically declined since the morning, and there was some general uneasiness as to whether there would be any music at all.

Michael Lang tuned into the undulating pulse of the crowd and prepared to head off an adverse reaction that would mar the euphoria of his manmade paradise. He had to come up with some way of whetting their appetites, something truly revolutionary, that would boost the audience's spirit until Sweetwater arrived to dispel any rumors of closing down the show.

John Morris sat across from him in the trailer, his ear seemingly glued to the telephone. Morris had been trying for over an hour to convince the White Lake fire marshall to send in a truck so they could hose down the crowd. He forgot, however, that it was impossible to get an engine either in or out of the site because of the snarled road situation.

"Son," the marshall replied, "I wouldn't know what to tell you if you called me and said your entire carnival over there was on fire. It's that bad a mess."

"Hey—cut it out, will you." Michael waved Morris off the phone. "Hang up, man. Listen, I know what we're going to do."

Morris slammed the receiver down on the hook. "This has gone a little too far, Michael. You've got a dangerous situation heating up out there."

"Don't worry about it, man. I know how to handle this. Trust me." It was an old line, but it always seemed to do the trick.

*   *   *

Twenty minutes later, John Roberts was fighting his way through the lines in front of the refreshment stands. He had come there out of desperation to present Jeffrey Joerger with a piece of paper turning 100 percent of the concession profits over to Food For Love, but so far he had been unable to locate him among the disorganized ranks. He was just about to try the location trailer when he heard the announcement over the public address system.

"Ladies and gentlemen"—it sounded like John Morris, but he couldn't be sure—"the promoters of this concert, Woodstock Ventures, have declared this a free festival. A free festival," the voice repeated. "The show's on us—" A vocal explosion rampaged across the bowl. It was so deafening an acclamation that Roberts had to cup his hands over his ears. "We'll be getting it on at four this afternoon, so please be patient with us till then."

Almost at once, Roberts felt lightheaded, and he leaned against the side of the concession trailer to steady himself until the dizzyness passed. That was it, he thought—the whole ball game. He had nervously been stringing himself along since Wednesday on the slim notion that some tie-dyed angel of mercy would swoop down on White Lake and rescue his investment from obliteration. Now, it was too late for any miracle.

And yet, Roberts was struck by a morbid sense of relief knowing that further attempts to salvage the wreck would be in vain. The festival had gone bust, and that's all there was to it. He'd survive. He'd learn from this experience and climb back out of debt because he had learned a little bit about what he could accomplish with the right help. He had also come to learn more about himself and, oddly enough, had acquired a newfound respect for his own ingenuity. It might take a few years for him to get back on his feet, but he would—he had no doubt about that. And now, it seemed there was nothing left for him to do but sit back for the next two and a half days and enjoy the show.

"Has anybody heard from Bert Cohen?" one of the press representatives from Wartoke inquired of a production assistant. Cohen had started out from New Jersey the night before in an enormous tractor-trailer carrying 100,000 copies of a festival program that the promoters intended to distribute for free. By 3:30, he had still not arrived, nor did anybody backstage seem to know the whereabouts of the festival's "advertising specialist" or his cargo. "We've got 300 members of the international press corps waiting for that material. Could you have someone check on it for me?"

The assistant returned to her trailer and made a series of calls to information centers scattered around the site. Forty-five minutes later she skipped back to the press tent wearing an impish grin on her face. "Pick a day and a time, and give me two dollars," she sportively instructed the publicist.

"There's no time for games right now. Have you located Bert?"

"Oh yeah." Her eyes twinkled. "I've got a pretty good idea of where he's at this very moment. That's why I'm smiling. I think I'm going to win the pool."

The publicist was losing her patience. "What are you talking about?"

"Bert's somewhere on the Thruway between Spring Valley and Suffern," she tittered. It was nearly sixty miles south of Bethel. "He's been calling in every hour giving us his location, and so far he's only moved three miles in the last four hours. The traffic's so fucked up that he might sit there to next March. That's one of the reasons I'm smiling like I am. Joel started a pool among the staff to guess when Bert shows up—winner take all—and I've got Sunday at 2:30. It's no contest!"

— 3 —

At 4:35, Sweetwater's equipment truck was spotted from the air. A helicopter pilot, accompanied by two production assistants, had made a number of sweeps over the immediate area before making a positive identification of it. It was wedged in on all sides by invulnerable columns of traffic, three miles from the West Shore Road intersection to Yasgur's farm. A team of state troopers was dispatched to free the truck and clear a narrow path leading to the service entrance behind the stage. However, they radioed back to security, "It could take hours."

The festival executive staff had made a career out of buying time at a premium. Lee Mackler resourcefully located another four helicopters in an upstate aviation-school hangar and added them onto the payroll at a cost of $80 an hour for each one. The Federal Aviation Agency prohibited all scheduled planes from flying less than 2,500 feet over the festival site to provide the helicopters with unobstructed and safe access for emergencies. Within twenty minutes, the new reserves hovered over Sweetwater's van while three roadies lugged equipment to a grassy plain on the other side of the highway, preparing for the airlift.

In any event, Sweetwater wouldn't be ready to go on until seven o'clock that evening, and John Morris, wrapped in his third white bush jacket (the first two had wilted), began to articulate his panic.

"We've gotta get somebody on stage quickly," he rumbled, "otherwise we're going to have a mutiny on our hands. Those kids have been sitting out there all day in sweltering ninety-degree weather. I don't know how they've managed to have kept their heads so far—maybe we've just been lucky bastards—but it can't last if we don't find something to distract them with. That jackknife was as close a call as I want to see in my lifetime."

Ten minutes before, a Konglike hippie had climbed up the side of the 80-foot scaffolding that supported the sound system while 200,000 voices egged him on. "Jump! Jump! Jump!" they chanted, not knowing what to expect from the bearded daredevil once he made it to the top. He sped toward the final section of railing with the same determination he had when he set out. "Jump! Jump! Jump!" Pulling himself onto the uppermost platform, he blessed the crowd with a peace sign, gratefully bowed to their applause, and then suicidally flung himself over the side.

"That kid should have broken his neck," Morris said in disbelief, "but he walked away without so much as a scratch! It's got me fooled. All I know is—it can't last. We've gotta make a move while we still can."

Michael Lang agreed.

Together, the two production coordinators combed the performers' pavilion until they came across Richie Havens who was in the process of tuning his guitar.

"Richie—look, man, we got a problem," Lang told him, pulling up a chair and straddling it. "Sweetwater hasn't made the scene yet. We got 'em comin' in by copter, but it's gonna take too long. How about openin' the show for us?"

"C'mon, man, don't do that to me." Havens explained that he wasn't concerned about the crowd. Years before, he had played in front of 17,000 people at the Newport Folk Festival, and as far as he was concerned, "that was the whole world." Once you see 17,000, he told them, you forget about numbers. "I just don't think I can get ready in time."

"You're the only guy who can save us, Richie," Morris said. "We don't have all the amplifiers ready to go yet, but that shouldn't interfere with your performance anyway. It'll give us time, man."

"Well, wait a minute now. What do you mean? Tim Hardin's here too, y'know." He pointed to the entertainer sitting across the way from them. "He's got an acoustic guitar."

"He won't do it, man. He's scared shitless."

Havens laughed. "What can I say? Okay—give me a couple minutes to get ready and to round up the rest of the group. I'll do it."

Not waiting around to hear another word, Lang and Morris rushed off to alert the stage crew. It was 5:01 P.M.

*　　*　　*

Chip Monck stood off to one side of the stage with a clipboard, and performed a final check of the production facilities.

"Lights," he spurted into a crooked mouthpiece, pointing to the typed word at the top of his list with a ballpoint pen.

"All set," a voice whistled over his headset. He paused for a moment, not fully satisfied with the response. "It's okay here, too," another person confirmed. Monck scratched an "x" in front of the descriptive heading and moved his pen down the page.

"Levels?"

"Tested and approved. Six mikes working center stage, two on standby."

To his left, Monck heard the familiar gnashing of sound technicians adjusting the height on the microphone stands. A quartet of stagehands moved the equipment for Richie Havens's backup group into position. A gooseneck microphone was contorted into the shape of a rollercoaster in order to properly amplify a set of congas, and a boom was angled to pick up Richie's guitar.

"Recording?"

"Rolling," came the affirmative reply, and he marked another "x" next to the remote crew's entry.

Monck lifted his eyes and stared at the mixing platform that seemed to levitate a few feet above the crowd in front of the stage. "Console?"

The boy seated behind the computerized board met Chip's eyes and nodded. "Picking it all up beautifully."

Monck made his last notation on the sheet, and scanned each of the production stations around the bowl that were patched into his network with amused interest. "Well, friends—if that's the case"—his voice was one decibel above a whisper—"then I think we're about to have ourselves a festival."

More than 150 people jammed the back lip of the stage as John Morris escorted Richie Havens and his accompanists across the bridge from the performers' area to where they waited for the elevator to be sent down to them. Everyone on stage—the electricians, construction crew, sound men, stagehands, Steve Cohen, Jay Drevers, Ticia Bernuth, one of Michael's Black Shirt heavies, and a sizeable gang of invited friends—anxiously held their breath in anticipation of the climactic moment of truth. No one was really sure how, or even *if*, all the elements they had labored over would jive together. But they'd find out in just a few short seconds.

A contingent of photographers and journalists was led into the cramped pit just below the bandstand. Cameras and pens were poised in an effort to capture the first notes of the festival they had written about months before when it was but an abstract idea.

Michael Lang leaned against a railing behind the communications board, grinning. This was it, he thought. The colossal party was about to begin. He had orchestrated its planning with fine-tuned syncopation, and now the Nation he first dreamed about in Coconut Grove with Ellen was about to experience its spiritual awakening. A minute before, while Chip was double-checking the equipment, Michael had passed among the crew, rewarding each man with a packet of cocaine as a personal expression of gratitude for their support. It would provide them with a well-deserved lift to keep them going for the next two and a half days.

Richie Havens stood behind the production crew as John Morris strode to the stage-front microphone. "Well, this is another one of those here-I-go-again opening 'trips,'" he thought. "What am I going to do out there to make everybody happy, to put everyone at ease?"

He did not have a long time to arrive at a solution.

"Well, it's time for the music to begin," Morris's voice surged over the marvelously accurate sound system. This time, he did not wait for the applause to die down. "Let's welcome Mr. Richie Havens!"

Morris skipped off to the side of the stage, next to Michael, as the applause burst into 250,000 cheers of welcome. Havens, wearing a majestic ochre caftan and white bell-bottom pants, very calmly stalked forward carrying his nicked, oversized Guild guitar. He propped his foot on the ribbing of a wooden stool and began strumming in his patented, disjointed rhythm. "Thank you very much." He nodded to the crowd. "I hope it was worth the wait."

Morris checked his watch. It was 5:07—just over an hour late. Not bad, considering all the headaches of the past four months. He poked Lang in the ribs and pointed with his head in the direction of the audience. "It's outta sight, huh?"

Lang nodded, transfixed by Havens's driving guitar vamp. Without taking his eyes from the singer, he said, "You better not hang around here too long, man. How're you intendin' to keep the show rolling?"

Morris turned pale. "Holy shit! You're right. I gotta find someone else to follow Havens!" he sputtered, and darted down the steps leading to the production trailers.

The phone on his desk was ringing when John reached the trailer. All the assistants had been treated to a half-hour's leave so they could watch Richie

Havens open the festival. Morris toyed with the idea of ignoring the call, but finally succumbed to curiosity. "Production," he announced.

The call was from Iron Butterfly's manager. The group had just landed at Kennedy Airport and wanted to know how they were supposed to get from the airport to the Holiday Inn in Newburgh.

"C'mon, man," Morris said restively, "don't hang this on me now. You guys were supposed to have this all figured out ahead of time."

They had, indeed, the manager pointed out, *until* they got to New York and were bombarded with news bulletins about the state of extreme crisis in White Lake. They couldn't risk spending two days sitting in traffic or being squeezed onto a crowded train for a mere couple thousand dollars. That might be satisfactory for some of the other groups who counted on the exposure to boost their careers, but it certainly was *not* the case for international stars like Iron Butterfly. The promoters would have to come up with some alternate means of transportation if they wanted his group to perform.

"What's wrong with the limousines we have waiting for your group in front of the terminal?" Morris asked. "They have a direct hookup with our security command center and know which back roads to take to shoot you directly in here. We've been having nothing but success with the other performers on the bill."

The manager couldn't rely on just *anybody* to insure his artists' safety. No, they had another plan worked out, and they wanted Morris to put it immediately into effect. They would walk over to the airport's heliport and wait for a festival helicopter to pick them up. They expected to be shuttled directly to the site, where the band would perform upon arrival, and, upon completing their set, board the same helicopter for a return trip to Kennedy. That was it, he said. There were no other conditions under which Iron Butterfly would play.

"But your band isn't scheduled to appear until Sunday afternoon, man. We've got to take care of a lot of acts who have been here for the last two or three days and are willing to wait their turn. This isn't the goddamn amateur hour you're talking about. Now, how about being reasonable and hopping one of our limos?"

The manager repeated that he wouldn't hear of it. It was the helicopters or nothing.

"Well then, you're gonna have to give me some time to make the proper arrangements and to clear the flight with the FAA. Why don't you give me the number of the phone you're using, and I'll get back to you as soon as I know more of the details." John took down the ten-digit number on a slip of paper and repeated it to make sure he had it right. "Okay, man—keep your guys cool until I can work things out." He hung up the phone, and sat perfectly still while he contemplated the situation. What a crock of shit, he thought. Who the hell did they think they were, anyway? Iron Butterfly was a glorified bar band compared to the other artists on the bill and they were the only group with the balls to complain about the accommodations. He held up the tiny piece of paper with their phone number written across it, smiled to himself, and then crumpled it into a ball. Fuck 'em, he decided, and tossed it into the wastepaper basket.

Morris still needed someone to follow Richie Havens on stage. He scanned the list of Friday's acts to see who was available, and found his options were relatively bleak. Ravi Shankar was back at the hotel and the Incredible String Band needed too much time to set up, and he only had about ten minutes in which to get them on. No one had seen Bert Sommer yet. Arlo Guthrie and Joan Baez were headliners, and they'd have to be saved until last if he wanted to build the show's momentum properly. Tim Hardin was going to have to swallow his fear and go on next. There was no other way out.

Morris jogged around to the back of the stage, across the service road, and into the performers' pavilion. The tent was comparatively empty, except for a few stragglers huddled in conversation and a disgruntled crew of electricians still fighting nature to connect the power for the refrigeration. John pulled up short in front of the serving table. He was distracted by a familiar face in the process of pouring itself a cup of coffee.

Bill Belmont juggled a second steaming cup in his hand as he walked toward his friend. "I thought that was you streaking past. How's the show progressing?"

"Sensational," Morris said sarcastically. "It's about to come to a deathly halt if I don't produce another act out of thin air in the next five minutes. Have you seen Tim Hardin around?"

"He cut outta here right after you hit him with going on first," Belmont snickered. "I think he took it as an omen and made himself scarce in case you got any other bright ideas—like putting him on second. Hey—wait a second. Don't tell me that's what you're up to?"

"Would you grant a condemned man a last request?"

"That bad, huh? Sure. Name it."

"Organize a posse to bring Hardin in—dead or alive. Better make that *alive*. He's gotta be able to do about twenty minutes; after that, he's on his own." Belmont said he would recruit a few of the stagehands to help out. "You're a lifesaver, man. Look, if you come upon him before I do, don't waste any time looking for me. Hustle him right over to the stage and let Lang know what the story is. Hopefully he'll put two and two together and will handle it."

"All right. Just let me take this over to Joe"—Belmont nodded to one of the cups—"and I'll be on my way."

"Joe?"

"You know, man—McDonald."

"Country Joe's here—*in the performers' pavilion*?" Morris asked, doing a quick pan of the premises.

"He's right over there." Belmont motioned to the back of a curly red head partially obscured by the master electrician. "Want to say a quick hello before you split?"

"Hold it! Just hang on a second. Look, is Joe still considering a solo career?"

"It's way off, man. I don't know."

"Well, we just might push the calendar ahead a few years," Morris said, scratching the back of his head. "I might have the makings of a brainstorm here, or it might be total lunacy, but do you think we could convince Joe to go out there and do a few numbers?"

Belmont grinned his approval. "It's a hell of an idea. Let's go ask him."

Country Joe McDonald was a spidery, modishly daft man who looked more like a high school misfit than an extremely clever and perceptive political satirist. Disguised in an army field jacket, orange pleated slacks, and a baseball cap pulled down over his eyes, a skirt of reddish hair flowing across his shoulders, he was a zany poet forever lost in thought or—as a long-time friend observed—"a scholar on sabbatical from the human race." Along with the Fish, whom he had toured with since 1963, McDonald was a mainstay of the Berkeley anti-Establishment movement, showing up for every rally, demonstration, and sit-in, prepared to sing. McDonald was best known for salting his eclectic arrangements with topical, acid-tipped lyrics, interweaving a sense of the absurd with Bolshevist commentary on the Vietnam war, police, drug laws, and politics. But as the revolution melted into another liberal country-club phenomenon, McDonald's career began to slide. By 1969, his brand of parody was considered passé and Country Joe and the Fish were recognized as artifacts of the fickle record-buying public. That Country Joe and the Fish had even been invited to play at Woodstock seemed more a tribute to their past than an acquiescence to current demand.

"Hey, guys—what's happenin'?" McDonald flashed the peace sign as Morris and Belmont sallied over to his table.

Morris placed a fatherly hand on the entertainer's shoulder. "I need a favor, Joe. I've got no one to follow Richie and I wondered if you'd go on and do something?"

"Whoa, man! Like, I'd be glad to help you out, but I don't have a guitar with me. Can't sing without a guitar." He grinned.

"We'll get you one!" Morris pulled McDonald to his feet. "C'mon, man, let's get over to the stage. Bill"—he turned to Belmont who was still balancing the coffee cups in one hand—"you work on getting a guitar. I've gotta get Joe on stage. And please be quick about it."

Richie Havens could be heard finishing the stanza of a song as Morris dragged Joe McDonald into the backstage elevator and hit the Start button.

> "Hey looka yonder, tell me what do you see
>   marchin' to the fields of Vietnam?
> Looks like Handsome Johnny with an M-15 in his hands,
>   Marchin' to the Vietnam war."

"We don't have much time," Morris fussed, as he and McDonald stepped out onto the back side of the stage. "If there is a God, will you please see that little Billy Belmont gets a guitar for Christmas six months early?" he joked, looking up into a slowly fading sky. A strip of clouds had masked off the sun, providing partial relief to those who had been sitting under its blazing rays all afternoon. In the distance, he could see a continuous stream of people pouring through the gates. The pasture was evenly coated with people as far as he could see, like a field of wild dandelion. Why, there must be close to 300,000 bodies out there, he thought, wondering how much longer they could go without somehow restricting the population. It was truly a frightening scene.

Even more alarming was the sudden thunderous audience response that signaled Havens's ending of the song. Without missing a beat, the black guitarist began strumming the introduction to his next number. This *had* to be Richie's closing tune, Morris deduced.

"How's this?" a voice asked from behind him. Morris spun around in time to see Bill Belmont lift his trophy into the air. It was a wooden Yamaha guitar whose condition suggested it had seen better days.

McDonald snatched it out of his hands and lightly ran his fingers across the strings. "Yeah, yeah, that'll do," he approved. "But I can't play without a strap."

Morris threw up his hands in frustration, but Belmont saved him from further panic by ripping a piece of rope off the stage railing and lacing it to either end of the guitar. "Witness: a strap!" he exclaimed, impressed by his own split-second ingenuity.

"Very neat, Belmont," McDonald applauded. "But I seem to have left my picks back at the motel. I guess that puts a lid on my going on next."

Belmont put his hands on his hips and shook his head. "Don't give me that shit, Joe. Do I have to remind you how many times I watched you do a set using a matchbook cover for a pick? C'mon, man, no more excuses."

Morris watched this whole drama with mild apprehension. He had gotten McDonald this far; there was no way the singer wasn't going on next.

"Just get me a capo, and everything'll be cool."

Belmont put two fingers on his forehead. A capo was a piece of elastic which wrapped around the neck of a guitar and allowed the artist to transpose a song into his proper vocal key. He knew that it was impossible for Country Joe to go on without it. "I'll be right back," he said. He tapped Morris reassuringly on the shoulder. "Don't worry, man, I'll find a capo. Stall Havens for a few minutes." And he disappeared down the steps.

Morris caught Lang's attention and pointed to Joe McDonald's head. Lang chuckled and nodded his approval. Now, all Morris had to do was to endure Belmont's capo hunt, time it to Havens's finish, and he'd succeed.

On stage, Richie Havens was whipping the crowd into a mushrooming frenzy. He had half-risen from the stool and was bent over the microphone in uninhibited emotion. A string on his guitar had snapped, but he played on.

"Sometimes I feel like I'm almost gone,
Sometimes I feel like I'm almost gone,
Sometimes I feel like I'm almost gone,
Yeah, a long, long, long way from my home."

"Oh shit! He's on his way off!" Morris checked over his shoulder, but there was no sign of Belmont. Havens took two steps back, and then launched into another improvised chorus of the song, which had begun four minutes earlier as a freedom chant. Morris knew he had no longer than another minute or so before he had to go out on that stage and announce the next act. "Doesn't Richie have a capo?" Morris asked McDonald.

"No, man. He plays in an open tuning and uses his thumb to bar across the frets."

Havens had now stepped off to the side of his two musicians and was slowly backing off the stage. Still beating his guitar in time to the congas, Richie stepped behind a group of stagehands in front of the communications console. Morris wrapped an arm around the singer's perspiration-drenched robe and moved his mouth toward Havens's bobbing head. "You gotta go back!" he pleaded, not sure whether Richie even heard him.

Havens continued keeping time to the two-man percussion section. His eyes were closed, and he resembled a victim of a voodoo trance. After completing a four-bar progression, Richie's head lolled forward. "Can't go back," he said breathlessly.

"You *gotta* go back, man."

"Can't go back."

Without further debate, Morris put a hand in the small of Richie Havens's back and gently shoved him out on stage. Havens re-emerged to an overwhelming ovation from the crowd, but it was clear that he did not intend to do an encore. He finished out the song, waved his thanks, and marched triumphantly off the stage. At that precise moment, Morris caught sight of Bill Belmont waving a capo over his head as he hustled up the flight of steps. John caught Havens by the arm and hugged him. "You were sensational, man," he said, nearly in tears. Before he could release Richie from his grasp, Joe McDonald wandered out onto stage, wrestling the capo onto the neck of his guitar, and saluted the audience.

"Gimme an F!" he screamed. A quarter-million voices responded obediently. "Gimme a U! Gimme a C! Gimme a K!" The bowl had erupted in jubilation. "What's that spell?"

"Fuck!" the audience shouted.

"What's that spell?"

"Fuck!"

"What's that spell?"

"Fuck!"

"What's that spell?"

"Fuck!"

McDonald reared back his head and laughed while he introduced the opening bars of a song on his hand-me-down guitar.

> "Come on all of you, big strong men,
> Uncle Sam needs your help again.
> He's got himself in a terrible jam
> 'Way down yonder in Vietnam . . ."

Morris and Belmont slapped each other on the back and yelled their support to McDonald, who was thoroughly enjoying himself.

> "And it's one, two, three, what are we fightin' for?
> Don't ask me, I don't give a damn,
> Next stop is Vietnam;
> And it's five, six, seven, open up the pearly gates,

Well, there ain't no time to wonder why,
Whoopee! we're all gonna die."

"He's outta sight, man. They love him." Morris whistled, jamming two fingers inside his mouth. He wiped his hand on a shirtsleeve and motioned Belmont to follow him down the steps toward his trailer.

The inside of the cabin was still empty, and Morris imagined that the assistants were enjoying themselves too much to return to work. He closed the miniature window, cutting off a fraction of the droning cacophony. He offered Belmont a soda and opened one for himself. "I need you back at the Holiday Inn," he said. "I don't know how the fuck I'm going to stay on my feet at this pace, so it'd be much simpler if we kept the groups coming in time for their set."

"How do you propose to pull that off with the roads closed?" Belmont asked.

"Helicopter. There's no other way. In fact, I'm going to ship you over there now by helicopter so you can round up the next three acts. I'll want to get Bert Sommer, Sweetwater, and the Incredible String Band over here as soon as possible. How long is Joe good for?"

"The way he's going—about a half hour, forty-five minutes, depending on the crowd."

"That'd be terrific," Morris said hopefully. "I'll hook Tim Hardin for the next spot, and that should give us about an hour and a half to put our shuttle into effect. You've got the number for the direct line to the stage, right?" Belmont said that he did. "Okay then. Just keep 'em coming until I tell you to stop. Every forty-five minutes should do the trick."

Morris called the security office to make sure he had a helicopter at his disposal and walked Belmont over to the launching pad. Afterwards, he made his way back to the performers' pavilion to see who, if anyone, was around and available to play.

A young man with sandy hair, wire-rimmed glasses, and dressed from head to toe in tie-dyed clothing walked into the tent just ahead of him, carrying a guitar. It didn't take Morris more than a flickering glance to recognize John Sebastian.

Nearly two years had passed since Sebastian had dropped out of the public eye. After nine hit singles—including such rock classics as "Daydream," "Do You Believe In Magic," "You Didn't Have To Be So Nice," and "Summer In The City"—on which he sang lead vocals and played both the autoharp and harmonica, the Lovin' Spoonful had split up, and Sebastian took up exile in Woodstock. The Spoonful were one of the few East Coast bands with universal appeal between 1965 and 1967 when a band emanated from either Liverpool or California. But they pulled up their Greenwich Village roots like a bouquet of four-leaf clovers and rose to skyscraping heights alongside such western counterparts as the Byrds, the Mamas and the Papas, the Righteous Brothers, the Turtles, and the Buffalo Springfield. A drug bust had cut their reign short—or, not so much the bust as the allegations that arose from it. It was reported in the underground press that drummer Joe Butler and lead guitarist Zal Yanovsky had fingered their drug source to the San Francisco police in exchange for their freedom, and that had been enough to seal their death sentence. Sebastian's resurfacing now, especially at the festival, was news—*big* news—and a potential treat, if Morris had his way.

Morris chatted with the singer for a few minutes and learned that Sebastian had spent a considerable portion of his time in retirement writing new material for a solo album. "That's wonderful, man. But, tell me—are you willing to play?"

"No thanks. I just came to hang out with some friends." Sebastian smiled politely.

"C'mon, man. If those kids knew you were back here and holding out on them, they'd be snorting fire. How about doing a few numbers and letting everyone know what you've been up to these last two years?"

Morris took him firmly by the arm and led Sebastian toward the elevator. The whole way across the rickety footbridge and onto the lift, Sebastian repeated with staunch conviction his reluctance to perform as a solo artist. It was too soon, he said, standing his ground. He had to rehearse for several months, pick up a few sidemen perhaps. He wasn't even sure that he knew all the words to his new songs.

As they disembarked at stage level, Sebastian's protests became more vehement. And then Chip was at the microphone announcing the special visit of "an old friend" and it was as if he had never been away. Something magical transformed the stage when John Sebastian ambled out, waving at his fans, and it was at that moment, Morris thought, that the Woodstock Music and Art Fair truly became a festival.

— **4** —

John Roberts spent the early evening hours in a corner of the Bethel security office talking, long distance, to newspapers, radio stations, television commentators, and community leaders across the nation, urging kids *not* to come to Woodstock, to turn back "if they have any common sense at all."

Roberts had watched the growing colonization of Yasgur's farm with terrifying concern. There was truth in numbers, and the statistics he had been quoted by the police and state agencies concerning movement in the direction of Sullivan County foretold his personal undoing. He was about to rival the New York Social Services Department of Welfare as the state's most prominent charity. As the corporation's sole financier, not only would he be obliged to pick up the admission for each festival goer, but, once they were inside the ravaged gates, he'd be responsible to provide for their well-being, which was starting to approach the luxury accommodation rates at the Plaza. None of the kids were coming to White Lake prepared. They weren't carrying any money. Nor had the latecomers packed food or brought along changes of clothing. Their cars had run out of gas and needed servicing. Many had no way of returning home. It was madness that he stared in the face, and there seemed no way out of it without bringing about the total suffocation of his assets.

Independent contractors had begun stopping by Roberts's desk during the late afternoon demanding full or partial payment for their services. Some, whose functions were required throughout the weekend and who were essential to the very life-sustaining systems that had, so far, proved effective, threatened to walk off the job unless they received cash in advance of their forthcoming shifts. No one would accept a check drawn on the Woodstock Ventures account. The implications had become all too clear. The promoters were in an insurmountable pinch, and tomorrow their checks wouldn't be worth the paper they were written on. They'd take cash, they said, or a personal IOU from John Roberts—but *only* from Roberts, no one else would do.

Late Friday night, the worsening situation began to overwhelm Roberts. His complexion had developed an unearthly pallor, which distressed many of his co-workers. "Keep an eye on John," they cautioned one another, "he may go over the edge." But he held fast through the heavy sledding, meeting each successive crisis with a predictable moan and a gesture of nightmarish distress.

Around 11:00, he slipped away unnoticed, ducking into a vacant room in the back of the building while Joel, Don Ganoung, Lee Mackler, and an assistant manned the continuously ringing phones. Roberts picked up the phone and dialed Paul Marshall at his home in Harrison, a man whose evenhanded counsel and experience he regarded with confidence. Marshall treated Roberts as an adult, a professional, and John liked that. He'd fill him in on what had transpired since they last communicated and see if Marshall could offer him guidance.

There is some discrepancy about what was said during that phone call. Roberts admits to a faint recollection of speaking to Marshall that night, but cannot, for the life of him, remember a word of their conversation. The lawyer, on the other hand, remembers what was said as if it were an important piece of evidence in a case.

"He called up and began to cry," Marshall said pensively. "John said he'd gone through everything. There was no money, and they were asking him to sign bad checks. I told him, 'You can't do that. You know there's no money, and that's a potential criminal liability.' But he said he had signed them anyway, knowing the consequences. I asked him, 'Why? What did you go and do that for before consulting me?' I had warned him about signing his name to *anything* without the advice of counsel. But it was apparently too late for that. He cried more uncontrollably now, and said: 'All these people here, Paul, they're like my guests.' And he hung up the phone without another word."

At about the same time, Lee Mackler decided it was time she was spelled by a replacement before succumbing to weakness. "I've gotta get something to eat before I die," she told Don Ganoung, slumping across her littered desk. "Anybody up for trying to reach civilization?"

A bearded man in a staff T-shirt whom she had never seen before volunteered to guide her through traffic, and together, they slipped through the congestion and roadblocks to the Holiday Inn in Liberty where Woodstock Ventures had put up many of the performers.

"It was like paradise," she noted with amusement, "like a wonderful dream in which one's friends and heroes were present. I remember sitting down with a few kids from the staff and ordering a banquet, seven courses, which we simply signed for. Janis Joplin was there, and so was Grace Slick and two or three of the Grateful Dead—the revolutionaries dining on T-bone steaks and French champagne. We were hysterical, because we knew damned well that come Saturday or Sunday night, these people would change into their oldest torn jeans and sing to 'the people' about poverty and starvation.

"It was absolutely decadent. We had heard about the pitiful conditions out at the site, how the food was low, and the medical tents were bursting with patients, like a modern-day Gettysburg. But nobody gave a shit. We were on an expense account, and that was really all that mattered to most of the people in that dining room. I knew what I wanted all along. I didn't want to return to that godawful mess in the security building. I wanted the comforts of home. So when I was told there was no way I'd get back to White Lake that night, I submitted without a whimper. I spent the night in a room in the Holiday Inn with air-conditioning, a color television, and a Magic Fingers—which, after all, is what everyone knows peace, love, and life is all about."

The $4,500 Joshua Light Show spectacular, which John Morris had insisted upon booking over his employer's objections, lasted for a meteoric streak of brilliance before fizzling out over White Lake for good.

As soon as it had gotten dark enough to commence with the projection, right after Sebastian finished, Josh White hung his gigantic screen from the back of the stage and proceeded to flash a series of colorful, formless splotches behind the Incredible String Band's silky performance. The crowd hailed the familiar exhibit, another "old friend" in this unusual, new environment. Most of them had experienced White's famous show at the Filmore East or had witnessed several imitations of the psychedelic art form at one concert or another in their hometown. Its pageantry, coming in the middle of Friday night's show, was taken for granted, much the same way one expects the "Star-Spangled Banner" to be sung before a sports event begins.

Something, however, was not working properly—the images were not lucid enough or as fluid as the artist wanted them to appear—and the temperamental White stomped off in the direction of the trailer compound in search of a new projector lamp.

Steve Cohen had had enough of both White and the light show and told two of his stagehands to keep an eye out for Josh while he had a look behind the stage. Maybe, he leered, there was some way he could give White a hand and locate the source of trouble.

With the help of a staff carpenter and one of the Bastard Sons, Cohen disengaged the backdrop from its flimsy frame and disappeared with it underneath the orange scaffolding.

Twenty minutes later, White returned, carrying a gunmetal tool box and a carton of tempera paint. He seemed more relaxed, more composed, than he had been previously. He had brought everything he needed along with

him on this trip from the production area. Nothing else could give him cause
to interrupt his show again.

As he ascended the steps to the stage, he knew, at once, that something
was out of place. He couldn't quite put his finger on it, but he sensed that
something had been tampered with, someone had intruded upon his territory. Then it dawned on him.

"Hey! My screen, man—what's happened to the screen?" A stagehand
shrugged his ignorance of the situation and went back to watching the show.
"I can't fuckin' believe it!" He flexed his arms like a weightlifter and then
brought them down with a hard slap against his thighs. No one paid his ti-
rade any attention and White sensed a conspiracy among the production
staff, which only infuriated him more. "My screen—who the fuck's stolen my
screen? I'm gonna nail someone to the wall if I don't get my screen back!"

White ranted and searched for fifteen minutes without much luck. The
Joshua Light Show had come to a spiteful, inconsiderate end. It was not until
later that night that the show's creator learned of the catastrophe which had
befallen his curtain. One of the electricians had found it while replacing a
cable beneath the stage. It had somehow come loose from its mooring, the
man proposed, but he could not explain how it came to be wrapped neatly
in a blanket—nor could he come up with a theory about how or why it had
been slashed to ribbons.

The Incredible String Band was a traditional, folk-oriented ensemble who
had miraculously hung on to their loyal audience during the Liverpool up-
rising of the mid-1960s. While the Beatles, the Stones, the Dave Clark Five,
the Yardbirds, and the Who, among others, banished the folkies to life along
the coffeehouse circuit, the String Band conformed to the flower-generation's
milieu, adapting their unique blend of exotic instrumentals to that of trendy
experimental drug lore. Michael Lang had been quick to hire the English
band, replete with their richly textured robes and transcendental stage paraphernalia. However, by the time the festival rolled around, the quaint duet
had been expanded into an unwieldy five-piece pop band. Much of their
esoteric veneer had been diluted by the group's development, although their
hour-and-twenty-minute set commanded a splendorous response from the
crowd.

Tim Hardin finally took a turn on stage after the Incredible String Band.
It was a few minutes past nine o'clock, a logical transition in the show—the
String Band, a stunning orange sunset, then Hardin's sauntering to the
mike—and the crowd's well-timed composure helped cushion the songwrit-

er's stage fright. Tim was a familiar face to the Woodstock musical community; his friends included John Sebastian, Eric Andersen, and the Band. He was a descendant of outlaw John Wesley Hardin and it is believed that his ancestry inspired Dylan to build an album around the desperado's turbulant mystique. Tim, however, had a mystique all his own, a lush, silky voice that fluttered over jazz/blues compositions such as "If I Were A Carpenter," "Reason to Believe," "Lady Came From Baltimore," and "Misty Roses." For nearly an hour, Hardin spun gentle, convincing renditions of his classics. One could almost see his fear melt away as the set progressed, and by the time Tim Hardin returned to the performers' pavilion, he was but a vestige of his former nerve-wracked self.

Food For Love was holding its own on the hill overlooking the stage. Despite the estimated 300,000 people in attendance—nearly three times the number for whom they had planned—and an inexperienced labor force working the stands, no one had to wait more than ten or twenty minutes in line to be served. In contrast to their business tactics, Food For Love's organization seemed conscientious and well mannered.

Some of the pressure of feeding so many people had been taken off their shoulders, of course, by the Hog Farm's Free Kitchen. Word of their existence spread quickly, and before long the campground facility was swamped with requests for meals far in excess of their ability to dish them out. Volunteers offered their assistance behind the counters ungrudgingly, where they chopped vegetables, stirred the boiling vats or carried pails of festering slop to the garbage-disposal area without demur.

The electricians had given up all hope of wiring the performers' pavilion for refrigeration, and an aggravated David Levine reluctantly donated his mountain of beefsteak to the Hog Farm's stew before it putrified. Only four weeks before, the commune had demanded the strict observance by everyone on the staff of their vegetarianism. Now, they disavowed any allegiance to their meat-free diets. As one Hog Farmer so aptly put it: "How can anyone in their right mind turn down a gift of great-looking steaks, man? It's just not human."

The only post on the verge of becoming a critical juncture for the promoters was the medical operation that, on inspection, proved to be a churning vortex of disorderliness.

"It's not an emergency situation yet," Dr. Abruzzi argued with a reporter from the New York *Post* just after the sun had gone down, "but we're almost at the breaking point. We simply can't cope with the medical needs of what amounts to a large city packed into a field."

Abruzzi's chief concern was that the promoters had only contracted for a medical staff until eight o'clock each night, resuming again at ten the next morning. "We're understaffed," he mentioned to another newspaperman. "Wait a minute—did I say understaffed? I meant under siege."

By the time Tim Hardin was finally coaxed on stage for his set, Abruzzi's short-handed team of physicians and nurses had already treated close to 400 people for minor injuries—most conspicuously cut feet (as very few kids came to White Lake with anything on their feet) and broken toes and fingers resulting from falls in the playground. A few teen-agers bounded into the trailer screaming that they were being attacked by bug-eyed monsters or God, and they were immediately chaperoned to the Hog Farm's waystation on the other side of the woods, where someone sat by their side and talked them down from the bad trip. Otherwise, Abruzzi took down their vital statistics, provided them with a thorough examination, tended their injuries, and steered them back into battle.

The more complicated cases were airlifted to one of the local hospitals that, along with the state police, cooperated in evacuating and caring for the seriously ill patients. Abruzzi, or one of the eighteen residents who had reported for duty, diagnosed two ruptured appendixes, five incomplete abortions, three cases of noncommunicable hepatitis, and three of ulcers of the eye as a result of excessive contact lens use, as well as a dozen or more instances of food poisoning.

As of late Friday afternoon, Liberty and Monticello hospitals were filled to capacity, and Middletown hospital was admitting ten to fifteen patients from the festival per hour.

That afternoon, the Red Cross had telephoned Charles Rudiger, the superintendent of schools for the Monticello district, requesting that the Rutherford School, an elementary school a mile down the road from Community General Hospital, be opened as a field medical center for "the festival wounded." Rudiger had already received permission from the building's administrators to provide it as a dormitory for the National Guard if the situation required that troops be sent in, but, as Rudiger remembered, "I could see that wasn't going to be necessary, so we just bent the rules a bit."

One hundred fifty cots and mattresses were set up in the gym, which became the school's main treatment center, and a pair of army helicopters set down in the blacktopped play area behind the parking lot. The temporary hospital's operation was spontaneous; whatever needed to be done was performed without the least subjection to carelessness or argument. And, for a while, it looked like the Rutherford School would be enough to handle the load.

— 5 —

Ravi Shankar was in the middle of his instrumental set when the storm hit. No one had been forewarned of its approach. The moonless sky was a raven-black curtain of darkness until bolts of lightning set the night ablaze, reveal-ing a cloud-capped firmament. By then, it was too late to lay the necessary groundwork to offset the rain.

At 10:35, Shankar and his accompanist were ushered offstage to one of the adjoining trailers as eight shirtless hippies worked furiously to unravel the ball of plastic that was draped over the equipment. Two others scampered across the platform on their haunches pulling plugs out of amplifiers and tucking musical instruments under the covering.

"Surface shield!" Jay Drevers screamed, barely able to hear his own voice above the din of excitement. "Will somebody please run over to the equip-ment trailer and get the surface shield!" A stagehand in the midst of slipcov-ering the revolving platform (which had ceased to function after the first amplifier was thrust upon it) gave Drevers the high sign and bounded over to the supply area. Surface shield was a canned liquid that displaced water and did not conduct electricity. Ideally, it was used to spray every sparkling appliance to prevent an electrical fire—that was, if it was handy during a storm. Much good it did them to have the case of surface shield locked away when they needed it most.

The storm continued to rage for fifteen minutes before slowing to a steady drizzle. Like the scene of a gypsy convention, the amphitheatre was dotted with bonfires, and sections of the audience huddled around them, deter-mined to ride out the inconvenience. Most of them were soaking wet; their blankets and sleeping bags were drenched with mud and thoroughly useless to them for shelter. But nobody seemed to mind. Those who were fortunate enough to have tents made room for their neighbors. Some of the hippies strung their parkas together for a rainshield or built primitive huts out of hay and garbage. The rest, however, sat unprotected in the open field, just happy to be there, thrilled to be part of the spiritually thriving Woodstock Nation.

*   *   *

Most of the performers who waited to go on that night—Ravi Shankar, Melanie (who dropped by unexpectedly and consented to perform), and Arlo Guthrie—were crowded into one of the production trailers, drinking coffee and bucking the moisture to keep their instruments from sliding out of tune.

"It's outta sight, man," Guthrie drawled to a sidekick who turned out to be a writer from the *Rat*. "This here festival, y'know—it reminds me of J.C. on the Mount, but more receptive." Guthrie said he was "wired," and looking forward to facing the "children of the earth."

Ravi Shankar reacted exactly the opposite, having faced a much smaller, yet equally mindboggling, following at Monterey. "I am frightened in case something goes wrong with so many people," he confided to Al Aronowitz moments before he was called to resume his portion of the show. The Indian sitarist chose to pass the rest of the unscheduled intermission in deep thought and retired to a corner of the trailer.

Joan Baez, who was to close Friday's extravaganza, excused herself from the stuffy room. Tucking her guitar under her arm, she walked unnoticed through the woods, out beyond the fences, and waited her turn in the rain so that she could perform for the handful of kids who were gathered in front of the free stage.

Three amateur bands preceded Baez, playing vigorously to hearty encouragement from the audience. To the trained ear, they were strictly unendowed artistically; as a matter of fact, they could hardly carry a tune. But creative genius was not a prerequisite as far as the small audience was concerned. All that mattered to them was the performer's desire to get up and entertain, to share some time with the People. That, they claimed, was cause enough for celebration.

Baez gave lovingly of herself, playing a selection of songs about America's changing social structure, poverty, union leaders, and about her husband, journalist David Harris, who was serving time in a Federal prison for refusing to answer his draft call. "*This* is what we live for," she said between numbers, pointing to the wide-open countryside and the covey of tents on the other side of the road. "It's why we're fighting together right now—for our right to be heard, and the right to remain free."

Baez played for forty minutes until her road manager found her and respectfully informed the folksinger that she had to fulfill her obligation on stage for the festival's promoters.

For those who sat on the wet grass and applauded her thoughtfulness and professional kindness, the show was reason enough for their optimism. If

Joan Baez had taken the time out to play for those unable to get close to the main stage, they reasoned others would obviously follow. The Jefferson Airplane or the Dead or Crosby, Stills and Nash—they were all champions of the People's Revolution and would eventually get around to putting in an appearance. It was only a matter of time before Joan related her experience and they came.

The free stage became a forum for the voice of the underground throughout the remainder of the weekend. Anyone who wished to have the spotlight was given a slot on the bill. Jugglers, poets, movement leaders, and orators took turns at the mike, some of the young men destroyed their draft cards in protest of the Vietnam war, two marriages were performed, even a striptease was enacted by one *very* stoned girl from Philadelphia. A good time, as the old show business slogan goes, was had by all. In fact, the small group of diehards who shunned the amphitheatre for the free stage enjoyed themselves so much that, by Monday morning, when it was time to leave for home, hardly any of them realized that the superstars had failed to come by.

CHAPTER ELEVEN

Saturday, August 16, 1969

Here were the Israelites, nearly half a million struggling to
survive in a sea of mud, and Moses had lost the map.
—*Liberation News Service*

— 1 —

The Woodstock Generation's first night as a full-fledged nation passed
without incident. When Chip had hesitantly pulled the plug on the music
a few minutes after two o'clock, the majority of the audience reacted in the
one way the producers *hadn't* anticipated: they went to sleep.

In the past, at most of the other summer rock festivals, the show's finale
had been a signal for all hell to break loose. And, indeed, Wes Pomeroy had
entertained some discussion as to whether it might not be better to keep the
performers on stage all night rather than to run the risk of a violent outbreak.
There had also been talk of sending Hugh Romney on stage to recite fairy
tales to those who needed some form of recreation to keep them out of trouble.

In the final analysis, however, it had been so pure an action, a mere formality, which succeeded as a nightcap to the musical jamboree. No apologies
were made to the audience for cutting off the entertainment. Chip simply
took center stage after Joan Baez finished her encore, and said, "Well, that's
it for tonight, gang. All of you get a good night's sleep, and we'll see you tomorrow around ten o'clock. Peace and good night."

In the morning, the field was motionless, like a piece of sculpture com-
memorating a historical event. Mel Lawrence awoke around six o'clock, just
before sunrise, and tumbled out of his trailer, not at all prepared for the
spectacle that stretched before him.

"At first, I was overcome by the eerie silence, and then I panicked," he recalled some years later. "I saw all of those young, beautiful bodies, twisted in the grass and mud and garbage—there was junk scattered all over the place—and I wasn't sure whether they were asleep or dead. For all I knew, they could have been hit by lightning during the night. My trailer was grounded, so a disaster like that would have bypassed me completely. Who the hell knew *what* might have happened out there while I was in bed. The whole scene just sort of stuck in my throat."

After his eyes adjusted to the low light, Lawrence could make out faint activity stirring in remote areas around the site. Near the left field fence (what remained of it), two boys stepped over bodies in an attempt to revive the smoldering campfires every fifteen or so feet, careful not to wake anyone in the process. Groups of hippies sat in circles, talking and passing joints to newly acquired friends, scraps of food were shared, canteens passed so that everyone could take a sip of water. Lines had already begun forming in front of the Johns, and Lawrence decided to have a look at their condition before performing an overall inspection of the site.

The portable toilets located near the concession stands at the top of the hill were, in Lawrence's words, "in real bad shape . . . they were filthy and disgusting. I really had to control myself to keep from throwing up when I went in one of them." From what he could determine, the problem there was twofold: excessive use, and lack of servicing. He hadn't calculated such a heavy demand, nor had he counted on the breakdown of their servicing operation. Two sanitation trucks, their tanks filled with human waste, were barricaded behind the facilities, unable to move through the surrounding people. Even had they been able to maneuver the trucks out to Hurd Road, it would have been impossible to drive them off the site to a dumping station because of the abandoned cars. But something had to be done soon, because the toilets were starting to overflow. A muddy discharge had begun to seep through the floorboards and collect in puddles around the already soggy area. As soon as the sun hit the field, they'd have a monumental problem on their hands. Lawrence grimaced. He'd have to find Bill Reynolds, who was in charge of sewage disposal, to see what could be done about averting such a problem.

The toilets in the campgrounds were in much better condition. The service road leading from the rows of Port-O-Sans out to West Shore Road had miraculously remained free of vehicles, and a truck had been able to tend to that compound during the night. Lawrence hadn't the foggiest idea where the truck had gone to dump the waste, but he decided against asking any questions that might prevent it from happening again.

On his way back to the command trailer, Lawrence noticed that twenty cots had been set up in the employees' mess hall. The large tent had been summarily converted into a provisional field hospital for the increasing number of incapacitated. Friday night, after the rain had let up, a contingent of volunteer doctors from the Medical Committee For Human Rights cornered Stanley Goldstein in the campgrounds and threatened to call the governor's office for the purpose of having him declare White Lake a disaster area unless certain demands were met to elevate the festival's health standards. Don Goldmacher, a young bearded psychiatrist from New York City and the group's fiery spokesman, informed Goldstein they were on the verge of an unmanageable medical tragedy that could explode at any time.

"There's close to a half million people here, but you don't have running water or good sanitation facilities," Goldmacher argued. "We don't know what's sterile and what's not. That stinks! And on top of that, there aren't sufficient medical supplies to care for these kids. I don't care what Abruzzi told you he had—he *doesn't* have what we need or anywhere near what these kids need." Goldmacher, although thoroughly disgusted with the setup, said he was restraining several members from the MCHR staff from taking official action against the promoters. "We're going to provide you with a list of things we want—no, we *need* to have—and if you don't see we get these things immediately, then we'll just have to call Rockefeller's office and ask for military assistance.

"Here's what we want: We want you to charter a plane out of LaGuardia Airport tomorrow morning and have it fly to Sullivan County Airport. We'll call our people in New York, get a lot of them out of bed, and tell them they've got to fly up here tomorrow. We'll also give you this list of supplies we want, and you'd better make sure they're on the plane." He handed Goldstein an enumerated list of intravenous supplies, minor surgical equipment, and medication, which the festival co-ordinator studied with divided interest.

Looking up from the piece of paper, Stanley asked, "And where, might I ask, do you expect us to come up with this equipment in the middle of the night?"

Goldmacher harrumphed his scorn. "I don't give a shit how you find it or how you get it here, as long as you do it right away. Be reasonable. We're talking about the safety of these kids, not extra guitar strings or champagne. Don't try to cut any corners on this, or we'll all lose in the end."

Goldstein knew that the picture the doctor presented to him was a fairly accurate assessment of the situation. If he resisted the demands, he'd only be arguing against his own case, and that was self-defeating. Without debating it any longer, he had security order the plane. Then, he called one of the production trailers and told a purchasing agent to transform the mess hall into a medical tent so the new recruits would have a place to operate.

Penny Stallings, who was seated at a desk across from the purchasing agent when he took the call, watched his reaction with a sinking malaise. "It was harrowing," she reminisced much later. "He just went out, he went to sleep, he didn't want to be there any longer. I knew the urgency of the order, and had to go see if I could get it started on my own."

Along with an assistant, a woman named Ingrid Von Wilsheim, Stallings communicated the verdict to Peter Goodrich, under whose authority the tent functioned as a mess hall. "Peter went crazy," she said in retrospect. "He accused me of conspiring against him, of ruining his food operation. He wouldn't hit me, but he certainly came close at that moment, and he said that he forbade us from taking over the tent because that was where people had to eat."

Penny took a look around the tent, saw that it was virtually empty, and decided to stand up to Goodrich, a man twenty years her senior. "If you think the kids on the staff are going to be able to take breaks and come have a nice little box lunch here, you're out of your mind!" she screamed. "Don't you see what's going on? We've got a crisis on our hands and it's a helluva lot more important than feeding a few stagehands."

Goodrich, a man who no longer had a rational perspective, instructed her not to touch a thing in the mess hall until he could come back with Lang or Lawrence.

As soon as Goodrich was out of sight, Penny and Ingrid began preparing the tent for the hospital it was inevitably going to become. Stallings enlisted two of Chris Langhart's assistants and had them "borrow" sheets of plywood from a stack in back of the stage so they could lay a floor. Langhart diverted water and electricity from a nearby facility into the tent, hung lamps on surgical hooks, and reinforced the building's frame while Ingrid located bunks and laundry supplies. In less than two hours, the employees' mess hall had gone from cafeteria to casualty ward and was ready for occupancy before Joan Baez got off the stage.

Mel inspected the women's skillful results with admiration. From what he had seen of Abruzzi's and the Hog Farm's overtaxed facilities, they had prepared the new hospital none too soon. The doctors' flight was expected from LaGuardia about 10:30 A.M. There wasn't a moment or an empty cot to spare.

Before returning to the top of the hill, Lawrence thought he might take a couple of minutes to appoint someone to provide the awakening masses with a few encouraging words. He realized that, for many of the kids, this was their first morning away from home. There was every chance that some of them had suffered through an emotionally restless night and perhaps he could reduce the edge of insecurity many of them would feel when they got up in unfamiliar surroundings. However, when he approached the front of the stage, there wasn't a staff member in sight to handle the assignment, so he decided to make the announcement himself.

It took Lawrence practically fifteen minutes to find someone from the sound crew who was both awake and authorized by Bill Hanley to turn on the power for the microphones. Feeling ill at ease, Mel walked slowly toward the live mike, his head bowed, rehearsing the "casual" remarks he intended to pass on to his guests like "Good morning, everybody, rise and shine. We're going at it again today. Let's clean up our areas." He flashed on his earlier days in the Catskills when the director of the summer camp he went to started each morning with almost those identical words. Now here he was twenty-five years later—Uncle Mel—counselor at the most spaced-out kiddie show the Catskills had ever experienced. And probably the most expensive.

It would have been a piece of cake for him had he looked up and seen fifty eager faces hedged with crew cuts wearing Camp Mohawk T-shirts. He could have been cool about it then, perhaps he would have tossed in a stale joke or two to liven up his address. But when he looked out on 300,000 people his heart jumped about two city blocks and his salutation burst forth with an ear-splitting swell. "GGOOO-OOD MOOOR-NINGGG!" he blurted, stumbling backwards as 300,000 heads vaulted up in unison. Those troubled souls who had succeeded in sleeping off their insecurity felt the old alarm come rushing back with a new, improved vitality. "Sorry about that," he laughed, embarrassed by his faux pas. "Let's try that one again. Good morning," he said, softly. If it was scientifically inconceivable for 300,000 to applaud in a state of drowsiness, the kids in Max Yasgur's pasture provided the exception to the rule. "Thank you," Mel beamed. "Listen, last night was incredible, and we just wanted to let you know that everything's okay. No hassles. We're going to have another groovy day today and into the night and tomorrow." He paused, waiting for the roar to die down. "I just need your help with this one small favor. We're going to pass out these bags now so that we can keep our home clean. We'll hand 'em out to those of you on this side of the bowl," he said, pointing to the group closest to the woods, "and I'd appreciate it if all of you over there will toss your junk in and pass the bag on until it gets over to the other side of the field. Some of the guys from the

Peace Service Corps will pick them up over there and get rid of that stuff for you. We've gotta keep this place livable so we can prove to the rest of the world that we can make it together in peace and in comfort. And we're gonna do it, too." Again, he received a unanimous vote of applause from the crowd, and this time he knew enough to quit while he was ahead. One of the technicians threw on a tape of Love's *Da Capo,* and Lawrence shuffled down the steps to supervise the cleanup, confident that the world was on his shoulders.

Day Two had gotten off to an auspicious start.

Joel Rosenman woke up in a chair in the telephone office with an inflamed case of hives. Instead of waking his partner, who was snoring away on a cot across the room, Joel took a twelve-hour antihistamine cold capsule, hopped on his Honda, and rode over to a police roadblock, where he directed traffic before heading over to the Diamond Horseshoe to have breakfast with the staff.

He found the hippies' reaction to the "travesty" at Yasgur's farm exactly the opposite of his own. None of them had any idea of the financial straits the promoters were in, and his impression was that even had they known what was going down, they probably would not have cared. Nothing mattered as long as the People were happy. Their share-the-wealth philosophy, however praiseworthy as a platonic thought, was an economic illusion; their sense of political upheaval even more romantic. Any serious revolutionary knew that to change the system, one first had to cope with it, infiltrate its administration. But these kids didn't care a damn about political evolution, Joel thought, as long as they could be part of this magnificent game called the Counterculture, rebels without a justifiable cause. Their morality was as sincere as the moment, as potent as their own pleasure. The whole generation had begun to offend him, and he drifted off to sleep in a lobby armchair as an effective way of keeping his distance from them before breakfast was served.

When he woke up (for the second time that day) a half hour later, the hives had disappeared. Without waiting around for the second sitting of pancakes, he hopped back on his bike, zig-zagged through the anchored line of cars, and arrived back at the security office in time to witness his partner's being served with a summons.

"Are you Roberts?" a stout, balding man in a rumpled Eisenhower jacket and baggy pants asked John. Receiving an affirmative nod, the man pulled out an envelope and held it upright, just out of the boy's reach. "Are you authorized to accept papers on behalf of Woodstock Ventures?" Again, Roberts said he was. "Then it is my duty to give you this." He handed the envelope across to Roberts and walked out of the building without waiting for a response.

"You want to let me in on it?" Joel asked, after a genteel amount of time had lapsed.

"Oh, yeah. Sorry." He shook his head in a way that could only be interpreted as pathetic. "I just never thought it would all come at us at once like this. We're being sued, Joel. Monticello Raceway claims we're into them for three hundred grand for failure to provide adequate access to the festival. As a result of our 'negligence' in allowing the roads to be blocked, most of their potential customers weren't able to reach the betting windows last night. We're going to have to make good on all those losing two-dollar tickets. Jesus Christ! Do you believe this? Everybody wants a piece of our action."

"Take it easy, man," Joel said comfortingly. "It's probably nothing. Give Marshall's office a call, and ask someone there what we should do about it."

Instead, Roberts called Richard Gross at his home in Liberty, who advised him to put the complaints in his pocket along with all the others he would undoubtedly receive before the weekend was out. "I guess you're going to need a pretty large pocket," the attorney joked, and said that he'd follow up on the subpoenas on Monday, after the festival was over.

Wes Pomeroy stopped by the office to pick up the neatly ribboned packets of cash so that he could pay the ten o'clock security detail, or, as he affectionately had taken to calling them, those thieves. "You'd think they'd at least work for this booty," he grumbled, waving the money in the air, "but most of them are too busy dragging teen-age girls off to the barn for a quick lay." Lee Mackler handed him a payroll sheet, which each cop was to sign before receiving his salary. "This isn't going to do us a helluva lot of good. They're all using those damned aliases, and there's no telling one from the other."

Pomeroy said that after he paid the cops, he'd take a quick walk around the site, pay a visit to the Yasgur house, and then head back to his cottage for a short nap. Fabbri would be in touch with the office while he was away.

"This has turned into a farce," Roberts commented, after his chief of security left the building. "The cops are screwing the chicks, the local merchants are screwing the kids, the kids are screwing the residents, and *everybody* is screwing us. The kids, the cops, Michael and Artie, Food For Love, Monticello Racetrack—we're not being screwed, we're being riveted into the ground."

"Well, look on the brighter side," Joel wisecracked, "it can't get any worse."

Predictably, though, it could. Lawrence called a few minutes later with perhaps the most depressing news since the festival began. A seventeen-year-old boy named Raymond Miszik, from Trenton, New Jersey, had been asleep in his sleeping bag when a tractor rolled over him. Miszik was rushed to the helicopter where doctors, awaiting transportation for the boy to a local hospital, administered artificial respiration with a small hand pump. He died, however, before one of the helicopters landed. They were informed that the boy's body had already been removed to a hospital in Monticello pending notification of the parents.

Roberts and Rosenman were distraught. The likelihood of death— a *youngster's* death—was something they hadn't even considered for a moment. Suddenly their responsibility had transcended the bounds of reality; they were plunged into a preposterous black comedy whose savage improprieties seemed to have no end.

"I can't believe this is happening to us," Roberts grieved. "We've never fucked anybody in our lives. And now this. If I had not financed this festival, come to this site, done everything I had done, this person would not have died. I hold myself personally responsible for this boy's death." Tears welled up in John's eyes and he appeared on the verge of nervous collapse.

Joel led his friend into the back office and closed the door. "You can't do this to yourself, man, and you've got to pull yourself out of it. Hell, I don't like it any better than you do. Neither of us ever dreamed that we'd be linked to anybody's death. But it happened, and we've got to deal with it until this thing is over." He paused for a moment, and listened by the door in case someone was eavesdropping on their conversation. Satisfied what they were saying was confidential, he continued. "Look, John, there must be around 500,000 people out there—all around us. In any given group of 500,000, how many people do you think die over a three-day period? You know as well as I do that the answer to that is a lot more than one person. I think we're ahead of the game." He realized the callousness of his statement, and qualified it. "I'm blown away by it too, man, but we owe it to the rest of those kids to keep our heads and see they get out of here all right. You think Michael and Artie give a shit about their welfare? They're vacationing on some other planet and my opinion is that we leave them there—forever, if possible."

Roberts laughed at Joel's observation of their spaced-out partners and wiped at the corners of his eyes. "They'd have the whole crowd on a cosmic vacation if they could. Kalaparusha!" he mimicked, and they both broke up.

"You got it, man," Joel slapped him on the shoulder and stood up. "C'mon, we'd better get out there before they have Ticia or one of their other cronies selling tickets for seats on the first psychedelic space shuttle."

Roberts weakly pulled himself out of the chair, and, together, they went back into the main office prepared to fend off the further consequences of their first business venture.

Water pressure had been the most erratic of utilities since the festival opened on Wednesday. In any given span of time, the pumping gauges could read normal, dip to a trickle, and shoot up to near bursting to the utter horror of the county health inspector sent to monitor the supply.

The plastic pipes had been breaking at a faster rate than the crews were able to repair them. The difficulty wasn't so much in tying off the leaks as it was in locating them. Kids who stepped through a pipe, fearing they would be held responsible for a gross misdemeanor and sent home, ran the other way instead of notifying a festival official. Morris had made an announcement the night before begging people who had "accidentally" stepped on a pipe to report it as soon as possible, but guilt feelings obviously outweighed those of responsibility. No one heeded Morris's advice.

Langhart and his crew of engineers and college professors had been up all night following the water lines. Wherever a leak was spotted, they radioed for assistance and a backup unit was dispatched with the proper equipment to do the job. Mud had clogged some of the pipes preventing the water from being pumped uphill, and they had to be dismantled and cleaned out. Pumping mechanisms were inspected for wear and tear, and frayed parts were replaced. At one juncture, Langhart encountered two pipes, with sixty to seventy pounds of water in each, laid right over a rock. "That's rather idiotic," Langhart remarked to a friend as he climbed out of the jeep to reroute the duct. "If they get banged against the rock or someone drops something on them, they'll split in two." In another location, he came upon a tent pitched over the water line. Somebody had to have been unconscious to sleep on top of a plastic connecting joint holding seventy-five pounds of water in it. Again, Langhart stopped to untangle the pipes and move the tent off to the side. "If that pipe had gone off under the tent," Langhart told his assistant, "it would have had the entire lake pumped up there in less than an hour." He scratched the back of his head and looked at his work. "The problem is that nobody has any idea what's going on here. They're just in bliss, and it's just wonderful. That's the trouble with this generation—they're so used to having things done for them, with everything being so rosy. Let's just hope that nothing drastic goes wrong here this weekend. These kids wouldn't know what to do if their life depended on it."

— **2** —

The music had resumed at 12:15 P.M. with an unknown group from Boston named Quill. The band's manager was someone whom Lang had hung out with in Miami, and the two musical "movers" had cooked up a plan to introduce the group to a captive audience of 300,000 potential album buyers in hope of cashing in on it afterwards. Depending upon how the group went over, they, as Quill's managers, could demand a heavy recording advance and bill them as the new band that had been invited to play at Woodstock *before* making it on the charts. It was a slot that had been originally reserved for the now defunct Train.

Ironically, Lang's formula for creating a rock legacy was more innovative than Quill's ability as a band deserved. They were a mediocre talent at best, who would be hard pressed to captivate the most tepid pop-music listener, much less the connoisseurs of undiluted acid rock who at present sat in deliberation on the group's future. In an attempt to ingratiate themselves from the opening chord, Quill took the stage and tossed maracas into the crowd. Failing to draw an energetic response with that weary device, they began flinging anything else they could get their hands on to help them knock out the audience. Nothing, however, improved their status. Following a less-than-respectable performance, they were demoted to the free stage where they were expected to earn their keep for the remainder of the weekend before lapsing into certain obscurity.

Keef Hartley followed Quill with a hard-driving set of English blues, only to relinquish the spotlight to yet another newcomer on the rock scene. The Santana Blues Band had been the bright stars of the Atlantic City Pop Festival in June and were emerging as a vital musical force out of the Bay Area, a locale that had just about run its course as an international music capital. But, otherwise, their distinctive brand of Latin rock wasn't widely known and they were regarded as intruders on a bill of established gods. The band's Mexican-born leader, Carlos Santana, the son of a Mariachi musician, had been a standout on one of the year's most heralded albums, *The Live Adventures of Mike Bloomfield and Al Kooper,* and was a noted session man on the San Francisco club circuit. When Santana formed his own band in 1969, he added a conga player named Mike Carrabello and Jose "Chepito" Areas—Central America's poll-winning percussionist—to a standard rhythm section of friends he had worked with in the past, and their debut album on Columbia Records had been released a few weeks prior to the festival.

Santana's appearance at Woodstock proved to be one of the festival's uncontested highlights. Their searing performance took the audience by complete surprise, and, some say, was responsible for keeping the event peaceful. By the time Quill had crept offstage, the temperature had climbed to ninety-two degrees with a ninety-seven percent relative-humidity chaser. The bowl had turned into a sauna, and emotions, fueled by the boredom emanating from the stage, began to heat up. Halfway through Keef Hartley's set, the sauna evolved into a pressure cooker. Hartley, the former drummer for John Mayall's Bluesbreakers, had kicked around the hard-rock stratosphere for some time without finding his niche of commercial acceptance. Now, the crowd decided, wasn't the right time for Hartley to make his move, and they tuned him out in favor of getting high. But they were still trapped in the amphitheatre, in the sweltering heat and mud, and one could sense the crowd's growing discomfort swell into a human time bomb. Many hippies had woken up cranky from a restless night's sleep, their clothing was damp and uncomfortable, and hunger pangs whipped impatience into a case of jangled nerves. It was an exact reenactment of a pricklish situation Pomeroy had described to the staff back in June, which they had striven to avoid. When Chip announced Santana, the staff held its breath. They knew that the next act would hold the key to the festival's rocky future, and Santana wasn't exactly a hands-down favorite to save the day.

From the first drum roll, however, Santana disarmed the crowd and forced a breath of fresh air into that muggy bowl. Their sound was a novel approach to rock, and Carlos's sassy guitar whistled at the crowd like a snake charmer sounding his Svengali-like tune. Santana brought the crowd to its feet, culminating in a frantic version of "Soul Sacrifice," which became a focal point of festival gossip and catapulted the group to instant stardom— Bill Graham's original prediction.

When Santana turned the stage over to Mountain, the near-hysteria created by the rock neophytes mellowed into inextinguishable rapture. Leslie West, a New York favorite, fed the crowd's rock and roll appetites until they were sated and set the tone for the rest of the day's entertainment. The best, as the audience knew only too well, was yet to come.

Lee Mackler, who had been stranded at the Holiday Inn, called Roberts at the security office with a proposition. "Well, I'm in Liberty," she said tamely. She knew they'd be swamped with work. "There's no getting through anymore—not even on the back roads. If you want me back, you're going to have to ransom me."

"Ah, that sounds remotely familiar," Roberts kidded. "Let me see—

you're from the Hog Farm? No, that's not it—wait, ransom . . . ransom. . . . You've got to be a friend of Lang's. Okay—I'm licked," he surrendered. "How much is it gonna cost me?"

"C'mon, John! I'm serious. How am I going to get back there to help you guys?"

He advised her to find a ride to Grossinger's. The roads between the motel and the resort were clear, and they had a helicopter on the roof, which Jennie Grossinger had been kind enough to let Woodstock Ventures use for emergencies. "This is an emergency," Roberts said. "I'll send a helicopter for you."

An army jet helicopter was waiting when Lee arrived and whisked her back to White Lake. "It was one of the most incredible experiences of my life, seeing all those people from the air," she recalled, describing the view of Bethel and its surrounding communities. "All one could see for miles, or so it seemed at the time, was bodies. I looked down at one point and felt that it was like Auschwitz. Everyone was crammed together, and they seemed to be holding each other. It sent a chill through me. And when we landed, it looked like the helicopter was swooping down on top of people. I remember thinking, well, we're going to hit thirty or forty kids and nobody'll know the difference."

Artie Kornfeld came in on a helicopter right behind Mackler's. That morning he had concluded a deal for the movie rights with Fred Weintraub at Warner Brothers that gave the studio distribution for a token $1-million advance against royalties. The deal involved absolutely no risk for the movie company. The newspapers had set the festival's attendance (however incorrectly) at 500,000 people. If Warner's did absolutely *no* advertising for the film and merely counted on those who had attended the festival to buy a $4 ticket to the movie, they'd double their investment. And that was without taking television rights into account. The deal was money in the bank for Warner's. Of course, producer's points had yet to be negotiated, and John and Joel would have to agree on the terms before the deal was valid, but that, as far as Artie cared, was a formality. He had already discussed the terms of the agreement with Paul Marshall who had given it his blessing. Roberts and Rosenman valued Marshall's opinion as if it were the almighty word. On Monday, they'd bank a cool million, Artie surmised, and he'd be a wealthy man.

Food For Love spent most of Saturday afternoon in anguish as they watched their fortune being dissipated by disorganization and squalor.

From the moment they opened for business, Joerger suspected that not everything was being handled aboveboard as far as their sales were concerned. To control the flow of money, they had set up two booths, manned by Pinkerton guards, where tickets were sold for refreshments. The tickets, in turn, could be used at any of Food For Love's sixteen stands. That delivered his young vendors from the temptation of handling cash, but not necessarily from evil, as Joerger soon discovered. He had spotted tickets being turned in that were caked with mud or mustard or hot chocolate, which moved him to investigate their origin; it was inconceivable that his ticket salesmen managed to spill so much food in booths where no food was allowed. Of course, it didn't take him long to catch on to what was happening. Instead of ripping the tickets in half and dropping the pieces into the slots of their aprons, his vendors were stuffing handfuls of whole tickets into their pockets and passing them on to their friends. Joerger estimated that about fifty percent of Food For Love's sales were from tickets they had already redeemed. He fired the perpetrators whenever he caught one of them red-handed and hired replacements. But it didn't take long before the new workers were up to the same thing. No one worried about the consequences. Being fired from concession work became a status symbol. They only had to depend on three days' employment anyway, so they played it for what they could take, and if they were caught—so what?

Occasionally, Joerger observed his employees waiting in line at the Johns to relieve themselves of more than nature's complaint. He interrupted the call of more than one of his vendors only to find that the kid had emptied the contents of his or her apron on the floor of the toilet. A friend, waiting next in line, would retrieve the tickets and sell them at half-price to eager customers in the woods.

Joerger tried to have himself or one of his associates police the area, making sure the workers ripped the tickets in half, but that soon gave way to other, more urgent matters, which necessitated their immediate attention.

Coca-Cola had sent Food For Love approximately 500 cases of soda with cans that were only half-filled, and kids were angrily returning them, claiming they had been "ripped off by capitalist pigs."

The concessionaires had ordered an additional six refrigerated tractor-trailers of frankfurters and hamburger meat at the last minute and the caravan had miraculously made it through the traffic late Friday night. By midafternoon, they had run out of fuel for the refrigeration and had no way of getting an oil truck into the site to refill the tanks. Within two hours after the depletion, a forty-foot tractor-trailer full of frankfurters began to spoil.

The stench was unbearable, although it was not quite as repulsive as the malodor from a newly excavated septic pool behind the command trailer that wafted across the hilltop. Lawrence had found the Johnny-On-The-Spot representative earlier in the day and presented him with the problems of disposing of the wastes from the portable toilets. Most of the units, by this time, had overflowed, and the swill was polluting not only the air but the earth. Puddles of putrid sewage collected in the mud and notched furrows in the ground that headed downhill. They had to find some way of curtailing the seepage before it ran into the bowl.

"There's only one thing we can do," explained the sanitation engineer, "and it's not what I'd call the most civilized answer to the problem."

"*Anything*," Lawrence pleaded, "we'll do anything you say. Just make it go away, man."

"Well—you dig a ditch, you pump all the shit in it, and you cover it over with dirt."

"*That's it?*" Lawrence was incredulous.

"What did you want me to say—that we'll hire helicopters to airlift it out in paper bags?"

"Well, no . . . I just thought . . ."

"That's your only alternative. Otherwise, it'll just get worse. Especially in the heat. And forget about it if it rains. We'll be swimming in crap."

That was all Lawrence needed to hear. He ordered Bill Reynolds to gather his crew together, picked a spot behind his office, and had them dig a ditch eighty feet long by eight feet deep with a backhoe, into which they emptied the tanks from each unit. They dumped an enormous quantity of chemicals into the pit before covering it over to keep the intensity of the smell down, but the chemicals were generally overpowered by its potency.

"Now it was a city dump," the New York *Post* decreed. "The flies clung to your arms. The stink attacked your stomach." The *News* was equally severe in its criticism, describing the site as "a morass of mud, music, and misery." It went on to note that "police feared a major medical crisis because of the nightlong rain which created huge pools of mud."

Once the papers hit the newsstands, Lawrence's trailer was inundated with calls from alarmed parents whose children had gone to White Lake "and had not been heard from since."

"Don't worry about them," Lawrence told each caller. "They're fine. Everything's beautiful, groovy. Your kid has never been in a more secure atmosphere in his life. Don't believe everything you read in the papers." But each parent wanted to know if it was safe for his or her child. "Safe?" Lawrence scoffed. "Where's your kid from? . . . New York City! Lady—what would your kid know about safe? You think he's gonna be mugged in a pasture full of hippies? Take it easy. You'll see him on Monday morning, and you'll probably wish he'd take another three-day vacation like this one."

The board of health called, too, wanting to know more about the "major medical crisis" they were reading about. Their inspector, who had been assigned to spend the weekend on the grounds, had made the mistake of bringing his teen-age daughter along with him. They became separated as soon as the crowds started arriving, and the man spent most of his waking hours attempting to find her. Every so often the inspector poked his head into the command trailer to find out if his daughter had surfaced. Mel insisted the man first call his regional office and give the festival a clean bill of health before he provided the information.

"Everything's fine here," the inspector reported to his supervisors in Albany. "There's no need for you to implement supplementary action at this time. There appears to be plenty of food and water in reserve, good sanitation facilities. We've checked the medical centers, and the staff seems to have the situation well under control." After hanging up, the man would beseechingly ask Lawrence about his daughter's whereabouts.

"Sorry, nobody's seen or heard from her," he'd reply, upon which the inspector would frantically vanish into the crowd for another two hours.

"Our only hope of staying afloat," Lawrence told an associate, "is that the chick is banging her brains out in some motel room. As long as she stays out of sight until Monday, we'll keep the board of health off our back."

About three o'clock, in the middle of Santana's set, Michael Lang made his one and only call to the security building that weekend. Someone handed the phone to John Roberts and backed off, not wishing to get caught in the certain exchange of verbal gunfire.

Michael was calling, he said, from some far-off cosmic heaven. "Hey, man, it's beautiful here. You really oughta come down."

"Hey, man, it's *not* beautiful here," Roberts snapped. "*You* really should come over. Michael, seriously—we're going nuts over here. This thing has gotten out of hand, and we're trying desperately to dig ourselves out from under this mess. We sure could use your help. We have no way of knowing what you promised everybody and, therefore, it's been impossible assessing what our obligation is to them. All afternoon, people have been barging in here demanding money, threatening to sabotage the festival unless we turn over a great deal of cash to them. The governor's office calls every fifteen minutes wanting to send in the National Guard. It's a goddamn zoo. Really—how about coming over here and giving us a hand?"

"Aw, man, y'see that's where you and Joel have got it all wrong," Lang complained. "You cats are out of it. Y'know, you're too uptight about all that money shit. We've done the incredible, man. We pulled off the biggest fuckin' party anyone in our generation's ever seen. It's beautiful. We've got some-thin' like 400,000 people groovin' on the music. We're heroes, man. Dig it. You gotta get into the vibes. Look, close up that office and make it over here. This is for all of us to enjoy."

"We can't do that, Michael. We've got too much at stake here," Roberts said aggravatedly.

"Suit yourself, man. I gotta split. Hey—hang on a second! Artie wants to lay a few words on you."

Roberts suppressed the urge to tell Lang what he wanted to lay on Artie. Why waste his breath, he thought.

"Whoooah! Man! How's it goin', guys?" Artie was orbiting the earth on some unknown stellar energy. "Hey! Yeah—this is really great!"

Roberts cupped his hand over the mouthpiece and yelled for everyone else in the office to get on an extension. "You've gotta hear this. But don't you *dare* laugh," he said, already chuckling.

"How are you, Artie? We haven't heard from you in—oh, it must be months."

"Right on, man! This is really great. It's incredible here. All our friends are here, man. My *God*—I'm freaking out!"

"Well, get ahold of yourself, Artie, and tell me what it is you wanted to say."

"Oh yeah—right. Look, man, I need six cases of Coke right away. Six cases—you got that?"

"I got it. What do you need six cases of Coke for?"

"What do I need it for?" Artie repeated softly. "Uh, let me see . . . oh yeah, like Creedence is here, man, and they're real thirsty. How 'bout sendin' a messenger over with it right away?"

"Well"—Roberts stalled for time while he motioned for the security as-sistants to stop their shrieking—"I'll see what I can do, Artie. You do realize that it's a little inconvenient right now."

"No sweat, man. I'll send a limo for it."

The office was in hysterics at that, and Roberts had a difficult time hear-ing. "Good idea!" he spurred him on. "You do that. We'll wait for it to get here, and then we'll put your sodas on the back seat and speed them right back to you. Oh, and speaking of speed, Artie—take it easy, will you. You're liable to break the sound barrier in your condition."

"Out-ta sight!" Artie hollered, and hung up.

"We ought to consider ourselves lucky," Joel said, helping one of the assistants who had rolled onto the floor back up to her feet. "I took the last 'Artie Call' and it was for imported champagne. I think he's finally beginning to realize and appreciate the value of a dollar."

"God! I hope they don't hurt themselves over there," Lee cried, wiping away the tears from her eyes. "They're in bad shape."

Mackler, in fact, had been given the inside track as far as Michael and Artie's physical conditions were concerned. A half hour earlier, Penny had called her from the stage and said, "You'll never guess what those assholes are doing. They're tripping!"

"I don't believe it!" Lee told her.

"I swear. They each did a tab of acid in the midst of all this delirium," Penny said. "Listen, the reason I'm calling is that someone told me they were running all over the place trying to find Thorazine for Artie. What in the hell is Thorazine?"

Lee explained that it was a drug used in bringing kids down from a bad trip. It was used after more conventional methods—like talking someone down—failed. "I believe you now, kid," Lee said. "Just stay away from him for the time being, okay? It'll wear off if people leave Artie alone."

John Morris had also called Lee with an update on the show and told her to forget about Lang and Kornfeld for the rest of the weekend. "They just dropped another tab for good luck. We should get a postcard from them from Mars sometime next month."

Morris recounted a stunt that Artie had pulled that, according to John, set staff relations back about six months. A production supervisor had gone out of his trailer in search of wellheads for Langhart's field crew, and, when he returned, found all of his belongings piled on the ground outside. Artie and his wife had moved into the trailer, kicking the supervisor out of a place he'd been living in and working from for the last five weeks. It was as insensitive and inconsiderate an act as anyone had experienced since coming together to work on the festival, and it served to alienate Artie from a large segment of the executive staff who were informed of the incident. "The supervisor just took off for the city," Morris said, "and I don't think he plans on coming back."

Artie's frantic calls to the security office began coming about as frequently as Bert Cohen's (who was still marooned somewhere on the Thruway between Middletown and Monticello). He wanted them to rush the order on that soda (Creedence wanted their Coke) or to find some crystal wine glasses from which the Band could sip champagne or to enclose a packet of blank Woodstock Venture checks so he could draw on petty cash. And with each phone call, Artie's voice grew more detached, as though he was slipping off into his own insular world. At first, whoever picked up one of Artie's calls tried to humor him, but after a while, it became too time-consuming and Joel had them ignore his "partner" completely, placing the phone receiver on a desk for a length of time before simply hanging up. Two of the original Four Musketeers, Joel decided, had drawn their last word.

Around four o'clock, Morris made another call to the security office for the purpose of realigning the concert. He thought it might be wise to have the bands play extended sets so that each day's show would end the following morning. That would eliminate all the kids having to be on the road at night. But it would also require their clearing it first with the artists' managers so that contracts would not be violated. Roberts and Rosenman concurred with his reasoning and agreed to gently broach the subject with one of the groups' representatives in order to "feel them out before throwing it open to negotiation."

"Is there any group in particular whom you think we should talk to?" they asked him.

Morris hardly afforded the question a moment's thought. "No doubt about it—the Grateful Dead. I've seen those guys go all night at the Filmore, and the crowd loves them. They're also sympathetic to things like this. They play free shows in People's Park all the time."

Rosenman located the Dead's road manager at the Holiday Inn at Liberty and asked him politely whether or not his group would mind playing for a longer period of time than was stipulated in the performance contract.

Their manager, a young man with an intimidating tone of voice, sounded a bit cautious about discussing business over the phone. His manner was presumptuous, and he acted as though Joel were setting him up for a string. "What's the matter, man? You guys in trouble?"

"Not at all," Joel insisted. "Everything's going quite smoothly."

"I mean bread trouble."

Joel emphatically denied the implication and explained Morris's theory aimed at keeping kids off the road. "We're also overcrowded," Joel added, "and we want to avoid people roaming around and getting into trouble because the stage is dark. Morris told me that the Dead are one of the few groups who can do an extra hour or two with no trouble. So, I'll restate the question: Will your guys play another set or what?"

"We're not gonna play at all, man."

Joel felt all the muscles in his body tense, and he threw himself forward in his chair. "What are you talking about?"

"You heard me," he said impertinently. "You guys are in some kind of trouble. We're not going on stage without our money."

"Without your money? *Without your money?*" Rosenman shouted into the phone. His hand swept across the desk in anger, and he knocked a half-filled cup of coffee onto the floor. "What the fuck are you talking about? You'll get your money just like everybody else, pal."

"Yeah? How's that?"

"By check, when your band goes on."

The manager's tone remained unchanged. "That's not good enough."

Joel assured him that every other act had been and would continue to be paid that way. It was the only system for which they were set up.

"Fuck the other acts, man. We want cash. I'm convinced that you're in some kind of trouble, and I'm here to make sure the Dead don't get burned."

"Cash! Where the hell do you expect me to get cash on a Saturday night in the middle of Sullivan County?"

The manager said that raising money was Woodstock Ventures' problem; his was getting the group to the gig and making sure they got paid—in cash.

"Listen, forget the whole thing," Rosenman backed off. "Forget I called you. Have the Dead just play their normal set, and . . ."

"Bullshit! You want us to go on, you'd better get that second fifty percent in cash or a certified check." Otherwise, he said in no uncertain terms, the group would be on the next plane out of Sullivan County International Airport. Then he hung up.

Rosenman checked the Dead's contract. The payment was $7,500—about $5,000 more than they had on hand in cash. If they gave in to the demand, it would leave them without a cent for any one of the hundred or so other emergencies that were bound to crop up in the next two days. They also had to pay the police. No, it was out of the question. He called John Morris back and filled him in on the new developments.

"It stinks!" Morris agreed.

"Yeah, well there's no way in hell we're going to be able to lay our hands on that kind of cash. So tell me this: What'll happen if I tell this guy to go fuck himself and the Dead doesn't go on?"

"The crowd'll tear us to pieces."

"Thanks for your discretion, John. But that's what I thought you'd say. Okay, look, I'm going to give it the old college try. If their manager asks you anything about our arrangements with the Dead, tell him I'll be there with the bread. Don't let them leave. And, for God's sake, don't let him mention a thing about this to any of his pals from the other acts we've got booked. If a thing like this gets out, it could snowball, and if it snowballs, more than our assets will be frozen."

At practically the same time, Ticia Bernuth was engaged in a similar confrontation with John Wolff, the Who's manager, who had been reluctant to let his group appear at Woodstock in the first place. Ticia had been on her way from the performers' pavilion to the stage when the irate Wolff accosted her on the bridge. He demanded the rest of the Who's money up front and in cash.

"Hey, man, like, y'know—that's not my bag," Ticia said. Wolff's volatile disposition frightened her, and she wanted to get away from him as quickly as possible. As she went to move around him, he blocked her path.

"If you fuckin' don't get Michael Lang to pay me, I'm not going to let my group go on!" he screamed.

Not knowing what else to do, Ticia started to cry. Wolff pushed her out of his way and stomped off toward the food tent.

In reality, it had been partly Ticia's fault that none of the festival's creditors had been able to get hold of Lang to discuss finances. Michael did not want to hear about money matters as long as there was music on stage, and Ticia spent a lot of time hiding Michael, moving him from trailer to trailer, until the person trying to find him just gave up and went away. This time, however, she thought she should tell him about Wolff's ultimatum.

"Fuck it," he said. "Those guys are gonna play if it's the last thing they do. All we do is get up and tell everybody that the Who won't play because they didn't get paid yet. This place'll go nuts." He smirked at Ticia, and leaned back against the stage railing to enjoy one of his favorite bands. It was dusk, and Canned Heat was doing to the crowd what any respectable Los Angeles band would do to a group of 400,000 people on a Saturday night at dusk: they were singing the blues.

Lawrence was in his trailer when Canned Heat launched into an off-key, static version of "On The Road Again." Bob "The Bear" Hite's voice sounded strained and lost in the cavernous amphitheatre. Nonetheless, the crowd was on its feet and bouncing up and down in time to the pulsating beat of the bass guitar.

Peter Goodrich knocked on the door of Lawrence's trailer and entered, looking very pale and withdrawn. The colonies, once loyal to his burgeoning fast-food empire, had fallen away from him like defensive tackles meeting the unexpected blitz—and in less than seventy-two hours. First, Food For Love had Goodrich deposed as their partner-in-grime, then the employees mess hall was abruptly pulled out from under his control, and he was ultimately relieved of his command in the performers' pavilion. Now, he had additional woes, and all he felt like doing was lying down on a cot and sinking into sleep.

"There's a group holing up in the woods who want to liberate the food," Goodrich said dejectedly. "What do you want to do about it?"

"What are you talkin' about, man? What group and what food? And what the hell does liberation have to do with ten thousand putrid franks and a couple of half-filled cans of Coke?"

"It's one of those half-cocked power-to-the-people groups, about fifty troublemakers who are screaming themselves silly about taking back what's by rights theirs and distributing it among the underprivileged. Are you kidding me?" he scoffed. "Underprivileged—at this bash? That's a laugh."

Lawrence got up from his desk and looked out the window at the concession stands, all of which seemed to be doing brisk business. "I'm not laughing. Go and get Lenny down by the stage, and tell him to get his Black Shirt security guys up here in a jiffy. I don't want any fucking 'liberating the food' going on now. Not after we've been this lucky."

The group was called the Up-Against-The-Wall Motherfuckers, a collection of mostly apolitical New York hellraisers who got their kicks out of inciting a crowd to riot and picking over the spoils. Word had spread through the staff that a few of them were Hell's Angels and had come to Bethel that afternoon at the invitation of the Hog Farm, but nobody knew for sure.

Lawrence, Goodrich, Lenny and his task force of bruisers, and a hand-picked entourage of the more muscular stagehands descended on the Up-Against-The-Wall Motherfuckers' camp in the woods and confronted the group's spokesman, a rather meek-looking college type more suited to the SDS than a Harley-Davidson 1000. "We're gonna liberate the food," he reaffirmed, looking apprehensively from one festival representative to the next.

"That's just peachy," Lawrence said. "What are you going to do with it once you get it? And whaddya mean you're going to liberate it?"

The boy stood his ground. "We're going to give it out to the people."

"I'm gonna punch 'em out, man," Lenny growled, taking a step toward the leader.

"Hang on a minute." Mel restrained the Black Shirt with a gentle, but firm, arm on his cannonball bicep. He turned back to the agitator. "Do you have any idea how many people are out there, man? Give the food to the people—that's bullshit! What are they going to get? I'll tell you: nothing. You fuckers want it for yourselves. Now, I'm going to give you a choice. Either you guys lay off and go back to playing revolution, or I'm going to let Lenny and his friends take you apart."

Lenny smiled, as if that appealed to him more than a peaceful settlement. "You'd better believe it. You guys—if you ever try something like that, you're going to be dead men."

Fifteen minutes later, after Mel and his own motherfuckers had departed, Abbie Hoffman told Lang and Morris that the group had decided to carry out its original plan and were getting ready to burn down the concession stands and everything in them. "And, oh yeah"—Hoffman fluttered his hands—"you didn't hear this from me."

Lang got on the phone and called Jeffrey Joerger in the concession trailer. "You'd better get your security up," Lang said.

"What're you talkin' about, man. What security? We don't have any security here other than a few ticket guards."

"Well, man, you better tell the people that are workin' for you to be careful. There's somebody comin' up there to take over the stands."

"Aw shit. Then let 'em do it. I give up, anyway. Let 'em take over whatever they want. Whatever they take over, we'll just eliminate." Joerger was fed up with all the nonsense he'd been through since he arrived at White Lake. Without waiting to find out what was going to happen, he picked up the phone, called Albany, and requested of Governor Rockefeller's office that they declare the Woodstock Music Festival a disaster area.

Charles Baxter was the first of Food For Love's principals to see the detachment of Up-Against-The-Wall Motherfuckers come charging up over the hill, and he knew right away what had to be done. Baxter ran back to the trailers and forced those of his staff who were inside to evacuate at once. "If they start to push over the trailers, then join in and help them. Don't act like you're a part of the concession staff. That's the only way we're gonna get through this thing without being beaten to a pulp."

Stan Goldstein and Hugh Romney came shooting over the rise in a dune buggy as the Motherfuckers reached their destination. Baxter rushed out to meet them, found himself caught between the two factions, and was made to answer for the concessionaires' "crimes against the people." The Up-Against-The-Wall Motherfuckers accused Food For Love of everything from selling horsemeat hamburgers at a premium to making a 300-percent profit on a 35-cent hot dog to purposely not paying for fuel so the People would have to eat cold meat.

Baxter vehemently denied each of the accusations, but suggested to Goldstein that Food For Love would donate a quantity of the food to the group's cause and the Hog Farm could dispense it as they saw fit.

Hugh Romney was offended by Baxter's offer. He gestured with his arm at the mass of people sitting in the bowl and said, "We couldn't possibly feed your food to these people. They're all vegetarians."

But Goldstein, not wanting to stand by and watch hand-to-hand combat surge across the plateau, talked Romney into accepting the gift. Then he advised the concessionaires to consolidate their holdings into a few booths because, like it or not, the Up-Against-The-Wall Motherfuckers were probably going to set a torch to their stands, and they might as well salvage what they could.

By 9:30 Saturday night, Food For Love's sixteen stands were reduced to four, their nonperishable stock was heavily depleted by sales, decay, and charity, and their once-palatial grouping of twelve decorated stands had been burned to the ground.

The following rolled off the Hog Farm mimeograph machine soon after the fire and was distributed to the crowd:

SURVIVE-SURVIVE—BE HIP SURVIVE-SURVIVE BULLETIN. . . . *** 8 P.M. Saturday

Welcome to Hip City, U.S.A. We are now the third largest city in New York, and like New York City basic services are breaking down. Gov. Rockefeller has declared us a disaster area. The situation now: limited food, a great scarcity of water, crowded but improving medical facilities, the N.Y. City press reports hiways will be clogged until Tuesday. Meanwhile everyone is cooperating and our spirits are good. With the mud, traffic and breakdowns we could be here several days.

The festival promoters have been overwhelmed by their own creation. They've created a great free festival, but we can't remain passive music consumers; we must take care of ourselves. Everything might seem groovy now, but think about tomorrow. Life could get hard. If you're hip to the facts below, pull together in the spirit of the Catskill mountain guerilla, and share—everything will be cool. We've had virtually no cops, and there's been no violence. We can take care of ourselves. Dig it!

ACCESS—/// The hiways leading to the festival site are now blocked. Cars are being turned back in an effort to clear hiway 17-B which is now reported moving slowly in both directions. It's suggested that people head west (right) on 17-B to Rt. 52 and turn right toward Liberty and the Quickway.

SANITATION—Please stay off the roads. Garbage trucks need clear rights-of-way to pick up trash. Either burn trash or dump it in bags along the road (Use the heavy green bags). We must clear up our own areas or there will be a severe health hazard.

MEDICAL—There are three medical stations. Minor stuff (cuts and bruises) can be taken care of at the South Station in the Hog Farm, or at the health trailer at the main intersection (behind the stage). A plane load of doctors has been airlifted from New York City. Medical supplies have been flown in and patients are being flown out every fifteen minutes. Serious injuries will be treated at the large red and white tent behind the information booth located at the west corner of the stage area. Drug freakouts will be tended by Hog Farm people (red armbands). Any trained medical personnel should report to the above medical centers. // Many freakouts. Do not take any acid from strangers, and understand that taking strong dop may be a drag when your help is needed. // Don't run naked in the hot sun for any period of time (do it in the shade). You're risking water loss and severe blisters. // Cuts on bare feet getting quickly infected if not treated. // People using chronic medications should report to medical centers for refills, but don't wait.

WATER—Try to boil all drinking water or use prepared beverages. New mains are being readied. Black and white pipes are water pipes; don't walk on them, they break easily. The lake is now the main source of water. Swimming will fuck things up. Share and conserve all water.

FOOD—Food is being airlifted into the festival grounds. Free food in the concession area; and the Hog Farm will continue to serve free meals in South camping area.

HINTS—Organize your own camping area so that everyone will make it through uncomfortable times ahead. Figure out what you must do and the best way to get it done.

VOLUNTEERS AND PEOPLE WHO CAN HELP DISTRIBUTE THIS LEAFLET SHOULD COME TO MOVEMENT CITY AREA IN THE SOUTH CAMPGROUND (ACROSS FROM ENTRANCE TO HOG FARM) READ AND PASS ON.

Saturday night's audience seemed to be comprised of two very distinct types of people: the healthy and the wounded, and no one was really sure which group was in the majority. The hospital tents averaged a turnover of nearly two hundred bodies every hour (about five percent of whom were airlifted to Sullivan and Orange County hospital facilities better geared for the patient), and the line outside Abruzzi's trailer resembled one waiting to get into a blockbuster movie in New York City. The demand for free medical care might have put Blue Cross in hock up to their stethoscopes had that company insured the patients. Instead, Woodstock Ventures underwrote the complete cost of treatment on bad checks, sending out regularly for new shipments of supplies to meet the inflated market.

Abruzzi's staff had sewn and bandaged close to 2,500 cut feet. Most of the mishaps were attributed to kids running around barefoot in the mud, although those who had slipped on the rocks around the lake were beginning to give the cut feet a good run for their money. Cleaning the wounds was time-consuming but considered absolutely essential to prevent infection resulting from foreign matter mixed in with the mud. If the wound was deep and looked as though it might reopen, the doctors wrapped the patient's foot in a plastic bag to keep it dirt free. Otherwise gauze and Ace bandages proved satisfactory until the kids returned home and saw their private physicians for a thorough examination. Several cases of insulin shock were treated (it seemed that, for some inexplicable reason, the entire hippie community of diabetics hadn't considered bringing their medication with them when they left for the weekend away from home), and attacks of bronchial asthma ran high on the "casualty" list, but broken limbs and more serious injuries had diminished since Friday's medical onslaught occurred.

The tents—especially those in the campgrounds—had been overrun by kids who were bummed out on trips. The sharp rise in freakouts was due in part to heavy sales competition going on in the woods, which had lowered the prices of psychedelic drugs considerably. A cap of acid or mescaline had dropped from a Thursday afternoon high of six dollars to three or four dollars, depending upon where it was purchased. (Grass, which had been scarce in the United States throughout the summer, remained at fifteen dollars an ounce, and there was plenty of it around for sale.) But as the price of acid dropped, so did its quality. Scores of kids staggered into the tents Saturday night doubled over in pain. Most thought they had been poisoned; others were too scared to venture a guess, especially when it was their own physical conditions on which they were speculating.

The acid that was supposed to be causing the problems, flat blue tabs, was taken off one of the disabled patients and rushed over to the Hog Farm "laboratory" for a quick analysis. By 9:30, they had arrived at an opinion, and rushed it over to the stage so that a general announcement could be made to the crowd.

John Morris followed Canned Heat's performance with the Hog Farm's authoritative verdict. "You aren't taking poison acid," he said, waiting for the applause to subside. "The acid's not poison. It's just badly manufactured acid. You are not going to die. We have treated three hundred cases and it's all just badly manufactured acid. So, if you think you've taken poison, you haven't. But if you're worried, just take half a tablet."

The Hog Farm's method of treating freakouts was referred to as "body contact"—talking to and holding the victims, assuring them that they were all right until they had come down and realized where they were. It was a practice they used successfully among their own family, and they subsequently taught it to whoever assisted them in the tents.

A specific case that night involved a young boy who was covered in mud and wandered into Big Pink mumbling, "Miami Beach, 1944 . . . Joyce, Joyce . . ." Hugh Romney snatched him away from a doctor who was frocked in a white coat, shirt, and tie.

Bending down so that he could look into the boy's deeply troubled face, Romney pointed to his own forehead. "Think of your third eye, man, just center on your third eye." He put an arm around the boy's shoulder and smiled.

"Miami Beach, 1944 . . . Joyce, Joyce . . ." He seemed locked into a thought pattern from which he couldn't escape.

Romney led the boy over to a cot and helped him sit down. "What's your name, man?"

"Miami Beach."

"No, man. I mean what's your name? Your real name?"

The boy stopped to consider the question. "Paul?" he asked, looking at Romney for some sort of confirmation.

"Hey—Paul! Your name is Paul." The boy responded with a wide, elastic grin. "Paul what? You've gotta have a last name, Paul. Paul what?"

"Brown," he mumbled, then let loose with an agreeable endorsement. "Paul Brown! I'm Paul Brown, man."

"Where are you from, Paul Brown?"

"New Jersey."

Romney stood up, still maintaining "body contact" with the boy's shoulder. "Your name is Paul Brown and you're from New Jersey. Outta sight! Guess what, Paul? Well, you just took a little acid, a little LSD, and you know somethin'—it's gonna wear off. Now, I'm gonna be around here, man, and if you need me for anything, just gimme a call. Why don't you keep cool, lay down or somethin' for a while. You're gonna be all right."

When the boy had recovered and prepared to leave the tent, Romney grabbed him and said, "Hold it, man. See that guy comin' through the door? Well, that was you an hour ago and now you're the doctor. Take over." And before long, there was a volunteer staff of former trippers talking their friends down to earth. Occasionally John Sebastian, Rick Danko, or Bobby Neuwirth would stroll through the tent with their guitars, playing for the patients. Abbie Hoffman also rolled up his sleeves and participated in getting kids back on their feet.

In the other tent just across the road, where the Medical Committee For Human Rights had their field hospital, the doctors were torn between performing medical procedures and patiently sitting with those who were tortured by bad reactions to LSD.

At one point during the early hours of evening, Don Goldmacher looked up from setting a broken finger on a young girl and was confronted by "a very paranoid guy who looked very near the breaking stage."

"I have this knife, man," he said, opening a Swiss utility knife with a rusted blade, "and they're after me."

Goldmacher moved very slowly toward the boy, careful not to make too sudden a move that might seem menacing to him. "Who's after you?"

"Oh shit, they're all around, man. If you look, man, you'll see 'em."

Goldmacher nodded sympathetically and resumed his approach. He was a certified psychiatrist and this type of psychotic person was his specialty. "Okay. I'll go look. But tell me—what are they after you about?"

"Everything. They're really after everything, man." The boy jumped back about six feet, and Goldmacher froze. "Don't come any closer, man."

"All right," the doctor assured him. "Don't get uptight. Look, I want to explain something to you. In this tent, nobody's going to hurt you. You're safe here. We'll make sure of that. Do you trust me?"

The boy nodded, unsure of the situation but willing to listen.

"Okay—now, all these people that you see here are working with me. I know all of them, and they won't hurt you. They're our friends. I'm a doctor, and I'll protect you from whoever is out there." Goldmacher studied the weapon in the boy's hand. "What do you want to do with that knife, man?"

"I gotta protect myself!" His attention was drawn back to the pocketknife open in his hand, and it seemed to startle him. "Uh, I better hang on to it for now."

"Fine. You hold on to it. But go over to that cot and rest for a while. Keep the knife under your pillow and just let me know if you have any problems. If anybody's hassling you, don't hurt them, man. Just come and get me, and I'll get them off your back. Okay?"

The boy nodded again and curled up on the stretcher while Goldmacher went back to work on others who were anxiously waiting to see him. There was a rash of upper respiratory infections throughout Saturday night— probably due to people's sleeping on the wet ground—and several hundred head colds, which he treated with antibiotics and aspirin. By morning, patients were backed up for an hour's wait and beds were a rarity.

Goldmacher's knife-wielding tripper lay awake all night. Every so often, he'd dart outside to see if any of his enemies were in sight and then slink back onto the cot in abject depression. Goldmacher sat down with him from time to time, inquiring as to whether or not he had seen any of his tormentors. The boy's answer was always the same: "They're comin', man, I know they're comin'." As the sun came up, however, he became more relaxed. Finally, he popped outside for a quick check of the premises and never came back. Goldmacher was a little concerned for his patient's welfare, but knew that if the boy encountered any problems, he would streak back to the tent. It was safe there, so much so that the boy had left his knife under the pillow for safekeeping.

Joel had gotten ahold of a man named Charlie Prince, the branch manager of the Sullivan County National Bank where Woodstock Ventures had its account, at his home around eleven o'clock. With Canned Heat gone, Creedence halfway through their set, and the Dead scheduled to go on next, Rosenman didn't have a minute to spare and therefore explained his predicament in the most abbreviated account possible. If Prince was a perceptive individual, he'd detect the panic in Joel's voice and interpret it for himself.

Prince and his wife had been following the course of events at the festival on the radio, and the branch manager said he'd be glad to do anything in his power to help the promoters out. His hands were tied, however, when it came to putting up money as there wasn't any cash in the bank for which the boys could write a check, and all other negotiable bonds—bank certified checks, security vouchers, stock—were stashed away in a time-lock vault set to re-open on Monday morning. Even if he had the combination, there was no way of getting inside until then.

Rosenman had all but given up hope of raising the cash to pay the Grateful Dead and was preparing to put out an alert for Wes Pomeroy when Prince called him back. There was an outside chance, Charlie said, that he had forgotten to put away a book of certified checks before leaving the bank on Friday. If that was the case—and it would be a fluke because he had *never* done that before in his entire career at Sullivan National—then the checks were still in his desk drawer.

Rosenman radioed the landing strip behind the stage and had them send a helicopter immediately over to pick up Prince at his home and take him to the bank. Then he waited. And waited. Ten minutes passed, and still there was no word from either Prince or his wife. Another five minutes passed, and *nothing*. Hadn't Prince understood the life-and-death urgency of the situation? Had he misjudged the banker's perspicacity? He hoped not, but then what in the hell was taking Prince so damned long in getting back to him?

As Rosenman pulled out the security directory to look up Pomeroy's number, the phone rang.

It was Charlie Prince. "I'm in the bank, Joel," he said. "Now, I haven't even checked the drawer yet. Keep your fingers crossed."

Another agonizing minute passed during which Rosenman grappled with his own threshold for prayer. He was not a devoutly religious person, but there was no time like the present to come to terms with faith. In sixty seconds' time, Joel made reparation with his Maker for past transgressions and promised to keep his nose clean from here on in if only those checks turned up in Charlie Prince's drawer.

"They're here, Joel! I've got them."

Rosenman looked up at the ceiling and mouthed a silent thank you. "Don't move a muscle, Charlie. Stay right where you are. I'm on my way over."

— **3** —

The generation's crown princes and heirs had been granted the daylight stage to make their bid for ascendancy, and, in most cases, their presentations had been well received. Now, however, the darkness caused the stage to radiate with the majesty of a crystal chandelier, and the loyal subjects hungrily awaited the appearance of their kings and queens. The names were pure magic to the audience—Grace Slick, Marty Balin, Roger Daltry, Peter Townshend, Sly Stone, and, of course, the beaded Persephone, Janis Joplin, who was expected to cast her spell over the crowd as soon as Jerry Garcia pranced the Dead offstage.

"Janis was in a very bad way at the festival as far as drugs were concerned," recalled Myra Friedman, Joplin's long-time friend and biographer. "And on top of that, she was freaked by the crowd. She stared out across that field and thought the audience at Woodstock was made up of too many people for her to reach. 'Too abstract,' Janis kept saying to me before she went on. 'It's just too abstract, Myra.'"

Janis and Grace Slick watched Canned Heat's performance from the back of the stage with petrified intensity. Both women seemed more intent on what lay beyond the footlights, the hundreds of thousands of dancing heads, than Bob Hite's gyroscopic performance only a few feet away from them. "Janis Joplin stood tensely motionless, her mouth set hard," *Rolling Stone* reported, and, indeed, the description was an accurate portrait of her increasing dread of having to entertain the crowd.

From what is known about Janis's movements preceding her segment of the concert, the crowd apparently had a demoralizing effect on her. (Judging from filmed footage of the Airplane's performance, the same can probably be said about Grace Slick.) Janis retreated to the performers' pavilion while the Dead were on stage where, according to John Morris, "she had bottles of vodka and tequila in each hand and was popping them off like crazy."

Morris and Joplin had known each other from the Filmore, and it was John who had suggested she vacation at his house in St. Thomas earlier in the summer. They hadn't seen each other since—John had been tied up with the festival and Janis had been on the road—and she walked over to him while waiting to go on to thank him for the use of the house.

"She was very drunk," Morris remembered, "and very depressed. But she said something to me that night which made my hair stand on end. I hugged her and said, 'How are you, honey? How was St. Thomas?' To which Janis replied, 'Oh yeah, man, thanks. But it was just like anywhere else—I fucked a lot of strangers.'"

Joplin's performance reflected a combination of her blue funk and the misgivings she had about reaching the audience. She clearly lacked the raw enthusiasm for which she was so well known; her intoxicating voice was more liquored than whiskey-hoarse. About all that can be said of her contribution to the festival is that Janis sang her songs and got off quickly. The audience, not about to be patronized, was less than kind in its response.

Myra Friedman walked over to her afterwards as Janis came across the bridge, and informed her that a reporter from *Life* had requested a few minutes of her time for an interview.

"Fuck him, man," Janis said, "and fuck the world." After which she disappeared into an adjoining tent and shot her veins full of junk.

* * *

Throughout Janis Joplin's performance, John Morris made a series of trips between the stage and a trailer situated behind the mess hall-cum-medical tent where Sly Stone was changing into his outfit. Sly was scheduled to follow Janis onstage, but Dave Kapralik, his manager, informed Morris that Sly wasn't going on "until the spirit moves him."

"What the hell kind of mumbo jumbo is that?" Morris asked, nervously checking his watch. "I've got to have him out there in ten minutes. Get him ready to go."

Kapralik replied that ten minutes should just about do it, but when Morris returned, there was still no sign of the star. "Sly's not in the mood yet," Kapralik said.

Morris began to understand Lang's reluctance to sign Sly when the subject first came up. The black singer's reputation as an extraordinary showman had been undermined by temper tantrums and what the rock periodicals referred to as "overdramatized star trips." But Morris and Lang had been assured by associates close to the performer that Sly had turned over a new leaf. Some leaf, Morris thought; it was probably poison ivy.

"Okay, look—Janis is still on, but in fifteen minutes it's going to be Sly's turn. So, could you possibly get him 'in the mood' in fifteen minutes?"

Morris had a sneaking premonition that he hadn't heard the last of Sly Stone's impetuosity and, ten minutes later, sent a stagehand over to the trailer for a progress report. The boy returned in a flash with an instant replay of Morris's previous encounters. "Kapralik met me outside the trailer, man, and said that Sly wasn't in the mood. Do you believe this shit?" The stagehand gawked.

Morris believed it, all right. He had been warned about it occurring, waved it off, and was about to pay the price for his faith. He waited another ten minutes before stalking back to the trailer. Kapralik was outside, waiting for him.

"Get him on stage. Let's go!" Morris barked, without waiting to hear the manager's pretense.

"I told you, man, he can't go on until the spirit moves him. Hey, listen—you can't do this to him. He's Sly Stone, man."

"I don't care if he's a sly-fuckin' fox," Morris yelled. "Get that fucking act of yours onto the goddamn stage! There's half a million people out there, and you, my friend, are in the minority!"

With that, the trailer door swung open, and the elusive Sylvester Stone poked his head outside.

"Hey—what's this noise, man? Mah concentration's bein' disturbed. It ain't happenin' for me, baby!"

Sly jiggled down the steps to where Morris and Kapralik were squared off. If he was not acting the part of a star, he certainly looked like one. Dressed from head to toe in a white fringed and beaded jumpsuit, a thick gold chain around his neck, his smooth face covered by hawk-shaped glasses, Sly Stone was a lanky, ebony god in a state of irritation.

In his own distress, John Morris was no mortal match-up. "Are you ready to go on, Sly?"

"Hey man, I thought I told you." He looked at Kapralik. "I can't swing it until the vibes are right."

Morris lost his temper. "Don't give me that shit! Now I've got 400,000 people out there who think you're a star—for now. If you're not on that stage in five minutes, they're going to think you're a piece of shit, and it's gonna be me that tells 'em that. Don't fuck around with me, man. You'd better be out there and ready to do your show whether you're in the spirit or not!"

No one can really say for sure what it was that motivated Sly Stone, but when he showed up on the stage just after 1:30 in the morning, he was *in the mood* and left little doubt that he intended to transmit some of that electric intensity with which he was charged to the audience.

Morris felt it too, and suddenly, bygones were bygones. Stepping to the mike, he said, "Sly's about to come out and destroy your minds, but it's so dark out there we can't see you, and you can't see each other. So when I say 'three,' I want every one of you to light a match. Okay? Everybody got your matches ready? One . . . two . . . three!"

In the fraction of an instant it takes for a spark to produce light, the amphitheatre was transformed from a dark, spacial infinity to a penumbra of human emotion. A mass consecration of 400,000 candles lit up the hillside in a hallowed oblation to the spirit of Woodstock. The energy, the anticipation, and the hope of a generation were manifest in the transcendental glow that welcomed Sly and the Family Stone onto the Aquarian stage. And Sly returned the love in kind. He turned in what eventually became known as the most outstanding performance of the entire festival, keeping his promise: "I want to take you higher."

The Who followed Sly at 3:30 A.M., after John Wolff collected a certified check for $11,200 from Joel Rosenman. Michael Lang and Abbie Hoffman stood at the side of the stage and watched Roger Daltry leap through the air as the band did a medley from *Tommy*. Abbie had worked in the medical tent most of the night and, afterwards, had done some acid to "help him relax." But as the Who incited the crowd with their specialized brand of theatrical fireworks, Abbie began frothing with political cogitation.

"Oh, man, this is bullshit," he complained to Lang. "I mean, we're headed in the wrong direction again, man. I gotta go up there and make a speech."

"Hey, cool it, man. Now's not the time."

"It's never the time as far as you hippies are concerned," Hoffman said, tormented and perspiring. "No, man, I gotta go up there. I gotta tell everybody about John Sinclair, man. We gotta fight for that cat." Sinclair was the leader of the White Panther Party and manager of a Detroit-based rock group, the MC-5, who had been arrested and given a nine-year prison sentence for possession of two joints. "It's too important, and it can't wait."

Before Lang could react, Abbie dashed across the stage. Stepping in front of Peter Townshend, he lowered the guitarist's microphone. "This festival is meaningless as long as John Sinclair's rotting in prison!" Abbie screamed. Townshend had no idea who the speaker was who had the audacity to interrupt the Who's performance, but he wasn't about to let him continue. He lifted his guitar in the air, wound up, and swatted Hoffman into the photographers' pit—a revolutionary mosquito laid to rest.

Abbie picked himself up. He blasted Townshend with a torrent of obscenities and ran screaming up the side of the hill, never to return to White Lake.

The Who's set lasted well into Sunday morning, and as the sun rose over the trees behind the stage, Townshend smashed his guitar to smithereens in a madcap finale to the evening's musical mayhem.

At 8:30 A.M. the Jefferson Airplane took to the stage with a particularly dull and uninspired set of their well-worn songs. The group was visibly spent from having had to wait around backstage all night. Grace Slick's voice, frail under the best of circumstances, cracked repeatedly as she strained to overcome the fear and exhaustion that had taken its toll on her stage presence. Nevertheless, she looked unusually ravishing in a tight-fitting fringed white dress revealingly laced up the front. Marty Balin and Jorma Kaukonen traded vocals on the opening few numbers, struggling to pick up the pace of their show, but it wasn't until much later that Grace broke it open with "White Rabbit." By then, however, it was too late. Two thirds of the audience had passed out on the ground, worn out from too much of a good thing. The hits kept on coming—"Somebody To Love" and "Volunteers" built toward a redeeming climax—but they attracted scant applause. By 10:00 Sunday morning, after the Airplane jetted into the sunrise, all anyone could think about was sleep. For many in the audience, the show was already over.

CHAPTER TWELVE

Sunday, August 17, 1969

And the night shall be filled with music,
And the cares, that infest the day,
Shall fold their tents like the Arabs,
And as silently steal away.
                    —*Henry Wadsworth Longfellow "The Day Is Done"*

— 1 —

"**G**ood morning!" Hugh Romney screeched from the foot of the main stage, his hoarse voice barely audible, even over the ear-splitting sound system. It was fast approaching noon, and the music was slated to resume at 1:30. "What we have in mind is breakfast in bed for 400,000." About ten percent of the crowd had already set out in search of their cars, but those who decided to stick it out to the end responded with renewed vitality. "Now, it's gonna be *good* food and we're going to get it to you. It's not just the Hog Farm, either. It's everybody. We're all feedin' each other. We must be in heaven, man! There's always a little bit of heaven in a disaster area." A volley of whistles and exultant shouts drowned out Romney's parched cough. "Now, there's a guy up there—some hamburger guy—that had his stand burned down last night. But he's still got a little stuff left, and for you people that still believe capitalism isn't that weird, you might help him out and buy a couple hamburgers." His voice trailed off as he leaned back and stole a quick glance behind the stage. There, from around the side of the production trailers, came a quartet of Hog Farm women, marching toward the stage with wagonloads of cold mush, three or four ladles, and a veritable forest of paper plates. "Okay," Romney warned the crowd, "here it comes!"

A scantily clad young man jumped on the platform and blew an off-key mess call on a scrap-pile bugle. One of the stagehands remarked that it was a fortunate thing that Max's cows didn't stampede the amphitheatre. However, after getting a closer look at the "breakfast," he retracted his statement.

While the women distributed the food, Muskrat, an aptly nicknamed hippie from New York, read the front page of the Sunday *New York Times* to the "hippest brunch set this side of Fifth Avenue." The feature news item was about how 300,000 people at a "folk-rock fair camp out in a sea of mud."

Not everything at the festival, however, was taking place with such storybook results. The rest rooms were disgusting, and hygienic conditions continued to deteriorate despite the regular application of chemicals and disinfectants. A good many of the kids avoided using the toilets altogether and relieved themselves in the corn field. Much to the consternation of local residents, their back yards served as clandestine comfort stations, and one hippie went so far as to tell an irate homeowner that he had fertilized the man's flower beds. "You oughta be lucky I don't send you a bill for it, asshole," the boy yelled over his shoulder as he was chased from the yard. Gas stations and restaurants were overrun with mud-drenched teenagers who waited in line to use their facilities, and many of them opted to shut down for the day and to take a financial loss.

On the whole, however, area merchants found the patrons of the Aquarian Exposition the "most polite, most behaved . . . and the best-mannered customers" they had ever seen. A Monticello restaurant owner confessed to a reporter, "I sure have changed my opinion of these kids since I have had the opportunity to come into contact with them . . . they are so polite." And a housewife from Liberty covered the kids' activities on a turf she claimed to know better than most: the local supermarkets. "They are so quiet—not like the vacationers—and don't push their grocery carts into your back to get you out of their way." She recounted an incident on Friday afternoon when one of the shoppers in her aisle dropped a bag of groceries. Within ten seconds, the shopper was surrounded by hippies who offered to help the woman pick up her belongings. "This response would never come from the ordinary shopper I have seen."

Medical and drug-related problems continued to mount. Dr. Abruzzi estimated that his clinics had treated as many as 3,000 people since the festival got underway. At his request, the Sullivan County sheriff had put out an emergency alert Saturday night for additional medical assistance. "Immediate precedence" messages were relayed to Aerospace Command Headquarters in Colorado Springs and to the Pentagon for authorization of U.S. Army Air Force task force pilots to fly rescue missions over the

festival site. Two Army UH-1D (Huey) helicopters, the type used for evacuating the wounded in Vietnam, were dispatched from Stewart Air Force
Base in Newburgh to airlift emergency food supplies and to transport the
injured to an army emergency medical aid facility that had been set up in
Monticello.

Sunday morning at 6:35, an eighteen-year-old Marine home on leave,
identified as Richard Beiler of Holbrook, Long Island, died of an apparent
overdose of heroin, making him the second festival casualty. Three other
men, all under the age of twenty-five, were listed in critical condition at a
hospital in Middletown.

One of them, a student from New Jersey, was found unconscious in the
middle of the night and carried to Bill Abruzzi's trailer where he was diagnosed as a victim of an overdose and "close to death." Abruzzi ordered the
boy to be immediately flown to Horton Hospital in Middletown; closer medical centers, he said, lacked the intensive care facilities such as an artificial
kidney machine necessary to save his patient's life.

At 2:30 A.M., a helicopter, which had been requested by Abruzzi to evacuate the boy to Horton, attempted to land behind the stage but missed the
pad the first time around. On the copter's following attempt, it set down next
to the hospital tent and the student was placed on board, ahead of a patient
with a ruptured appendix and another with a broken ankle.

"Just forget about everyone else, and get this kid to Horton," Abruzzi told
the pilot. "He doesn't have much time."

"I can't," the pilot shouted above the whirring of the propeller. "Not
enough fuel. I can take him as far as Monticello."

"Monticello won't do. This man is near death and in fourth degree car-
diac failure. How soon can you get another helicopter here?"

The pilot emphatically shook his head. "Forget it. The entire fleet's short
on fuel and there's no one at the airport to pump gas."

Tri-Co's radio operators finally located another helicopter idling at
Grossinger's. It landed at Yasgur's farm within ten minutes of the call, and
the boy was rushed in the nick of time to Horton, where a team of specialists
determined that he was suffering from alcohol poisoning. By noon, after
having undergone a stomach pump and dialysis treatment, the patient was
resting in satisfactory condition and he was expected to recover in time to be
sent home on Tuesday.

Another crisis that loomed on the horizon was food. No one knew how
long the current supply would last or if indeed it would keep in the stifling
heat. In addition, the state police were predicting that it might be necessary
for them to detain a large portion of the audience at the site for several days

in order to clear the roadblock. That would certainly create a food shortage, especially since trucks couldn't get into the area to replenish their stock.

Mel Lawrence and four assistants got on the phones early Sunday morning and called the Catskills resort hotels to appeal for food. The first helicopter carrying 1,300 pounds of food hovered over the site at 11:00 A.M. and requested landing directions. In order to keep the heliport clear for medical emergencies, Lawrence instructed it to set down on the grass to the right of his trailer. Utilizing the "buddy system," he organized a circle of teen-agers and had them join hands so that the helicopter had a target in which to land. Fifteen volunteers unloaded the plane, separating its cargo into perishables (which were immediately consumed), and items that could be saved for future use. Lawrence looked at some of the packages that came off the helicopter with curiosity. Four packets of Kool-Aid, two jars of Mother's gefilte fish, eleven boxes of lime Jell-O, a sixteen-ounce can of julienned carrots—he couldn't understand how anyone in his right mind could expect them to provide nourishment for half a million people in a muddy pasture with supplies like those. "Get a load of this," a girl said, holding up a carton of one-pound boxes of Mueller's spaghetti.

The tomato sauce came on the next helicopter.

The emergency menu became more practical, however, and, by mid-afternoon, the outlook was much brighter. The Women's Auxiliary of the Monticello Jewish Community Center prepared over 30,000 meat, cheese, and peanut butter-and-jelly sandwiches, which, in the spirit of the event, were handed out by twelve sisters from the Convent of St. Thomas. Dr. Rudiger of the Rutherford School had spent most of the morning rounding up donations from the big hotels. After borrowing a truck from the Concord, he followed a path cleared for him by the state police and drove 1,000 dozen eggs, 300 pounds of fried chicken, and 500 pounds of fresh vegetables into the campgrounds where it was whisked off to the Free Kitchen. Max donated cheese, milk, and butter, another neighbor contributed several hundred loaves of bread, Food For Love gave away thousands of uncooked hot dogs, and before long, anybody who wanted something to eat was able to tap one of the many food sources around the grounds.

Joe Cocker opened Sunday's show around 2:00. For most people at the festival, it was the first opportunity they had to see Cocker perform, and his epileptic contortions provided an entertaining diversion to the frantic, husky vocals that kept the crowd on its feet throughout most of the show.

Lawrence watched Cocker's opening number from below the side of the stage. Mel was startled by the singer's striking similarity to Ray Charles's style of blues, breathlessly squeezing out the last few syllables of a refrain while sliding right into the next line with a surging, yet short-winded, growl. But, while Cocker's vocal inflections paid tribute to his American mentor, the visual show was an invention all his own. Cocker arched his shoulders and pumped the microphone with his chest in time to the bass runs. Occasionally he stumbled backward, dipped, then sprang toward the mike to deliver the next swell of sound with an almost animalistic intensity. Cocker's own inimitable trademark, however, was the way he accompanied his backup group, the Grease Band, on an imaginary guitar. He would spasmodically slap at its invisible strings while twisting his pretzel-like body into rhythmically responsive contortions. Each song seemed to be a totally enervating experience for the tortured Cocker, yet he bounced back with the resilience of a prizefighter conditioned to go the distance.

Ten feet away, Artie Kornfeld humped a motorcycle in time to "Delta Lady," and wept uncontrollably into the bend of his arm. "This is just great! Outta sight! Oh man, look what we've done, look what we've done. This is forever," Artie wailed. He collapsed over the handlebars, sobbing, as Mel cut around him and headed up the hill toward his trailer.

The director of operations hadn't slept since Friday. "I *feel* the way Cocker *looks*," he thought, and decided to sneak off somewhere for an hour of uninterrupted peace and quiet. On his way past concessions, Lawrence picked up a young staff member with whom he had been intimate and invited her to accompany him to a room at the Howard Johnson's Motel in Newburgh, which he had reserved in case such an opportunity presented itself. After calling around the site to make sure everything was functioning as smoothly as could be expected, he took a helicopter ride to their hideaway, enjoyed the luxury of a hot shower, and settled into some serious lovemaking.

The sharp, whiplike crack sounded for the third time before Lawrence reacted to it. After a fourth outburst, he threw the covers off the bed, scampered over to the window, and peeked through the blinds.

"Oh—fuckin'-A!" he winced.

"What is it, Mel?" his companion asked, sitting up in bed.

"Honey—you wouldn't believe it if I told you. Just get dressed as fast as you know how. We're gettin' out of here."

John Morris saw it at the same moment and shuddered. It had come upon them suddenly, two fingerlike, black storm clouds reaching over the sea of heads with alarming velocity. From the stage, it resembled a giant pinwheel hurtling toward the crowd. The clouds spun across the pink sky and left splotches of tumultuous paste on the spectral horizon. In less than ten minutes, that complexion bled into a solid screen of charcoal gray, then faded to black. The crowd shuddered in unison.

Joe Cocker grabbed the bottle of beer at his feet, tucked it under his arm, and fled to safety. There was no time for apologies or long, drawn-out good-byes. He disappeared into the service elevator with the rest of the Grease Band close on his heels.

"Hit the power!" someone screamed from behind a bunker of amplifiers.

The stormtroopers, armed with their balled-up plastic slipcovers and cans of surface shield, galloped across the stage for the second time that weekend. One could almost sense their sophistication this time around, their nimble proficiency. Only those close enough to get a good look at the crew's faces realized the full meaning of the term 'stagefright.' If the storm hit before they had a chance to complete their missions, those in the vicinity stood a better than average chance of being electrocuted.

"Hey! No fuckin' around, man—cut that power!" By now, the eighty or so privileged guests and technicians who had, only an hour before, lined the rear of the bandstand, were squared away in the tents and trailers behind the stage. "There's a master beneath the performers' elevator. Shut it off and get the hell outta here!"

"No!" The sharp directive billowed across the open field like an expatiate shock wave. It was so sudden, so spontaneous, he wasn't sure that it had come from his throat. "Leave the power on. *Just leave the power on* and get outta here."

Staring frantically into the face of destruction, everyone left on the stage stopped what they were doing and turned toward the commanding voice.

At the foot of the stage, John Morris faced the crowd, paralyzed, bathed in perspiration, and confronted their inevitable destiny. His white knuckles were wrapped around the live microphone held two inches away from his lips; his short legs, spread slightly apart, were locked in fear.

"Go. Go ahead," he told them without looking over his shoulder. "I can handle it." The rapid movement behind him warned him of the crew's departure. At his feet, Michael Wadleigh was perched on his elbows supporting a minicam, capturing the whole wretched scene. The gentle whirring of the hulking metal machine was an ironic, sweet lullaby in direct contrast to the jangling panorama before him. The drama of misery, he thought. An indelible print of human blunder.

The winds took over. Rising out of the east, they swept into the natural amphitheatre and played havoc with the temporary plywood architecture.

Garbage swirled through the air. To Morris's utter horror, the latticework towers holding the massive sound speakers began to sway out over the crowd. A follow-spotlight tumbled off one of the raised stands and disappeared in the audience.

"Would you *please* get away from the towers!" he cried into the microphone. "*Please! Clear away before someone gets hurt!*" Morris detected a note of hysteria in his voice and knew he had to somehow gain control of himself. At that point, he felt like the director of the most realistic disaster film in history; the least he could do, he decided, was to give it a touch of dignity. Collecting his runaway passion, he said in a more controlled tone: "Let's keep it nice and cool. Just sit down and be cool." Thunder drowned out the remainder of his soothing words.

"It looks like we're gonna get a little bit of rain so you'd better cover up. If it does—if we should have a slight power problem, just cool it out. We'll sit here with you. You'll be okay."

Thunder blasted a last-second warning before the heavens gave way. The rain, like skeins of metal pellets, stung everything in its line of fire.

"Wrap yourself up, gang. That's it—open up your newspapers." It wasn't working. He could see it reflected in their faces, the crazy smiles plastered from ear to ear. He could feel it in their movement. Their dreams of peace and love were being engulfed by mud. "*Hey!*" he shouted, trying any device to boost their spirits. "If you think really hard enough, maybe we can stop this rain!" The undulating applause was a nervous release of the crowd's frustration.

The thunder boomed again. "That's it!" he repeated. "We've got to ride this out."

Out of the corner of his eye, he focused on the towers again as they leaned out over the crowd and then sprang back like ladders in a Chester Conklin comedy. "Okay—everybody sit down. Let's go." Scores of kids crawled through the scaffolding holding up the sound towers; others were wrapped in its monkey-bar frame playing daredevil games and laughing. "Please come down off those towers, gentlemen. Everybody just sit down. Right. Sit down."

It seemed hopeless. The towers shook like knobby, stick knees. He gazed up at their support platforms and watched as thousands of pounds of speakers shifted with each movement. It was only a matter of time before they either toppled off or the towers snapped. It would be utter chaos. Hundreds could be hurt, killed. Idiocy. Fault—whose fault? Mine? Maybe. "*Keep your eyes on those towers!*" He wondered if that was his voice; he couldn't be sure anymore.

"No rain, no rain, no rain, no rain. No rain, no rain, no rain, no rain."

It had begun softly from off to the left of the stage and swelled to all ends of the arena. The crowd chanted between claps of thunder.

"No rain, no rain, no rain, no rain. No rain, no rain, no rain, no rain."

It reminded Morris of the fearless band of men who sang on the deck of the *Titanic* in *A Night to Remember* as the ship went down. "Keep thinkin' it!" he encouraged them. *"Hey*—get off those towers."

Just then, Morris felt a tremendous shove from behind, his legs buckled, and he grabbed onto the microphone stand to keep from falling. "What the . . . !" He whirled around. There was no one behind him. That's weird, he thought. Was he losing his coordination? He couldn't cave in—not now. He had to control himself. He had to remain strong for all those kids. He wiped his brow and stood up, but it happened again. *No!* he cried to himself. *It wasn't possible! It just could not be possible!* But it was. The stage foundation had loosened in the mud and was sliding down the steep enbankment.

He stumbled to his feet and stared out into the crowd—200,000; 300,000; 400,000. The numbers had lost their significance. It *was* really happening. Not just to him, but to all of them. There, huddled together awaiting—what? A catastrophe? Who knew anymore. It was his own personal nightmare.

His eyes swept the scene again and came to rest on two young kids swinging each other gleefully in the mud. In back of them, a myriad of teen-agers had joined hands and were dancing a hora. Others skated through the mud in front of the photographers' pit. Could this really be happening? he wondered as the stage moved another two inches downhill.

"Dear God," he prayed silently, *"what have we done?"*

Nobody in the large medical tent behind the stage saw the storm coming before it struck. Blinded by the moon-shaped canvas flaps hanging down from the bigtop, they were taken completely by surprise and the team of doctors and nurses were shaken with unrelenting force. Pharmaceutical supplies toppled off carts into pools of mud. Cots were caught by the crosswind and blown clear across the service road. Patients who had been lying on the ground remained where they were, oblivious of the downpour; for many, their wills had been broken long before the rain began.

Rikki Sanderson, Abruzzi's chief nurse, held onto the wobbly center pole of the tent while her staff of nurses and paramedicals scrambled to protect the bandages. If their supplies became wet, they'd no longer be considered sterile. That would be the clincher—especially after what the storm would do to the audience. They'd need every last piece of gauze they could get their hands on.

The wind kicked up its strong arm once again and pulled at the canvas covering with all its might. Sanderson maintained her grip and resisted the traction, defying the inevitable. There were sick children in that tent, victims of this carnival of horrors, and she'd be damned if she'd allow them to be emotionally hurt any more than they already had been. She looked at the thirty-five kids doused with mud and thought, "This is what war must be like." It was a detestable situation. She reached up to wipe the rain from her face and realized she was crying. Was this the way it was meant to be? she cried. "We've got to stick together," she called to a tentful of patients, most of them her children's age. "We've got to fight this!"

"Right on!" someone called back.

It was at that moment Rikki Sanderson knew they'd pull through.

Roberts and Rosenman had been sitting on the lawn outside the security office when the first flashes of lightning pierced the sky. Blind impulse moved them to laugh. After all, wasn't it John who, only minutes before, had joked that the only calamity that hadn't beset them was a thunderstorm. There hadn't been a cloud in the sky at the time. And now—*this!* It was the crudest joke of all.

John's face lost all of its expression as they squeezed through the office door. "It's going to rain. All those people . . . what are we going to do? *Oh my God!*"

The four of them—Roberts, Rosenman, Lee Mackler, and John Fabbri—pressed up against the window while the storm flooded Lake Street. The trees blew backwards as strong gusts of wind slapped high-tension wires through the air like flimsy kite-tails. "I didn't read anything about a hurricane in this area," Lee remarked.

"It's the tail end of Hurricane Michael," Fabbri said with a straight face. "Somebody ought to declare it a disaster area."

"Somebody already has," Joel said.

"The stage isn't covered, is it?" Roberts asked Lee.

"Well—yes and no. Some of it has a roof overhead."

"The part with the electrical instruments?"

"Yes"—she thought about it for a few seconds—"and no. It depends on how you look at it. Let's put it this way: if you're asking me if the stage has a place where one can go to stay out of the rain, the answer is yes; if you're asking me whether or not it's possible for that person to keep dry, the answer is no."

"Either way, we lose." John put his head in his hand.

"Not exactly," Joel reminded him. "Remember that rain insurance policy we took out with Lloyds? Well, I think it's going to pay us off for this little inconvenience. If I remember correctly, this is considered peak time, and during peak time Lloyds is on the hot seat instead of us. I never thought I'd get the chance to say this, but, John m'boy, we're going to be coming into a little money."

"Great," Roberts mumbled with little apparent interest. "We'll need every cent we can get our hands on to pay back all of our debts."

As suddenly as the rain had started, it stopped. The storm had lasted for a period of not longer than twenty minutes before pulling back over the campgrounds and then vanishing in what actually appeared to be a purple haze.

Michael Lang had spent part of that time on the phone arranging for a special gift to be delivered to the Woodstock Nation. When the sun reappeared, so too did a plane he had hired to spray flower petals across the beleaguered site. "Michael's magic dust," Ticia called it. It was an enchanting moment—the calm after the storm. Now, all Michael had to do was to figure out a way to make Jimi Hendrix materialize in White Lake and his mission would be nearly completed. The man who put Outer Space on the map was holed up in Woodstock, freaked by the crowd reports, and as of 4:00 Sunday afternoon, he remained adamant about cancelling his appearance.

While it looked as though the weather was prepared to come to terms with Sunday's presentation, the rain had certainly taken its toll on the site. The lush, emerald field that had stood there only four days before was a solid body of mud held together by a mucilage of garbage and human excrement. What remained of the concession stands could hardly be described as more than a few wooden planks nailed together with shreds of canvas clinging to their horizontal beams like the moth-eaten cloak of a lost civilization. Flies and gnats battled overhead to determine which insect would be awarded territorial rights once the humans moved on.

The stage, which had slid a total of six inches downhill, was temporarily restrained by Jay Drevers and a crew of stagehands who drove stakes into the downhill side of the mud plates "to slow it down." Drevers insisted that the foundation had jarred loose in the mud and was not strong enough to hold the various bands, their equipment, and people who "happened along to hang out." Above and beyond that, the weight of the audience pushing against the front had caused that portion of the bandstand to tip forward

ever so slightly. It was a first-rate hazard. When he was asked what it would
take to reduce the stress and the risk of further downhill movement of the
stage, Drevers answered, "The elimination of the combined weight of nine
million friends should do it." Someone took his advice seriously. To reduce
needless traffic, the steps were torn off the side of the stage. Everyone who
wished to go topside was forced to take the elevator, and that meant first
passing the scrutiny of an ornery carpenter named Leo whose lionlike disposition was not to be tested.

Mel Lawrence had convinced a helicopter pilot that it was safe to fly him
from the Howard Johnson's in Newburgh back to the site. He got there just
in time to inspect the damage done to the stage and to chat with Michael
Lang about the incredible durability of the crew.

Michael stopped him halfway through a testimonial to the Hog Farm
and muttered, "Don't look now, man, but here comes Max, and he looks
blown-out."

"Oh shit! *Not now* of all times. I just know he's gonna lay into me about
his field or cows or alfalfa, and I don't have the time. I've got too many other
things on my mind."

Lawrence pivoted around to confront the farmer head-on and stopped
dead in his tracks. Max looked awful. His stubbly face was ashen and his eyes
bulged out of their fleshy sockets like two soft plums. Unbeknownst to his
young associates, Max had spent all of Saturday night in his office with his
son, Sam, and another man from the dairy, armed with rifles in anticipation
of a motorcycle-gang raid. An anonymous call had tipped him off to their
arrival and they decided to surprise the bikers. Max had been on and off
oxygen ever since and was exhausted.

"Holy shit," Lawrence whispered, "this thing's gonna kill Max. We've
gotta figure out some way to cheer him up. I've got an idea, Michael. Whaddya say we get Max up on stage to say a few words to the kids? That ought
to cool him out."

Michael grinned. "It's a great idea, man. Do it."

But they had misread Yasgur's expression, which, as he came closer to
them, became more apparent.

"Fuckin' Max is in heaven, man," Lawrence giggled. "Take a look at that
shit-eating grin. He's really diggin' this."

And, indeed, Max was. "This is incredible! I don't know what to say,
boys. The kids are so nice and polite. I never thought this could happen."
Max twirled 360 degrees, overcome by sheer emotion.

Mel pumped his hand and held it while they looked into each other's eyes.
"Max, why don't you go onstage and tell the people how you feel? I think it'll

be real good for the festival for them to know that you're behind them and that they're welcome on your land."

Yasgur was apprehensive about going before so many people, but after some gentle prodding by Michael and Mel, he allowed Chip and Mel to escort him up in the elevator to say a few words.

The stagehands had just about swept all the water off the stage. As a result of the downpour, they had to pierce the canvas roof in order to avoid its caving in from the weight. Max waited patiently on the side, out of their way, obviously fascinated by the crew's industriousness and the spectacle of his hillside.

When they were finished, Chip put an arm around Max's shoulder and guided him to the front of the stage.

"This is the man whose farm we're on—Mr. Max Yasgur," Chip said, stepping back to start the applause.

Max leaned into the mike and spoke to his guests with heartfelt sincerity. "I'm a farmer," he said. "I don't know how to speak to twenty people at one time let alone a crowd like this. This is the largest group of people ever assembled in one place, but I think you people have proven something to the world—that a half a million kids can get together and have three days of fun and music and have nothing *but* fun and music!" The tears welled up in his eyes as he shouted over the applause, "*And I God-bless you for it!*"

Penny Stallings had been having trouble getting back into her production trailer all afternoon. Every time she put her foot on the metal steps, Penny was thrown off by a charge of electricity that shot through her body and sent her sprawling on the wet ground. She finally pulled the master electrician aside, and he informed her the main terminal for the site was nearby the trailer. "We're keeping an eye on it, especially with this wet ground. I don't want to frighten you, but with all those kids climbing over the scaffolding . . . well, I'd hate to think what'd happen if one of those towers fell over into the wires."

The situation grew progressively worse. By 6:00 Sunday night, the dirt that covered one of the main feeder cables to the stage had washed away, and the crowd's constant tramping over it had worn out part of the rubber insulation. It was no longer simply a matter of exercising caution; the situation had exploded into a full-blown emergency, and the electrician called security for his orders on how to handle it.

Fabbri took the call, and then immediately summoned Roberts and Rosenman to a conference in the back office. "He says that with all those kids being drenched and packed together the way they are—if the insulation goes, we're going to have a mass electrocution." They had a choice, he said. They could continue to feed the stage on the same line and pray that the kids wouldn't remove what was left of the rubber tubing or they could cancel the remainder of the show. "It's not what I'd consider to be an ideal spot for us to be in," Fabbri said solemnly.

"What does the electrician want us to do?" Joel asked.

Fabbri looked at his feet. "He wants us to shut down for a while."

"That's impossible! We can't do that," Roberts pitched in. "It'll be mayhem, for sure. A half million freaked-out rabid kids running around with nothing to do will just about finish us off."

"Well, somebody's got to make a decision before those kids do it for us," Fabbri said. "Its up to you—whatever you decide."

The three men sat painfully still in the back office, each one examining his own conscience, not daring to look at his two associates for fear of backing down from a decision. A few minutes went by unnoticed. Every so often Roberts whimpered, but no one said a word. The silence was ultimately broken by Joel Rosenman who jumped up and dialed the phone. Without faltering, he ordered the electrician to keep the music running continuously and to investigate methods of rerouting the power to protected cables. He saw by Fabbri's face that the policeman disagreed with his decision; John Roberts was catatonic. "I want you to work on a switchover without losing one minute of music. And *please* give us a call as soon as you know anything further."

In the front room, Lee Mackler took a call from John Morris, who had been consulted by the electrician before security became involved in the life-or-death option.

"Fuck it—we're gonna turn the power off," Morris said. "If we don't, we're gonna have French-fried musicians on that stage. It'll be one big disaster." Lee could detect in his voice that Morris was overcome with grief. "You gotta see it to believe it. All of the wires are exposed. It's drizzling again. The lives of hundreds of thousands of people are at stake. For God's sake—turn the fuckin' power off!"

"Take it easy, John," Rosenman said, grabbing the phone out of Lee's hand. "We're handling it. I've talked to an electrician and the odds are heavily in our favor—otherwise I wouldn't have made such a quick decision. Whatever you do, don't tell anybody what's going on or else we'll have a panic that'll be harder to control than the electricity. Sit tight. I'll call you back."

Joel hung up the phone and slumped against the wall. Lee suggested that he call Wes for advice, and after some deliberation, Joel tracked down the chief of security on the mobile phone. Pomeroy told Joel that he felt he had done the right thing. Wes was having a difficult time at the festival and had receded from a role of major importance in executive decision-making to that of an aged figurehead whose time was past. Pomeroy had spent most of Friday and Saturday following up complaints by Max's neighbors about hippies trespassing on the property. The final blow to his professional ego had come early Sunday morning when he took a call from Max's wife placing the entire blame for the festival on Wes's shoulders.

"Pomeroy, this is all your fault," she accused him, "everything that's gone on here. It wouldn't have happened if it weren't for you. And if anything happens to Max because of it—I'll hold you responsible!"

Wes lay down to catch a few hours' sleep after taking the disturbing call, and, according to a close associate, "he never woke up. He watched something that he worked so long and hard on be torn apart by incompetence and emotion, and he didn't know how to deal with it. Wes was a man to whom honor came above everything else. He could deal with honorable people better than anybody else on the face of the earth, but he was defenseless against deceit. The cops' treachery did him in. And he just couldn't compete with Mrs. Yasgur's love for her husband; he didn't even want to try."

Joel found his partner in the same position he had left him in in the back room before taking Morris's call. Roberts was taking it harder than even he thought possible, but it was understandable nonetheless. For three days John had sat by helplessly as his inheritance was snuffed out, writing bad check on top of bad check to keep the festival afloat. He'd have to account for the money sooner or later, and Roberts intended to cover each piece of paper personally endorsed by him over the weekend. He had to; his family reputation was at stake. But this—the possible mass electrocution of anywhere from 300,000 to 500,000. He couldn't cope with it.

"What's going on here?" John stared up at his partner, in a state of shock. "What does this mean to our lives—that we could make such a callous decision?"

Joel tried to find the words to answer him, but could not.

"What can we possibly do in the next twenty-four to forty-eight hours? If we survive it! And then where do we go from here? God, Joel, I don't understand this thing at all."

The two of them decided that whatever course of action they took in the next two days, it was going to have a lot to do with the quality and nature of the rest of their lives. They wouldn't spare any expense or effort to see that the power lines were switched safely, and they would do everything within their ability to pay their creditors and preserve their reputations.

"You mean—*if we* make it," Joel said.

"If we make it," John conceded.

Years later Roberts would remember that precise moment and the philosophy he chose to embrace. "I think I had very clearly decided at that time, as a concept, that if thousands and thousands of people were electrocuted, I was going to find a reasonably swift and painless way to take care of myself. It wasn't a suicide pact of any kind, but it was something that I knew I would never be able to live with."

An hour passed, then another, and finally the electrician was on the phone saying that the transfer had been made without a hitch. The stage had all the power it would need for the next two weeks, and the frayed cables had been uprooted. Joel collapsed in his chair. John slumped across his desk and sobbed tearlessly. The operation had been a success.

While Roberts and Rosenman were huddled in the back office pondering the outcome of their decision, another fate had been determined. Bert Cohen had arrived with the program books. The tractor-trailer had finally gotten through the traffic and he was ready to unload them on a table by the main gate.

His truck had rolled into Sullivan County at 4:42 P.M. Sunday afternoon paying the winner of the pool $37.50.

Country Joe and the Fish had demanded to take to the stage during the energy crisis despite warnings from the stagehands that the "electrifying" performance they intended to put on might be just exactly that. It was raining, he said, and there were "these problems."

Barry Melton, lead guitarist for the Fish, overruled the stagehand's objections. "We wanna play, man. We wanna play *now*. We don't need electricity." And they proved the impossible. In front of a crowd that spanned six hundred acres of open farmland, where a distance of ten feet was considered to be well out of earshot, Country Joe and The Fish pantomimed their set with acoustic instruments and nonelectric microphones—*and the crowd got off on it!* Joe McDonald dashed into the performers' pavilion in the middle of the group's show and returned carrying six-packs of beer, a few bottles of champagne, and oranges, all of which were tossed from the stage into the crowd. A male dancer from the audience was yanked up on stage by an electrician where he proceeded to strip naked and wiggle back and forth across the bandstand in time to the music. It was a perfectly resilient display of impromptu showmanship that held the audience's rapt attention while the rest of the crew insulated the stage. The Fish (and Country Joe McDonald for the *second* time during the weekend) rescued the day.

"They reminded one of the brave rodeo clowns that run into the pit when a rider's hurt and the bull's ready to trample him," a writer from *Rolling Stone* interpreted the Fish's heroics. "They came through."

So did Alvin Lee and Ten Years After, who took to the stage around eight o'clock, and tore through a two-hour set of gut-wrenching progressive blues. Most of the kids sitting in the damp amphitheatre had seen the group before, Ten Years After holding the distinction of having toured the United States more than any other of the British blues breakers. But Alvin Lee had come to play—and *play* he did. Dressed in a black short-sleeved T-shirt, jeans and white leather boots, wide studded leather straps lashed to his right wrist, Lee stepped into the spotlight with his cherry-red guitar and exhibited the technique that had earned him his reputation as "the Fastest Fingers in the West." His small hands effortlessly performed formidable lead riffs like a well-oiled machine, a thin adequate voice pulsating in counterpoint to the astonishing fingerwork. If, indeed, Lee's back was aggravating him, it certainly was not affecting his playing. Opening with three seemingly identical versions of twelve-bar blues, Ten Years After eased into some of their more well-known anthems, icing the cake with a nine-minute rendition of "Goin' Home."

At 10:30, the Band took over, making as inconspicuous an entrance as anyone could have imagined. Looking much like a collection of moonshiners on leave from the Ozarks, they slipped behind their instruments and simply began to play a medley of their legendary compositions. Michael and Artie glowed throughout the Band's relaxed set—Michael because to him the Band represented the soul of the Woodstock Music and Art Fair, its down-home sensitivity, its intelligence; and Artie because he had fought so hard to bring them to national attention during his stint at Capitol Records. That most of the crowd waited for Bob Dylan to walk out and join them in a few numbers was a foil to their interpretive genius and songwriting ability. (Dylan, who had planned to sail for Europe over the festival weekend, had returned to his home in Woodstock on Friday to be with his ailing son.) But the Band hadn't been up for the show, and it soon became evident to those in the bowl. Their set was flat and spiritless, with none of the folksy, grinning demeanor usually associated with their music. Nor did they try to compensate by pushing their personality to the fore. It was as if they hid behind their tight arrangements, intimidated by the clamor of public expectation that preceded their appearance.

Just after midnight, while Blood, Sweat and Tears' road men set up the group's equipment on the front end of the revolving platform, Michael and Artie went back to their trailer and took care of some last-minute business.

Much to his relief, Lang discovered that Mike Jeffries had finally lured Jimi Hendrix to the site where he was afforded the luxury of an attended private trailer behind what was once the employees' mess hall. Hendrix was still in a panic over the "cave of despair" he had heard so much about on the news, but Jeffries assured the promoters there was nothing to worry about. If Jimi hadn't intended to perform, he never would have consented to making the trip. "Just give him some time to relax and get adjusted. He'll be ready in time to close the festival."

John Morris sat across from them, frantically attempting to convince Ed Goodgold, Sha Na Na's skittish manager, that his group couldn't possibly be assured they'd go on in the dark. In fact, it looked pretty good that they wouldn't. Sha Na Na was virtually unknown to even the *au courant* of rock lore. A few months before, they had been students at Columbia University who had banded together for fun to parody the doo-wop classics of the 1950s. Lead by a spunky guitarist named Henry Gross, from Queens, New York, they became a local phenomenon and turned professional to satisfy the growing demand for their uproarous personal appearances. "My boys' show is strictly visual," Goodgold insisted. "If they can't be guaranteed a spot at night, they might as well not go on."

"Suit yourself, man," Morris said. "Look, I've got a half dozen top acts in line to go on and, frankly, Sha Na Na is shit compared to their reputations. They'll go on when I can fit 'em in."

As Goodgold forlornly slunk away from the production trailer, Lang went over the remaining bill with his production manager. The rest of the evening's acts were all present and accounted for, including the unexpected arrival of Paul Butterfield who brought his band of blues journeymen by for an unannounced show. All that in order, Michael and Artie rode over to the heliport where they boarded a plane to take them into New York City, along with a few of the junior production staff. They were scheduled to be interviewed by veteran talk-show host David Susskind at Metromedia Studios, and their mutual decision was that to hang around for any length of time after the Band performed could only result in a king-sized downer. For Lang/Kornfeld, the wild ride—from Woodstock, to Wallkill, then on to White Lake—was about to conclude its final leg. The gig had gone down in style. Tomorrow was another day.

Approximately two thirds of the audience sadly followed Michael and Artie's lead between midnight and 3:00 A.M. Monday morning. Leaving most of their worldly possessions behind in the mud, standing tearfully beneath the boundless, star-lit sky, the Children of Woodstock bade new friends goodbye and joined the silent exodus out the main gate and along either Hurd or West Shore Road to search for a way back home. They had fleetingly tasted their cherished freedom, experienced life as it had been meant to be lived during their brief stay at Yasgur's farm. Their metamorphosis had come full cycle; they had spread their wings and soared, and now, they would return to their respective homes to attempt to build on what they had learned in flight.

The state police had restricted traffic on Route 17-B to outbound vehicles and emergency equipment heading for the festival site. Roads slowly became unclogged, abandoned cars were towed to the shoulders, and by sunrise, the Quickway was reported to be moving toward New York City with only minor delays.

John Roberts and Joel Rosenman knew when it was time to stop pressing their luck. They had survived a near-riot of 400,000 hippies, a gargantuan medical disaster, an underground revolt, what was thought to be a certain holocaust, a massive food shortage, and mass electrocution—not bad for a three-day celebration of peace and music. By midnight, both young men admitted that they had suffered enough, and they began transferring the contents of their desks to the trunk of the green Porsche.

Conferences had been called with their executive staff, and a timetable had been worked out which would allow for a smooth and gradual transition at the close of the show. Mel Lawrence agreed to remain behind in White Lake to supervise the clean-up detail until Max was reasonably satisfied that his land had been returned to its "rightful" state. He'd have the Hog Farm to assist him until Tuesday night, and then the salvage companies would take over. The Red Cross and Salvation Army had been alerted to stand by so that they might sift through the rubbish and recondition the discarded sleeping bags for their own profit; a local Boy Scout troop had volunteered to rake the land of trash and begin a program for planting new grass. Wes would close up the administrative office with Don Ganoung and Lee Mackler, settling selected accounts with the corporation's last six thousand dollars which Roberts had slipped him in an envelope. Likewise, Bill Abruzzi would stay on the site with a skeleton staff for as long as he was needed, evacuating all those who were unable to get home by themselves or were in need of additional medical transition. The entire process was expected to take no longer than a week.

Goodbyes were exchanged with long-faced affection, addresses and phone numbers passed on tiny slips of paper, promises hastily made, regards extended to other staff members, thanks expressed in no uncertain terms—it had been an incredible experience. The family was breaking up; the Children of Aquarius stood together for perhaps the last time. It was an uncomfortable moment, better cut short. With no more than a wistful smile of farewell, Roberts and Rosenman slipped out the front door of the security building and joined the anonymous string of cars out of the city they had helped to create. The ride back to New York City took them nearly four hours and was passed in unmitigated silence. Neither of them knew what to say.

John Morris and Chip Monck handled the stage chores for the remainder of the concert. The early morning hours were devoted to the blues, with two of America's most proficient interpreters of the idiom on hand to demonstrate its soulfulness: Johnny Winter and Paul Butterfield.

Winter was an albino from Beaumont, Texas, who, along with his brother, Edgar, had recently emerged as one of the most influential rural blues guitarists on the scene. Johnny's first album was only months old, but it was rapidly gaining the type of following usually bestowed upon legends. Paul Butterfield, the harp player most responsible for the Chicago blues revival, had been recording in the city and brought his band to White Lake for a possible jam with some of the other virtuosos. John Morris begged him to do a long, drawn-out show to hold the audience until morning. Morris wasn't sure how long Crosby, Stills, Nash and Young and Jimi Hendrix would play, and he knew "Butter" could filibuster anywhere from two to five hours if necessary.

By 3:00 A.M., however, it became evident that the balance of the acts were good for another six or seven hours of music—especially since Sha Na Na had finally consented to perform a daylight show. Crosby, Stills and Nash became Crosby, Stills, Nash and Young at 3:30 after the trio opened with "Suite: Judy Blue-Eyes." Neil Young had been added to the group at the suggestion of Ahmet Ertegun, president of Atlantic Records, to allow Stills to double on keyboards, thus reuniting the two ex-members of Buffalo Springfield for the first time in over two years. Crosby, Stills, Nash and Young's performance at Woodstock became, for many, the musical symbol of the festival. Theirs was a new sound, a soft, harmonious blending of voices that resounded above the cries of revolution and the vociferousness of acid rock. It was also, according to rock historian Charlie Gillett, "a new advance in the genealogy [of folk music] which went from the Weavers, through the Kingston Trio, Peter Paul and Mary, and Simon and Garfunkel, to the Mamas and Papas."

At 6:00 A.M., following a now-historic set of their songs and a venerative ovation from the audience, Crosby, Stills, Nash and Young jubilantly retired to the performers' pavilion to toast their newly consecrated fellowship. A few minutes later, Chip Monck departed on a helicopter headed for Manhattan, along with Stephen Stills, David Crosby and Grace Slick. They were due at ABC-TV Studios on West Fifty-seventh Street at 11:00 that morning to tape a segment of the Dick Cavett Show.

Sha Na Na went on as the sun rose behind the stage, providing the fledgling group with a more dramatic backdrop than even they had hoped for at night. The audience looked puzzled at the troupe of fifties greasers, not quite knowing what to make of their antics. It had to be someone's idea of a joke!

John Morris, looking shell-shocked and a bit silly in his sixth white bush jacket, introduced Jimi Hendrix at 8:30 Monday morning to a small gathering of 30,000 who had remained until the end. Hendrix epitomized the Electric God–image conferred upon him by a hardcore group of adoring fans. He was splendidly attired in a beaded, white leather vest, blue jeans, miles of gold chain, and a red scarf tied, crownlike, in his bristly Afro. If Janis Joplin was the pearl, Hendrix was unquestionably the diamond in the rough, the patron saint of psychedelic rock.

Hendrix surprised everyone there with a free-form version of "The Star-Spangled Banner" leading into "Taps." Before anyone knew what was happening, they were on their feet for an equally supercharged version of "Purple Haze." Then, he suddenly brought the crowd's emotions back to earth with an instrumental prayer—a final tribute to the Nation that had breathed a moment of eternity and passed out of the picture forever.

Afterword

On Monday morning, August 18, 1969, John Roberts and Joel Rosenman arrived precisely at ten o'clock for their cheerless appointment with officials from the Bank of North America. Billy Roberts had gotten there ahead of them and discovered that, in all the confusion, the bank's lawyers had neglected to formalize Woodstock Ventures' "Line of Credit" agreement. That oversight empowered the promoters to simply declare bankruptcy and walk away, leaving the bank legally responsible to cover the outstanding checks with its own funds.

The overdraft was estimated to be somewhere around $1,600,000, not including refunds which the attorney general deemed should be made to ticket holders who were not able to reach the site. The bank was appalled. All that its president, officials from the CIT, and a full team of bankruptcy attorneys wanted to know was: "What do you intend to do about it?"

Billy Roberts volunteered the solution. The Roberts family, he said, intended to assume the debt in full; there was never any intention of declaring bankruptcy, nor would they involve the bank in scandal. On behalf of his father, Billy agreed to secure the entire amount by signing the lien agreement against John's trust fund. It was a matter of family pride. "You can lose your money a dozen times," John explained to a reporter, "but you can only lose your name once."

One of Alfred Roberts's stipulations, which had to be complied with before he guaranteed the liability, was that Woodstock Ventures enter into an immediate agreement with Warner Bros. Pictures in order to recoup a portion of the loss. Warner's received exclusive distribution rights to the Woodstock film in return for a flat sum of $1 million plus a fractional participation in the net box office receipts. It was a wretched deal for Woodstock Ventures, considering they had a finished product that was rumored to be "dynamite" and fifty percent of all profits going into the negotiating meeting. As of January 1979, the movie had chalked up a worldwide box office gross of over $50,000,000 and was about to be re-released. Needless to say, none of the promoters got rich off their percentage.

Six weeks after the Roberts family indemnified the Bank of North America, Michael Lang and Artie Kornfeld negotiated a fairly hefty settlement of their own. Relations with their more conventional partners had broken down completely, and they wanted their wings. Until Roberts and Rosenman reached some kind of financial terms with them, Michael and Artie refused to co-sign any corporate checks or agree to the reconciliation with the bank. In typical festival tradition, they had Roberts and Rosenman over a barrel. Each dissenting partner was eventually paid $31,250 (Michael also got the Tapooz property in Woodstock, underneath which he had buried a nine-pound block of hash he claims to have had imported at John and Joel's request) to relinquish all shares in Woodstock Ventures Inc. and any claim to the Woodstock name. Roberts and Rosenman agreed to repay John's family and were subsequently free to exploit the festival to their hearts' desire. Four months later, following a vigorous licensing campaign, they had broken even, and two years after that, Michael and Artie sued them for $10,000,000.

Approximately eighty lawsuits were filed against the festival. Three were settled out of court (including a substantial payment to Food For Love); the rest were dropped quietly. John Roberts, in what must have been a moment of nostalgic folly, placed the following ad in a Sullivan County newspaper:

> By accepting those of us with long hair and peculiar garb, you set an example for the world to follow. You, as a community, looked beyond our exteriors to our actions and found there bonds of fellowship.
>
> To you who opened your hearts and your homes, we convey our gratitude and the gratitude of thousands of young people across the country.
>
> Peace and Love,
> John Roberts, President, Woodstock Ventures.

In 1972, a few weeks before the statute of limitations elapsed, Woodstock Ventures was sued by the Town of White Lake for having disturbed the peace and having caused property damage. Such was the impression gratitude and fellowship had left on a community when opportunity availed. The suit was eventually dropped.

But regardless of all the torment and aggravation heaped upon the promoters, the havoc wrecked on the citizens of White Lake, Town of Bethel, New York, despite the economic philandering or the conflicting interests disguised as some superhip jingoistic philosophy, the Woodstock Music and Art Fair stands as a reminder of how close we came to utopia, and of our ongoing gamble with the vicissitudes of fortune.

Two days after the Woodstock Nation dispersed and set out in search of their starry-eyed legacy, Max Yasgur, a dairy farmer, stood on the lawn of his farm home, and read meaning into the inexplicable, remarkable episode that had taken place just a few miles down the country road.

He had come to terms with his life, he said, having experienced a dramatic victory for the spirit of peace, good will, and human kindness. "If a half million young people at the Aquarian Festival could turn such adverse conditions—filled with the possibility of disaster, riot, looting, and catastrophe—into three days of music and peace, then perhaps there is hope, that if we join with them, we can turn those adversities that are the problems of America today into a hope for a brighter and more peaceful future. . . ."

Acknowledgments

I wish to express my sincere gratitude to all the friends and associates whose advice, assistance, and support throughout the preparation of this manuscript were a source of immeasurable wealth. I am deeply indebted to their generous contributions and hope that this treatment of the festival lives up to their expectations.

Perhaps the most arduous task that confronted me at the start of this book was locating the original Woodstock staff. Nearly a decade had elapsed, and people had scattered, lost touch with one another, gone underground, started families, disappeared—a microcosm of evolution. Stanley Goldstein, assuming a role not unlike that of his festival assignment, helped to lay all the groundwork for me. He spent hours vividly reconstructing the events which took place between April and September 1969, and then wonderfully produced phone numbers, addresses, contacts, friends of friends, and informants, all of whom dusted off their memorabilia and invited me into their lives. For weeks—months!—after our initial conversations, Stanley's calls, beginning with: "I just thought of someone else you should see" or "There's someone passing through town who you must talk to," were met with both enthusiasm and curiosity. His patience and understanding were the foundation of my research; my life will be richer as a result of our friendship.

Two of the first sources whom Stanley suggested I contact were Al and Ethel Romm from the *Times Herald Record* in Middletown, New York.

"They're holding a few clippings which may be of interest to you," was how he had put it. In fact, their "few clippings" turned out to be a concise scrapbook of newspaper accounts surrounding the festival that had been considered for a Pulitzer Prize in journalism and which Ethel had updated over the years. They insisted I be a guest in their home while conducting research in the Middletown-Wallkill area, afforded me credibility in a community whose memories of the festival were less than fond, and gave me complete access to both the paper's and their private files. Additionally, the Romms provided me with a copy of the scrapbook, which is directly responsible for the proper sequencing of events.

As my preliminary investigation progressed, I discovered that the festival underground was, indeed, still very much alive. One staff member led me to another until almost everyone had been accounted for. I found that the Woodstock Festival staff remains a very closely knit family, and I am grateful to them for entrusting me with their story.

The four promoters were tremendously accessible to my innumerable phone calls and visits. For John Roberts and Joel Rosenman, the recollections were often painful, often amusing; at no time, however, did their personal interests interfere with a candid and forthright record of the facts. Because of Joel's busy schedule, information about many of the events described herein was imparted by John Roberts; however, this does not diminish Joel's role. They made available to me the complete Woodstock Ventures files, including thousands of memos exchanged by the staff and a full financial accounting of expenditures. I owe heartfelt thanks to them, as well as to the staff of Media Sound Studio. Michael Lang treated me to a series of rare, illuminating interviews, including one that took place on a coast-to-coast trip. Artie Kornfeld, whose wife, Linda, died suddenly during my research, miraculously stood up to the ardors of soul-searching at a time in his life when it was more advantageous for him to forget. Their part in this work is beyond measure.

Wes Pomeroy, whose initial conversations with me took place at his office in the White House, showed me a compassionate side of law enforcement I never dreamed existed. He is a remarkable man and an inspiration, not only to me, but to most of the people who worked alongside of him at the festival.

Mel Lawrence, Lee Mackler Blumer, John Morris, and Penny Stallings endured countless interviews in order that the facts and incidents contained in this story might be presented with accuracy and reflect the spirit of Woodstock. Mrs. Miriam (Yasgur) Mass and Sam Yasgur shared their memories of Max with enormous verve and a profound sense of loss. Additionally, I am obliged to Carol Green, Chip Monck, Chris Langhart, Bill Abruzzi, Bert

Cohen, Bill Hanley, Ticia Bernuth, Bill Ward, Jean Ward, Jeff Joerger, Hugh Romney, Bonnie Jean Romney, Bill Belmont, Lisa Law, Renee Levine, Judy Bernstein, Harold Cohen, Charles Baxter, Barry Secunda, Peter Loeds, and Rufus Friedman, all of whom contributed their accounts of the festival freely and without reservation.

Wherever I traveled, I was shown hospitality and unbiased cooperation. In Wallkill: Jack Schlosser, Howard Mills, Jr., Pat Mills, Samuel W. Eager, Jr., Karen Eager, Jules Minker, Dennis Cosgrove, and Irma Sattarelle, the town clerk, who provided me with complete transcripts of the town meetings. In Bethel: Louis Ratner, Harold Pantell, Richard Gross, Dr. Charles Rudiger, Robert Flynn and the Monticello Sherrifs Department, Mrs. Rikki Sanderson, and the Sullivan County Board of Supervisors.

Richie Havens, Country Joe McDonald, and Myra Friedman filled in the behind-the-scenes details involving the performers and their managers. Pat Costello and Jane Friedman of the Wartoke Concern, Dick Gersh, Mr. and Mrs. Harry Lang, Miles Lourie, Paul Marshall, Tom Rounds, Michael Wadleigh, Ellen Lemisch, Don Keiter, Bob Lenox, and Bill Reid also provided me with their remembrances, as well as personal correspondence, clippings, and photos.

Trish McPhail, my research assistant, amassed a veritable treasure of library information, catalogued the facts, and transcribed hundreds of hours of taped interviews that ultimately became *Barefoot in Babylon!*

The people at Viking have been overwhelmingly supportive of a "small book" that mushroomed into an epic none of us knew was there. My thanks to Tom Guinzberg and Becky Singleton who firmly believed there was a story to be told; and to my editor, Vicky Stein, who inherited a cumbersome manuscript, poured her soul into it, gave it shape and me encouragement. She was an ideal editor for a project about the festival; she knows about things like peace and love, and also happens to be a consummate rock and roller. Additionally, I want to thank Connie Sayre, Nanette Kritzalis, Deborah Harris, and Beth Tondreau for their publishing expertise and creative input.

Lastly, I am indebted to Starling Lawrence at W.W. Norton for his continued support of my writing and for an abiding fondness for this book, which inspired him to republish it.

BOB SPITZ

Credits

Map by Paul J. Pugliese, GCI

Photograph on front of jacket and paperback cover: John Dominis, Courtesy *Life* magazine

A portion of this book, in slightly different form, originally appeared in *Penthouse.*

Alkatraz Corner Music Co.: "I Feel Like I'm Fixin' to Die Rag," © 1965, 1968 by Joe McDonald, Alkatraz Corner Music Co. (1977).

Garland Publishing Inc.: "Ode," by Arthur W. E. O'Shaughnessey.

Jondora Music: "Lodi," words and music by J. C. Fogerty. Copyright © 1969 Jondora Music, Berkeley, Ca. Used by permission.

Luvlin Music and Akabestal Music: "Rain, the Park and Other Things," written by Artie Kornfeld and Steve Duboff. © 1967, Luvlin Music and Akabestal Music. All rights reserved. Used by permission.

Macmillan Publishing Co., Inc., Michael Yeats, and A. P. Watt: "The Second Coming," from *Collected Poems* of William Butler Yeats. Copyright 1924 by Macmillan Publishing Co., Inc., renewed 1952 by Bertha Georgie Yeats.

MCA Music: "Born to Be Wild," words and music by Mars Bonfire. © Copyright 1968 by Manitou Music, a division of Revue Studios Limited. Sole selling agent Duchess Music Corporation, New York, New York 10022. Used by permission. All rights reserved.

John Roberts and Joel Rosenman: from *Young Men with Unlimited Capital*.

Gail Sheehy: from "The Woodstock Story," by Gail Sheehy. (Originally appeared in *New York* magazine.) Copyright © 1969 by Gail Sheehy. Used by permission.

United Artists: "Handsome Johnny," by Richie Havens and Louis Goussett. Copyright © 1967 Unart Music Corporation.

Index

ABC-TV, 435
Abraham, Morris, 249, 252–54, 262–64, 265, 385
Abruzzi, Dr. William, 290–92, 307, 331, 352–55, 378–79, 386–87, 407, 417–18, 423, 433
Adler, Lou, 86–87
Albany, N.Y., 142, 349, 397, 404
Aldon Music, 23
All-State Bus Corporation, 217
Amatucci, Daniel J., 265–66, 281
American Airlines, 197, 294
Andersen, Eric, 378
Angels, 23
Annenberg School of Communications, 8, 11
Anthony, Dee, 163
Apollo 11, 262
Aquarian Crafts Bazaar, 308
Aquarian Music and Arts Fair, 67–68, 125, 132, 136, 137, 144, 150, 160, 175, 178, 188, 199, 209, 212, 220, 222, 227, 234, 237, 244, 255, 261, 278, 359, 414, 417, 439
Areas, Jose "Chepito," 392
Armstrong, Neil, 263
Aronowitz, Al, 335, 381
Atlantic Records, 434
Auerbach, Leon, 159
Avatar, 177

"Bad Moon Rising," 72
Baez, Joan, 100, 158–59, 367, 381–82, 383, 386
Balin, Marty, 411, 415
Band, The, 15, 18, 25, 35, 47–48, 93, 161, 378, 399, 431–32
Bank of North America, 71, 101, 437–38
Barb, 177
Barsalona, Frank, 163
Bastard Sons, 308–9, 325, 376
Beach Boys, 25
Beacon Hospital, 292
Beat Generation, The, 89
Beatles, 14, 25, 29, 47–48, 73, 93, 162, 377
Beck, Jeff, 163, 318
Beiler, Richard, 418
Belafonte, Harry, 86
Belmont, Bill, 334, 367–72
Bender, Max, 306
Bernuth, Ticia, 108–10, 116, 180–81, 205, 244–45, 250–52, 315, 324, 364, 390, 402, 425
Berry, Chuck, 22, 34, 60
Bethel, N.Y., 244–45, 248–49, 251, 257, 260, 264, 265–66, 267–69, 277, 281, 282–84, 286, 287, 293, 301, 312, 324–27, 342–44, 351, 362, 374, 394, 439
Bethel Businessman's Association, 282–83
Bethel Medical Center, 284

Bethel town and zoning boards, 265, 287
Big Pink. *See* medical
Black Shirts, 324, 333, 364, 403
Block, Alexander, 5
Block Drugs, 5
Blood, Sweat and Tears, 100, 124, 161, 431
Board of Health, 57, 95–96, 97, 153, 172,
    235, 282, 391, 397
"Born on the Bayou," 72
Boston, Mass., 95, 132, 216, 329–30, 392
Boston Globe, 343
Brandt, Jerry, 203
Bridges, Beau, 11
Bright, Kimberly, 93
Bronx, N.Y., 23, 40
Brooklyn, N.Y., 23, 26, 32, 58
Brown's Hotel, 245
Buffalo Commune, 197
Buffalo Springfield, 373, 434
Bullville, N.Y., 120, 127
Burger King, 119–20, 222
Burrelle's Clipping Service, 102
Butler, Joe, 373
Butterfield, Paul, 60, 432, 485
Byrds, 373

Cafe Au Go Go, 203
campgrounds, 96, 122, 137–38, 153, 171–72,
    176, 193, 196, 198, 233, 285, 287, 289,
    294, 296–97, 303, 328, 359, 384–85,
    406–7
Canned Heat, 60, 81, 402, 408, 410, 412
Cannon Films, 281
capitalism, 70, 80, 88, 147, 149, 150, 178,
    301, 395, 416
Capitol Records, 14–16, 24–27, 30, 35, 36,
    37, 46–48, 52, 53–54, 84, 431
Carnegie Tech, 156
Carrabello, Mike, 392
Catskill Mountains, 94, 120, 175, 193, 252,
    277, 283, 306, 387, 405, 419
Cavett, Dick, 435
Central Intelligence Agency, 257
Central Park, 177
Challenge International, Ltd., 12, 13, 14, 18,
    35, 103
Charles, Ray, 4, 420
Charleston, N.C., 19
Chicago, Ill., 95, 110–13, 146
Chicago Transit Authority, 124, 219
Chip Monck Industries Corp., 89
Chock Full o'Nuts, 225
Christians for Social Action, 115
Christopher, Warren, 112
Circleville, N.Y., 222

Circleville Inn, 145
City College, 285
Clapton, Eric, 163
Clark, Ramsey, 75, 111–13
Clayton-Thomas, David, 124
Clean-up. *See* sanitation
Clergy Assistance Program, 293
Cobb, George L., 283–84
Cocker, Joe, 46, 162, 419–21
Coconut Grove, Fla., 26, 32–33, 365
Cohen, Bert, 58, 62, 66–70, 79, 81–85, 92,
    148, 155–57, 361, 399, 430
Cohen, Ralph, 203, 218, 285
Cohen, Steve, 92, 156–58, 232, 234, 269,
    270–71, 300, 315, 364, 376
Cole, Nat King, 14
Columbia Medical School, 290
Columbia Pictures, 315
Columbia Records, 10, 46, 213–14, 392
Columbia University, 432
Community General Hospital, 379
Concerned Citizens Committee, 219, 221,
    238, 255–56, 294
Concert Hall Publications, 58, 66–67, 69–70,
    82, 148, 156
concessions, 39, 58, 94, 96–98, 124, 143,
    186–87, 193, 225–26, 229, 269, 288,
    300–302, 303, 305, 308, 309–10, 324–
    25, 332, 339–42, 352, 360–61, 378, 384,
    386, 394–95, 402–6, 416, 418–19, 420,
    425, 433
Concord, 245, 419
construction, 97, 122, 125–26, 145, 181, 189,
    215, 233–34, 268, 270–71, 297, 300,
    303–4, 305–7, 308–10, 315, 364
Cook, Bruce, 89
Cordell, Denny, 162
Cosgrove, Dennis, 145–46
Country Joe and the Fish, 60, 334–35, 368,
    370, 430
Cow Palace, 115
Cowsills, 24
Crazy World of Arthur Brown, 34
Cream, 46
Creedence Clearwater Revival, 72, 159, 160,
    398, 399, 410
Criteria Sound Studios, 47, 62
Crosby, Stills and Nash, 131, 271, 382, 434
Crosby, Stills, Nash and Young, 434–35

Daley, Mayor Richard J., 111–13
Daltry, Roger, 411, 414
Danko, Rick, 409
Dave Clark Five, 377
David's Potbelly, 158

Davis, Clive, 213–14
Davis, Rennie, 111–12
"Dead Man's Curve," 23
"Delta Lady," 420
Democratic National Convention, 111
Diamond Horseshoe Hotel, 277–78, 307, 344, 388
Dion, 23
Domino, Fats, 22
Donovan, 159
Doors, The, 61
Dow, Richard, 132, 136, 140, 240
Drake, Bill, 60
Drevers, Jay, 271, 296–97, 307–8, 329, 335, 364, 380, 425
Driscoll, Tom, 60–61, 62–63
drugs, 7, 27, 32, 33–34, 35, 42, 46, 83–85, 102, 106, 129, 137, 147, 166, 175–77, 181–83, 190, 191, 195, 219–20, 286, 291–93, 295, 307, 312, 322, 326–27, 329, 344, 352–54, 358–59, 365, 368, 373, 379, 384, 399, 407–9, 412, 414, 438
Dulles International Airport, 74
Dunbrook, Harrison F., 222
Dylan, Bob, 15, 18, 29, 35, 47, 73, 93, 100, 133, 159, 214, 335, 378, 431

Eager, Karen, 320
Eager, Samuel W., Jr., 151–54, 185, 188, 206, 236–42, 320
East Village Other, 177, 294
Elder, Boyd, 97
Electric Circus, 203
electricity, 49, 97, 122, 143, 232, 233, 272–73, 328, 356, 364, 367, 378, 380, 386, 421, 427–30, 433
Electric Kool-Aid Acid Test, The, 122
Elektra Records, 213
El Monaco Motel, 245–47, 252, 255, 262, 269–70, 272
Emerick, George, 61
Ertegun, Ahmet, 434

Fabbri, John, 114, 200–202, 204, 217–19, 224–25, 320, 338, 343, 350, 389, 424, 428–29
Fabrikant, Herbert F., 236–37
Fantasy Fair and Magic Mountain Music Festival. See rock festivals
Federal Aviation Agency, 95, 362
Federal Bureau of Investigation, 257, 339, 351–52
"Feelin' Alright," 162
Feliciano, Jose, 60
Fifth Dimension, 59

Filippini, William, 311
Fillmore East, 68, 83, 85–86, 87, 92, 99, 148, 155, 158, 161, 177, 203, 271, 273, 335, 376, 400, 412
Fillmore West, 87, 212
Fink, Joe, 203, 218, 285–86, 322–23, 336
Flatt and Scruggs, 60
Fleetwood Mac, 60
Food For Love, 230–32, 293, 309, 325, 332, 340, 343, 351, 361, 378, 389, 394–95, 403, 404–5, 419, 438
Forad, Jim, 180
Foreman, Michael, 66–67, 79, 155–56
Fosburgh, Lacey, 344
Foster, Paul, 296
Free Kitchen, 80–81, 172, 194–95, 196, 297, 328, 378, 419
Freer, Herbert, 238, 240–41
Free Stage, 80, 181, 297, 381–82, 392
Friedman, Jane, 156
Friedman, Myra, 411–12
Fulbright, Sen. James W., 7

Ganoung, Don, 114–15, 131–32, 138–39, 141, 166, 168, 176, 199, 201–2, 204, 216–19, 222, 223–24, 227, 232–33, 238–39, 284–85, 286–87, 291–93, 295, 337, 343, 433, 474–75
Garcia, Jerry, 411
Gaye, Marvin, 60
Gersh, Dick, 103
Gillett, Charlie, 434
Goffin, Gerry, 23
"Goin' Home," 431
Goldmacher, Donald, 385, 409–10
Goldstein, Stanley, 47–52, 55–58, 62, 67–68, 70, 74–90, 93–94, 96, 99–100, 102, 108–10, 113, 115–16, 123, 127, 130–32, 134–41, 143–44, 150–51, 153, 166–68, 172–74, 186, 188, 193–99, 206, 232–36, 238, 245–46, 263–64, 273, 281, 293, 295, 297–99, 316, 385, 404–5
Goodgold, Ed, 432
Goodrich, Peter, 34, 98, 224–25, 229–32, 309, 325, 330, 332–33, 340, 341, 386, 402–3
Goshen, N.Y., 150, 216, 235, 273
Graham, Bill, 85–88, 159–61, 163–65, 393
Grand Central Station, 293
Grant, James, 195, 198
Grateful Dead, 59–60, 159–60, 375, 382, 400–401, 410
Grease Band, 420
Green, Carol, 191, 276
Greenfield, Howard, 23

Greenhill, Manny, 100
Greenwich Village, 26, 32, 90, 91, 104, 146, 150, 177, 203, 230, 373
Grimm, Tom, 301
Gross, Henry, 432
Gross, Richard, 266, 320, 389
Grossinger, Jennie, 394
Grossinger's Hotel, 245, 394, 418
Grossman, Albert, 93
Gulf Stream Racetrack, 34, 60
Guthrie, Arlo, 100, 159, 367, 381

Haight-Ashbury, 79
Hallendale, Otis, 144
Hammond, John, Sr., 10
Hanley, Bill, 51–52, 62, 86, 316, 329–30, 355, 387
Hanley Sound, 330
Happy Avenue, 250–53, 258
Hardin, Tim, 15, 73, 159, 335, 363, 367, 372, 377–78
Harris, David, 381
Hart, Malcolm, 312
Hartley, Keef, 392–93
Havens, Richie, 30, 60, 159, 160, 335, 363–67, 369–70
head shops, 32–33, 68, 238, 308–9
helicopters, 95, 102, 204, 288–89, 349, 362, 366, 372, 379, 390, 394, 396, 411, 418–19, 420, 426, 432
Hell's Angels, 121
Hendrix, Jimi, 34, 47, 55, 73, 100, 162, 163, 165, 334–35, 425, 432, 434–35
hippies, 15, 25, 32, 42, 46, 48, 60, 68–69, 76, 85–86, 88–90, 94, 111, 121–23, 126–29, 132–33, 135, 137, 138–39, 146, 152, 166–67, 169, 173, 175–77, 189–92, 193, 194, 198, 200–204, 205, 209, 219, 220–21, 227–28, 231, 239–40, 260, 266, 276, 278, 282–83, 285–86, 290, 294, 299, 303, 308, 312, 315, 320, 322, 326, 338, 342–44, 353, 357, 359–60, 363, 380, 384, 388, 393, 397, 407, 415, 417
Hirsch, Howard, 310
Hite, Bob "The Bear," 402, 412
Hoffman, Abbie, 83, 133, 146–50, 159, 404, 409, 414–15
Hoffman, Judge Julius, 146
Hog Farm, 79–81, 172, 177, 194–99, 215, 233, 276, 293–99, 308, 324–25, 328, 352–55, 358, 378–79, 386, 394, 405–6, 407–8, 416, 426, 433
Holiday Inn, 235, 334–35, 350, 356, 366, 372, 375–76, 393, 400
Holly, Buddy, 22

Holzman, Jac, 213
Hooker, John Lee, 34
Horton Memorial Hospital, 290, 418
Howard, Lee, 230–31, 325–26, 332–33, 341, 352
Howard Johnson's, 98, 420, 426
Hubbard, L. Ron, 59
Humphrey, Hubert H., 113
Hurd Road, 268, 273, 276, 285, 288, 302, 303, 318, 327, 384, 433

"If I Were A Carpenter," 378
Incredible String Band, 100, 159, 335, 367, 372, 376–77
Indian artists, 293, 295, 310, 318, 358
Ingrassia, Louis, 206, 208–9
Institute of Indian Art, 215
Intermedia Systems, 217, 287, 317
International Association of Police Chiefs, 75, 108
Iron Butterfly, 20, 60, 131, 366–67
It's a Beautiful Day, 160
Itzla, Henry, 206, 209
Ivy 3, The, 23

Jefferies, Michael, 162, 335, 432
Jefferson Airplane, 46, 55, 59, 73, 87, 159, 160, 382, 412, 415
Joerger, Jeffrey, 230–31, 324–25, 332–34, 341–42, 352, 361, 395, 404
Johnson, Lyndon B., 7, 75, 113, 358
Joint Productions, 34
Jones, Brian, 211
Joplin, Janis, 73, 159, 310, 334, 375, 411–12, 435
Joshua Light Show, 376–77
Juke Savages, 79, 197

Kapralik, David, 413–14
Kaukonen, Jorma, 415
Keiter, Don, 28, 34–35
Kenmore Hotel, 282–83
Kennedy, Sen. Edward, 256
Kennedy International Airport, 57, 62, 163, 289, 293–94, 366
Kesey, Ken, 79, 172
Kettle, 80
Kimble, Joseph, 176–77, 200, 202, 204, 320
King, Carole, 23
King, Martin Luther, Jr., 291
Kingston Trio, 434
Kirshner, Don, 23
Knapp, Whitman, 200
Komancheck, Louis, 282

Kooper, Al, 124
Kopechne, Mary Jo, 256
Koppelman, Charles, 23–24
Koppelson, Arnold, 103
Kornfeld, Artie, 4, 14–30, 35–36, 40, 42, 44, 46–48, 52–54, 64, 68, 69–72, 83–85, 90–91, 100–108, 148, 162, 214, 230, 232, 239, 258–59, 278, 281, 312, 314, 320, 389–90, 394, 420, 431–32, 438
Kornfeld, Linda, 27, 30, 399
Kramer, Eddie, 355
Kutcher's Hotel, 245

LaGuardia Airport, 109–10, 289, 385–86
Landlord, The, 11
Lang, Michael, 4, 14–21, 25–40, 42–50, 52–55, 57–58, 62–63, 67–73, 78, 80, 83, 85, 87–94, 96, 98–111, 112–16, 121–24, 128, 130–32, 141, 143, 146–50, 153–62, 165–66, 172–73, 178–81, 182, 185, 188–89, 191, 194, 201, 204–6, 210, 212–17, 225–27, 229–32, 235–37, 238–40, 242, 243–47, 250–60, 261–65, 269–70, 271, 278, 279, 282, 304, 307–8, 312–13, 314–16, 319–20, 324, 328, 332–36, 340–42, 345, 352, 356, 360, 363, 365, 370, 377, 386, 389, 391–92, 394, 397–99, 402, 404, 413, 425, 432, 438
Langhart, Chris, 92, 99, 155–58, 172–73, 269, 272–76, 277–78, 289, 297, 300–301, 303, 310–11, 316–17, 321, 328, 386, 391, 399
Law, Tom, 358
Lawrence, Mel, 58–63, 66, 70, 89–91, 93–101, 120–32, 144, 152–53, 155, 158, 166, 170–71, 188–89, 190, 192, 198–99, 205–6, 207, 217, 224, 232–33, 235–36, 238, 241–42, 243–46, 251–55, 265, 267–71, 272, 274, 276–77, 302–3, 305, 317, 319, 321–22, 328–32, 350–51, 355–57, 383–84, 386–88, 390, 396–97, 402–4, 419–20, 426, 433
Lax, George, 81
Leary, Commissioner Howard, 203, 322–24, 337
Led Zepplin, 219
Lee, Alvin, 163, 431
Leeds, Peter, 181, 310
Lembke, Al, 176
Lemon, Burton, 282
Lennon, John, 93, 162
Lenox, Bob, 53–54
Lettermen, 25, 27, 30
Levine, David, 158, 356, 378
Levine, Renee, 82–83, 90

Levitt, John, 97
Lewis, Mort, 159
Liberty, N.Y., 266, 375, 389, 393, 400, 406, 417
Liberty Hospital, 379
Life magazine, 178, 339, 412
lighting, 48–49, 56, 62, 76, 86–88, 96–98, 122, 124, 143, 155, 269–73, 301, 322, 335, 364
Liis, Ron, 172–73, 268, 359
Lincoln Tunnel, 194
Lindsey, Mayor John V., 173, 324
Little Richard, 22
Live Adventures of Mike Bloomfield and Al Kooper, The, 392
Livingston, Alan, 24–25
Los Angeles, Calif., 47, 53, 60, 95, 175, 215, 402
Lourie, Felix, 142
Lourie, Miles, 4–5, 13, 20, 37, 40, 42, 45–46, 52, 64, 69, 97–98, 100, 103, 141–42, 185–86, 228–29
Love, 388
Lovin' Spoonful, 15, 372

Macaluso, Charles, 302
Mackler, Lee, 121, 130, 190, 232, 285–86, 322–23, 337, 350, 355, 362, 374, 375, 389, 393–94, 399, 424, 428, 433
Madison Square Garden, 57, 225
Makeba, Miriam, 86
Mamas and the Papas, 373, 434
Mandor Beekman, 35
Mann, Barry, 23
Margetz, Michael, 312
Marshall, Paul, 100, 186, 228–31, 278, 279, 281, 375, 383–84, 389, 394
Mayall, John, 60
Mayall's Bluesbreakers, John, 393
Maysles Brothers, 281
McDonald, Country Joe, 334, 368–72, 430
McManus, George P., 201, 203, 218
Media Sound, 4, 13, 17, 103, 320
medical, 139, 143, 176–77, 192, 195, 204, 234, 269, 287, 290–92, 297, 303, 330–31, 352–55, 376, 378–79, 385–86, 396–97, 405–10, 414, 417–18, 423, 433
 Big Pink, 297, 352–55, 408–9
Medical Committee For Human Rights, 385, 409
Melanie, 335, 381
Melton, Barry, 430
Mercury Records, 24
Meredith, James, 291
Merry Pranksters, 79, 172, 233, 296

Metromedia Studios, 432
Meurice, Bob, 313
Miami, Fla., 20, 26, 28, 32–34, 47, 58, 60–
    61, 129, 198, 238, 268, 290, 357–58,
    392, 408
Miami Herald, 61
Miami Pop. See rock festivals
Michaels, David, 293
Middletown, N.Y., 41, 64, 95, 98, 100, 120,
    126, 127–28, 131, 135, 141, 151–52, 173,
    185, 188, 192, 199, 218, 223, 233, 256,
    286, 291, 299, 353
Middletown Fire Dept., 226
Middletown State Hospital, 216, 379, 418
Mills, Howard, 41–45, 64, 65, 70, 95, 97–99,
    121, 125, 127, 130–31, 135, 137, 140,
    141, 143–45, 153, 156, 167–69, 187–88,
    221, 236–37, 243, 257, 279
Mills, Jacob, 43
Mills, Pat, 144, 167–69
Mills Heights, 42–44, 95, 99, 121, 125–28,
    135, 144, 150, 153, 156, 167, 172–73,
    174, 188–89, 192, 210, 217, 221, 222,
    233, 238, 240, 242, 244, 255, 269, 273,
    276, 285
Minker, Jules, 145–46, 150, 208, 221, 237
Mitchell, Jim, 212, 232, 234, 269, 279, 289
Mitchell, Joni, 60
Mitchell, Joyce, 91, 93, 164, 232
Mitchell Samuel, 206, 208–9
Mizsik, Raymond, 390
Monahan, John A., 327
Monck, E. H. Beresford "Chip," 62, 86–92,
    97, 99, 155–58, 189, 215, 232–33, 269,
    270–73, 300, 322, 335–36, 364, 373,
    383–84, 393, 427, 434–35
Monterey Pop. See rock festivals
Monticello, N.Y., 216, 247, 315, 318, 327, 331,
    339, 344, 350, 399, 417–18
Monticello General Hospital, 292, 379
Monticello High School, 175
Monticello Jewish Community Center, 419
Monticello Raceway, 262, 389–90
Moody Blues, 100, 131, 161–62
Morales, Hector, 55, 72, 87
Morris, Betsy, 331
Morris, John, 87–89, 90–94, 99, 102, 121,
    156, 158–62, 163–65, 213–15, 232,
    234–35, 269, 271, 301, 310, 315, 330,
    334–36, 344–45, 360–61, 362–73, 376,
    391, 399–401, 404, 408, 412–14, 420–
    23, 428–29, 432, 434–35
Morrison, Jim, 61
Mothers of Invention, 34
Mountain, 393

Nashville, Tenn., 100
Nathan's Famous, 98, 225
Nation, 189
National Guard, 349–50, 379, 397
Neuwirth, Bobby, 409
Newburgh, N.Y., 224, 228, 232, 366, 418,
    420, 426
Newport Jazz Festival, 19, 220
Newsweek, 7, 178
New York Carting, 302
New York City, 5, 9–10, 13, 23, 41, 47–48,
    62, 66, 74, 79, 81, 90, 128, 141, 145, 146,
    150, 155, 161, 166, 173, 177, 194, 200–
    201, 213, 217, 221, 244, 258, 274, 285,
    293, 298, 311, 329, 385, 396, 405–7,
    432–33
New York Daily News, 295, 396
New York magazine, 343
New York Police Department (NYPD), 200–
    203, 218–19, 234, 285–86, 288, 320,
    322, 326, 337–38
New York Post, 295, 335, 342, 345, 378–79,
    396
New York Quickway, 41, 119, 152, 249–50,
    281–82, 288, 344, 406, 433
New York State Council on the Arts, 142
New York State Department of Transporta-
    tion, 222–24, 287–88
New York State Police, 224, 318, 326–27,
    337, 343, 379, 419, 433
New York State Thruway, 39, 40, 326, 362,
    399
New York Times, 12, 103, 160, 211, 220, 344,
    417
New York University, 31, 92, 156, 173, 248,
    278
Nixon, Richard, 61, 75, 207, 220, 358
No Vietnamese Ever Called me Nigger, 313
Nowack, Mr. and Mrs. Martin, 150

O'Connor, Keith, 83, 86, 99
Odetta, 86
O'Gorman, Judge Edward M., 232, 237, 266
"On the Road Again," 402
Orange County, N.Y., 62, 96, 141–43, 150,
    175, 188–89, 193, 208–9, 227, 237, 267,
    407
Orange County Fair, 65, 153, 188–89
Osborne, Lee, 355
Owen, Joseph, 143, 207, 237–40

Pacific Gas and Electric, 219
Palisades Parkway, 62
Papuga, Mr. and Mrs. Adam, 150

Paramount Pictures, 315
parking, 98, 122–23, 143, 171, 186, 199, 202, 217, 223–24, 233, 270, 287–88, 318, 327–28, 339, 343
Patrolmen's Benevolent Association, 218
Paul, Steve, 73
Peace Service Corps, 171–72, 182, 202, 204, 218, 234, 284, 321, 338, 388
Pentagon, 96, 417–18
Peoples Park, 400
performers' pavilion, 157–58, 234–35, 305, 325, 329, 330, 356, 363, 367, 372, 378, 402, 412, 430, 435
Peter, Paul and Mary, 86, 434
Philadelphia Folk Festival, 156, 271
Pinkerton guards, 395
Plastic Ono Band, 93
Plaza Hotel, 62, 328, 374
Pomeroy, Wes, 74–78, 108–14, 115–16, 128, 131, 133–34, 138, 165–66, 168–72, 176–77, 181–83, 185, 193, 194–95, 198–206, 216–18, 222–24, 227, 232, 234, 265–66, 271, 285–88, 290, 294, 296, 302, 320, 323–24, 327, 336–37, 343, 351–52, 383, 389, 393, 410–11, 429, 433
Pompili, Jerry, 99
Port Authority Bus Terminal, 344
Premier Talent, 163
Prince, Charlie, 410–11
Princeton Club, 148
Princeton Trio, 10
Princeton University, 9–10
"Proud Mary," 72
publicity, 58, 81, 91, 101, 102–3, 121, 141, 176–80, 185, 212–13, 219, 230, 255–56, 269–70, 278–79, 295, 334, 362
Public Service Commission, 301
Puff, Arnold, 199, 224
"Purple Haze," 435

Queens, N.Y., 23, 432
Queens College, 23
Quicksilver Messenger Service, 25
Quill, 216, 392

"Rain, the Park, and Other Things," 24
Rat, 177, 183, 381
Ratner's Dairy Restaurant, 161
RCA Records, 46
Realist, 177
Red Cross, 379, 433
Red Top, 189–90, 192, 262, 276
Reischman, Barry, 82
Republican National Convention, 75, 111, 115
Restaurant Associates, 225, 229

Reynolds, Bill, 384, 396
Reynolds, Cliff, 145–46, 150, 176, 204, 210, 221–22, 235, 237, 240–41, 244
Righteous Brothers, 373
Rismiller, Brent, 145
Roberts, Alfred, 5–6, 257, 319, 437–38
Roberts, Elizabeth, 5–6
Roberts, John, 3–21, 36, 39–46, 48, 53, 55, 64–66, 68–72, 81–84, 89–91, 100–108, 131, 141–42, 143, 150, 166, 172, 180, 185–88, 190, 205, 210, 227, 236, 239, 244, 251, 255–59, 261–62, 278, 281, 311–15, 318–23, 332–34, 336, 339–41, 350–52, 356–57, 361, 374, 388–91, 393–94, 397–400, 424–25, 427–30, 433–34, 437–38
Roberts, Keith, 5–6
Roberts, William, 5–6, 12, 71, 318, 437–38
Rockefeller, Nelson D., 142, 324, 350, 385, 397, 404
rock festivals, 59–60, 66, 68, 93–94, 95–96, 138–39, 219, 234, 383
Atlanta Pop, 219
Atlantic City Rock Festival, 392
Fantasy Fair and Magic Mountain Music Festival, 59
Fort Lauderdale, 139
Miami Pop, 47, 60–62, 63, 66, 97, 125, 155–57, 162
Monterey Pop, 19, 60, 86, 281, 381
Newport Folk Festival, 363
Northridge, 175–76, 179
Rolling Stone, 412, 431
Rolling Stones, 211, 377
Romm, Al, 174–75, 188
Romm, Ethel, 359
Romney, Bonnie Jean, 235–36, 296–97
Romney, Hugh, 79–80, 194, 196–98, 295–97, 383, 404–5, 408, 416
Rosenberg's, 120, 125, 127, 189
Rosenman, Douglas, 6, 8
Rosenman, Joel, 3–6, 9–21, 36, 39–46, 48, 52–53, 55, 64–70, 72, 82–84, 89–91, 100–108, 131, 141–42, 147–49, 166, 172, 187–88, 190, 205, 210, 227–28, 230, 232, 236, 238–39, 255, 261, 278, 281, 285, 287, 297, 311–13, 320, 322–23, 338–40, 362, 374, 388–90, 394, 398–401, 410–11, 414, 424–25, 428–30, 433–34, 437–38
Ross, Jewell, 202, 285, 320
Rounds, Tom, 59, 62–63

Sainte-Marie, Buffy, 60
Salvation Army, 433
Sanderson, Rikki, 331, 354, 423–24

San Francisco, Calif., 24, 59–60, 75, 86, 114–15, 133, 159, 161, 285, 320
sanitation, 39, 56–57, 95–97, 139, 143, 152–53, 187, 198, 210, 234, 282, 284, 297, 302, 305, 340, 384, 395–97, 417
  clean-up, 96, 171, 293, 302, 387–88, 406, 433
Santana, 160, 162, 392–93, 397
Santana, Carlos, 392–93
Saugerties, N.Y., 39
Schadt, Frederick W. V., 266, 281
Schenectady, N.Y., 273
Schlosser, Jack A., 132, 134–37, 139–40, 151, 153–54, 173, 186, 189, 206–9, 279
Scotchtown, N.Y., 131–32, 188
Sebastian, John, 372–73, 376, 378, 409
security, 76–79, 80, 108–9, 110, 113–14, 115–16, 135, 138, 143, 150, 165–66, 168, 169–71, 176, 182, 193, 199–200, 202–5, 210, 211, 216, 218–19, 222–24, 233, 239, 269, 284–87, 288, 290–91, 293, 295, 300, 319–24, 327, 336–38, 343, 350–51, 355, 360, 362, 366, 372–73, 376, 388–89, 393, 397–98, 399–400, 404
  policemen, 33, 61, 108–11, 113–14, 129, 138–39, 166, 175–76, 182, 187, 191, 244, 268, 331, 336–38, 343, 368, 389, 401, 428–29
Sedaka, Neil, 23
Seger, Bob, 25
Shaler, 39–40
Sha Na Na, 432, 434–35
Shankar, Ravi, 100, 159, 367, 380–81
Shea Stadium, 225
Sheehy, Gail, 342
Shirelles, 23
Short Line Bus Company, 344
Simon, Paul, 4
Simon and Garfunkel, 159, 434
Sinclair, John, 415
Skolnick, Arnold, 212–13, 279
Slick, Grace, 375, 411–12, 415, 435
Sly and the Family Stone, 29, 124, 162, 220, 235, 411–14
Smokey Robinson and the Miracles, 220
"Somebody To Love," 415
Sommer, Bert, 335, 367, 372
"Soul Sacrifice," 393
sound, 48–51, 76, 86, 97, 254, 269–71, 305, 316, 329–30, 355, 364–65, 387
South, Joe, 25
Soza, Billy, 215
stage, 92, 96–97, 122, 155–58, 237, 241, 268, 269–70, 296, 302, 305–8, 318, 319, 321–22, 329, 412–13, 423–28, 430, 434

Stallings, Penny, 91, 94, 121–22, 128–29, 190, 232, 241, 261, 276, 294, 296, 386, 399, 427
"Star Spangled Banner," 376, 435
Steppenwolf, 60
Stevens, Harry M., 225, 229
Stewart, Rod, 163
Stills, Stephen, 358, 434–35
"Suite: Judy Blue Eyes," 434
Sullivan County, N.Y., 189, 244, 247, 265, 268, 283, 306, 315, 320, 343, 374, 401, 407, 430, 438
Sullivan County National Bank, 410–11
Susskind, David, 432
"Suzie Q," 72
Sweetwater, 124, 335, 356, 360, 362–63, 372

Tanglewood, 163–64
Tapooz, Alexander, 70, 438
Ten Years After, 163, 431
Tesuque Indian Reservation, 194
Thayler, Dr. Ed., 100
Thornton Memorial Hospital, 291
tickets, 68–69, 81–82, 83, 91, 123, 130, 170–71, 211–12, 214, 228, 236, 243–44, 255–56, 259, 269, 278–79, 285, 293, 297, 302, 312, 318–21, 327, 336, 339, 357, 437
Tieber, Elliott, 245, 246, 252, 260
Time, 178, 215
Times Herald Record, 131–32, 141, 143, 150, 174–76, 188–89, 205, 209, 220–21, 240, 243, 260, 266, 281–82, 359
Toch, Hans, 189
Tommy, 414
Townshend, Peter, 163–64, 411, 415
Train, 16, 26–27, 28, 35, 47, 52–55, 101, 392
transportation, 76, 94–95, 123–24, 152, 187, 199, 202, 206, 216–17, 222–23, 235, 239, 282, 287–88, 318, 326–28, 334, 342–45, 349, 362, 366, 375, 388, 405, 433
Tremper, Margaret, 227
Tri-County Citizens Band Radio Club, 199, 224, 234, 418
Turtles, 60, 373

Ulster County, 227
UNICEF, 213
University of Miami, 33, 62, 80–81, 97, 121, 170, 181, 268
University of Pennsylvania, 6, 7
Up-Against-The-Wall Motherfuckers, 309, 403–5
U.S. Army, 96, 417–18

Van Loan, Ken, 283, 302
Vidockler, Murray, 217
Vidockler, Stu, 287
Vietnam, 7, 8, 76, 111, 181, 182, 285, 368–69, 371, 382, 418
Village Gate, 86, 178, 185
Village Voice, 79, 215
Volunteers, 415
Von Wilsheim, Ingrid, 386

Wadleigh, Michael, 312–15, 421
Wadleigh-Meurice Productions, 313
Wallkill, N.Y., 41, 45, 64–65, 66, 77, 78–79, 80–81, 94, 99, 102–3, 114, 115–16, 119, 125, 127, 132, 134–35, 136–38, 140–41, 144–45, 147, 150–52, 154–55, 160–62, 165, 169, 173–74, 176, 177, 186, 188–89, 195, 201, 204–7, 208–9, 214–20, 223, 226–28, 232–33, 236, 237–38, 240–41, 243–44, 249–52, 254, 255–56, 263, 265–66, 268–69, 273, 278–79, 285, 287, 290, 294, 302, 306, 312, 331
Wallkill Town Council, 64, 130, 132, 136, 139–41, 142, 143, 151–53, 154, 165, 174–75, 185–88, 206, 207–9, 211, 212, 215–18, 227, 234, 237–38, 241–42
Wallkill Town Fire Advisory Board, 187, 227
Wallkill Town Hall, 65, 134
Wallkill town meetings, 134–40, 205–8, 237–41
Wallkill Zoning Board of Appeals, 64–66, 128–29, 131, 139–41, 154, 177, 187, 206–7, 210, 221, 232–33, 237–40, 241, 243–44, 267
Wall Street Journal, 12
Wappingers Falls, N.Y., 290, 331
Ward, Bill, 97, 121, 125, 144–45, 193, 233, 268, 290
Ward, Jean, 97, 121, 125–26, 144, 193, 233, 268, 290
Warner Brothers Pictures, 281, 315, 394, 438
Wartoke Concern, 99, 103, 141, 156, 177–79, 211, 361
Warwick, Dionne, 59
Washington, D.C., 7, 75, 78, 96, 110, 113, 114
water, 93, 96, 97, 98, 122, 143, 147, 153, 172–73, 186, 196, 210, 222, 234–35, 270, 273–76, 288, 311, 316, 328, 385, 386, 391, 405–6
Weil, Cynthia, 23
Weingrad, Stephen, 230, 325, 340, 352
Weintraub, Fred, 394
West, Leslie, 393
West Shore Road, 268, 288, 310, 362, 384, 433

White, Joshua, 86, 88, 335, 376–77
White House, 74
White Lake, N.Y., 244, 247–48, 250–51, 256, 261–62, 266, 268, 270, 277–79, 285, 286–87, 291, 296, 300, 301, 306, 317–18, 321, 327, 337, 349, 357, 360, 366, 374, 376, 379, 385, 394, 396, 404, 415, 425, 432–34, 439
White Lake Daily Weirdness, 296
White Panther Party, 415
"White Rabbit," 415
Who, the, 46, 48, 100, 163–65, 377, 402, 414–15
Wilkens, Roger, 111–13
William Morris Agency, 55
Wilson, Brian, 23
Wilson, Malcolm, 142
Wine, Toni, 23
Winter, Edgar, 434
Winter, Johnny, 73, 161, 434
Wolff, John, 164–65, 402, 414
Woodstock, N.Y., 15–17, 20, 26, 28, 31, 34–35, 40–41, 48, 70, 214, 235–36, 307, 324, 335, 372, 432, 438
Woodstock Kalaparusha Management, 53, 390
Woodstock Music and Art Fair, 19, 21–22, 45–48, 50, 52–53, 62–63, 67–68, 70–71, 73, 74–75, 81–82, 86–88, 92–93, 102–3, 105–6, 108, 110, 113–14, 120, 121–22, 125–28, 129–30, 131, 134–36, 137–39, 140–43, 147, 150–52, 153–54, 155–56, 157–58, 160–65, 171, 174–75, 177–84, 186, 188, 189–90, 192–94, 196–98, 199–201, 203–5, 206, 210, 212–14, 215–16, 217–21, 224–29, 233–38, 241, 244, 246–47, 254–55, 258–61, 263–64, 265–66, 268–72, 278, 281–83, 287, 289–91, 293–94, 295, 298–99, 306, 315–24, 327–28, 330, 338, 340–42, 343–45, 439
Woodstock Ventures Inc., 37, 43, 45, 55, 62–63, 67, 69–70, 71, 79, 81–82, 84, 89, 99–101, 121, 127, 131–32, 136, 141, 143–46, 150–51, 154, 156, 160, 167, 170, 176, 177–79, 185, 186–87, 189, 190, 194, 197–98, 200–201, 206–7, 208, 210–11, 213–15, 216, 221–25, 228–29, 231–32, 237, 239, 241, 243, 256, 258, 260, 264, 265, 279, 283–84, 286, 287–89, 292, 293, 301, 303–4, 311–12, 314, 320, 326, 338–39, 341, 356, 360–61, 374–75, 389, 394, 399–400, 401, 407, 410, 437–38

Yale Law School, 10
Yankee Stadium, 57, 158, 225

Yanovsky, Zal, 373
Yardbirds, 163, 377
Yasgur, Max, 247–54, 256–61, 263–66, 267–68, 272–76, 279, 281–83, 284–85, 287–88, 298–300, 303–4, 306, 310–11, 315–16, 317, 320, 328, 330, 349, 362, 374, 387–89, 418–19, 426–27, 429, 433, 439
Yasgur, Miriam, 248–49, 260–61, 304, 306, 429
Yasgur, Sam, 275, 426
Young, Neil, 434